Wales

John King

LONELY PLANET PUBLICATIONS
Melbourne • Oakland • London • Paris

ENGLAND

IRISH SEA

ST GEORGES CHANNEL

CARDIGAN BAY

ELEVATION

- 900m
- 600m
- 300m
- 0

LLANDUDNO
An old-fashioned seaside resort with great Victorian architecture and its own dramatic peninsula

LLANGOLLEN
A family-friendly town with a 13th-century abbey, whitewater rafting and Thomas Telford's spectacular aqueduct

CAERNARFON
With a UNESCO-listed castle, the most imposing of several built by Edward I to keep the Welsh under his thumb

MT SNOWDON
The highest peak in England and Wales, its summit accessible by train or on foot

GLYNDŴR'S WAY
A long-distance footpath following the trail of national hero, Owain Glyndŵr

THE CENTRE FOR ALTERNATIVE TECHNOLOGY
Europe's best eco-centre, near Machynlleth

THE VALE OF RHEIDOL RAILWAY
The most scenic of Wales's many narrow-gauge railways, from Aberystwyth to Devil's Bridge

BLAENAFON
Memorial to the best and worst of the Industrial Revolution, and now a UNESCO World Heritage Site

HAY-ON-WYE
A town built on books

CARDIFF
Europe's youngest capital city, with its own fantasy castle, a world-class fine arts museum, the UK's finest sports stadium and Wales' most switched-on nightlife

LLANWRTYD WELLS
With fine cycling, walking and riding, and a calendar of oddball events

THE PEMBROKESHIRE COAST PATH
FROM ST DAVID'S TO CARDIGAN
With wild sea-cliffs, Neolithic monuments, puffin colonies and some of the world's oldest rocks

THE NATIONAL BOTANIC
GARDEN OF WALES
Twice the size of London's Kew Gardens, with a gigantic, high-technology domed greenhouse

ST DAVID'S CATHEDRAL
Wales' holiest place, dedicated to its patron saint

ENGLAND

BRISTOL CHANNEL

CAMBRIAN MOUN...

Mynydd Eppynt

Brecon Beacons National Park

Pembrokeshire Coast National Park

Carmarthen Bay

Cardigan Bay

Mouth of the Severn

Offa's Dyke Trail

Elan Valley

Black Mountains
Waun Fach (811m)

Pen-y-Fan (886m)

Fan Brycheiniog (802m)

Black Mountain

The Mumbles

Gower Peninsula

Towns and places:
Aberystwyth, Llanbadarn Fynydd, Llandewi Ystradenny, Llandrindod Wells, Rhayader, Pontrhydfendigaid, Devil's Bridge, Ponterwyd, Llanidloes, Kington, Knighton, Willersley, Hereford, Hay-on-Wye, Glasbury, Clyro, Talgarth, Crickhowell, Gilwern, Brynmawr, Abergavenny, Monmouth, Raglan, Usk, Caerleon, Newport, Chepstow, Caldicot, Tintern, Penarth, Cardiff, Barry, Rhoose, Cowbridge, Bridgend, Porthcawl, Port Talbot, Neath, Aberdare, Merthyr Tydfil, Pontypridd, Caerphilly, Abertillery, Blaenavon, Ebbw Vale, Aberafan, Porth, Glyn Neath, Glynneath, Blaengarw, Maesteg, Ystradgynlais, Pontardawe, Ammanford, Llandovery, Llandeilo, Llanwrtyd Wells, Builth Wells, Brecon, Llangammarch Wells, Llangynidr, Llanwrthwl, Myddfai, Swansea, Llanelli, Llandybie, Pontarddulais, Laugharne, Carmarthen, Newcastle Emlyn, Llandysul, Lampeter, Llanybydder, Aberaeron, New Quay, Temple Bar, Synod Inn, Aberaeron, Cardigan, Newport, Fishguard, St David's, Newgale, Broad Haven, Dale, Milford Haven, Neyland, Pembroke Dock, Pembroke, Haverfordwest, Narberth, Saundersfoot, Amroth, Tenby, Manorbier, Ramsey Island, Skomer Island, Caldey Island, St Bride's Bay, Preseli Hills, Barafundle Bay, Oxwich, Port Eynon, Rhossili

To Rosslare
To Cork

0 7.5 15mi
0 15 30km

N

Wales
1st edition – October 2001

Published by
Lonely Planet Publications Pty Ltd ABN 36 005 607 983
90 Maribyrnong St, Footscray, Victoria 3011, Australia

Lonely Planet Offices
Australia Locked Bag 1, Footscray, Victoria 3011
USA 150 Linden St, Oakland, CA 94607
UK 10a Spring Place, London NW5 3BH
France 1 rue du Dahomey, 75011 Paris

Photographs
Many of the images in this guide are available for licensing from
Lonely Planet Images.
Web site: www.lonelyplanetimages.com

Front cover photograph
Tintern Abbey, Monmouthshire (Jon Davison).

ISBN 1 86450 126 X

Printed by SNP SPrint (M) Sdn Bhd
Printed in Malaysia

Although the authors
and Lonely Planet try
to make the informa-
tion as accurate as
possible, we accept
no responsibility for
any loss, injury or
inconvenience sus-
tained by anyone
using this book.

Contents – Text

SOUTH-EAST WALES & THE BRECON BEACONS 155

PEMBROKESHIRE & CARMARTHENSHIRE 198

MID WALES 235

SNOWDONIA & THE LLŶN 260

ANGLESEY & THE NORTH COAST 296

Contents – Maps

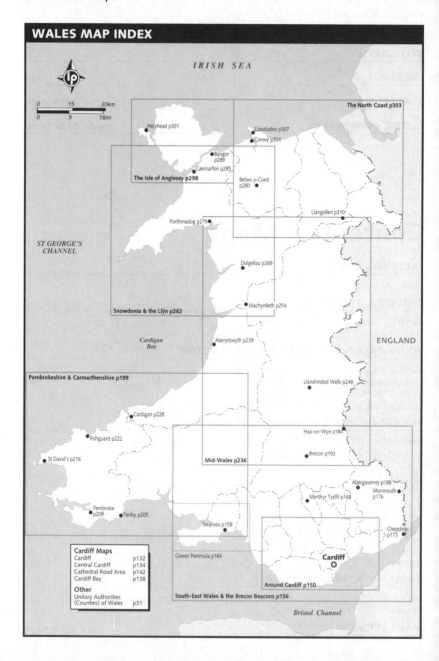

WALES MAP INDEX

IRISH SEA

The North Coast p303

Holyhead p301

Llandudno p307
Conwy p304

Bangor p289
Caernarfon p285

The Isle of Anglesey p298

Betws-y-Coed p280

Llangollen p310

Porthmadog p275

ST GEORGE'S CHANNEL

Dolgellau p269

Machynlleth p254

Snowdonia & the Llŷn p262

Cardigan Bay

Aberystwyth p239

ENGLAND

Pembrokeshire & Carmarthenshire p199

Llandrindod Wells p248

Cardigan p228

Hay-on-Wye p184

Fishguard p222

Mid-Wales p236

Brecon p193

St David's p216

Abergavenny p188
Monmouth p176

Merthyr Tydfil p168

Pembroke p209
Tenby p205

Swansea p158

Chepstow p173

Gower Peninsula p164

Cardiff

Around Cardiff p150

South-East Wales & the Brecon Beacons p156

Bristol Channel

Cardiff Maps	
Cardiff	p132
Central Cardiff	p134
Cathedral Road Area	p142
Cardiff Bay	p138
Other	
Unitary Authorities (Counties) of Wales	p31

0   15   30km
0   9   18mi

The Author

John King

John grew up in the USA, and in earlier 'incarnations' has been a university physics teacher and an environmental consultant. In 1984 he headed off for a look at China, ended up living there for half a year, and never quite came home. John took up travel writing in 1988 with the 1st edition of Lonely Planet's *Karakoram Highway*. He is also co-author of Lonely Planet's *Pakistan*; *Czech & Slovak Republics*; *Prague*; *Portugal*; and *South-West France*; and was co-author of early editions of *Russia, Ukraine & Belarus* and *Central Asia*. He is also a contributor to *Western Europe* and *Mediterranean Europe*. John lives with his wife Julia Wilkinson and their two children in south-west England.

From the Author

Before I'd even started this book I was in debt to Bryn Thomas for his affectionate text on Wales in Lonely Planet's *Britain*, and for his interest in this project.

Several people have made contributions that raise the calibre of this book. For helping me get to grips with Welsh history I'm especially grateful to Dr Eryn White, Lecturer in Welsh History, Department of History & Welsh History at the University of Wales (Aberystwyth). For essential guidance through the rich tradition of Anglo-Welsh literature I am indebted to Tony Curtis, Professor of Poetry at the University of Glamorgan; Prof Curtis also contributed the boxed text 'The Visual Arts in Wales'. Eddie Butler of the *Observer* and the BBC contributed the boxed text 'A Peculiar Passion', about Welsh rugby. The aside about Richard Booth, self-styled king of Hay-on-Wye, is by Patrick Horton.

On the visual side, painter Peter Prendergast has very generously allowed us to embellish this book with his work.

Glenda Davies of the Welsh Tourist Board repeatedly came to the rescue with information and contacts, and I'm grateful for her support and enthusiasm. Thanks also to her colleague, Heledd Llewelyn, for her help – especially on the subject of the eisteddfodau – and her networking. Nicola Mills and Lowri ap Robert at Cardiff Marketing were equally skillful on the subject of Cardiff. Hannah Thomas of Cadw provided timely help on several occasions.

Another master of networking was Sion Llewelyn of Cardiff Backpackers. Thanks to Steve Roberts at Hamilton Guest House (Fishguard) for Pembrokeshire tips; Sarah Cole, production manager at the Sherman Theatre, for a view of Cardiff's theatre and gay scene; Dave Berry (Sgrîn) and Andrew Offiler (Siriol) for a look at Welsh animation; and Sarah Jenkinson for information on the Centre for Alternative Technology (Machynlleth). Jock

Smith at Cardiff Parks Services helped me sort out Bute Park, and archaeologist Peter Dorling at the Brecon Beacons National Park told me about the *crannog* at Llangorse Lake.

Unsung staff at scores of Tourist Information Centres went out of their way to track down information. Nia Lynn Powell-Jones and Nêst Thomas of the Caernarfon Record Office were generous with information on and pictures of David Lloyd George. And cheers to Maria Kingsbury at Arriva Cymru for a hundred thousand bus fares.

Support from Lonely Planet was widespread. Rachel Suddart and Finola Collins (London) struggled to keep a straight face during research on Cardiff's nightlife. Authors David Else and Pete Cruttenden shared much information on walking in Wales, and Tom Hall (London) helped me sort out Wales' sports scene. Dora Chai and Emily Coles (Melbourne) interrupted their production schedules to furnish text on cycling and walking in Britain.

This book owes much to the editing of Samantha Trafford and the cartographic skills of Angie Watts, and to the logistical support and extreme forbearance of Amanda Canning and Tim Fitzgerald.

Finally and most importantly, love and *diolch in fawr iawn* to Julia, who single-handedly kept me afloat throughout this project, in more ways than one.

This Book

This book was researched and written by John King and is based on the relevant chapters of Lonely Planet's *Britain* guide.

From the Publisher

This 1st edition of *Wales* was produced in Lonely Planet's London office. Sam Trafford, Emma Sangster and Amanda Canning coordinated the editorial side, with invaluable assistance from Imogen Franks, Abigail Hole and Jenny Lansbury. Angie Watts coordinated the cartography and design, assisted by James Ellis, Ed Pickard and David Wenk in London and Marcel Gaston, Joelene Kawalski, Louise Klep et al in the Melbourne office. The cover was designed by Andrew Weatherill, illustrations were drawn by Jane Smith and Asa Andersson and the climate charts were produced by James Ellis. Thanks to Emma Koch for her linguistic expertise, to Tom Hall for being the fount of all sporting knowledge, to Rachel Suddart for knowing how to get there and then come back again and to Tim Ryder and Sara Yorke for stepping in with last-minute help. Final thanks go to John King for remaining enthuastic and involved throughout production.

Foreword

ABOUT LONELY PLANET GUIDEBOOKS

The story begins with a classic travel adventure: Tony and Maureen Wheeler's 1972 journey across Europe and Asia to Australia. Useful information about the overland trail did not exist at that time, so Tony and Maureen published the first Lonely Planet guidebook to meet a growing need.

From a kitchen table, then from a tiny office in Melbourne (Australia), Lonely Planet has become the largest independent travel publisher in the world, an international company with offices in Melbourne, Oakland (USA), London (UK) and Paris (France).

Today Lonely Planet guidebooks cover the globe. There is an ever-growing list of books and there's information in a variety of forms and media. Some things haven't changed. The main aim is still to help make it possible for adventurous travellers to get out there – to explore and better understand the world.

At Lonely Planet we believe travellers can make a positive contribution to the countries they visit – if they respect their host communities and spend their money wisely. Since 1986 a percentage of the income from each book has been donated to aid projects and human rights campaigns.

Updates Lonely Planet thoroughly updates each guidebook as often as possible. This usually means there are around two years between editions, although for more unusual or more stable destinations the gap can be longer. Check the imprint page (following the colour map at the beginning of the book) for publication dates.

Between editions up-to-date information is available in two free newsletters – the paper *Planet Talk* and email *Comet* (to subscribe, contact any Lonely Planet office) – and on our Web site at www.lonelyplanet.com. The *Upgrades* section of the Web site covers a number of important and volatile destinations and is regularly updated by Lonely Planet authors. *Scoop* covers news and current affairs relevant to travellers. And, lastly, the *Thorn Tree* bulletin board and *Postcards* section of the site carry unverified, but fascinating, reports from travellers.

Correspondence The process of creating new editions begins with the letters, postcards and emails received from travellers. This correspondence often includes suggestions, criticisms and comments about the current editions. Interesting excerpts are immediately passed on via newsletters and the Web site, and everything goes to our authors to be verified when they're researching on the road. We're keen to get more feedback from organisations or individuals who represent communities visited by travellers.

Lonely Planet gathers information for everyone who's curious about the planet – and especially for those who explore it first-hand. Through guidebooks, phrasebooks, activity guides, maps, literature, newsletters, image library, TV series and Web site we act as an information exchange for a worldwide community of travellers.

Research Authors aim to gather sufficient practical information to enable travellers to make informed choices and to make the mechanics of a journey run smoothly. They also research historical and cultural background to help enrich the travel experience and allow travellers to understand and respond appropriately to cultural and environmental issues.

Authors don't stay in every hotel because that would mean spending a couple of months in each medium-sized city and, no, they don't eat at every restaurant because that would mean stretching belts beyond capacity. They do visit hotels and restaurants to check standards and prices, but feedback based on readers' direct experiences can be very helpful.

Many of our authors work undercover, others aren't so secretive. None of them accept freebies in exchange for positive write-ups. And none of our guidebooks contain any advertising.

Production Authors submit their raw manuscripts and maps to offices in Australia, USA, UK or France. Editors and cartographers – all experienced travellers themselves – then begin the process of assembling the pieces. When the book finally hits the shops, some things are already out of date, we start getting feedback from readers and the process begins again...

WARNING & REQUEST

Things change – prices go up, schedules change, good places go bad and bad places go bankrupt – nothing stays the same. So, if you find things better or worse, recently opened or long since closed, please tell us and help make the next edition even more accurate and useful. We genuinely value all the feedback we receive. A well travelled team reads and acknowledges every letter, postcard and email and ensures that every morsel of information finds its way to the appropriate authors, editors and cartographers for verification.

Everyone who writes to us will find their name in the next edition of the appropriate guidebook. They will also receive the latest issue of *Planet Talk*, our quarterly printed newsletter, or *Comet*, our monthly email newsletter. Subscriptions to both newsletters are free. The very best contributions will be rewarded with a free guidebook.

Excerpts from your correspondence may appear in new editions of Lonely Planet guidebooks, the Lonely Planet Web site, *Planet Talk* or *Comet*, so please let us know if you *don't* want your letter published or your name acknowledged.

Send all correspondence to the Lonely Planet office closest to you:

Australia: Locked Bag 1, Footscray, Victoria 3011
USA: 150 Linden St, Oakland, CA 94607
UK: 10a Spring Place, London NW5 3BH
France: 1 rue du Dahomey, 75011 Paris

Or email us at: talk2us@lonelyplanet.com.au

For news, views and updates see our Web site: www.lonelyplanet.com

HOW TO USE A LONELY PLANET GUIDEBOOK

The best way to use a Lonely Planet guidebook is any way you choose. At Lonely Planet we believe the most memorable travel experiences are often those that are unexpected, and the finest discoveries are those you make yourself. Guidebooks are not intended to be used as if they provide a detailed set of infallible instructions!

Contents All Lonely Planet guidebooks follow roughly the same format. The Facts about the Destination chapters or sections give background information ranging from history to weather. Facts for the Visitor gives practical information on issues like visas and health. Getting There & Away gives a brief starting point for researching travel to and from the destination. Getting Around gives an overview of the transport options when you arrive.

The peculiar demands of each destination determine how subsequent chapters are broken up, but some things remain constant. We always start with background, then proceed to sights, places to stay, places to eat, entertainment, getting there and away, and getting around information – in that order.

Heading Hierarchy Lonely Planet headings are used in a strict hierarchical structure that can be visualised as a set of Russian dolls. Each heading (and its following text) is encompassed by any preceding heading that is higher on the hierarchical ladder.

Entry Points We do not assume guidebooks will be read from beginning to end, but that people will dip into them. The traditional entry points are the list of contents and the index. In addition, however, some books have a complete list of maps and an index map illustrating map coverage.

There may also be a colour map that shows highlights. These highlights are dealt with in greater detail in the Facts for the Visitor chapter, along with planning questions and suggested itineraries. Each chapter covering a geographical region usually begins with a locator map and another list of highlights. Once you find something of interest in a list of highlights, turn to the index.

Maps Maps play a crucial role in Lonely Planet guidebooks and include a huge amount of information. A legend is printed on the back page. We seek to have complete consistency between maps and text, and to have every important place in the text captured on a map. Map key numbers usually start in the top left corner.

> Although inclusion in a guidebook usually implies a recommendation we cannot list every good place. Exclusion does not necessarily imply criticism. In fact there are a number of reasons why we might exclude a place – sometimes it is simply inappropriate to encourage an influx of travellers.

Introduction

A visit to Wales has a bit of 'Alice in Wonderland' about it: here, within the mother of English-speaking nations, is an entire country where you might have to ask *Ydych chi'n siarad saesneg?*, 'Do you speak English?'.

Centuries of London-centredness has left the world thinking of Wales as a land of pious, hard-working but quarrelsome country folk out on the fringes of England. It's little wonder that this image persists: a people tends to be set apart by its language, and for 4½ centuries the Welsh have been aggressively weaned off of theirs. But peel away the PR and something richer emerges.

The Celts had occupied the whole of Britain for five centuries before the Romans arrived, and more or less continued to do so under Roman rule. But after the Romans left about AD 410, Angles and Saxons moved in, severing the Celts from their European roots and pushing them into the corners of the land.

Isolated and compressed, these once-diffuse Britons became something new, distinct, solid to the touch: Welsh (and up north, Scots). Their stories began to solidify into legends, their ancient beliefs into religion, their entertainments into art, their warrior bands into armies. An intense, highly durable culture was born, and Saxons and other invaders began to meet resistance.

With overwhelming military might the Normans put many Welsh rulers out of business and eventually pushed right across to the sea, but they never managed to make the land Norman. Even after being hammered by some of the most intense industrialisation the West has ever seen, Wales won't lie down.

This sense of a culture so concentrated as to be indestructible is something that makes Wales fascinating. Faced with the vanishing hope that it might ever become a *state*, Wales stubbornly remains a *country* – united, more or less, by territory and traditions, and a language that refuses to die.

The most profitable way to prepare for a journey to Wales is by getting to grips with its history. Wherever you go in Wales, history talks – the landscape talks, with its references to Arthur and Offa, with the outlines of Stone Age tombs, Celtic earthworks and holy wells, with the disfigured hillsides and rusting machinery of the Industrial Revolution; towns talk, with their medieval squares, stout walls, dour chapels and sad graveyards; and people talk, about their saints, their princes, their national heroes.

Travel through Wales with its history in mind and you'll see it as the perfect stage for a Tolkienesque saga of romance and bravery, treachery and danger. You may also find it easier to understand Welsh anger and longing, Welsh pride in the new-born National Assembly and in the first signs of a resurgence of the language.

But there's more to the place than abstractions. Wales is heavily rural and gorgeously green, a country that looks good even when it's soaking wet, as it often is. In its small space it has a range of landscapes to please almost everybody, especially with its 600 splendid miles of coastline, which is nowhere more than about 50 miles away. Some of the finest coastal and mountain countryside is protected within three national parks, though the Gower and Llŷn peninsulas and parts of Anglesey are just as deserving. Some parts have not been so lucky, with sections of the north coast ruined by shoddy bungalows and ugly caravan parks.

Wales' cities and towns tend to be less inspiring, though there are some prominent exceptions, from rustic settlements seemingly frozen in time to the buzz of Cardiff, Wales' vibrant capital city. You can gorge on medieval castles – with some 600 of them, mostly built to keep a lid on the Welsh, Wales is Europe's most densely fortified country. Edward I built a string of them in the north-west, and four – Caernarfon, Conwy, Beaumaris and Harlech – share

a listing as a UNESCO World Heritage Site. You can wonder at the dignified bleakness of the old mining towns; here too, at Blaenafon, Unesco has recognised the role they played.

The best way to appreciate the great Welsh outdoors is by walking, cycling or boating through it. Away from the bigger towns, public transport can sometimes be sparse, and you'll be happier with a car or the odd taxi for day-trips. Basing yourself at a small town or farmhouse B&B and exploring the surrounding countryside for a few days is much preferable to a linear, day-by-day slog by bus or train.

Wales is perhaps as upbeat and proud as it has been since Owain Glyndŵr's 15th-century near-revolution. 'Every day when I wake up I thank the Lord I'm Welsh' run the endlessly quoted lyrics from Catatonia's now-classic album, *International Velvet*. This is a good time to visit and dispel the cobwebbed stereotypes of the place.

Facts about Wales

HISTORY
Prehistory & the Celts

Much of Wales' early history remains unknown. The earliest evidence of human habitation dates from some 250,000 years ago. Stone monuments and burial chambers dating from the Neolithic Age, such as Pentre Ifan in Pembrokeshire, dot the landscape. These are often referred to, mistakenly, as Celtic.

'Celtic' in its general sense refers to a Europe-wide confederation of tribes, linked by language, who made iron tools, rode horses, shared strong artistic traditions and eventually came to be quite powerful. It was only after around 600 BC that the influence of the Celts was felt in the British Isles, probably spread by bands of adventure-warriors and their druids or priests. Hill forts such as Dinorben and Pendinas testify to the Celtic presence in Wales, although much of what is known of Celtic civilisation in Britain has been through the eyes of later Roman occupiers, and its remains are obscured by those of the Romans.

The Romans

By the time Julius Caesar landed in Britain in 55 BC, Wales was inhabited primarily by the Silures and Dematae tribes in the south and the Ordovices and Deceangli in the north. The Ordovices and Silures in particular resisted the Roman advance, both of them at some point led by Caradog (Caractacus). Caradog was eventually defeated in AD 51 and taken to Rome in chains, where he was released by the Emperor Claudius and, according to tradition, made a moving speech, demanding 'Why do you, who possess so many palaces, covet our poor tents?'

By AD 60, Roman legions had invaded Mona (Anglesey), the centre of druid power, to stamp out continued resistance. Even so, Wales was not easily subdued nor completely Romanised, despite the establishment of garrisons at Caerleon and Chester

---

The Red Dragon

You can't go anywhere in Wales without seeing its national symbol, the red dragon. No one really knows when it first appeared here, though it's been around at least since the time of the Romans, who probably first heard about the beast from the Parthians. And they may well have been inspired by stories of Alexander the Great's journeys to India and the later trade with China.

At any rate the Anglo-Saxon King Harold, and Cadwaladr, 7th-century king of Gwynedd, liked it so much they used it for their standards in battle. Featured in legends (see the Myths & Legends special section), the red dragon became a powerful symbol and by the 14th century was recognised as the emblem of Welsh archers. It was the quarter-Welsh Henry Tudor (later King Henry VII) who made the dragon part of the Welsh flag in the 15th century.

---

and further settlements – eg, at Caernarfon and Carmarthen – along with villas in the fertile south. Some roads were built, but much of the interior held little attraction, save for mining enterprises such as the gold mines at Dolau Cothi.

With the Roman empire facing growing problems towards the end of the 4th century AD, the connection between Rome and Britannia was finally severed in AD 410. In the wake of the Roman withdrawal, migration from Germany seems to have increased. Despite doubts about whether or not King Arthur should be considered a historical figure, it appears that a British leader, possibly of that name, emerged and proved victorious against Saxon invaders, before being killed or disappearing at the battle of Camlan around AD 515.

The Birth of Wales

The Roman exit seems a reasonable point to take for the beginnings of a Welsh nation. This was the only part of the western Roman empire not immediately overrun when the Romans left. A number of separate kingdoms evolved, chief amongst them Powys, Dyfed, Ceredigion, Ystrad Tywi, Brycheiniog, Morgannwg and Gwent, names which in many cases were later revived as the names of counties. Dyfed, in the south-west, faced many Irish invasions.

For many of the other kingdoms the connection with the 'Old North', the Brythonic kingdoms of Rheged and Gododdin in what is now Scotland and Cumbria, was vital. Around AD 400 a leader named Cunedda is said to have arrived from Gododdin to drive Irish invaders from north-western Wales. His memory survives in the name of the kingdom (and the present-day county) of Gwynedd.

The earliest surviving Welsh literature, the poems of Taliesin and Aneirin, were probably composed in the late 6th and early 7th centuries in the northern kingdoms. By the late 6th century a distinct Welsh language seems to have emerged from its Brythonic ancestor. Its closest Celtic relations are Cornish and Breton. The word *Cymry* for the land and its people was first used around 580.

By the 8th century, the Brythons had been cut off by invaders from their compatriots in Cumbria. Territorial scuffles led Offa, ruler of the powerful Anglo-Saxon kingdom of Mercia (757–96), to build his famous dike from Prestatyn to Chepstow to mark the borders of his kingdom.

During the period after the Roman withdrawal, a monastic form of Christianity had gained ground in Wales, introduced via sea routes from Ireland, France and elsewhere in Europe, and grafted onto old Celtic beliefs. The names of the early saints – Dyfrig, Illtud, Teilo and Dewi (David) amongst them – are echoed in a host of place names, particularly those beginning with *llan* (church). Only reluctantly did the Celtic Church eventually yield, in the 8th century, to the authority of Canterbury and Rome.

Early Welsh Rulers

The 9th and 10th centuries witnessed a period of savage coastal attacks in the south by Danish and Norse pirates. These Viking attacks were one factor that led the small kingdoms of Wales to begin cooperating. Two early rulers who united several kingdoms under their authority were Rhodri Mawr (Rhodri the Great, d.878) and his grandson, Hywel Dda (Hywel the Good, d.950). Hywel is believed to have consolidated Welsh Law, a system based mainly on relations between kinship groups, and affording women and children greater respect than other legal systems of the time. For instance, a woman had the right to divorce her husband on the grounds that he was impotent, a leper or had bad breath!

Ironically, as Wales was becoming a recognisable entity, so did it fall further under the aegis of the English crown. In 927, faced with the destructive onslaught of the Vikings, the Welsh kings recognised Athelstan, Anglo-Saxon king of England, as their overlord in exchange for an alliance against the Vikings.

Wales Under the Normans

By the time the Normans arrived in England in 1066, the Welsh had returned to their warring, independent ways. To secure his new kingdom William the Conqueror set up powerful, feudal barons – called Lords Marcher – along the Welsh borders at Chester, Shrewsbury and Hereford, from where they repeatedly raided Wales in the 11th and 12th centuries, eventually occupying most accessible lowland areas in South and Mid Wales.

Curiously enough, this time of troubles is also a seminal time for Welsh literature, with court poets, the *gogynfeirdd*, honing their craft, and *The Mabinogion*, a collection of fantastic tales with roots in oral tales of the Celtic gods, soon to be transcribed. The oldest surviving manuscript in the Welsh language is the 12th-century *Black Book of Carmarthen*, now in the National Library of Wales at Aberystwyth.

One of the greatest Welsh leaders in the south arose at this time – Rhys ap Gruffydd, known as Lord Rhys, based at Dinefwr, near Llandeilo. After the English King Henry II seized great tracts of his land in 1157, Rhys fought back and by 1166 had regained most of it, and set up a new court at Cardigan. It was here that he convened the first-ever *eisteddfod* (see under Arts later in this chapter for more on this bardic and musical competition).

Llywelyn ab Iorwerth, also called Llywelyn the Great (d.1240), ruler of Gwynedd, attempted to set up a Welsh state along feudal, hereditary lines, although the English Crown proved reluctant to acknowledge the situation. After internal struggles, his grandson Llywelyn ap Gruffydd (Llewellyn II or Llewellyn the Last) took control of Gwynedd. In 1258 he adopted the title 'Prince of Wales', the first leader to do so, and in the 1267 Treaty of Montgomery was recognised as such by Henry III of England.

But Llywelyn's triumph was short-lived, and by 1277 he had lost much of what he had achieved. He was plagued by financial problems and by struggles with other Welsh princes, some of whom preferred to pay homage to Henry's powerful successor, Edward I. When Llewelyn's brother Dafydd went to war against Edward in 1282, he was forced to back him, with disastrous consequences.

The campaign ended abruptly on 11 December 1282 when Llewelyn was killed by an English soldier at Cilmeri, a few miles from Builth Wells – whether by accident, ambush or treachery is not clear. His head was despatched to London and his body was buried at Cwmhir Abbey. Said one chronicler, 'And then all Wales was cast to the ground'. Poets greeted his death as the end of the world.

Edward mopped up the remaining Welsh resistance, including Llywelyn's brother, Dafydd, who was executed in brutal fashion in Shrewsbury in 1283. Llywelyn's infant daughter, Gwenllian, surely one of the most forlorn figures in Welsh history, was placed in a nunnery in Norfolk until her death in 1337. Edward confirmed his conquest of Gwynedd with the 1284

Statute of Rhuddlan, which divided Wales between the Principality (Llywelyn's former territories, now directly controlled by the Crown), and the remaining semi-autonomous Marcher lordships.

Edward, so the story goes, promised to give the Welsh a prince who didn't speak English. In the event he named his infant son – the future Edward II, born at Caernarfon and at that point not speaking any language at all – as Prince of Wales, a practice that the British royal family maintains to this day with the eldest son of the reigning monarch.

The country's most imposing castles are the product of Edward's campaign against Llywelyn. Flint, Rhuddlan, Aberystwyth and Builth were built in 1277 and the remarkable castles at Conwy, Caernarfon, Harlech, Cricieth and Beaumaris – designed by James of St George, an architect from Savoy – during and after the 1282–3 campaign. They can be seen either as symbols of the subjugation of the Welsh, or as evidence of the strength perceived necessary to overcome Welsh resistance. Perhaps symbolically, Conwy castle was built over the original tomb of Llywelyn the Great.

Boroughs were established alongside the castles. Those of Conway, Caernarfon and Beaumaris in particular were intended as English colonies, with the bulk of the inhabitants imported from the English border counties with promises of rent-free land for 10 years. The lands around these boroughs were cleared of their native population, who were relocated in order to provide farmland for the newcomers. Similar but smaller clearances occurred in some rural areas, such as the Vale of Clwyd. English settlers remained a minority and many of their descendants were assimilated into local communities over time.

The Welsh were a conquered people and were treated as such.

Owain Glyndŵr
Simmering resentment boiled over in the Glyndŵr rebellion of 1400. Owain ap Gruffydd (Owen Glendower to the English), lord of Glyndyfrdwy, although a descendant of the royal house of Powys, was

an unlikely rebel. He had been educated in London and was at one time squire to Henry of Bolingbroke, later King Henry IV.

His initial rising stemmed merely from a quarrel over land with his Marcher neighbour, Lord Grey of Ruthin. He took Grey to court but the case was dismissed, apparently with the words 'What care we for barefoot Welsh dogs?' Following the first skirmishes, Henry passed a series of penal laws, forbidding the Welsh from bearing arms, holding public office and trading in land in the English boroughs.

These may have actually increased support for the rebellion, which gained momentum during the early years of the 15th century, backed by many of the Welsh gentry. By 1404 Glyndŵr controlled most of Wales and, proclaiming himself Prince of Wales, summoned a parliament at Machynlleth. He gave the English a wake-up call by capturing the fortresses of Harlech and Aberystwyth, and began forming alliances with foreign powers such as Scotland and France, whose enmity with England made them natural allies.

But things turned shaky when Prince Henry, son of Henry IV and hero of the Battle of Agincourt, defeated the Welsh at Grosmont and Usk. In 1406 Glyndŵr retreated north, and gradually the English regained control. After that, Glyndŵr, who had come as close as anyone ever had to uniting the country, simply disappeared. Speculation about his death and his burial place continues to this day.

The ruins of his home at Sycharth are barely discernible, but the parliament house at Machynlleth – or one very like it – still stands. For many years Glyndŵr was dismissed as a renegade and a rebel by Tudor and Stuart historians, but during the 18th century was rehabilitated as a national hero, a status he has maintained ever since.

The Tudors & the Acts of Union

The remainder of the 15th century saw the Welsh and English in many ways learning to coexist, though old tensions remained, as is evident from an English verse of the period – 'Beware of Wales/Christ Jesus may us keep/Lest it make not/Our child's child to weep'. Welsh poets wrote of a second Arthur or Owain, a *mab darogan* (son of prophecy) who would restore the fortunes of the Welsh race and lead them to victory over the English.

Most agreed that Henry Tudor best fit the role, after his victory at Bosworth in 1485. Henry was a quarter Welsh by blood, a descendant of the Tudor family of Penmynydd in Anglesey who had once supported Glyndŵr. One of their number, Owain ap Maredudd ap Tudur, acquired a post in the royal household and won the affections of Henry V's widow, Katherine de Valois. Their eldest son, Edmund, married into the House of Lancaster, through which his son Henry acquired an admittedly shaky claim to the throne.

Henry emerged as the most prominent Lancastrian claimant in opposition to Richard III. In reality, he gained the throne by defeating Richard in battle, aided by his Welsh supporters. After fleeing his native Pembroke in 1471, at the age of 14, for 14 more years of exile in Brittany, he landed on the Welsh coast near Milford Haven and marched through Wales towards Bosworth, gaining support along the way. Tradition has it that one of his Welsh supporters, possibly Rhys ap Thomas, struck the blow that killed Richard III.

The Tudor dynasty reigned until the death of Elizabeth I in 1603, though it must be said that Henry VII was the only one who seemed aware of his Welsh roots. St David's Day was celebrated at his court, and his Welsh supporters flocked there in the hope of preferment. But his priority was to secure the throne for his descendants and he needed to concentrate on his power base in England.

Little attention was paid to Wales until the reign of his son, Henry VIII, when the Acts of Union finally incorporated Wales and England in 1536 and 1543. The Welsh were henceforth to be regarded as equal citizens and were granted parliamentary representation. Welsh Law was abolished and the country was divided into thirteen counties, administered on the English model. Despite the objective of uniformity, the

Acts in effect created a border between England and Wales, where English counties met the new Welsh ones.

English was declared the official language of law and administration in Wales, and no one without knowledge of English could hold public office. In the long term, this clause in the 1536 Act may have contributed to the notion that English was the language of success and prestige, and may have encouraged the gentry to gradually turn their backs on the Welsh language. The gentry – already in the main bilingual – were most likely to hold public office, and they leapt at the chance to enhance their status and influence as members of parliament, justices of the peace, high sheriffs and a host of other roles. Their ancestors might have fought with Glyndŵr but they saw the advantages of cooperation with the Tudor dynasty. In effect they were entrusted with the day-to-day governance of the country on behalf of the Crown.

Part of the motivation behind the Acts of Union was to find a solution to the abiding problem of the Welsh March, created by the Statute of Rhuddlan in 1284. The March had become a byword for lawlessness as of the semi-independent power of its lords and the lack of uniform law and jurisdiction made it easy for felons to escape justice by fleeing from one lordship to another, or from principality to March. Although the power of the Marcher lords was waning by the early 16th century, their anomalous position could not continue into the era of European nation-states. The Crown sought to tighten its hold over the farthest reaches of the realm, and the union with Wales can be seen as part of the move towards centralisation.

It may also have been prompted by a desire to ensure that the new religious changes were effectively implemented in Wales, since Henry VIII's reign also witnessed the break with Rome and the Catholic Church.

The Welsh Church & the Welsh Language

The Church in Wales came under the jurisdiction of Canterbury, thus Protestantism was introduced via legislation passed by Henry VIII and his descendants. There was no strong resistance to the new faith in Wales, despite the dissolution of abbeys such as Valle Crucis, Neath and Strata Florida, which had been centres of Welsh culture for centuries, and despite the introduction of an English Prayer Book. Yet there is little evidence that the Welsh welcomed the religious changes, and every evidence that they quietly clung to familiar Catholic practices such as praying to the saints and visiting shrines and holy wells. Only three Protestant martyrs died for their faith under the Catholic Mary Tudor: Rawlins White, a fisherman from Cardiff, William Nicholl of Haverfordwest and Robert Ferrar, former Protestant bishop of St David's.

Despite these unpromising beginnings, in the long term Protestantism would come to be regarded as an essential element in Welsh national identity, particularly after the translation of the Bible into Welsh. Elizabeth I assented to the 1563 Act for the translation of the Scriptures as a result of petitions from Welsh Protestants and humanists who argued that it was impossible to convert the people of Wales without a version of the Bible they could understand. The translated New Testament, chiefly the work of the brilliant humanist scholar from Denbighshire, William Salesbury, appeared in 1567 and the complete Bible, the work of William Morgan, vicar of Llanrhaeadr-ym-Mochnant, appeared in 1588.

Welsh was the only non-state language in Europe to produce a translation of the Scriptures within a century of the Protestant Reformation, and this did much to root Protestantism as the national religion – and to prop up the Welsh language. This, along with the achievements of humanists in producing grammars and dictionaries during this period, helped preserve Welsh as a literary language. As a spoken language, its position was unassailable, and it would remain the language of the majority until well into the 19th century. But had it not also been established in the 16th century as a language of public worship and as a medium for the written word, it might eventually have experienced a decline similar to that which befell its Celtic cousins, Cornish and Manx.

Welsh loyalty to the Tudors was inherited by their descendants, the Stuarts, who united the crowns of Scotland and England in 1603, although a formal union was not confirmed until 1707. James I exchanged the Welsh dragon, which Henry VII had incorporated into the royal coat of arms, for the Scottish unicorn. But the Welsh remained loyal to the Crown throughout the Civil War of the 17th century (as a result of which Wales is full of the ruins of perfectly sound castles wrecked by the Roundheads so they couldn't be used again), and resented the period of Commonwealth government in the 1650s. They fervently welcomed Charles II and the Restoration of the monarchy in 1660.

Education & Nonconformism

The late 17th century and early 18th century witnessed the first attempts to educate the mass of the Welsh population. Grammar schools established from the 16th century onwards had provided schooling mainly for the sons of the gentry and more affluent farmers. With the lapse in 1695 of licensing laws which restricted the printing of books to London, Oxford and Cambridge, printing presses were established in Wales – the first by Isaac Carter in Adpar near Newcastle Emlyn in 1718 – and a huge increase in the number of books printed in Welsh followed. Most of these were religious works, aimed at instilling saving knowledge of the Gospel.

A similar religious motivation fuelled the educational initiatives of the period, including the work of the Society for the Promotion of Christian Knowledge and the circulating schools of Griffith Jones. Jones, rector of Llanddowror in Carmarthenshire, founded the system of circulating schools in the 1730s and made the pioneering decision to use Welsh as the medium of instruction. At a time when an estimated 70% of the population were monoglot Welsh speakers, this decision ensured the success of the schools. By the time he died in 1761 over 200,000 men, women and children had learnt to read the Bible in his schools. Efforts to provide instruction in Welsh continued with the work of the Sunday Schools into the 19th century.

The 1730s also saw the birth of the Methodist Revival, centred on the vast, impoverished diocese of St David's in the south. Under the leadership of Daniel Rowland, Howel Harris and William Williams, the influence of Methodism gradually spread throughout the country, gaining a firm hold in the north and in the new industrial communities of the south by the end of the century.

Ultimately this changed the religious complexion of Wales for good, not only by establishing a new denomination in 1811, but also by reinvigorating Nonconformist groups such as the Independents and the Baptists. By the 19th century the majority of Christian worshippers in Wales no longer chose the Established Church – a fact which would lead to deep dissatisfaction about the compulsion to pay tithe to the Church, and to increasing calls by the 20th century for the disestablishment of the Church.

The Revival also sparked off Wales' great hymn-writing tradition, its best-known exponent being William Williams of Pantycelyn, author of the famous 'Guide me, O Thou Great Jehovah', a favourite of rugby-watching crowds for generations.

Romantic Wales

Towards the end of the 18th century the influence of the Romantic Revival helped make Wales popular with tourists for the first time. Napoleon was making European travel difficult, and so the wilder landscapes of the British Isles became popular with the genteel traveller. Landscape painters such as Richard Wilson did much to popularise the rugged mountains and ruined castles. Wales was the ideal location for those enamoured of Gothic romances.

At the same time, Romanticism also influenced a new sense of Welsh identity based on the rediscovery of Celtic and druidic traditions. This was very much the

Madog

As part and parcel of Wales' Romantic renaissance, the story of Madog, said to have discovered America in 1170, gained popularity. Used during Queen Elizabeth's reign to justify the colonisation of America, it was now deployed to gave the Welsh a sense of pride in their past. It was widely believed that Madog and his followers had intermarried with native Americans, and an expedition to find the Welsh Indians set off in 1796. Its leader, John Evans, helped map the River Missouri in his search, but was disappointed not to find any Welsh speakers along its banks.

🐪🐪🐪🐪🐪🐪🐪🐪🐪🐪🐪🐪🐪🐪

work of Edward Williams – Iolo Morganwg to give him his bardic name – who was responsible for the creation of the Gorsedd of Bards which met for the first time in Primrose Hill in London in 1792. In 1819, in the back yard of the Ivy Bush Hotel in Carmarthen, Iolo's Gorsedd met as part of the first 'modern' eisteddfod.

The tradition of the *eisteddfod* (literally 'session', a meeting of bards and musicians to compete with each other) dates back centuries – the one called by Lord Rhys in Cardigan in 1176 is frequently cited as the first 'national' eisteddfod – but it made a comeback in the late 18th century as part of the cultural revival of the period. Scholars were increasingly concerned about the need to preserve the culture and heritage of their country, which seemed in danger of being lost with the end of the tradition of household bards maintained by the gentry. Efforts were made to collect and publish literature such as the work of the gifted 14th-century poet, Dafydd ap Gwilym.

Romantic Wales continued to flourish with the efforts of Augusta Hall, Lady Llanover (whose husband, Benjamin Hall, was the industrialist after whom Big Ben was probably named). It was she who invented the Welsh national costume which generations of schoolgirls have been condemned to wear on St David's Day ever since! It was based on fashions out of date in England for

years but still worn in Wales and considered picturesque by Lady Llanover.

Industrialisation

The Welsh economy had long been based on agriculture and especially reliant on the drovers who took animals to be sold in English markets and returned with hard cash (which is one of the main reasons why Wales' first banks were founded in connection with the droving trade). This system of trade across the border helps explain why the main lines of communication run from east to west. North–south travel has always been more difficult.

But from the mid-18th century another major development was to change the face of Wales. The growth of industry was centred on the north-east and south-east, primarily associated with the development of the iron industry. Ironworks proliferated along the northern rim of the South Wales coalfield, particularly around Merthyr Tydfil. This led to a concentration of population in the counties of Glamorgan and Monmouth, the growth of industrial communities and urbanisation, and the construction of roads, canals and tramways to cope with the transport needs of the new industry.

The industrial dynasties of the Guest and Crawshay families came to dominate life in the new communities just as landowners had dominated rural life. Although in the initial stages of industrialisation most of the workforce migrated from rural Wales, by the second half of the 19th century the numbers of non-Welsh speakers would swell and prove a threat to the continued dominance of the language, especially in the south. From the mid-19th century the iron industry would decline and coal come to be of greater importance.

Industrialisation also created an emerging working-class consciousness which led to protest, unrest and the growth of trade unions. The first half of the 19th century was characterised by protests, as calls for parliamentary reform to give the vote to more people grew, along with discontent with the Poor Law Amendment Act of 1834 enforcing the building of Dickensian-style workhouses throughout England and Wales.

The Merthyr Rising of 1831 was the first time the red flag of revolution was flown in Britain, and the execution of Richard Lewis, or Dic Penderyn, for allegedly assaulting a soldier during the rising still invokes strong feeling. There is little doubt that he was wrongly convicted and many novels, songs and poems record the injustice of his fate. The bloody Chartist march on Newport in November 1839 may or may not have been an attempt to establish a 'Silurian Republic' in the south-east, but it certainly frightened the authorities.

With the rural south-west being ravaged by the Rebecca Riots from 1839–43, it is small wonder that Wales seemed a hotbed of malcontents and revolutionaries to the government in London. The 'Daughters of Rebecca' took out their anger at tolls levied on roads controlled by the Turnpike Trusts by blackening their faces, dressing in women's clothes and acting out a pantomime which resulted in the tollgates being smashed. 'Mother Rebecca' would command her children to tear down the gate which blocked her way and they would eagerly comply. The movement took inspiration from traditions of community justice and its name from a verse in Genesis: 'And they blessed Rebecca, and said unto her, Thou art our sister, be thou the mother of thousands of millions, and let thy seed possess the gate of those which hate them'.

Tensions between the Established Church and Nonconformity also increased with the 1847 Commission on Education, better known in Wales as the Treason of the Blue Books. The commission's findings (published in blue-covered reports) on the poor state of education were fairly accurate, but what incensed people was its statements about the morality of the Welsh in general and their women in particular. That the commissioners, who were English and Anglican, attributed this alleged immorality to the influences of Nonconformity and the Welsh language, only stoked the fires of Welsh anger. For the remainder of the 19th century,

Nonconformist leaders seemed obsessed with disproving the accusations by peddling an image of Wales as a country of unimpeachable character and morality, the 'Land of White Gloves', so-called after the habit of assize judges of drawing on a pair of white gloves when there were no cases before the court.

Politics & Depression

The second half of the 19th century saw Liberalism gaining a firm hold in Wales, particularly after reform acts in 1867 and 1888 extended the vote to the majority of adult males. The 1868 election was seen as something of a turning point, with the election of Henry Richard as the first radical member of Parliament in Merthyr Tydfil. Some tenant farmers who voted Liberal against the wishes of their Tory landlords found themselves evicted from their lands, giving rise to protest which helped lead to the passing of the Secret Ballot Act of 1872.

Liberal Nonconformity held sway over much of Wales during the late 19th and early 20th century, even producing a prime minister in David Lloyd George (see the boxed text 'The Rise of Lloyd George'). But in 1900 Merthyr Tydfil returned Keir Hardie as its second member of parliament (MP), and Wales' first Labour MP. As the 20th century progressed, South Wales in particular was to adopt Labour as its politics, and rugby as its national sport (for more on rugby, see the boxed text under Spectator Sports in the Facts for the Visitor chapter).

Rural and industrial Wales suffered the results of economic depression in the interwar period. Thousands were driven to emigrate in search of employment. After WWII the Labour government tried to restructure the Welsh economy, but even after nationalisation in 1948, the numbers employed in the coal industry continued to fall. The latter part of the 20th century saw the decline of traditional industry, in particular the closure of the majority of coal mines. The Miners' Strike of 1984–5 was a bitter struggle which ended in defeat for the National Union of Miners and, if anything, hastened the closure of the pits.

The Rise of Lloyd George

David Lloyd George was born in Manchester on 17 January 1863, son of an English schoolteacher father and a Welsh mother. When his father's health declined the family moved to a Pembrokeshire farm, and when his father died his mother moved with her three children to the home of her brother, a Baptist minister in the small town of Llanystumdwy, on the Llŷn Peninsula.

The young David was a model student at the local (Anglicised) church school, and went on to become an attorney in 1878. His political inclinations led him to join the Liberal Party, and in 1890 he was elected the MP for the Caernarfon Boroughs, defeating the local Tory squire by just 18 votes. He was to keep this seat for 55 years, and before long had made a name for himself in the House of Commons.

Appointed president of the Board of Trade for the new Liberal government in 1905, within three years he was Chancellor of the Exchequer, a position from which he launched a broad programme of social reforms, including old age pensions, a 1909 budget that taxed the wealthy to fund services for the poor, and the 1911 National Insurance Act to provide health and unemployment insurance.

During WWI he was Minister for Munitions, and in 1916 was made Secretary of State. Shortly afterwards he replaced Herbert Asquith as Prime Minister, and in this capacity played a major role in the Peace Conference at Versailles. But domestic politics – especially problems in Ireland, postwar industrial unrest and economic reconstruction – wore him down, and in 1922 he bowed out of politics for good.

AMGUEDDFA LLOYD GEORGE MUSEUM

In 1943, two years after the death of his wife Margaret, Lloyd George – at the age of 80 – married Frances Stevenson, his longtime personal secretary and mistress. He died in 1945 at Llanystumdwy, where there is now a small museum devoted to his life (see the Snowdonia & the Llŷn chapter).

Nia Lynn Powell-Jones

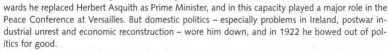

Welsh Revival?

In the 20th century Wales acquired some national institutions, and national feeling began to grow. The University of Wales had been established in 1893 from the constituent colleges of Aberystwyth, Cardiff and Bangor. In 1907 charters were granted to the National Library in Aberystwyth and the National Museum in Cardiff. Half a century later Cardiff would be declared the country's capital city.

In 1925, during the national eisteddfod at Pwllheli, six young men got together in a hotel room and formed Plaid Cenedlaethol Cymru (the Welsh Nationalist Party), to campaign for self-government. It failed to gain wide support for some years, but nationalism would gain greater support during the second half of the century. By the A487 south of Aberystwyth is a dilapidated wall bearing the painted slogan *cofiwch Dryweryn* ('remember Tryweryn'). This graffiti has remained in place for some 40 years, evolving into a familiar landmark and even forming the subject of a painting by artist Aneirin Jones. It commemorates one of the most emotive events in 20th-century Welsh history. This Tryweryn is the lake, near Bala, created by the inundation of the village of Capel Celyn and the surrounding valley, to provide water for the city of Liverpool. Despite fervent campaigning, including a march by the villagers through the streets of Liverpool itself, the project went ahead. Not one Welsh MP voted in favour of the measure in the House of Commons in 1957, but there were too few of them to make any difference, which to Plaid Cymru signified their failure to represent Welsh opinion and influence Welsh affairs in parliament.

The sixties was a decade of protest in Wales, accompanied by a flourishing of the pop scene and moves to establish Welsh publishing houses and record labels. In 1962 Cymdeithas yr Iaith Gymraeg (the Welsh Language Society), a pressure group campaigning for bilingual road signs, legal status for the language and Welsh-medium radio and television, was founded. Protests were particularly vociferous in 1969, the year of the investiture of Prince Charles as Prince of Wales in Caernarfon. The 1960s also saw the brief appearance of the Free Wales Army, a paramilitary group which did more posturing than damage, but whose Irish echoes gave the English palpitations.

In 1964 the Labour government appointed Jim Griffiths as the first Secretary of State for Wales, with cabinet rank. In 1966 the first Plaid Cymru MP was elected to Westminster when Gwynfor Evans won the Carmarthen by-election. The Welsh Language Act of 1967 began the process of recognition for the language in public life. Further electoral successes by Plaid Cymru in the 1970s may have started people thinking about a measure of Welsh self-government.

Although the numbers who spoke the Welsh language declined from census to census, by the 1990s the numbers would start to stabilise at around 20% of the population. Welsh-medium education became more widely available with the establishment of nurseries, primary and secondary schools and university courses. After a long campaign, the Welsh-medium television channel S4C began broadcasting in 1982 (see the boxed text 'Sianel Pedwar Cymru' in the Facts for the Visitor chapter).

Devolution

On St David's Day in 1979 a devolution referendum was put before the Welsh people. The result was a resounding 'No' vote. Little had been done by Plaid or Labour to ensure public support for the measure; indeed, although it was a Labour policy, prominent Labour MPs (including Neil Kinnock) campaigned against devolution.

By September 1997, when devolution was introduced again by the Labour government, there was greater solidarity in the Labour ranks and a greater spirit of cooperation with Plaid and the Liberal Democrats on this issue. In a nailbiting finish, a narrow majority voted in favour of a National Assembly.

The Assembly was duly established in Cardiff in 1999. Although lacking the legislative powers granted to the Scottish parliament, it took over many of the duties which had previously fallen to the Welsh Office. The election of Assembly members resulted in a slender Labour majority, with Plaid Cymru in second place, gaining some astonishing victories in traditional Labour strongholds such as Rhondda and Islwyn.

The establishment of the Assembly, the building of the Millennium Stadium in time to host the rugby world cup and the success of rock bands such as the Manic Street Preachers and Catatonia seemed to herald a new period of confidence and optimism regarding the new millennium. On the other hand, the loss of jobs in the steel industry, problems in the agricultural sector and continued concerns regarding the Welsh language suggest that the Assembly will be faced with many challenges.

GEOGRAPHY

Covering some 8017 sq miles, Wales is approximately 170 miles long and 60 miles wide. Surrounded by sea on three sides (with over 600 miles of coastline), its border to the east with England still runs roughly along Offa's Dike, the giant defensive earthwork constructed in the 8th century.

Wales has a mostly mountainous but very diverse landscape, moulded largely by the great ice sheets of the last Ice Age. It has three major mountain systems: the Black Mountains and the rounded Brecon Beacons in the south and the more rugged mountains of Snowdonia in the northwest which lie at the northern tip of the Cambrian Mountains running north–south throughout much of central Wales. These glaciated mountain areas are deeply cut by narrow river valleys and feature lakes of glacial origin.

Wales' most prominent peaks are Snowdon – at 1113m the highest peak in England and Wales – and 895m Cader Idris near Dolgellau, while the dour moorland heights of Plynlimon (754m), east of Aberystwyth, are the source of five rivers (Severn, Wye, Dulas, Llyfnant and Rheidol). Rolling upland moorlands between 180m and 600m stretch from Denbigh in the north to the Glamorgan valleys in the south, ending on the western coast in spectacular cliffs and the plains of river estuaries. Inland, among the foothills, are waterfalls, rivers and bogs and remnants of ancient forest, while the eastern border with England is characterised by a rolling, pastoral landscape.

GEOLOGY

Wales can boast one of the richest and most diverse geological heritages in the world. As early as the 17th century, geologists were drawn to the mysteries of this mountainous land whose rippled rocks – appearing in some places to be folded, elsewhere stretched or squashed or bent – bear intriguing signs of ancient floods, volcanoes or rivers of ice, of tropical seas and equatorial swamps.

Edward Lhuyd was one of the earliest geologists to cast some light, identifying fossils (known nowadays as trilobites) here in 1698. More significant discoveries followed in the 19th century by Adam Sedgwick, Professor of Geology at Cambridge and the first to apply the term 'Cambrian' to rocks in northern Wales dating back 500 million years. Sedgwick's contemporary, Roderick Murchison, coined 'Silurian' (after the Silures, an ancient Welsh tribe) to identify another epoch (some 400 million years ago) while 'Ordovician' (after the Ordovices tribe) now identifies rocks of 440 to 500 million years ago. Other Welsh place names (eg Llanvirn and Llandovery) are also now common geological terms.

Most of Wales features very old rocks indeed, from the pre-Cambrian to Jurassic era (180 million years ago); some of the oldest exposed rocks in the world are around St David's Head. The causes of Wales' extraordinary geology lie in those Cambrian times when a huge ocean, the Iapetus, separated the southern half of Britain, together with Wales, from the northern half. The dramatic continental collision (lasting millions of years) which closed this ocean caused molten rock to burst out and congeal into rounded 'pillows' (typically evident today in south-western Anglesey). Volcanic eruptions entombed marine life (there are fossil shells on the summit of Snowdon), the immense pressures creating the folded, squashed rock effects and deposits of slate. Huge mountains created by the collision were then split up by extreme temperatures, some eventually petering out to be eroded and washed away into the rock layers known as Old Red Sandstone which form the relatively flat Brecon Beacons and Black Mountains.

Wales' limestone landscapes were formed by layer after layer of algae and coral reefs piling up on the ocean floor over millions of years; its rich deposits of coal were formed by forests submerged in equatorial swamps, buried under sand and sea and mud in times of tropical heat. After the heat came the ice, with the last Ice Age (ending some 15,000 years ago) carving out Wales' broad river valleys, its glaciers scouring the landscape.

CLIMATE

Although Welsh weather is as difficult to second-guess as anywhere else in the UK, it is probably fair to say that it suffers from an excess of rainfall: around 1350mm annually, with January regularly soaking in at least 150mm. In 2000 excessive autumnal rain caused widespread floods in Wales. Westerly and south-westerly winds can also make life pretty miserable, especially when it is raining as well. But, the closeness of the mountains to the coast means that you can encounter very different climatic conditions within a relatively short distance.

Average temperatures range from around 5°C in winter (the uplands can be considerably colder, with frequent snow) to 16°C in summer.

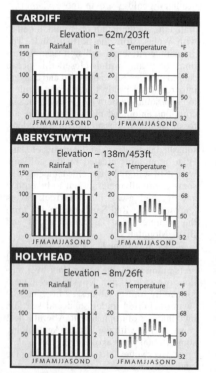

ECOLOGY & ENVIRONMENT

Wales has vast areas of environmentally precious countryside. Its three national parks (see the Flora & Fauna section later for details) and five Areas of Outstanding Natural Beauty or AONBs (Gower Peninsula, Anglesey Coast, Wye Valley, Llŷn Peninsula and Clwydian Range) constitute about a quarter of Wales' total area. There are also 64 National Nature Reserves, 999 Sites of Special Scientific Interest (SSSIs), 40 Local Nature Reserves, six Environmentally Sensitive Areas, 10 Wetlands of Designated International Importance and over 40 Special Areas of Conservation and 13 Special Protection Areas (both EU designations in the 'Natura 2000' network), not to mention over 311 miles of coastline defined as Heritage Coast (outstanding, undeveloped stretches of coastline requiring special management) and a Marine Nature Reserve in Pembrokeshire.

Wales' efforts to improve or preserve its less-protected areas have shifted into high gear in recent years. For example, the number of its beaches to achieve Blue Flag status (Europe's highest accolade for clean beaches) has risen from two in 1995 to 22 in 2000. And anyone returning to South Wales who'd last seen the place in its coal-mining days would scarcely recognise the valleys now. The mines have closed, many of the ugly slagheaps have been grassed over and the air is cleaner than it's been for centuries.

Much of this transformation is thanks to the Welsh Development Agency (WDA) which has spent £400 million in the last 25 years to reclaim or transform previously derelict or industrial land and invigorate local communities. Among its major success stories are the clean-up of the notoriously polluted River Taff; the removal of tipped deposits in Pentre in the Rhondda Valley; and the development of a Forest Park in North Wales where the Parc Lead mine previously posed serious erosion problems. Had such a hands-on approach applied earlier, the Aberfan disaster (see Around Merthyr Tydfil in the South-East Wales & the Brecon Beacons chapter for details) might never have happened. Certainly, safety regulations and environmental concerns have increased greatly since then. The WDA's Web site is at www.wda.org.co.uk.

But there have been notable disasters too – notably the massive spill from the *Sea Empress* (see the boxed text). As in the rest of the UK, other environmental problems include overuse of pesticides, destruction of hedgerows and an ever increasing number of vehicles on the roads (a 20% increase in Wales between 1986 and 1996). The expected increase in the number of households in Wales, from 1.18 million in 1996 to 1.32 million in 2016, will also increase pressure on land and other resources.

Several problems which are particularly acute in Wales arise from livestock production, its main form of farming: it has the highest density of sheep in the EU (numbers have doubled in the past 25 years) and overgrazing seriously erodes soils. Sheep-dip pesticides also pollute an estimated 750 miles of streams, while slurry and silage pollution from dairy farming are serious in west and north-west Wales. Wales' industrial legacies continue to cause pollution too, notably discharges from some 40 metal mines and various abandoned coal mines. The spread of opencast mining in South Wales has also become a major concern.

Tourism is taking its toll, too. The growing tourist traffic in the national parks has led to serious footpath erosion, especially in the Brecon Beacons and Snowdonia. A massive fund-raising effort was launched in the 1990s (see the boxed text, 'Save Snowdonia: Enter Hopkins, Stage Right' in the Flora & Fauna section later) to help maintain this area's delicate balance between the demands of public access, agriculture and wildlife conservation.

Organisations

The government's Environment Agency Wales (☎ 0845 933 3111, fax 029 2079 8555), Rivers House, Fortran Rd, St Mellons, Cardiff CF3 0EY, has a brief that ranges from improving the quality of air, land and water to coping with environmen-

Sea Empress

In February 1996, Pembrokeshire hit the world news when the supertanker *Sea Empress* broke up off the Pembrokeshire Coast National Park, releasing 72,000 tonnes of light crude oil into the sea – the UK's third worst oil spill ever. More than 120 miles of coastline were covered with oil, and damage to wildlife was widespread.

The official tally by the Marine Conservation Society was 1035 dead birds and 2831 oiled birds that received treatment, but more than 6900 oiled birds of at least 28 different kinds were actually collected, and unofficial estimates suggest that 20,000 birds probably died at sea. Most affected were sea ducks (scoters), guillemots, razorbills, shags and cormorants, as well as grey seals and dolphins. Less headline-grabbing was the complete destruction of the rare, green rock-pool starfish (Asterina phylactica) in West Angle Bay, and effects on limpets and periwinkles, barnacles and seaweeds, and contamination of mussels and clams. It was only thanks to a massive clean-up effort by 950 people, 50 boats, 19 aircraft and 24 different organisations that the damage was not more serious.

Three years later the courts fined Milford Haven Port Authority £4 million for allowing an inexperienced pilot to guide the supertanker into the harbour. Many are still uneasy: as long as there's an oil refinery at Milford Haven, in the centre of the Pembrokeshire Coast National Park, the risk of further damage remains.

tal disasters. Its comprehensive Web site at www.environment-agency.wales.gov.uk documents the good, the bad and the ugly throughout Wales.

The Countryside Council for Wales (CCW; ☎ 01248 385500), Plas Penrhos, Ffordd Penrhos, Bangor, Gwynedd LL57 2LQ, is the national wildlife conservation authority and the government's statutory adviser on sustaining Wales' natural beauty and creating opportunities for its enjoyment. Among its many jobs is overseeing an agri-environment stewardship scheme called Tir Gofal, which encourages farmers and landowners to manage their land in an environmentally friendly way. In 1999, together with the Forestry Commission, the CCW published a comprehensive snapshot of the state of the Welsh natural environment *(A Living Environment for Wales)* which provides a valuable appraisal of species, habitats and landscape. See the Web site at www.ccw.gov.uk.

A notable umbrella organisation promoting sustainable, environmentally sensitive tourism in Wales is the Festival of the Countryside (☎ 01686-625384, fax 622955, e foc@foc.org.uk), Frolic House, Frolic St, Newtown, Powys SY16 1AP. Its free annual *Festival of the Countryside* booklet details hundreds of 'green' events – special walks and walking festivals, art workshops, fairs and more – plus ramblers' associations, specialist touring services, museums, galleries and nature centres. See also the Web site at www.foc.org.uk.

Campaigning more vociferously on a variety of rural issues are the Campaign for the Protection of Rural Wales (☎ 01938 552525, fax 552741, e hq@cprw.org.uk), with a Web site at www.cprw.org.uk; and the Wales Green Party (☎ 01443-741242, e jmatthews@headweb.co.uk), online at www.walesgreenparty.org.uk. Other national organisations with specific agendas for Wales include the National Trust (NT; ☎ 01492-860123), Web site nationaltrust.org.uk; Friends of the Earth (☎ 020-7490 1555), Web site www.foe.co.uk; The Wildlife Trusts (☎ 01522-544400), Web site www.wildlifetrust.org.uk; and the Ramblers' Association (☎ 0171-339 8500), Web site www.ramblers.org.uk.

Energy

Wales has become a world leader in the development of clean and sustainable energy. Water power, wind power, solar power and biomass (energy from plant debris) – Wales has it all.

If all goes to plan, a revolutionary, £500 million tidal-power scheme, featuring a 20-sq-mile artificial island off the north coast, would become the UK's largest renewable energy scheme, generating almost 15% of Wales' electricity by 2003 (only about 1% of Wales' needs currently come from renewable sources). Tidal Electric, the developer behind the scheme, has also proposed a smaller scheme for Swansea Bay. Check out its Web site at www.tidalelectric.com.

Such ecofriendly projects are nothing new for Wales, which has some of the best wind and water resources in Europe and has long put them to good use. Aberdulais Falls near Neath has powered industrial activities since 1584, while engineers built hydropower schemes in Wales over a century ago. The Sustainable Energy Group in the Welsh National Assembly now adds government support to encourage all forms of sustainable energy. Nuclear power hardly features: Wales' only nuclear power station is at Wylfa on Anglesey's north coast (the Trawsfynydd nuclear station – built, incredibly, within one of Snowdonia's most beautiful areas – closed in 1993).

Wind farms, which first appeared in the early 1990s, constitute most of Wales' renewable-energy facilities. The 56-turbine, 33MW Carno Wind Farm in Powys has the largest production capacity in the UK, while the nearby Penrhyddlan & Llidiartywaun Windfarm, the largest in Europe when it was built in 1992, has 103 turbines. You can find out more about these and other Welsh wind farms from the Web sites of National Wind Power, PowerGen Renewables Ltd and British Wind Energy Association, at www.natwindpower.co.uk, www.powergen.co.uk and www.bwea.com respectively. There's growing opposition, however, to what many see as insensitively sited, profit-motivated schemes which blight the landscape. For the full blast of the argument, check out the Web sites of Campaign for the Protection of Rural Wales and the Wales Green Party (see Organisations earlier). Both have campaigned vigorously against a proposed 253-turbine facility at Cefn Croes on environmentally sensitive land in Mid Wales, which would be the UK's largest yet.

Pumped-storage power stations may not be as fashionable as wind farms but they are put to dramatic service in Wales. The best known is the Dinorwig station (nicknamed Electric Mountain) near Llanberis in North Wales, where six giant pump-turbines within the underground cavern of a former slate mine can provide full output in just 16 seconds, the fastest response time of any pumped storage power station in the world. Its Web site is at www.electricmountain .co.uk. The UK's first such facility, at nearby Blaenau Ffestiniog (built in 1963), is still capable of producing 360MW of electricity within a minute.

The Centre for Alternative Technology (CAT) near Machynlleth (see the Mid Wales chapter) is a pioneer in the application of solar technology. Now one of Wales' biggest tourist attractions, CAT's visitor centre demonstrates a variety of renewable-energy facilities including wind and water turbines, and a 13.5kW photovoltaic roof, the largest in the UK. Its Web site is at www.cat.org.uk.

Another interpretative centre open to visitors is the West Wales ECO Centre at Newport (see the Pembrokeshire & Carmarthenshire chapter).

A *Guide to Renewable Energy in Wales*, detailing these and other facilities in Wales, is available from CAT.

FLORA & FAUNA
Flora

Much of Wales was once covered by forest, mainly sessile oak, though very little remains and of that none is virgin growth. Most has long since been cleared for agriculture, or chopped down for shipbuilding, charcoal burning or construction – not least for pit props in the mines. Woodland now covers about 12% of the land, two-thirds of it non-native conifers such as Sitka spruce. This is popular with plantation owners seeking a quick-growing source of timber, but far from ideal as habitat for native birds and mammals (apart from the sturdy pine marten).

Soil types vulnerable to erosion by cultivation or overgrazing are widespread in Wales, and soil erosion has damaged some habitats. Overgrazing also makes it hard for

new oak saplings to take root; in Snowdonia the rampant spread of wild rhododendrons prevents them even seeding; imported oaks, such as the Turkey oak, seem to fare better. Pengelli Forest, 3 miles east of Newport in Pembrokeshire, is as close as you'll get to untouched Welsh woodland nowadays.

Ash trees are also native to Wales, and are common everywhere, especially along rivers and in woods and thickets in the Gower peninsula and the Brecon Beacons. In their shade grow primroses, common dog violets and several species of orchid. Hornbeams were once restricted to south-eastern Wales but are now found elsewhere. You'll see plenty of wild cherry trees and field maples, and churchyards often harbour yew trees, as in England.

A great way to enjoy Wales' woodlands is to visit one of the 17 areas managed by Forest Enterprise Wales (the agency responsible for managing the Forestry Commission's land and the largest provider of outdoor recreation), where activities range from theatrical events and mountain bike rallies to beer festivals and husky racing. The Coed Y Brenin Visitor Centre near Dolgellau (see the Snowdonia chapter for details) is one of seven such centres. Details of others are available from Forest Enterprise (☎ 01970 612367, fax 625282, Victoria Terrace, Aberystwyth, Ceredigion, SY23 2DQ) or Tourist Information Centres (TICs).

Wales' mountainous terrain makes it a perfect breeding ground for fragile alpine-Arctic plants, including the unique Snowdon lily which brightens the slopes of Mt Snowdon between late May and mid-June. Easier to spot are saxifrage and moss campion growing on the rocks. Amid coastal sand dunes you may find evening primrose, sea spurge, sea bindweed and marram grass, while the Gower peninsula is a good place for thrift, samphire and sea lavender. Around Tenby you might even find the unique Tenby daffodil, while the delicate fen orchid – one of Europe's rarest plants – is being closely protected in the Kenfig National Nature Reserve near Port Talbot.

Wales has an unrivalled variety of bogs and peatland sites, harbouring everything from bog mosses and myrtle to crowberry and the rare slender cotton grass (which particularly likes Crymlyn Bog near Swansea, despite its proximity to an oil refinery and a rubbish tip). At Rhos Goch near Painscastle in Powys you can find sphagnum mosses in the raised bog areas and more fen-like plants in the swampy sections. Cwm Cadlan, near Penderyn, is another soggy area, a wet grassland boasting meadow thistle and butterwort, bog pimpernel and the globeflower.

On firmer ground, Wales' most exciting floral attraction is the National Botanic Garden, east of Carmarthen (see the Pembrokeshire & Carmarthenshire chapter for details). Inside a massive domed glasshouse designed by Lord Foster you can experience everything from a Mediterranean landscape to an interactive exhibit on the life cycle of a giant plant, while outside are wild meadows, native woodland and a geological 'timewalk' through Wales.

Fauna

Wales' lengthy coastline guarantees a sizeable seabird population. Grassholm Island harbours one of the world's largest gannet colonies, with 30,000 breeding pairs. Wales also has 150,000 pairs of Manx shearwaters, 30% of the world's population. The rock faces of Skomer and Skokholm islands are crowded with colonies of guillemots, razorbills, storm petrels, kittiwakes and puffins. There are also a few pairs of rare choughs on Ramsey and Bardsey islands; passing migrants include the occasional great northern diver.

Kite Country

The striking, chestnut-coloured red kite *(Milvus milvus)*, with its distinctive 2m-long wing span, agile flight and amazing aerobatics, was once common throughout the UK. It even enjoyed royal protection in the Middle Ages. But with the growth in agriculture during the 16th century, it was declared vermin (although it is primarily a scavenger, preying only on small mammals and birds) and mercilessly hunted. By the 19th century only a few pairs were left, in the Tywi and Cothi valleys of Mid Wales.

On the brink of extinction, the kite was saved by a group of committed landowners, rural communities and organisations who launched an unofficial protection programme that was to last 100 years, the longest-running protection scheme for any bird in the world. Despite persistent threats from egg-hunters and poisoned baits (meant for crows or foxes) there are now over 200 pairs throughout Wales, their survival supported by the Kite Country Project. This ecotourism initiative was launched in 1994 to encourage visitors to Mid Wales to see the red kite in action, either in the wild or at six Kite Country Centres (two are noted in the Mid Wales chapter) where you can watch kites being fed at close range, along with buzzards, ravens and other birds.

Kites nest and roost in woodland, and hunt over open country. Courting and nesting take place in March; babies hatch in early May, take their first flights in July and are independent by the end of summer. For more information contact Kite Country (☎/fax 01686 625090, ℮ info@kitecountry .co.uk), Frolic House, Frolic Street, Newton, Powys SY16 1AP, with a Web site at www.kitecountry.co.uk; or the Welsh Kite Trust, The Stable Cottage, Dolwdowlod, Llandrindod Wells, Powys LD1 6HG.

In general, the Welsh inland bird population mirrors that of England, although with an exceptional number of red kites in the southern Cambrian Mountains of Mid Wales (see the boxed text 'Kite Country').

The mammal population is also similar to England's, although the greater horseshoe bats is now confined to Wales and corners of south-western England, and Skomer Island boasts a unique species of vole. Red squirrels are vanishing fast throughout the UK, but a few survive around Lake Vyrnwy. Otters, once very rare, are re-establishing themselves along the River Teifi and in the border area of northern Powys. A colony of grey seals is breeding successfully on Ramsey Island.

With so many fast-flowing rivers, it's hardly surprising that Wales has a wide variety of fish, although salmon (once common in the Usk and Wye) are declining, as in other north-eastern Atlantic countries; and even its sea trout and brown trout are diminishing, due to pollution or man-made barriers to their migration sites. Llyn Tegid (Bala Lake) in Snowdonia National Park is the only home of the gwyniad, a species of whitefish trapped there at the end of the last Ice Age, and cockles are still harvested at low tide in the Burry Inlet on the Gower peninsula.

Endangered Habitats & Species

The UK Biodiversity Action Plan, which identifies habitat and species in need of conservation (a response to the 1992 Rio de Janeiro Earth Summit), had recognised 37 habitats and 185 species in Wales by the end of 1999. They range from raised bogs to upland hay meadows, fens to yew woodland, the hornet robber fly to the harbour porpoise, the dormouse to the otter, and the lesser horseshoe bat to the pearl-bordered fritillary butterfly. The factors responsible for their decline or destruction include intensive farming, loss of habitat and acidification. The idea is to set targets for their conservation (or restoration and expansion of the habitats) but, inevitably, the financial resources for such work (largely carried out by the CCW) are still severely lacking.

Among the CCW's success stories so far is the discovery of Wales' only known roost of rare Barbastelle bats (at Pengelli Forest National Nature Reserve in north Pembrokeshire) and of one of the world's rarest plants, the shore dock, which only grows in the Celtic countries and has been rediscovered on the Pembrokeshire coast.

The EU, too, is pushing its own conservation agenda with the so-called Habitats Directive which requires the UK to submit a list of sites for consideration as Special Areas of Conservation (SAC), to be included in a EU-wide series of protected areas known as Natura 2000. So far, 44 candidate SACs have been identified in Wales (with more expected by 2002), including the greater and lesser horseshoe bat (which like Wales better than anywhere else in the UK), the bottle-nosed dolphin, and various marine reefs and sand-dune systems.

National Parks

The three national parks in Wales, designated during the 1950s, could not be more different from one another, although they all feature some of the most spectacular landscapes in Wales. In the south-east (see the South-East Wales & the Brecon Beacons chapter) are the high plateau and rolling hills of the Brecon Beacons National Park. In the south-west (see the Pembrokeshire & Carmarthenshire chapter) is the UK's only coastal park, the Pembrokeshire Coast National Park; while the dramatic mountains and ridges of Snowdonia National Park dominate the north (see the Snowdonia & the Llŷn chapter).

In addition to these major protected areas there's a confusing array of other protected sites such as Special Areas of Conservation (see the Ecology & Environment section for other categories) that may fall within the national park areas. The NT, too, owns tracts of land within the parks (eg parts of Snowdonia), although the majority of park land is privately owned. Since 1996 the parks have become independent, largely self-regulating authorities.

Save Snowdonia: Enter Hopkins, Stage Right

When the National Trust (NT) launched its Snowdonia Appeal in 1990, the aim was to raise funds for countryside projects and work programmes on all the NT's properties in the area. But in 1998 a huge chunk of land on the mountain's southern flank – right up to the summit – came up for sale. The NT needed to raise some £4 million in 100 days in order to prevent it from being sold to commercial developers.

Welsh-born actor Sir Anthony Hopkins, president of the appeal, flung it into high gear by personally donating £1 million. Within four months, over £5 million had been secured and Snowdonia was saved. Hopkins had played his finest Welsh role.

Sadly, his halo was tarnished two years later when he took out American citizenship, to the disgust of many in his home town of Port Talbot. He made matters worse by appearing in a TV promotion for Barclays Bank just as the bank was announcing plans to close small branches all over the UK.

GOVERNMENT & POLITICS

Wales is technically a principality, and since 1302, when Edward I invested his son as Prince of Wales, the British sovereign's eldest son has been given this title. In 1969, Prince Charles was formally proclaimed Prince of Wales at Caernarfon Castle. It goes without saying that few Welsh Nationalists appreciate this state of affairs.

In 1997, the people of Wales voted to be governed by a National Assembly for Wales, rather than from the House of Commons in London – a decision which took effect in May 1999 with the first elections to the Assembly and the transfer of devolved powers from the Secretary of State for Wales.

The 60-member Assembly has responsibility for such national portfolios as education, health, housing and language, but has no authority on international affairs, defence or taxation. Controversially, its budget is still set in Westminster. Laws passed in Westminster also still apply to Wales although the Assembly has powers to make secondary legislation to meet specific Welsh needs. There is still a Secretary of State for Wales in the London cabinet and Wales retains full representation in the House of Commons.

Elections to the Assembly are held every four years: 40 of its 60 members are elected from each constituency in Wales (corresponding to those for the House of Commons) and the remaining 20 by a system of proportional representation from each of five electoral regions corresponding to European parliamentary constituencies. The Assembly's first secretary appoints a cabinet of eight secretaries responsible for particular areas of policy. All are accountable to the Assembly. A new, purpose-built chamber for the Assembly is due to open in 2003 at Cardiff Bay.

The country is resoundingly Labour in its attitudes. But although Labour won the largest number of seats (28) in the 1999 Assembly elections, Plaid Cymru took a spectacular 17 seats. Rather than run a minority administration, Labour in October 2000 joined forces with the Liberal Democrat party (which won six seats) in a coalition government. The deal gave the Lib Dems two seats in the cabinet as well as an agreed policy program (notably, increased spending on health and education). The other big bloc in the Assembly is the Conservative party (nine seats).

The Assembly's first secretary (or first minister, as the Welsh prefer to call him) is Labour leader Rhodri Morgan; his Lib Dem colleague and deputy first minister is Mike German. About 42% of Assembly members are women (only Sweden has a higher proportion); five women are Cabinet members and one is a deputy minister.

There are 40 Welsh MPs in the Westminster parliament (34 Labour,x four Plaid Cymru and two Liberal Democrat) and five

MEPs in the European Parliament (two each from Labour and Plaid Cymru, and one Conservative).

For purposes of local government, the country is divided into 22 'unitary authorities' or councils, administered by 1268 councillors. Most are Labour-controlled but the Independent Party (with a total of 269 councillors) outnumbers Labour in six councils, and Plaid Cymru (208 councillors) in three, notably Gwynedd.

The likelihood of Wales emerging as a nation independent of the rest of the UK is currently small. Even Plaid Cymru has denied it wants an independent Wales, claiming that self-government in Europe is the goal.

ECONOMY

The Welsh economy has traditionally been based on agriculture and, since the 18th century, on the coal, steel and slate industries. During the Industrial Revolution, rich deposits of coal in the south-east and slate in the north-west were intensively exploited, and factories for producing steel were established in the south to meet the growing demand for bridges and railways. By the 1920s a quarter of a million people were employed in Wales' coal industry; 50 pits employed 40,000 men in the Rhondda Valley alone. At Llanwern steelworks (opened in 1961) over 10,000 were employed. In Ebbw Vale, the tinplate factory offered jobs to 13,000. But all that is changing, fast.

In the 1950s, light manufacturing began to replace some of these industries; and in the 1980s the most drastic cuts to the now-nationalised but increasingly inefficient coal industry began. By 1989, only 11 pits remained. Today, there are no large working pits left. The Thatcher years of privatisation also led to drastic cuts in the manufacturing and steel industry. The resulting massive unemployment led to widespread social disruption. Meanwhile, too, agriculture was facing its own problems, with hill farmers eking out an increasingly precarious existence.

Today, Wales' economic profile and prospects are very different from even 50

UNITARY AUTHORITIES

1	Anglesey (Ynys Môn)	8	Ceredigion	16	Rhondda Cynon Taff
2	Gwynedd	9	Pembrokeshire	17	Merthyr Tydfil
3	Conwy	10	Carmarthenshire	18	Caerphilly
4	Denbighshire	12	Neath Port Talbot	19	Blaenau Gwent
5	Flintshire	13	Bridgend	20	Torfaen
6	Wrexham	14	Vale of Glamorgan	21	Newport
7	Powys	15	Cardiff	22	Monmouthshire

| | 11 | Swansea | | |

years ago. The most significant first step to recovery was the establishment, in 1976, of the Welsh Development Agency (WDA) to help Wales make the awkward transition to new sources of employment. Recently merged with the Development Board for Rural Wales and the Land Authority for Wales, the WDA is now a powerful body, promoting economic and community regeneration across the whole of Wales.

One of the WDA's biggest successes has been to attract £13 billion worth of inward investment since 1983 (16% of the total for the whole of the UK), particularly from the EU (213 companies have set up operations here), the USA (143) and Japan (55, including Sony, National Panasonic, Aiwa and Toyota). Indeed, Wales has the highest concentration of Japanese companies in western Europe. Such investment has led to 175,000 jobs being created or safeguarded.

Wales Fights the Westminster Poodle

Wales has always disliked the way it's controlled by Westminster mandarins, and with devolution has come a sharp drop in Welsh patience. When Alun Michael, a junior minister in London (and, briefly, the Secretary of State for Wales), was foisted on Wales by Tony Blair and the Labour leadership as their choice for Wales' Labour leader, there were accusations that he was 'Blair's poodle'. He barely found the votes to become First Secretary in the new National Assembly.

Unsurprisingly, he was soon in trouble. By February 2000, faced with a vote of no-confidence over his apparent inability to obtain Westminster funds that would have made Wales eligible for a substantial EU grant, he resigned. In his place came the man Wales wanted in the first place: the widely popular and populist MP, Rhodri Morgan, who went on to form a coalition with the Liberal Democrat party.

These companies have spearheaded the rapid growth in Wales' more varied manufacturing and industrial sectors such as electronics, automotive engineering, food, aerospace, telecommunications and financial services. Manufacturing now accounts for 29% of gross domestic product (GDP) in Wales (the UK average is 22%), followed by financial and business services (16.4% of GDP). Even struggling agriculture (which nevertheless accounts for a greater percentage of GDP than the UK average) is getting support to develop the agri-food sector via such initiatives as the Rural Partnership for Wales.

But it's not all looking rosy. Until recently the steel industry was still a major economic player, accounting for 42% of the UK's steel output. But in February 2001 the Anglo-Dutch steel group Corus announced that 6050 jobs would be cut – half of them in Wales, notably at Llanwern, Shotton, Bryngwyn and Newport. The once-thriving Ebbw Vale tinplate plant, beaten by competition from cheaper Spanish slate, closed completely. Some 10,000 jobs have now been lost at Llanwern alone in the past decade, and more losses are predicted.

Counteracting such blows is a huge job for agencies such as the WDA. It will take plans such as its Entrepreneurship Action Plan (to support a stronger entrepreneurial culture in Wales) years to see economic and social benefits. Despite optimism about what Wales can achieve, even the WDA admits that the nation still faces 'significant economic challenges'.

Meanwhile, the EU remains a vital aid provider, especially in west Wales and the valleys, which have been designated Objective 1 areas (ie seriously lagging behind the EU average) and therefore qualifying for maximum EU funding to the tune of £1.2 billion for 2000–6. This massive investment (which is controversially supposed to be matched by funding from Westminster) can actually be used to help any region of Wales, and is likely to significantly boost development in many previously deprived areas. With Wales' other main traditional industry – agriculture – at an all-time low, and further devastated in early 2001 by the UK's Foot & Mouth disease epidemic, such aid will be vital.

POPULATION & PEOPLE

Wales has a population of around 2.9 million, about 5% of the population of the UK (on 8.6% of its land). The largest population centre is Cardiff, with 320,000 people. Swansea and Newport, also in South Wales, are the other main centres. Mid Wales is the least densely populated region – although the population of Powys, the emptiest area (62 people per sq mile) actually grew between 1981 and 1991 as people deserted the cities for the countryside and an alternative lifestyle. The average population density is 365 per sq mile (compared to the UK average of 627). In many places there are considerably more sheep than people (in Snowdonia the ratio is 25:1, on Anglesey 4:1).

The caricature Welshman of English imagination was a coal miner who went to chapel on Sunday and spent his spare time singing or playing rugby. His wife wore long skirts with a pinafore and shawl and a tall black hat. The 1980s and 1990s saw the mining part of this picture laid to rest, and the chapel-going too has died as much in Wales as in England. The only places you're likely to see women in national costume nowadays are at the *eisteddfodau* or the Welsh Folk Museum. That said, the Welsh do remain a people apart, if only because their language is still very much alive.

You'll notice the difference in the predominantly Welsh-speaking enclaves of the north-west. The so-called Landsker line, roughly along the present-day A40 through Pembrokeshire, is considered something of a cultural divide between the 'Welshry' and the coastal 'little England'. You're unlikely to experience hostility even in the Welsh heartlands, although the Welsh anywhere can be as reserved as the English when it comes to introducing themselves to strangers.

The indigenous Welsh are mostly of Celtic stock. During the Industrial Revolution the population balance shifted as wealthy investors moved to Wales to take advantage of its mineral wealth, recruiting in their wake a large non-Welsh workforce. It was at this time that the Welsh language began a decline that is only slowly being halted.

Wales has a small ethnic-minority population, mainly concentrated in Cardiff, Newport (where there's a large mosque) and Swansea. A sizeable number of English people live in Wales, running B&Bs, craft centres, cafes and other tourist attractions. During the rise of nationalism from the 1960s to 1980s, resentment against such English 'invaders' became heated, with an outbreak of anti-English slogans and graffiti. It culminated in the firebombing of English-owned holiday homes by a radical underground organisation, which did much to harm the nationalists' cause, although it won the support of outspoken patriots such as the late poet RS Thomas (see the Literature section later), who believed that English speakers were ruining Welsh culture.

Today such feelings are far less acute, although by no means gone: in 1998 when it was revealed that David Beckham and Spice Girl Victoria Adams had bought a luxury holiday home in North Wales, the Welsh Language Society protested that 'outsiders' were pricing local people out of the housing market.

EDUCATION

In most ways the Welsh education system mirrors the English one: schooling is compulsory for those aged five to 16, with free education available to those aged 18. Wales has one of the UK's highest proportions (over 75%) of three- and four-year-olds receiving primary education. But over 10% of school leavers have no GCSEs (nationally recognised qualifications for 15- and 16-year-olds), over 20% of the working-age population has low numeracy skills and one in six has low literacy skills. Such findings led to a record increase in educational spending in 2000: some £360 million up to 2003, including £12 million in 2003–4 to expand nursery provision for three-year-olds. More money has been earmarked to ensure that all schools are connected to the Internet by 2002.

The major difference in Welsh education is, of course, the revival of interest in the Welsh language. The 1944 Education Act marked the first shift in official attitudes to Welsh language teaching. The first state-funded Welsh-medium primary school opened three years later and by 1949 there were nine more. Today there are over 450 primary schools (27% of the total) in which Welsh is the main or sole medium of instruction. Over 50,000 children – around one in four – are now educated in Welsh. English is treated as a second language to be introduced at about age seven.

This has led to a similar increase in Welsh-medium secondary schools: around 22% of secondary schools now teach Welsh as both a first and second language. In 50 schools, more than half the foundation subjects are taught wholly or partly through Welsh. This rise in Welsh language education has also been boosted by the 1993 Welsh Language Act which put Welsh and English on an equal basis in public life in Wales, and the 1998 Government of Wales Act which required the Assembly to treat both languages as 'official' (see the Language chapter for more about the Welsh language).

At university level, there are 13 higher educational institutes hosting over 87,000 students. The biggest player is the 'federal' University of Wales which collectively has some 50,000 students at universities or universities colleges in Aberystwyth, Bangor, Cardiff, Lampeter, Newport and Swansea. There's also a university in Glamorgan (Pontypridd). Cardiff University, with 15,600 students, is the largest in Wales and the second-largest in the UK, and particularly strong in advanced technology.

ARTS

For years the Welsh arts scene – particularly theatre – has been in turmoil, largely because of controversy over the way the Arts Council of Wales (ACW) – the major funding body, whose Royal Charter makes it unanswerable to the National Assembly – runs the show. In 2000 there were calls for an enquiry following a row over the ACW's

The Visual Arts in Wales

A visit to the National Museum and Gallery of Wales in Cardiff will offer ample evidence that Wales has a long tradition of decoration and the visual arts, from Celtic stone crosses to the fine examples of work by Augustus John (1878–1961) and Gwen John (1876–1939), Frank Brangwyn (1867–1956), David Jones (1895–1974) and Ceri Richards (1903–71), and contemporary paintings and installations in the changing exhibitions of its Art in Wales Gallery. Thanks to the patronage of the Davies Sisters of Gregynog, the museum also holds some of the finest examples of European impressionist and postimpressionist art – major works by Monet, Manet, Renoir, Cezanne, Sisley, Rodin, as well as Bacon, Spencer and Magritte.

Wales became the most fashionable place to visit for landscape painters at the end of the 18th century, when the French Revolution effectively closed Europe to British artists. Those seeking a romantic engagement with nature discovered the closer delights of one of the most beautiful countries in terms of mountains, lakes and coastline. Richard Wilson and Paul Sandby and, later, JMW Turner and David Cox painted that Wales. There are fine examples of their work in Cardiff and in many of the world's major galleries.

Nonconformity in religion and society and the furious expansion of the Industrial Revolution meant that the art of Wales in the 19th century was largely untutored and naïve. However, the famous 1913 Armory Show in New York, which introduced the exciting new art of Europe to Americans, included JD Innes (1869–1914), Augustus John and his sister Gwen. Augustus, it would appear, more than any other created the 'Bohemian' figure in painting. He was a beautiful draughtsman, open to the influences of postimpressionism from Europe and as outrageous in his private life as the younger Dylan Thomas whose portrait he painted and to whom he introduced his future wife Caitlin, having first seduced her. Gwen John went to Paris and became Rodin's lover; after his death she became more solitary and converted to Catholicism. Her small portraits of nuns, cats and women friends are more admired now than Augustus' big, bold canvases, and she has been canonised by feminist critics.

Ceri Richards, influenced particularly by Matisse, is the most notable figure from the mid-20th century, and the Glynn Vivian Gallery in Swansea has a room dedicated to his work. Other 'Neo-Romantics', the notable English painters John Piper and Graham Sutherland, also lived in and painted the landscape and castles of Wales. Industrial Wales, particularly the coal valleys, was the subject of handling of school theatre contracts and proposed cuts to fund new drama. In February 2001 a review of its operations was launched. Not surprisingly, the Assembly is itching to take over control.

In January 2001, in a kind of declaration of independence of the Welsh arts world from London, the Assembly's culture minister launched Cymru'n Creu (Wales Creates), a consortium of public agencies from the arts to sport to tourism, aimed at encouraging Wales' 'creative industries', some of which are growing twice as fast as the rest of the economy, such as filmmaking, pop music and cultural tourism. This was partly a response to the first major Wales-initiated report for the Assembly, *A*

Culture in Common, whose 104 proposals are aimed at creating a culturally diverse, creatively rich and entrepreneurial ethos. The Assembly, though stalling on some fronts (eg the establishment of a national art gallery), is nevertheless supporting the vision to the tune of an extra £7.85 million in arts spending over the next three years.

Arts Centres

Wales' two most important arts centres are in Aberystwyth and Cardiff. The Aberystwyth Arts Centre (☎ 01970-623232), on the university campus, is Wales' largest, and Mid Wales' most important, arts venue. It houses a concert hall, gallery space, theatre and cinemas and runs a busy

The Visual Arts in Wales

PETER PRENDERGAST 1982. PRIVATE COLLECTION

Bethesda Quarry by Peter Prendergast

a number of fine artists in the second half of the century – Cedric Morris (1889–1982), Leslie Moore (1913–76), Esther Grainger (1912–90), Evan Walters (1893–1951), Will Roberts (1910–2000) and the 'Rhondda Group' – Ernest Zobole (1927–99), Charles Burton and Glyn Jones. Important too was the influence of immigrants such as Heinz Koppel (1919–80) and Josef Herman (1911–2000), who brought with them a central European sense of colour and the figure of the working man.

Since WWII the dominant figure in Welsh landscape has been Sir Kyffin Williams, whose thickly-layered oils on canvas – mountains, lakes, hill-farmers – have been highly sought after in Wales and London. Younger artists such as Kevin Sinnott and Peter Prendergast have brought a new vigour to the sights and figures of South and North Wales respectively, while Iwan Bala, Ivor Davies and David Garner are at the cutting edge of political engagement with issues of language and postindustrial Wales in their more radical art.

Wales currently has more energy, inspiration and experimentation in the visual arts than at any time in its history. The tradition is well represented in three University of Wales books in *The Visual Culture of Wales* series. Interviews with artists are in *Welsh Painters Talking* and *Welsh Artists Talking* (Seren Books) and contemporary art can be viewed at www.gallery4wales.com.

Tony Curtis
University of Glamorgan

program of performances, exhibitions and arts festivals.

In Cardiff, the Chapter Arts Centre (☎ 029-2030 4400) is one of Europe's most dynamic centres, with an innovative program of over 150 contemporary arts events monthly. It focuses on the work of small companies and serves as home to a variety of theatre companies, professional artists and craftspeople. It has two cinemas, three theatres, a gallery, dance studio, and film, video, animation and photography facilities. Check out the Web site at www.chapter.org.

Music

Wales has a reputation as the home of lusty male voice choirs, pretty female harpists and mysterious music festivals. Even rugby fans sing in the terraces. Why this passion for song? Celtic culture has always put as high a value on vocal (particularly choral) music as on the written word. Composers, musicians, singers and poets held annual contests – eisteddfodau – as long ago as the 12th century, and they're still doing it (see the boxed text 'The Eisteddfod' in the following Literature section).

Even puritan Nonconformists of the 18th and 19th centuries couldn't stop the singing, though hymns were the only thing on the menu. Gymanfa Ganu were local festivals of hymn singing, when denominations put aside their differences and joined in song; there are still regional versions, and a Gymanfa Ganu session at the National Eisteddfod. Other forms of music-making were sustained by a revival of interest in Celtic culture, Arthurian legends and Welsh folklore during that period. Wales' trademark male voice choirs were born of the community spirit forged in the mines, quarries and ironworks, and are still hugely popular (see the boxed text).

Wales also has an international following for two other musical extremes – explosive rock (see the following section on that) and angelic pre-teen singers. Aled Jones was the darling of the 1980s and today it's Charlotte Church. Check out Charlotte's CD, *Song of an Angel*, for sweet renditions of old Welsh

---

Male Voice Choirs

The Welsh male-voice choir *(cor meibion)* is something of an institution, and most closely associated with the coal-mining towns of the South Wales valleys. It was the Nonconformist sects, particularly Methodism, that breathed life into these choirs, so their repertoires are stronger on hymns than might be anticipated.

You'd think the collapse of the old coal-mining communities would present a threat to the survival of the choirs, but so far they're hanging on, with about 100 choirs still singing their hearts out. The Wales Tourist Board booklet *Welsh Male Voice Choirs* lists rehearsal nights for village choirs that are happy to host visitors (some may even invite you to join them at the pub afterwards!). It's advisable to call ahead to check times.

You'll find choirs in all the main towns, but the largest concentration is in the south. As a sign of the times, some of them now boast female singers, too.

---

songs and lullabies which capture something of the enigmatic quality of her homeland.

Folk Music While the annual eisteddfodau are the highlights of Wales' traditional music scene, you can hear informal Welsh-language folk music any time of year at dozens of pubs, folk clubs and other, mainly northern, venues. English-language folk music predominates in the south. Excellent festivals dot the calendar, notably the Welsh-language Gŵyl Werin y Cnapan every July in Ffostrasol, near Cardigan.

Traditional Welsh music has several unique instruments, notably the triple harp which evolved in the 17th century (although harps were a feature of Welsh music well before that). The leading triple harpist today is Robin Huw Bowen (check out his *Harp Music of Wales* CD). Other popular harpists are Elinor Bennett and Delyth Evans; the latter has produced gorgeous renditions of traditional Welsh harp sounds in an album entitled *Delta*. Other medieval instruments making a comeback are the *crwth* (a stringed instrument which can be bowed or plucked), the *pibgorn* reed instrument, and a bagpipe known as the *pibacwd*.

Equally ancient are the themes of Welsh folk music, most commonly *hiraeth*, an untranslatable expression of nostalgia, longing and emptiness; lullabies and love songs are also popular. Many tunes in the minor key bear a close resemblance to traditional Breton versions; some are thought to have been deliberately transposed into a major key to make them easier to dance to. Look out for groups such as Ar Log, Fernhill and Mabsant, and solo work by Dafydd Iwan. Recordings by the now-defunct Aberjaber band are worth tracking down.

The Cardiff-based Welsh Folk Song & Dance Society (Cymdeithas Ddawns Werin Cymru; ☎/fax 029-2055 5055) is one of Wales' leading folk organisations. Its Web site at www.welshfolkdance.org.uk includes a useful listing of events. ECTARC, the European Centre for Traditional and Regional Cultures (☎ 01978-861514, fax 861804, ⓔ ectarc@aol.com), organises regular events at its centre in Llangollen. An excellent range of recordings is available on the Sain label. Its Web site is at www.sain.wales.com.

Classical Music Classical music enjoys a high profile here: the BBC National Orchestra of Wales, founded in 1928, has showcased Welsh composers such as Alun Hoddinott and William Mathias, and is on its finest form during the Welsh Proms, held in Cardiff's St David's Hall each June.

Naturally opera holds a special place. The Welsh National Opera (WNO), founded by keen amateurs in 1943, became fully professional 30 years later. Since 1986, when it won rave reviews for performances of *Otello* and the *Ring* cycle (the latter, at Covent Garden, marked the first time a British regional opera company had appeared there), it has been recognised as one of the UK's finest companies. It does most of its main productions in Cardiff's New Theatre.

Among opera singers whose careers the WNO has fostered – Helen Field, Donald Maxwell, Anne Evans, Catrin Wyn-Davies – the hot name these days is Bryn Terfel. This energetic, popular bass-baritone has risen meteorically from Welsh sheep-farm beginnings to the world stage since winning the London Guildhall School of Music's 1989 gold medal for best singer, and the Lieder prize the same year in the Cardiff Singer of the World Competition. After his 1990 debut with the WNO, he was invited to perform throughout Europe. His 1998 Metropolitan Opera debut was reported on the front page of the *New York Times*.

Pop Music Baby-boomers will recognise two of Wales' earliest and biggest (English-language) pop stars: Tom Jones and Shirley Bassey. And they're not over the hill yet: Cardiff-born Bassey (perhaps best known for the theme tune to *Goldfinger*) made her latest big stage appearance in 1999 at the Voice of a Nation concert. Jones (who also made a few hearts flutter at that concert) has now found a younger audience, thanks to a successful album of classic pop covers and collaborations with high-profile bands.

But rock puts Wales on the map these days. The last decade has seen the emergence of a potent pop culture, with indie guitar bands such as the Manic Street Preachers, Super Furry Animals, Stereophonics, Gorky's Zygotic Mynci and Catatonia gaining international recognition. Formidable rockers, the Manics paved the way with a series of successful albums after *Generation Terrorists* (1992) established them as a key 1990s British band. The three-piece Stereophonics followed with a string of infectious singles, many derived from their Welsh roots. The bilingual cult band Super Furry Animals is as popular for its alternative approach as for its infectious tunes. Cardiff-based Catatonia, fronted by female vocalist Cerys Matthews, shot to stardom after

International Velvet (1998) sold over 750,000 copies.

At concerts in Wales these groups inspire passionate patriotism, with thousands of fans waving Welsh flags. Catatonia's now-classic concert anthem includes the refrain: 'Every day when I wake up I thank the Lord I'm Welsh'. For a great early compilation, listen to the 1997 *Dial M for Merthyr* on the Fierce Panda label. For some good old 1970s rock-'n'-roll, try Budgie, or the Sunsets. A well-established rockabilly band is the Rimshots.

David Gray and Katell Keineg are making their mark as singer-songwriters, and a host of younger bands are now tuning up; one to watch is Big Leaves. Less commercially successful are specifically Welsh-language bands such as punks Anhrefn and rappers Y Tystion; you can hear these and other groundbreakers on the equally outlandish Ankst label (☎ 029-2023 5453, ℮ emyr@ankst.co.uk). See the Web site at www.ankst.co.uk.

Literature

Of course Wales has two literary traditions because it has two languages. Literature in the Welsh language can be traced back to AD 600 and a bardic poem called *Y Gododdin* celebrating a battle in what is now the north of England, near York. This most ancient of literatures may be sampled in translations such as Anthony Conran's *Welsh Verse*.

In the early 19th century the bardic traditions of communal arts festivals (eisteddfodau; see the boxed text) were reintroduced and substantially re-invented by Edward Williams (1747–1826), who called himself Iolo Morganwg. In the mid-19th century Lady Charlotte Guest published her widely influential translations of *The Mabinogion* (1838–49), some of the oldest myths associated with the west of Britain (for a look at some of them, see the Myths & Legends special section).

However, the literature of Wales in English only really comes to full strength in the 20th century. Gerard Manley Hopkins, the Jesuit priest best known for his *The Wreck of the Deutschland* (1897), is sometimes listed as a Welsh poet, though he was resident in Wales for only a short time. But his remarkable 'sprung-rhythm' poetic effects were probably derived from the Welsh-language tradition of *cynghanedd* (essentially the framing of a poetic idea within the constraints of a carefully balanced, almost chanting repetition of sound-sequences).

The 20th century in literary Wales is dominated by the Thomases – Edward, Dylan, Gwyn and Ronald Stuart – and English-language Welsh writing rests heavily on their reputations.

Edward Thomas (1878–1917) was a London Welshman who wrote evocative prose about the beauties of nature, until he met the American poet Robert Frost in 1913 and was persuaded to direct his sensibilities and talents towards poetry. Remarkably, in the four years before his death in action in WWI, he produced some of the finest work of the Georgian period in English poetry. Poems such as *Adlestrop* have become part of the English poetry canon.

Edward Thomas's work now far overshadows that of his friend WH Davies (1871–1940), whose work was popularly acclaimed, especially after the success of his bestselling *The Autobiography of a Super-Tramp*, recounting his experiences as a hobo in the USA. Still, his 'What is this life if, full of care,/ We have no time to stand and stare?' still claims a place in English verse.

Dylan Marlais Thomas (1914–53) is, of course, the best known of writers from Wales. His reputation as a 'roaring boy' from the 'ugly, lovely town' of Swansea continues to hold mythic force – though his Swansea friend Vernon Watkins (1906–67) was also a fine lyrical, visionary poet. You can visit the Dylan Thomas Centre in Swansea where there is a permanent exhibition.

Dylan wrote half a dozen of the greatest poems in the English language – Do not go Gentle, Fern Hill, The Force that Through the Green Fuse, A Refusal to Mourn the

The Eisteddfod

The unique Welsh cultural jamboree known as the **eisteddfod** (pronounced ey-**steth**-vot; plural **eisteddfodau**, ey-**steth**-vuh-dye; literally a gathering or session) is the descendant of ancient bardic tournaments in which poets and musicians competed for a seat of honour in the households of noblemen – a highly prized position since poets depended on patronage for their livelihood.

The first genuinely regional tournament seems to have been held in 1176 at Rhys ap Gruffydd's castle in Cardigan, though references exist to earlier gatherings. Eisteddfodau grew less frequent and less lively following the Acts of Union, a process accelerated in the 17th and 18th centuries as dour Nonconformism took hold. But in the late 18th century Edward Williams (better known by his bardic name, Iolo Morganwg) reinvented the eisteddfod as a modern festival, and an early, informal one took place in Carmarthen in 1819.

The first Royal National Eisteddfod was held in 1861, and has since become Europe's largest festival of competitive music-making and poetry-writing, attracting over 150,000 visitors and some 6000 competitors. It's held during the first week of August, alternately in North and South Wales (in 2002 it will be at St David's; in 2003 in Meifod, Powys).

What makes this gathering unique is that it takes place solely in Welsh – although non-Welsh speakers need not be put off. There's music, dance, handicrafts, clothing, food and souvenirs, and simultaneous translation for bigger events. Indeed there is usually a sizeable non-Welsh contingent, including Americans fascinated by their own Welsh ancestry. Fringe events include Welsh bands and artists, giving the festival a bit of Woodstock/Glastonbury atmosphere; aspiring bands often premier their work here, or time new releases for the occasion.

For more information on the Royal National Eisteddfod, call ☎ 029-2076 3777.

Wales has other eisteddfodau too. The Urdd National Eisteddfod (☎ 01970-623744) is a festival of performing and visual arts for children (*urdd*, pronounced irth, is Welsh for youth). Held every May (in 2002 in Llandudno; in 2003 probably at Neath/Port Talbot), it brings together some 15,000 performers chosen from all over Wales during local and regional eisteddfodau. Most self-respecting young adults, however, head for the fringe activities of the Royal National Eisteddfod.

The International Musical Eisteddfod (☎ 01978-860236), held each July in Llangollen, is a bit different. Started in 1947 with the aim of promoting post-WWII understanding, the week-long event attracts 2500 competitors from over 40 countries. In addition to daily music, singing and dancing competitions, there are gala concerts in the evenings. This, of course, is not a Welsh-only event.

If you'd like to see an eisteddfod but can't make any of the big ones, it's still worth contacting the Welsh Tourist Board for its events booklet, which also lists local contests.

JANE SMITH

Death of a Child, Poem on His Birthday and The Hand that Signed the Paper. He was, too, the author of one of the greatest radio plays *(Under Milk Wood)*, and some of the wittiest stories of childhood and youth *(Return Journey, Portrait of the Artist as a Young Dog* and *A Child's Christmas in Wales)*. He was mad, bad and dangerous to know, as well as being a charming womaniser, a wonderful performer of his own and others' work, and a highly skilled scriptwriter for radio and war-time film documentaries.

Thomas burst upon an unsuspecting Literary London in 1934, at the age of 20. His prize-winning *18 Poems* announced the arrival of a poet as original and spiritual as Gerard Manley Hopkins and as modern and engaged as Eliot or Pound. He left the Swansea of his youth and innocence and went to London, returning to live variously in New Quay (north Pembrokeshire) and Laugharne (near Carmarthen). A visit to The Boathouse in Laugharne, where Thomas and his wife Caitlin lived and fought, is highly recommended.

Both villages helped to shape his hugely comic play for voices, *Under Milk Wood*, in which characters such as Polly Garter, Organ Morgan and Mrs Pugh strut their moments on the stage for one day observed by the blind Captain Cat. There's a good film version starring Peter O'Toole and that original and famous Welsh-American couple, Richard Burton and Elizabeth Taylor. (Welsh people often have striking accents, regional and distinct in their enunciation: Richard Burton's renditions of Thomas and of Shakespeare are high points in recorded spoken English.)

Thomas died as he had lived, outrageously, after a monstrous drinking bout in the Chelsea Hotel in Manhattan on the last of his great USA reading tours. The New York doctor pronounced 'an insult to the brain'.

Dylan Thomas had little to say about the industrial Wales which fed its coal and iron down to the coastal ports of Newport, Cardiff, Barry and his home-town of Swansea. But the birthplace of the industrial revolution was rooted in the mineral-rich valleys of South Wales and the slate quarries of North Wales, and a literature of pain and politics inevitably grew out of the huge migrations of workers and their families from the early 19th century to WWI.

The first notable poet of these experiences was Idris Davies (1905–53) whose two long sequences of poems, *Gwalia Deserta* and *The Angry Summer* reflected on the suffering and courage brought about by the Depression years in the coal valleys. His 'Oh what can you give me?/ Say the sad bells of Rhymney' was given new life as a 1960s pop-folk hit (though not by Bob Zimmerman, who changed his name to Dylan in homage to the Welsh poet).

The hardships and suffering of the South Wales coalfields were communicated to the wider world not by any of these notable poets, but rather by a romantic rollercoaster of a novel written by a Welshman with dubious credentials. Richard Llewellyn (1906–83) may have had little direct experience of the valleys' coalfields but his 1939 novel *How Green was my Valley* was one of the bestsellers of the war years and won an Oscar when filmed by John Ford. It's a popular and powerful gathering of all the myths, cliches and truths of the industrial valleys and remains in print today. But this fictive opera needs to be balanced with a reading of the work of Glyn Jones, Gwyn Jones, Bert Coombes, Lewis Jones and Alun Richards.

In the postwar years the comic novelist and radio personality Gwyn Thomas (1913–81) gave an ironic twist to the cliches of valley life. His characters are often referred to as 'the voters' and his situations throw satirical barbs at the failings of politics and laws in the face of industrial forces. For this particular Thomas, the Welsh are the victims of a huge capitalist joke. From *The Dark Philosophers* (1946) through his successful play *The Keep* (1962) to *The Lust Lobby* (1971), Gwyn Thomas worried away at any sign of pretension or hypocrisy in South Wales society.

In the post-industrial Wales of the last quarter of the 20th century, a number of writers developed more realistic, socially-rooted works. Christopher Meredith's novel *Shifts* (1988) deals with the last days of the steel industry in Gwent, while his former student at the University of Glamorgan, Richard John Evans, has produced the most notable treatment of the post-industrial, drug-dissipated valleys' youth culture in his darkly comic novel *Entertainment* (2000).

Poetry in Wales at the beginning of the new century has lost the final major Thomas, RS Thomas (1913–2000), the poet-priest twice nominated for the Nobel Prize.

'RS' was a deeply spiritual, deeply questioning Christian who found more solace, more evidence of God in the natural beauty of Wales than in any of its churches. There is a huge body of work, often short, meditative poems that ask more questions than they could find answers for.

But RS Thomas was also more politically controversial than any other Welsh writer, criticising the spread of English holiday cottages and English language and culture in rural, Welsh-speaking areas. He also publicly protested against the building of a government nuclear bunker in Carmarthen. His autobiography was published in Welsh and had the title *Neb*, which means 'No one' – RS Thomas was as reserved in his private life as Dylan had been outrageous in his. The reputation of this recently deceased poet can but increase in the years to come.

The postwar generations of Welsh writers are dominated by poets, though one of the finest of these, Dannie Abse, has also written a wonderful autobiographical novel, *Ash on a Young Man's Sleeve* (1954), about a young Jewish boy growing up in Cardiff as clouds of menace gather over 1930s' Europe. Other notable poets are Leslie Norris and Glyn Jones, both of whom also have stories about the valleys. John Ormond (1923–90) was a fine poet who also produced memorable films for the BBC about Wales' writers and artists.

Women writers came to the fore in the later 20th century – novelists Sian James and Catherine Merriman, for example, and poets such as Gillian Clarke, Sheenagh Pugh, Catherine Fisher and Gwyneth Lewis, who has produced fine work in both English and Welsh.

Contemporary writers have become increasingly part of a global literature in English, influenced by writing from the USA: Robert Minhinnick (editor of *Poetry Wales*, who also writes travel essays), Tony Curtis (director of the Masters in Writing program at the University of Glamorgan), Peter Finch, Duncan Bush, Niall Griffiths, John Davies and Stephen Knight. These contemporary writers, together with many mentioned earlier, can be enjoyed online at the Web sites www.academi.org and www.seren-books.com.

Theatre

Wales is awash in theatre, from amateur Welsh-language shows in rural hired halls to top English-language productions with world-class stars in Cardiff. There are some 20 major theatre companies and a host of smaller community and educational groups. Attempts to establish a Welsh national theatre have become tangled in the controversies surrounding the Arts Council of Wales.

Wales' leading English-language professional company is Theatr Clwyd (☎ 01352-756331, ✉ drama@celtic.co.uk) at Mold (Flintshire), attracting top names such as Sir Anthony Hopkins, Julie Christie and Janet Suzman. One of its main aims is to put new Welsh writing on an international stage (half the company's 12 annual productions go on tour throughout Wales and the UK).

Cardiff's acclaimed Sherman Theatre Company (☎ 029-2039 6844) performs in its own theatre (South Wales' major producing and presenting venue for young audiences) and on tour: its 1993 production of Dylan Thomas' *Under Milk Wood* even reached the USA.

Two big names on the Welsh-language stage include Cwmni Theatr Gwynedd (☎ 01248-351707) in Bangor; and Dalier

Sylw (☎ 029-2023 6650), at the Chapter Arts Centre in Cardiff. Cwmni Theatr Gwynedd produces mainstream productions including new plays, Welsh classics and translations from international works. It has also toured with English adaptations of work originally performed in Welsh.

Dalier Sylw is known for its new and challenging productions. Launched to promote only new Welsh-language works, it now commissions English-language and bilingual plays, and translations of classical and contemporary European texts. Its touring venues are just as eclectic, ranging from main theatres to clubs and warehouses.

The Chapter Arts Centre is also home to several experimental companies. Made in Wales (☎ 029-2034 4737) develops and produces new works for professional English-language Welsh theatre, with emphasis on minority cultural experience in Wales. Geared more to original work with a Welsh voice is The Fiction Factory (☎ 029-2064 4521), concentrating in particular on the energetic, often black humour of award-winning playwright Edward Thomas, its own artistic director. The distinctive all-woman Alma Theatre (☎ 029-2034 1239) has also established itself as a leading exponent of experimental theatre in Wales.

Finally, watch out for Green Ginger. Under director Terry Lee (an ex-puppeteer for Spitting Image), this bizarre experimental group (☎ 01834-842746) based in Tenby produces street and fringe shows as absurd as they are memorable.

Cinema

Welsh cinema – comprehensively traced in Dave Berry's *Wales & Cinema; the First 100 Years* – took off in the 1930s and 1940s with a clutch of films on life in the coal valleys, most famously *The Citadel*, *The Proud Valley* and *How Green Was My Valley*, which gave the world a stereotypical image of Wales that has been slow to go away. But these were hardly 'Welsh' films, featuring non-Welsh actors, English or American directors and few if any Welsh locations.

Sir Ifan ab Owen Edwards' 1935 *Y Chwarelwr* (The Quarryman), the first Welsh-language sound film, was the only prominent exception. Arguably the first genuinely Welsh film didn't come along until 1977 – Welshman Karl Francis' *Above Us the Earth*, based on the true story of a colliery closure, and featuring an all-amateur cast in real valley locations.

Television gave screenwriters, directors and actors a new platform, and S4C, the Welsh-language channel (see the boxed text under Radio & TV in the Facts for the Visitor chapter), has rejuvenated Welsh cinema with its support and commissions. One of these, Karl Francis' 1985 Welsh-language *Milwr Bychan* (Boy Soldier), was a fair commercial success. S4C's greatest success story has probably been the Welsh-language docu-drama *Hedd Wyn*, about Ellis Humphrey Evans, a farmer's son from Trawsfynydd (Snowdonia), conscripted into WWI and killed in the trenches of the Somme before learning that he had been awarded a chair at the 1917 Birkenhead Eisteddfod – the highest honour for a poet. The film, directed by Paul Turner, was nominated in 1994 for an Oscar for Best Foreign Language Film.

Another Welsh film nominated in the same category – this time in 1999 – was Paul Morrison's *Solomon and Gaenor*, a story of forbidden love set against the backdrop of the South Wales coalfields at the turn of the century.

The emergence of film workshops (notably Cardiff's Chapter House and smaller outfits such as Pontypridd's all-female Red Flannel cooperative) was another vital ingredient. In 1989 S4C and BBC Wales set up the features studio Ffilm Cymru (succeeded in 1993 by the Wales Film Council). The 1990s BBC Wales series Wales Playhouse revealed more hidden talent.

Many films (mostly for TV) are starting to focus on contemporary Wales and Welsh life. Independent production is thriving in Cardiff (a local light is Taliesin), Bangor and Caernarfon. With the arrival of the Welsh media agency, Sgrîn, in 1997, to champion, promote and develop Welsh film, TV and new media industries, even the funding picture is improving.

The status of Welsh cinema has risen sharply both internationally and within Wales, and 1988 saw the launch of the International Film Festival of Wales. This annual 10-day event screens new Welsh and international releases, and honours a Welsh-born or Wales-resident director with Europe's biggest short-film prize, the £25,000 DM Davies Award. In 1991 Wales BAFTA launched its own awards ceremony in an acknowledgment of indigenous talent; and in 1992 a Wales Film Archive was established at Aberystwyth.

Wales has also seen success in animation. From work such as Joanna Quinn's *Girls' Night Out* and *Tea at No 10* to cartoons such as *Fireman Sam* and the BAFTA-winning *SuperTed*, Welsh animation has gained strings of international awards, and Welsh-based animators are recognised as among the best in the world.

Architecture

It won't take you long to notice Wales' most striking architectural asset: its castles. There are around 600 of them, giving Wales the dubious honour of being Europe's most densely fortified country. Now in various states of ruin or repair, they were mostly built along the coasts and border areas in medieval times by the Anglo-Norman kings to keep a lid on the Welsh. They've been a sore point among patriotic Welsh ever since ('the magnificent badge of our subjection', as the writer Thomas Pennant put it).

The finest are those built by Edward I in North Wales – Caernarfon, Harlech, Conwy and Beaumaris, jointly listed as a UNESCO World Heritage Site – but wherever you go there's a castle not far away. Most are cared for by Cadw, the Welsh historic monuments agency (see under Useful Organisations in the Facts for the Visitor chapter). Cardiff boasts two rather different 'castles' – Cardiff Castle and Castell Coch – designed by William Burges, a Victorian specialist in love-it-or-hate-it repro-Gothic.

Castles aside, Wales is not particularly famous for architecture. The history of Christianity in Wales stretches back to the 5th century, but medieval Wales never shared in the prosperity that gave rise to England's splendid churches and cathedrals. The exceptions are St David's Cathedral and a clutch of ruined Cistercian abbeys at Tintern (lower Wye Valley), Neath (near Swansea), Strata Florida (south-east of Aberystwyth in Ceredigion) and Valle Crucis (near Llangollen).

There are also some pleasing towered churches in Pembrokeshire and Monmouthshire, but the real boom in Welsh church building came during the Industrial Revolution, which coincided with the surge of interest in Nonconformist religion. Wales is scattered from end to end with small, plain Methodist, Baptist and Congregationalist chapels – many now boarded up or converted to some wholly irreligious function.

On the secular side, there are several fine country houses, including Tredegar House outside Newport, Williams Hall at Bodelwyddan on the North Coast (now home to the National Portrait Gallery's Victorian collection) and Plas Newydd, the half-timbered former home of the Ladies of Llangollen (see under Llangollen in the Anglesey & North Coast chapter). This and several other outstanding properties in Wales (including five castles) are owned and managed by the National Trust (NT; see Useful Organisations in the Facts for the Visitor chapter).

Not surprisingly, Wales has an abundance of industrial architecture, and attitudes to this have changed enormously: where once the great colliery towers and winding gear were regarded as eyesores, they're now valued as tourist attractions, vital remnants of history and sources of national pride. In November 2000, the South Wales town of Blaenafon received the ultimate accolade, as a UNESCO World Heritage Site, for its 'Industrial Landscape' of ironworks, quarries and workers' houses (see Blaenafon in the South-East Wales & the Brecon Beacons chapter for details).

Other industrial sites worth visiting are the Rhondda Heritage Centre (see Around Cardiff) and the old slate quarries at Llanberis and Blaenau Ffestiniog (see the Snowdonia & the Llŷn chapter).

Three superb engineering works by Thomas Telford are worth mentioning – the spectacular Pontcysyllte Aqueduct (1805) near Llangollen and his suspension bridges over the Menai Strait and over the River Conwy (both 1826).

Notable contemporary works are rare, although the NCM Building at Cardiff Bay and Richard Rogers' Electrotech plant at Newport have raised some appreciative eyebrows.

SOCIETY & CONDUCT

Wales expresses its Welshness most passionately at the eisteddfodau, not only with music and poetry but with handicrafts, clothes, food and a variety of locally produced fringe events. See the boxed text in the preceding Arts section for more details.

At other times, you're most likely to be reminded you're in Wales when the language you hear isn't English. The stronghold of the Welsh language is in the north-west (especially Anglesey and the Llŷn Peninsula) and to some extent in the Swansea Valley and eastern Carmarthenshire. Especially in those areas, an attempt to speak the language goes down very well. Wherever you go you'll find some degree of nationalist feeling, though it's rarely threatening unless mixed with ignorance and alcohol. An honest attempt to see the Welsh point of view on matters of language and history is all you need to feel welcome here.

Probably the greatest insult you can give the Welsh is to refer to their country as 'England' (see the boxed text 'What's in a Name?').

Alternative Culture

In the 1980s, parts of Mid Wales in particular became popular refuges for people in search of an alternative lifestyle. At its most extreme, this has meant teepee camps in remote valleys; at its most moderate, a pro-

---

What's in a Name?

England dominates the UK to such an extent that not only the English but most of the world tends to say 'England' when they mean the UK. The island of Britain (England, Scotland and Wales) together with Northern Ireland make up the country whose official name is the United Kingdom of Great Britain and Northern Ireland.

It may seem an obvious point but it's important to get it right. The Welsh – like the Scots and the people of Northern Ireland – find it deeply insulting if you tell them how much you like being 'here in England' when you're in their part of the UK.

---

fusion of alternative bookshops and restaurants in small towns such as Llanidloes and Machynlleth.

The Centre for Alternative Technology (CAT) near Machynlleth has concentrated these cravings for something new, wholesome, non-destructive and sustainable: organic farming, energy from sun, wind and water, and the recycling of virtually everything, all in a communal setting – and managed to make a tourist attraction out of it as well.

RELIGION

Christianity is believed to have arrived in Wales in the 5th century, going its own ascetic, monastic way and revering its own saints until the time of the Reformation, when the Welsh Church was reorganised as part of the established Anglican Church. In 1588, William Morgan translated the Bible into Welsh (see the earlier Literature section).

As the population grew in the 18th century, the new industrial working classes were fertile ground for various Nonconformist Protestant denominations, particularly Baptists, Methodists and Congregationalists. An 1851 survey discovered that almost 80% of the population was Nonconformist. In 1920 the Anglican Church effectively ceased to be the established church in Wales.

The Nonconformist tradition brought a puritanical strain to Welsh life that might account for the rather dour image of its people. Until recently, it wasn't just shops that stayed shut on Sunday in Wales, but pubs as well.

But all that has changed, and now it would be hard to argue that Wales is any more actively religious than the rest of the UK. The most recent survey found 108,400 people identifying themselves as members of the Anglican Church, 60,600 as Roman Catholics and 220,300 as Methodists, Baptists and assorted other nonconformists.

See the boxed text under St David's in the Pembrokeshire & Carmarthenshire chapter for a look at Wales' own patron saint, David.

LANGUAGE

The one thing that marks Wales out from the rest of the UK is the survival of Welsh as a living language. Despite its weird, seemingly unpronounceable double 'l's and consecutive consonants, Welsh is an Indo-European language, a Celtic offshoot whose closest linguistic cousins are Cornish and Breton.

During the Roman occupation, people in positions of authority probably spoke Latin, even if everyone else spoke Welsh. Gradually, a bilingual Latin/Welsh-speaking population emerged, and the influence of Latin on Welsh is clear, as is the influence of French (from the Norman period) and English. The language as it is spoken today seems to have been more or less fully developed by the 6th century, making it one of Europe's oldest languages.

Following the Acts of Union (1536 and 1543), people were forbidden to hold high office unless they spoke English as well as Welsh. But within a century of the Protestant Reformation there was a full translation of the Bible in Welsh, which not only helped Protestantism take root but helped to keep the language alive. For more on this historical symbiosis, see The Welsh Church & the Welsh Language in the preceding History section.

But the Industrial Revolution brought a whole new class of industrial landlords, employers and workers, few of whom spoke Welsh. From then on, the number of native Welsh speakers went into steep decline. At the start of the 19th century, 80% of the population probably spoke Welsh, but by 1901 this had sunk to 50%. Today only about 20% of the population speak Welsh as their mother tongue, mainly in the northwest (especially Anglesey and the Llŷn Peninsula, where up to 80% of the people in a given locality may speak it) and to some extent in the Swansea Valley and eastern Carmarthenshire. By contrast, less than 3% of people living in Monmouthshire know more than the odd word.

Reasons for the decline in the number of people speaking Welsh are not hard to find: television, better communications, emigration, mixed marriages and tourism are just some of those commonly cited. Perhaps what is more surprising is that so many people have continued to speak the language.

Since the 1960s the importance of Welsh has been officially recognised, and in 1967 the Welsh Language Act ensured that Welsh speakers could use their own language in court. Since then an increasing number of publications are bilingual, and it's rare now to see a road sign in just one language. In 1982, Channel 4 set up S4C, which broadcasts Welsh television programs daily and has made several feature films (see the boxed text in the Facts for the Visitor chapter). Radio Cymru also transmits in Welsh, and roughly 400 books a year are published in the language.

In 1988, a Welsh Language Board was set up to advise the Welsh Office on everything to do with the language. In 1994, a new Welsh Language Act gave equal status to Welsh as a language for public-sector business. There is some evidence that the number of Welsh speakers has bottomed out and is again on the rise, especially among those under about 15 years of age.

If all this sounds too good to be true, there are those who would argue that is the case and that the cause of the Welsh language has been espoused by middle-class interlopers as a way of ensuring grants and jobs. There are also English visitors who get very hot under the collar when they visit Welsh-speaking areas and find themselves unable to understand what is being said.

For a compendium of useful Welsh words and phrases, and some help on how to get your mouth around them, see the Language chapter.

MYTHS & LEGENDS

landscape rich in natural wonders and artefacts of the past is an obvious breeding ground for myths and legends. Wales is richer than most, featuring in its relatively small area a horde of prehistoric caves and Bronze Age tumuli, cairns, *cromlechs* (burial chambers) and standing stones, Iron Age forts and Roman remains, grand peaks and wild passes, ancient abbeys and ruined castles.

This has always been a nation of small, self-reliant communities, close-knit and sociable, traditionally dependent on story-telling as a form of entertainment, along with songs and festivals, verse and riddles. The pride and enthusiasm generated by its centuries-old celebrations of Welsh literature and culture, the *eisteddfodau* (see the boxed text under Literature in the Facts about Wales chapter), testifies to the continuing importance attached to this tradition.

But here it's not just the landscape that makes people tell tales of giants, saints and fairies, King Arthur and the Devil, mythological beasts and supernatural events. Wales' long history is itself rich and dramatic enough to have inspired many a story. From the time of the Celts and their druid priests, through the Roman era to the struggle against the Saxons, to the arrival of Christianity during the 5th and 6th centuries, there was always ample fodder for a God-fearing, death-fearing audience who had been invaded, suppressed and occasionally treated to moments of glorious victory.

As early as the 9th century, a collection of tales featuring everything from mysterious lakes and stones to the heroic King Arthur had appeared in *Historia Brittonum* written by one Nennius, thought to be a monk at Bangor. Throughout the Middle Ages, professional story-tellers carried on the already ancient tradition of boosting the morale and massaging the self-esteem of their noble patrons with tales full of all the favourite themes: battles against evil (notably the devil or foul witches), the adventures of heroic leaders, tales of magic, mystery and enchantment, full of fairies and ghosts.

Few of these stories were ever written down by the Welsh in their own language, so most have either been dressed up almost unrecognisably in the clothes of other cultures or have been lost. But a handful of fantastic tales derived from myths of the Celtic gods have survived in two remarkable 14th-century compendia called *The White Book of Rhydderch* and *The Red Book of Hergest*, together known as *The Mabinogion*. (The latter title – meaning something like 'Tales of a Hero's Youth' – was only bestowed by their 19th-century English translator, Lady Charlotte Guest.) It is *The Mabinogion* that today provides us with the clearest window into Welsh mythology, an insight into a magical, and sometimes rather terrifying, pagan Celtic world.

By the 15th century, with the addition of specifically Welsh heroes to the cast of characters (Llewelyn the Great, his grandson Llywelyn ap Gruffydd, Owain Glyndŵr and others – all seen as leading the resistance against the English conqueror), the source material was richer than ever.

Illustrations: Jane Smith

Stones, Lakes & Holy Wells

Some of the most enchanting Welsh myths step straight from the world of fairy tales, featuring locales that feel strange and mysterious even today.

Llyn y Fan Fach, a small alpine lake of dark waters in the Black Mountain area of eastern Carmarthenshire, is the setting for the best known of Wales' many Lady-of-the-Lake stories. A farmer's son falls in love with a fairy-woman from the lake, and is permitted to marry her on condition he does not strike her three times in anger. Inevitably he does so and back she goes, leaving behind only her knowledge of local medicinal herbs and an appeal to their son to heal the sick (for more on this legend, and its connection with a real family of medieval physicians in the area, see the boxed text 'The Physicians of Myddfai' under Llandovery in the Mid Wales chapter).

Water is associated in a curious way with many of Wales' prehistoric standing stones (menhirs). These megaliths – invariably said to have been thrown into their positions by giants, saints, King Arthur or Merlin – often have the added mystery of allegedly wandering off for a drink at certain times. Samson's Stone (near Kenfig, South Wales) goes down to the River Sker on Christmas morning; the immense Fish Stone (near Crickhowell in southern Powys) pops into the River Usk for a Midsummer Eve's swim; the four standing stones at Old Radnor (east of Llandrindod Wells in southern Powys) sip from Hindwell Pool when the village church bells ring at night.

Strange markings on many of these stones, and on equally ancient burial chambers, are taken to be finger marks of the devil, King Arthur etc, when they threw the stones. Perhaps the chamber with the spookiest association is at St Lythan's (5 miles south-west of Cardiff), set in the so-called Accursed Field (where nothing can grow) and whose capstone is said to spin round three times on Midsummer's Eve.

The many ancient burial mounds scattered throughout Wales have their own genre of legends: some as the graves of giants (or of Roman soldiers, as with the Twyn Tudor mound on Mynydd Islwyn in South Wales), some to have been deposited by the devil. Treasure-seekers or

Death & Disaster

Scoff if you like, but don't say we didn't warn you. Here are a few myths to ignore at your peril:

Cader Idris If you spend the night on the 889m summit of this peak in southern Snowdonia (its name means Chair of Idris , referring to a mythical giant who lives on the mountain)) and you'll wake up either blind, mad or a poet.

Maen Du'r-arddu In a version of Cader Idris's warning, a couple who sleeps by this boulder, also in Snowdonia, will find by morning that one has become a poet and the other mad.

Tinkinswood, near St Nicholas, Cardiff Don't dance round this Neolithic burial chamber on a Sunday or you'll end up like the group of women who once did so and were turned into the stones that now surround it.

Twyn Tudor, Mynydd Islwyn, South Wales If you dig into this mysterious mound for treasure you'll provoke a terrific thunderstorm.

Twmbarlwm Hill, near Risca, Gwent Don't meddle with this mound (said to be the site of a former druid court of justice) or you'll be attacked by a swarm of bees (as happened in 1984 to a group of workmen trying to restore the mound).

Llyn Irddyn, North Wales Walk on the grass round this lake and malicious fairies will come and get you (keep a blade of grass in your pocket as a safeguard).

others with the temerity to poke around on these mounds often meet with misfortune or disaster (see the boxed text 'Death & Disaster'). There is a nugget of truth in some of the stories. For years the so-called Mound of the Goblins (Tomen yr El-lyllon, near Mold in North Wales) was said to be haunted by a horseman in gold armour. When it was excavated in 1833, lo and behold, a man's skeleton was found, wrapped in a gold cape some 3500 years old.

A good many other Welsh legends – notably those about floods and submerged cities – are probably based on fact. The most famous of these concerns Cardigan Bay, said to have once been dry land – a fertile region called Cantref Gwaelod (The Lowland Hundred). The legend recounts how Sei-thenyn, keeper of the dikes that kept the sea at

bay, got drunk one night and forgot to shut the sluice gates, and the land, together with 16 cities, was inundated. Even today, so the stories go, you can hear the tolling of sunken church bells (this buried-city legend is so popular it has also travelled elsewhere, complete with church bells – eg, to Llangorse Lake near Brecon).

The arrival of Christianity in Wales gave a new slant to many ancient stories: markings on stones, previously attributed to a giant, or Arthur's horse, became the footprints of saints; mysterious mounds were said to have been miraculously elevated as pulpits from the surrounding land by preachers. Most commonly, wells once worshipped in pagan rites, and supposedly guarded by dragons or huge eels, acquired associations with Christian saints and amazing curative powers. The best known is St Winifred's Well, around which the town of Holywell (in North Wales) has flourished. A 7th-century chieftain called Caradoc, when rejected by Winifred, niece of St Beuno, expressed his displeasure by decapitating her. From the spot where her head fell there appeared a spring, one with healing power of course – even for Caradoc's own descendants, who were cursed by St Beuno to bark like dogs unless they immersed themselves in its waters. To round out this tale, St Beuno managed to join Winifred's head back to her body with a prayer, and she later became an abbess.

Arth Fawr the Bear

No other figure has inspired more legends, folk tales and curiosities, nor given his name to more features of the landscape in Wales, than King Arthur. And no other hero has had a story so interwoven with myth and mystery, folklore and fiction. Was he a giant of superhuman strength or a dwarf king who rode a goat instead of a horse? Was he a Celtic god associated with the constellation called Ursa Major, the Great Bear (Arth Fawr in Welsh), also known as Arthur's Plough (Aradr Arthur)? Or was he, as most historians suspect, a 5th- or 6th-century cavalry leader who led the early Britons in a dozen major battles against the Saxon invaders, and whose story became increasingly romanticised?

One of the earliest, most tantalising descriptions about such a hero appears in the *Historia Brittonum*. By the 9th century Arthur's fame as a fighter against the Saxons had reached every corner of the British Isles. Legends crop up from Cornwall to Scotland, associating him with local caves (where he and his knights are said to be sleeping, waiting to fight again), ancient megaliths (named Arthur's Chair, Arthur's Table or Arthur's Quoit), mountains (battle scenes and troves of treasure) and lakes (the magical source of his great sword).

Prose romances and epic poems soon transformed Arthur into a heroic king of marvels and magic deeds, at the head of a phalanx of other famous heroes and aided by the wise magician Myrddin (Merlin; see the following section). Arthur is there in the 12th-century *Llyfr Du Caerfyrddin* (The Black Book of Carmarthen), the oldest surviving Welsh manuscript. In the centuries that followed, other writers – most recently and perhaps most famously the Victorian poet Alfred Lord Tennyson – climbed on the bandwagon, weaving in love stories, Christian symbolism and medieval pageantry to create the romance that surrounds Arthur today.

Tintagel in Cornwall has the strongest claim to be Arthur's birthplace, Cadbury Castle in Somerset as the site of Camelot, his court, and Glastonbury Abbey as his burial place, but Wales – especially southern Wales – makes many fervent claims of its own. The 12th-century historian-novelist Geoffrey of Monmouth (see the boxed text under Monmouth in the South-East Wales & the Brecon Beacons chapter) claimed that a grassy mound at Caerleon, near Newport in Gwent, was the site of Arthur's first court, describing it as populated with hundreds of scholars, astrologers and philosophers as well as many fine knights and ladies. And why not? Caerleon had already been favoured by the Romans, serving as headquarters of the elite, 6000-strong Second Augustan Legion. The remains of its amphitheatre are still visible today (doing double duty in the mind's eye as Arthur's great Round Table).

Camlan, the site of Arthur's final battle (curiously well pinpointed at around AD 542), may

have been in Cornwall, Somerset or Cumberland but Wales has at least two candidates: Camlan hill in Cwm Cerist in the north-west, and Maes Camlan in Mid Wales. As for Avalon (Avallach in Welsh) – the blessed 'island of apples' where the dying Arthur was taken by Merlin – could it not be Wales' saintly Bardsey Island (off the tip of the Llŷn Peninsula)?

Many other places in Wales have used natural features or curiosities to suit the Arthurian legends, notably the Preseli Hills of northern Pembrokeshire – the source of the 'bluestone' megaliths that form the inner circle of Stonehenge in England and the site of many Neolithic monuments bearing Arthur's name. The Gower Peninsula's scattered megaliths have been drafted in – notably a massive burial chamber on Cefn Bryn near Reynoldston (see The Gower Peninsula in the South-East Wales & the Brecon Beacons chapter) whose 25-ton capstone is well known as Arthur's Stone. Castell Dinas Brân at Llangollen is said to hide the Holy Grail – the vessel used by Christ at the Last Supper and imbued with supernatural qualities – which Arthur and his knights sought obsessively in later stories.

More intriguingly, some locales have directly inspired Welsh versions of the hero's exploits. The Pembrokeshire coast is where – according to the 10th-century story *Culhwch and Olwen*, earliest of all the Welsh-language Arthurian tales, and part of *The Mabinogion* – Arthur and his knights started the hunt for a ferocious magic boar. On Mt Snowdon, Arthur slew Rita Gawr, a giant notorious for killing kings and making coats of their beards. Snowdon also provides an alternative version of the king's death and burial, following a fierce battle at Bwlch-y-Saethau (Pass of the Arrows), after which his knights took refuge in a nearby cave called Ogof Lanciau Eryri (Cave of the Lads of Eryri) – although, of course, other Welsh caves, including Craig-y-Ddinas in South Wales, also lay claim to this role.

Ultimately, in most stories Arthur and his followers end up in a cave – not dead, perish the thought, but in a kind of mythical cold storage – asleep until the Once and Future King is again called upon to defend Britain.

Merlin the Magician

The story of this great Welsh wizard is probably modelled on a 6th-century holy man named Myrddin Emrys (or Ambrosius), thought to have been born near Carmarthen (whose Welsh name, Caerfyrddin, means Merlin's City) during the time of Vortigern, a legendary leader of the Roman British against the Saxons.

It's said that Myrddin's mother was a strict Christian and his father an evil man of magical powers: Myrddin inherited the wizardry minus the wickedness and became famous for his prophecies (a specifically Welsh angle to the legend says he had acquired his prophetic skills while wandering for 50 years in the Scottish Lowlands in the company of wild animals). By the 10th century these prophecies were common currency across western Europe, and gave hope to many Welsh princes in their struggles with the Anglo-Normans. One of the most potent of these early rallying prophecies concerns two dragons, one red and one white, revealed by Myrddin to be lurking in a cave beneath a place where Vortigern had tried unsuccessfully to build a tower, on Dinas Emrys in Snowdonia. The dragons started fighting, Myrddin explaining to the king that the struggle symbolised the fight between Britons (or the Welsh) and Saxons. Naturally the red dragon – symbolising Wales – won (and Myrddin kept Dinas Emrys as the site for his own fortress).

Geoffrey of Monmouth, the Benedictine monk whose colourful *Historia Regum Britanniae* (The History of the Kings of Britain) became a 12th-century bestseller, changed Myrddin's name to Merlin (in order, so it's said, to spare the delicate sensibilities of his Norman French readers from any association between 'Myrddin' and *merde*) and shamelessly embellished the old stories.

He presented Merlin as the wise wizard and advisor to Arthur's father, King Uther Pendragon. Among his (as it were) seminal acts was to disguise Uther one night as Duke Gorlois, to enable Uther to spend the night with the duke's wife Ygerna, who duly conceived Arthur. It was Merlin, too, who planted the prediction that Uther Pendragon's true heir would draw a sword from a stone, and who advised Uther to establish a fellowship of

knights (and who actually made the famous Round Table at which those knights would eventually sit). These stories would become essential ingredients in the highly romanticised Arthurian legend which developed in the following centuries, most notably in the hands of the French poet Chrétien de Troyes in the 12th century, and in the English-language *Morte d'Arthur*, written by Sir Thomas Malory in the 15th century.

As Arthur's own counsellor, Merlin continued to be the pivot around which all revolved. It was through Merlin, of course, that Arthur obtained his miraculous sword, Excalibur – from another Lady of the Lake (one of many lakes to claim this role is the lily pond at Bosherston, in south Pembrokeshire). It was Merlin who predicted Arthur's demise, and it was thanks to Merlin that his remaining knights afterwards found safety on the Scilly Isles.

Merlin himself appears to have come to an ignominious end, trapped by that same Lady of the Lake in a cave on Bryn Myrddin (Merlin's Hill) just east of Carmarthen – where groans and the clanking of iron chains are still part of local lore. Other versions sustain the hopes of believers by insisting that Merlin is not dead but held in a trance in Brittany (where many Britons had indeed found refuge from the Saxons in the 5th century) or in a glass house on Bardsey Island, where he guards the Thirteen Treasures of Britain (including a magical cloak, a cauldron, a robe, a ring and a chessboard with pieces that play themselves).

Tales like this still have a grip of some kind on the Welsh imagination. The stump of a 17th-century oak tree, nicknamed 'Merlin's Tree', once stood inconveniently in Carmarthen's Priory St. One of Merlin's well documented prophecies was that

When Myrddin's tree shall tumble down/Then shall fall Carmarthen town.

The tree died of old age and was removed in 1978, and Carmarthen is still there – although some years after the tree died, the River Tywi burst its banks and flooded the town. Pieces of the tree are still kept under glass at Carmarthen's civic centre.

Readers interested in knowing more about Wales' ancient stories should check out Robin Gwyndaf's detailed bilingual *Chwedlau Gwerin Cymru; Welsh Folk Tales*, or the Wales chapter of the Reader's Digest anthology, *Folklore, Myths and Legends of Britain*.

Facts for the Visitor

HIGHLIGHTS
Here's a list to help you find the best of everything in Wales:

Outdoor Activities
Coasteering
High-adrenaline coastal cliff exploration (North Pembrokeshire)

Mt Snowdon
Scramble, stroll or ride to unbeatable views from the highest point in England and Wales (Snowdonia)

Mawddach Trail
Through woodlands and wetlands from Dolgellau to Barmouth, along one of Wales' loveliest estuaries (Snowdonia)

Coed y Brenin Forest Park
Some of Britain's finest cycle trails, near Dolgellau (Snowdonia)

River Treweryn
Wales' biggest rapids, near Bala (Snowdonia)

Pontcysyllte Aqueduct
Canal boating across Thomas Telford's engineering masterpiece (near Llangollen)

Castles & Walled Towns
Caernarfon
The most intimidating of Edward I's many castles (Snowdonia)

Conwy
One of Europe's finest walled towns (North Coast)

Caerphilly
Wales' biggest and most powerful castle (near Cardiff)

Historic Cities & Towns
Victorian seaside resorts
Big beaches, genteel accommodation and old-fashioned entertainment at Tenby (South Pembrokeshire), Aberystwyth (Ceredigion) and Llandudno (North Coast)

Llandrindod Wells
Wales' handsomest Victorian spa town (Mid Wales)

Industrial/mining sites
The heavy tracks of the Industrial Revolution in Wales, at Blaenafon (South-East Wales) and Blaenau Ffestiniog (Snowdonia)

Cathedrals, Churches & Abbeys
St David's Cathedral
Wales' holiest place, dedicated to its patron saint (North Pembrokeshire)

Tintern Abbey
Serene remnants of a once-powerful Cistercian abbey, in the lower Wye Valley (South-East Wales)

Cathedral Church of St Deiniol
Ancient seat of Britain's oldest diocese, Bangor (Snowdonia)

Museums & Galleries
National Museum & Gallery of Wales
Wales' pride and joy, with a superb collection of impressionist paintings (Cardiff)

Techniquest
One of Britain's best hands-on science museums, and very child-friendly (Cardiff)

Museum of Welsh Life
History made real, in the form of old churches, mills, homes, barns and other buildings rescued and reconstructed at St Fagans (near Cardiff)

Big Pit Mining Museum
A chance to go down into a genuine coal mine with the miners who once worked it, Blaenafon (South-East Wales)

Centre for Alternative Technology
One of Europe's premier ecocentres, near Machynlleth (Mid Wales)

Gardens
National Botanic Garden of Wales
A world-class attraction rivalling London's Kew Gardens and twice its size, with the world's largest single-span glass house (Carmarthenshire)

Bodnant Garden
One of the UK's finest gardens, a riot of rhododendrons, camellias and magnolias in spring, roses and water-lilies in summer, and hydrangeas in autumn, near Conwy (North Coast)

Powis Castle
Spectacular terraced gardens, overhung with yew hedges, Welshpool (Mid Wales)

Stackpole Estate
Lily ponds, footpaths, causeways and a handsome eight-arched bridge, Bosherston (South Pembrokeshire)

Coastline
Worm's Head
Wave-blasted tidal islands at Rhossili, beside Rhossili Bay, the biggest and finest beach on the Gower Peninsula, near Swansea (South Wales)

St David's to Cardigan
The wildest stretch of Britain's only coastal national park, with dramatic clifftop scenery, some of the world's oldest rocks, and seabird sanctuaries (North Pembrokeshire)

Newborough Warren
A National Nature Reserve around one of Britain's finest coastal sand-dune systems (Anglesey)

Islands

Skomer Island
Seals, seabirds and an Iron Age settlement (South Pembrokeshire)

Caldey Island
Cistercian monks, grey seals and seabirds, near Tenby (South Pembrokeshire)

Bardsey Island
The 'Isle of 20,000 Saints' (Llŷn Peninsula)

Isle of Anglesey
Last refuge of the Celts in Britain, and still one of the most determinedly Welsh parts of Wales

Prehistoric Remains

Castell Henllys
A restored Iron Age settlement with an imaginative range of events and activities that brings the ancient Celts to life (North Pembrokeshire)

Pentre Ifan
A 4500-year-old Neolithic burial chamber, thought to be the finest and best-preserved such chamber in Wales, Preseli Hills (North Pembrokeshire)

Barclodiad y Gawres
Wales' most important Neolithic site, a burial chamber featuring ceremonial art of the time (Anglesey)

Roman Sites

Caerleon
Wales' most important Roman site, one of Roman Britain's three principal military bases, complete with a 6000-seat amphitheatre, near Newport (South-East Wales)

Segontium
The westernmost Roman legionary fort in the Roman Empire, from where Anglesey was conquered, near Caernarfon (Snowdonia)

Train Journeys

Heart of Wales Line
Across the remote and beautiful centre of Wales, from Swansea to Llandrindod Wells (Mid Wales)

Vale of Rheidol Railway
A gorgeous 12-mile journey from Aberystwyth to Devil's Bridge (Mid Wales)

Cambrian Coaster
Prime coastal scenery from Machynlleth to Pwllheli (Snowdonia)

Ffestiniog Railway
Scenic 14-mile route of the line once used to haul slate from Blaenau Ffestiniog to port at Porthmadog (Snowdonia)

Snowdon Mountain Railway
The easy way to reach the summit of Mt Snowdon, highest point in Wales (Snowdonia)

Festivals

Royal National Eisteddfod
Annual August jamboree of Welsh poetry, music and more, the descendant of ancient bardic tournaments

Cardiff Festival
Three-week, midsummer bash with concerts, dance, comedy, food and drink, culminating with Britain's biggest open-air free festival, July/August (Cardiff)

Llanwrtyd Wells
Bog-snorkelling and other oddball events all summer (Mid Wales)

Festival of Literature
The highlight of the year in the town with two score and more bookshops, May/July, Hay-on-Wye (Brecon Beacons)

Sports Events

Millennium Stadium
Any event here, a three-tiered monster with a sliding roof – probably Britain's finest sports venue (Cardiff)

Youth Hostels

Llangollen Youth Hostel
Occupying its own rural Victorian mansion (North-East Wales)

Pwll Deri Youth Hostel
Perched at the edge of a 120m cliff above the roaring sea (North Pembrokeshire)

Penycwm Youth Hostel
Wales' only five-star hostel, child-friendly and comfortable (South Pembrokeshire)

SUGGESTED ITINERARIES

The itineraries described in this section cover most of Wales' worthy destinations, leaving you to work out local excursions. They assume a total of one day each week in transit.

One Week

Cardiff & Around – Cardiff town centre, Cardiff Bay, National Museum (three days), Castell Coch and Caerphilly (one day), Museum of Welsh Life and Rhondda Heritage Park (one day), Newport and Caerleon (one day)

Swansea & the Brecon Beacons – Swansea and the Gower Peninsula (two days), to Llandrindod Wells on the Heart of Wales Line (one day), Brecon and Brecon Beacons walks (two days), via Merthyr Tydfil to Swansea (one day)

Pembrokeshire – Tenby and Manorbier (one day), Pembroke and Stackpole (one day), St Bride's Bay and trip to Skomer Island (one day), St David's (one day), Fishguard (one day), Newport and Nevern (one day)

Snowdonia Sampler – Conwy (one day), Betws-y-Coed with local walks (one day), Blaenau Ffestiniog and Porthmadog with visit to Portmeirion (one day), Llanberis with a trip up Snowdon (two days), Caernarfon (one day), back to Conwy

Two Weeks

Cardiff (two days), Brecon and Brecon Beacons walks (two days), via National Botanic Garden of Wales to St David's (two days), Aberystwyth, Vale of Rheidol Railway and Devil's Bridge (one day), Porthmadog, Portmeirion, Blaenau Ffestiniog and Betws-y-Coed (two days), Llanberis and Mt Snowdon (two days), Caernarfon (one day)

One Month

Cardiff & Around (three days), Chepstow, Tintern and Monmouth (two days), Abergavenny, Blaenau, Brecon and Brecon Beacons walks (four days), the National Botanic Garden and Tenby (two days), St David's, Fishguard, Newport and the Preseli Hills (four days), Aberystwyth and Devil's Bridge (one day), Machynlleth and the Centre for Alternative Technology (one day), Dolgellau and Barmouth (one day), Porthmadog and Portmeirion (one day), Blaenau Ffestiniog and Betws-y-Coed (one day), Llanberis and Caernarfon (two days), Bangor, Holyhead and south Anglesey (two days), Conwy and Llandudno (one day)

PLANNING
When to Go

Settled weather – sunny or otherwise – is rare in Wales, with rain likely at any time. Even in midsummer you may go for days without seeing the sun, and you'd be crazy to go out without an umbrella or raingear. But rural Wales is beautiful even in the rain; after all, that's what makes it so lush and green!

The least hospitable months are November to February, with cold, wet (or frosty) weather and startlingly short days (less than eight hours of daylight in December). Winter occasionally blankets the north picturesquely in snow, and many hotels and bed & breakfasts (B&Bs) offer reduced rates then; but many attractions, Tourist Information Centres (TICs) and B&Bs close from October to around Easter, and some mountain passes get snowbound.

March brings daffodils in the south, but it's not warm yet. October is acceptable, with moderate temperatures and marginally stabler weather, which means you can get good spells of sun (or rain).

In July and August, attractions, accommodation and roads get choked with visitors, and even the kindest of local people grow annoyed with the crush. Spring and early summer (especially May and June) and autumn (especially September) are the finest times to go, when the landscape bursts into colour, the roads are empty, and accommodation is plentiful in every price range.

See also the Climate section in the Facts about Wales chapter.

What Kind of Trip

Wales may be small but there are no fast roads, apart from the M4 across the south and the A55 along the north coast. Trying to nip round ticking off the sights will just drive you crazy. The remoter parts of Wales are best appreciated on a longer stay. One way to relax and maximise your pleasure is to base yourself in a small village, a farmhouse B&B or a hostel near one of the national parks.

There are some appealing options for long-distance rail travel, particularly the Heart of Wales line and the Cambrian Coaster. You can take Arriva's TrawsCambria coach all the way from Holyhead to Cardiff (and on to Bristol), but coach transport – though cheaper than trains – tends to be chopped up by county, requiring frequent changes. There are several hop-on, hop-off coach tours tailored to backpackers; see the Getting Around chapter for details.

With three national trails and hundreds of miles of sublime coastline, Wales is a fine place for walking. There is also a trans-Wales bicycle route, Lôn Las Cymru, and many local multi-use trails. Indeed one of the pleasures of Wales is its menu of outdoor activities of all types. See the Activities section later in the chapter.

Maps

Two useful countrywide maps, updated annually by the Wales Tourist Board (WTB), are available at nearly every TIC. The *Wales Tourist Map* (£2.50) presents all major roads and major sights, national parks, towns with TICs (and a list of those open in winter), several town plans, and suggested car tours. The free *Wales Bus, Rail and Tourist Map & Guide* manages to map just about every bus and train route in Wales with more than about three services per week, plus the essentials of bus, train and ferry connections into Wales, along with tables of frequencies and information numbers.

Free regional transport booklets, with complete maps and timetables, are also available at TICs, and train stations stock free timetables provided by each train operator.

For walkers and cyclists, most TICs and local bookshops stock the UK-government-published Ordnance Survey (OS) maps covering their regions, including the useful 1:50,000 (about 3cm to the mile) Landranger series at about £5.25, the excruciatingly detailed 1:25,000 (about 6.5cm to the mile) Outdoor Leisure series at £6.50 and the Explorer series at £5.50. OS Pathfinder Walking Guides cover short walks in popular areas, and Outdoor Leisure maps cover the national parks, both at 1:25,000.

On a more general scale, look for the OS Routemaster series at 1:250,000. A to Z publishes 1:200,000 *North Wales* and *South Wales* road maps (£4.25), with useful detailed town indexes. Many TICs also have free or inexpensive leaflets on local walks available.

Maps can be ordered on-line at the OS Web site at www.ordsvy.gov.uk.

What to Bring

Just about everything you need is available in high-street chain shops and national supermarkets, so pack light and pick up extras as you go along.

A travelpack – a combination backpack and shoulder bag – is the most sensible way to carry your gear, especially if you plan to do any walking. Its straps zip away inside when not needed, making it easy to handle in airports and on crowded public transport. Most travelpacks have sophisticated shoulder-strap adjustment systems and can be used comfortably, even for long hikes.

Only diehard campers need bring a tent: the weather hardly encourages camping, and long-distance walks are well served by hostels, bunkhouses and B&Bs. A sleeping bag is useful in hostels and when visiting friends. A sleeping sheet with pillow cover is preferred, and sometimes required, at Youth Hostel Association (YHA) hostels; if you don't bring one you might have to hire or purchase one.

A padlock may be needed to secure your hostel locker, and – especially with a light, case-hardened chain – is handy for locking your bag to a train or bus luggage rack. A Swiss Army knife (or any pocketknife with a bottle opener and strong corkscrew) is useful for all sorts of things. For city sightseeing, a small daypack is harder for snatch thieves to grab than a shoulder bag.

Other possibilities include a compass, an alarm clock, a torch (flashlight), an adapter plug for electrical appliances (see Electricity later), sunglasses and an elastic clothesline.

Raingear is absolutely mandatory in Wales. Whether it's waterproof outwear or an umbrella or both, bring whatever you need because you can expect rain at anytime anywhere. An umbrella is easier to deploy than a high-tech raincoat in brief showers. If you're walking, bring not only a waterproof jacket but also waterproof overtrousers since it may be windy as well as rainy. In summer a swimming costume is also useful; the sea can be surprisingly warm.

Toiletries are easily purchased. Use plastic carrier bags to keep things organised inside your bag or backpack (and dry in case it's left sitting in the rain). Airlines lose bags from time to time, but there's a better chance of getting yours back if it's tagged with your name and address – inside as well as outside.

RESPONSIBLE TOURISM

Wales – even its rural and mountainous corners – gets desperately crowded during the peak tourist season. Traffic on narrow roads in popular spots can come almost to a standstill, and visitors can do residents and themselves a favour by using public transport.

Mountain bikers should stick to roads or designated bike tracks as considerable damage has been done to mountain paths (eg, in Snowdonia) by cyclists. If you're rough camping make sure you ask the permission of the landowner first and take care not to damage crops or leave any litter.

TOURIST OFFICES

The Wales Tourist Board (WTB; ☎ 029-2047 5298, fax 2047 5345) has its headquarters in Brunel House, 2 Fitzalan Rd, Cardiff CF2 1UY. Check out its Web site at www.visitwales.com.

Outside Wales, the WTB is represented by the British Tourist Authority (BTA; ☎ 020-8846 9000, fax 8563 0302), Thames Tower, Black's Rd, London W6 9EL. In London, visit the Wales desk at the Britain Visitor Centre (☎ 020-7808 3838, fax 7808 3830), 1 Regent St. The BTA's Web site is at www.visitbritain.com.

Local Tourist Offices

Every town of any size has its own TIC, usually run by the local council. In towns in or around one of Wales' three national parks, the TIC may be run by the park, although it still dispenses local as well as park information. TICs usually have lots of free brochures on local and regional attractions, and also sell a range of OS and other maps, books and sometimes souvenirs.

Most TICs are staffed by local people, happy to chat about their town or region – especially first thing in the morning before the crowds have worn them down. You can book accommodation with them – both locally and for your next few stops under the Book-A-Bed-Ahead (BABA) scheme – for a nonrefundable £1 fee plus a 10% deposit which is deducted from what you pay your host. Most TICs, however, will only tell you about accommodation that meets the requirements of the WTB, often overlooking some good bottom-end bargains.

Most TICs are open at a minimum from 10 am to 5.30 pm on weekdays, with longer hours and more open days in high season and/or at popular destinations. Many in smaller towns close or keep limited hours during the winter season, typically November to Easter. Even when they're closed you might find a map and information on accommodation and other services posted in the window.

Tourist Offices Abroad

Following are the addresses of some overseas BTA offices:

Australia
(☎ 02-9377 4400, fax 9377 4499, ⓔ visitbritain aus@bta.org.uk) Level 16, The Gateway, 1 Macquarie Place, Circular Quay, Sydney, NSW 2000

Canada
(☎ 905-405 1840, toll free 888-847 4885, fax 905-405 1835) 5915 Airport Rd, Suite 120, Mississauga, Ontario L4V 1T1

France
(☎ 01 44 51 56 20, fax 01 44 51 56 21) Maison de la Grande Bretagne, 19 rue des Mathurins, 75009 Paris

Germany
(☎ 069-971123, fax 9711 2444, ⓔ gb-info@bta .org.uk) Westendstrasse 16–22, 60325 Frankfurt-am-Main

Ireland
(☎ 01-670 8000, fax 670 8244) 18–19 College Green, Dublin 2

Netherlands
(☎ 020-689 0002, fax 689 0003, ⓔ britinfo.nl@ bta.org.uk) Stadhouderskade 2, 1054 ES Amsterdam

New Zealand
(☎ 09-303 1446, fax 377 6965) 17th floor, Fay Richwhite Building, 151 Queen St, Auckland 1

USA
Chicago: (☎ 800-462 2748, @ travelinfo@bta
.org.uk) 625 N Michigan Ave, Suite 1001,
Chicago IL 60611 (personal callers only)
New York: (☎ 800-462 2748, @ travelinfo@bta
.org.uk) 551 Fifth Avenue, Suite 701, New
York, NY 10176

There are over 40 BTA offices worldwide;
for other addresses see its Web site at www
.bta.org.uk.

VISAS & DOCUMENTS

Unlike many other European countries,
people in the UK are not required by law to
carry identification, but it's always a good
idea to have your passport or some other
photo ID with you.

Passport

Your most important travel document is a
passport. Its validity date should be well
past the date when your trip is to end; if it's
just about to expire, renew it before you go.

Getting or renewing a passport can take
from a few days to several months, so don't
leave it until the last minute. Bureaucracy
usually grinds faster if you apply in person
rather than by mail or through a passport
agency. Be sure to take everything you need
when you apply – eg, passport photos, birth
certificate, population register extract, signed
statements, exact payment in cash.

Australian citizens can apply at post offices or at the passport office in their state
capital; New Zealanders can apply at any
district office of the Department of Internal
Affairs; Canadians can apply at regional
passport offices; and US citizens must
apply in person (but may usually renew by
mail) at a US Passport Agency office or at
certain courthouses and post offices.

Citizens of certain European countries
may not need a passport to travel to the UK.
A national identity card may be sufficient,
and usually involves less paperwork and
processing time. Check with your travel
agent or the British embassy.

Visas

No visas are required if you arrive in Wales
from within the UK. If you arrive directly
from any other country, British regulations
apply.

At present, citizens of Australia, Canada,
New Zealand, South Africa and the USA
are given 'leave to enter' the UK at their
point of arrival for up to six months, but are
prohibited from working. If you're a citizen
of the European Union (EU), you don't
need a visa to enter the country and may
live and work here freely. However, visa
regulations are always subject to change, so
check with your local British embassy, high
commission or consulate before leaving
home.

The immigration authorities in the UK
are tough. Dress neatly and be prepared to
prove that you have sufficient funds to support yourself. A credit card and/or an onward ticket will help.

Visa Extensions Tourist visas can only be
extended in clear emergencies (eg, an accident). Otherwise you must leave the UK
(eg, by going to Ireland or France) and
apply for a fresh one, although this tactic
will arouse suspicion after the second or
third visa. To extend (or attempt to extend)
your stay in the UK, contact the Home Office's Immigration & Nationality Department (☎ 020-8686 0688), Lunar House, 40
Wellesley Rd, Croydon CR2 2BY, before
your existing visa expires. It opens 10 am to
noon and 2 to 4 pm Monday to Friday. You
can also ring the Visa & Passport Information Line on ☎ 0870 606 7766.

Student Visas Nationals of EU countries
can enter the UK to study without formalities. Otherwise you must be enrolled on a
full-time course of at least 15 hours a week
of weekday, daytime study at a single educational institution to be allowed to remain
as a student. For more details, consult the
British embassy, high commission or consulate in your own country.

Work Permits EU nationals don't need a
permit to work in the UK, but everyone else
does. If the main purpose of your visit is to
work, you must be sponsored by a British
company.

However, if you're a citizen of a Commonwealth country and aged 17 to 27 inclusive, you may apply for a Working Holiday Entry Certificate, which allows you to spend up to two years in the UK and take work that is 'incidental' to a holiday. You must apply to the nearest UK mission overseas: Working Holiday Entry Certificates are not granted on arrival in the UK, and you cannot switch from being a visitor to a working holiday-maker. When you apply, you must satisfy the authorities that you have the means to pay for a return or onward journey and that you will be able to maintain yourself without recourse to public funds.

Visiting students from the USA who are at least 18 years old and studying full time at a college or university can get a permit allowing them to work for six months. It costs US$200 and is available through the Council on International Educational Exchange (☎ 212-661 1414), 205 East 42nd St, New York, NY 10017; its Web site is at www.ciee.org. The British Universities North America Club (BUNAC; ☎ 020-7251 3472, fax 7251 0215, ℮ enquiries@bunac .org.uk), 16 Bowling Green Lane, London EC1R 0QH, can also help you organise a permit and find employment. Its Web site is at www.bunac.org.

If you have any queries once you're in the UK, contact the Home Office's Immigration & Nationality Department (see the earlier Visa Extensions section).

Travel Insurance

Whichever way you're travelling, make sure you take out a comprehensive travel insurance policy that covers you for medical expenses and luggage theft or loss, and for cancellation of (or delays in) your travel arrangements. Ticket loss should also be included, but make sure you have a separate record of all the details, or better still, a photocopy of the ticket.

The international student travel policies handled by STA Travel and other student travel organisations are usually good value. Some policies offer lower and higher medical expense options; unless you're eligible for free NHS treatment (see the Health sec-

tion later in the chapter), go for as much as you can afford. Other policies are cheaper if you forgo cover for lost baggage.

Buy insurance as early as possible. Otherwise you may find you're not covered for flight delays caused by strikes or other industrial action. Always read the small print carefully for loopholes.

Paying for your ticket with a credit card often provides limited travel accident insurance, and you may be able to reclaim the payment if the operator doesn't deliver. In the UK, credit card providers are required by law to reimburse consumers if a company goes into liquidation and the amount in contention is more than £100.

Driving Licence & Permits

Your normal driving licence is legal for 12 months from the date you last entered the UK; you can then apply for a British licence at post offices. The International Driving Permit (IDP) is not needed in the UK. For more on driving to and around Wales, see under Car & Motorcycle in the Getting There & Away and Getting Around chapters.

Camping Card International

Your local automobile association can issue a Camping Card International, which is basically a camping ground ID card. They're also issued by local camping federations, and sometimes on the spot at camp sites. They incorporate third party insurance for damage you may cause, and many camping grounds offer a small discount if you sign in with one.

Hostel Cards

If you're travelling on a budget, membership of the YHA or Hostelling International (HI) is a must (£12 adult, £6 under-18). There are at least 37 hostels in Wales, and members are also eligible for all sorts of discounts. See the Accommodation section later in the chapter for more information about hostelling in Wales.

Student & Youth Cards

Most useful of these is the International Student Identity Card (ISIC), a plastic ID-style card with your photograph that costs

£5 in the UK and provides cheap or free admission to museums and sights, inexpensive meals in some student restaurants and discounts on many forms of transport.

There's a worldwide industry in fake student cards, and many places now stipulate a maximum age for student discounts or simply substitute a 'youth discount' for a 'student' one. If you're aged under 26 but not a student, you can apply for a GO25 card issued by the Federation of International Youth Travel Organisations (FIYTO) or a Euro 26 Card, which give much the same discounts for the same fee as the ISIC.

All these cards are issued by student unions, hostelling organisations and student travel agencies. For more information on Euro26 see its Web site at www.euro26 .org. Further information on ISIC, ITIC and Go25 is at www.counciltravel.com.

Seniors Cards

Many attractions reduce their admission price for those aged over 60 or 65 (sometimes as low as 55 for women); it's always worth asking even if it's not posted. Travellers aged 50 and over get 30% off standard National Express coach fares with the Discount Coach card (£8; see Bus Passes & Discounts in the Getting Around chapter); those aged over 60 get 33% off most rail fares with a Senior Railcard (£18; see Railcards in the Getting Around chapter).

Travel Cards

If you plan to travel a lot by bus and/or train, Wales offers some good-value travel passes, especially those marketed under the name Flexi-Pass; see the Getting Around chapter for more on these. Another good bargain is the Cardiff Card (see the Cardiff & Around chapter). Most local bus operators also offer day and family passes.

Heritage Passes

Several passes offer good value to anyone keen to see lots of the castles, stately homes, ruined abbeys and other properties owned by Wales' heritage trusts, Cadw and the National Trust (NT). See under Useful Organisations later in the chapter for information on these organisations and for details on buying the passes.

Other Documents

If you're visiting the UK on a Working Holiday Entry Certificate (see Visas earlier) bring any course certificates or letters of reference that might help you find a job.

Copies

All important documents (passport data page and visa page, credit cards, travel insurance policy, air/bus/train tickets, driving licence etc) should be photocopied before you leave home. Leave one copy with someone at home and keep another with you, separate from the originals.

You can also store details of your vital travel documents in Lonely Planet's free on-line Travel Vault. Your password-protected Travel Vault is accessible on-line anywhere in the world – create it at www .ekno.lonelyplanet.com.

EMBASSIES & CONSULATES
British Embassies, High Commissions & Consulates

British missions overseas include those listed below. If you need the details of others, consult the Foreign & Commonwealth Office Web site at www.fco.gov.uk.

Australia
High Commission: (☎ 02-6273 3236, fax 6270 6653) Commonwealth Ave, Yarralumla, Canberra, ACT 2606
Consulate: (☎ 02-9247 7521, fax 9233 1826) Level 16, The Gateway, 1 Macquarie Place, Sydney, NSW 2000
Web site: www.uk.emb.gov.au

Canada
High Commission: (☎ 613-237 1530, fax 232 2533) 80 Elgin St, Ottawa, Ontario K1P 5K7
Consulate: (☎ 416-593 1290, fax 593 1229) Suite 2800, 777 Bay St, College Park, Toronto, Ontario M5G 2G2
Web site: www.britain-in-canada.org

France
Embassy: (☎ 01 44 51 31 00, fax 01 44 51 31 28) 35 rue du Faubourg St-Honoré, 75008 Paris
Web site: www.amb-grandebretagne.fr

Germany
Embassy: (☎ 030-201 840, fax 201 84158)

Unter den Linden 32–4, 10117 Berlin
Web site: www.britischebotschaft.de
Ireland
  Embassy: (☎ 01-205 3822, fax 205 3890) 29
  Merrion Rd, Ballsbridge, Dublin 4
  Web site: www.britishembassy.ie
Netherlands
  Embassy: (☎ 070-427 0427, fax 427 0345)
  Lange Voorhout 10, 2514 ED The Hague
  Consulate: (☎ 020-676 43 43, fax 676 10 69)
  Konigslaan 44, 1075 AE Amsterdam
  Web site: www.britain.nl
New Zealand
  High Commission: (☎ 04-472 6049, fax 471
  1974) 44 Hill St, Wellington 1
  Consulate: (☎ 09-303 2973, fax 303 1836)
  17th floor, Fay Richwhite Building, 151
  Queen St, Auckland 1
  Web site: www.brithighcomm.org.nz
South Africa
  High Commission: (☎ 021-461 7220, fax 461
  0017) 91 Parliament St, Cape Town 8001
  Consulate: (☎ 011-325 2133, fax 325 2132)
  Dunkeld Corner, 275 Jan Smuts Ave, Dunkeld
  West, Johannesburg 2196
  Web site: www.britain.org.za
USA
  Embassy: (☎ 202-588 6500, fax 588 7850)
  3100 Massachusetts Ave, NW, Washington,
  DC 20008
  Consulate: (☎ 212-745 0200, fax 745 3062)
  845 Third Ave, New York, NY 10012
  Web site: www.britainusa.com/bis/embassy/
  embassy.stm

Embassies & Consulates in Britain

It's important to realise what your own embassy – the embassy of the country of which you are a citizen – can and can't do to help you if you get into trouble. Generally speaking, it won't be much help if the trouble you're in is remotely your own fault; remember that you're bound by the laws of the country you're in. Your embassy will not be sympathetic if you end up in jail after committing a crime locally, even if such actions are legal in your own country.

In genuine emergencies you might get some assistance, but only if other channels have been exhausted. For example, if you need to get home urgently, a free ticket home is exceedingly unlikely – the embassy would expect you to have insurance. If you have all your money and documents stolen,

it might assist with getting a new passport, but a loan for onward travel is out of the question.

The only foreign consular offices in Wales are a handful of consulates in Cardiff, including the following:

Ireland (☎ 029-2066 2000) Brunel House, 2
  Fitzalan Rd, Cardiff CF24 0EB
Italy (☎ 029-2034 1757) 14 Museum Place,
  Cardiff CF10 3BH
Netherlands (☎ 029-2082 4405) NCM Building, 3 Harbour Drive, Cardiff CF10 4WZ

For the embassies or high commissions of most other countries, you'll have to go to London. Some foreign missions in London include:

Australia
  High Commission: (☎ 020-7379 4334, fax
  7240 5333) Australia House, Strand WC2
Canada
  High Commission: (☎ 020-7258 6600, fax
  7258 6333) 1 Grosvenor Square W1
France
  Embassy: (☎ 020-7838 2050, fax 7838 2046)
  58 Knightsbridge SW1
Germany
  Embassy: (☎ 020-7824 1300, fax 7824 1435)
  23 Belgrave Square SW1
Ireland
  Embassy: (☎ 020-7235 2171, fax 7245 6961)
  17 Grosvenor Place SW1
Netherlands
  Embassy: (☎ 020-7590 3200, fax 7590 3458)
  38 Hyde Park Gate SW7
New Zealand
  High Commission: (☎ 020-7930 8422, fax
  7839 4580) New Zealand House, 80
  Haymarket SW1
South Africa
  High Commission: (☎ 020-7451 7299, fax
  7451 7284) South Africa House, Trafalgar
  Square WC2
USA
  Embassy: (☎ 020-7499 9000, fax 7495 5012)
  24 Grosvenor Square W1

CUSTOMS

On entering the UK, if you have nothing to declare go through the green channel; if you may have something to declare go through the red channel. If you arrive from an EU country you go through a third, blue, channel.

Like other EU nations, the UK has a two-tier customs system: one for goods bought duty-free and one for goods bought in another EU country where taxes and duties have already been paid.

Duty Free

Duty-free sales to those travelling from one EU country to another were abolished in 1999. For goods purchased at airports or on ferries outside the EU, you are allowed to import 200 cigarettes or 250g of tobacco, 2L of still wine plus 1L of spirits over 22% or another 2L of wine (sparkling or otherwise), 50g of perfume, 250cc of toilet water, and other duty-free goods (including cider and beer) to the value of £136.

Tax & Duty Paid

Although you can no longer bring in duty-free goods from another EU country, you can bring in goods from another EU country, where certain goods might be cheaper, if taxes have been paid on them. If you purchase from a normal retail outlet, customs uses the following maximum quantities as a guideline to distinguish personal imports from those on a commercial scale: 800 cigarettes, 200 cigars, 1kg of tobacco, 10L of spirits, 20L of fortified wine, 90L of wine (of which not more than 60L are sparkling) and 110L of beer.

Pets

To protect its rabies-free status, the UK has long had draconian pet quarantine policies that required any animal brought into the UK to be placed in quarantine for six months.

The rules thawed slightly in 2000 when a pilot scheme was introduced for dogs and cats from certain countries: Andorra, Austria, Belgium, Denmark, Finland, France, Germany, Gibraltar, Greece, Italy, Liechtenstein, Luxembourg, Monaco, Netherlands, Norway, Portugal, San Marino, Spain, Sweden, Switzerland and the Vatican. Said animals must not have been outside those countries in the six months before travel to the UK, must have an identity microchip implanted, and must have various vaccinations, tests and certifications. The process is complex, but at least it is a thaw from the previous no-exceptions policy.

If you're contemplating bringing your pet to the UK, contact your nearest UK embassy or consulate for the latest details on the quarantine situation.

MONEY

Wales has the same currency and the same major banks as the rest of the UK.

Currency

The UK currency is the pound sterling (£), which is divided into 100 pence (p). Coins of 1p and 2p are copper; 5p, 10p, 20p and 50p coins are silver; and the bulky £1 coin is gold-coloured. The £2 coin, introduced in 1997, is gold-coloured on the edge with a silver centre. Notes come in £5, £10, £20 and £50 denominations and vary in colour and size. The £50 notes can be difficult to change, so try to avoid them.

By 2002, most of the EU will have a single currency called the euro. The pound will continue to be the unit of currency in the UK as the British government has decided not to adopt the euro for the time being.

Exchange Rates

Exchange rates at the time of going to print were:

country	unit		pounds
Australia	A$1	=	£0.37
Canada	C$1	=	£0.45
euro zone	€1	=	£0.61
Japan	¥100	=	£0.57
New Zealand	NZ$1	=	£0.30
USA	US$1	=	£0.69

Exchanging Money

The UK's major banks are represented throughout Wales, though smaller towns may only have one or two banks. Nearly all these banks have automatic teller machines (ATMs). Most also have a bureau de change service, where foreign currency holders can change money. Most post offices in larger towns also have a bureau de change service, at reasonable rates.

Cash Nothing beats cash for convenience – or risk. It's still a good idea, however, to travel with some cash in pounds sterling, if only to tide you over until you get to an exchange facility. There's no problem if you arrive in the UK cashless: the country's international airports have good-value exchange counters open for incoming flights.

Travellers Cheques & Eurocheques

Travellers cheques offer protection from theft. Ideally your cheques should be in pounds and preferably issued by American Express (AmEx) or Thomas Cook, which are widely recognised, well represented and don't charge for cashing their own cheques.

Bring most cheques in large denominations. It's only towards the end of a stay that you may want to change a small cheque to make sure you don't get left with too much local currency. Travellers cheques are rarely accepted outside banks in the UK, so you need to cash them in advance.

Eurocheques, available if you have a European bank account, are guaranteed up to a certain amount. When cashing them, you will be asked to show your Eurocheque card bearing your signature and registration number as well as your passport or ID card. Eurocheques are not as commonly used in the UK as they are in continental Europe, and many places refuse to accept them. Some people may have never even seen them before.

Lost or Stolen Travellers Cheques Keep
a record of the numbers of your cheques and which cheques you have cashed, so if they're lost or stolen you'll be able to tell the issuing agency exactly which cheques have gone. Keep this list separate from the cheques themselves.

As soon as you realise any cheques are missing, contact the issuing office or the nearest branch of the issuing agency. AmEx (☎ 029-2066 6111) and Thomas Cook (☎ 01733-318950), both of which operate 24 hours a day, seven days a week, can often arrange replacement cheques within 24 hours.

ATMs Plastic cards make perfect travelling companions – they're ideal for major purchases and let you withdraw cash from selected banks and ATMs. ATMs are usually linked to international systems such as Cirrus, Maestro or Plus, so you can use your card for instant cash, just as if you were at home. But ATMs aren't fail-safe, especially with cards issued outside Europe, and it's always safer to deal with a human teller. It can be a major headache if an ATM swallows your card.

Debit cards, which you use to withdraw money directly from your bank or savings account, are widely linked internationally – ask your bank at home for advice. Credit cards, on the other hand, may not be hooked up to ATM networks unless you specifically ask your bank to do this for you and request a PIN number. AmEx cards are accepted in many ATMs as well. Note that some UK banks charge an extra fee if you use a card not issued by them in one of their ATMs.

Not all major banks are represented in all towns (eg, there are few Lloyds TSB branches in Snowdonia), so you may have to plan ahead with your withdrawals.

Credit Cards Visa, MasterCard, AmEx and Diners Club cards are widely accepted in the UK, although small businesses such as B&Bs prefer cash. Businesses sometimes make a charge for accepting payment by credit card so this isn't always the most economical way to go. You can get cash advances using your Visa and MasterCards at many banks. If you have an AmEx card, you can cash up to £500 worth of personal cheques at AmEx offices in any seven-day period.

If you plan to use a credit card make sure you have a high enough credit limit to cover major expenses such as car hire or airline tickets.

If you're going to rely on plastic, go for two different cards – an AmEx or Diners Club with a Visa or MasterCard. Better still, combine cards and travellers cheques so you have something to fall back on if an ATM swallows your card or the bank won't accept it.

Lost or Stolen Cards If a card is lost or stolen you must inform the police and the issuing company as soon as possible – otherwise you may have to pay for the purchases that the thief has made using your card. Here are some numbers for cancelling your cards:

AmEx	☎ 01273-689955
Diners Club	☎ 01252-516261
MasterCard	☎ 01702-362988
Visa	☎ 0800 895082

International Transfers If you instruct your bank back home to send you a draft, be sure you specify the bank and the branch to which you want your money directed, or ask your home bank to tell you where a suitable one is. The whole procedure will be easier if you've authorised someone back home to access your account.

Money sent to you by telegraphic transfer should reach you within a week; by mail, allow at least two weeks. When it arrives, it will most likely be converted into local currency – you can then take it as is or buy travellers cheques. The charge for this service is usually around £20.

You can also transfer money using AmEx or Thomas Cook or by post office MoneyGram. Americans can also use Western Union (☎ 0800 833833), although it has fewer offices in the UK from which to collect, and charges 10% plus commission.

Other Methods Personal cheques are still widely used in the UK, in conjunction with a cheque guarantee card. Increasingly, retail outlets are linked to the Switch and Delta networks, which allow customers to use debit cards (deductions are made directly from your UK current account).

If you plan to stay a while in the UK, you may want to open a bank account, but it's no simple matter. Building societies (like savings & loan associations in the USA) tend to be more welcoming than banks and often have better interest rates. You'll need a permanent UK address, and it smooths the way if you have a reference or introductory letter from your bank manager at home, plus bank statements for the previous year. Owning credit/charge cards also helps. Get a 'current account', which usually pays a microscopic bit of interest, and includes a debit card and/or a cheque book and cheque guarantee card, and ATM access.

Security

Whichever way you decide to carry your funds, it makes sense to keep most of it out of easy reach of thieves in a money belt or something similar. It always makes sense to keep something like £50 apart from the rest of your cash for use in an emergency.

Never leave wallets sticking out of trouser pockets or daypacks and never leave bags hanging over the back of chairs in pubs and restaurants. Also watch out on buses and around popular tourist attractions.

Costs

Britain is a fairly expensive place to travel, though prices in general average around 5% to 10% less in Wales than in England. Fresh food costs roughly the same as in Australia or the USA.

Leaving long-distance transport aside, if you stay in hostels and the occasional cheap B&B, and go easy on the beer, you can get by on £25 per day: youth hostels cost from £7 to £14, cheaper B&Bs £15 to £20; add at least £6 for food, a few pounds for admission charges, and a few more for miscellaneous supplies, film, books and telephone calls.

Again leaving long-distance transport aside, if you stay in B&Bs, eat one sit-down meal a day and don't stint on admission fees, you'll need £55 to £65 per day: most modest B&Bs cost £20 to £25 per person, and dinner will be about £8 to £15; add £5 for lunch and snacks, and around £7 to £8 for admission fees and miscellaneous supplies.

If you're travelling by car you'll probably average a further £8 to £10 per day on petrol and parking – plus at least £20 per day if you're hiring the car. Alternatively, figure around £5 per day if you hire a taxi or a bike every few days for local jaunts, or buy a transport pass.

Food and accommodation prices are noticeably higher in the Cardiff area and Snowdonia than elsewhere. B&B rates often drop by around £5 per person in winter.

Throughout this book admission costs are, unless otherwise specified, given as adult/child. Admission fees for kids and seniors are usually around half to two-thirds of those for adults; kids aged under five often get in free. Most museums and attractions offer good-value family tickets too.

Tipping & Bargaining

Outside Cardiff and a few other big towns, tipping doesn't seem to be expected, though 10% is always appreciated in restaurants, if the service warrants it. Table staff are often paid derisory wages on the assumption that the money will be supplemented by tips. A few upper-end restaurants include a service charge in the bill, though this must be clearly advertised; you needn't add a further tip in this case. You never tip to have your pint pulled in a pub. Taxi drivers expect a gratuity of 10% or so.

Bargaining is virtually unheard of, even at markets, although it's fine to ask if there are discounts for students, young people, seniors or YHA/HI members. You might succeed in talking the odd B&B price down a bit in the off season.

Taxes & Refunds

Value-added tax (VAT) is a 17.5% sales tax levied on most goods and services except food and books. Restaurants must by law include VAT in their menu prices.

It's sometimes possible for visitors to claim a refund of VAT paid on goods – a considerable saving. You're eligible if you've spent fewer than 365 days out of the two years prior to making the purchase living in the UK, and if you're leaving the EU within three months of making the purchase.

Not all shops participate in the VAT refund scheme, called the Retail Export Scheme or Tax-Free Shopping, and different shops will have different minimum purchase conditions (normally around £75 per shop). On request, participating shops will give you a special form (VAT 407), which must be presented with the goods and receipts to customs when you depart (VAT-free goods can't be posted or shipped home). After customs has certified the form, it should be returned to the shop for a refund (minus an administration/handling fee), which takes eight to 10 weeks.

POST & COMMUNICATIONS
Post

Although post-office queues can be long, the Royal Mail (☎ 0845 600 0606) delivers a pretty good service. Post office hours vary, but most open 9 am to 5.30 pm weekdays and 9 am to 1 pm Saturday.

First class domestic mail (27p per letter) usually arrives in one or two days; 2nd class (19p) may take longer. Air-mail letters cost 36p to other European countries, and 45/65p (up to 10/20g) to the Americas and Australasia. An air-mail letter generally takes around a week to reach Australia or New Zealand, and less to the USA or Canada.

If you don't have a permanent address, mail can be sent to a poste restante in the town or city where you're staying. A reliable Wales address for poste restante is Cardiff's main post office, The Hayes, Cardiff CF10 2SJ. AmEx Travel offices will also hold card-holders' mail free of charge.

Telephone

Wales' country code is the same as that of the rest of the UK; to call from abroad, dial your country's international access code, then 44 (the UK country code), then the area code (dropping the initial 0) followed by the phone number.

Britain's famous red phone boxes survive only in conservation areas. More common these days are glass cubicles with phones that accept coins, prepaid phonecards and/or credit cards. British Telecom phonecards for £2, £5, £10 and £20 are widely available from retailers, including post offices and newsagents. A digital display on the telephone indicates how much credit is left on the card.

Some special phone codes worth knowing are:

☎ 0500	toll-free
☎ 0800	toll-free
☎ 0808	toll-free
☎ 0845	local call rate applies
☎ 0870	national call rate applies
☎ 0891	premium rate (49p per minute)
☎ 09064	premium rate (49p per minute)

Codes beginning with ☎ 07 indicate a mobile phone, which is considerably more expensive to call than a conventional phone.

Local & National Calls & Rates Local calls are charged by time alone; national calls are charged by both time and distance. Daytime rates apply from 8 am to 6 pm on weekdays; considerably cheaper rates apply from midnight to 8 am and 6 pm to midnight on weekdays, and the cheapest rates from midnight Friday to midnight Sunday.

For directory enquiries (which provides telephone-number information) call ☎ 192. These calls are free from public phones but cost 25p from a private telephone. For an operator, dial ☎ 100.

International Calls & Rates To call someone outside the UK, dial 00, then the country code, the area code (you usually drop the initial zero if there is one) and the number. International direct dialling (IDD) calls to almost anywhere in the world can be made from almost all public telephones.

To make a reverse-charge (collect) call, dial ☎ 155 for the international operator; these calls are more expensive than direct dialling. For international directory enquiries dial ☎ 153 (50p from private phones).

For most countries (including Europe, the USA and Canada) it's cheaper to phone overseas between 8 pm and 8 am, and all day at weekends; for Australia and New Zealand, however, it's cheapest from 2.30 to 7.30 pm and from midnight to 7 am every day. The savings are considerable.

A number of international phonecards now on the market offer – at certain times and for certain destinations – cheaper international rates than British Telecom's, and can be used from any telephone by dialling a special access number and a PIN. One is Lonely Planet's eKno global communication service, aimed at independent travellers and offering competitive international rates, free messaging services, email and travel information. You can join on-line at www .ekno.lonelyplanet.com, or by phone from the UK at ☎ 0800 169 8646; to use eKno from the UK, dial 0800 376 2366 (not available from all payphones) or ☎ 0845 085 0855. Check the eKno Web site for updates on local access numbers and new features.

None of these cards is very good value for local calls.

Mobile Phones The UK uses the GSM 900/ 1800 protocol, compatible with the rest of Europe and Australia but not with the North American GSM 1900 or the totally different system in Japan (though some North American GSM 1900/900 phones do work here). If you have a GSM phone, ask your service provider about using it from the UK. Note that domestic calls on these phones are often routed internationally and can therefore be very expensive.

For calls just within the UK, the simplest and cheapest option may be to buy one of the pay-as-you-talk phones sold from seemingly every other shop in the high street. For under £70 you get a phone with its own number and a fair amount of airtime. As you use up your airtime, you simply buy more; there are no contracts or billing hassles. All four big mobile phone companies in the UK – Orange, Vodaphone, One 2 One and BT Cellnet – have variations on this scheme.

Fax
Many newsagents and tobacco shops offer fax services. Ask at a TIC or just look for signs.

Email & Internet Access
If you have a Web-based email account such as Hotmail at www.hotmail.com or Yahoo! Mail at www.yahoo.com, you can check your email anywhere that offers Internet access. Many public libraries offer

access, in blocks of an hour, though it's advisable (sometimes essential) to book ahead; rates range from free to about £4 per hour. This book notes opening hours (often convoluted) at libraries with access. Cybercafes charge £4 to £5 per hour, though they're not plentiful in Wales; TICs can often point you to one. Many YHA/HI and independent hostels also have access, at similar rates.

If you've got your own laptop/palmtop and modem, and your Internet service provider (ISP) at home has global roaming service (access via local telephone numbers in countries where you'll be travelling), you might succeed in logging on from your hotel room. Major ISPs such as CompuServe, AOL, Earthlink and AT&T Global, with Web sites at www.compuserve.com, www.aol.com, www.earthlink.net and www.attglobal.net respectively, have dial-in numbers throughout the UK; download these numbers before you leave home.

With luck your telephone will be connected by a socket at the wall, though you'll need an adapter cable between your computer (usually USA standard, RJ-11) and UK standard wall jacks. Hotels aimed at business travellers often have RJ-11 sockets as well. Be sure the hotel doesn't have a digital telephone exchange, which can blow your modem; you can always plug safely into an analogue data line such as the hotel's fax line. Many B&Bs are still computer-shy and may refuse to let you plug in anywhere.

A line tester will ensure that the line is safe to use with a modem. Line testers, telephone and power adapters, and other accessories are available from Web-based dealers such as Konexx at www.konexx.com, TeleAdapt at www.teleadapt.com and Road Warrior at www.warrior.com, and from most home-town electrical shops.

PCMCIA card-modems may not work once you leave your home country, and you won't know for sure until you try. The safest options are to carry a reputable global card-modem, or to buy one in the UK if you'll be staying for a while.

It's also possible to access the local email service you use at home, but you must carry three pieces of information with you to do this: your incoming (POP or IMAP) mail server name, your account name and your password. Your ISP or network supervisor can tell you these. Armed with this information, you should be able to access your email account from any Internet-connected machine in the world, provided it runs some kind of email software (remember that Netscape and Internet Explorer both have mail modules). It pays to become familiar with the process for doing this before you leave home.

DIGITAL RESOURCES
Web Sites
The World Wide Web is a rich resource for travellers. Towns, tourist boards, individual attractions, B&Bs, hotels and transportation companies across Wales have their own Web sites; you'll find many listed throughout this book. You can also chat with locals and other travellers about the best places to visit (or avoid!).

There's no better place to start than the Lonely Planet Web site at www.lonelyplanet .com. Here you'll find succinct summaries on travelling to most places on earth, postcards from other travellers and the Thorn Tree bulletin board, where you can ask questions before you go or dispense advice when you get back. You can also find travel news and updates to many LP guidebooks, and the subWWWay section links you to useful resources elsewhere on the Web.

Following are several very good sites dealing with Wales as a whole:

Welcome to Wales The Web site of the Wales Tourist Board (WTB), with history basics, regional tours, shopping tips, and information on WTB-approved accommodation; you can also order specialist brochures on walking, cycling, fishing, golf etc.
Web site: www.visitwales.com

Go Britannia! Guide to Wales, a site developed with Welsh-Americans in mind, with a prodigiously detailed archive on history, language and literature, plus virtual tours.
Web site: www.britannia.com/celtic/wales

Total Wales A business-oriented site with current news, sports, entertainment, weather, even jobs.
Web site: www.totalwales.co.uk

Data Wales A marvellous miscellany of cultural titbits about the country.
Web site: www.data-wales.co.uk

BOOKS

Most books are published in different editions by different publishers in different countries. As a result, a book might be a hardcover rarity in one country while it's readily available in paperback in another. Fortunately, bookshops and libraries search by title or author, so your local bookshop or library is best placed to advise you on the availability of the following recommendations.

Lonely Planet

If your travels will take you to other parts of the UK, have a look at Lonely Planet's *Britain*, *England* or *Scotland* guides. Another angle is provided by Lonely Planet's *Walking in Britain*, with chapters on Wales' three national long-distance trails and a host of smaller walks. *Cycling Britain* takes you through Wales' national parks and its serenely beautiful countryside by pedal-power. And the *British phrasebook* has a section on the Welsh language.

Guidebooks

You'll come across a wide range of detailed guidebooks and books on Welsh life as you travel around Wales. Many are stocked by larger TICs, town bookshops and shops at tourist attractions and the many heritage sites managed by Cadw, the NT and the National Museums & Galleries of Wales (NMGW).

The WTB (see Tourist Offices earlier in the chapter) publishes its own reliable, if not totally comprehensive, listings of hotels, B&Bs, farmhouse accommodation, self-catering apartments and camp sites; plus booklets on walking, cycling, fishing, riding, golf and other outdoor pursuits; and others on beaches, gardens, farm and countryside holidays and Welsh food. Local tourism authorities also publish their own accommodation listings.

Travel

Daniel Defoe's 1720s classic *A Tour Through the Whole Island of Great Britain* includes

---

Gerald of Wales

Wales' earliest travel writer was probably a quarter-Welsh monk, scholar, gossip and self-publicist named Giraldus Cambrensis (Gerald of Wales), who wrote about his journey around the country with Archbishop Baldwin of Canterbury in 1188, in search of recruits for the Third Crusade. The originals, *The Journey Through Wales* and *The Description of Wales*, are heavy going, but the Welsh heritage agency Cadw (see Useful Organisations later in this chapter) has published a fine annotated, illustrated paperback look at Gerald and his journey, called *A Mirror of Medieval Wales*. It's sold at most Cadw sites, and many Tourist Information Centres (TICs) and bookshops, for about £4.

During his full-to-brimming life Gerald also served as tutor to both Richard the Lion-Heart and King John, served as rector of several churches in Wales – including Tenby and Brecon – and waged an ultimately vain campaign to have St David's declared a bishopric independent of the English church.

---

a modest look at Wales. Thomas Pennant travelled round Wales on horseback a few decades later, and wrote lovingly of its wild landscapes in *A Tour in Wales*.

George Borrow was a writer-traveller from Norfolk who mounted his own walking tour of Wales in 1854. He taught himself Welsh before leaving, allowing him a much better understanding of Welsh places and people than most other visitors. His *Wild Wales: Its People, Language and Scenery* remains evocative and illuminating, if a bit condescending, even after 1½ centuries. A modern travelogue in this mould is Anthony Bailey's *A Walk Through Wales*.

History & Politics

The Welsh have been looking back at themselves for at least several centuries, and there's a wide choice of histories to choose from. 'Whatever the 20th century Welsh will be remembered for, they will be remembered for their historians', as one of them, Gwyn Williams, put it in his own *When Was Wales?*, a lively, very readable look back at the Celts and the Welsh.

Authoritative, wide ranging and detailed, John Davies' *A History of Wales* – translated by the author from his own Welsh-language version – is probably the most widely admired academic history of the country. In paperback it's small enough to tote along. Smaller yet is Heini Gruffudd's pocket-size *Real Wales*, a feisty booklet that hurtles through the centuries charting the rise and fall and rise of the Welsh by the strength and survival of their language.

At the other end of the scale, for those with a truly obsessive interest, is the six-volume *Oxford History of Wales*. For a look at the last five centuries of Welsh history in a European context, see Philip Jenkins' *A History of Modern Wales 1536–1990*. A study of some 60 major historical personalities is *Welsh Nation Builders* by Gwynfor Evans, leader of Plaid Cymru for 36 years and its first MP in 1966. *Land of My Fathers* is Evans' own passionate, partisan history of Wales.

The best available account of Owain Glyndŵr's 'if-only' uprising in the early 15th century is RR Davies' *The Revolt of Owain Glyndŵr*.

General

Travel writer Jan Morris, half Welsh by birth and wholly Welsh by temperament, has written her own unabashed hymn to the country, *Wales: Epic Views of a Small Country* (originally published as *The Matter of Wales*) – affectionate, richly impressionistic and pretty spot-on. This is a good candidate for the book to take along. Morris and her musician son Twm have also written a three-part, bilingual vision of Wales' past, present and an arresting future, in *A Machynlleth Triad*.

If you want to get to grips with Welsh mythology, start with *The Mabinogion*, a collection of fantastic tales with their origins in traditional oral tales of the Celtic gods – transmitted for centuries by storytellers, first written down only in the 13th and 14th centuries, and first translated into English (and

named) by Lady Charlotte Guest in 1838–49. A modern translation is *The Mabinogion*, by Gwyn Jones and Thomas Jones.

Edward Thomas mused on the Welsh and scorned the English in his *Wales*, a collection of random, poetic and opinionated essays published in 1905 (out of print). For a wide-ranging look at what people have said about the Welsh, and what they've said about themselves, over two millennia, see *A Most Peculiar People: Quotations about Wales and the Welsh*, a collection of over 2300 quotations, kind and unkind, edited by Meic Stephens.

A quirky book to look out for in northeast Wales is Elizabeth Mavor's *The Ladies of Llangollen*, about the equally quirky lesbian couple who eloped dramatically from Ireland and settled down at Llangollen, there to be feted, gifted and visited by many of the 18th century's great and good.

Bruce Chatwin's acclaimed, elegant novel *On The Black Hill*, following the lives of twin brother-farmers, evokes the joys and hardships of rural life on the English-Welsh border.

For a look at the works of Welsh writers, see under Arts in the Facts about Wales chapter.

FILMS

Wales' oldest claim to cinematic fame is as a location. Its stunning landscapes have been popular with directors since the 1920s, when 26 silent movies were made here. North Wales has provided backdrops for home-grown productions such as the Oscar-nominated *Hedd Wyn*, as well as *First Knight*, *Hilary and Jackie*, *Merlin*, and *The Englishman Who Went Up a Hill but Came Down a Mountain* (starring Hugh Grant and directed by Welshman Chris Monger). The WTB's *Wales Film Location Map* will tell you where these and dozens of other films were shot.

A series of films produced in the 1930s, 1940s and later, mythologising working-class life in the hard-hit coal valleys of South Wales, was responsible for the world's images of Wales for two generations. Ironically, they were all produced outside Wales. They include King Vidor's *The Citadel* (1938), based on the best-selling novel by AJ Cronin about medical hypocrisy in the valleys; *Proud Valley* (1940), about the reopening of a colliery; and the film that probably annoys the Welsh more than any other, *How Green Was My Valley* (1941), based on Richard Llewelyn's novel of the same name describing the life of a boy growing up in a mining community. Many more films, too numerous to mention, have been partly or wholly set in Wales purely for its luxuriant rural scenery.

The founding of the Welsh-language television channel S4C (see the section on Radio & TV later) produced a renaissance in Welsh-made films; for more details of Welsh cinema, see Arts in the Facts about Wales chapter.

NEWSPAPERS & MAGAZINES
Newspapers

Wales' only 'national' English-language daily newspaper is *The Western Mail* (along with its Sunday stablemate *Wales on Sunday*), though it's quite south-centred. In the west and north you're more likely to find people reading the *Daily Post*. Both offer a mix of local news, features and sport. In Swansea, check out the *Swansea Evening Post*, not because it's a lively read but because it's the paper where Dylan Thomas cut his journalistic teeth.

You can also buy all the standard London dailies and weeklies in Wales, although they won't give you much news (or gossip) about the area you're in.

Magazines

Wales' main national magazine is *Golwg* (Vision), full of current events and features; unfortunately it's only in Welsh.

In any sizeable newsagent's you can see that the UK seems to have a magazine for almost every interest, with whole shelves of computer magazines, trainspotting magazines, heritage magazines and so on. *Time* and *Newsweek* are readily available, though *The Economist* remains the best news weekly of all.

RADIO & TV
Radio

BBC radio caters for most tastes. BBC Radio 1 (1089kHz and 1053kHz MW; 97–99MHz FM), the main public pop/indie music station, features Welsh bands on its Session in Wales every Thursday from 8 to 10 pm.

Radio 2 (88–90.2MHz FM) leans towards 1980s and older tracks. Radio 3 (1215kHz MW; 91.3MHz FM) sticks with classical music and drama, while Radio 4 (198kHz LW; 720kHz MW; 93.5MHz FM) offers a mix of drama, news, current affairs and chat. On Radio 5 Live (693kHz MW) you'll find sports, current affairs and chat.

'The Beeb' also has local services in Wales: BBC Radio Wales (93.9–95.9MHz and 103.9MHz FM; 882kHz MW; 1125kHz MW in Mid Wales; 657kHz MW in northeast Wales) offers English-language news and features about Wales, while BBC Radio Cymru (92.4–96.1MHz, 96.8MHz and 103.5–105.0MHz FM) transmits much the same in Welsh. Radio Wales also broadcasts on Sky Digital.

In Wales you'll also find a range of commercial stations – mainly English-language – with everything from pop to elevator music to classical. These include Red Dragon Radio (97.4MHz or 103.2MHz FM), Real Radio (105–106MHz FM) and Valleys Radio (999kHz and 1116kHz MW) around Cardiff and the Brecon Beacons; Swansea Sound (96.4kHz FM; 1170kHz MW); bilingual Radio Ceredigion (96.6MHz, 97.4MHz and 103.3MHz FM) in west Wales; Radio Maldwyn (756kHz AM) in eastern Mid Wales; Marcher Coast Radio in the northeast (96.3MHz FM); and Champion (103MHz FM) in the north-west.

TV

There are currently five regular TV channels – BBC1 and BBC2 are publicly funded by a TV licence and don't carry advertising; ITV and Channels 4 and 5 are commercial stations and do. Of these, Channel 4 has the most interesting programming. These stations are up against competition from Ru-

Sianel Pedwar Cymru's Success

Currently receiving a subsidy of £78 million a year, making it the world's most heavily subsidised public television channel, Sianel Pedwar Cymru (S4C; the name is Welsh for 'Channel 4 Wales') might not sound like a success story. But the benefits of this Welsh-language TV service, on the air since the early 1980s, are becoming clear to its former critics, who thought the money could be better spent elsewhere.

S4C came into being not through the benevolence of the British government, but after heavy campaigning by Cymdeithas yr Iaith Gymraeg (the Welsh Language Society), including a 1979 hunger strike by Gwynfor Evans, Welsh nationalist and father-figure of Plaid Cymru. Since then the channel has played a major part in rejuvenating the Welsh language, and it's now estimated that about one-third of children in Wales – some of them from English-speaking homes – can speak at least some Welsh. And the channel's benefits are not only cultural. S4C has sold many of its programs to other channels, and film makers from abroad are starting to use Wales-based production companies.

The long-running Welsh soap opera *Pobol y Cwm* (People of the Valley) has been transmitted with subtitles to the rest of Britain on BBC2. Other acclaimed productions have included the children's cartoon *SuperTed*, now a global star. S4C's greatest film success to date is *Hedd Wyn*, nominated for an Oscar in 1994 for Best Foreign Language Film.

pert Murdoch's satellite TV company, BSkyB, and assorted cable channels. Cable churns out mostly missable rubbish but Sky is slowly monopolising sports coverage and has pioneered pay-per-view screenings of the most popular events.

Wales has its own alternative to Channel 4 – Sianel Pedwar Cymru or S4C (see the boxed text), broadcasting mainly Welsh-language programs daily. S4C Digital is now giving the station a wider audience.

VIDEO SYSTEMS

If you want to record or buy video tapes to play back home, you won't get a picture if the image registration systems are different. The UK uses the PAL system, which is incompatible with both the French SECAM system and the North American and Japanese NTSC system. Australia and most of Europe use PAL.

PHOTOGRAPHY & VIDEO
Film & Equipment

Although print film is widely available, slide film can be more elusive; if there's no specialist photographic shop around, Boots, the high-street chemist chain, is the likeliest stockist. Print film (36-exposure) costs from £3.50 for ISO 100 to £5 for ISO 400.

Technical Tips

With dull, overcast conditions common, high-speed film (ISO 200 or ISO 400) is useful. Contrast between light and shadow is harshest at high noon; try to get out in the early morning or just before sunset for the gentlest light.

Video cameras have amazingly sensitive microphones. Filming beside a busy road may produce only a deafening roar as a soundtrack when you replay it at home. Try to film in long takes and not move the camera around too much.

Lonely Planet's full-colour *Travel Photography: A Guide to Taking Better Pictures*, by internationally renowned travel photographer Richard I'Anson, is designed to be taken on the road.

Restrictions

Many tourist attractions either charge for taking photos or prohibit it altogether. Use of flash is frequently forbidden to protect delicate pictures and fabrics. Video cameras are often disallowed because of the inconvenience they can cause to other visitors.

Airport Security

Carrying unprocessed film in checked baggage, even in a lead-lined 'filmsafe' pouch, is inviting trouble. Several international airports now use 'smart' CTX 5000 scanners for checked baggage. These scan first with a mild beam, then zero in ferociously on anything suspicious. A lead pouch would not only be ineffective but would invite further scans, and film inside is certain to be ruined.

By contrast, airport scanners for carry-on bags are relatively harmless. You will have to put your camera and film through one of these at all British airports. There are no plans yet to use the CTX 5000 for carry-on luggage. The moral of the tale is obvious: carry unprocessed film in your carry-on bags, and if possible get officials to hand-inspect it.

TIME

All of the UK is on GMT/UTC in winter and GMT/UTC plus one hour during summer. Clocks are set forward by an hour on the last Sunday in March and back on the last Sunday in October.

Most public transport timetables are based on a 24-hour clock.

ELECTRICITY

The standard voltage in Wales (and throughout the UK) is 240V AC, 50Hz. Plugs have three square pins and adapters are widely available.

WEIGHTS & MEASURES

In theory Wales has, by EU directive, moved to metric weights and measures, although nonmetric equivalents are still widely used. Supermarkets now tend to use both metric and imperial measurements on their price labels.

The EU has granted a permanent exemption for speed and distance measurements – for example, on road signs and car odometers. Pubs are permitted to continue pulling pints, and milkmen may go on leaving the morning pint on the doorstep, though most other liquids are now sold in litres. For conversion tables, see the inside back cover of this book.

This book uses miles to indicate road distances.

LAUNDRY

Every high street has its laundrette. The cost for a single load (wash and dry) is about £4. Bring soap powder with you; it can be expensive if bought in a laundrette.

TOILETS

Although many conveniences are still pretty grim (graffitied or rendered vandal-proof in solid stainless steel), those at train stations, bus terminals and motorway service stations are generally good, usually with facilities for disabled people and those with young children. Elsewhere, you can try your charms on publicans or lose yourself in the anonymity of large department stores.

Many toilets for disabled people can only be opened with a special key that can be obtained from some tourist offices or by sending a cheque or postal order for £2.50 to RADAR (see the Disabled Travellers section later in the chapter), together with a brief description of your disability.

HEALTH

Travel health largely depends on predeparture preparations, day-to-day health care while travelling and how you handle any medical problem or emergency that does develop. Wales is a healthy place to travel. Hygiene standards are high and there are no unusual diseases to worry about.

Predeparture Planning

Immunisations Although no immunisations are required, it's recommended that everyone keep up-to-date with diptheria, tetanus and polio vaccinations.

Health Insurance Make sure you have adequate health insurance. See Travel Insurance earlier in the chapter for details.

Other Preparations Make sure you're healthy before you start travelling. If you are going on a long trip make sure your teeth are OK. If you wear glasses take your prescription.

If you require medication, take along the packaging showing its generic name, rather than the brand, which will make getting replacements easier and cheaper. To avoid any problems, it's wise to have a legible prescription or doctor's letter to show that you legally use the medication.

Basic Rules

Care in what you eat and drink is the most important health rule; stomach upsets are the most likely travel health problem (between 30% and 50% of travellers in a two-week stay experience this) but the majority of these upsets will be relatively minor.

Water Tap water is always safe unless there's a sign to the contrary (eg, on trains). Don't drink straight from a stream – you can never be certain there are no people or cattle upstream.

Environmental Hazards

Heat Exhaustion Wales may not seem like a place to worry about heat exhaustion, but complacency can lead to problems. Dehydration or salt deficiency can cause heat exhaustion. In hot conditions and if you're exerting yourself make sure you get sufficient nonalcoholic liquids. Salt deficiency is characterised by fatigue, lethargy, headaches, giddiness and muscle cramps. Vomiting or diarrhoea can rapidly deplete your liquid and salt levels.

Hypothermia Too much cold can be just as dangerous as too much heat. In much of Wales you should always be prepared for cold, wet or windy conditions, even if you're just out walking or hitching. Every year people set out for walks on mild days – especially in upland areas of Snowdonia and Brecon Beacons national parks – and end up in trouble when the weather suddenly changes.

Hypothermia occurs when the body loses heat faster than it can produce it and the core temperature of the body falls. It's surprisingly easy, on a day's jaunt, to progress from chilly to dangerously cold due to a combination of wind, wet clothing, fatigue and hunger, even if the air temperature is above freezing. It's best to dress in layers; silk, wool and some of the new artificial fibres are all good insulating materials. A hat is important as much heat is lost through the head. A strong, waterproof outer layer is essential, and a 'space' blanket is wise for emergencies. Carry basic supplies, including food containing simple sugars to generate heat quickly and fluid to drink.

Symptoms of hypothermia are exhaustion, numb skin (particularly toes and fingers), shivering, slurred speech, irrational or violent behaviour, lethargy, stumbling, dizzy spells, muscle cramps and violent bursts of energy. Irrationality may take the form of sufferers claiming they are warm and trying to take off their clothes.

To treat mild hypothermia, first get the person out of the wind and/or rain, remove their clothing if it's wet and replace it with dry, warm clothing. Give them hot liquids – not alcohol – and some high-kilojoule, easily digestible food. Do not rub victims: instead, allow them to slowly warm themselves. This should be enough to treat the early stages of hypothermia. The early recognition and treatment of mild hypothermia is the only way to prevent severe hypothermia, which is a critical condition.

Infectious Diseases

Fungal Infections To prevent fungal infections, wear loose, comfortable clothes, wash frequently and dry carefully. Always wear flip-flops (thongs) in shared bathrooms. If you get an infection, consult a chemist (pharmacy). Expose the infected area to air or sunlight as much as possible and wash all towels and underwear in hot water as well as changing them often.

Diarrhoea Simple things such as a change of water, food or climate can cause a mild bout of diarrhoea, but a few dashes to the loo with no other symptoms does not indicate a major problem.

Dehydration is the main danger with any diarrhoea, particularly in children or the elderly, who can become dehydrated quickly. Under all circumstances fluid replacement (at least equal to the volume being lost) is the most important thing to remember. Weak black tea with a little sugar, soda water, or soft drinks allowed to go flat and diluted 50% with clean water are all good. With severe diarrhoea a rehydrating solution is preferable to replace minerals and salts lost. Drink small amounts often. Stick to a bland diet as you recover.

HIV & AIDS Infection with the human immunodeficiency virus (HIV) may lead to acquired immune deficiency syndrome (AIDS), which is a fatal disease. Any exposure to blood, blood products or body fluids may put the individual at risk. The disease is often transmitted through sexual contact or dirty needles – vaccinations, acupuncture, tattooing and body piercing can be potentially as dangerous as intravenous drug use. HIV/AIDS can also be spread through infected blood transfusions, though these are screened and safe in the UK.

Sexually Transmitted Diseases HIV/AIDS and hepatitis B can be transmitted through sexual contact. Other sexually transmitted diseases (STDs) include gonorrhoea, herpes and syphilis; sores, blisters or rashes around the genitals and discharges or pain when urinating are common symptoms. In some STDs, such as wart virus or chlamydia, symptoms may be less marked or not observed at all, especially in women. Chlamydia infection can cause infertility in men and women before any symptoms have been noticed. Syphilis symptoms eventually disappear completely but the disease continues and can cause severe problems in later years. While abstinence from sexual contact is the only 100% effective prevention, using condoms is also effective. The treatment of gonorrhoea and syphilis is with antibiotics. The different STDs each require specific antibiotics.

Women's Health
Gynaecological Problems Antibiotic use, synthetic underwear, sweating and contraceptive pills can all lead to fungal vaginal infections, especially when travelling in hot climates. Fungal infections are characterised by a rash, itch and discharge, and can be treated with a vinegar or lemon-juice

douche or with yoghurt. Nystatin, miconazole or clotrimazole pessaries or vaginal cream are the usual prescribed treatment. Maintaining good personal hygiene and wearing loose-fitting clothes and cotton underwear may help prevent these infections.

STDs are a major cause of vaginal problems. Symptoms include a smelly discharge, painful intercourse and sometimes a burning sensation when urinating. Medical attention should be sought and male sexual partners must also be treated. For more details see the section on Sexually Transmitted Diseases earlier in the chapter. Besides abstinence, the best thing is to practise safer sex using condoms.

Medical Services
Reciprocal arrangements with the UK allow residents of Australia, New Zealand and several other countries to receive free emergency medical treatment and subsidised dental care through the National Health Service (NHS); they can use hospital emergency departments, general practitioners (GPs) and dentists (check the Yellow Pages phone directory). Long-term visitors with the proper documentation will receive care under the NHS by registering with a specific practice near where they live. Again, check the phone book for one close to you. EU nationals can obtain free emergency treatment on presentation of an E111 form, validated in advance in their home country.

Travel insurance, however, is advisable as it offers greater flexibility over where and how you're treated and covers expenses for an ambulance and repatriation that won't be picked up by the NHS (see the Travel Insurance section under Documents earlier in the chapter). Regardless of nationality, anyone will receive free emergency treatment if it's a simple matter such as bandaging a cut.

Chemists (Pharmacies) Chemists can advise on minor ailments such as sore throats, coughs and earache. There's always one local chemist open somewhere at any hour; other chemists should display details in their window or doorway (or you can look in a local newspaper). Since all standard medications are readily available either over the counter or on prescription, there's no need to stock up before you travel.

WOMEN TRAVELLERS
Attitudes Towards Women

Women will find Wales fairly enlightened. There's nothing to stop women going into pubs alone, although not everyone likes doing this; pairs or groups of women blend in more naturally.

Safety Precautions

Solo travellers should have few problems, although common-sense caution should be observed in big cities, especially at night. Hitching is never wise.

Condoms are now often sold in women's toilets as well as men's. Otherwise, all chemists and many service stations stock them. In the UK, the contraceptive pill is only available on prescription. Emergency contraception (the 'morning-after' pill; actually effective for up to 72 hours after unprotected sex) is now available over the counter in many chemists, but it's expensive at around £20. It's still free on prescription.

Organisations

Most big towns have a Well Woman Clinic or Centre that can advise on general health issues. Find its address in the local phone book or ask in the library. Should you suffer an atrack, Rape Crisis Centres can offer support.

GAY & LESBIAN TRAVELLERS

In general the UK is tolerant of homosexuality; certainly it's possible for people to acknowledge their homosexuality in a way that would have been unthinkable 20 years ago. But tolerance only goes so far, as a glance at any tabloid newspaper will confirm.

The battle by the Labour government to lower the homosexual age of consent from 18 to 16, in line with that for heterosexuals, was won in November 2000 when – after three defeats in the House of Lords – the government invoked the Parliament Act to pass the Sexual Offences (Amendment) Bill into UK law.

Cardiff has an active gay and lesbian scene, and there are also small above-the-parapet gay communities in Swansea and in the university towns of Aberystwyth and Bangor, although overt displays of affection may not be wise beyond acknowledged venues. These two University of Wales campuses also have limited but regular social events for gay and lesbian students (and visitors); see under those towns for further information.

Wales' biggest gay/lesbian/bisexual bash is Cardiff's Mardi Gras festival on the first Saturday of September (see the Cardiff chapter). There's also a Mardi Gras page at the Gay Wales Web site (see the following Organisations section).

Organisations

British gay periodicals such as the *Pink Paper*, *Boyz* and *Gay Times* and lesbian publications such as *Diva*, have very limited information on Wales. The best Wales-specific resource – with news, events, listings and helplines – is the Gay Wales Web site at www.gaywales.co.uk.

University of Wales campuses at Bangor and Aberystwyth have lesbian-gay-bisexual student 'officers' who can be contacted for information and help; Aberystwyth also has a gay and bisexual hotline. See under those towns for further information.

A London resource is the 24-hour Lesbian & Gay Switchboard (☎ 020-7837 7324), which can help with most enquiries, general and specific. London Lesbian Line (☎ 020-7251 6911) offers similar help but only on weekdays from 7 to 10 pm (Monday and Friday from 2 pm).

DISABLED TRAVELLERS

Most new buildings in Wales – including hotels and recent tourist attractions – are designed with wheelchair access in mind. But most B&Bs and guesthouses are in hard-to-adapt older buildings, so travellers with mobility problems can end up paying over the odds for accommodation.

Newer buses and trains sometimes have steps that lower for easier access (though it's always wise to check before setting out); older ones don't. Wales & West offers sizeable discounts on full-fare tickets to wheelchair-bound passengers. A Disabled Persons Railcard gives wider rail-fare discounts; see under Trains in the Getting Around chapter for details.

Most TICs and tourist attractions reserve parking spaces near the entrance for the disabled. Most TICs in Wales are wheelchair accessible, have counter sections at wheelchair height and have information on accessibility in their particular area. Many ticket offices, banks etc are fitted with hearing loops to assist the hearing impaired; look for the ear logo.

The 1995 Disability Discrimination Act makes it illegal to discriminate against people with disabilities in the provision of services. Under Part 3 of the Act, barriers to access have to be removed by 2004. This includes introducing physical features such as ramps and automatic doors, so the situation for wheelchair users should slowly improve.

Organisations

The Royal Association for Disability and Rehabilitation (RADAR) publishes an annually updated survey, *Holidays in Britain & Ireland; A Guide for Disabled People* (£7.50). Contact RADAR (☎ 020-7250 3222, fax 7250 0212), 12 City Forum, 250 City Rd, London EC1V 8AF.

The Holiday Care Service (☎ 01293-774535), 2nd floor, Imperial Buildings, Victoria Rd, Horley, Surrey RH6 7PZ, publishes *A Guide to Accessible Accommodation and Travel for Britain* (£5.95), and can offer general advice.

The WTB publishes *Discovering Accessible Wales*, a free booklet with useful information on accessible attractions, accommodation, restaurants and transport.

Shopmobility is a UK-wide scheme under which wheelchairs or electric 'scooters' are available at central points for access to shopping areas in certain towns. The scheme is run as a charity in Cardiff; in other Wales towns – including Swansea, Newport, Merthyr Tydfil and Wrexham – it's council-run, with modest rental fees involved. For more information contact the National Federation of Shopmobility (☎/fax 01905-617761, e nfsuk@lineone.net), 85 High St, Worcester WR1 2ET.

SENIOR TRAVELLERS

Seniors are entitled to some discounts on public transport and admission fees if they present proof of their age. Sometimes a special pass is needed. The minimum qualifying age is generally 60 to 65 for men, 55 to 65 for women. See the Getting Around chapter for details on senior discounts and discount cards.

Organisations

In your home country, travellers as young as 50 may be entitled to special travel packages and discounts (on car hire, for instance) through organisations and travel agents catering to senior travellers. Start hunting at your local senior citizens advice bureau.

SAGA Holidays (☎ 0800 096 0085) is a reliable UK tour operator specialising in holidays for travellers aged over 50, with a Web site at www.saga.co.uk; see the Organised Tours section in the Getting Around chapter.

TRAVEL WITH CHILDREN

The media may dote on celebrities with kids, but travellers with kids don't get the same treatment. If you're seeing Wales with children, be prepared for some hotels, B&Bs and upper-end restaurants that don't want them (save yourself the headache by asking when you book whether children are welcome).

On the whole, however, cafes and middle- and lower-bracket restaurants are quite tolerant of little people. Many pubs now lay on playgrounds and children's menus. Most hotels and some B&Bs can rustle up a baby cot or heat up a bottle for you. Most supermarkets, bigger train stations, motorway service stations and major attractions have toilets with baby-changing facilities.

Preschool children usually get into museums and other sights free, and those aged up to about 16 get in for one-third to one-half off the adult price. Some rail companies have launched separate 'family carriages' where you needn't cringe when your tots enjoy themselves at volume.

Wales presents no major health risks for kids other than cold mountains and the occasional hot beach. Restaurant food is quite safe. Also see the Health section earlier in the chapter.

For more detailed and wide-ranging suggestions (not all of them necessary in Wales), pick up Lonely Planet's *Travel with Children*.

USEFUL ORGANISATIONS

Between them, Wales' two big nonprofit heritage organisations, Cadw and the National Trust (NT), care for hundreds of spectacular historical sites. Most of these cost around £3 to £4 to enter, so if you're planning to see a lot of stately homes, castles, ruined abbeys and/or other historical buildings, it may be worth joining one or both organisations, since membership gives you free admission to all their properties, as well as maps and printed material about them. Another significant 'heritage' property owner is the National Museums & Galleries of Wales (NMGW).

In this book, a Cadw/NT/NMGW property is indicated by one of these names in parenthesis, usually following the telephone number.

Cadw

Cadw (**ka**-doo; a Welsh word meaning 'to preserve') is the Welsh historic monuments agency, responsible for looking after most of Wales' ruined abbeys and castles, plus many prehistoric, Roman, post-medieval and industrial sites. These include the four castles (Caernarfon, Harlech, Conwy and Beaumaris) in North Wales and the industrial sites at Blaenafon in the south, which have been designated as World Heritage Sites by UNESCO.

A year's Cadw membership costs £25 for adults, £17/30 for one/two seniors, £16 for young people aged 16 to 20 or £12 for under-16s. A family membership costs £44. You can join at any staffed Cadw site, or contact Cadw's Heritage in Wales membership department (☎ 0800 074 3121, fax 2082 6375) at Freepost CF1142/9, Cardiff CF24 5GZ. Cadw has a Web site at www.cadw.wales.gov.uk.

Wheelchair users and the visually impaired, together with their assisting companion, are admitted free to all Cadw monuments.

National Trust

The NT cares for properties in England, Wales and Northern Ireland, most of them stately homes, gardens and prehistoric sites. As part of its ongoing Neptune Coastline Campaign, the NT has, since 1965, purchased some 600 miles of coastal land in Wales and elsewhere in the UK, with the aim of preserving it for public use.

A year's NT membership costs £30/15 for those aged over/under 26, £51 for an adult couple and £57 for a family. You can join at most major sites; or by contacting the NT (☎ 020-8315 1111), PO Box 39, Bromley, Kent BR1 3XL; or through the NT for Wales (☎ 01492-860123, fax 860233), Trinity Square, Llandudno LL30 2DE; or online at www.nationaltrust.org.uk.

The NT also has reciprocal arrangements with its counterparts in Scotland, Australia, New Zealand and Canada, and with the Royal Oak Foundation in the USA.

National Museums & Galleries of Wales

The NMGW has seven historical sites open to the public: the National Museum & Gallery (Cardiff), the Museum of Welsh Life (St Fagans), the Turner House Gallery (Penarth), the Roman Legionary Museum (Caerleon, near Newport), the Museum of the Welsh Woollen Industry (Dre-fach Felindre), the Welsh Slate Museum (Llanberis) and the Segontium Roman Museum (Caernarfon). The Big Pit Mining Museum at Blaenafon may soon come under the NMGW banner too.

A year's NMGW membership costs £17.50/27 for an adult/couple, £10 for students and those aged 19 to 21, and £32.50 for a family. Those aged up to 19 or at least 60 are admitted free to all NMGW sites. You can join at any of these museums or galleries, or by contacting the NMGW (☎ 029-2057 3472, fax 2057 3144, ⓔ post@ nmgw.ac.uk), Cathays Park, Cardiff CF10 3NP. The NMGW's Web site is at www .nmgw.ac.uk.

Heritage Passes

For visitors who are unlikely to be in the country for more than a few weeks, Cadw sells a three/seven-day Explorer Pass for £9/15 per person, £16/25 for two people or £21/30 for a family – though you'd probably have to use it about every other day to recoup the cost.

The Great British Heritage Pass, marketed by the BTA (see Tourist Offices earlier in the chapter), gives free access to all 580 properties under the care of Cadw, NT and English Heritage (and NT Scotland). A seven/15/30-day pass costs £35/46/60, irrespective of age. But it's available only to non-British citizens – in the UK at many international airports and seaports (though none in Wales), from the BTA's Visitor Information Centre in London, and in Wales from Cardiff and Caernarfon TICs; in the USA and Canada through Rail Europe (see under UK Rail Passes in the Getting Around chapter for contact details).

DANGERS & ANNNOYANCES
Weather

Never, in Wales, assume that just because it's midsummer it will be warm and dry. Always pack an umbrella or raingear, even for a jaunt around town.

The general wetness aside, it's even more important to treat the Brecon Beacons and Snowdonia national parks with respect. Mist can drop with a startling suddenness, leaving you dangerously chilled and disoriented. Never venture onto the heights without checking the weather forecast and without being sensibly clad and equipped. Ideally, make sure someone knows where you're heading if it's off the beaten track or in dubious conditions. See Hypothermia

under Health, and Walking under Activities for more advice.

Crime

Wales (and the UK in general) is remarkably safe considering the national disparities in wealth. But common sense is still in order when hitching or walking in city centres at night. The Cardiff Bay area used to have a reputation for drunken violence but has been considerably cleaned up now.

The obvious things to guard are your passport, papers, tickets and money. It's always best to carry these items next to your skin or in a sturdy leather pouch on your belt. Pack your own padlock for hostel lockers. Don't leave valuables lying around in your hotel room or B&B.

Never leave valuables in a car, and remove all luggage overnight. This is especially true in seemingly safe rural locations: while you're out tramping about the countryside, someone may well be tramping off with your belongings. Look for secure parking areas near TICs and national park visitor centres.

Report thefts to the police and ask for a statement, or else your travel insurance company won't pay out.

Drunks

The sight of a bleary-eyed lad of 20 ordering four pints of beer 15 minutes before closing time is a sign of trouble to come. Brawls are not uncommon as tanked-up louts are all tossed onto the streets simultaneously at closing time. The best you can do is give these yobs a wide berth.

Beggars

Cardiff has its share of panhandlers. Give them something if you wish, but don't wave a full wallet around – carry some change in a separate pocket. Your money may go further if you give it to a recognised charity. Shelter (☎ 020-7505 2000), 88 Old St, London EC1, helps the homeless and gratefully accepts donations. Also consider buying the *Big Issue* (£1), a weekly magazine available from homeless street sellers who benefit directly from sales.

Hostility & Loneliness

Anti-English sentiment certainly exists throughout Wales, especially in the heavily Welsh-speaking north-west, though it's rarely out in the open and almost never angry or violent. Some English visitors work themselves into a quite unnecessary frenzy over the 'unfriendliness' of native Welsh speakers. You might have the misfortune to bump into a raving nationalist, ready to take issue with anyone who ventures the wrong opinion in the wrong place, but it's pretty unlikely. For the most part, the Welsh are as welcoming as anyone, especially if you visit in the off-season when the slower pace of life leaves more time for honest chat.

However, the Welsh can be slow to warm up, and a solo visitor may find it hard to break the ice in pubs and elsewhere. Here's a trick that might help: sit down with your beer in a cheerful, well lit pub and open a road map (you don't have to be lost, nor to be looking for anything at all). Before long you'll probably be surrounded by locals, offering suggestions, arguing with one another and generally looking after you.

EMERGENCIES

The national emergency services number throughout the UK is ☎ 999, good for all police, fire and medical emergencies. The Europe-wide emergency number, ☎ 112, can also be used.

LEGAL MATTERS
Drugs

Illegal drugs of every type are widely available, especially in clubs. But all the usual dangers associated with drugs apply and there have been several high-profile deaths associated with ecstasy, the purity of which is often dubious. Possession of small quantities of cannabis usually attracts a small fine (still a criminal conviction) or a warning; other drugs are treated more seriously.

Driving Offences

The laws against drink-driving have got tougher and are treated more seriously than they used to be. Currently you're allowed to have a blood-alcohol level of 80mg/100mL. The safest approach is not to drink anything at all if you're planning to drive. For information about current speed limits and parking violations, see Car & Motorcycle in the Getting Around chapter.

Fines

In general you rarely have to cough up on the spot for an offence. The main exceptions are on trains and buses where people who can't produce a valid ticket for the journey when asked to by an inspector can be fined there and then: £5 on buses, £10 on trains, no excuses accepted.

BUSINESS HOURS

Offices are generally open 9 am to 5 pm weekdays. Shops may stay open longer, and most open all day Saturday. An increasing number of shops also open on Sunday, perhaps from 11 am to 4 pm. Evening shopping is usually on Thursday or Friday.

Many small and/or country towns have a weekly early-closing day – different in each region of the country, usually Tuesday, Wednesday or Thursday afternoon – though not all shops honour it. Early-closing is more apparent in winter. Pubs no longer have to close on Sunday (see the boxed text 'The End of Dry Sunday').

The End of Dry Sunday

'Dry Sunday', the prohibition against drinking alcohol on the Sabbath, goes back over two centuries to the time of the religious revivals (see under History in the Facts about Wales chapter). Many arriving visitors seem to think it's still in place.

As often as a referendum could be held on the subject, regular campaigns were mounted in the 20th century for an end to Dry Sunday. The first of the now-gone Welsh districts to vote for an end to the practice did so in the 1970s, but it was not until 1995 that the last of them – Dwyfor, essentially all of the Llŷn Peninsula – went 'wet'. Sunday is no longer dry anywhere in Wales.

If someone tells you a place opens daily, they almost always mean 'daily except Sunday'.

PUBLIC HOLIDAYS & SPECIAL EVENTS
Public Holidays

Most banks, businesses, a few museums and other places of interest are closed on public holidays. A 'bank holiday' is indeed a holiday for banks, but refers more generally to a weekday closure which is defined generically (eg, the first Monday of May) rather than associated with a particular calendar date or religious festival.

The UK's official public holidays are New Year's Day (1 January), Good Friday, Easter Monday, May Day Bank Holiday (first Monday in May), Spring Bank Holiday (last Monday in May), Summer Bank Holiday (last Monday in August), Christmas Day (25 December) and Boxing Day (26 December). If New Year's Day, Christmas or Boxing Day falls on a weekend, the following Monday is also a bank holiday.

Most museums and other attractions in Wales close on Christmas and Boxing Day but stay open for the other holidays. Exceptions are those that normally close Sunday; they're quite likely to close on bank holidays too. Some smaller museums close Monday and/or Tuesday.

Special Events

Eisteddfodau Wales' biggest annual events are its *eisteddfodau* (singular *eisteddfod*), described in detail under Literature and Society & Conduct in the Facts about Wales chapter. They range from little village songfests to three vast annual cultural gatherings: the International Music Eisteddfod, held at Llangollen every July; the Royal National Eisteddfod, which moves between North and South Wales each August; and the Urdd Eisteddfod for under-25s, which also alternates between sites in North and South Wales each May.

Dates and venues for upcoming Royal National Eisteddfodau are 3–10 August 2002 in St David's (Pembrokeshire) and 2–9 August 2003 in Meifod (Powys). Those for future Urdd Eisteddfodau are 27 May to 1 June 2002 in Llandudno, and 26–31 May 2003, probably in Neath and Port Talbot. If you'd like to see an eisteddfod but can't make any of the big ones, contact the WTB (see under Tourist Offices earlier for details) for its free annual events booklet, which also lists local contests.

Shakespeare in the Castles Another appealing series of events are the July and August performances (£7.50/5), by the Wales Actors' Company, of Shakespeare's *A Midsummer Night's Dream* at many of the old castles and other properties managed by Cadw. Contact Cadw (see Useful Organisations earlier in the chapter) for a timetable of these and other events at Cadw sites.

Festival of the Countryside This isn't a festival at all, but an umbrella organisation promoting environmentally sensitive tourism in Wales. Its free annual *Festival of the Countryside* booklet details hundreds of eco-friendly events across the country – special walks and walking festivals, art workshops and exhibitions, fairs and more. See under Ecology & Environment in the Facts about Wales chapter for contact details.

Other Events Among many interesting regular events around Wales are the following:

February/March
Six Nations Rugby Championship – the most important event in the Welsh rugby calendar; Millennium Stadium, Cardiff; match dates vary

Early May
FA Cup Final – England's premier football knock-out tournament, to be held in the Millennium Stadium for as many years as London's Wembley Stadium is under reconstruction; Cardiff

May/June
Urdd Eisteddfod (Youth Eisteddfod) – changing venues; six days in late May or early June
St Davids Cathedral Festival – festival of classical music; St David's; Spring Bank Holiday weekend

Hay Festival – festival of literature in the town of bookshops; Hay-on-Wye; one week

June

Man vs Horse Marathon – a lunatic cross-country race with a £21,000 prize; Llanwrtyd Wells; first Saturday in June

Gregynog Music Festival – festival of classical music, including a Welsh night; Gregynog, near Newtown; one week in mid-June

July

International Music Eisteddfod – international festival of music; Llangollen; runs for six days in early July

Morris in the Forest – morris dancing, ceilidhs, walks and workshops; Llanwrtyd Wells; three-day weekend in early July

Chepstow Festival – art exhibits, Shakespeare in the castle, medieval pageantry; Chepstow; most of July in even-numbered years

Royal Welsh Show – Wales' biggest farm and livestock show; Builth Wells; runs for most of a week in late July

Fishguard International Music Festival – chamber, orchestral, choral music and jazz; Fishguard; one week in late July

Sesiwn Fawr Festival – free Celtic folk festival; Dolgellau; third weekend in July

Country & Western Music Festival – Welshpool; third Sunday in July

The Big Cheese – street theatre, folk dancing, medieval costumes and food; Caerphilly; last weekend in July

July/August

Cardiff Festival – Europe's biggest free arts festival, with street theatre and music around the city; Cardiff; two weeks culminating on the first weekend in August

August

Royal National Eisteddfod – national cultural festival; changing venues; eight days in early August

United Counties Show – major agricultural show and family entertainment, classic cars; Carmarthen; Thursday and Friday in mid-August

Brecon Jazz Festival – one of Europe's leading jazz festivals; Brecon; one weekend in mid-August

Pembrokeshire County Show – agricultural fair with livestock, food, music and dancing; Haverfordwest; three days in mid-August

Race the Train – quirky all-terrain race against the Talyllyn steam train; Tywyn; Saturday in mid-August

Miri Madog – Welsh rock festival; Porthmadog; third weekend in August

Victorian Festival – a week of fun and Victorian dressing-up; Llandrindod Wells; mid- to late August

World Bog Snorkelling Championships – competitors swim two lengths of a murky, 60 yard bog, for their five minutes of fame; Llanwrtyd Wells; Summer Bank Holiday Monday

September

North Wales Hot Air Balloon Festival – Llangollen; first weekend in September

Tenby Arts Festival – street theatre, samba bands, classical and pop concerts; Tenby; nine days in late September

September–November

Swansea Festival – drama, opera, film, ballet, jazz and classical music; Swansea; runs for six weeks

Late November

Mid Wales Beer Festival – scores of real ales in the town's pubs, plus off-road foot and cycle races fuelled with beer; Llanwrtyd Wells; runs for 1½ weeks

ACTIVITIES

Wales is working hard to promote itself as the place to visit for activity holidays, and for good reason. The opportunities for outdoor activities are enormous, and there are activity centres all over the place to help you do them. You can walk, cycle, ride, climb, boat, surf, fish, golf, bird-watch and otherwise indulge yourself almost year-round.

The three-fold reward of these activities is that, first, they'll coax you off the beaten track into some of Wales' most beautiful corners; second, they'll give you a sense of pitching in rather than just looking on; and third, most of them will cost relatively little. Following is an overview of the possibilities.

Local trails, activity centres and other facilities are identified in the regional chapters. TICs will have further details of what's possible in their vicinity. The WTB publishes the free *Activity Wales*, a roundup of activities and WTB-approved operators across the country, as well as several specialist booklets noted in the following sections.

For details of riding Wales' many narrow-gauge steam trains see the Getting Around chapter.

Walking

Every weekend, people take to the parks and countryside of Wales in their thousands. Seen at long range, rural Wales appears frozen in time, its damp and deeply green hills speckled with sheep, punctuated with white farmsteads and often topped with fairytale castle ruins. No wonder so many directors like to set their films here.

Walkers are well cared for here. There are thousands of miles of popular trails, the most challenging of them in Snowdonia and Brecon Beacons National Parks. Serious walkers can choose from three official National Trails and at least seven long-distance paths (LDPs), created by linking existing paths and developing new ones where there are gaps. Most of the LDPs – regional routes mainly developed by county councils – are well organised and have good information available.

Every village and town is surrounded by footpaths, and it's quite feasible to base yourself in one interesting spot (perhaps in a self-catering cottage, youth hostel or camp site) and spend a week exploring the surrounding countryside.

Access People's right of access to land – even privately owned land – is jealously protected in Wales. The countryside is criss-crossed by countless 'rights of way', most of them over private land, which may be used by any member of the public. They may cross fields, moors, woodlands, even farmhouse yards.

These public footpaths and bridleways (the latter can be used by horse riders and mountain bikers) have existed for centuries, sometimes millennia. They're marked on maps, and are often signposted where they intersect with roads. Some have special markers along their length (yellow arrows for footpaths, blue for bridleways, or other markers if they're part of a particular walk). Some are completely unmarked, so a good map – and the ability to use it – can be essential. If a path is overgrown or obstructed, walkers may remove enough of the obstruction to pass. The need for discretion is obvious: no farmer will appreciate damage to property.

Some rights of way cross land owned by the Ministry of Defence (MoD) and used occasionally by the army. When manoeuvres or firing is underway, access is denied and red flags are put up to warn walkers.

There are some areas – clearly signposted – where walkers can move freely beyond the rights of way. The NT (see Useful Organisations earlier in the chapter) has become one of the UK's largest landowners, and many of its properties are open to the public.

Perhaps surprisingly, national parks are *not* necessarily open to unlimited access; these parks were set up by the Countryside Commission to protect the finest landscapes and to provide opportunities for visitor enjoyment, but much of the land remains privately owned and farmed. It is almost always necessary to get permission from a landowner before pitching a tent.

Other officially protected areas, such as Areas of Outstanding Natural Beauty and Sites of Special Scientific Interest (see under Ecology & Environment in the Facts about Wales chapter for more on these and other protected areas), may likewise not have unlimited access.

Maps & Guides Lonely Planet's *Walking in Britain* is a detailed guide and includes the three National Trails in Wales, a dozen other long-distance paths and a wide selection of shorter walks and day-hikes.

The Countryside Agency, with Aurum Press and the OS, publishes excellent official guides for many trails, with detailed notes and relevant sections of OS 1:25,000 Explorer maps. TICs, newsagents, bookshops and outdoor equipment shops stock these, plus scores of books on everything from heritage trails to trans-Wales expeditions. The WTB publishes the free *Walking Wales*, an introduction to the best long and short walks, with a huge list of publications on local walks and which TICs stock them.

The OS publishes several series of excellent, widely available maps covering all of Wales; see under Planning at the start of the chapter.

Guided Walks & Luggage Services All three national parks organise guided day-walks during the summer, and there are numerous private adventure and activity centres in and around the parks with day-walk and longer programs. Some recommended outfits are noted in the sections on each park.

Scores of private companies offer multi-day walking tours in every corner of Wales. Some also offer luggage services, sending travellers' bags ahead to their next destination, leaving them unencumbered and free to enjoy their walks. Purists may scoff, but this is just the ticket if you're doing a long-distance walk as part of a larger, non-walking trip. See the local chapters for more details.

Long-Distance Walks The energetic and the impecunious should definitely consider a multiday walk or two. Civilisation is never far away in Wales so it's easy to assemble a walk connecting with public transport and punctuated by hostels or bunkhouses, and villages. A tent and cooking gear are rarely necessary. Warm, layered clothing with a waterproof outer layer (and a hat and gloves), sturdy footwear, lunch and some high-energy emergency food, a water bottle (with purification tablets or resin filter), first-aid kit, whistle, torch (flashlight), and map and compass are all you need. Check the weather forecast with the TIC or the Met Office (☎ 0891 500449), and always leave details of your route and return time with someone trustworthy.

There are three official National Trails – open to walkers, cyclists and horse riders, and waymarked with the familiar acorn symbol – through some of the country's finest landscapes. These are the Pembrokeshire Coast Path, hugging the sea-cliffs of the Pembrokeshire Coast National Park; Offa's Dyke Path along the Wales–England border; and Glyndŵr's Way, which cuts right across Mid Wales and back again.

The longest of the waymarked LDPs – more rugged and demanding, and less well known, than the others (thus less heavily used) is the Cambrian Way, running all the way from Conwy to Cardiff through much of Wales' highest, wildest and most gorgeous terrain.

Walk these trails from end to end, or pick a segment that fits your holiday. Other major ones are:

The Taff Trail (55 miles) from Cardiff up the Taff Valley and across the Brecon Beacon National Park to Brecon

The Usk Valley Walk (50 miles) from Newport and the Severn Estuary up the Usk Valley to Abergavenny and Brecon

The Wye Valley Walk (144 miles) from Chepstow up the valley of the River Wye (in England in its middle reaches) via Builth Wells to the Mid-Wales market town of Rhayader

The Severn Valley Way (210 miles) along the entire course of the River Severn, largely in England but in Wales in its upper reaches from Welshpool to the river's source in the Cambrian Mountains

The Dyfi Valley Way (108 miles) from Aberdovey to Llyn Tegid (Bala Lake) and back along the other side of the valley to Borth, north of Aberystwyth

The North Wales Path (48 miles) along the north coast from Bangor via Llandudno to Prestatyn

The Pembrokeshire Coast Path Lying entirely within the Pembrokeshire Coast National Park, this 186-mile cliff-top coastal trail – most of it, at any rate – is quite simply one of the UK's most beautiful walking routes. It includes Wales' finest beaches and best coastal scenery, passes through tiny fishing villages, skirts secluded coves, and crosses some areas surprisingly empty of people. Distractions include St David's (the UK's smallest city, with its fine cathedral) and charming Tenby, plus ruined castles, Iron Age forts and tranquil nature reserves – not to mention pubs, many of them right beside the trail. It's a seabird-watchers' heaven. The rocks here are among the world's oldest, and their spectacular patterns and colours are another constant attraction.

The route also shows you the other side of Wales – ugly towns, oil refineries and a power station – and some middle sections, around Pembroke and Milford Haven, are definitely worth skipping. The only other town of any size on the route is Fishguard, although there's rarely any shortage of modest accommodation options close to the path.

The continual steep ascents and descents where it crosses river valleys make this walk more challenging than the mileages would suggest. South to north is the preferred direction, allowing you to limber up in the south for wilder walking in the north, and keeping the sun – and usually the wind – at your back. If all went well you could do the whole trail in about 15 days, though you'd be crazy not to add a few days for side trips to nearby islands and other places of interest. There are several possible shortcuts en route, though most involve heading away from the coast, thus missing the whole point of the trail.

If you're tight on time, stick to the northern half, from Sandy Haven or Marloes to Cardigan. If you've only got a day or two, zero in on the scenic, accessible section between Dale and Martin's Haven, near Marloes. This is also on the route of the park's excellent Puffin Shuttle bus service, which runs twice daily all summer between Milford Haven and St David's, stopping almost anywhere to pick up or drop off walkers and other visitors.

The national park publishes *Coast Path Accommodation* and *Public Transport Guide* booklets, and produces a good range of cheap leaflets and trail cards on the path and adjacent walks. These are available from local TICs, or by post from the National Park Information Centre (☎ 01437-764636, e pcnp@pembrokeshirecoast.org), Winch Lane, Haverfordwest SA61 1PY. The official trail guide, *Pembrokeshire Coast Path* by Brian John, includes detailed route descriptions, OS map extracts and colour photos. More useful is *The Pembrokeshire Coastal Path* by Dennis Kelsall, which runs in the preferred south to north direction and includes detailed descriptions, background information, line maps and an accommodation list.

The route is covered by just two OS Outdoor Leisure 1:25,000 maps – No 35 (North Pembrokeshire) and No 36 (South Pembrokeshire).

Offa's Dyke Path Offa's Dyke was a grand earthwork project, conceived and executed in the 8th century by Offa, king of Mercia – probably as a mutually agreed border with neighbouring Welsh princes. This ambitious earthwork, mostly in the form of a bank and adjacent ditch, was pivotal in the subsequent history of the region known as the Welsh Marches. Even though only 80 miles of the Dyke remains, it still roughly defines today's Wales-England border.

The 178-mile Offa's Dyke Path runs from the Severn Estuary at Chepstow in the south, through the beautiful Wye Valley and Shropshire Hills to end on Wales' north coast at Prestatyn. It doesn't stick religiously to the Dyke but veers between England and Wales, detouring along quiet valleys and up sharp ridges, through an astonishing range of scenery and vegetation – possibly the most varied of any long-distance trail. You'll walk from river flatland to hill country, through oak forests, heathland and bracken, across high moors and the more exacting mountainous conditions of the Clwydian range in the north. The region's turbulent history is reflected in ruined castles and abbeys, ancient hillforts and surviving sections of Roman road.

The trail is best done south to north, putting the sun and wind at your back; most guidebooks describe the walk this way. You could do it all in about 12 days with the weather on your side, but two weeks will give you some rest days for taking in some off-trail attractions, including Tintern Abbey and Powis Castle. This is a strenuous walk, with some testing gradients and over 700 stiles to climb, and making use of a local baggage-transfer service will increase your enjoyment.

The Offa's Dyke Association (ODA; ☎ 01547-528753, e oda@offasdyke.demon .co.uk), West St, Knighton, Powys LD7 1EN, publishes several helpful booklets and pamphlets, including the indispensable

Offa's Dyke Path – Where to Stay, How to Get There & Other Useful Information, South to North Route Notes and a set of strip maps. Some of these are also available at TICs along the route. The Offa's Dyke Web site, at www.offas-dyke.co.uk, has general route information, critiques of maps and route guides, and luggage-transport and accommodation services.

The official, two-volume guide, *Offa's Dyke Path* by Ernie & Kathy Kay & Mark Richards, is the best on offer, with straightforward route notes, a taste of the history, colour OS map extracts and suggested circular walks. For a sense of the trail's rich heritage, you can't beat *Walking Offa's Dyke Path – A Journey Through the Border Country of England and Wales* by David Hunter.

The best maps are the OS Explorer and Outdoor Leisure 1:25,000 series. You'll need Outdoor Leisure maps No 14 (Wye Valley and Forest of Dean) and No 13 (Brecon Beacons – Eastern Area), and Explorer maps No 201 (Knighton Presteigne), No 216 (Welshpool & Montgomery), No 240 (Oswestry), No 256 (Wrexham & Llangollen) and No 265 (Clwydian Range/Bryniau).

Glyndŵr's Way Glyndŵr's Way – Wales' newest national trail, officially opened in April 2001 – is named after Owain Glyndŵr, the Welsh warrior-statesman who led a spirited but ultimately ill-fated rebellion against English rule in the early 15th century. The 132-mile route makes a great zig-zag from Knighton to Machynlleth and back to Welshpool, passing many sites connected with the rebellion.

The area covered by the trail is sandwiched between the better-known walking regions of Snowdonia and the Brecon Beacons. The landscape is predominantly low moor (some of it rather bleak) and farmland, with lakes, gentle hills and beautiful valleys. Although quite undulating, the route – mainly on good paths and farm tracks – never rises above about 500m and rarely drops below 200m. A highlight is its impressive range of birdlife, including buzzards, kingfishers, woodpeckers, red kites, peregrine falcons, flycatchers and wrens.

Most people tackle the walk in eight to 10 days. The hilly terrain and multitude of cross-paths can mean slow going, so it's wise to allow more time than you might for a more established trail. For those who don't want to do it all, Machynlleth has good transport connections. If you don't intend to camp, plan your route around the available accommodation, which is scarce on some sections.

Owain Glyndwr's Way by Richard Sale is the route's only dedicated guidebook, but it's now out of print and out of date. The Powys County Council publishes a set of 16 leaflets called *Glyndŵr's Way*, describing the route and its history and offering some wildlife notes; these and an accommodation list are sold as a package (£4) at TICs along the route (Knighton, Llanidloes, Machynlleth, Lake Vyrnwy and Welshpool). The council has a full-time National Trail project manager (☎ 01654-703376) who can provide advice and information on the new route.

The OS Explorer 1:25,000 maps are the best option: No 201 (Knighton & Presteigne), No 214 (Llanidloes & Newtown/Y Drenewydd), No 215 (Newtown/Y Drenewydd & Machynlleth) and No 239 (Lake Vyrnwy, Llyn Efyrnwy & Llanfyllin) cover the entire route except the last half-mile as you enter Machynlleth.

The Cambrian Way Winding through Wales from Conwy to Cardiff, and taking in just about every bit of high, wild landscape on the way, is the 274-mile Cambrian Way. It's billed as a 'mountain connoisseur's walk', and it is indeed only for the experienced, dedicated walker. It covers the Carneddau, Snowdon, the Rhinog Mountains, Cader Idris, the remote heart of Mid Wales including the Plynlimon uplands (source of the Rivers Wye and Severn), the Black Mountains and an east-west traverse of Brecon Beacons National Park.

The route lacks the infrastructure and resources associated with the national trails, which is at once its beauty and its biggest drawback. Among the few books dedicated to the trail is *The Cambrian Way* by A Drake. Several enterprising hoteliers along the route have banded together to offer walking holidays and accommodation on each of five segments; for details contact Nick Bointon at Llanerchidda Farm (☎ 01550-750274, e nick@cambrianway .com) or check out the Web site at www .cambrianway.com.

Cycling

The backroads of Wales offer some superb cycling, at least outside the traffic-choked months of July and August. You can hire bikes all over the place (sources are noted throughout this book) and make up your own day trips, or bring your own machine and ride clear across the country.

Bikes are not allowed on motorways. A-roads tend to be busy and are best avoided. B-roads are usually quieter and many are pleasant for cycling. The best roads for cyclists are the quiet, unnumbered country roads or lanes between villages. In Wales, bicycles can be ridden on any track identified as a public right of way on OS maps. The right to cycle does not, however, usually exist on a footpath.

Information Lonely Planet's new *Cycling Britain* has details of the best bike routes, information on places to stay and eat and a useful section on bicycle maintenance.

The Cyclists' Touring Club (CTC; ☎ 01483-417217, fax 426994, e cycling@ ctc.org.uk), 69 Meadrow, Godalming, Surrey GU7 3HS, offers comprehensive information (free to members) about cycling in the UK and overseas – including suggested routes, local contacts, accommodation tips, organised cycling holidays, a bike-hire directory, and mail-order OS maps and books. Annual membership costs £25 (those aged under 26 and seniors £15). Some cycling organisations outside the UK have reciprocal membership arrangements with the CTC. Check out the Web site at www.ctc.org.uk.

Better regional TICs have information on local cycling routes and bike-hire outfits. The WTB publishes *Cycling Wales*, a free introduction to Wales' long-distance and regional routes (road rides, traffic-free trails and mountain biking), with an annual supplement listing tour organisers, cycle-hire outlets, useful regional publications and events.

Tours As with walking, many specialist tour companies cater for cyclists in Wales. For its members, the CTC (see the preced-

---

Sustrans & the National Cycle Network

The National Cycle Network is a project to create 10,000 miles of cycle routes around the UK, with the network passing within two miles of the homes of half the population, by 2005. Half the network is to be on traffic-free paths (including cycle lanes, forestry roads, canal towpaths and disused railway lines), to be shared with walkers, and the rest along quiet minor roads. In 2000, the first 5000 miles of routes were officially opened.

The driving force behind this vision is a Bristol-based civil-engineering charity called Sustrans ('*sustainable transport*'). When Sustrans announced its plans in 1978 it was barely taken seriously, but the growth in popularity of bicycles, coupled with near-terminal road congestion, has focused much attention on the idea of cycle paths. The charity picked up £43.5 million from the Millennium Commission, and has had frequent pats on the back from the government and numerous high-profile public figures.

Sustrans' *Official Guide to the National Network* (£9.99) details 29 one-day rides around the network. Maps are available for all the routes (free for shorter paths, £3.99 to £5.99 for map-guides to the national routes). For further information, contact Sustrans (☎ 0117-929 0888, e info@ nationalcyclenetwork.org.uk), 35 King Street, Bristol BS1 4DZ. Its Web site is at www.sustrans.org.uk.

ing section) offers good-value tours all over the UK, some with vehicle support, for as little as £200 per week.

For a week-long itinerary with most tour operators, figure upwards of £300 to £400 (self-guided), or £1000 (with support and quality accommodation). Some reliable Wales-based operators are listed in the local chapters.

Cycling Routes There are two long-distance routes, both part of the National Cycle Network (see the boxed text). Their end-points are on the rail network, so you can go out by bike and back by train, or vice-versa. Sustrans publishes a two-map set (at 1:100,000; £5.99 per map) for each route.

Lôn Las Cymru ('Greenways of Wales', the Welsh National Route; Sustrans route No 8) stretches for some 260 miles – about a week's hilly, moderately hard riding – right across Wales, from the Anglesey port of Holyhead, via Snowdonia, the Cambrian Mountains and the Brecon Beacons National Park, to Cardiff. From Brecon to Cardiff the trail coincides with the Taff Trail (see the preceding Walking section). An alternative route (No 42) runs through Abergavenny to Chepstow.

Lôn Geltaidd ('the Celtic Trail'; corresponding to Sustrans routes No 4 and 47) presently runs from near Chepstow, via Newport and Swansea, to Kidwelly, and by 2002 is meant to stretch for a total of 186 miles as far as Fishguard. Local routes such as the 100-mile Pembrokeshire Park Cycle Trail are gradually being integrated with the Celtic Trail. This trail also has its own office (information hotline ☎ 0800 243731, ☎ 01792-781212, fax 781300, e celtic -trail@tsww.com), c/o Tourism South & West Wales, Charter Court, Enterprise Park, Swansea SA7 9DB.

A third trail, the North Wales Coastal Route (Sustrans route No 5), is in the planning stages, though its Anglesey segment and the traffic-free seaside-promenade ride from Colwyn Bay to Prestatyn are already in place.

The long-distance routes also have alternative high-level sections specifically for mountain bikes. The best purpose-built mountain-bicycle tracks in Wales are at Coed Y Brenin Forest Park, near Dolgellau in Snowdonia National Park. Other good ones, also in the national park, are in Gwydyr Forest Park near Llanrwst (Conwy Valley) and in Beddgelert Forest Park.

Many of the trails referred to under Walking are also open to cyclists.

Surfing

Wales may not be the first place that comes to mind when someone says 'surfing in the UK', but the south-west coast does have some pretty good surfing, backed up by lots of splendid coastal scenery.

Summer waves tend to be small and unreliable; peak season is September to April, though this can also mean minimal crowding at many spots. With the Irish Sea emptying and filling twice a day, the tidal range along the Wales coast is immense – 4.5m to over 7m – which means you may find a completely different set of breaks at low and high tides. Waves tend to be biggest and best on the incoming tide.

Wales' beaches are some of the cleanest in the UK. Sea temperatures run from a maximum of about 16–17°C in summer to a minimum of around 7–8°C in winter, so you'll need a wetsuit in any season (and possibly boots, hood and gloves in winter).

Best Breaks The south coast is the favoured area. Popular south-eastern beaches are at Llantwit Major and Porthcawl. The Gower Peninsula is the home of Welsh surfing, probably because of the wide choice in a small area; good spots include Langland Bay, Oxwich Bay, and Llangennith at the northern end of Rhossili Bay.

South Pembrokeshire's best breaks are at Tenby South Beach, Manorbier, Freshwater West and West Dale Bay; along St Bride's Bay, try Broad Haven South and Newgale. St David's immense Whitesands Bay is good, but popular with everybody. Along Cardigan Bay, check out Aberystwyth's Harbour Trap.

Coasteering & Sea-Kayaking

Coasteering is a high-adrenaline sport, more or less invented on the Pembrokeshire coast. Essentially it's rock-climbing with the sea snapping at your feet. Equipped with wetsuit, flotation jacket and helmet, you make your way along the wave-thrashed coastal cliffs by a combination of climbing, traversing, scrambling, cliff jumping and swimming.

It's a demanding, fairly risky activity and should only be done in the company of qualified leaders with a good knowledge of coastline, water and weather conditions. Participants need to be reasonably fit, capable swimmers.

At present two reliable activity centres in north Pembrokeshire offer coasteering trips, by themselves or as part of residential, multiactivity programs: TYF at St David's, and Preseli Venture near Fishguard. For details of their programs, see under Pembrokeshire Coast National Park in the Pembrokeshire & Carmarthenshire chapter.

Both also offer program modules in sea kayaking. The Pembrokeshire coast is one of the UK's finest sea kayaking areas, with powerful tidal currents creating huge standing waves between the coast and offshore islands. Two other organisations doing sea-kayak courses and trips are the Plas Menai National Watersports Centre at Caernarfon (see the Snowdonia and the Llŷn chapter) and the Anglesey Sea & Surf Centre near Holyhead (see the Anglesey & North Coast chapter).

NICK HURST, PRESELI VENTURE

The best the Llŷn Peninsula has to offer is at Porth Neigwl (Hell's Mouth); other possibilities are at Aberdaron and Porth Oer (Whistling Sands). On Anglesey's southwest coast you may find modest breaks at Cable Bay and Rhosneigr.

Information Coldswell's Web site at www.coldswell.com is a good one for UK and Ireland surfers, with weather, live video images, and a beach guide where surfers post their own reviews of breaks. A1 Surf's Web site at www.a1surf.com has comprehensive links and surf reports from around the UK. For surfing and weather reports ring ☎ 0839 505697 (premium-rate number).

For further information, contact the Welsh Surfing Federation (WSF; ☎ 01639-886246), 71 Fairway, Port Talbot SA12 7HW. The WSF, affiliated to both the British and European Surfing Federations, is responsible for organising National Championships and selecting teams to represent Wales at an international level.

The Stormrider Guide: Europe is *the* atlas of European surfing. It's sold for £25 by Low Pressure (☎/fax 01288-359867, ℮ mail@lowpressure.co.uk), 2 Efford Farm, Bude, Cornwall EX23 8LP; and at the Low Pressure shop (☎ 020-7792 3134), 23 Kensington Park Rd, London W11 2EU.

Surf Schools If you fancy a few lessons, you could try the WSF's own surf schools (☎ 01792-386426), Hill End, Llangennith (North Gower); Porthcawl Marine (☎ 01656-

784785), 20 New Rd, Porthcawl; West Wales Wind, Surf & Sailing (☎ 01646-636642, e sports@surfdale.co.uk), Dale; or Haven Sports (☎ 01437-781354), Marine Rd, Broad Haven.

Watersports

With scores of inland lakes and sheltered bays, Wales has plenty on offer for 'flatwater' enthusiasts, including sailing, windsurfing and flatwater canoeing. Some bigger activity centres for these sports include:

Plas Menai (☎ 01248-670964, fax 029-2030 0628, e plas.menai@scw.co.uk) Llanfairisgaer, Caernarfon LL55 1UE. The National Watersports Centre offers courses in dinghy and keelboat sailing, cruising, navigation theory and windsurfing. Web site: www.plasmenai.co.uk

Anglesey Sea & Surf Centre (☎ 01407-762525) Porthdafarch, Trearddur Bay, Holyhead LL65 2LP. This centre runs modular programs in sailing, windsurfing and dryside activities.

West Wales Wind, Surf & Sailing (☎ 01646-636642) Dale, Pembrokeshire SA62 3RB

White-Water Sports Despite Wales' substantial rainfall and mountainous terrain, the opportunities for white-water rafting and canoeing here are somewhat limited, for a combination of climatic and legal reasons. Not all steep-gradient river stretches have a reliable summertime flow. And those that do are often inaccessible, thanks to legal precedents in some areas that give owners of riverside land the ownership of the river out to its midpoint: thus permission to launch on one section of a river doesn't entitle you to pass through downstream sections without permission there.

The Welsh Canoeing Association (WCA), with a Web site at www.welsh-canoeing .org.uk, and fishery owners have negotiated agreements allowing canoeing by WCA and British Canoe Union members on designated sections of certain rivers at certain times of year and/or under certain flow conditions. On the River Wye upstream of Builth Wells, world-famous for its fishing, boating is off the agenda between April and October. The frisky River Dee can only be

run for about a mile, near Llangollen, which has consequently carved itself a niche as a canoeing centre.

In 1965 – to the anger of many Welsh people – the Llyn Celyn dam was completed on the River Treweryn near Bala, in part to regulate downstream flow into the Dee, the main source of drinking water for the city of Liverpool. A side-effect has been that the Treweryn and Dee below the dam are among the few Welsh rivers with big, and fairly predictable, summertime white water. Other northern rivers with good rapids include the Conwy, Eden, Glaslyn, Llugwy, Mawddach and Ogwen.

On a 1½-mile stretch of the Treweryn, the National Whitewater Centre (☎ 01678-521083, fax 521158, e welsh.canoeing@virgin.net), Frongoch, Bala, Gwynedd LL23 7NU, runs skills and safety courses and rafting trips; see under Bala in the Snowdonia & the Llŷn chapter for details. The WCA, which has its headquarters here, is a source of information on canoeing clubs and courses throughout Wales.

Two other national recreation centres offering white-water safety and skills courses are Plas y Brenin, the National Mountain Centre (☎ 01690-720214, fax 720394, e info@pyb.co.uk), Capel Curig, Gwynedd LL24 0ET; and Plas Menai, the National Watersports Centre (see the beginning of the Watersports section).

The WTB's free *Activity Wales* (see the introduction to the Activities section) lists a score of private operators offering white-water trips, and this book identifies several in the local chapters.

Canal Travel

A network of elegant canals spread rapidly across the UK during the Industrial Revolution. As a way of moving freight (passengers were always secondary) they were a short-lived wonder, stilted by railways and killed off by motorways. By WWII, much of the system was in stagnant, terminal decline. But in the 20th century a growing number of canals were reincarnated as tourist attractions, thanks partly to the same volunteer enthusiasm that put narrow-gauge railways back on the map.

Canal travel is a peaceful, rewarding way to explore a landscape of quiet villages, pretty countryside and colourful waterside pubs. Modern narrow boats for cruising still follow the traditional style but come equipped with all mod cons, from refrigerators to televisions. They can be rented from numerous operators and, for a family or a group, offer a surprisingly economical combination of transport and accommodation.

Early canal boats were pulled by horses, walking on towpaths beside the canals. Steam power and eventually diesel power replaced horsepower, but towpaths themselves have been reborn as popular routes for walkers and cyclists.

The canal system also demonstrates the reach of the Industrial Revolution's visionary engineers, who threw flights of locks up steep hillsides or flung amazing aqueducts across wide valleys (the most famous of these is Thomas Telford's immense Pontcysyllte Aqueduct, near Llangollen). They built their projects to last too – the locks you 'work' as you travel along the canals are often well over a century old.

Narrow Boats A typical narrow boat is 12m to 21m long and no more than about 2m wide. Narrow boats are usually equipped with bunks and double beds, kitchen and dining areas, fridge, cooker (stove), flush toilet, shower and other conveniences. Usually they're rented out by the week, though shorter periods may be available.

Food supplies are just about all you need to worry about, and there are plenty of shopping opportunities along the waterways. Alternatively, careful planning can see you moored at a riverside pub or restaurant for most meals.

Boats can accommodate from two or three people up to a party of 10 or 12. Costs vary with the size of boat, the standard of equipment and the time of year. At the height of the summer season, a boat for four can vary from around £500 to £1000 per week. Larger boats work out cheaper per person; a boat for eight might cost £1000

per week. This means canal travel can cost not much over £100 per person for a week's transport and accommodation, a terrific travel bargain.

No particular expertise or training is needed, nor is a licence required to operate a narrow boat. You're normally given a quick once-over of the boat and an explanation of how things work, a list of rules and regulations of the waterways and a brief foray out onto the river or canal and then you're on your way.

When you're chugging along with only the occasional lock to be worked, this will seem like the most painless means of transport imaginable. But on a steep section where one lock follows another, progress can be a combination of aerobics (keys to be wound, paddles to be raised and lowered), weight lifting (heavy lock gates to be pushed open and closed) and jogging (the lock crew runs on ahead to prepare the lock before the boat gets there). Canal travel is great if you have children – and they're sure to be exhausted by the end of the day!

Boat Hire Wales' three main canal systems are the Monmouthshire & Brecon Canal (see under Abergavenny and Brecon in the South-East Wales & the Brecon Beacons chapter); the Llangollen Canal (see under Llangollen in the Anglesey & North Coast chapter); and the Montgomery Canal (see under Welshpool in the Mid Wales chapter).

There are independent boat operators on all of them, and this book mentions several reliable ones. Among agencies handling bookings for many individual companies, one of the biggest is Hoseasons Holidays (☎ 01502-501010, fax 514298), Sunway House, Raglan Rd, Lowestoft, Suffolk NR32 3LW. See the Web site at www .hoseasons.co.uk.

If you only want a taste of the canal system, some firms run day trips.

Information The Inland Waterways Association (☎ 01923-711114), PO Box 114, Rickmansworth, Herts WD3 1ZY, can provide information on the canal system. It publishes *The Inland Waterways Guide*

(£3.25), a general guide to holiday hire with route descriptions. Its Web site is at www.waterways.org.uk.

Approximately two-thirds of UK waterways are operated by the British Waterways Board (☎ 01923-226422), Willow Grange, Church Rd, Watford, Herts WD17 4QA. It publishes the free *Waterways Code for Boaters*, packed with information and advice; also available is a complete list of boat-hire companies.

Horse Riding & Pony Trekking

Seeing the country from the saddle is highly recommended, even if you're not an experienced rider. There are riding schools catering to all levels of proficiency, many of them in national park areas.

Pony trekking centres are spreading like wildfire in rural Wales, as shrinking EU subsidies force farmers to find alternative uses for their land. Many pony trekkers are novice riders, so most rides are at walking speed with the occasional trot. A half-day should cost around £10 (hard hats included). If you're an experienced rider there are numerous equestrian centres with horses to hire. This book identifies some, and TICs have details of others.

For more information, see the WTB's free, regularly updated *Riding Wales* booklet. The British Horse Society (☎ 01926-707700, @ enquiry@bhs.org.uk), Stoneleigh Deer Park, Kenilworth, Warks CV8 2XZ, publishes UK-wide and regional listings of riding centres; the Web site is at www.bhs.org.uk.

Fishing

Fish are normally referred to as either game fish – because of the difficulty of catching them and the struggle they put up – or coarse fish.

Dry-fly fishing, in which an artificial lure resembling an insect is gently dropped on the water, is considered by its proponents the highest form of the sport. Fly fishing is used for that most cautious of game fish, the trout – found wild in over 100 upland lakes, and stocked in hundreds of small lowland fisheries. Many still-water fisheries also offer good coarse fishing.

There are some 240 rivers and streams for anglers to choose from, with brown trout in spring (on the Usk and Teifi, as well as the Wye, Dee, Seiont and Taff); Wales' own shy sewin in spring and summer (on the Towy, Teifi, Rheidol, Dyfi, Mawddach and Conwy); salmon in autumn (on the Usk, Teifi and Conwy); and grayling in autumn and winter (on the Wye, Dee and upper Severn).

Along one of Europe's most productive coastlines, you may also angle – from the rocks or from a chartered boat – for sea fish.

Rules & Regulations Fishing is fairly tightly regulated in the UK. Many prime stretches of river are privately owned, and fishing there can be amazingly expensive.

The Environment Agency (EA; ☎ 0870 166 2662) administers licences for rod fishing in Wales and England. A one-year licence (April to March) for nonmigratory trout and coarse fishing costs £19 per adult (£9.50 youth or senior); an eight-/one-day licence costs £6.50/2.50. Prices for salmon and sea trout are roughly triple this.

Rod licences are available from post offices, bankside agencies and EA regional offices. Tackle shops are good places to make enquiries. Before fishing anywhere you need the correct licence and the permission of the owner or tenants of the fishing rights.

During a statutory close season (15 March to 15 June) coarse fishing is banned on all rivers and streams – different rules apply on canals, lakes, ponds and reservoirs. The actual dates for close seasons vary by region.

Information Fishing in Wales, with a Web site at www.fishing-in-wales.com, is a first-rate Web site chock full of detail on everything from river access to accommodation to wildlife. The EA has a useful Web site at www.environment-agency.gov.uk/fish with all the fishy details on getting a rod licence; you can even order one on-line. The

WTB publishes *Fishing Wales*, a free book-let on where to fish for what, with a regu-larly updated supplement on clubs, tackle shops and trout fisheries; WTB's fishing Web site at www.fishing.visitwales.com has roughly the same information.

Golf

Wales has over 170 golf courses, many of them championship standard. For information on any of them, contact the Welsh Golfing Union (☎ 01633-430830). For a look at the best of them, and a listing of upcoming events, pick up a copy of WTB's free *Golf Wales* book-let. A Web site with information on most of Wales' golf clubs is at www.golfeurope .com/clubs/wales.htm.

If you're more interested in watching than playing, see Golf under Spectator Sports, later in the chapter.

COURSES

The obvious subject – and one you'd be hard pressed to study anywhere else – is the Welsh language. Courses are taught throughout Wales from March to Septem-ber, including three- or four-day family courses, weekend- to week-long intensives, and residential courses for those prepared to spend one to six weeks immersed in the lan-guage. Most immersion courses are based on a program called *Wlpan* (ool-pahn), an adopted Hebrew word for the Hebrew-language program on which they're based.

Major centres include University of Wales campuses at Aberystwyth, Bangor, Cardiff, Lampeter and Swansea; and other centres at Abergavenny, Builth Wells, Conwy, Dolgellau, Fishguard, Harlech, Mold, Newport and Pontypridd.

The Welsh Language Board (Bwrdd yr Iaith Gymraeg; ☎ 029-2087 8000, fax 2087 8001, e ymholiadau@bwrdd-yr-iaith.org .uk), Market Chambers, 5–7 St Mary St, Cardiff CF10 1AT, publishes a leaflet with details of summer and residential courses. For further information, contact them or see the Welsh for Adults page at their Web site at www.bwrdd-yr-iaith.org.uk/html/adults/ index-e.html.

The year-round National Language Cen-tre (Nant Gwrtheyrn; ☎ 01758-750334, fax 750335, e nantgwr@aol.com), Llithfaen, Pwllheli, Gwynedd LL53 6PA – in Wales' Welsh-speaking heartland on the Llŷn Peninsula – caters for all levels and is ideal for families and others who would also like to spend time in Snowdonia. Have a look at the Web site at www.marketsite.co.uk/wlc.

Typical Nant Gwrtheyrn prices for a two/five/12-day course range from £70/ 150/300 (nonresidential) to £116/265/576 (full board). Each month of a two-month Wlpan intensive through the University of Wales, Cardiff, costs £150 for registration (£75 for EU residents) plus £425 for ac-commodation.

For those keen to plug into the language before arriving, there are beginners' corre-spondence courses on offer through the Lan-guages Department of the University of Glamorgan (☎ 01443-480480, e aengland@ glam.ac.uk), Treforest, Pontypridd, Rhondda Cynon Taff CF37 1DL; and Powys Commu-nity Education (☎ 01686-626521, e nedh@ powys.gov.uk), The Old College, Station Road, Newtown SY16 1BE. For information on an on-line beginners' course, contact the University of Wales, Lampeter (☎ 01570-424754, e l.thomas@lamp.ac.uk), Lam-peter, Ceredigion SA48 7ED.

WORK

If you're prepared to work at menial jobs for long hours and relatively low pay, you're sure to find work in the UK – but those with-out skills will have trouble making enough money to save. You're probably better off saving ahead in your home country.

Unskilled visitors have traditionally worked in pubs and restaurants, and as nan-nies or au pairs. Both jobs may provide live-in accommodation, but hours are long, the work is exhausting and the pay isn't bril-liant. Live-ins will be lucky to get £130 per week, others £180. Before you accept any job, be clear about terms and conditions, es-pecially how many (and which) hours you're expected to work. A minimum wage of £3.60 per hour (£3 for those aged 18 to 21) was introduced in 1999 but if you're working under the table no one's obliged to pay you even that. Look for au pair and nanny work in *The Lady* magazine.

Accountants, health professionals, journalists, computer programmers, lawyers, teachers and clerical workers with computer experience stand a better chance of finding well-paid work. Even so, you'll probably need some money to tide you over while you search. Don't forget copies of your qualifications, references (which will probably be checked) and a CV (résumé). Qualified teachers should contact the education departments of individual county or borough councils.

To work as a trained nurse you must register with the UK Central Council for Nursing (UKCCN). Registration can take up to three months. The application fee is £70 (for overseas-trained nurses), plus £56 to be admitted to the register once the application is accepted. Contact the Overseas Registration Department (☎ 020-7333 9333, fax 7636 6935, ℮ update@ukcc.org.uk), UKCCN, 23 Portland Place, London W1N 4JT. The UKCCN Web site is at www.ukcc.org.uk. If you aren't registered you can still work as an auxiliary nurse.

Check the government-operated Jobcentres in most larger towns (listed under Employment Services in the Yellow Pages). Whatever your skills, it's worth registering with several temporary agencies.

For details on all aspects of short-term work pick up *Work Your Way Around the World* by Susan Griffith. Another good source is *Working Holidays*, published by the London-based Central Bureau for Education Visits & Exchanges.

Tax

As an official employee, you'll find income tax and National Insurance automatically deducted from your weekly pay-packet. Deductions are calculated on the assumption that you're working for the entire financial year (which runs from 6 April to 5 April); if you aren't, you may be eligible for a refund. Contact a regional office of the Inland Revenue for information (find them in the local telephone directory).

Volunteer Work

The NT runs a program of outdoor 'working holidays' of two to 10 days, in which volunteers (who must be aged at least 17 years) help with everything from rebuilding dry stone walls to installing eco-friendly reedbed sewage treatment systems. For contact details see Useful Organisations earlier in the chapter.

ACCOMMODATION

Aside from a possible long-distance air fare, accommodation will almost certainly be your single greatest expense. Even camping can be expensive at official sites.

For travel on the cheap, the main options are hostels and B&Bs. Over the past few years several independent 'backpacker' hostels have opened and the number is growing. At mid-range, good B&Bs and guesthouses are often in fine old buildings. If money's not a concern there are some first-rate hotels, the most interesting of them in converted castles and mansions.

The WTB operates a complex, and not always very revealing, grading system based on both facilities and quality of service. Participating hotels, guesthouses, B&Bs and camping grounds usually display their star-rating prominently. Even youth hostels are graded here (Wales has one five-star hostel, at Penycwm in Pembrokeshire).

In practice there's wide variability within each classification, and some one-star guesthouses are far more pleasant than the three-star hotel around the block. Some excellent B&Bs don't participate in the system at all because they have to pay to do so. TICs are rarely broad-minded enough to mention good nonparticipating places, or may simply dismiss them as 'not approved'. In the end actually seeing a place, even from the outside, will give the best clue as to what to expect. Always ask to look at your room before deciding.

The worst-value accommodation tends to be in big towns where you often pay extra for inferior quality (abrupt service, chaotic decor, ropey fittings). Cheap B&Bs are rare in city centres, which means those without cars are stuck with bus services that tail off just when they're getting ready to go out in the evening.

Single rooms seem to be in short supply everywhere.

Many budget places, and nearly all at mid-range and up, accept at least Visa or MasterCard credit/debit cards, although it's wise to check first. All accommodation prices in this book include VAT.

TIC Reservations

Most TICs will book accommodation for you, for a £1 fee plus a 10% deposit (the latter is then deducted from your accommodation bill). For the same charges, most can also book your next two nights' accommodation anywhere in the UK, under the Book-A-Bed-Ahead (BABA) scheme. Outside opening hours, many TICs put a list of local places with available beds as of closing time. These services are particularly worthwhile over weekends and the July–August peak season.

Camping

Free camping is rarely possible. Camp sites vary widely in quality; most have reasonable facilities, but can be tricky to reach without your own transport. Local TICs will have information on nearby sites, as well as free catalogues of camping grounds all around their region. The WTB publishes an annual guide (£3.95) to approved self-catering facilities, including caravan and camp sites. Another useful reference is the RAC's *Camping & Caravanning in Britain*.

Those planning to camp extensively, or tour with a van or caravan, should consider joining the Camping & Caravanning Club (☎ 024-7669 4995), Greenfields House, Westwood Way, Coventry CV4 8JH. The world's oldest camping and caravanning club runs many of its own sites, from quiet backpacker patches to vast holiday parks. Annual dues of £27.50 entitle you to discounted rates, a guide to several thousand sites across Europe and other useful services. See its Web site at www.campingandcaravanningclub.co.uk.

Camping is possible at some NT properties (see Useful Organisations earlier in the chapter), and at facilities run by the Forestry Commission (☎ 0131-334 0066, e fe.holidays@forestry.gsi.gov.uk); see the Web site at www.forestholidays.co.uk. Camping grounds in Wales tend to be concentrated in the national parks and along the coast. Expect to pay about £6 a night for two people plus a tent, although on some sites prices go much lower, especially in low season. Most sites are only open from March or April to October, so phone before going out of your way at other times.

YHA/HI Youth Hostels

Membership of an Hostelling International (HI) affiliated association, such as the Youth Hostels Association (YHA) for England and Wales, gives you access to 37 hostels across Wales, and you don't have to be young or single to use them.

The advantages of youth hostels are price (though the difference between a pricier hostel and cheaper B&Bs isn't huge) and the chance to meet other travellers. The disadvantages are that you're often locked out from 10 am to 5 pm, and locked in after 11 pm, you usually sleep in bunks in single-sex dormitories, and many hostels close in winter. YHA hostels are rarely in town centres – fine if you're tramping the countryside or have your own transport, a pain otherwise.

UK residents can join the YHA – in advance or on arrival at most hostels – for £12.50 for adults, £6.25 for under-18s and £25 for a family (two adults, with all those under 18 free). Overseas visitors without an international membership can join through a system of 'welcome stamps', available at most hostels: a £2 stamp is purchased at each of their first six hostels, after which they become HI members.

Nightly rates for a dorm bed in Wales range from about £7 to £14 for adults, £6 to £11 for under-18s (in this book hostel prices are given as adult/under-18s). Holders of Flexi-Pass travel passes (see the Getting Around chapter) get a £1 discount. Bed linen is included in the price.

Most hostels have TV rooms and social areas, and some have separate family rooms

Leading the way in Snowdonia

Builth Wells, famous for fishing

Glyder Fawr – one of many stunning peaks around Snowdon

Strong legs are needed for some of the cycle routes in Gwynedd.

Sea kayaking in Pembrokeshire

Old steam trains traverse stunning countryside.

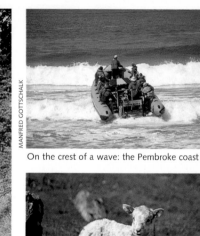

On the crest of a wave: the Pembroke coast

Don't mention mint sauce to this local.

One for the photo album: traditional costume

Pup from the colony at Ramsey Island: ah, bless

Time for a chat at Monmouth cattle market

with keys and all-day access. Eight in Wales also offer camping facilities at half the adult rate (no concessions). All have facilities for self-catering, and all offer a cooked breakfast for £3.30 extra; some offer other meals too. The hostels at Cardiff, Bangor, Conwy and Pen-y-Pass open all day, and Broad Haven and Llangollen open from 1 pm.

The England-Wales YHA (☎ 0870 870 8808, ☒ customerservices@yha.org.uk) is at 8 St Stephen's Hill, St Albans, Herts AL1 2DY, and has a useful Web site at www .yha.org.uk. It publishes a guide to all its hostels, free to members and on sale at YHA/HI Adventure Shops and many hostels. If you plan to use hostels a lot you should get one, as it includes exact directions to each place, plus the often complex opening times. If you just want a list of Welsh hostels, contact YHA Wales (☎ 029-2039 6766), 4th floor, 1 Cathedral Rd, Cardiff CF1 9HA.

It's essential to book ahead for busy periods: May to September, Easter and Christmas/New Year. You can do so by telephone, and you can secure a reservation with full payment by Visa or MasterCard. Even if you don't want to plan ahead, it's worth ringing the hostel on the day to check availability. Unsecured reservations made less than a week in advance will be held until 6 pm. Most hostels will book your next hostel stop for you at no cost.

To book any number of hostels in west Wales – up to two weeks ahead, at 50p per person per night – contact the West Wales Booking Bureau (☎ 0870 241 2314).

Independent Hostels

A slowly growing network of private hostels offers the opportunity to escape curfews and lockouts for around £10 to £15 per night. Like YHA hostels these are great places to meet other travellers, but they tend to be in town centres, which will suit the nonwalking fraternity. Ambience and facilities vary from anarchic to professional, but the atmosphere tends to be relaxed, the service attentive and the owners very knowledgeable about their turf. Bed linen is supplied, as well as a basic breakfast. A few have small, licensed bars.

At last count Wales had perhaps eight or nine of what could really be called independent hostels. For a look at the best of them, check out www.hostelswales.com or the Wales page at www.hostelseurope.com on the Web.

The Independent Hostel Guide (£4.95) is an all-Europe directory of indie hostels, along with bunkhouses and camping barns (see the following section). It's available from some TICs and bookshops, or from Backpackers Press (☎/fax 01629-580427), 2 Rockview Cottages, Matlock Bath, Derbyshire DE4 3PG.

Camping Barns & Bunkhouses

A camping barn – usually a converted farm building – is a spartan place for walkers to stay for around £5 per night. Several notches up are bunkhouses, with dormitory accommodation, hot showers, drying rooms, stoves for heating and cooking, and usually a social area of some sort. You're expected to bring your own sleeping bag and food supplies and generally look after yourself.

Both are aimed at walkers, and tend to be out in the countryside, often in spectacular settings but with little public transport and few places to go for a bite or a beer. The majority of those in Wales are in or around the Brecon Beacons National Park. Bunkhouses tend to get block-booked by groups in summer, but can usually accommodate individuals during midweek and outside peak season. Always call ahead.

The best of the bunkhouses are like no-frills hostels, with beds as cheap as £7. Many are in handsome renovated traditional-style farm or village buildings. This book notes some of the better-value ones.

The line-up changes from year to year, but a listing of Wales bunkhouses (and links to some of them) is at the Web site of the Association of Bunkhouse Operators, www .hostels-wales.com. Many are also listed in *The Independent Hostel Guide* (see the preceding section on Independent Hostels).

University Accommodation

Many University of Wales campuses offer student rooms to visitors during the holidays:

usually for three weeks over Easter and Christmas and from late June to late September. Rooms tend to be comfortable, functional singles, but many nowadays have en-suite bathroom. Full-board, half-board, B&B and self-catering options are often available; B&B normally costs from £18 to £25 per person.

We note some options in this book. For more general information, contact Venuemasters (☎ 0114-249 3090, fax 249 3091, @ info@venuemasters.co.uk), The Workstation, Paternoster Row, Sheffield S1 2BX; or visit the Web site at www.venuemasters .co.uk.

B&Bs & Guesthouses

Almost anywhere you go in Wales you'll find reasonably priced, comfortable B&Bs – essentially just private houses with bedrooms to let, with prices from around £13 to £25 per person. Outside Cardiff, Swansea and Snowdonia, you're unlikely to have to pay more than £17, even in high season.

Some of the finest and most family-friendly B&Bs are in rural farmhouses. Many around the national parks are well used to the muddy boots and big appetites of walkers, cyclists and climbers.

Guesthouses, which are often just large converted houses with half a dozen rooms, are an extension of the B&B idea. Prices range a bit higher than B&Bs. In general, they're less personal than B&Bs, more like small budget hotels.

Rooms usually have central heating, TV, tea-making equipment and a wash basin with hot and cold water. Better places have at least some rooms with private (en-suite) toilet and shower/bath. Double rooms will often have twin beds, so you don't have to be too familiar to share! Prices in this book are generally for en-suite rooms unless otherwise noted.

Traditionally the British prefer baths to showers, and lower-end B&Bs may have only a bathtub, or a fiddly shower contraption dispensing an unpredictable flow at unpredictable temperatures. It's worth getting some instruction on these diabolical things well before you find yourself struggling, naked, with them first thing in the morning.

You may not regard fried eggs, fried sausages, fried potatoes, fried tomatoes and even fried bread as high cuisine, but most B&B and guesthouse breakfasts (which also include cereal, juice, toast and tea/coffee) are at least very generous. Nobody seems to have heard of fresh fruit.

Many (but not all) of these places are listed in the WTB's annually updated *Bed & Breakfast* or *Hotels, Guesthouses & Farmhouses* booklets (each £3.95); though listed establishments are WTB-approved, the descriptions are provided by proprietors.

Hotels

The term 'hotel' is used with abandon, and may refer to anything from a pub to a castle. In general, hotels tend to have a reception desk, room service and other extras such as a licensed bar. Many offer weekend-break and other promotional rates, so if you're booking ahead, ask if they offer any discounts.

Many country pubs offer mid-range accommodation, though they vary widely in quality. Staying in a pub or inn can be good fun as it places you at the hub of the community, but they can be noisy and aren't always ideal for solo women travellers. They usually have a lounge where cheap meals are served; some also have decent restaurants.

Shading gradually upscale from pubs are former coaching inns in many towns, offering what Brits like to call an 'oldey-worldy atmosphere'. But the atmosphere at such places tends to inflate the prices, and you're best to check out the room no matter how elegant the front desk looks.

The very best hotels are magnificent places, often with restaurants to match. In rural areas you'll find country-house hotels set in vast grounds, and castles complete with crenellated battlements, grand staircases, oak panelling and the obligatory rows of stags' heads. For these you can pay from £60 to well over £100 per person, though many also offer weekend-break and other promotional discounts.

Two Web sites with select lists of country-house hotels and inns are Welsh Rarebits at www.welsh.rarebits.co.uk and the slightly

more modest Great Little Places at www
.wales.little-places.co.uk.

Short-Term Rentals

Staying in one place gives you an opportunity to get a real feel for a region and a community. There's plenty of rental accommodation around Wales, much of it of a high standard, though some must be booked by the week. A cottage for four can cost as little as £125 per week.

Outside weekends and July/August, it's not essential to book a long way ahead, in which case the nearest TIC can often help you find a place. A few such places are listed in the WTB's £3.95 catalogue, *Self Catering*, updated every year.

Among really splendid possibilities are rural properties owned by the NT (see under Useful Organisations earlier in the chapter) and let as holiday cottages for weekly rates as low as £190/450 (winter/summer). For a catalogue to drool over, contact the NT's Holiday Booking Office (☎ 0870 458 4422, fax 458 4400, e cottage@smtp.ntrust.org.uk), PO Box 536, Melksham, Wiltshire SN12 8SX; or visit the Web site at www.nationaltrust.org.uk/cottages.

The Landmark Trust (☎ 01628-825925, fax 825417, e bookings@landmarktrust.co.uk), Shottesbrooke, Maidenhead, Berkshire SL6 3SW, is an architectural charity which rescues unique old buildings, often in conjunction with the NT, and supports the work by renting them out. Wales properties include a tower of Caernarfon's walled town, and the blockhouse of a 19th-century fort at Milford Haven. The trust's Web site is at www.landmarktrust.co.uk.

For a little something out of the ordinary, how about a self-catering cottage at Portmeirion, Clough Williams-Ellis' Italianate fantasy estate near Porthmadog? For more information see under Around Porthmadog in the Snowdonia & the Llŷn chapter.

FOOD

It can hardly be said that Welsh cuisine has a high profile outside Wales. Pressed, people might recall lamb, leeks or rarebit, but that's about it. Taste of Wales is a promo-

tional organisation set up in 1988 to try and change all that. Its *Taste of Wales Gazetteer*, available at bigger TICs, lists some 400 restaurants where you can eat good food with a Welsh tang, and delicatessens and markets selling traditional Welsh produce.

Traditional Welsh dishes include cawl, a robust vegetable broth flavoured with lamb and possessing superior warming qualities in chilly wet weather; and laverbread, which is not bread at all but seaweed mixed with oatmeal and bacon, and usually served on toast – an acquired taste for some, but surprisingly good. Welsh rarebit is a sophisticated variant of cheese on toast, with the cheese seasoned and flavoured with butter, milk and sometimes a little beer.

Upland Welsh lamb and beef are known well beyond Wales. Glamorgan's famous sausages are made from cheese, breadcrumbs, herbs and chopped leek, so vegetarians can enjoy them too. A traditional dish in the south is cockles (a shellfish harvested along the coast).

There's little Caerphilly cheese being made in Caerphilly these days, but cheesemaking in general is undergoing a revival. Cheese-freaks should comb the delis for Caws Ffermdy Cenarth, Llanboidy, Llangloffan, Skirrid, St Illtyd or Y Fenni.

Welsh cakes are fruity little griddle scones. *Bara brith* is a spicy fruit loaf made with tea and marmalade along with the more conventional ingredients.

Beyond the home, and a minority of switched-on bistros and restaurants, English stodge still dominates the scene – especially in pubs – with red meat, gravy and cooked-to-death vegetables, perhaps a bit of lettuce or coleslaw on the side, and chips-with-everything.

Where to Eat

There are takeaways in all but the smallest towns – fish and chips, Chinese, kebabs, curries and pizzas. Ubiquitous snack items are the jacket potato – just a baked potato slathered with some sort of flavoured gloop – and baguettes stuffed with tuna mayonnaise or other fillings.

Cafes are abundant in larger towns. Even the seediest of them are usually warm, friendly places, and invariably serve cheap breakfast fry-ups and plain, filling lunches. Some cafes in tourist areas have mutated into twee tearoom/giftshops. A very few stand out with food prepared with care and imagination. Some are 'bistro-style', which here seems to mean they have sparky service and serve drinks from a little bar at the back.

These days most pubs also serve meals, during limited hours. At the cheaper end pub grub hardly differs from cafe food; at the pricey end it can be splendid. Lasagne or shepherd's pie (mince and mashed potato) are often the cheapest offerings, easily microwaved by untrained staff. A filling 'ploughman's lunch' of bread, cheese and pickle rarely costs more than £4. Blackboard specials tend to be good value.

Most bigger towns in Wales do have a handful of expensive but professional-quality restaurants, with fresh seafood, roasts and other dishes. Happily, vegetarianism has taken off in a big way; most places have at least one token vegetarian dish, sometimes several. As anywhere, vegans will find the going tough.

In smaller towns, the only food available on Sunday may be the popular, pricey Sunday roast served at pubs and hotel restaurants.

Self-Catering

The cheapest way to eat is to cook for yourself. Every town has at least one small supermarket, and many have open-air markets. Even if you lack great culinary skills, you can buy good-quality pre-cooked meals.

DRINKS

Takeaway alcoholic drinks are sold from neighbourhood off-licences (liquor stores) rather than from pubs. Opening hours vary; some stay open to 9 or 10 pm daily. Alcohol can also be bought at supermarkets and smaller Spar stores. Most restaurants are licensed to sell alcoholic drinks, especially wine, though they're always expensive.

Pubs

Pubs in Wales vary enormously in decor, atmosphere and what's on draught. In country areas you'll find cosy watering holes with big fires, inviting menus and the TV tuned to S4C. In high season so many tourists pass through that local people keep pretty much to themselves; but at other times you may find people happy to chat. In Cardiff and other big towns you'll need to pick and choose: some town-centre places are decidedly uninviting, especially for solo women travellers.

Given how much pubs epitomise the UK for many visitors, it's odd how unenthusiastic the breweries seem to be about hanging onto them. Many urban pubs are simply disappearing, while others are reinventing themselves as Irish (eg, O'Neill's) or Australian (eg, Walkabout Inns) theme bars.

Most pubs are licensed to serve alcohol only until 11 pm, with the bell for last orders ringing at about 10.45 pm, though some in Cardiff centre are licensed to stay open until 1, 2 or 4 am. On Sunday most open noon to 3 pm and 7 to 10.30 pm, though many stay open all day.

Nonalcoholic Drinks

The British national drink is undoubtedly tea, but coffee is now just as popular. Many cafes and restaurants offer the option of filter (cafetiere) coffee, and it's not hard to find somewhere in town for a cappuccino or espresso. A few cafes have herbal teas on the menu.

Alcoholic Drinks

Beer Welsh pubs generally serve an impressive range of beers – lagers, bitters, ales and stouts. What New Worlders know simply as 'beer' is actually lager and – much to the distress of local connoisseurs – lagers (including Fosters and Budweiser) now take a huge chunk of the market. Fortunately traditional ales are fighting back, thanks to the Campaign for Real Ale (CAMRA) organisation – look for its endorsement sticker on pub windows.

Traditional beers range from very light and lager-like to extremely strong and trea-

Welsh Hootch

Whisky was once produced throughout Wales, but the temperance movement within the influential Nonconformist churches (see under History in the Facts about Wales chapter) led to the closure of all the Welsh distilleries, the last one at Ffrongoch in North Wales in the 1890s.

A few years ago a new distillery was founded, ostensibly to revive the tradition and compete with considerably better-known Scottish and Irish brands. After much fanfare it was discovered that the folks at the Welsh Whisky Co weren't actually distilling anything, but only blending and bottling stuff made elsewhere. The powerful Scotch Whisky Association, which regulates the Scots industry, was not amused, and the company was shut down.

Recently a group of Welsh businessmen bought its assets and name, and set about building a real distillery, Wales' first for a century. The site, at Penderyn, 10 miles west of Merthyr Tydfil in South Wales, was apparently chosen for the high purity and slight peaty taste of the local water. Production has begun, using locally produced malted barley, but at the time of writing the product hadn't matured for quite the obligatory three years on oaken casks.

Stay tuned.

cly. They're usually served at room temperature, which may come as a shock if you've been raised on ice-cold lager. But if you treat these as something new, you'll discover subtle flavours that a cold, chemical lager can't match. The best are handpumped from the cask, not carbonated and drawn under pressure. Stout is a dark, rich drink; Guinness is the most famous brand.

Beers are usually served in pints (570mL; from £1.60 to £2.50), but you can also ask for a 'half' (half pint or 285 mL). Among favoured Welsh brews is Brains SA, brewed in Cardiff.

Wine Good wine is widely available. Wine bars became popular in the 1980s and, while the concept is old hat now, it did force many pubs to broaden their selection of wines by the glass. Restaurants tend to have decent wine lists, and if you're looking for something for a picnic, the chain supermarkets have large selections at reasonable prices.

ENTERTAINMENT

As everywhere in the UK, pubs tend to be the focal point of local social life. See the preceding section on Drinks for more about pubs. Only Cardiff, regional capitals and the university towns have substantial nightlife beyond pub-life. Cardiff has a vibrant club scene, and plays host to many up-and-coming Welsh indie and rock bands. Folk music is alive and well, and you'll find live performances in everything from pubs to concert halls.

Cardiff has several good venues for classical music: the Welsh National Opera performs most of its mainscale productions at New Theatre, and the BBC National Orchestra of Wales usually performs at St David's Hall, said to have some of the best acoustics in Europe. In line with a British tradition of quality theatre, Cardiff, Bangor, Mold and Milford Haven have their own well regarded theatre companies. Regional capitals have modern cultural centres offering everything from comedy to dance to first-run films.

For a rundown of major local events, see under Public Holidays & Special Events earlier in the chapter, and under entries for individual towns.

SPECTATOR SPORTS

A clever sportswriter once said the difference between football and rugby is that football is a gentlemen's game played by hooligans, while rugby is a hooligan's game played by gentlemen. Both these sports hold Wales in their grip. Roughly speaking, rugby is big in the south, football in the north.

For the purpose of international football and rugby union competitions, Wales is a country in its own right. All home matches of the national rugby and football teams are played in Cardiff's new, city-centre Millennium Stadium, arguably the UK's finest international sports arena. This is a source of great pride to many Welsh, and attendance at international matches has jumped substantially since it was built.

Rugby Union

Rugby takes its name from Rugby School in Warwickshire, where the game originated when William Webb Ellis picked up the ball and ran off with it during a football match in 1823. Rugby union, the traditionally amateur, 15-player form of the game, is Wales' de facto national sport (see the boxed text 'A Peculiar Passion').

Tickets for some international fixtures are easy to get, and at reasonable prices (around £10 to £25; ☎ 0870 558 2582 for details). Big events – especially the Six Nations championships starting in January, and the Rugby World Cup, which takes place every four years – sell out months in advance. The last Rugby World Cup, in 1999, was hosted by Wales (who made it to the quarter-finals); the next one is in 2003, in Australia.

You can catch club matches between September and Easter. The best club sides are (with their club venues): Cardiff (Cardiff Arms Park), Llanelli (Strady Park), Swansea (St Helens), Newport (Rodney Parade), Pontypridd (Sardis Rd) and Neath (The Knoll). Most of the former mining-valley towns also have their own sides.

For information and news about Welsh Rugby Union, visit the official Web site at www.wru.co.uk. There is also a Welsh women's rugby movement, with its own page at this site.

Rugby League

Rugby league, the traditionally professional, 15-player version of the game, has

A Peculiar Passion

Rugby arrived in Wales by rail. In the 19th century a vast workforce came in search of employment, and they brought with them the games they played. Thus, association football (soccer) travelled from Liverpool and Manchester into North Wales, and rugby union came from the West Country of England into the coalfields of the South.

And since the trains do not run north-south in Wales, that's the way it remained. Rugby is the sport of the industrial, densely populated south, a game brought in by Englishmen but quickly appropriated by the Welsh as an ex-

JANE SMITH

pression of defiance against their neighbours and overlords.

The very physical nature of 19th-century rugby, where just about anything went, bonded rough, tough working communities and gave them a focus: here was a chance for exploited Wales to take on England, literally, on a level playing field.

Rugby has always been more than a healthy pursuit in Wales. It is a barometer of the Welsh mood. Or moodiness. Because in recent times, things have not been going very well.

The coal mines have shut and now the last of the giant steelworks are threatened. Welsh rugby entered a period of decline in the 1980s and there is no sign that anything is improving in its new professional age.

For over a hundred years Wales adhered to the amateur principles of rugby union. They did not wish to lose that opportunity of playing against England, even if the notion of a game to be played for no reward by chaps with time on their hands was completely at odds with the vision of rugby in a pit-village of the Gwendraeth Valley.

its main stronghold in the north of England. In Wales it's completely overshadowed by rugby union, although there are both club and international teams. In this case the 'national' team is Great Britain. For more on rugby league, check out the Web site at www.rleague.com.

Football

Football (soccer) is very much second fiddle to rugby, though internationals still bring the crowds out.

At the club level, the season lasts from August to May, with most matches on Saturday afternoons. Tickets, at £12 to £40, are usually hard to buy on the day, so try to book them well ahead. The best clubs (and their venues) are Swansea City (The Vetch) and Wrexham (The Racecourse), both 2nd division, and Cardiff City (Ninian Park), 3rd division; all are members of the English

Football League. A separate, semi-pro League of Wales is dominated by Barry. Tickets to see Cardiff, Swansea and Wrexham will not be hard to come by, as they are lower division sides (except maybe for Cardiff-Swansea derby matches). Tickets for these games won't cost more than £10–16 (Cardiff and Swansea) and £11–17 (Wrexham).

Although the Welsh national team has underachieved in the last decade, several well-known Welsh players play for top UK Premiership teams, including Ryan Giggs (Manchester United), Robbie Savage (Leicester City) and John Robinson (Charlton Athletic). Ex-player Mark Hughes is now coach of the national team.

Wembley Stadium was where the English team played its home internationals each season, and where the FA Cup Final (English football's biggest do) took place

---

A Peculiar Passion

Worse still, when professionalism finally arrived in 1995, England emerged more intact from the chaos of turning rugby into commerce than Wales. Famous clubs such as Cardiff, Swansea, Llanelli, Pontypridd and Newport have all twinkled briefly on the grand new stage of pan-continental competition but none has threatened to win rugby's grail, the European Cup. English clubs have won it twice.

And in the most important international tournament for Wales, the annual Six Nations Championship between themselves, England, Ireland, Scotland, France and Italy, it is England who have become the perennial team to beat. For 28 years between 1963 and 1991 England did not win once in Cardiff. Now they win there almost at will, even at the new super-home of the Welsh game, the Millennium Stadium.

Welsh rugby is going through a bad patch. But it has been through them before. There is no fear that this love affair with rugby is over. Because it is not really love at all. It is hysterical obsession. Wales is shackled to rugby as tightly as she is stuck to England by her border.

So, as long as England is there, Welsh rugby will be there. And a dip into the hysteria is well worth the experience. Nobody moans and groans more entertainingly than the Welsh. The hysteria expresses itself in highly charged outpourings of noise and laughter – song and dollops of bleak, black Welsh humour. Tickets are like gold dust for Six Nations games at the Millennium Stadium but you never know...

Club games, especially in the European Cup, are easier to attend, and are just as vibrant because the frenzy of the national game is replaced by the element of local jealousy. Which is a story in itself. Suffice to say that the Welsh and their rugby form an archive of bizarre tribal customs. Wonderfully peculiar.

Eddie Butler,
The Observer **and BBC Sport**

each May. But rebuilding at Wembley – and the likelihood that Manchester United would play in any final, thus ruling out Old Trafford – has led to the decision to stage the FA Cup at Cardiff's Millennium Stadium from 2001 to at least 2003. Cardiff, of course, is over the moon about it (Cardiff City is the only club ever to take the FA Cup out of England, beating Arsenal in 1927).

SHOPPING

The recent revival of craft industries in centres all over Wales has provided plentiful shopping fodder for visitors with a yen for anything from carved-wood dressers to knitwear, tartan and lace. Indeed, there can be hardly a visitor attraction left that doesn't have its shop selling commemorative T-shirts, pencils, stationery, books and souvenir fudge. Even the industrial sites have got in on the act, hawking repro miner's lamps, coal sculptures and similar artefacts. Prices are often high, and quality variable, but amongst the furry red dragons there are some classy items to be had.

Two of the most famous items are Portmeirion pottery and the ubiquitous lovespoon (see the boxed text).

Portmeirion pottery is the creation of Susan Williams-Ellis, daughter of the late Welsh architect Sir Clough Williams-Ellis, creator of the village of Portmeirion (see the Snowdonia & the Llŷn chapter). A trained artist, she started designing pottery in the 1960s for the village gift shop. The simple, functional shapes and innovative, symbolic designs became immediately popular, but it was her 1970s Botanic Garden pattern that made the name internationally famous, becoming one of the world's biggest selling tableware patterns and still accounting for over half the company's sales. Find out more on Portmeirion's Web site at www.portmeirion.co.uk.

Lovespoons

All over Wales, craft shops turn out wooden spoons with contorted handles in a variety of different designs, at a speed that would have left their original makers – village lads with their eyes on a lady – gawking in astonishment. The carving of these spoons seems to date back to the 17th century, when they were made by men to give to women to mark the start of courtship.

Various symbols were carved into the spoons; the meanings of a few of them are as follows:

Anchor – I'm home to stay; you can count on me
Balls in a cage, links in a chain – captured love, together forever; the number of balls or links may correspond to the number of children desired, or the number of years already together
Bell – marriage
Celtic cross – faith; marriage
Double spoon – side by side forever
Flowers – love and affection, courtship
One heart – my heart is yours
Two hearts – we feel the same about one another
Horseshoe – good luck, happiness
Key, lock, little house – my house is yours
Vines, trees, leaves – our love is growing
Wheel – I will work for you

If you want to see carving in progress, the Welsh Folk Museum at St Fagans can usually oblige. Any number of shops will be happy to sell you the finished product.

ASA ANDERSSON

Getting There & Away

Wales has its own international airport at Cardiff, but the vast bulk of international connections (and the best bargains) to Wales come through London, a global transport hub. The birth of 'no frills' discount carriers has increased competition on flights to/from Europe and Ireland – routes once characterised by ridiculously high fares.

Fast train services run to Cardiff from London, Birmingham, York and Newcastle. You can also take the train to North Wales (including Llandudno, Bangor and Holyhead) from London, via Birmingham and Chester.

There are international seaports at Swansea, Pembroke, Fishguard and Holyhead, with passenger services to/from the Republic of Ireland. For connections by sea from continental Europe – with or without your own car – you're spoilt for choice, but only to English ports. Continental ferries are getting a run for their money from the Channel Tunnel, and have been forced to drop prices and lay on more services. Prices and times are improving on the Ireland routes too.

The cheapest option from Europe and Ireland is usually bus travel, though it's bone-crunching and exhausting, and the savings over no-frills air fares are no longer very impressive.

AIR

Unless otherwise noted, fares quoted here are approximate return fares during peak air-travel season, based on advertised rates at the time of writing. None of them constitutes a recommendation for any airline.

Airports & Airlines

Wales' only international airport is Cardiff International Airport (☎ 01446-711111), heavily used for holiday charter flights but with a number of scheduled flights as well. It has a Web site at www.cial.co.uk. The main international hub serving Cardiff is Amsterdam. International airlines flying direct to Cardiff include home-grown Air Wales (Cork and Manchester); British Airways (BA; Aberdeen, Belfast, Brussels, Dublin, Edinburgh, Glasgow, Newcastle, Guernsey and Paris); KLM (Amsterdam); Manx Airlines (Jersey); and Ryanair (Dublin). See the boxed text 'Airline Booking Numbers' overleaf for these carriers' contact details.

Most of the world's major airlines fly to London. Most international flights to London arrive at Heathrow or Gatwick airports, with many from European centres going to London City, Stansted or Luton airports. Of the UK's many other airports with international connections, those conveniently close to Wales are Manchester, Birmingham and Bristol; other major ones are at Glasgow and Edinburgh.

Warning

The information in this chapter is particularly vulnerable to change: prices for international travel are volatile, routes are introduced and cancelled, schedules change, special deals come and go, and rules and visa requirements are amended. Airlines and governments seem to take a perverse pleasure in making price structures and regulations as complicated as possible. You should check directly with the airline or a travel agent to make sure you understand how a fare (and ticket you may buy) works. In addition, the travel industry is highly competitive and there are many lurks and perks.

The upshot of this is that you should get opinions, quotes and advice from as many airlines and travel agents as possible before you part with your hard-earned cash. The details given in this chapter should be regarded as pointers and are not a substitute for your own careful, up-to-date research.

Airline Booking Numbers

Following are UK-wide reservations numbers for international airlines with scheduled flights serving Cardiff airport:

Air Wales (☎ 0870 013 3151)
Web site: www.airwales.co.uk
British Airways (☎ 0845 773 3377)
Web site: www.britishairways.com
KLM (☎ 0870 507 4074)
Web site: www.klmuk.com
Manx Airlines (☎ 0845 725 6256)
Web site: www.manx-airlines.com
Ryanair (☎ 0870 333 1231)
Web site: www.ryanair.com

Buying Tickets

World aviation has never been so competitive, making air travel better value than ever. But you have to research the options carefully to make sure you get the best deal.

The Internet is a useful resource for checking air fares, as most travel agencies and airlines now have Web sites. There is also an increasing number of online agents such as www.travelocity.co.uk and www.deckchair.com. But a close watch on good old-fashioned newspaper travel ads will turn up short-term bargains too.

In general there's little to be gained from going directly to the airlines. They release discounted tickets to selected travel agents and discount agencies, and these are often the best deals. For short-term travel you'll save by travelling mid-week, staying away at least one Saturday night or going for promotional offers. Many discounted tickets for long-term travel are valid for 12 months, allowing multiple stopovers with open dates. Another money-saving tactic is an indirect flight with a third-country carrier. Some airlines offer student/youth fares. Round-the-World (RTW) tickets are comparable in price to ordinary long-haul return flights.

On European routes, travel agents are now facing stiff competition from 'no-frills' airlines, which mostly sell direct – by telephone or online – and often for knock-down prices. At the time of writing, Ryanair was the only no-frills carrier serving Wales (to/from Dublin only), though Virgin Express (☎ 020-7744 0004) uses London Heathrow; Buzz (☎ 0870 240 7070) and Go (☎ 0870 607 6543) use Stansted; and easyJet (☎ 0870 600 0000) flies into London Gatwick and Luton. Check out the Web sites at www.ryanair.com, www.virgin-express.com, www.buzzaway.com, www.go-fly.com and www.easyjet.co.uk.

You may find some very cheap flights advertised by obscure agencies. Most such firms are honest and solvent, but there are some rogue outfits, so keep your eyes open. If you feel suspicious about a firm, steer clear – or pay only a deposit until you get your ticket, then ring the airline to confirm that you're actually booked on the flight before paying the balance.

Paying by credit card generally offers protection since most card issuers provide refunds if you don't get what you paid for. Similar protection can be obtained by buying a ticket from a bonded agent, such as one covered by the Air Travel Organiser's Licensing (ATOL) scheme in the UK. Established agencies such as those mentioned in this book offer more security and are about as competitive as you can get.

Travellers with Specific Needs

If you have special requirements – you're in a wheelchair, taking the baby, vegetarian, terrified of flying – let the airline know when you book. Restate your needs when you reconfirm, and again when you check in at the airport.

With advance warning most international airports can provide escorts from check-in to the plane, and most have ramps, lifts, wheelchair-accessible toilets and telephones. Major carriers can provide wheelchairs. Aircraft toilets present problems for wheelchair users, who should discuss this early on with the airline and/or their doctor. The disability-friendly Web site, www.everybody.co.uk, has a directory of facilities offered by various airlines.

Guide dogs for the blind must often travel in a specially pressurised baggage

Airport Connections to Wales

Each London airport has shuttle services into London for onward connections to Wales.

Heathrow – Heathrow Express train to Paddington station (trains to South Wales); Airbus or Piccadilly underground train to Euston station (trains to Mid and North Wales)

Gatwick – Gatwick Express train to Victoria station (coaches to Mid and North Wales), from where Victoria underground trains run to Euston station. Gatwick also has its own train station, with connections by Thames Trains west to Reading (which has easy train connections to South Wales)

Stansted – Stansted Express train to Liverpool St station, and from there by Stationlink bus or Circle Line underground train to Paddington or Euston stations; Flightline bus to Victoria coach station.

Luton – Luton Flyer bus to Airport Parkway train station, from there by Thameslink train to King's Cross station, and from there to Paddington or Euston stations; Green Line bus No 757 to Victoria coach station.

National Express Flightlink No 201 is a daily coach service from both Heathrow (terminal 3, 4 and central bus station) and Gatwick (both terminals) to South Wales (including Newport, Cardiff, Port Talbot and Swansea), with departures every 1½ to 2¼ hours from 6 am to midnight. Flightlink No 202 runs from Heathrow to Cardiff every two hours from 8 am to 1 am. Heathrow–Cardiff (3½ hours) costs £30/24 adults/concession, and Gatwick–Cardiff (four hours) £34/27. For information and booking call ☎ 0870 575 7747.

All other international airports in the UK have shuttle services of some kind into the city centre. For more on long-distance coaches and trains into Wales, see the Bus and Train sections later in the chapter.

compartment with other animals, though smaller guide dogs may be admitted to the cabin. They're subject to the same stiff quarantine laws as any other animal entering or returning to rabies-free countries such as the UK. Recent changes to UK quarantine laws allow animals arriving from elsewhere in the EU via certain routes to avoid quarantine, provided they meet strict vaccination and other requirements and have been tagged with an ID microchip (for details contact the UK Department for Environment, Food & Rural Affairs at ☎ 0870 241 1710, fax 020-7904 6834, ⒺⓅⒺⓉⓈ pets@ahvg.maff.gsi.gov.uk).

Children under two years normally travel for around 10% of the standard fare, as long as they don't occupy a seat. They don't get a baggage allowance. Bassinets or 'skycots' can usually be provided by the airline if requested in advance, and the better international carriers usually have an on-board stock of nappies (diapers) and other supplies. Children aged between two and 12 years can usually occupy a seat for half to two-thirds of the full fare, and do get a baggage allowance. Pushchairs can often be taken as hand luggage.

Departure Tax

All UK domestic flights and those from the UK to destinations within the EU carry a £10 departure tax each way. For flights to other cities abroad you pay £20. This is usually factored into the price of your ticket.

Elsewhere in the UK

Flights to Wales from other parts of the UK are expensive. For the short distances involved they're barely worth considering.

Services to Cardiff include Air Wales from Manchester (from about £100 return, 45 minutes, daily except weekends); and roughly daily links from the following airports with BA (with BA's own best advance-purchase fares at the time of writing): Aberdeen (about £195, 2½ hours), Belfast (£135, one hour), Edinburgh (£130, 1½ hours), Glasgow (£130,

Air Travel Glossary

Alliances Many of the world's leading airlines are now intimately involved with each other, sharing everything from reservations systems and check-in to aircraft and frequent-flyer schemes. Opponents say that alliances restrict competition. Whatever the arguments, there is no doubt that big alliances are the way of the future.

Courier Fares Businesses often need to send urgent documents or freight securely and quickly. Courier companies hire people to accompany the package through customs and, in return, offer a discount ticket which is sometimes a bargain. However, you may have to surrender all your baggage allowance and take only carry-on luggage.

Fares Airlines traditionally offer 1st class (coded F), business class (coded J) and economy class (coded Y) tickets. These days there are so many promotional and discounted fares available that few passengers pay full fare.

Lost Tickets If you lose your airline ticket, an airline will usually treat it like a travellers cheque and, after inquiries, issue you with another one. Legally, however, an airline is entitled to treat it like cash and if you lose it then it's gone forever. Take good care of your tickets.

Onward Tickets An entry requirement for many countries is that you have a ticket out of the country. If you're unsure of your next move, the easiest solution is to buy the cheapest onward ticket to a neighbouring country or a ticket from a reliable airline which can later be refunded if you do not use it.

Open-Jaw Tickets These are return tickets where you fly out to one place but return from another. If available, this can save you backtracking to your arrival point.

Overbooking Since every flight has some passengers who fail to show up, airlines often book more passengers than they have seats. Usually excess passengers make up for the no-shows, but occasionally somebody gets 'bumped' onto the next available flight. Guess who it is most likely to be? The passengers who check in late. If you do get 'bumped', you are normally offered some form of compensation.

Reconfirmation Some airlines require you to reconfirm your flight at least 72 hours prior to departure. Check your travel documents to see if this is the case

Restrictions Discounted tickets often have various restrictions on them – such as needing to be paid for in advance and incurring a penalty to be altered or cancelled. Others are restrictions on the minimum and maximum period you must be away.

Round-the-World Tickets RTW tickets give you a limited period (usually a year) in which to circumnavigate the globe. You can go anywhere the carrying airlines go, as long as you don't backtrack. The number of stopovers or total number of separate flights is decided before you set off and they usually cost a bit more than a basic return flight.

Ticketless Travel Airlines are gradually waking up to the realisation that paper tickets are unnecessary encumbrances. On simple one-way or return trips, reservations details can be held on computer and the passenger merely shows ID to claim their seat.

Transferred Tickets Airline tickets cannot be transferred from one person to another. Travellers sometimes try to sell the return half of their ticket, but officials can ask you to prove that you are the person named on the ticket. On an international flight, tickets are compared with passports.

1½ hours), Newcastle (£110, 1¼ hours) and Guernsey (£100, 55 minutes). Manx Airlines flies from Jersey five times weekly (£135, 45 minutes).

Flying out of the UK Discount air travel is big business in London. Cheap international fares appear in the weekend broadsheet papers and, in London, in *Time Out*, the *Evening Standard* and the free *TNT* magazine.

The UK's best known bargain-ticket agencies are Trailfinders (Europe line ☎ 020-7937 5400, long-haul line ☎ 020-7938 3939), Travel CUTS (☎ 020-7792 3770) and STA Travel (☎ 020-7361 6161). All have branches throughout the UK. One of the best Web sites – where you can also track down, book and pay for flights – is STA's at www.statravel.co.uk.

Some other reliable bargain-hunters are:

Bridge the World (☎ 020-7734 7447)
  Web site: www.b-t-w.co.uk
Flightbookers (☎ 020-7757 2000)
  Web site: www.ebookers.com
North-South Travel (☎ 01245-608 291)
  This company donates part of its profits to projects in the developing world
  Web site: www.nstravel.demon.co.uk
Travel Bag (Australasia ☎ 020-7287 5556, North America ☎ 020-7287 5559)
  Web site: www.travelbag.co.uk

SAGA Flights Service (☎ 01303-773 532) has some air-fare bargains for travellers aged over 50. Its Web site is at www.saga.co.uk.

Ireland

The no-frills carrier Ryanair has daily flights between Dublin and Cardiff (about €83 return, one hour), as does BA (BA's best advance-purchase fare about €127). Air Wales flies from Cork (from about €127, 1¼ hours) every Monday, Wednesday and Friday.

Elsewhere in Europe

There's little variation in air-fare prices for departures from the main European cities. Most major airlines offer some sort of deal, as do a lot of travel agents, so shop around.

The only direct connections to Cardiff from European centres are daily or almost-daily flights with BA from Paris (€282 return, 1¼ hours) or Brussels (€285 return, 1¼ hours) and with KLM from Amsterdam (€239, 1¾ hours). For flights to other points in the UK, expect to pay the equivalent of about £100 to £200 for a discounted return ticket with a major airline; no-frills carriers charge from about £50 to £150 for their destinations, which usually happen to be the most competitive markets.

For air-fare information in Amsterdam, try the official student travel agency NBBS Reizen (☎ 020-620 5071), with branches in most cities and a Web site at www.nbbs .nl; or Malibu Travel (☎ 020-626 3230). In Brussels, go to Acotra Student Travel Agency (☎ 02-512 86 07) or usit Connections (☎ 02-550 01 00) with a Web site at www.connections.be; in Antwerp try WATS Reizen (☎ 03-226 16 26). In Germany try Frankfurt-based STA Travel (☎ 069-70 30 35) or Cologne-based usit Campus (☎ 0221-925 9670) with a Web site at www.usitcampus.de.

Bargain-flight specialists with branches around France include AJF (☎ 01 42 77 87 80) and OTU Voyages (☎ 01 44 41 38 50) with a Web site at www.otu.fr. Others in Paris are usit Connect (☎ 01 43 29 69 50) and STA affiliate Voyages Wasteels (☎ 08 03 88 70 00). General agencies offering good deals are Nouvelles Frontières (☎ 08 03 33 33 33), on the Web at www.nouvelles-frontieres.com, and Voyageurs du Monde (☎ 01 42 86 16 00).

The USA & Canada

Since the late 1990s there has been a permanent price war on the USA–London axis, the world's busiest transcontinental route. Fares on all major airlines flying from the East Coast have fallen as low as US$300 in winter, US$400 in spring and autumn, and US$600 in summer; fares from the West Coast are about US$100 higher. There are no direct flights from North America to Wales.

Discount travel agents in the USA and Canada are called consolidators, and can be

Discount travel agents in the USA and Canada are called consolidators, and can be found in the *Yellow Pages* or major newspapers. Ticket Planet is a leading consolidator and you can visit its Web site at www.ticketplanet.com. The *Los Angeles Times,* the *New York Times,* the *Examiner* (San Francisco), *Chicago Tribune,* the *Globe & Mail* (Toronto), the *Toronto Star,* The *Gazette* (Montreal) and the *Vancouver Sun* all have weekly travel sections with ads and information.

Given how low advertised fares are, you might do well by contacting the airlines directly. Should you prefer an agent, two air-fare specialists in the USA are STA Travel (☎ 800 777 0112) and Council Travel (☎ 800 226 8624). Canada's best bargain-ticket agency is Travel CUTS/Voyages Campus (☎ 888 838 2887). All three have offices countrywide and Web sites at www.statravel.com, www.counciltravel.com and www.travelcuts.com respectively.

Australia & New Zealand

Competition is high on routes between Australasia and Europe. Cheap flights generally go via South-East Asian capitals, with stopovers at Kuala Lumpur, Bangkok or Singapore. Flights from New Zealand sometimes stop at Honolulu, Australia or one of the Pacific Islands. The very cheapest flights may be on carriers such as Emirates which entail two stops. If a long stopover between connections is necessary, transit accommodation is sometimes included in the price of the ticket.

Expect to pay anywhere from A$1800 in the low season to A$3000 in the high season for a return ticket to the UK. RTW tickets are often real bargains, and it can sometimes work out cheaper to keep going right round the world on a RTW ticket than to do a U-turn on a return ticket. RTWs that include London start at about A$1720/1940 or NZ$2150/2200 for students/non-students.

Check travel agency ads in the *Yellow Pages*, and the Saturday travel sections of the *Sydney Morning Herald,* the *Age* (Melbourne) or the *New Zealand Herald.*

STA Travel and Flight Centres International, both with offices across Australia and New Zealand, are major dealers in cheap air fares. For the nearest office, call either STA (☎ 131 776 Australiawide), with a Web site at www.statravel.com.au, or Flight Centres (☎ 131 600 Australiawide) with Web sites at www.flightcentre.com.au and www.flightcentre.com/nz/.

Asia

Although most Asian countries now offer fairly competitive air-fare deals, Bangkok, Singapore and Hong Kong are still the best places to shop around for discount tickets. Talk with other travellers though, as there are some bad eggs among the hundreds of honest travel agencies.

Khao San Rd is the budget zone in Bangkok. STA Travel (☎ 02-236 0262), 33 Surawong Rd, is a reliable place to start. In Singapore STA Travel (☎ 737 7188) in the Orchard Parade Hotel, 1 Tanglin Rd, offers competitive fares. Chinatown Point shopping centre, New Bridge Rd, has a good selection of travel agents.

In Hong Kong, many travellers use the Hong Kong Student Travel Bureau (☎ 2730 3269), 8th floor, Star House, Tsimshatsui; and Phoenix Services (☎ 2722 7378), 7th floor, Milton Mansion, 96 Nathan Rd, Tsimshatsui.

India

You can get cheap tickets in Mumbai (Bombay) and Calcutta, but Delhi is the centre for wheeling and dealing.

In Delhi, Connaught Place has lots of discount travel agencies but, as always, be careful before handing over your cash, and then double-check with the airline to confirm the booking. STIC Travels (☎ 011-332 5559), an agent for STA Travel, has an office in Room 6 at the Hotel Imperial in Janpath.

In Mumbai, STIC Travels (☎ 022-218 1431) is at 6 Maker Arcade, Cuffe Parade. Another recommended Mumbai agent is Transway International (☎ 022-262 6066), 2nd floor, Pantaky House, 8 Maruti Cross Lane, Fort.

Middle East

The best air-fare deals in the Middle East are likely to be the airlines' official excursion fares. Some travel agencies will drop the price by up to 10% if you're persistent, but may then tie you to fixed dates or less popular airlines.

The nearest thing to a discount travel ticket market is offered by some travel agencies in Israel and Istanbul. The Israel Student Travel Association (ISSTA) has branches in Tel Aviv (☎ 03-524 6322) at 128 Ben Yehuda St and in Jerusalem (☎ 02-625 2799) at 31 HaNevi'im St. In Istanbul, the Overseas Travel Agency (☎ 216-513 4175), Alemdar Caddesi 16, Sultanahmet, is recommended.

Africa

Nairobi and Johannesburg are the best places in East and South Africa to buy tickets. Flight Centres (☎ 02-210024) at Lakhamshi House, Biashara St, Nairobi, has been in business for years. In Johannesburg, the South African Student's Travel Services has an office (☎ 011-716 3045) at the University of the Witwatersrand, and STA Travel (☎ 011-447 5551) is on Tyrwhitt Ave, Rosebank.

West Africa's main international airports are at Abidjan, Accra, Bamako, Dakar and Lagos. Travel agents' fares are generally equivalent to those offered by the airlines, but agents may be more helpful if anything goes wrong. In Abidjan (Le Plateau), Saga Voyages (☎ 32 98 70) is opposite Air Afrique, and Haury Tours (☎ 22 16 54, fax 22 17 68, ✉ haury@africaonline.co.ci), 2nd floor, Chardy Bldg, is an affiliate of the French travel group Nouvelles Frontières. In Accra try Expert Travel & Tours (☎ 021-775498), Ring Rd East, near the US embassy.

In Bamako, reliable agencies include ATS Voyages (☎ 22 44 35), Ave Kassa Keita, and TAM (☎ 23 92 00, ✉ tvoyage@sotelma.net) on Square Lumumba. Agencies in Dakar include Senegal Tours (☎ 823 31 81), 5 Place de l'Indépendance, and SDV Voyages (☎ 839 00 81), 51 Ave Albert Sarraut. In Lagos there are many agencies in the Race Course Rd complex on Tafawa Balewa Square, Lagos Island; try L'Aristocrate Travels & Tours (☎ 01-266 7322), on the corner of Davies and Broad Sts, or Mandilas Travel (☎ 01-266 3339) on Broad St.

South America

Venezuela has the cheapest and most convenient air links with Europe. In Caracas, IVI Tours (☎ 02-993 60 82), Residencia La Hacienda, Piso Bajo, Local 1-4-T, Final Avenida Principal de las Mercedes, is an agent for STA Travel.

Rio de Janiero is Brazil's most popular international gateway, with no shortage of travel agents. The Student Travel Bureau (☎ 021-259 0023), an affiliate of STA Travel, is at Rua Visconde de Piraja 550, Ipanema.

The best connections to Europe from Argentina are from Buenos Aires. ASATEJ (☎ 011-4315 14570), Argentina's nonprofit student travel agency and an agent for STA Travel, is on the 3rd floor, Oficina 319-B, at Florida 835.

LAND
Bus

Coaches are slower and less comfortable than trains for long-distance travel, though you usually get reclining seats and on-board toilets, and sometimes air conditioning. They're cheaper than trains, especially if you qualify for a youth or senior discount, or take advantage of frequent promotional fares.

For travel from elsewhere in the UK, National Express – by far the largest national network – has frequent services between most major cities. For travel from outside the UK, the two major options are Eurolines and Busabout.

National Express Services of National Express (☎ 0870 580 8080) feed into Wales from all around the UK:

From London and Bristol into South and west Wales (Newport, Cardiff, Swansea, Carmarthen and Pembroke Dock).

From London and Birmingham via Shrewsbury into Mid Wales (Aberystwyth) and into north-east Wales (Wrexham), and via Chester into North Wales (Llandudno, Bangor, Pwllheli and Holyhead).

From Scotland and northern England via Birmingham into South and west Wales, and via Manchester and Liverpool into North Wales.

Following are some sample routes, approximate single economy fares, trip durations (hours); all these services run daily:

journey	fare (£)	hours
Bristol–Cardiff	5	1¼
London–Aberystwyth	22.50	7
London–Cardiff	16	3¼
London–Llandudno	21	8
Birmingham–Aberystwyth	18.50	4
Birmingham–Cardiff	17	2½
Edinburgh–Wrexham	28	11½
Manchester–Llandudno	10	4
Shrewsbury–Aberystwyth	13.50	2¼

Return tickets usually cost 20% to 50% more than singles, with some discounts if you book a week ahead and/or don't travel on Friday.

It's worth booking your seat on any journey to/from Wales a few days ahead. You can book at main bus stations, by telephone, or online at www.nationalexpress.co.uk or www.gobycoach.com.

Arriva Cymru Once a day from late May to late September, the TrawsCambria service of this major Wales operator runs from Bristol, via Newport, Cardiff, Swansea and Carmarthen, to Aberystwyth (£15/24 single/return, 5½ hours). See the Getting Around chapter for more on this service.

Eurolines An association of companies that together form Europe's largest international bus network. Eurolines booking offices in Europe include:

Amsterdam
  Eurolines (☎ 020-560 8788) Rokin 10
Brussels
  Eurolines (☎ 02-274 1370, ℮ info@eurolines .be) rue du Progrès 80

Dublin
  Eurolines (☎ 01-836 6111) Broadstone
  Web site: www.buseireann.ie
Frankfurt
  Deutsche Touring (☎ 069-790 350) Am Römerhof 17
  Web site: www.deutsche-touring.com
Paris
  Eurolines (☎ 08 36 69 52 52) Gare Routière Internationale de Paris, 128 rue du Général de Gaulle, Bagnolet
  Web site www.eurolines.fr

In the UK you can book directly with Eurolines (☎ 0870 514 3219, ℮ welcome@ eurolines.co.uk), through any National Express office, and at many travel agencies. See also the main Eurolines Web site at www.eurolines.com.

Some sample single/return fares to London in July and August (seven-day advance booking) include: €50/61 from Amsterdam (nine hours), €51/50 from Dublin (11 hours), €50/63 from Brussels (seven hours), €89/112 from Frankfurt (15 hours) and €49/59 from Paris (nine hours). All have multiple daily services. Fares outside July and August are about 10% lower. Typical discounts are approximately 40% for children aged four to 12, and 10% for travellers aged under 26 and over 60 (these vary with season and destination, and senior discounts are not available on all services). UK connections include a crossing by ferry/hovercraft in the price.

If you're travelling widely in Europe by coach, the Eurolines Pass gives you unlimited travel between 45 European cities, plus a limited amount of domestic travel (but not to Wales). In the UK, a 30-day pass costs £245/195 for adults/concessions (youth and senior) and a 60-day pass costs £283/ 227, in high season (July, August and mid-December to early January). The equivalent low-season prices are £175/139 for 30 days and £219/175 for 60 days.

Busabout UK-based Busabout is a hop-on-hop-off network linking some 70 European cities. Coaches run from April to October, and travellers can move freely around the network using one of two passes. The

Consecutive Pass is good for a set period from two weeks (£169 in the UK; £149 for youth or student card holders) to seven months (£699/629). The Flexi-Pass lets you choose the number of travel days you want, from 10 days within two months (£259/229) to 30 days within four months (£659/599).

Passes are available in the UK from Busabout (☎ 020-7950 1661, fax 7950 1662, e info@busabout.co.uk), 258 Vauxhall Bridge Rd, London SW1V 1BS, with a Web site at www.busabout.com; or from suppliers such as usit Campus and STA Travel.

Coach stops are near hostels and camping grounds, and coaches pass by every two days. The only UK stop is at the Busabout office, and the nearby St Christophers Village Hostel, 165 Borough High St, London. Travellers joining the network from London pay an extra £30 for a return-trip shuttle to Paris by coach and ferry.

Every coach has an on-board guide who can answer questions and make computerised travel and hostel arrangements en route.

Train

Trains are a popular way to get around Europe – comfortable, frequent and generally on time – and they're a good place to meet other travellers. But unless you have a rail pass (see European Rail Passes later in the chapter, or UK Rail Passes in the Getting Around chapter) or a Railcard (see Railcards in the Getting Around chapter), a train fare can be almost as expensive as an air fare.

Despite the damage wrought by privatisation in the Thatcher years, the UK rail service remains impressive – if you're using it as a tourist rather than a commuter, at any rate. And connections to London are abundant – via Paris, Lille and Brussels – from the European rail network.

If you plan to travel widely by train, consider buying the *Thomas Cook European Timetable*, which gives a complete listing of train (and ferry) schedules, supplements and reservations information. It's updated monthly and is available from Thomas Cook outlets worldwide; or order it online at www.thomascookpublishing.com/books.

Elsewhere in the UK First Great Western's hourly Intercity service will take you from London's Paddington station to Cardiff in two hours (£34/37, 2nd-class SuperSaver single/return, hourly). There's also a line to Cardiff from London's Waterloo station but journey times are considerably longer (almost three hours).

From London's Waterloo station, the terminus for Eurostar services from continental Europe (see the next section), Wales & West's Alphaline service goes daily to Cardiff (£34/37, 3½ hours), and on as far as Carmarthen. Frequent fast Intercity trains, run by Central Trains and by First North Western, also link South Wales with Birmingham, York and Newcastle.

Virgin Trains' twice-daily Intercity service runs from London's Euston station to North Wales (including Llandudno Junction and Bangor), reaching Holyhead (£49.50/50.50) in 4½ hours. For connections to Mid Wales, go with Virgin Trains from London Euston to Birmingham (£14/15, 1½ hours), transferring there to Central Trains' Cambrian Line via Shrewsbury to Aberystwyth (£16/30, 3 hours).

See the Getting Around chapter for further details on services, fares and discounts. It's advisable to book journeys to/from Wales at least a few days ahead.

For enquiries about rail services within the UK, call the countrywide enquiries number, ☎ 0845 748 4950 (from outside the UK, ☎ 44 1332-387601). Other ways to obtain train information are listed in the boxed text 'Call 'Em Up: Rail Companies', under Train in the Getting Around chapter.

Europe via the Channel Tunnel Two services operate through the Channel Tunnel: the railway companies of France, Belgium and the UK operate Eurostar, a high-speed passenger service linking London with both Paris and Brussels; and Eurotunnel runs a rail shuttle service for cars and other vehicles between France and the UK (see Car & Motorcycle later in the chapter).

Eurostar trains travel to London's Waterloo International Terminal via Lille and Calais from Paris (Gare du Nord; three hours, about 16 daily) or Brussels (2¾ hours, about 11 daily); journey times should drop by half an hour when the high-speed track through Kent is completed. Immigration formalities are usually completed on the train; UK customs is at Waterloo.

The normal Paris–London return fare is an arresting €396, but various special offers and/or advance purchase can reduce this to €152 or less. You can buy tickets from travel agencies, larger mainline stations or directly from Eurostar (☎ 0870 518 6186 in the UK, ☎ 08 36 35 35 39 in France, ☎ 0900-10366 in Belgium). Eurostar's Web site at www.eurostar.com often has special deals.

Europe via Rail-Sea-Rail There are some cheaper but longer rail connections to London (Charing Cross or other stations) involving a Channel crossing by ferry or SeaCat – such as Paris–London (about €107 for a 2nd-class adult return, nine hours) via Sealink ferry from Dieppe to Newhaven. Tickets can be purchased from travel agents or larger mainline stations; in the UK you can also get them from Connex South Eastern (☎ 0870 001 0174); see the Web site at www.connex.co.uk.

See the Sea section later in the chapter for details on sailings.

European Rail Passes There are several passes for use on the European rail system, but note that none of these are valid in the UK! For UK passes, see Train in the Getting Around chapter. Even with a pass you must still pay for seat and couchette reservations and express-train supplements.

The Inter-Rail Pass is available to anyone resident in Europe for at least six months before starting their travels. There are eight passes, each for a different zone; eg zone E includes France, Belgium, the Netherlands and Luxembourg. A pass for 22 consecutive days travel costs the equivalent of £229 (£159 for those aged under 26). Multi-zone passes, valid for one month, are better value: all eight zones costs £349 (£259).

The EuroDomino Pass is good for three, five or 10 consecutive days within a specified month, in a specified European country. Adult/youth prices for a 10-day pass range from £129/79 (Netherlands) to £249/199 (Spain).

For non-European residents, the Eurailpass is valid for unlimited travel (1st/2nd class for those aged over/under 26) in 17 European countries. Standard versions are good for 15 days (US$610) to three months (US$1714); 'flexi' versions allow a certain number of travel days per longer period. Eurailpasses are meant to be purchased before you get to Europe, although you can buy them at a limited number of European locations (including through Rail Europe; see UK Rail Passes in the Getting Around chapter) for about 10% more, provided your passport shows you've been in Europe for under six months.

Another pass for non-Europeans is the Europass, with versions good for five to 15 days of unlimited travel within two months. It's a little cheaper than the Eurailpass because it covers fewer countries.

Car & Motorcycle

Motorways from all the main ferry ports and from the Channel Tunnel converge on the M25 motorway, the multilane 'bypass' that circles London. You can use this (often clogged) artery to get round the city and on to other destinations.

From here the M4 motorway runs west to the Severn Bridge – across the estuary of the River Severn, at the southern end of the England–Wales border – and into Wales, past Cardiff (150 miles; about three hours from London) and Swansea (190 miles; about 3½ hours). Get your coins ready: the Severn Bridge, at three miles Britain's longest, had a whopping £4.20 toll at the time of writing (though only westbound).

The main route into North Wales is the M56 from Manchester to Chester and the coastal A55 from there across to Bangor. There are no major roads to get you easily into Mid Wales; the best you can do is take the scenic, mostly two-lane A44 to Aberystwyth from Worcester on the M5.

Bringing Your Vehicle from Europe

Your car or motorcycle can travel to the UK by ferry; for more information on ferries, see under Sea later in the chapter.

It can also arrive through the Channel Tunnel. Specially designed trains operated by Eurotunnel (☎ 0870 535 3535) serve as a kind of round-the-clock vehicle conveyor belt, departing up to four times hourly during the day and hourly at night. Customs and Immigration formalities take place before you drive onto the train. Terminals, at Calais and Folkestone, are linked to motorway networks on both sides; the trip takes 35 minutes and motorway-to-motorway time is an hour (it's 2½ hours for the shortest ferry trip). Check out the Web site at www.eurotunnel.com.

A car and all its passengers costs from £270, with day-trip fares of £69 or less. You can book ahead or pay by cash or credit card on arrival.

Paperwork Drivers of vehicles registered to other EU countries will find bringing a car or motorbike into the UK fairly straightforward. The vehicle must have registration papers and a nationality plate, and the driver must have insurance and an international drivers' permit. Although an International Insurance Certificate ('green card') is no longer required in the UK, it still comes in handy as proof of coverage.

SEA

There are ferry links from Ireland to four seaports in Wales: from Dublin and Dun Laoghaire to Holyhead; from Rosslare to Pembroke Dock; from Rosslare to Fishguard; and from Cork to Swansea.

There's a bewildering array of services to other UK ports from mainland Europe. Competition from Eurotunnel and no-frills airlines has kept fares down, but they're not simple. Each operator has a welter of fares depending on season, time of day, ticket validity, and the size of your vehicle if you're driving. The cost for a car may include several passengers at no additional cost, so if you can hitch a ride in a less than full car it will cost you and the driver noth-

---

Seaport Connections to Wales

Nearly all seaports in south-east England have shuttle services into London or other centres for onward connections to Wales. Remember that if you're a coach passenger – eg with Eurolines – your service carries on from the ferry to London's Victoria coach station.

Dover Shuttle bus to Dover Priory train station, from there by train to London's Charing Cross station, and from there to Paddington station (trains to South Wales) or Euston station (trains to Mid and North Wales)

Folkestone Taxi to Folkestone Central train station, from there by train to London's Charing Cross station, and from there to Paddington or Euston stations

Harwich Adjacent Harwich Parkeston Quay train station, with services to London's Liverpool Street station, and from there to Paddington or Euston stations

Newhaven Train to London's Victoria station, from there to Paddington or Euston stations

Plymouth Taxi to Plymouth train station, from there on direct Alphaline trains (Wales & West) to Newport and Cardiff

Poole Shuttle bus to Poole train station, from there by train to Southampton, and from there on direct Alphaline trains to Newport and Cardiff

Portsmouth Shuttle bus to Portsmouth Harbour train station, and from there on direct Alphaline trains to Newport and Cardiff; or taxi to Portsmouth coach station with connections to London's Victoria coach station

Other international seaports in the UK have shuttle services or taxis into the city centre. For more on long-distance coaches and trains into Wales, see the Bus and Train sections earlier in the chapter.

---

ing extra. On longer crossings there are options for cabin accommodation.

Some sample fares are listed in the following sections – though with advance planning you can beat these with special offers at all but the busiest times. Rail passes aren't valid for most ferry travel, but some discounts are available for students and young people.

Pleasure cruises on the Bristol Channel are awkward as one-way transport because of their seasonality and their dependence on weather and on demand. But you can do it, for about two-thirds of a return fare; see the following sections.

Ferries to Wales

All direct crossings to Wales are from Ireland. Unless otherwise noted, listings here give the cheapest high-season return fare (usually a five-day return) for one foot passenger and for one car plus driver, plus crossing times and frequencies. As stated earlier, prices vary widely according to season, day and time of crossing, and length of stay. Promotional (eg advance booking) and family fares are often available.

Cork–Swansea
Swansea Cork Ferries ferry £68/315 (car plus up to five passengers), 10 hours, four to six weekly from mid-March to early November

Rosslare–Pembroke Dock
Irish Ferries ferry £20/189, four hours, two daily

Rosslare–Fishguard
Stena Line Superferry £44/184, 3½ hours, two daily
Stena Line Catamaran £60/219, two hours, two to four daily

Dublin–Holyhead
Irish Ferries slow ferry £44/209, 3¼ hours, two daily
Irish Ferries fast ferry £56/249, 1½ hours, three daily
Stena Line Superferry £-/199 (no foot passengers), 3¾ hours, two daily

Dun Laoghaire–Holyhead
Stena Line Superferry £56/244, 1¾ hours, four daily

Ferries to Elsewhere in the UK

Only routes to UK ports with straightforward onward links into Wales are noted here. Listings give standard high-season return fares for a single foot passenger and for one car plus driver, crossing times and frequencies.

Ireland
Dublin–Liverpool
Sea Containers SeaCat catamaran £44/236, 3¾ hours, one daily

Call 'Em Up: Ferry Companies

A general Web site offering good deals on ferry fares is www.ferrysavers.co.uk.

Brittany Ferries (☎ 0870 536 0360)
Web site: www.brittany-ferries.com
Condor Ferries (☎ 01305-761 551)
Web site: www.condorferries.co.uk
DFDS Seaways (☎ 0870 533 3000)
Web site: www.dfdsseaways.co.uk
Hoverspeed (☎ 0870 240 8070)
Web site: www.hoverspeed.co.uk
Irish Ferries (☎ 0870 517 1717)
Web site: www.irishferries.ie
P&O Irish Sea (☎ 0870 242 4777)
Web site: www.poirishsea.com
P&O North Sea (☎ 0870 129 6002)
Web site: www.ponsf.com
P&O Portsmouth (☎ 0870 242 4999)
Web site: www.poportsmouth.com or www.poferries.com
P&O Stena Line (☎ 0870 600 0612)
Web site: www.posl.com or www.po ferries.com
Sea Containers (☎ 0870 552 3523)
Web site: www.steam-packet.com
SeaFrance (☎ 0870 571 1711)
Web site: www.seafrance.co.uk
Stena Line (☎ 0870 570 7070)
Web site: www.stenaline.co.uk
Swansea Cork Ferries (☎ 01792-456116)
Web site: www.swansea-cork.ie

Northern Europe
Esbjerg (Denmark)–Harwich
DFDS Seaways ferry £228/338 (including berth in economy cabin), 20 hours, two to three weekly

Hamburg (Germany)–Harwich
DFDS Seaways ferry £228/338 (including berth in economy cabin), 19½ hours, three weekly

Hoek van Holland (Netherlands)–Harwich
Stena Line fast ferry £50/270, 3¾ hours, two daily
Stena Line slow ferry same price, 6¼ hours, one daily

Oostende (Belgium)–Dover
Hoverspeed SeaCat £28/245, two hours, two to three daily

Northern France
Calais–Dover
P&O Stena ferry £26/195, 1¼ hours, every hour or less

SeaFrance ferry £17/175, 1½ hours, every one to two hours
Hoverspeed SeaCat £24/245, 40 minutes, four to seven daily

Normandy

Dieppe–Newhaven
Hoverspeed SeaCat £28/265, two hours, two to three daily from late April to early September

Cherbourg–Poole
Brittany Ferries ferry £56/190, 4¼ hours, one to three daily
Brittany Ferries fast ferry £60/266, 2¼ hours, one daily from June and September

Cherbourg–Portsmouth
P&O Portsmouth ferry £70/196, five hours (5½ to seven hours overnight), six daily

Le Havre–Portsmouth
P&O Portsmouth ferry £70/196, five hours (eight hours overnight), three daily

Ouistreham (Caen)–Portsmouth
Brittany Ferries ferry £45/190, six hours, two to three daily

Brittany

St Malo–Portsmouth
Brittany Ferries ferry £48/216, nine hours, one to two daily

St Malo–Poole (via Guernsey and Jersey)
Condor Ferries catamaran £47/209, 4½ to 5½ hours, one daily

Roscoff–Plymouth
Brittany Ferries ferry £46/200, six hours, one to three daily (one weekly from mid-November to March)

Spain

Bilbao–Portsmouth
P&O Portsmouth ferry £250/555 (including obligatory cabin), 29 to 35 hours, twice weekly

Santander–Plymouth
Brittany Ferries ferry £112/436 (including reclining seats), 24 hours, twice weekly from mid-March to mid-November

Pleasure Cruises

From May to October the *PS Waverley*, the world's last seagoing paddle steamer, or its more conventional sister ship the *Balmoral* tootle out from several South Wales ports – mostly Penarth, also Newport, Swansea and Porthcawl – for day or evening cruises on the Bristol Channel. Every few days one ties up on the other side – mostly Ilfracombe in Devon or Minehead in Somerset – and you can ride these one-way for around £10 to £15, ie about two-thirds of the full excursion fare.

But flexibility and a relaxed attitude are essential, since these cruises are subject to cancellation in the event of low demand, high seas or bad weather. For information and bookings call ☎ 029-2070 4520, or contact Waverley Excursions (☎ 0141-243 2224, fax 248 2150), Waverley Terminal, Anderston Quay, Glasgow G3 8HA. You can also buy a ticket on board, or at Cardiff Bus in Cardiff, or at TICs in Cardiff, Newport, Merthyr Tydfil, Caerphilly, Swansea or Porthcawl.

Getting Around

UK government policy in the 1980s and 1990s was openly hostile to public transport. Car ownership was favoured and local rail and bus services suffered. The government in London has promised to reverse the trend, but it will take years for the effects to be felt. This is bad news for visitors without their own wheels, as transport to the more remote areas is limited.

Despite the short distances involved, transport in Wales is a mixed bag. Regional roads and transport connections, especially along the north and south coasts, are better than those between North and South Wales. County transport authorities fall over themselves with timetables and maps but – with the exception of coastal roads – going between North and South Wales is often easiest via England. Nonstop coach services are almost nonexistent, and regional coordination is limited. Interior Mid Wales is a semi-void, transport-wise. Wales has no internal air connections.

It's worth considering car rental for at least part of your trip. But if you aren't in a hurry, you can patch together an odyssey by public transport, the odd taxi, walking and bicycle hire, through most of what is really appealing about Wales. There are several superb train journeys, and while coverage is limited, the landscape can be sublime.

Buses are nearly always the cheapest way around, though with advance booking and discount passes, trains can be competitive. There's rarely any need for bus or train journeys within Wales to be booked ahead to ensure a seat. But it can be as complicated as finding a cheap airline ticket, with a plethora of ticket types and prices. Single tickets tend to be poor value, costing nearly as much as return tickets. For many, the convenience of a travel pass outweighs any potential savings from bargain-hunting.

Note that road signs, and all information at bus and train stations, are now bilingual within Wales.

Information

A must-have for anyone getting around Wales by public transport is the free *Wales Bus, Rail & Tourist Map & Guide*, a compact, high-density compendium of information – maps, telephone numbers and tables of routes, journey times and frequencies, though not individual timetables nor fares. It's updated annually by the Welsh Tourist Board (WTB) and available at all Tourist Information Centres (TICs).

Many local authorities produce their own more exhaustive maps or booklets containing bus and train timetables, available free at relevant TICs – though you might have to ask for them. There are also UK-wide bus and rail enquiry telephone numbers, and individual operators and county councils have their own enquiry numbers and Web sites; see the separate Bus and Train sections later in the chapter.

Travel Passes

Those planning a lot of travel by public transport will save money with one of four very good-value travel passes marketed under the name Flexipass, good for free travel, in designated regions of Wales and immediately adjacent areas of England, on all rail routes and nearly all intercity bus routes.

The passes, with high/low season prices (high season being from late May to late September; those aged between 5 and 15 and Senior Railcard holders get one-third off), are:

Freedom of Wales 15-day Flexipass Fifteen days bus travel plus any eight days train travel, throughout Wales (£92/75)

Freedom of Wales 8-day Flexipass Eight days bus travel plus any four days train travel, throughout Wales (£55/45)

Freedom of South Wales 7-day Flexi-Rover Seven days bus travel plus any three days train travel in South Wales (£35/30)

Freedom of North and Mid Wales 7-day Flexi-Rover Any three days of bus and train travel in North and Mid Wales (£28 year round)

The passes also get you £1 discounts at Youth Hostels Association (YHA) and Hostelling International (HI) hostels in Wales; free or discounted travel on narrow-gauge railways (see the boxed text 'Wales Heritage Railways' under Train later); 20% discount on admission to several properties owned by the National Trust (NT), the National Museums & Galleries of Wales (NMGW) and Cadw; and a discount for Guide Friday's Cardiff, Llandudno and Conwy tours.

The passes are sold online at www .travelwales-flexipass.co.uk, and over the counter at:

- All staffed train stations and rail-accredited travel agencies in Wales
- TICs at Abergavenny, Aberystwyth, Bangor, Brecon, Cardiff, Carmarthen, Fishguard, Haverfordwest, Holyhead, Llandudno, Llangollen, Merthyr Tydfil, Monmouth, Porthmadog, Pwllheli and Tenby
- YHA/HI hostels in Bangor, Cardiff, Chester, Conwy and Llangollen (as well as Bath, Bristol, Shrewsbury, and Liverpool in England)

See the separate Bus and Train sections in this chapter about other passes, though most are worthwhile only if you practically live on trains and buses. Good-value local passes – for example, for a day's unlimited bus travel – are mentioned under Cardiff and a few other towns. Most transport authorities also offer youth/student and senior passes and/or discounts.

BUS
Limited connections within Wales are possible with National Express (☎ 0870 580 8080) coaches to/from London, Bristol, Hereford, Shrewsbury and a few other English cities; see the Getting There & Away chapter or the Web site www.gobycoach.com. But the vast majority is offered by a web of some 70 private bus companies within Wales; each chapter highlights the most important companies in its area. Another big carrier, especially in rural Mid Wales, is the Royal Mail (see under Postbus later in the chapter).

Long-distance express buses are usually called coaches, and some towns have separate bus and coach stations.

Unless otherwise stated, bus prices quoted in this book are for economy single tickets.

Bus Information
Many bus operators and county councils have their own enquiries numbers (answered during normal business hours), and wherever possible these numbers have been provided.

Traveline (☎ 0870 608 2608), the new UK-wide national bus enquiries service, is intended to be a one-stop shop for all information on fares, timetables, journey times and discounts. At the time of writing it was still in the teething stage, though you'll be transferred if they don't have what you want.

Bus Passes & Discounts
As noted under Travel Passes at the start of this chapter, the best pass to have in your pocket if you're going to do a lot of Wales travel by public transport is one of the four Flexipasses.

There are literally scores of other regional and local bus passes, with names such as Rover, Explorer and Wanderer. The majority are only worthwhile if you're going to spend a lot of time on buses in one area. Most can be bought from bus stations or from drivers as you board. Worthy ones are noted in the local chapters.

National Express has several passes, though they won't save you anything unless you'll be travelling widely throughout the UK. Various discount coach cards (all £9), good for 30% off standard adult fares, are available to full-time students and those aged between 16 and 25 or over 50 (you'll need a passport-size photo and proof of status and age). The Tourist Trail Pass allows unlimited coach travel within a specified period – two days out of three (£49/39 adult/discount), five days out of 10 (£85/ 69), seven days out of 21 (£120/94) or 14 days out of 30 (£187/143).

Regular Services
The biggest intercity operators are Arriva Cymru (☎ 0870 608 2608) in the north and west; First Cymru (☎ 01656-728393) in the

south-west; and Stagecoach (☎ 01633-244744) in the south-east.

The only real through coach service between North and South Wales is Arriva's TrawsCambria (No 701), running between Holyhead and Cardiff (£20/32 single/return; nine hours; daily from late May to late September) via Bangor, Caernarfon, Portmadog, Dolgellau, Machynlleth, Aberystwyth, Carmarthen and Swansea. An additional, shorter version from Aberystwyth to Cardiff (£11.35, four hours, daily from late May to late September) continues to Newport and Bristol. There's also a Sunday-only TrawsCambria service between Bangor and Holyhead.

Few other through services could be called 'trans-Wales'. National Express services No 419 (from London and Birmingham) and No 420 (from Shrewsbury) each run from Welshpool to Aberystwyth (£9.50, 1¾ hours, once daily). National Express No 508 (from London) runs from Swansea to Haverfordwest (£6, 2½ hours, twice daily) via Carmarthen, Tenby and Pembroke.

Arriva Cymru has a few inter-regional services, including No 94 Barmouth–Wrexham (£4.30, 2½ hours, seven times daily Mon-Sat, twice daily on Sun); No 522 Machynlleth–Newtown (£2.80, 1¼ hours, three times daily); and No 550 Cardigan–Aberystwyth, jointly with Richards Bros (£3.60, two hours, with a change of bus near New Quay, hourly).

See the table below for a sampling of other inter-regional fares (single), trip durations (hours) and frequencies (per day; daily except Sunday unless otherwise noted).

Postbus

Royal Mail postbuses – minibuses holding four to 10 passengers – provide a reliable, if somewhat circuitous, service to remoter towns and villages, especially in Mid Wales. They run through some beautiful areas and can be useful for walkers (but cannot usually carry bicycles).

For information and timetables contact local post offices, the Postbus Helpline (☎ 01246-546329) or Royal Mail Customer Services (☎ 0845 774 0740). County council transport booklets (available at many TICs) usually have postbus timetables too. For a free *Postbus Guide to England & Wales* contact Postbus Services (☎ 020-7490 2888), Post Office HQ, 130 Old St, London EC1V 9PQ.

National Park Bus Services

Each of Wales' national park authorities runs or organises dedicated bus services aimed at walkers and cyclists trying to get around the parks. Many routes include transport for bicycles. These services are described in more detail in the local chapters.

Stray Travel

Stray Travel runs low-budget UK tours, though their extreme flexibility qualifies them as 'transport' as well. For details see Organised Tours at the end of this chapter.

TRAIN

Following privatisation of the UK's railways in the Thatcher years, the rail system has become more chaotic and less reliable than under the single nationalised company that was known as British Rail. Services are now provided by a host of train operating companies (TOCs) – at least five just within Wales. Each can set its own fares, and passengers can only use their tickets on ser-

Inter-regional Bus Journeys

journey	fare (£)	duration (hours)	frequency	operator/route
Cardiff–Abergavenny	4.20	2¼	hourly	Stagecoach No X4
Swansea–Brecon	5.45	1¼	3 per day	Stagecoach No 63
Machynlleth–Dolgellau	2.45	1¼	half-hourly	Arriva No 32
Dolgellau–Caernarfon	4.35	1½	4 per day	ArrivaExpress No 1/2
Caernarfon–Llandudno	3.45	1½	hourly	Arriva No 5/5X

vices operated by the company who issued the ticket. Competing companies sometimes use the same routes. A separate company, Railtrack, owns and maintains all track and stations.

The main railcards (see the Railcards section) are accepted by all TOCs, and travellers can still buy a ticket to any destination from most train stations, though travel agents cannot always sell the full range of tickets.

Train Services in Wales

To a large extent, trains along Wales' north and south coasts serve to link the English rail network with seaports at Swansea, Pembroke Dock, Milford Haven, Fishguard and Holyhead. But there are some fine rail journeys across the middle of the country, and an amazing number of 'heritage' railways (mainly steam and narrow-gauge), survivors of an earlier day; see the boxed text 'Wales' Heritage Railways' later.

The main standard-gauge track networks are:

North Coast Chester-Holyhead and Llandudno Junction-Blaenau Ffestiniog (Virgin Trains, First North Western)
Heart of Wales Shrewsbury-Swansea (Wales & West)
Cambrian Shrewsbury-Aberystwyth and Machynlleth-Pwllheli (Central Trains)
South Wales Newport-Swansea (First Great Western, Wales & West) and Swansea-Pembroke Dock, Whitland-Milford Haven and Whitland-Fishguard (Wales & West)
Valley Cardiff-Rhondda, Aberdare, Merthyr Tydfil and Rhymney (Valley Lines)

Wales' most beautiful rail journeys fan out from Shrewsbury: the Heart of Wales through southern Mid Wales, the Cambrian across northern Mid Wales to Aberystwyth, and its spectacular branch line up the coast and along the Llŷn Peninsula. Another gem is the Conwy Valley line down through Snowdonia. Each is worth the fare just for the scenery and the hypnotic, clickety-clack pace.

Trains on the Heart of Wales line (see the boxed text under Llandrindod Wells in the Mid Wales chapter) run four times daily (once

Call 'em Up: Rail Companies

The best place to go for general UK rail enquiries is ☎ 0845 748 4950, or the Web site at www.nationalrail.co.uk. Another useful Web site, for fare information and on-line booking, is www.thetrainline.com – though it's often busy. Otherwise you can chase the individual train operating companies (TOCs):

Central (☎ 0870 000 6060)
　Web site: www.centraltrains.co.uk
First Great Western (☎ 0845 700 0125)
　Web site: www.great-western-trains.co.uk
First North Western (☎ 0845 700 0125)
　Web site: www.firstnorthwestern.co.uk
Valley Lines (☎ 029-2044 9944)
　Web site: www.valleylines.co.uk
Virgin Trains (☎ 0845 722 2333)
　Web site: www.virgintrains.co.uk
Wales & West (☎ 0870 900 0773)
　Web site: www.walesandwest.co.uk

Timetable information is also available at Railtrack's Web site, www.railtrack.co.uk.

on Sunday). Swansea-Llandrindod Wells (£12 return in summer) takes 3½ hours, for example, so return day-trips from Swansea are quite feasible. You could even go all the way to Shrewsbury and back (£16) in a day.

The Cambrian line negotiates the rugged Severn and Dyfi valleys from Welshpool to Aberystwyth (£8/15 single/return, 1½ hours) via Newtown and Machynlleth. You can take in prime coastal scenery from the Cambrian Coaster, running every two hours on weekdays, right along Cardigan Bay from Machynlleth to Pwllheli (£6/14, two hours), via Barmouth, Harlech Castle and Porthmadog, and with connections to several narrow-gauge lines.

The Conwy Valley line runs six times daily from Llandudno to Blaenau Ffestiniog (£4.80/5, 1¼ hours), where you can carry on to Porthmadog on the narrow-gauge Ffestiniog Railway.

Classes

There are two classes of rail travel: 1st class and what is now officially called 'standard'

Wales' Heritage Railways

The invention of the steam engine and the rapid spread of the railway to almost every corner of the UK transformed 19th-century life. But in the 20th century these lines declined in importance, and the infamous Beeching Report of 1963 led to the closure of many rural lines and stations. Five years later British Rail stopped using steam trains. For many people these two events brought the 'golden age of rail' in the UK to a sad end.

But it wasn't long before rail enthusiasts started buying up old locomotives, rolling stock, disused lines and stations, and restoring them – and financing their labour of love by offering rides and an old-time atmosphere, often with the help of the very people who worked the lines in pre-Beeching days. Today there are nearly 500 independent railways in the UK, many of them narrow-gauge, using steam or diesel locomotives from all over the world.

Wales' narrow-gauge lines are survivors from an industrial heyday when mine and quarry owners needed to move materials more quickly than horses could manage, and across terrain that defied normal standard-gauge trains. Most ran through glorious scenery, primarily in northern and Mid Wales, so their reincarnations are worth checking out even if you're not a rail buff. Many have a station in common with, or near, a standard-gauge mainline, so you can build them right into your rail journey.

Following is a list of the best of them, with the nearest sizeable town. Eight of them (starred * in this list) market themselves collectively as 'The Great Little Trains of Wales' (GLTW; ☎ 01938-810441, fax 810861), The Station, Llanfair Caereinion, Powys SY21 0BR, with a joint Web site at www.whr.co .uk/gltw/. These offer a joint 'Wanderer' pass giving four days travel in any eight days (£32/16 for adults/children) or eight days in any 15 (£42/21).

JANE SMITH

class. First class costs 30% to 50% more than standard and, except on very crowded trains, isn't worth the extra money.

Tickets

You can just roll up to a station and buy a standard single or return ticket for any time on the day you want, but this is the most expensive way to go. Like the airlines, each TOC has its own discount schemes and promotional fares, and the cheapest fares have advance-purchase and minimum-stay requirements, as well as limited availability. The main fare classifications are as follows:

Open Return For outward travel on a stated day and return on any day within a month

Saver Open return but with no travel during weekday peak-traffic periods

SuperSaver Open return but with no travel during weekday peak-traffic periods, nor on Friday at any time, nor on certain other high-traffic days (eg, during the Christmas and Easter holidays)

Wales' Heritage Railways

Brecon Beacons
Brecon Mountain Railway* (☎ 01685-722988, fax 384854), Merthyr Tydfil
  Web site: www.ukhrail.uel.ac.uk/bmr.html
Pontypool & Blaenavon Railway (☎ 01495-792263), Blaenavon

Pembrokeshire & Carmarthenshire
Gwili Steam Railway (☎ 01267-230666, e enquiries@gwili-railway.co.uk,), Carmarthen
  (standard-gauge)
  Web site: www.gwili-railway.co.uk/
Teifi Valley Railway (☎ 01559-371077), Newcastle Emlyn (near Cardigan)
  Web site: www.teifivr.f9.co.uk/

Mid Wales
Vale of Rheidol Railway* (☎ 01970-625819, fax 623769), Aberystwyth
  Web site: www.ukhrail.uel.ac.uk/vor.html
Welshpool & Llanfair Light Railway* (☎ 01938-810441, fax 810861), Welshpool
  Web site: www.wllr.org.uk/

Snowdonia & The Llŷn
Bala Lake Railway* (☎ 01678-540666), Bala
Fairbourne & Barmouth Steam Railway (☎ 01341-250362, fax 250240), Fairbourne (near
  Barmouth)
  Web site: www.fairbourne-railway.co.uk
Ffestiniog Railway* (☎ 01766-512340, fax 514715), Porthmadog
  Web site: www.festrail.co.uk
Llanberis Lake Railway* (☎ 01286-870549), Llanberis
Snowdon Mountain Railway (☎ 01286-870223, fax 872518), Llanberis
Talyllyn Railway* (☎ 01654-710472, fax 711755, e enquiries@talyllyn.co.uk,), Tywyn
  Web site: www.talyllyn.co.uk/
Welsh Highland Railway* (☎ 01766-513402, fax 514995), Caernarfon

Anglesey & North Coast
Llangollen Steam Railway (☎ 01978-860979), Llangollen (standard-gauge)
  Web site: www.llangollen-railway.co.uk/

The lines are described further in local chapters of the book. Most are open only from Easter to October, with complex timetables. Local Tourist Information Centres (TICs) have timetables for the routes nearest to them.

Cheap Day Return For outward and return journeys on the same specified day, with restricted outward travel time (eg, only after 9.30 am); often costs barely more than a single; a great deal for day-trippers

Apex For outward and return journeys not on the same day, but at fixed times and dates; the cheapest long-term return ticket, but must be booked well in advance, and has limited availability

Children under five travel free; those aged between five and 15 pay half-price for most tickets. However, when travelling with children it is almost always worth buying a Family Railcard (see Railcards later).

Unless stated otherwise, prices quoted in this book are for standard-class adult single tickets.

You can buy tickets from ticket offices and ticket machines at staffed stations, and from rail-appointed travel agencies. Some TOCs have telesales numbers, where you can buy tickets using a credit card number.

You may have to pay a transaction surcharge, and you must usually leave enough time for the tickets to be mailed to you. If you're unsure which TOC you want, any of them can help. Telesales numbers for TOCs in Wales include: Central (☎ 0870 000 6060); First Great Western (☎ 0845 700 0125); Wales & West (☎ 0870 900 0773); First North Western (☎ 0845 700 0125); and Virgin (☎ 0845 722 2333).

Railcards

Railcards entitle certain travellers to discounts of up to 33% on most rail (and some ferry) fares in the UK. Most stations have application forms; note that processing for some cards can take up to two weeks.

The Young Person's Railcard (£18) is for those aged between 16 and 25, or a full-time UK student of any age. The Senior Railcard (£18) is for anyone over 60. A Disabled Person's Railcard (£14) applies to its holder and one person accompanying them. A Family Railcard (£20) – a great bargain – allows discounts for up to four adults travelling together (only one needs to hold a card), and a flat fare of £2 each for up to four accompanying children.

UK Rail Passes

Rail passes usable on a Europe-wide trip are described under European Rail Passes in the Getting There & Away chapter, but none can be used in the UK.

BritRail passes can *only* be used in the UK – but they're available only to non-Brits and must be bought overseas. Most larger overseas travel agencies will have details; in the USA and Canada you can also get them through Rail Europe (USA ☎ 800 4 EURAIL, fax 432 1FAX; Canada ☎ 800 361 RAIL, fax 905-602 4198). The Web site is at www.raileurope.com.

The BritRail Classic is good only for consecutive travel, and you'd have to live on the trains to get your money's worth. Prices for adult 1st class, adult standard class, senior 1st class and youth standard class (the only options) range from US$400/265/340/215 for eight days to US$900/600/765/420 for 30 days. The better-value BritRail Flexipass stipulates the number of travel days out of 60 days – from US$350/235/300/185 for four days to US$770/515/655/360 for 15 days. BritRail pass-holders are also – like Eurail and Euro pass-holders – entitled to discounted fares on Eurostar trains.

As noted under Travel Passes at the start of this chapter, the best pass to carry if you're doing a lot of travel by public transport just in Wales is one of the multi-mode Flexipasses. If you're spending a good deal of time in just one area of Wales, check on local rail passes, some of which combine bus validity too.

CAR & MOTORCYCLE

From a visitor's standpoint, a car or motorcycle allows you to reach remote places and to travel quickly, independently and flexibly. This independence, on the other hand, tends to isolate you from your surroundings. What's more, cars are nearly always inconvenient in city centres. And at around 80p per litre (equivalent to about US$4.50 per US gallon) at the time of writing, petrol is expensive by American or Australian standards, with diesel only a few pence cheaper.

Despite its traffic density, the UK has the EU's safest roads. There are five grades of road. Motorways and main A-roads are triple or dual carriageways. They are fast – and dangerous in foggy or wet conditions. Lesser A-roads are single carriageways, apt to be clogged on weekdays with slow-moving trucks. Life is more relaxed and interesting on B-roads and unclassified minor roads, fenced by hedgerows, winding serenely through the countryside.

Getting around North or South Wales is easy, thanks respectively to the A55 and the M4. Elsewhere, roads are generally good but considerably slower, especially in the mountains and through Mid Wales. Wales may be just 170 miles long, but Llandudno to Cardiff by car – via the main north–south road, the A470 – still takes four hours. From the north-east to the south-east, it's quickest to go via England.

Higher roads are often snowbound in winter. Even when the snow clears, ice can

Road Distances in & near Wales (Miles)

1 mile = 1.61km

	Aberystwyth	Brecon	Bristol (England)	Cardiff	Fishguard	Holyhead	Llangollen	Shrewsbury (England)	Swansea
Aberystwyth	---								
Brecon	63	---							
Bristol (England)	125	67	---						
Cardiff	118	48	45	---					
Fishguard	56	85	149	111	---				
Holyhead	104	150	258	281	159	---			
Llangollen	68	90	159	134	123	74	---		
Shrewsbury (England)	76	77	130	105	131	104	31	---	
Swansea	74	43	79	49	67	177	131	124	---

make driving treacherous, especially on windy, narrow mountain roads, which are often single-track affairs with passing places at intervals.

Road Rules

Once accustomed to driving on the left side of the road, visitors are most often caught out by either speeding laws or parking regulations.

Legal speed limits are 30 mph (48 kph) in built-up areas – indicated, for example, by the presence of street lighting – 60 mph (96 kph) on single carriageways (two-lane roads) and 70 mph (112 kph) on motorways (expressways) and dual carriageways (divided highways). Exceptions to this – and there are plenty – are indicated by signs.

Parking a car in the wrong place, or failing to pay car-park charges, can cost you dearly. If your car is wheel-clamped and you must pay to retrieve it from a pound, you won't see much change from £100. On-the-spot fines are rare.

Yellow lines painted along the edge of the road mean there are parking restrictions, and these are set out on a sign somewhere nearby. A double yellow line means no park-

ing at any time; a single yellow line means no parking for at least an eight-hour period between 7 am and 7 pm; and a broken yellow line means there are some restrictions.

It's not a bad idea to read through the *Highway Code* (often available in TICs). Other important points are that front seat belts are compulsory, and if belts are fitted in the back they must be worn; and you must give way to your right at roundabouts (traffic circles), ie traffic already on the roundabout has the right of way. See Legal Matters in the Facts for the Visitor chapter for information on drink-driving rules.

Rental

A rental car can be useful if you want to reach beyond the public transport network. But bear in mind that busy roads can render cars a slower option than trains, and while trains usually deposit you near the centre of a town, rental cars often have to be returned to out-of-the-way places.

Rental cars are expensive in the UK, and parking is difficult in town centres; in fact it's increasingly rare to find free parking, and you can end a day's car sightseeing several pounds poorer from parking fees. If you think you'll be renting a car in Britain, consider arranging it before departure to take advantage of package deals on offer at home.

The best European car rental deals are offered by Web-based brokers such as Autos Abroad (UK ☎ 0870 066 7788) and Holiday Autos (UK ☎ 0870 400 0099). Sample rates from both at the time of writing – economy model, unlimited mileage, insurance and breakdown assistance – were about £250 for a two week rental within the UK. Worldwide rental companies are listed in the *Yellow Pages*. TICs usually have lists of local car-hire firms.

Insurance for damage or injury to other people is mandatory, but collision-damage waivers vary from company to company; policies offered by smaller companies may leave you liable for a deductible/excess cost of up to £800. If you're in an accident where you're at fault, or if the car is damaged and the guilty party is unknown, or if the car is stolen, this is the amount for which you're liable before the policy kicks in. Check the small print when you shop around.

All the major rental companies accept payment by credit card. All insist on a deposit; for this, some ask you to leave a signed credit card slip without a sum written in. If this makes you uncomfortable, have them make out separate slips for the rental and for the deposit, and see that the latter is destroyed when you return the car.

Motorcycle Touring

Wales is made for motorcycle touring, with good quality winding roads and stunning scenery. Just make sure your wet-weather gear is up to scratch. Crash helmets are compulsory in the UK. The Auto-Cycle Union (☎ 01788-566400, fax 573585), ACU House, Wood St, Rugby, Warwickshire CV21 2YX, publishes a very useful booklet about motorcycle touring in the UK.

Motoring Organisations

The UK's two largest motoring organisations, both of which offer 24-hour breakdown assistance, are the Automobile Association (AA; ☎ 0800 444999) and the Royal Automobile Club (RAC; ☎ 0800 550550). One year's membership starts at £44 for the AA and £39 for the RAC, and both can also extend their cover to include continental Europe. Your motoring organisation at home may have a reciprocal arrangement with one of them.

BICYCLE

Most sizeable towns have at least one shop where you can hire bikes from £10 to £12 per day, and almost anybody in reasonable shape can use these for a bit of local sightseeing. For long-distance travel around Wales, the hilly and often mountainous terrain is really for experienced cycle tourers. Options for bicycle travel around Wales – including on several branches of the National Cycle Network – are examined under Activities in the Facts for the Visitor chapter.

Transporting your Bicycle

Bikes can be taken on most trains, although each TOC has its own policy on this. Timetables usually have a symbol above each service on which bikes can be taken.

To be sure that you can take your bike, you should make your reservation (and get your ticket) and check bike carriage details at least 24 hours before travelling. A good place to start with this chore is the National Rail Enquiry Service (☎ 0845 748 4950), but you should also check with the train operator. With Wales & West, which runs many of Wales' intercity rail services, a reservation is essential on nearly all routes at all times, with a maximum of just two bikes per train. The reservation fee is £1 if you book at least two hours before departure, or £3 otherwise.

Bikes can usually be taken on local services free of charge on a first-come-first-served basis, though almost certainly not during rush hours.

HITCHING

Hitching is never entirely safe anywhere, and we don't recommend it. Travellers who hitch should understand that they are taking a small but potentially serious risk. Those who do choose to hitch will be safer if they travel in pairs and let someone know where they are planning to go.

It's against the law to hitch on motorways or the immediate slip roads; make a sign and use approach roads, nearby roundabouts, or service stations.

BOAT

You're most likely to use boats to reach the islands off the Pembrokeshire coast – Skomer, Skokholm and Grassholm (see under St Bride's Bay), Ramsey (see St David's) and Caldey (see Around Tenby) – or Bardsey off the Llŷn Peninsula. Charges vary according to the type of trip, but a day trip will cost around £10 to £20.

For another way to see Wales by boat, see Canal Travel under Activities in the Facts for the Visitor chapter.

LOCAL TRANSPORT

Most towns and cities in Wales are well equipped with public transport. The biggest problem for you may be sorting it out: in another of its anti-public transport initiatives, the former Conservative government privatised local buses throughout the UK – with often shambolic results. Local transport bodies were disbanded and private companies allowed to compete willy-nilly. In many towns today, no one seems quite sure who's running buses where.

Taxi

Taxis in Wales are quite reasonably priced – typically around £1.40 per mile – and definitely worth considering as a means of reaching out-of-the-way hostels, sights or trailheads. A taxi over a short distance is competitive with local buses, especially if three or four passengers share the cost. More importantly, when it's Sunday and you find that the next bus due to visit the charming town you've just hiked to is on Monday, a taxi can get you to a transport hub for a reasonable cost.

ORGANISED TOURS

Scores of local and regional outfits offer walking, cycling and multi-activity tours in their own areas. Many are mentioned under Activities in the Facts for the Visitor chapter, and more in local listings.

Stray Travel

Stray Travel (☎ 020-7373 7737, fax 7373 7739, e enquiries@straytravel.com), 171 Earls Court Rd, London SW5 9RF, runs budget UK 'tours' flexible enough to be considered 'transport'. Their buses run on fixed timetables on a six-day circuit with stops in London, Abergavenny and Caernarfon, as well as the English Lake District, Edinburgh and York, but your ticket allows you to get on and off as often as – and wherever – you like.

There are four options: a single day's travel (£24); three/four days' travel within two months (£79/99); and six days within four months (£129). Tickets can be purchased at STA, usit Travel and Flight Centre branches, at many independent agencies, or from Stray Travel directly or online at www.straytravel.com.

You can stay anywhere, though Stray has budget beds booked for its use; in Wales these are at two independent hostels, Blacksheep Backpackers in Abergavenny and Totters in Caernarfon.

Other General Tours

Haggis Tours (☎ 0131-557 9775, fax 558 1177), Scotland's own hop-on-hop-off tour company, runs a five-day guided tour from London to Edinburgh taking in selected bits of England, Wales and Scotland on the way. In Wales they spend the night at Llangollen's atmospheric YHA/HI hostel. The cost is £109 and there are weekly departures. You can visit its Web site at www.radicaltravel.com.

Companies with trips pitched at a young crowd include Contiki (UK ☎ 020-7637 0802, fax 7637 2121, Australia ☎ 02-9511 2222, NZ ☎ 09-309 8824); Insight (UK ☎ 020-7468 4141, fax 7468 4125, Australia ☎ 02-9512 0767, NZ ☎ 09-307 3871); and TracksTravel (UK ☎ 01797-344164, fax 344135). Contiki, Insight and TracksTravel have Web sites at www.contiki.com, www.insightvacations.com and www.tracks-travel.com respectively.

If you don't quite fit into this category, try Shearings Holidays (☎ 01942-824824, fax 230949), Miry Lane, Wigan, Lancashire, WN3 4AG, with a wide range of four-day to 12-day coach holidays. It has a Web site at www.shearingsholidays.com.

For travellers aged over 50, Saga Holidays (☎ 0800 300500), Saga Building, Middleburg Square, Folkestone, Kent CT20 1AZ, offers everything from coach tours to luxury cruises. Saga in the USA (☎ 617-262 2262) is at 222 Berkeley St, Boston, MA 02116, and in Australia (☎ 02-957 4266) at 10–14 Paul St, Milsons Point, Sydney 2061.

Its Web site, www.saga.co.uk, has more information.

Adventure Tours

London-based Bushwakkers (☎ 020-8573 3330, ⓔ info@bushwakkers.co.uk), 15 Chartwell Court, 145 Church Rd, Hayes, Middlesex UB3 2LP, offers weekend adventure trips to Wales by minibus. Prices are around £115, accommodation is in tents and activities include walking, mountain-biking, canoeing and horse riding. Visit their Web site at www.bush wakkers.com.

NEIL SETCHFIELD

We're on our way to the Millennium Stadium...

JOHN KING

Cardiff Castle's imposing neo-Gothic clock tower

MANFRED GOTTSCHALK

Caerphilly Castle once had six portcullises and three drawbridges – it's a bit easier to get in to today.

Animal Wall, Bute Park, Cardiff

The subtle fireplace in the Banqueting Hall, Cardiff Castle

Keep an eye out for invaders from the Norman Keep in the grounds of Cardiff Castle.

Just one of the 72,500-seat Millennium Stadium's many functions

Chartist sculpture, Newport

Cardiff & Around

Based on media reports, and on the history of south-east Wales as the locus of intense industrialisation in the late 19th and early 20th centuries, visitors may suspect that there is little here beyond disused docks, rusting railway lines and spoil tips.

Nothing could be further from the truth. Cardiff is Europe's youngest capital, a multicultural city with an eye on the post-industrial future, and plenty to enjoy both inland and down by the sea. The valleys to the north have turned their history – from Norman times to the coal age – into tourist attractions and are threaded with picturesque walking and cycling trails.

Cardiff (Caerdydd)

☎ 029 • pop 320,000

Almost to its own surprise, Wales' capital and industrial centre is in the process of being reinvented.

At the end of the 19th century Cardiff (Caerdydd in Welsh, pronounced **care**-duth) was the grimy nerve centre of the biggest coal-exporting region in the world, a playground for sharp English merchants, the place where the world's first million-pound cheque was written. Its pockets of serious Victorian architecture, its expansive parklands (over 120 hectares' worth, making this one of Europe's greenest cities), its marvellous mock-medieval castle and its vast former docklands testify to that era's heady prosperity.

Two world wars and the Great Depression brought the coal party to an end and nearly turned Cardiff into a backwater, but in 1955 the city was designated the capital of Wales – in a sense the first formal English acknowledgement in nine centuries that there was a country here to be capital of – and in the 1980s it got a grip on itself again. It has been wooing investment, redeveloping like mad, dressing up in some striking architecture and, with some justification,

Highlights

- Playing Norman nabob in the Banqueting Hall of Cardiff Castle
- Getting impressionistic at the National Museum & Gallery of Wales
- Catching a live band and a second pint of Brains SA at Cardiff's Clwb Ifor Bach
- Elevating yourself at Techniquest, the UK's best hands-on science discovery centre
- Letting go on The Big Weekend, the UK's biggest free festival
- Bagging a ticket to an international match at the Millennium Stadium
- Travelling through time at the Museum of Welsh Life, St Fagans

Central Cardiff p134
Cardiff Bay p138
Cathedral Road Area p142

Cardiff p132

Around Cardiff p150

promoting itself as 'Europe's fastest growing capital city'.

Cardiff Bay, once lined with smelly mudflats at low tide, is being turned into a giant freshwater marina. In a physical statement of the city's hopes for the future, the bay and the decaying docklands beside it are slowly morphing into a glossy office and commercial complex, its highest-profile tenant being the new National Assembly for Wales.

For their part, most Cardiffians seem prouder of the city's most visible new landmark, the gargantuan Millennium Stadium, completed for the Rugby World Cup in November 1999 and planted slap bang in the city centre. Another source of pride is the National Museum & Gallery of Wales, home to a superb art collection (including one of the biggest collections of impressionist paintings outside Paris).

Walk through the city centre and you'll notice another refreshing thing about Cardiff: faces and languages from all over the world, many belonging to descendants of those who flocked here during the coal boom to build the docks, work the ships and run the factories. A docklands primary school is said to have kids of 50 different nationalities (Cardiff has one of the biggest Somali communities outside Somalia).

The Cardiff campus of the University of Wales, and the University of Glamorgan about 10 miles to the north, provide youthful leavening and a lively nightlife, and have encouraged a healthy arts scene. With Welsh having achieved official parity with English in Wales, Cardiff is the UK's only genuinely, officially bilingual city.

Of course, as everyone will tell you, Cardiff could not be less like the rest of Wales, but that's no reason to bypass this eager, well-endowed, multicultural city. As Wales moves headlong into the European mainstream, many of its credentials for doing so are here.

It's easy to get to Cardiff, which sits beside the M4 motorway from Bristol and London, and enjoys good long-distance bus and train connections. Extensive, good-value regional transport also makes it a fair base for exploring a wide swathe of southeast Wales, including the lower Rhondda, Cynon and Taff valleys, whose iron and coal put the city on the map.

HISTORY

After a spell as a Roman military outpost, Cardiff slipped into obscurity for most of 1400 years, to be reincarnated only in the last two centuries as a world centre for coal export and, subsequently, as the capital of Wales.

The Romans settled this area, at the mouths of the rivers Taff and Ely, in AD 75, building a fort where their road from Caerleon crossed the estuary. The name Cardiff probably derives from Caer Tâf (Taff Fort) or Caer Didi (Didius' Fort, referring to a Roman general named Aulus Didius).

After the Romans left Britain the site remained more or less unoccupied until the Norman Conquest. In 1093 a Norman knight named Robert Fitzhamon (later earl of Gloucester) built himself a castle here – the remains stand within the grounds of Cardiff Castle – and a small town grew up around it. Ground was broken in 1120 for Llandaff Cathedral. Town and castle were damaged in a Welsh revolt in 1183, and the town was sacked in 1404 by Owain Glendŵr during his ill-fated rebellion against English domination.

The 1536 Act of Union put the English stamp on Cardiff, and brought a measure of stability. The town got its first royal charter in 1581. One of the few city-centre reminders of medieval Cardiff is St John's Church. But despite its importance as a port, boisterous market town and bishopric, old Cardiff failed to grow, and barely 1000 people lived here by the time of the 1801 census.

The city really owes its present stature to iron and then coal mining in the valleys to the north. Coal was first exported from Cardiff on a small scale as far back as 1600. In 1794 the Bute family (see the boxed text 'The Bute Family') – who owned much of the land under which Wales' coal was eventually to be found – completed the Glamorganshire Canal for the shipment of iron from Merthyr Tydfil down to Cardiff.

In 1840 this was supplanted by the new Taff Vale Railway. A year earlier the second marquis of Bute had completed the first docks at Butetown, just south of Cardiff,

The Bute Family

The Butes, an aristocratic Scottish family, arrived in Cardiff in 1766 in the shape of John, Lord Mountstuart, who had served briefly as prime minister under King George III. He married a local heiress, Charlotte Jane Windsor, in the process acquiring vast estates (including a run-down Cardiff Castle) and mineral rights.

Their grandson, the second marquis of Bute, essentially built modern Cardiff. He grew fabulously wealthy from coal mining, then in 1839 gambled his fortune in creating the first docks at Cardiff. His son, John Patrick Crichton-Stuart, third marquis of Bute, became in his time one of the richest people on the planet. He was an intense, scholarly man – said to be fluent in six languages – with a passion for history, architecture, ritual and religion. It was he and architect William Burges who transformed Cardiff Castle and Castell Coch into neo-Gothic masterpieces.

But the Butes had interests all over Britain, and had never spent more than about six weeks at a time in Cardiff. By the end of WWII they had sold or given away all their Cardiff assets. The present marquis, the seventh, lives in Mount Stuart House on the isle of Bute, in Scotland's Firth of Clyde; he's better known as Johnny Dumfries, the Formula 1 racing driver.

getting the jump on other South Wales ports. By the time it dawned on everyone what immense reserves of coal there were in the valleys – setting off a kind of gold-rush fever – the Butes were in a position to insist that it be shipped from Butetown. Cardiff was off and running.

The docklands expanded rapidly, the Butes grew staggeringly rich and the city boomed, its population mushrooming to 170,000 by the end of the century and to 227,000 by 1931. A vast, multi-tongued workers' community known as Tiger Bay grew up in the harbourside area of Butetown. In 1905 Cardiff was officially designated a city, and a year later its elegant Civic Centre was inaugurated. The city's wealth and its hold on

the coal trade persuaded Captain Robert Scott to launch his ill-fated expedition to the South Pole from here in 1910. In 1913 Cardiff became the world's top coal port, exporting some 13 million tons of the stuff.

But hard times returned all too soon, with the post-WWI slump in the coal trade and the Great Depression of the 1930s. The city was badly damaged by WWII bombing, which claimed over 350 lives. Postwar reconstruction is responsible for some of the centre's more dismal modern architecture, although in 1947 the Bute family donated its castle and grounds to the city.

Cardiff's designation in 1955 as Wales' capital – making it Europe's youngest capital – gave it a new lease of life, as Wales-related government agencies relocated here. But the docklands never recovered, and it wasn't until the creation of the Cardiff Bay Development Corporation in 1987 that a serious effort was undertaken to revive the area.

ORIENTATION

Cardiff's working-class heart in the days of the coal boom was the harbourside community of Butetown, where the Taff empties into the Bristol Channel. The city centre today is over a mile inland via four-lane Lloyd George Blvd, though the harbour area is being reinvented as the Cardiff Bay development (see Cardiff Bay later in the chapter).

Central Cardiff is compact enough to explore on foot. The most prominent landmarks here are the massive Millennium Stadium, by the river, and nearby Cardiff Castle. A compact shopping, entertainment and restaurant zone – laced with turn-of-the-century arcades – is bounded by the shopping precincts of High St, St Mary St and pedestrianised Queen St; and by Mill Lane, Bridge St and Charles St. City Hall and other government buildings occupy the Civic Centre, north of the castle.

Facing Central Square, near the southern end of St Mary St, are the Tourist Information Centre (TIC), the central bus station and Cardiff Central train station. Canton is the area north-west across the river with lots of B&Bs and laid-back cafes and restaurants.

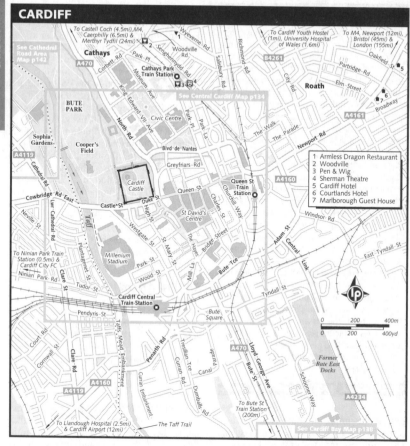

CARDIFF

1 Armless Dragon Restaurant
2 Woodville
3 Pen & Wig
4 Sherman Theatre
5 Cardiff Hotel
6 Courtlands Hotel
7 Marlborough Guest House

Many Cardiff streets change names in the middle – eg, High St and St Mary St (local people tend to call the whole thing St Mary St). The roads around Cardiff Bay seem to shift their very position by the week, as development continues.

INFORMATION
Tourist Offices

The TIC (☎ 2022 7281, fax 2023 9162, e enquiries@cardifftic.co.uk), 16 Wood St, opens 9 am to 5 pm (to 6 pm in July and August) Monday to Saturday, and 10 am to 4 pm on Sunday. It stocks the free *Cardiff 2001* (or its annually updated version), a detailed visitors guide.

Here you can also buy the great-value Cardiff Card (£11) which gives a day's unlimited travel with Cardiff Bus and Valley Lines trains, and free admission to a wide range of attractions including the National Museum, Techniquest, Castell Coch, Caerphilly Castle, Rhondda Heritage Park (see Around Cardiff later in the chapter) and the Big Pit Museum (see under Blaenafon in the Brecon Beacons chapter). It's also good for discounts at a few restaurants. See the Web site at www .cardiff-card.co.uk for more information.

Money

All major UK banks (with ATMs and currency desks) are represented along Queen St and/or High St.

Post

The main post office is on The Hayes, near St David's Shopping Centre. This is also the place for poste restante in Cardiff (postcode CF10 2SJ). A useful branch for those staying along Cathedral Rd, north-west of the centre, is at 91 Pontcanna St.

Email & Internet Access

Free Internet access is available at Cardiff Central Library (see under Libraries); booking is advisable. The 24-hour Cardiff Internet Café (☎ 2023 2313), 15–17 Wyndham Arcade, charges £1.50/£1/75p for the first/second/subsequent quarter-hour (£1/80p/45p from 11 am to 8 am); Youth Hostel Association (YHA), ISIC and other cards are good for discounts. Cardiff Cybercafé (☎ 2023 5757), upstairs at 9 Duke St, opens 10 am to 7 pm weekdays (to 6 pm Saturday, 11 am to 5 pm Sunday), and charges £1.25 per quarter-hour or £4.50 per hour.

Travel Agencies

There's a branch of usit Campus (☎ 2022 0744) inside the YHA Adventure Shop at 13 Castle St. STA Travel (☎ 2038 2350) is in the Duke St Arcade, 11 Duke St.

Bookshops

Cardiff's most complete bookshop is Blackwell's, 13–17 Royal Arcade. Waterstone's has two branches, at 2a The Hayes and nearby at 18–20 Hills St. The best source of specialist Welsh-language (and other) books is Oriel on High St.

Libraries

Cardiff Central Library (☎ 2038 2116) on Frederick St opens 9 am to 5.30 pm Monday to Saturday (to 6.30 pm Thursday and 5 pm Saturday).

Universities

The Cardiff campus of the University of Wales, near Alexandra Gardens, has about 15,000 students, most living in the neighbourhoods of Cathays and Roath, north of the city centre.

Laundry

There's a laundrette at 87 Pontcanna St, Cathedral Road area, open 9 am to 9 pm (to 6 pm weekends).

Left Luggage

You can leave luggage at the train station for £3 an item; the desk is staffed from 8 am to 6 pm (from noon on Sunday).

Medical Services & Emergency

The University Hospital of Wales (☎ 2074 7747) in Heath Park, 2 miles north of the Civic Centre (Cardiff Bus No 1 from the centre; 85p, 35 minutes), has an accident and emergency department. Next-closest is Llandough Hospital (☎ 2071 1711) in Penarth, about 3 miles south-west.

Pharmacies rotate late opening hours; check the regional *South Wales Echo* newspaper for details. Boots (☎ 2023 1291), 36 Queen St, opens until 8 pm Thursday.

Police headquarters (☎ 2022 2111) are on King Edward VII Ave in the Civic Centre.

Disabled Travellers

Cardiff Shopmobility (☎ 2039 9355) is a charity that provides wheelchairs and electric scooters for the disabled to get around the central shopping area. There's no charge but donations are welcome. It has its own entrance to the Oxford Arcade car park on Bridge St; its offices are also here.

The TIC can advise on disabled-friendly places to stay. A recommended taxi company is City Centre Cars (☎ 2048 8888).

Gay & Lesbian Travellers

Cardiff has Wales' most relaxed gay/lesbian community by a long way.

Three useful helplines are Friend South Wales (☎ 2034 0101), open 8 to 10 pm Wednesday to Friday; Lesbian Line (☎ 2037 4051); and Cardiff Aidsline (☎ 2022 3443 or 0800 074 3445, e aidshelpline@celtic.co .uk), open 10 am to 10 pm weekdays. Older

& Bolder, a contact group for lesbians aged over 35, meets on the first Saturday of each month at the Friends Meeting House on Charles St.

The nightlife scene is 'weekendy', with lots of people coming in from smaller towns in the region; see Entertainment later in the chapter. The biggest gay/lesbian event is the Mardi Gras festival on the first Saturday of September (see under Special Events later in the chapter). The city has one gay-run B&B – the Courtfield Hotel (see Places to Stay later in the chapter).

For much more Cardiff (and Wales-wide) information, see the Gay Wales Web site at www.gaywales.co.uk.

CENTRAL CARDIFF
Cardiff Castle

It would be hard to miss Cardiff Castle, which stands out almost incongruously from the shops across the road. Excavations indicate that the site was first occupied by the Romans in the 1st century AD, although the earliest substantial remains are an 11th-century Norman keep on a motte (hill) dominating the inner grounds.

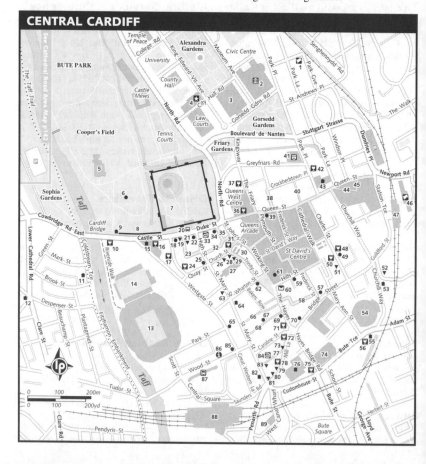

CENTRAL CARDIFF

A house was built here in the 1420s by the earl of Warwick, and extended in the 17th century by the Herbert family, the earls of Pembroke, but by the time the Butes acquired it a century later it had fallen into disrepair. The first marquis of Bute hired architect Henry Holland and Holland's father-in-law, the famous landscape architect Lancelot 'Capability' Brown, to get house and grounds into shape.

The present castle was designed for the third marquis by the Gothic Revival architect William Burges (1827–81). Both men were obsessed with things medieval, and the marquis gave Burges free rein with his eccentric fantasies (both here and elsewhere in the city). The splendid clock tower was his first project, completed in 1872 as a series of 'medieval' bachelor apartments for the young marquis.

The castle's interior is spectacular, though so over-the-top that it now seems more Hollywood than medieval. Only a few rooms – the huge Banqueting Hall (originally the castle's private chambers), the Islamic-inspired Arab Room and the fairy-tale Nursery – are open to the public, and only on a guided tour.

The castle (☎ 2087 8100) and grounds open 9.30 am to 6 pm daily, March to October, with hour-long castle tours at 20-minute intervals. Winter hours are 9.30 am to 4.30 pm, with five tours daily. A visit and tour costs £5/3 (adult/concession). A visit only to the grounds and a small museum devoted to South Wales' indigenous infantry, the Welch Regiment Museum, costs £2.50/1.50.

CENTRAL CARDIFF

PLACES TO STAY

9	West Lodge
11	Austin's Guest House
12	Cardiff Backpacker
15	Angel Hotel
43	Park Thistle Hotel
53	Ibis Hotel
55	Big Sleep Hotel
64	Sandringham Hotel; Café Jazz
76	Cardiff Marriott Hotel
82	Travelodge

PLACES TO EAT

19	Celtic Cauldron
21	Café Minuet
26	Topo Gigio
27	Cardiff Market
28	Cornish Bakehouse
29	Le Café Francais
51	Metropolis Restaurant & Bar
52	Thai House Restaurant
63	Oz Bar
73	Beaz Neez Café
79	Las Iguanas
80	Casablanca
81	La Brasserie; Champers
83	Servini's

PUBS, BARS & CLUBS

10	Callaghan's
16	Angel Tavern
17	Toucan Club
24	Clwb Ifor Bach
31	Owain Glyndŵr
36	Vision 2K
37	Bar Cuba
42	Scrum
48	Club X; The Edge
50	Exit Club
56	Out Bar; Atlantica
71	Duke of Wellington
72	King's Cross
75	Golden Cross
78	Continentals; Latino's

OTHER

1	Italian Consulate
2	National Museum & Gallery of Wales
3	City Hall
4	Police Headquarters
5	Remains of Blackfriars Priory
6	Gorsedd Stones
7	Cardiff Castle; Welch Regiment Museum
8	Animal Wall
13	Millennium Stadium
14	Cardiff Arms Park
18	usit Campus; YHA Adventure Shop
20	Guide Friday Tourbus Stop
22	Castle Welshcrafts
23	Castle Arcade
25	Oriel Bookshop
30	St John's Church
32	High Street Arcade
33	Cardiff Cybercafé
34	STA Travel
35	Duke Street Arcade
38	Dominions Arcade
39	Boots Chemist
40	Andrews Arcade
41	New Theatre
44	Capitol Arcade
45	Llandaff Arcade
46	Irish Consulate; Brunel House
47	Queen St Train Station
49	Friends Meeting House
54	Cardiff International Arena
57	Cardiff Central Library
58	Oxford Arcade
59	Waterstone's Bookshop
60	Main Post Office
61	St David's Hall
62	Waterstone's Bookshop
65	Ticketline
66	Morgan Arcade
67	Blackwell's Bookshop
68	Royal Arcade
69	Spiller's
70	Cardiff Shopmobility
74	Ice House
77	Wyndham Arcade
84	Cardiff Internet Café
85	Cardiff Bus Office
86	Tourist Information Centre
87	Central Bus Station
88	Cardiff Central Train Station
89	Jacob's Market

A bit of original Roman masonry can be seen below a line of red stone blocks in the outer wall – eg, near the south-east corner.

Bute Park

Vast, peaceful parklands north-west of the city centre include 56-hectare Bute Park, landscaped in the 1870s by Scots landscape architect Andrew Pettigrew and donated to the city by the Butes in 1947. This, and Sophia Gardens, Pontcanna Fields and Llandaff Fields across the river, form a 2-mile-long corridor of green along the river. All were part of Bute holdings that once extended all the way to Castell Coch (see Around Cardiff later).

A low wall with sculpted lions, seals, bears and other creatures climbing over it runs along the Castle St (south) side of the park. The 'Animal Wall' was designed by William Burges (see Cardiff Castle earlier) but only completed in 1892 after his death. The wall was extended and more animals added in the 1920s. A newspaper cartoon strip in the 1930s brought the animals to life, and many Cardiff kids grew up thinking the animals came alive at night.

In Cooper's Field, part of the park just behind the castle, is a stone circle – not Neolithic but *fin-de-siècle* – erected in 1899 when Cardiff hosted the Royal National Eisteddfod (see the Facts about Wales chapter for more on these festivals). Such so-called *gorsedd* stones are found all over Wales where eisteddfodau have been held.

Nearby are the foundations of the 13th-century Blackfriars Priory, destroyed in 1404 when Owain Glyndŵr attacked Cardiff and later rebuilt and finally vacated in 1538 when the monasteries were dissolved. West Lodge, a small gatehouse facing Castle St, is listed in the *Guinness Book of Records* as the world's smallest hotel; see Places to Stay later.

National Museum & Gallery of Wales

At Cathays (ka-**tice**) Park, a stately neoclassical ensemble of green lawns and white Portland stone buildings – looking for all the world like a Welsh New Delhi – is Cardiff's civic centre. Here are City Hall, the police station and law courts, crown offices, and the splendid National Museum & Gallery of Wales.

This is one of the UK's best museums, and a must-see, especially if you're here with kids. Most city museums have a bit on local history – Cardiff's reaches back to the dawn of time, with a first-rate multimedia astronomy/geology/archaeology exhibit that puts Wales into context in a big way. In the natural history section is the complete skeleton of a humpback whale that washed up near Aberthaw in 1982.

Pride of place goes to the museum's paintings, including a fine impressionist and postimpressionist collection bequeathed to the museum in 1952 (with more in 1963) by the Davies sisters, Gwendoline and Margaret, granddaughters of 19th-century coal and shipping magnate David Davies (for more on them, see Around Newtown in the Mid Wales chapter).

The museum's Glanely Gallery is a state-of-the-art interactive area where you can 'examine' items from collections not on display. There are numerous changing exhibitions, recitals and a holiday program of children's events.

The museum (☎ 2039 7951), run by National Museums & Galleries of Wales (NMGW), opens 10 am to 5 pm, Tuesday to Sunday, and on bank-holiday Mondays. Admission costs £4.50 (but is free to anyone aged under 19 or over 60).

St John's Church

Jutting up from the shopping precinct is the incongruously graceful Gothic tower of the 15th-century parish church of St John the Baptist – a retreat from the bustle outside and one of the city centre's few reminders of Cardiff's pre-Victorian past.

Millennium Stadium

Whether you're a sports fan or not, you'll have to admit that the Millennium Stadium is impressive. The Welsh certainly do: attendance at international matches has increased dramatically since this 72,500-seat, three-tiered monster venue with the sliding roof was completed in time to host the 1999 Rugby World Cup. The FA Cup final (English football's biggest event) was held here in 2001 and will be for at least the next two years (2002–3).

Not everybody likes it all the time. One architectural critic called it an 'absurdly overexcited structure...that rear[s] over the surrounding streets like a sumo wrestler'. It cost £110 million to build – money that some feel could have been better spent elsewhere in the city. And big matches paralyse the city centre, giving the emergency services fits. But when the singing starts in the stands, the whole city resonates and nobody minds.

The stadium has seven restaurants and 22 public bars (drinking is allowed during rugby matches but not football matches). The real grass turf is actually grown on thousands of palettes (at RAF St Athan in the Vale of Glamorgan), which can be taken up for big concerts.

Diehard sports fans can sit in a VIP box or walk down the tunnel to the pitch as part of guided tours (£5/2.50) available 10 am to 6 pm (to 5 pm on Sunday). For information dial ☎ 0870 558 2582 or visit on-line at www.cardiff-stadium.co.uk.

For details of matches see Spectator Sports later in the section.

Llandaff Cathedral

If Cardiff gets too busy for you, hop on bus No 25, 33 or 63 (£1.10, every 10–15 minutes) along Cathedral Rd to Llandaff, a peaceful, pretty northern suburb 2 miles from the centre, where Llandaff Cathedral sits in a dip in the landscape, on the site of a 6th-century monastery founded by St Teilo.

The present church dates from 1130, though it was largely rebuilt in the 19th century, and extensively restored after being damaged by a German landmine in 1941. The west-end towers epitomise the cathedral's fragmented history: one was built in the 15th century, the other in the 19th. Inside, a giant arch carries the organ and Sir Jacob Epstein's striking aluminium sculp-

ture *Majestas*. Fans of the Pre-Raphaelites will like the Burne-Jones reredos (screens) in St Dyfrig's chapel and the stained glass by Rossetti and William Morris' company.

CARDIFF BAY

As Cardiff's port declined in importance in the 20th century, the docklands decayed, cut off by the railway embankment and full of rundown housing and empty basins. The bay – with one of the highest tidal ranges in the world (over 12m) – was ringed for up to 14 hours a day by smelly, sewage-stained mudflats.

Since 1987 an ambitious project has been underway to bring the area back to life and – as the brochures like to say – reconnect Cardiff with its maritime past. The result is Cardiff Bay, a massive (1080 hectares) commercial redevelopment in the area of the old harbour and Bute East Docks.

Not that it looks anything like it once did. A £220-million tidal barrage now keeps the sea out, and when it's working properly will turn the mudflats into a 200-hectare freshwater lake (the thousands of wading birds that once fed on the mudflats will, it is hoped, find solace in a wetlands reserve being developed up the Severn Estuary towards Newport).

The highest-profile resident is the National Assembly for Wales, which will make its permanent home here. Restaurants, bars and scores of other commercial and leisure facilities have been coaxed in. On the drawing board is the Ferry Road Sports Village, to include a new stadium for the Cardiff City football team, a new rink for the Cardiff Devils ice hockey team and a swimming pool.

The proposed centrepiece was to be a dazzling opera house designed by architect Zaha Hadid, which might have done for Cardiff what the Opera House did for Sydney. But it fell victim to a 'no' campaign orchestrated by the local press, which called it elitist. Then the Millennium Commission decided to spend its money elsewhere (on the Millennium Stadium). At the time of writing, even its modest replacement – a multipurpose cultural venue to be called the Millennium Centre – was in doubt as harbour landowners grew impatient with political dithering.

In any case, the area is coming back to life and is worth half a day's exploration. A mile-long roadway and rail spur and several bus services, connect it to the city centre (see Getting There & Away later in the section).

Information

The Cardiff Bay Visitors Centre (☎ 2046 3833, fax 2046 8850), housed in an arresting silver tube on the eastern side of the harbour, has an immense model of Cardiff Bay and sells maps and booklets on the area and its history. It opens 9.30 am to 5 pm (from 10.30 am at weekends).

Inside the Pierhead Building (see the next section) is a new, high-tech information centre (☎ 2089 8200, fax 2089 8229) for the National Assembly, open 9.30 am to 4.30 pm weekdays (from 10 am on Friday).

Harbourside

At present the most appealing landmark is the **Pierhead Building**, a staid neo-Gothic confection in red brick, built with Bute money for the Cardiff Municipal Railway Co. This is one of the area's few Victorian survivors, now all alone in a sea of paving stones.

Hasty commercial development has given the harbourside **Mermaid Quay** a tacky feel, though it's well stocked with banks, restaurants and high-street shops. Nearby is the **Oval Basin**, a sculpted depression intended as an open-air performance area, overlooked by a silver phallus called the **Water Sculpture**.

The whitewashed **Norwegian Church** by the visitors centre was built in 1869 beside the now-gone Bute West Dock as a seamen's mission, modelled on the lines of a traditional Norwegian village church. It eventually fell into disrepair, but continued to serve as a place of worship until 1974. Children's

CARDIFF BAY

PLACES TO STAY
9   St David's Hotel & Spa

PLACES TO EAT
3   Baytree Café
5   Buff's Restaurant
12 Eli Jenkins Pub
13 Tiger Bay Café

OTHER
1   The Wharf
2   Butetown History & Arts Centre
4   Coal Exchange
6   Guide Friday Tourbus Stop
7   Guide Friday Tourbus Stop
8   Techniquest
10 Via Fosse
11 Mermaid Quay; Cardiff Cats Boat Tours
14 Water Sculpture
15 Site of Proposed Millennium Centre
16 Oval Basin
17 Pierhead Building
18 Future Site of National Assembly for Wales
19 Crickhowell House (National Assembly for Wales)
20 Cardiff Bay Road Train
21 NCM Building; Netherlands Consulate
22 Guide Friday Tourbus Stop
23 Cardiff Bay Visitors Centre
24 Norwegian Church; Arts Centre Cafe

author Roald Dahl, born in Cardiff, was christened here, and served as president of the preservation trust that dismantled and re-located the church. It has now been reincarnated as an arts centre (☎ 2045 4899) with a good cafe. It opens 10 am to 4 pm daily. Admission is free.

The plain red-brick structure east of the Pierhead Building is Crickhowell House, present home of the **National Assembly for Wales**. Members debate in a converted car park beneath it, but a striking new chamber is to be built in the space next door. The Assembly usually meets in plenary session from 2 pm on Tuesday and Wednesday, and seats in the public gallery are on a first-come-first-served basis. You can peek at the chamber when it's not in use, from 9.30 am to 4.30 pm weekdays (only until noon on Friday).

The box with the funny roof across the inner harbour is the £25-million **St David's Hotel & Spa**, owned by hotel and restaurant magnate Sir Rocco Forte (see also Places to Stay later in the chapter).

Techniquest

West of Mermaid Quay is Techniquest (☎ 2047 5475), the UK's biggest and best hands-on science and technology discovery centre, with everything from square bubbles and a machine that blows smoke rings to a planetarium and a science theatre. It opens 9.30 am to 4.30 pm weekdays and 10.30 am to 5 pm at weekends. Admission costs £5.50/3.80 (free with a Cardiff Card; see Tourist Offices under Information earlier).

Butetown

Mount Stuart Square, two blocks from the bay, is the Victorian heart of old Butetown. The old **Coal Exchange** in the centre was once the nerve centre of the Welsh coal trade, and for a time the place where international coal prices were set. It was here that a coal merchant wrote the world's first one million pound cheque, in March 1908. The Exchange is now an arts and performance venue.

The **Butetown History & Arts Centre** (☎ 2025 6757, fax 2025 5887, **e** info@bhac

.org), 5 Dock Chambers, Bute St, is a gallery and archive centre devoted to preserving oral histories, documents and images of the docklands. Its regular photographic exhibits are about the only way to visualise the area as it was. The gallery opens 11.30 am to 4.30 pm Tuesday to Sunday. See the Web site at www.bhac.org.

Getting There & Away

Roads around Cardiff Bay constantly mutate as development proceeds, so it's worth verifying the following before you go.

Cardiff Bus services (55p, about 15 minutes, four hourly) include No 7 (Wyndham Arcade on St Mary St to Mermaid Quay), No 8 (Wood St to Atlantic Wharf only) and No 6 (central station, rush hour only). With a Cardiff Card (see Information earlier), Guide Friday tour buses (see Organised Tours later) are a slow but free and entertaining way to get there.

Shuttle trains run from Queen Street station to Bute Street station (from £1.30 off-peak; three minutes; four hourly on weekdays, two hourly Saturday, none on Sunday), from where the harbour is a quarter-mile walk. From Central station the trip costs the same and takes 15 minutes with a change at Queen St. Future plans include a tram line from the centre beside Lloyd George Ave.

A taxi from the bus station costs about £4.

ORGANISED TOURS

From April to early November, open-top bus tours run by Guide Friday (☎ 2038 4291) circulate from the Civic Centre to Cardiff Bay. Buses depart from Cardiff Castle every half-hour from 10 am to at least 4 pm. You can hop off at any of about 10 points, snoop around and catch the next bus that comes along. The whole circuit, if you don't get off, takes an hour. Tickets cost £7/2.50 (£5.50 students; free with a Cardiff Card).

From Easter to October, Cardiff Cats (☎ 2048 8842, **e** yotty@msn.com) runs excursion boats on a 30- to 45-minute circuit of Cardiff Bay, stopping at Mermaid Quay (between Cadwalader's Ice Cream and the

Bosporus Restaurant) and at Penarth Marina near the tidal barrage. You can catch one about every 15 to 30 minutes from 7 am to 11 pm daily. Tickets (£3/2) are sold on board.

The Cardiff Bay Road Train (☎ 2075 1413, mobile ☎ 07977 905389) tootles around Cardiff Bay daily in July and August, and at weekends and school holidays the rest of the year. The half-hour excursion, starting in front of the NCM building, costs £2/1 (families £5).

SPECIAL EVENTS

The biggest thing on the calendar is the three-week, midsummer Cardiff Festival (☎ 2087 3690). Events include the Welsh Proms, 10 days of concerts at St David's Hall; two days of comedy acts at the Sherman Theatre; a Celtic Food & Drink Festival; two weekends of open-air music and street theatre on Queen St; and a carnival at Mermaid Quay with massed samba bands and dance troupes. The fun culminates with the UK's largest open-air free festival, The Big Weekend (the first weekend in August), with the Lord Mayor's Parade, a funfair and live bands at the Civic Centre.

Gŵyl Ifan (☎ 2056 3989) is the UK's biggest festival of folk dancing – a weekend in late June featuring troupes from Wales and other Celtic nations, a Twmpath (traditional Welsh barn dance) and an all-night bash at the Civic Centre on Saturday.

Mardi Gras is Cardiff's gay-pride festival, a 'family-friendly' event at Cooper's Field, behind the castle, on the first Saturday of September. For more information see the link from the Gay Wales Web site, www .gaywales.co.uk, or contact Cardiff County Council (☎ 2087 2000, fax 2087 3209).

The International Film Festival of Wales (IFFW), born in Aberystwyth but now relocated here, is a showcase for home-grown talent in both languages. A highlight is the £25,000 DM Davies Award for a Welsh-origin or Welsh-resident director of a short film. The festival takes place in late November, though at the time of writing the venue(s) hadn't been sorted out. For more information contact the IFFW at ☎ 2040 6220, or check out the Web site at www.iffw.co.uk.

PLACES TO STAY

When big sports events take place in Cardiff at the weekend, it can be hard to find a bed in the city centre, so if you're particular, call ahead.

Camping

Quiet but almost shouting distance from the city centre is the county-run *Cardiff Caravan Park* (☎ 2039 8362, Pontcanna Fields), off Cathedral Rd (enter via the Welsh Institute for Sport; see Hostels). Sample rates are £3 per person (no extra charge for a tent) or £11.60 for a caravan. It opens year round.

Hostels

Cardiff Backpacker (☎ 2034 5577, fax 2023 0404, 98 Neville St, Riverside) is a well run, popular independent hostel just over half a mile from the train and bus stations. The cheapest beds are in small dorms (£14); spartan singles/doubles/triples cost £21/34/41 (light breakfast included). They have a bar and a few secure parking spaces, and will collect you from the station if the weather's lousy or you're on your own. Booking ahead is advisable.

Another bargain is the *Welsh Institute for Sport* (☎ 2030 0500, fax 2030 0600, e wis@scw.co.uk, Sophia Gardens), just off Cathedral Rd. A plain en-suite double costs £25 with breakfast; other meals are available, and guests can use the pool and fitness room for free. It gets booked out for big weekend sports events so call ahead.

At the year-round YHA/Hostelling International (HI) *Cardiff Youth Hostel* (☎ 2046 2303, 2 Wedal Rd, Roath Park), a bed costs £13.50/10.20 with continental breakfast. The hostel is in the student area, 2 miles north of the city centre; take bus No 80 or 82 from the central bus station to the Wedal Rd stop (80p; four hourly, Sunday two hourly).

Student Accommodation

Cardiff University (☎ 2087 5508, fax 2087 4990, e groupaccom@cardiff.ac.uk) has some 4800 single bedrooms, half of them en suite, available June to September, with options for breakfast and self-catering. About 2000 rooms are within a 15-minute walk of the city centre. Prices range from £11.50 to £20.50 per night.

B&Bs & Hotels

Categories are muddled in Cardiff, so B&Bs and hotels are listed together here; hotels tend to have a reception desk, room service, licensed bar, off-street parking and other extras.

Accommodation in the centre tends to be top-end. Two neighbourhoods full of budget accommodation are tree-lined Cathedral Rd, across the river to the north-west, and more-downmarket Newport Rd, north-east from Queen Street station. Both are a 15- to 20-minute walk from the centre, or take a taxi for £3 to £4 from the train or bus station.

B&Bs & Hotels – Centre

The closest budget B&B to the centre is probably *Austin's Guest House* (☎ 2037 7148, fax 2037 7158, 11 Coldstream Terrace), across the Taff from the Millennium Stadium. Singles/doubles with shower cost £25/40, including a light breakfast.

Of many chain hotels, the *Ibis* (☎ 2064 9250, fax 2064 9260, Churchill Way), sterile but well run, has no-frills en suites for £42. The *Travelodge* (☎ 2039 8697, Imperial Gate, St Mary St) charges £50. The *Park Thistle* (☎ 2038 3471, Park Place), off Queen St, charges from £82, and the *Cardiff Marriott* (☎ 2039 9944, Mill Lane) £99. Breakfast is extra at all of these places; weekend rates are about 20% lower at some.

The most central hotel is probably the *Sandringham* (☎ 2023 2161, fax 2038 3998, 21 St Mary St), with well furnished but street-noisy en-suite singles/doubles for £40/49.

The high-rise *Big Sleep Hotel* (☎ 2063 6363, fax 2063 6364, ⓔ bookings@ thebigsleephotel.com, Bute Terrace) is a smart 'designer' hotel with huge, bright, minimalist rooms and long views. Doubles cost £58 mid-week or from £45 at week-

ends, including light breakfast; there's one splendid penthouse for £85. It's opposite the Cardiff International Arena, five minutes' walk from the centre, and has free off-street parking. View the rooms on-line at www.thebigsleephotel.com.

For something out of the ordinary, the castellated gatehouse near the castle is, according to the *Guinness Book of Records*, the world's smallest hotel; American hoteliers Bart and Iris Zuzik live at the *West Lodge* (☎/fax 2034 4896, Castle St) and let out one double room for £55 (including full American breakfast). The *Angel Hotel* (☎ 2064 9200, fax 2039 6212, ⓔ angel@ paramount-hotels.co.uk, Castle St), opposite the castle, was founded in 1883 by the third marquis of Bute. Doubles cost £130 (but £78 for weekend B&B, subject to availability).

B&Bs & Hotels – Cathedral Rd & Around

Leafy Cathedral Rd has a wide range of budget to mid-range accommodation, nearly all of it in restored Victorian townhouses; following are a few examples. Rooms have en-suite facilities except as noted, and prices include breakfast.

For singles/doubles from around £25/ 40, good choices are the *Penrhys Hotel* (☎ 2038 7292, fax 2066 6344, 127 Cathedral Rd) and nonsmoking *Anedd Lon Guest House* (☎ 2022 3349, fax 2064 0885, 157 Cathedral Rd), which has off-street parking. Others in this range include the *Georgian Hotel* (☎/fax 2023 2594, 179 Cathedral Rd) and *Maxine's Hotel* (☎ 2022 0288, fax 2034 4884, 150 Cathedral Rd), which has a few cheaper rooms with shared facilities.

The *Town House* (☎ 2023 9399, fax 2022 3214, ⓔ thetownhouse@msn.com, 70 Cathedral Rd) offers good value at £40/50, with comfortable, well furnished rooms, a generous breakfast and private parking. The gay-run *Courtfield Hotel* (☎/fax 2022 7701, ⓔ courtfield@ntlworld.com, 101 Cathedral Rd) has rather plain rooms for £45/55 and a few singles with shared facilities for £25. Both have off-street parking.

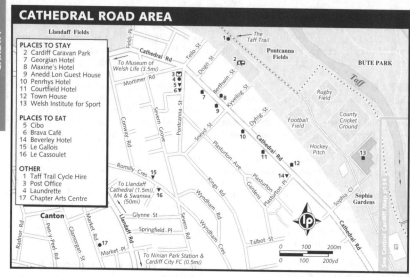

CATHEDRAL ROAD AREA

PLACES TO STAY
2 Cardiff Caravan Park
7 Georgian Hotel
8 Maxine's Hotel
9 Anedd Lon Guest House
10 Penrhys Hotel
11 Courtfield Hotel
12 Town House
13 Welsh Institute for Sport

PLACES TO EAT
5 Cibo
6 Brava Café
14 Beverley Hotel
15 Le Gallois
16 Le Cassoulet

OTHER
1 Taff Trail Cycle Hire
3 Post Office
4 Laundrette
17 Chapter Arts Centre

B&Bs & Hotels – Newport Rd

Every other house here seems to call itself a 'hotel', though not all are worth your money. A few reliable ones at the lower end – most with shared facilities and some private parking – are the basic *Cardiff Hotel (☎ 2049 1964, 138 Newport Rd)* with rooms from £21/33; *Courtlands Hotel (☎ 2049 7583, 110 Newport Rd)* at £30/40 (mostly en suite); and *Marlborough Guest House (☎ 2049 2385, fax 2046 5982, 98 Newport Road)* at £39/49 plus en-suite doubles for £55.

For more places farther out on Newport Rd, hop on bus No 30 (55p, three hourly).

Hotels – Cardiff Bay

The prestige address to bed down at here is *St David's Hotel & Spa (☎ 2045 4045, fax 2048 7056, Havanna St)*, with its striking, minimalist foyer. Every room looks out across the bay; a double costs £160 mid-week or £110 at weekends.

PLACES TO EAT

Amidst much run-of-the-mill food, Cardiff does have a few places which stand out for price, quality or both. Note that some quite pricey places have fairly affordable lunch

specials. Only a few places (noted here) open on Sunday, though you can usually find pub food somewhere if you don't leave it until late in the evening.

City Centre

Opposite the castle, the vest-pocket *Café Minuet (42 Castle Arcade)* delivers generous helpings of first-rate Italian food, carefully prepared by its proud and eccentric owner, to the sound of classical music. Of Cardiff's many Italian restaurants, this seems to be the best value in the centre.

Across the arcade, the little *Celtic Cauldron (☎ 2038 7185, 44 Castle Arcade)* presents adequate wholefood versions of traditional Welsh dishes such as laverbread, cawl (see Food in the Facts for the Visitor chapter) and oatmeal pancakes until 5 pm (4 pm on Sunday).

Appealing options around St John's Church include *Le Café Francais (☎ 2064 5188, Trinity St)*, where the baguette fillings are imaginative and the atmosphere laid-back; the *Cornish Bakehouse* on the corner of Trinity and Church Sts, with every kind of pasty, plus muffins and coffee; and lively *Topo Gigio (☎ 2034 5903, 12 Church St)*, serving pizza and pasta from about £7, noon to 11.30 pm daily.

A popular lunch spot is **Servini's** (*☎ 2039 4054, 10 Wyndham Arcade*), with big breakfasts, chicken curry or spicy Cajun chicken for £5, plus fresh salads. It opens daily except Sunday. For pub grub or an all-day meaty breakfast try the **Oz Bar** (*☎ 2066 8008, 112 St Mary St*).

Mill Lane is sometimes called Cardiff's Cafe Quarter. It's only 50m long but several lively places give it a vibrant atmosphere. **Las Iguanas** (*☎ 2022 6373, 8 Mill Lane*) is a Mexican joint offering one/two/three-course lunches for £4/5/6 and evening dishes (with live music) from £6. Moroccan/Iberian **Casablanca** (*☎ 2064 1441, 3 Mill Lane*) has tapas from £4 and tasty main courses from £10.

Around the corner (and cheaper), **La Brasserie** and **Champers** (*☎ 2037 2164, 2037 3363, 60–1 St Mary St*), neighbouring restaurants with the same owner, offer an arresting range of Spanish/French/Welsh dishes, including seafood – and a generous £6 set lunch.

The **Metropolis Restaurant & Bar** (*☎ 2034 4300, 60 Charles St*) is an easygoing bistro-bar with £4 stuffed baguettes, two/three-course set lunches for £9/11 (except Sunday) and imaginative dinner courses from £7 to £14. The bar stays open until 2 am Friday and Saturday.

The **Thai House Restaurant** (*☎ 2038 7404, 3–4 Guildford Crescent*) offers a change of pace with noodle and rice dishes from £5 at lunchtime. Evening meals are pricey, with a £15 minimum. It opens daily except Sunday.

Cardiff Market (*The Hayes*) is the city's handsome Victorian shopping arena, the place for bread, cheese, cold meats, laverbread and other picnic goodies.

Around Cathedral Rd

Popular, no-frills **Cibo** (*☎ 2023 2226, 83 Pontcanna St*) is a cafe-bar with Italian staff, Italian beer and wine and some very good Italian dishes to eat in or take away; it opens 10 am to 10 pm daily (from noon Monday). A few doors down, check out the desserts, smoothies and inventive sandwiches at **Brava Café** (*☎ 2037 1929, 71 Pontcanna St*), open 9 am to 6 pm (10 am to 4 pm on Sunday).

Cardiff's best French restaurant is probably sparky, trilingual **Le Gallois** (*☎ 2034 1264, 6–8 Romilly Crescent, Canton*), with pricey (one/two/three/four courses for £18/25/30/35) but superb contemporary Franco-Welsh concoctions. At lunch it's a bit cheaper; booking ahead is essential. It opens for lunch and dinner, Tuesday to Saturday. Down the road and in the same league is smaller, older **Le Cassoulet** (*☎ 2022 1905, 5 Romilly Crescent*).

If you're staying on Cathedral Road and everything else is closed, try the £3 dinner special at the **Beverley Hotel** (*☎ 2034 3443, 75 Cathedral Rd*), open every evening except Sunday.

Cardiff Bay

Everything is naturally overpriced out here, though not so much if you move away from the waterfront towards Mount Stuart Square.

The **cafe** (*☎ 2045 4899, Harbour Drive*) at the Norwegian Church, near the visitors centre, does excellent cakes, waffles, sandwiches and light lunches.

The **Baytree Café** (*☎ 2033 1020, 1–2 Mount Stuart Square*), chrome and clean, has a huge array of filled baguettes and other snacks for under £3. Nearby **Buff's Restaurant** (*☎ 2046 4628, 8 Mount Stuart Square*) is really a snug wine bar, with good salads and international cuisine (hot dishes from £5 to £6); it opens 11 am to 7 pm weekdays only.

A recommended choice is the **Tiger Bay Café** (*☎ 2049 3400, 5 Bute Crescent*), offering inventive mixtures of Mediterranean cuisines, including lots of vegetarian options, both as tapas/starters from £2.50 and as mains from £6. It's closed on Sunday and Monday.

A good pub in the neighbourhood is the **Eli Jenkins** (*7 Bute Crescent*). There are plenty of others with unexceptional grub.

Other Areas

For serious Welsh dining you must head north-east of the centre to the **Armless**

Dragon Restaurant (☎ 2038 2357, 97 *Wyeverne Rd, Cathays*), offering contemporary recipes – meat, game, fish and some seafood – with ingredients sourced in Wales. Main courses are around £10, with some cheaper daily specials. It opens for lunch from Tuesday to Friday and for evening meals daily except Sunday; call before you go.

Vegetarian

A remarkable number of restaurants have vegetarian choices on the menu.

A vegetarian/vegan cafe (with organic beer and wine) is the upstairs *Beaz Neez* (☎ 2033 1478, 35 *Wyndham Arcade*), with lots of salads and sandwiches for around £3; open evenings Tuesday to Saturday and for lunch on Sunday.

ENTERTAINMENT

Buzz is a useful, free bimonthly magazine with up-to-date event listings in the city, available from the TIC and elsewhere. For current gig, cinema and arts listings, check out the Virtual Cardiff Web site at www.virtualcardiff.co.uk.

Pubs & Bars

Cardiff's cultural richness is reflected in its diverse watering holes. From an after-match pint to a red-hot evening of salsa, there's everything you could want for either winding down or perking up. Expect big queues everywhere on Friday nights. Most bars tend to open midday to 11 pm (to 10.30 pm on Sunday), with exceptions noted. Don't forget to try the local Brains SA (which stands for Special Ale, Same Again or Skull Attack, depending on how many pints you've had), brewed by the same family concern since 1713.

A good place to begin is the area around Mill Lane, with a good range of pubs, restaurants and late-night cafe-bars – and chippies in Caroline St. Have your first Brains of the night at the *Duke of Wellington* (☎ 2033 7190, 42 *The Hayes*); this one closes at 7 pm on Sunday. Lively *Continentals* (☎ 2064 5000, 10 *Mill Lane*) attracts a broad clientele; the downstairs bar

closes at 11 pm but you can carry on in the upstairs club *Latino's* (to midnight Monday, to 2 am Thursday to Saturday). Packed out at weekends, it has a friendly atmosphere with music to suit all tastes. Nearby is the late-licence bar *Las Iguanas* (see Places to Eat earlier), whose intimate basement is popular with young clubbers. It opens to 2 am Thursday to Saturday.

Callaghan's (☎ 2034 7247, *Castle Street*) offers nightly live Irish music and stays open until 2 am (to midnight on Sunday). A lively atmosphere and a good selection of beers make this a popular venue with young and old.

The centrally located, recently renovated *Owain Glyndŵr* (☎ 2022 1980, 10 *St John's Street*) is modern and airy. Its wide range of guest ales and the local legends inscribed on its walls give it a Welsh flavour. It opens to 11.30 pm Monday to Thursday, to midnight Friday and Saturday. For an upmarket but laid-back and reasonably priced venue, head for the *Metropolis Bar & Restaurant* (see Places to Eat earlier), and don't be surprised if you spot the odd celebrity or two.

Scrum (☎ 2038 3471, *Park Hotel, Park Place*) is the place for live sports coverage. The walls are covered with sporting memorabilia and the novelty seating is highly sought after, though the music occasionally drowns out the commentary.

If you're after a more relaxing evening there are plenty of options. Tucked away near the railway bridge in Cathays, the *Pen & Wig* (☎ 2064 9091, *Park Place*) is a traditional-style pub favoured by an older crowd, with good food, good beer and board games on request; it opens to 11.30 pm (11 pm on Sunday). Near the castle, another good place to escape the bustle is under the Victorian eaves of the *Angel Tavern* (☎ 2064 9200, *Castle Street*). It opens 5 to 11 pm weekdays, 5 to 11.30 pm Saturday and closes on Sunday.

Away from the city centre, the area behind the student union has a wealth of pubs with cheap drinks and free admission. The *Woodville* (☎ 2064 9991, 1–5 *Woodville Road*) provides good daytime food, reasonably priced drinks and giant games –

although its cash-back facility can be dangerous to your bank balance (open till midnight Thursday to Saturday).

Cardiff Bay boasts a variety of posh, harbourside bars. The friendly staff at *Via Fosse* (☎ 2045 0947, Stuart St) welcome kids, and you can enjoy the view from comfy sofas. *The Wharf* (☎ 2040 5092, 121 Schooner Way) is another family pub, with a designated children's area. It opens until midnight Monday to Wednesday and 1 am Thursday to Saturday. Watch for regular events including comedy nights, quiz nights and live music; expect a door charge on entertainment nights.

Clubs

Cardiff does have big, mainstream club chains but the vibrancy of its club scene has more to do with unique, smaller venues.

Bar Cuba (☎ 2039 7967, The Friary) may be small in size but its heaving dance floor is the perfect place for a red-hot Latin evening. The resident DJ plays a selection of jazz, funk and dance, and there are salsa nights throughout the week. Open 11 am to 2 am Monday to Saturday and noon to 10.30 pm on Sundays, this is one of Cardiff's friendliest and most popular nightspots.

Centrally located *Vision 2K* (☎ 2066 4469, 43–5 Queen Street) is the most serious club Cardiff has to offer. Acclaimed as Wales' biggest clubbing venue, V2K attracts the big names, regularly featuring well-known guest DJs. Admission ranges from £2 to £11. Closing time depends on what's on; typically it opens until at least 4 am. Check out the Web site at www.enter-the-dragon.co.uk for the latest details.

Womanby St has several good clubs popular with students and locals. The labyrinthine *Toucan Club* (☎ 2021 5481, Womanby Street) has several rooms, each providing a variety of funk, Latin, jazz and dance. It promotes itself as a live-music club hosting touring bands as well as home-grown talent. Dress codes don't exist – punters can come in their pyjamas if they wish – although sports tops are out. It opens until 2 am Tuesday to Sunday. The Web site is at www.toucanclub.co.uk.

JANE SMITH

Directly opposite is *Clwb Ifor Bach* (☎ 2023 2199, 11 Womanby Street), Cardiff's first Welsh-language club, founded in the early 1980s. With its three dance floors, the club – also known as The Welsh Club – headlines both local, unsigned talent and some of the big names. Lots of young Welsh bands have got their break here. Closing time is usually 2 or 3 am. Admission varies between £2 and £8 and although you do have to be a member to get in, you can sign up at the door for £1. The Web site is at www.clwbifor.com.

For jazz enthusiasts, *Café Jazz* (☎ 2038 7026, Sandringham Hotel, 21 St Mary St) is a must. Here, at the home of the Welsh jazz society, there are live music events throughout the week, including the popular 'Jazz Attic' where budding amateurs can jam with the resident rhythm section. It usually opens 11 am to midnight on weekdays, to 1 am Saturday and 6 pm Sunday. Check out the Web site at www.cafejazzcardiff.com for more information.

Gay & Lesbian Venues

The centre of Cardiff's gay nightlife is around Charles St, and comes to life mainly at weekends. The following are the main venues – most or all gay-owned, all aimed at gay revellers (none specifically for men or for women), none hostile to straights.

The *Golden Cross* (☎ *2039 4556, 283 Hayes Bridge Rd)*, a handsome Victorian pub, is the only survivor from Cardiff's old open-air produce market. It opens to 11 pm Monday to Wednesday, to 1 am Thursday to Saturday.

King's Cross (☎ *2064 9891, Mill Lane)* opens normal pub hours daily (to midnight Friday and Saturday).

Club X (☎ *2040 0876, 35 Charles St)* is a downstairs club, open 10 pm to 2 am Wednesday and Thursday (to 3 am Friday and to 4 am Saturday); *The Edge* is the cafe-bar upstairs, open 6 pm until late daily.

Exit Club (☎ *2064 0102, 48 Charles St)* is a disco and bar; it opens 8 pm to 2 am (to midnight on Sunday). Admission costs £1.50 after 9.30 pm.

Out Bar (☎ *2022 4756, Harlech Court, Bute Terrace)* opens normal pub hours daily, with a club Wednesday to Saturday; next door, *Atlantica* cafe-bar, opens noon to 8 pm Wednesday to Sunday.

Music, Theatre & Cinema

St David's Hall (*box office* ☎ *2087 8444, The Hayes)*, designed for broadcasting and with one of Europe's best acoustic auditoriums, offers a full range of theatrical events and classical music concerts, including the 10-day Welsh Proms every July (see Special Events). Most of the BBC National Orchestra of Wales' performances are given here too.

There are occasional classical music concerts in Cardiff Castle, Llandaff Cathedral and St John's Church. The acoustics at the *Norwegian Church arts centre* (☎ *2045 4899)*, on the waterfront at Cardiff Bay make it one of Wales' best venues for early music, among other things. Nearby, the *Coal Exchange* (☎ *2033 0220, Mount Stuart Square)*, Butetown, has occasional gigs too.

The *Sherman Theatre* (*box office* ☎ *2064 6900, Senghennydd Rd, Cathays)*, one of four Wales venues with a resident company, has commissioned more plays than any other theatre in the UK. It also plays host to Music Theatre Wales and Mid Wales Opera. The *New Theatre* (*box office*

☎ *2087 8889, Park Place)* is the current home of the Welsh National Opera (☎ 2046 4666).

The most imaginative cinema and alternative theatre programs tend to be at the *Chapter Arts Centre* (*box office* ☎ *2030 4400, Market Rd, Canton)*, in the Cathedral Rd area; take bus No 33 from Central station or St Mary St (55p, 10 minutes, every 30 minutes).

The *Cardiff International Arena* (*box office* ☎ *2022 4488, Mary Ann St)* is the city's main pop venue, with regular concerts. The *Millennium Stadium* (*ticket office* ☎ *2023 1495)* hosts only the biggest ones.

SPECTATOR SPORTS

If you stand in Bute Park on certain Saturday afternoons you can hear the crowds roaring at three different sports grounds.

Cardiff Arms Park, just north of the Millennium Stadium, is the home pitch for the Cardiff Rugby Football Club (tickets ☎ 0870 013 5213), founded in 1876. Rugby union is this city's favourite sport, and the Blue-and-Blacks are Wales' richest, most star-studded club, having fed over 200 players into the national team.

Ninian Park, a mile west of the centre, is home to the Cardiff City Football Club (tickets ☎ 2022 2857). Fans still hark back to 1927 when the Bluebirds took the English FA Cup out of England for the first (and only) time – Welsh football's equivalent of Owain Glyndŵr's rebellion. Take Cardiff Bus No 1 (85p, hourly on Saturday) from the central bus station, or a Valley Lines Pontypridd-bound train (£1.20/1.70 single/return, half-hourly on Saturday) to Ninian Park station.

All national and international rugby and football matches take place at the Millennium Stadium (tickets ☎ 2023 1495). Tickets for international fixtures are impossible for ordinary mortals to get, but not so national ones. Football matches here are family affairs, with no drinking allowed inside during the match, and tickets for just £10/5. Rugby matches tend to be hairy-chested, beer-assisted events.

The Glamorgan County Cricket Club (tickets ☎ 2040 9380), the only Welsh club belonging to the England & Wales Cricket Board, plays at the County Cricket Ground in Sophia Gardens, 1.75 mile north-west of the centre. The city's newest sports team – founded only in 1986 – is the premier-league BT Cardiff Devils ice-hockey club (tickets ☎ 2064 5988), whose matches take place at the Ice House on Hayes Bridge Rd.

Tickets are sold at box offices or, at slightly higher prices, at Ticketline (☎ 2023 0130), 47 Westgate St; it opens daily.

SHOPPING

Cardiff's L-shaped shopping zone – within the angle formed by High St/St Mary St and pedestrianised Queen St – is threaded with well preserved Victorian- and Edwardian-era arcades, lined with small and often interesting shops and cafes. This is a charming and easily overlooked feature of the centre that may appeal even to dedicated non-shoppers. Those in need of retail therapy will like the massive modern St David's Centre and Queens Arcade.

A central source for antiques is the Royal Arcade. For period furniture, clothes, books and knick-knacks, try Jacob's Market, just south of the railway line at the western end of Bute Square; it opens most days but biggest on Friday, Saturday and Sunday.

Spiller's, 36 The Hayes, advertises itself as the world's oldest record shop, founded in 1894 when records were still cylindrical. It's a pretty rough-and-ready place but tends to undersell the chain shops, and is a good source for CDs by up-and-coming Welsh indie bands.

Finally, if it's lovespoons, stuffed dragons or Cardiff T-shirts you're after, the biggest, friendliest souvenir shop in the city is Castle Welshcrafts, directly opposite the entrance to the castle.

GETTING THERE & AWAY
Air

Cardiff airport (☎ 01446-711111) is 12 miles south-west of the centre, near the suburb of Barry. Cardiff Bus No X91 (£2.75, 30 minutes) runs hourly between the airport and the central bus station (berth C3). A taxi to/from the bus station costs about £16.

On most days there are direct flights to Cardiff from destinations around the UK and continental Europe; see under Air in the Getting There & Away chapter for details.

Bus

For information on intercity fares and timetables, contact First Cymru (☎ 01656-728393), Stagecoach (☎ 01633-244744) or National Express (☎ 0870 580 8080). Traveline (☎ 0870 608 2608), the new UK-wide national bus enquiries service, is meant to be a one-stop shop for all bus and coach information but has a long way to go.

All local and regional bus/coach companies use the central bus station.

First Cymru's Cardiff-Swansea Shuttle (£7 day return, 55 minutes) runs about hourly; bicycles are carried free. Arriva Cymru's TrawsCambria (No 701) service runs daily from late May to late September between Cardiff and Holyhead (£20/32 single/return, nine hours) via Swansea, Aberystwyth, Caernarfon and other points; an additional service goes to Aberystwyth (£11.35, four hours) and via Newport to Bristol (£4, 1¾ hours).

National Express runs to Cardiff from Bristol (£5 single, 1¼ hours) about hourly except Sunday; from Birmingham (£17, 2½ hours) six times daily except Saturday; and from London (£16, 3¼ hours) every two hours.

The Beacons Bus (route B3) also serves Cardiff (see Getting There & Around under Brecon Beacons National Park in the South-East Wales & Brecon Beacons chapter).

Train

Cardiff is served by direct trains from many other major UK cities such as London, Manchester, Birmingham and Nottingham; see the Getting There & Away chapter for details.

Portside connections include Holyhead via Crewe (£51/55 single/SuperSaver return), Pembroke Dock via Tenby (four hours, four daily), Milford Haven via

CARDIFF

Haverfordwest (three hours, six daily) and Fishguard (2¼ hours, one daily); all £14/19 single/Saver return.

InterCity trains run to/from Swansea (£8.20 cheap day return, one hour) every 20 minutes.

Trains run by Valley Lines link Cardiff Central, Queen Street and Cathays stations with towns all along the Llynfi, Rhondda, Cynon, Taff and Rhymney valleys. A Cardiff Card (see under Information at the start of the chapter) gives you two days' free travel on all Valley Lines trains. Valley Lines' one-day Day Ranger (see Getting Around) is cheaper than a single ticket to many places on the network.

Car & Motorcycle

The fastest access to Cardiff from the M4 is via the A48 (Eastern Ave) from junction 29 or 30 or, if you're coming from Swansea, the A470 (Northern Ave) from junction 32. The A4232 (Grangetown and Butetown Link) from junction 33 provides direct access to Cardiff Bay; this will eventually be extended north-eastwards to link up with the A48.

Car Rental Local offices of major car-hire companies include Avis (☎ 2034 2111), Budget (☎ 2066 4499), Europcar (☎ 2049 8978), Hertz (☎ 2022 4548) and National (☎ 2049 6256).

GETTING AROUND

If you're using public transport and plan to get around a lot, you'll save loads of money with a tourist pass or travel pass. The two-day Cardiff Card (see under Information for details) gets you two days of unlimited travel with Cardiff Bus and on Valley Lines trains, plus free admission to many places of interest.

There are a few one-day travel passes which work out cheaper than a single ticket to some of the destinations they cover: the Network Rider (£4.50/2.50), for all buses run by Cardiff Bus, Stagecoach and several other companies around south-east Wales (buy it on the bus); and Valley Lines' Day Ranger ticket (£6/3). Family versions of these passes are also available.

Cardiff Bus' City Rider is good for Cardiff and Penarth (£2.85/1.90/5.70 adult/child/family).

Bus

Orange and white Cardiff Bus services run all over town, though you're only likely to need them on trips away from the centre.

A single trip within the centre costs 55p/35p (adult/child) single or £1/70p day return. Fares beyond the centre cost more, though they're discounted a bit during off-peak hours (9.15 am to 3.45 pm weekdays). You must present either a travel card or exact change. Student, disabled and senior discounts are only available to local residents.

You can pick up timetables (though buses rarely run on time) and passes from the Cardiff Bus office (☎ 2066 6444) in St David's House, across Wood St from the bus terminal and just a few doors from the TIC. An excellent free map of local bus routes seems to have disappeared from the shelves, but it won't hurt to ask. The office opens 8.30 am to 5.30 pm weekdays and 9 am to 4.30 pm Saturday. See the Web site at www.cardiffbus.com.

Train

There are train stations at Queen St, Cathays, Llandaff, Ninian Park and Bute Rd. The only local service of much use is from Queen St to Bute St (see the earlier section on Cardiff Bay), though Valley Line trains are an excellent way to reach attractions outside the city (see Around Cardiff).

Limited services run south from Queen Street station to Bute Street station, near Cardiff Bay.

Car & Motorcycle

Most city-centre parking is severely restricted. In many areas you must display a voucher, to be purchased in advance from local shops; an 80p voucher lasts one hour.

Taxi

Cardiff has two kinds of official taxi. Those painted black with a white bonnet (hood), operated by various companies, can safely be hired off the street or at taxi ranks. Those of other colours are only for pre-booking; if you flag down one of these in the street you won't be insured in case of an accident.

City rates at the time of writing were £1.50 flagfall plus £1.10 per mile or 10p per 40 seconds of idling in traffic. Rates at night are higher. Among reliable taxi companies are A1 Cabs (☎ 2066 6566), B-Line (☎ 2071 1144), Capital Cars (☎ 2077 7777) and Dragon Taxis (☎ 2033 3333).

Bicycle
Taff Trail Cycle Hire (☎ 2039 8362), off Cathedral Rd, is by the Cardiff Caravan Park. Bike rental costs £8 per day. It has some adapted bikes for disabled cyclists.

Around Cardiff

There are lots of interesting ways to escape the city by bus, train or car journeys of under half an hour. You can go down to the sea at Barry or Penarth, explore the massive castle at Caerphilly or a cute neo-Gothic one at Castell Coch, step back in time at Rhondda Heritage Park or further back at the good Museum of Welsh Life at St Fagans, or further yet at the remains of a major Roman army base at Caerleon.

If you're going to do anything more than spend the day at Barry, you'd be crazy not to get a travel pass. The two-day Cardiff Card (see Information in the Cardiff section) gets you unlimited travel with Cardiff Bus and on Valley Lines trains, and free admission to many of the attractions listed in this section (the Museum of Welsh Life, Castell Coch, Caerphilly Castle and Rhondda Heritage Park).

Some one-day passes cost less than a single ticket to many of the places covered – eg, the Network Rider and the Day Ranger (see Getting Around under Cardiff for details).

MUSEUM OF WELSH LIFE
St Fagans, 4 miles west of central Cardiff, is a small village with one of South Wales' most appealing tourist attractions. The Museum of Welsh Life is a vast (40-hectare) collection of 30 reconstructed old buildings saved from demolition and brought here from the South Wales valleys and beyond. Examples include a tollhouse, a steam-powered woollen mill, a cock-fighting pit, an 18th-century Unitarian chapel, a row of Victorian shops and assorted houses and cottages.

It's a brilliant place for bringing history to life. Craftspeople work in many of the buildings, allowing visitors to see how blankets, clogs, barrels, tools and cider were once made. The woollen mill sells its handmade blankets for knock-down prices (£50 to £90) at the start of drier spring weather after they've been washed and dried. You can also see examples of peculiarly Welsh breeds of livestock and poultry.

It's a great place for kids, with a number of special summer programs. On public holidays the place gets desperately crowded with families tucking into their hot lamb sandwiches.

The museum (☎ 029-2057 3500; NMGW) opens 10 am to 5 pm daily. Admission costs £5.50 for adults or £3.90 for those aged 19 to 21; it's free if you're under 19 or at least 60. A £2 booklet has details on every exhibit. There's a cafe-restaurant in the visitors centre, and summer-only tea rooms at two other points.

Cardiff Bus No 32 or 320 (£1.10 off-peak, 25 minutes) runs once or twice hourly (hourly on Sunday) to a small gate at St Fagans Castle, 500m from the visitors centre. By car, take the B4258 (Cathedral Rd, Pencisely Rd and St Fagans Rd) for 4 miles, or the A4232 (Butetown and Grangetown Links) for 5 miles. There are no train services. A taxi from central Cardiff costs about £7.

PENARTH
☎ 029 • pop 21,000
Penarth is a prim seaside resort of the slow-moving, old-fashioned kind – pretty but madly boring – with a huge Victorian pier. The streets above its windblown esplanade are full of elegantly refurbished Victorian holiday homes.

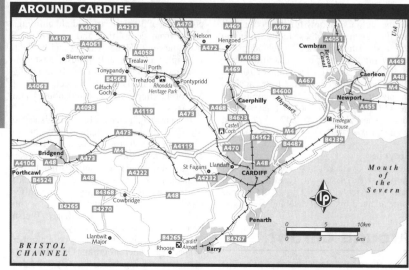

From Penarth train station or the bus stop at Windsor Arcade in the centre, it's a five-minute walk through Alexandra Gardens down to the esplanade. The TIC (☎ 2070 8849), at the pier, opens 10 am to 5.30 pm daily, for six months starting from Easter.

The red-brick Turner House Gallery (☎ 2070 8870; NMGW), on Plymouth Rd a block east of the train station, mounts good, temporary visual-arts exhibitions. It opens 10 am to 12.45 pm and 2 to 5 pm daily except Monday. Admission costs £1.25 (free for those aged under 19 or at least 60; and free to all on Sunday).

From May to October *PS Waverley*, the world's last seagoing paddle steamer, or its sister ship the *Balmoral* depart from Penarth pier three or four times weekly for day or evening cruises on the Bristol Channel. For information and bookings ask at the TIC or call ☎ 2070 4520. You can also buy tickets on board, or at the Cardiff Bus office in Cardiff.

The only food worth going out of your way for here is at *Tomlin's* (☎ 2070 6644, 46 Plassey St), a bright vegetarian restaurant with a few carefully prepared mains for around £10. It opens for lunch Friday,

Saturday and alternate Sundays, and for dinner Tuesday to Saturday. From the train station walk ¼ mile up Hickman Rd and Arcot St.

Penarth is at the end of a rail spur from Cardiff Central; trains (£1.80, 11 minutes) run about every 20 minutes. Cardiff Bus Nos P1–8 (95p off-peak, 20 minutes) run about every eight minutes to Penarth.

BARRY
☎ 029 • pop 45,000

Barry docks, 8 miles south-west of Cardiff, were built as competition to the Butes' enterprises by David Davies, a self-made dealer in transport and coal and grandfather to the Davies sisters (who endowed Cardiff's National Museum & Gallery with its breathtaking impressionist collection).

Present-day Barry is an uninspiring dormitory town for commuters to the capital. But for visitors with kids it boasts a Pleasure Beach, including a huge funfair and high-tech game centres. Trains from Cardiff run directly to the funfair (Barry Island station; £2.20, 17 minutes, three hourly), and Cardiff Bus No 354 (£1.10 off-peak, 40 minutes) runs hourly.

CASTELL COCH

Rising up among the beech trees on a hill in Tongwynlais, 5 miles north-west of central Cardiff, Castell Coch looks more like a red-brick Loire chateau than a Welsh castle. The fairytale summer retreat of the Bute family, it was (like Cardiff Castle) designed in high-camp Victorian Gothic by William Burges for the third marquis of Bute. Particularly interesting are the sitting room, with designs based on Aesop's *Fables*, the bedroom, with a sink on hinges, and the kitchen, with a fine Welsh dresser.

Castell Coch (☎ 2081 0101), run by Cadw, the Welsh historic monuments agency, opens 9.30 am to 5 pm daily, Easter to October (to 6 pm June to September) and to 4 pm the rest of the year. Admission costs £2.50/2 (free with a Cardiff Card; see Information in the Cardiff section). Cardiff Bus No 26 (£2.20 off-peak, 25 minutes) runs hourly to Tongwynlais, from where it's a 10-minute walk; the same bus continues to Caerphilly Castle (see later in the chapter), and the two castles make a good day trip.

CAERPHILLY

☎ 029 • pop 30,000

The biggest castle in Wales, and one of the most powerful in Europe, is just north of Cardiff at Caerphilly. The adjacent town is quite overshadowed by its castle, though there's plenty going on.

Most people know 'Caerphilly' as a type of cheese – mild and salty, once preferred by miners to replenish their salt levels. Not much of it is made here any more, although the town has a two-day Big Cheese festival near the castle at the end of July, with a medieval fair, Celtic costume events, cheese races, a crafts fair and live music.

Orientation & Information

Caerphilly sits in the picturesque Rhymney (**hrum**-ny) Valley, 9 miles north of Cardiff.

The TIC (☎ 2088 0011, fax 2086 0811, [e] tic@caerphilly.gov.uk) is on Twyn Square, opposite the castle – itself clearly visible ¼ mile north of Caerphilly train station (via Cardiff Rd). The TIC opens 10 am

to 6 pm daily, Easter to October; and to 5 pm the rest of the year. Downstairs are spanking-clean pay loos and a shop selling pricey Welsh food items, including souvenir-size rounds of Caerphilly cheese (though you can get essentially the same thing for less at the Safeway down the street).

Caerphilly Castle

Unlike most other castles in Wales, Caerphilly was never a royal castle. It was begun in 1268 by Gilbert de Clare (1243–95), Lord Marcher of Glamorgan and one of the most powerful of the English barons. Some 58 years in construction, it was among the first to use concentric fortifications and lakes for defence, state-of-the-art for its time; to reach the inner court one had to pass three drawbridges, six portcullises and five sets of double doors. With its elaborate water defences the castle occupies some 12 hectares.

A long dispute between Henry III and his nobles in the 1250s and 60s gave Llewelyn ap Gruffydd, prince of Gwynedd (and the last Welsh Prince of Wales), a chance to expand his holdings. Both he and de Clare sided with the nobles, but de Clare subsequently switched his allegiance to the king, drove out the local Welsh lord, Gruffudd ap Rhys, and set to work on Caerphilly. Llewelyn besieged the castle, but without success. Edward I's subsequent campaign against the Welsh princes put an end to local worries.

Caerphilly was beefed up but, overtaken by events, never again saw battle and slowly fell into ruin from the 15th century onward. Much of what you see today is the result of a 1930s restoration by the fourth marquis of Bute, who owned it by then. The effect is less magical than it might be because the castle is right across the road from the unremarkable town centre of Caerphilly. The trademark broken tower is the result not of battle but of subsidence.

The castle (☎ 2088 3143; Cadw) opens 9.30 am to 6 pm, June to September; to 5 pm in April, May and October; and to 4 pm (and from 11 am on Sunday) the rest of the year. Admission costs £2.50/2 (free with a Cardiff Card; see Information in the Cardiff section). A cassette audioguide can be rented for £1/50p. The tower beside the reception office contains an excellent, detailed exhibit on the castle's history.

Walking Routes

Caerphilly is surrounded by fine walking country. It's inside the 27-mile upland loop of the Rhymney Valley Ridgeway Walk, a patchwork of steep beech woodland and open fields which peaks at the 365m Mynydd Machen. If 27 miles sounds like too much for one day, you can take the train four stops north to Hengoed and walk back along either side of the loop. The trail's nearest approach is about 2 miles south of Caerphilly train station via Caerphilly Common, or more conveniently about 1 mile south-west of the town's other train station at Aber, just to the north. Aber station is also a good access point for the Taff Trail.

The TIC has maps and other information on these and other regional walks linked with them; or contact the Caerphilly Mountain Countryside service (☎ 2081 3356).

Places to Eat

Just north of the TIC and opposite the castle is *Glanmor's*, a cheerful sandwich shop with good homemade meals and fresh pastry.

Getting There & Away

The easiest way to reach Caerphilly from Cardiff is by train, on Valley Lines' Rhymney or Bargoed service (£2.50 return off-peak, 20 minutes, every half-hour). Cardiff Bus No 26 (£2.20 off-peak, 45 minutes, hourly) stops at the station and on Castle St near the TIC (this is the same bus that goes to Castell Coch, and the two castles make a good day trip). Drivers note: there's only limited parking by the TIC; the main car park is behind the castle, from where it's a half-mile walk to the castle gate!

RHONDDA HERITAGE PARK

If you're interested in the industrial history of the valleys, don't miss the Rhondda Heritage Park, 10 miles north-west of Cardiff, between Pontypridd and Porth. This was a major south-Wales coal centre, and the Heritage Park is built on the site of the Lewis Merthyr colliery, which closed in 1983. Here, an exhibition brings the old colliery buildings back to life and tries to explain what life was like for workers and their families.

You can descend in a cage to the coalface, with a retired miner as your guide. It's a mock-up, but pretty convincing (if you want to go down a real coal mine, visit the Big Pit Mining Museum at Blaenafon; see the South-East Wales & Brecon Beacons chapter).

The park (☎ 01443-682036) opens 10 am to 6 pm daily (except Monday, October to Easter), with the last tour at 4.30 pm. Admission costs £5.60/4.30 (free with a Cardiff Card; see Information in the Cardiff section).

It's a half-hour train ride from Cardiff Central station to Trehafod (£2.80 off-peak, three hourly) on Valley Lines' Treherbert line. Alternatively, take Stagecoach bus No 132 (£2.90 return, 55 minutes, two hourly except Sunday).

NEWPORT
☎ 01633 • pop 148,000

Newport, 12 miles up the Severn Estuary from Cardiff near the mouth of the River Usk, is one of Wales' busiest industrial and commercial centres. Most tourists head straight out to the Roman fortress at Caerleon (see Around Newport later). The town itself has more spirit than charm, though there are some unique attractions. Don't make the mistake of confusing this with the small Pembrokeshire town of the same name!

This Newport's fame is associated with the bloody Chartist riot of 1839. Chartism, a parliamentary reform movement during the early years of Queen Victoria's rule, was particularly strong in Wales, inspiring several local insurrections (see under History in the Facts about Wales chapter). On 4 November some 5000 men from the Usk, Ebbw and Rhymney valleys converged on the town, intent on taking control of it and sparking off a national uprising. They tried to storm the Westgate Hotel, where several Chartists were being held; police and infantrymen inside fired into the crowd, killing at least 20 people. Five men were subsequently imprisoned and three – including John Frost, a major organiser – deported to Australia.

Orientation & Information
The bus station is on the northern side of John Frost Square, at the heart of town. From the train station it's a 600m walk south along High St and Commercial St (the main shopping axis) to a passage into John Frost Square.

The TIC (☎ 842962, fax 222615, e newport-tic@tsww.com), at the southern end of John Frost Square, opens 9.30 am to 6 pm daily except Sunday (to 5 pm Thursday and Saturday).

Things to See & Do
The bullet-scarred **Westgate Hotel** is still here, on Commercial St, though in a sign of the times it's being redeveloped as a shopping and restaurant complex. Outside, amongst the hurrying shoppers, is an ensemble of angry bronze figures memorialising the Chartist riot.

The town centre is in fact an open-air museum of provocative sculpture. Northeast of the bus station by the river is the immense **Steel Wave** (1990) by Peter Fink, now almost a civic trademark, though not universally loved. In John Frost Square, **In the Nick of Time** is a hilarious clock tower that falls to pieces on the hour. **Stand and Stare**, a ghostly shrouded figure on Commercial St, is dedicated to local writer WH Davies, author of *The Autobiography of a Super-Tramp* (see Literature in the Facts about Wales chapter). **The Bell Carrier**, a huge ox near the bus station, recounts the vision of one St Woolos.

The **Transporter Bridge** is a remarkable 'aerial ferry' built in 1906 to carry traffic across the river above the high-masted ships of the time. Restored in 1995, it's one of only three left in the UK. It operates 8 am to 9 pm (1 to 9 pm on Sunday) in summer and 8 am to 6 pm (1 to 5 pm on Sunday) in winter. Pedestrians cross for free; vehicles cost 50p. From John Frost Square, it's about

a mile south along Commercial St and Commercial Rd (A4042).

Upstairs from the TIC the modest **Newport Museum** has displays on Caerleon (see Around Newport) and on local social history. It opens the same hours as the TIC, and admission is free.

Near the Steel Wave are the unremarkable ruins of the 13th-century **Newport Castle**, largely rebuilt after being trashed by Owain Glyndŵr in 1402. They are not open to the public.

Places to Stay & Eat
The town centre has little modestly priced accommodation. *Craignair Guest House* (☎ 259903, 44 Corporation Rd) – cross the Newport Bridge (by the castle), carry on for about 250m and turn right – offers B&B for about £16 per person.

Along the river-facing side of the municipal market (between the train and bus stations) is Dock St; here and along Commercial St you'll find lots of cafes for quick lunches. *Charlie's* (☎ 214121, 2a Skinner St) is a popular takeaway sandwich shop a stone's throw north of the Westgate Hotel.

Getting There & Away
The simplest and most frequent connections with Cardiff are by mainline train (£3.20 single, 14 minutes, at least four or five hourly). Newport Transport and Cardiff Bus jointly operate bus No 30 (£1.45 single, 45 minutes, three hourly, fewer on Sunday).

AROUND NEWPORT
Tredegar House
Tredegar (truh-**dee**-ger) House is a restored 17th-century mansion set in 36 hectares of gardens, 2 miles west of Newport town centre. It was built by the Morgan family, themselves the most interesting aspect of the place – Godfrey, Second Lord Tredegar, survived the Charge of the Light Brigade; Viscount Evan kept a kangaroo; Sir Henry was a pirate.

Done up with a playground, craft workshop, tearoom and gift shop, this makes a jolly half-day family trip. The house (☎ 01633-815880) opens for tours (£5/2.25)

11.30 am to 4 pm Wednesday to Sunday, Easter to September. Joint bus No 30 of Newport Transport and Cardiff Bus (see Getting There & Away under Newport) also calls here.

Note that Tredegar House is *not* in the town of Tredegar (which is some 20 miles away in the Rhymney Valley).

Caerleon Roman Fortress

At Caerleon, 4 miles north of Newport, is one of the most revealing Roman sites in Europe, and the most important one in Wales. Then called Isca Silurium, it was one of the three principal military bases in Roman Britain, headquarters from AD 75 of the elite Second Augustan Legion.

This wasn't just a military camp but a purpose-built township some 9 miles in circumference, complete with a 6000-seat amphitheatre and the Fortress Baths, a state-of-the-art 'leisure complex' with hot and cold baths, pool and exercise hall. Nearby are the foundations of the barracks, the only such site open to the public in Europe. An excellent Roman Legionary Museum offers a look at life for Roman soldiers in what was one of the Empire's most far-flung corners.

The splendid amphitheatre site – not surprisingly associated in local legends with King Arthur's Round Table – opens to the public at no charge. Joint admission to the baths (managed, along with the amphitheatre, by Cadw) and the museum (☎ 01633-423134; NMGW) costs £2.10 for adults; children can visit the baths for £1.25 and the museum for free. Museum and baths open 10 am to 5 pm daily (from 2 pm on Sunday).

Newport Transport's bus Nos 2 and 7 (75p, 15 minutes) run from Newport bus station to the museum every 10 to 15 minutes (hourly on Sunday). There's no direct service from Cardiff.

South-East Wales & the Brecon Beacons

The south-east has a reputation as Wales' overcrowded, over-urbanised, overindustrialised and over-anglicised corner. It's certainly crowded: along with Cardiff the region has half of the population of Wales and most of its industry. But the region is also dense with a rich, albeit sobering history, and beautiful, rugged landscapes. It was a foothold for the Normans, who built more castles per square mile here than anywhere else in Britain, and was a nerve centre for the Industrial Revolution – a heritage whose cultural importance has now been signalled with UNESCO protection at Blaenafon.

The mining valleys that run northwards into the Brecon Beacons and the Black Mountains are still coming to grips with the slow death of the iron and coal industries, and yet the bumper-to-bumper villages along each valley possess a stark beauty and people as warm-hearted and resilient as any in Wales.

Swansea, boyhood home of poet and writer Dylan Thomas, is the gateway to the Gower, a sparsely populated peninsula rimmed with cliffs, coves and beaches. Gower has some good spots for surfing, windsurfing and mountain biking, and is lovely enough to have been designated Britain's first Area of Outstanding Natural Beauty (AONB).

At the heart of the region is the Brecon Beacons National Park, a muscular, wind-blown landscape sculpted in the last Ice Age, and a paradise for walkers. One of Wales' finest long-distance walking and cycling trails is the 55-mile Taff Trail, climbing from Cardiff to Brecon and coinciding here with Lôn Las Cymru, the Welsh National Cycle Route.

Getting Around

The south-east's main intercity bus operators are First Cymru (☎ 01656-728393)

Highlights

- Trying your hand at the UK's finest pub crawl, Swansea's Mumbles Mile
- Visiting the dark heart of the Industrial Revolution at Blaenafon
- Playing King Arthur at Chepstow Castle
- Walking up the serene Wye Valley and looking into the past at Tintern Abbey
- Finding every book you ever wanted at Hay-on-Wye
- Riding a horse across the wind-blasted escarpments of the Brecon Beacons

Hay-on-Wye p184

Brecon p193

Abergavenny p188

Merthyr Tydfil p168

Monmouth p176

Swansea p158

Chepstow p173

Gower Peninsula p164

South-East Wales & the Brecon Beacons p156

and Stagecoach (☎ 01633-244744). Valley Lines (☎ 029-2044 9944) runs trains that link Cardiff with towns up in the Rhondda, Cynon, Taff and Rhymney valleys. Call National Rail Enquiries on ☎ 0845 748 4950 for information.

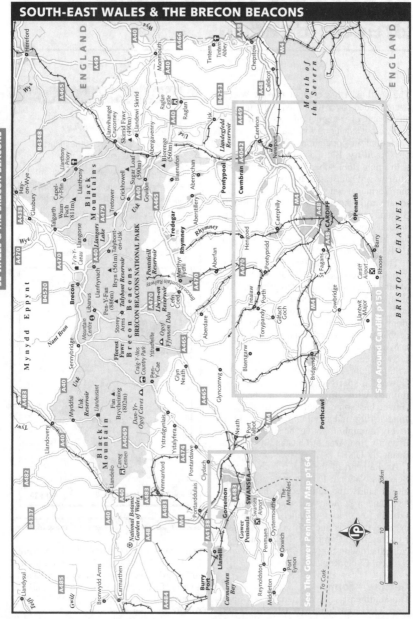

SOUTH-EAST WALES & THE BRECON BEACONS

If you'll be travelling a lot by public transport, you can save money with a travel pass. The one-day Network Rider pass (£4.50/2.50 for adults/children) can be used on all buses run by Cardiff Bus and Stagecoach as well as several other companies around south-east Wales.

The one-day Day Explorer ticket (£6/3, with 10% off for YHA/HI card holders) is good for all Valley Lines trains (except those on the Maesteg-Bridgend-Cardiff-Newport axis) and all Stagecoach buses, and for discounted admission to some attractions. Family versions are also available. These special tickets can be purchased on buses and at train stations.

Swansea & the Gower

SWANSEA (ABERTAWE)
☎ 01792 • pop 285,000

Swansea (pronounced **swan**-zee) is the gateway – or, one might say, the main obstacle – to the superb coastal scenery of the Gower Peninsula, and is the second-largest town in Wales.

Dylan Thomas grew up in Swansea and later called it an 'ugly, lovely town'. Its location beside Swansea Bay is decidedly lovely but some of its concrete developments are ugly indeed. However, there are a few things to make this rough-and-ready town worth a visit, including a first-rate maritime museum, the regenerated dockland area, a literary centre devoted to Dylan Thomas and, around the bay at Mumbles, one of the UK's finest pub crawls.

Don't come on Monday, when nearly everything touristy closes.

History
The Vikings named the area Sveins Ey (Swein's Island), probably referring to the sandbank in the mouth of the river.

The Normans built a castle here (of which little remains), but Swansea had to wait until the Industrial Revolution for its heyday, when it developed into a centre for copper smelting. Ore was first shipped in from Cornwall, across the Bristol Channel, but by the 19th century it was arriving from Chile, Cuba and the USA, in return for Welsh coal. This was Copperopolis – a world centre for the refining of nonferrous metals.

By the 20th century the heavy-industrial base had declined, although Swansea's oil refinery and smaller factories were still judged a worthy target by the Luftwaffe, which devastated the city centre in 1941.

Orientation
Swansea's Welsh name, Abertawe, describes its location at the mouth of the Tawe, where the river empties into Swansea Bay.

From Swansea train station it's a half-mile walk south-west along High St and The Kingsway into the town centre. The Tourist Information Centre (TIC) and bus station are in the centre, off West Way. Ferries arriving from Cork tie up to the east, across the Tawe.

The 'centre', if you can call it that, is a huge pedestrian shopping area bounded by The Kingsway, Castle St, West Way and Oystermouth Rd. In the middle is a mega shopping centre called The Quadrant. A long arm of the town reaches 5 miles south-west along the bay to include Mumbles Head and the village of Oystermouth.

Many Swansea streets have house numbers that run consecutively up one side and down the other.

Information
Tourist Offices The helpful TIC (☎ 468321, fax 464602, @ tourism@swansea.gov.uk), beside the bus station car park, opens 9.30 am to 5.30 pm Monday to Saturday, plus 10 am to 4 pm on Sunday from mid-July to August. There's another TIC (☎ 361302) on the seafront at Mumbles, open Easter to October; opening hours vary so call to check the latest times. For information on Swansea on the Web check out www.swansea.gov.uk.

Money Every bank in the UK seems to be represented in the streets between The Kingsway and The Quadrant shopping centre. All of them have ATMs.

SOUTH-EAST WALES

SWANSEA

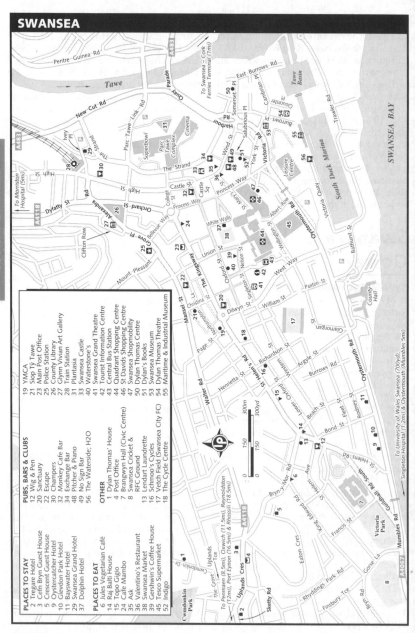

PLACES TO STAY
2 Tregare Hotel
3 Cefn Bryn Guest House
5 Crescent Guest House
9 Oystercatcher Hotel
10 Glevdon Park Hotel
11 Bayswater Hotel
29 Swansea Grand Hotel
37 Dolphin Hotel

PLACES TO EAT
6 Jules Vegetarian Café
14 Raj Balti House
15 Topo Gigio
24 Cafe Mambo
35 Ask
36 Valentino's Restaurant
38 Swansea Market
39 Gershwin's Coffee House
45 Tesco Supermarket
52 Indigo

PUBS, BARS & CLUBS
12 Wig & Pen
20 Sanctuary
22 Escape
30 Champers
32 Monkey Cafe Bar
34 Exchange Bar
48 Pitcher & Piano
49 No Sign Bar
56 The Waterside; H2O

OTHER
1 Dylan Thomas' House
4 Post Office
7 Brangwyn Hall (Civic Centre)
8 Swansea Cricket &
  RFC Ground
13 Lendart Laundrette
16 Schnoo's Cycles
17 Vetch Field (Swansea City FC)
18 The Cycle Centre
19 YMCA
21 Siop Ty Tawe
23 Main Post Office
25 Police Station
26 County Library
27 Glynn Vivian Art Gallery
28 Train Station
31 Plantasia
33 Swansea Castle
40 Waterstone's
41 Swansea Grand Theatre
42 Tourist Information Centre
43 Central Bus Station
44 Quadrant Shopping Centre
46 St Davids Shopping Centre
47 Swansea Shopmobility
50 Dylan Thomas Centre
51 Dylan's Books
53 Swansea Museum
54 Dylan Thomas Theatre
55 Maritime & Industrial Museum

Post & Communications The main post office is on The Kingsway. There is another post office on Uplands Crescent, west of the centre. Internet access is available at the county library (☎ 516757), Alexandra Rd, for £1.50 per half-hour. It opens 9 am to 7 pm Monday to Wednesday and Friday, and until 5 pm Thursday and Saturday. The YMCA (☎ 641398, e swanseaymca@hotmail.com), 1 The Kingsway, has a cybercafe charging the same; it opens 10 am to 6 pm weekdays and 9 am to 1 pm Saturday.

Bookshops Waterstone's on Oxford St has a modest Welsh-interest section. A shop specialising in Welsh-language books, music and gifts is Siop Tŷ Tawe (☎ 460657) on Christina St. For second-hand books go to Dylan's Books (☎ 655255) on Salubrious Place.

Laundry Lendart Laundrette, 91 Bryn-y-Mor Rd, is the most central do-it-yourself laundry. It opens 8 am to 8 pm weekdays and until 6 pm at weekends.

University The Swansea campus of the University of Wales, with some 8600 students, is 2 miles west of the centre on Mumbles Rd.

Medical & Emergency Services Morriston Hospital (☎ 702222), 5 miles to the north, has an accident & emergency department. For non-emergency services go to Singleton Hospital (☎ 205666), 2 miles west of the town centre. The police station (☎ 456999) is on Grove Place.

Gay & Lesbian Travellers Swansea has a Lesbian, Gay & Bisexual Switchboard (☎ 480044), which operates 7 to 10 pm Thursday. See Entertainment later for information on social venues.

Disabled Travellers For a small fee Swansea Shopmobility (☎ 461785) provides wheelchairs and electric 'scooters' for the disabled to get around the shopping area. It's on St David's Square, off Princess Way, and opens 9 am to 5 pm Monday to Saturday.

Dangers & Annoyances Park your car on Oystermouth Rd if you're staying at one of its guesthouses as the road is equipped with security cameras – but ask your host about the complex (and strictly enforced) parking regulations. Petty vandalism is a risk in the backstreets between Oystermouth Rd and St Helens Rd.

The Kingsway and adjacent streets can get a bit rowdy when the pubs close at 11 pm.

Maritime Quarter

The area around the old docks has been converted into a marina and an agreeable, squeaky-clean tourist area, with dockside apartments, two museums, several places with Dylan Thomas connections and a curious, seated statue of the man himself.

Two hundred centuries of local archaeology is on show at the **Swansea Museum** (☎ 653763) on Victoria Rd. This is Wales' oldest museum, founded in 1834; Dylan Thomas called it 'the museum that should be in a museum'. It opens 10 am to 5 pm daily except Monday. Admission is free.

Considerably more interesting is the **Maritime & Industrial Museum** (☎ 650351) charting the region's industrial history. In the main hall is Wales' first contribution to the global automotive industry, the fibreglass Gilbern Invader sports car. Upstairs is the world's first public passenger train, a tram that plied between Swansea and Mumbles from 1804 to 1960. Opening hours are the same as the Swansea Museum. Admission is free. Moored nearby are a lightship and a steam tug.

The focus of the **Dylan Thomas Centre** (☎ 463980) – also known as the National Literature Centre for Wales – is a permanent exhibition on the poet's life and work, called 'I, in my intricate image'. Other facilities include a theatre, exhibition galleries, bookshops, a restaurant and – fittingly – a bar. The centre, which is off Somerset Place, opens 10.30 am to 4.30 pm daily except Monday.

Plantasia

Eight hundred species of plant from around the world, plus attendant insects, reptiles, tropical fish, birds and tamarin monkeys are housed in the three climatic zones of Plantasia's striking pyramidal greenhouse. Plantasia (☎ 474555), off Parc Tawe Link Rd, opens 10 am to 5 pm daily except Monday. Admission costs £2.30/1.60.

Glynn Vivian Art Gallery

This gallery (☎ 655006), on Alexandra Rd, fairly claims to be 'one of Britain's liveliest provincial galleries'. The collection includes Welsh artists and old masters, Swansea china, European ceramics and clocks, and temporary exhibitions. It opens 10 am to 5 pm daily except Monday. Admission is free.

Swansea Castle

Swansea castle dates from the 14th century and was originally Norman. Most of it was destroyed by Cromwell in 1647 and what remained was used as a prison in the 19th century. The ruins – now reflected in the mirrored glass of the adjacent BT Tower – are not open as a tourist site.

Mumbles

Properly speaking, The Mumbles are two offshore rocks (one with a lighthouse), the name supposedly an anglicised/Welshified version of their nickname among visiting French sailors – *mamelles* (teats). 'Mumbles' has come to be used as a name for the village of Oystermouth.

Oystermouth Castle was the stronghold of the Norman lords of Gower, who built a wooden fort here in the 1180s and a stone castle in the late 13th century. The ruins, offering a fine view over Swansea Bay, open 11 am to 5 pm daily, Easter to September. Admission costs £1/80p. The castle is the focus of various summer events, including mock medieval battles and alfresco Shakespeare performances.

A 1-mile trek through the village and over the headland takes you to Langland Bay, facing out into the Bristol Channel. Farther west is Caswell Bay. Both have popular sandy beaches, with lifeguards and basic amenities in the summer.

See Getting Around for local transport to Mumbles.

Walking & Cycling Routes

The Swansea Bike Path is a 5-mile beach-front trail that runs out to Mumbles; it's also used by walkers. The Riverside Path is another cycle trail, running northwards along the River Tawe. The TIC has useful free booklets on cycling and walking in the area. See under Getting Around for local bike-hire shops.

Dylan Thomas in Swansea

Dylan Thomas' nondescript house at 5 Cwmdonkin Drive – virtually unchanged from the days when he lived there – opens for viewing by appointment with the Dylan Thomas Centre. It's also the venue for occasional evening literary events.

Two booklets – one on local sites associated with the poet and the other on local places he wrote about – are available from the TIC or the Dylan Thomas Centre.

Special Events

There is, of course, a Dylan Thomas Festival, during late October and early November, including poetry readings, talks and performances of *Under Milk Wood* at DT-related venues around the town. For information contact the Dylan Thomas Centre.

The annual Swansea Festival, running from late September to early November, features six weeks of drama, opera, film, ballet, jazz, classical music and dance competitions. For information call ☎ 475715.

Places to Stay

Just outside the train station, the *Swansea Grand Hotel* (☎ 650541, Ivey Place) has good-value singles/doubles for £18/25, although it's not looking very grand these days.

Oystermouth Rd is a strip of seafront guesthouses, but unless you really need to look at the sea, it's windblown and a bit cheerless. Among modest B&Bs with rooms (mostly with bathroom) for around £18 per person are the nonsmoking *Bayswater Hotel* (☎ 655301, 322 Oystermouth Rd), *Glevdon Park Hotel* (☎ 466737, 362 Oystermouth Rd) and *Oystercatcher Hotel* (☎ 456574, 386 Oystermouth Rd); the latter has a bar and optional evening meals.

The Victorian Pierhead in modern Cardiff Bay

The £25-million St David's Hotel, Cardiff Bay

Welsh history is brought to life at St Fagans.

1820s' water-driven wool-carding machine

Pass the time admiring the view in Cardiff's centre

A leisurely afternoon on Penarth's Victorian pier

Dylan Thomas surveys 'ugly, lovely' Swansea.

The fine beach at Rhossli Bay, Gower Peninsula

Bloody cranesbill...

...a shy hermit crab...

Swansea: which one is the 14th-century castle?

...and burnet rose brighten the Gower Peninsula.

In the more genteel neighbourhood of Uplands is a clutch of modest guesthouses charging £25 to £30 per person. These include the nonsmoking *Cefn Bryn Guest House* (☎ 466687, 6 Uplands Crescent), quiet *Crescent Guest House* (☎ 466814, 132 Eaton Crescent) and *Tregare Hotel* (☎/fax 470608, 9 Sketty Rd).

The centre offers more upmarket choices, including the business-oriented *Dolphin Hotel* (☎ 650011, White Walls), right in the central shopping district, charging £55/60 during the week and £45/55 at weekends.

Out at Mumbles, two B&Bs with bay views from about £20 per person are the friendly *Coast House* (☎ 368702, 708 Mumbles Rd) and the *Beach House Hotel* (☎ 367650, 734 Mumbles Rd). The deceptively plain-looking *Hillcrest House Hotel* (☎ 363700, 1 Higher Lane) has an excellent restaurant and posh 'themed' en-suite rooms from £50/70 (the £90 Safari Room boasts a four-poster bed, an imitation leopard-skin bed cover and African bush decor).

Places to Eat

In the shopping area, sedate *Gershwin's Coffee House* (☎ 474000, 14 Nelson St) has tasty blackboard specials, all-day breakfasts, cream teas and good coffee.

Wind St (pronounced as in 'wind me up') is Swansea's cafe quarter. *Valentino's Restaurant* (☎ 644611, 66 Wind St) is a traditional Italian eatery with pizza and pasta dishes from £7. Good £5 lunch specials at the *Pitcher & Piano* (see Pubs & Bars in the Entertainment section) include a drink. Trendy *Ask* (☎ 477070, 6 Wind St) has a good selection of pasta dishes from £6. Just off Wind St, in an alley encouragingly named Salubrious Place, is *Indigo* (☎ 463466), a popular Mediterranean bar-bistro that also does Welsh dishes from £5 and cheap tapas.

The *Monkey Cafe Bar* (see Pubs & Bars in the Entertainment section) serves baguettes, fruit lassis and beer during the day, plus main courses from £6 and a good selection of vegetarian dishes from £3.50. Colourful *Cafe Mambo* (☎ 456620, 46 The Kingsway) has an eclectic menu with vegetarian main courses from £8 and meaty

dishes from £10, as well as tapas and great cocktails.

Handy for those staying in Uplands or on Oystermouth Rd, St Helens Rd has half a dozen Indian restaurants with immense menus and dishes costing £5 to £8; the *Raj Balti House* (☎ 645383, 81 St Helens Rd) has a daily all-you-can-eat dinner for about £6. The nearby *Wig & Pen* (see Pubs & Bars in the Entertainment section) has pretty good food all day every day.

Cheerful *Topo Gigio* (☎ 467888, 55 St Helens Rd) has pasta dishes for around £5 and meaty choices from £10. It opens evenings Tuesday to Saturday evenings, plus Friday lunch time. *Jules Vegetarian Café* (☎ 412752, 68 Bryn-y-Mor Rd) offers light lunch dishes for £3 to £4, daily except Sunday.

Two good choices in Mumbles are *Hanson's at Hillcrest* (☎ 363700, 1 Higher Lane), at the Hillcrest House Hotel (see Places to Stay earlier), with carefully prepared dishes from £9 to £13; and *L'Amuse* (☎ 366006, 93 Newton Rd), a good French restaurant with set two-course lunches from £11.

Self-caterers will like the *Swansea Market*, a vast cacophonous covered market with stalls selling fresh foods and Welsh delicacies such as cockles. It has operated at the same site (between White Walls and Union St) since 1830 and is opens daily except Sunday. The most central supermarket is a vast *Tesco*, south-east of the bus station.

Entertainment

Pubs & Bars In central Swansea, *No Sign Bar* (56 Wind St) is a laid-back cafe-bar. The cool *Monkey Cafe Bar* (☎ 480822, 13 Castle St) has two floors and various DJ club nights; it opens Wednesday to Saturday (see Places to Eat). *Pitcher & Piano* (☎ 461312, 59 Wind St) is a spacious, airy bar with sofas and wooden floors. *Cafe Mambo* (see Places to Eat) is where Swansea's youth take their early-evening cocktails.

Near Oystermouth Rd and Uplands, the *Wig & Pen* (☎ 466519, 134 St Helens Rd) is a big, family-friendly pub.

At weekends, students flock to the pubs lining Mumbles Rd in Oystermouth, which is

SOUTH-EAST WALES

certainly the liveliest place to drink. Earn your 'Mumbles Mile' T-shirt by having a drink in each of the 11 pubs between Newton Rd and Bracelet Bay; work your way from the *White Rose* via the *Knab Rock* rock 'n' roll pub to the clubs, *Cinderella's* or *Neptune's*. The pub where Dylan Thomas used to drink, now called *Dylan's Tavern*, is fairly touristy.

Clubs Swansea's answer to Ibiza, *Escape* (☎ 652854, Northampton Lane) is a large house/garage club open 10 pm to 4 am at weekends. Admission costs £8 to £12. The newest venue is *Sanctuary* (☎ 366511, The Kingsway), which has a mix of funk, garage and house with local and guest DJs playing two floors on Friday and Saturday.

Check out *Buzz* magazine (available from the TIC or bars) for comprehensive club and live music listings.

Gay & Lesbian Venues Three congenial Swansea spots, keeping conventional pub hours, are *Champers* (☎ 655622, 210 High St), a pub and wine bar, *The Waterside* (☎ 648555, 18 Anchor Court, Victoria Quay), and *Exchange Bar* (☎ 645345, 10 The Strand). The *H2O* club, above The Waterside, opens 10 pm to 2 am Monday to Thursday and until 4 am Friday and Saturday.

Theatre & Classical Music The town's main theatre is *Swansea Grand Theatre* (☎ 475715, Singleton St), hosting everything from pantomimes to ballet. The *Dylan Thomas Theatre* (☎ 473238, Gloucester Place) is a favourite venue for Thomas' works. *Taliesin Arts Centre* (☎ 296883, Singleton Park) at the Swansea campus of the University of Wales, 2 miles west of the centre on Mumbles Rd, mounts a varied program of music, theatre, dance and film. Handsome *Brangwyn Hall* (☎ 635489, Guildhall Rd South) in the Civic Centre has the acoustics for classical choral and orchestral programs.

Spectator Sports
Swansea Rugby Football Club, the 'All-Whites', is among Wales' top six rugby

clubs. It plays at the Swansea Cricket & RFC Ground, west of the centre on the Mumbles Rd. The 'Swans', Swansea City Football Club, play at 'the Vetch' (Vetch Field) just west of the town centre. Both are soon to be relocated to a big new sports complex north-east of the centre.

Getting There & Away
First Cymru's comfortable Swansea-Cardiff Shuttle bus (£7 return, 55 minutes) runs hourly (every two hours on Sunday). The Beacons Bus (route B1) also serves Swansea (see Getting There & Around in the Brecon Beacons National Park section later).

Trains from Swansea run via Cardiff (£9 day return, 50 minutes) and Bath on the main line to London Paddington. There are also direct trains to Fishguard (£10, one hour 30 minutes, two daily) for ferries to Ireland.

Swansea is the southern terminus for Wales & West's gorgeous Heart of Wales line, which skirts the Brecon Beacons National Park and crosses southern Mid Wales. Day trips as far as Llandrindod Wells are possible; see Llandrindod Wells in the Mid Wales chapter for details.

Swansea Cork Ferries (☎ 456116) sails to/from Cork (Ireland) four to six times weekly from mid-March to September. In the high season single tickets for foot passengers cost £34 (£159 for a car and driver). The terminal is across the River Tawe, about a mile east of the town centre. The company runs a bus from the bus station via the train station to the ferry terminal about an hour before each departure, and returns with arriving passengers.

Getting Around
Bus First Cymru runs an efficient, colour-coded network of local services. Bus Nos 2, 2A, 3 and 3A run between Swansea and Oystermouth bus stations (£1.50) every 10 minutes (every half-hour in the evening) Monday to Saturday and every 30 minutes (every hour in the evening) on Sunday. During term-time, bus No 80 plies between the university and Oystermouth every half-hour all evening; the last bus back, at 11.45 pm, continues to The Kingsway.

A Swansea Bay Day Out ticket offers all-day bus travel in the Swansea and Mumbles area for £3.80/2.65. Tickets can be purchased on board.

Car Rental firms include Avis (☎ 460939) on Orchard St or Europcar (☎ 650526) on Lower Oxford St. Street parking is metered in the city centre.

Taxi For a taxi try Yellow Cabs (☎ 644446). It costs about £6.50 to go from the train station to Mumbles.

Bicycle Two bike-hire shops are within a block of one another in the centre: The Cycle Centre (☎ 410710), on Wyndham St, rents bikes for £12 per day and Schmoo's Cycles (☎ 470698), on Lower Oxford St, charges £10 per day. Schmoo's will deliver and collect bikes.

THE GOWER PENINSULA
☎ 01792

Stretching west from The Mumbles for 15 miles, 'the Gower' (Y Gŵyr) became the UK's first officially designated AONB (see Ecology & Environment in the Facts about Wales chapter) in 1956, and it well deserves the title. This is one of the most unaffectedly beautiful corners of the country, with miles of scenic cliffs and sandy beaches, serene rolling farmland and windblown uplands. It's fine walking country and was a favourite haunt of Dylan Thomas.

West of The Mumbles is a sequence of small bays and rugged headlands, culminating at Pwlldu Head. In the 18th century, smugglers landed brandy and tobacco from France here. The seas are treacherous: over 250 boats have been lost off the Gower.

The big beach at Oxwich Bay is protected on the west by its own huge headland. Beyond this is Port Eynon Bay, with a beachside youth hostel. The Gower's western tip is known as Worms Head, an apt name for this elongated, rocky headland. Beside it stretches the longest and finest of the Gower's beaches, at Rhossili. Less well known are Broughton Bay and the dunes of Whiteford Burrows farther north, part of

which is a National Nature Reserve. Much of the Gower's northern coast is salt marsh that faces the Burry Inlet, an important area for wading birds and wildfowl.

As part of its far-sighted Neptune Campaign to keep the UK's coastline accessible to the public, the National Trust (NT) now owns about three-quarters of the Gower's coast, mainly in a thin seaside area totalling about 26 miles of shoreline – NT staff joke about the 'Gower Marathon'. Some of this land is jointly managed with the Countryside Council for Wales (CCW) and the Glamorgan Wildlife Trust.

Being so accessible, the peninsula is naturally popular and gets very crowded in summer. Accommodation tends to be more expensive than in Swansea and gets booked out well in advance.

Information
Gower has no TICs beyond The Mumbles, although the Swansea TIC has information, including listings of B&Bs, camp sites and other places to stay.

The NT runs a good, year-round visitor centre at Rhossili (see Rhossili later), stocked with maps and booklets on walking, including the useful *Circular Walks in Gower*. It also publishes a series of free, detailed leaflets on its Gower holdings. Alternatively, contact the NT Warden for Gower (☎ 01792-390636) at Little Reynoldston Farm, Reynoldston, Gower SA3 1AQ.

The CCW publishes *National Nature Reserves*, with details of nature reserves all over Wales (there are three on the Gower), and *Nature at its Best*, with contacts for guided walks in these reserves. Contact the CCW (☎ 01248-385500) at Plas Penrhos, Ffordd Penrhos, Bangor, Gwynedd LL57 2LQ.

A very useful Web site devoted to Gower history, sights and practicalities is at www.explore-gower.co.uk. The Gower is covered by both the OS Pathfinder map No 1126 and the OS Explorer No 164.

Getting There & Around
First Cymru buses (£4.20 day return) from Swansea bus station to the Gower include No 16 to north Gower, including Llanrhidian

SOUTH-EAST WALES

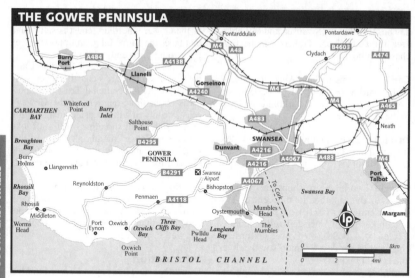

THE GOWER PENINSULA

and Llangennith (1¼ hours, four daily), No 18 to Penmaen and Oxwich (50 minutes, every two hours) and No 18A to Reynoldston, Port Eynon and Rhossili (one hour, every two hours). Nos 48 and 49 go all around Gower from Easter to October. All buses run Monday to Saturday, with very limited Sunday services.

You could do better with a bus pass: a Day Saver (£4.50/3.50) is good for a day's unlimited travel on any of First Cymru's services except the Swansea–Cardiff Shuttle. A family ticket costs £9. If you're planning to linger, a Gower & City Rider (£12/8.20) gives you a week's travel around Swansea and the Gower. Both tickets can be purchased on board.

Penmaen & Three Cliffs Bay

From Pwlldu Head the limestone Pennard Cliffs, honeycombed with caves, stretch westwards for 2 miles to Three Cliffs Bay – the closest sizeable beach to Swansea, though really a vast, sandy cove as the name suggests.

On Penmaen Burrows, the headland on the bay's west side, are the remains of a medieval church (and the buried remains of

a village known as Steadworlango, perhaps a Viking settlement), fragments of a Norman tower, a Neolithic burial chamber and a limekiln used until just a century ago for the production of quicklime fertiliser. Access is on foot from Penmaen.

The no-frills *Three Cliffs Bay Caravan Park* (☎ 371218, North Hills Farm), on a working farm at the east end of Penmaen, also has tent sites for £4.50 (one adult) to £10.50 (family) per night and self-catering cottages (from £220 per week for two people) in restored farm buildings on a spectacular location above the bay. It opens Easter to October.

Oxwich

Oxwich Castle (☎ 390359), run by Cadw, the Welsh historic monuments agency, is on a headland above Oxwich Bay, and is actually the remains of a 16th-century, mock-military Tudor mansion built on the site of a 14th-century castle, beside a working farm. It opens 10 am to 5 pm, late April to late September. Admission costs £2/1.50.

The 289-hectare Oxwich Nature Reserve, home to a variety of birdlife, dune plants, and oak and ash woodlands, is a favourite of ecology students and researchers. Windy Oxwich Bay is prime windsurfing territory. Gower Windsurfing (☎ 391686) on the beach give lessons for beginners and experts; for more information and surf/windsurf reports check out their Web site at www.gowerwindsurfing.com.

At *Oxwich Camping Park* (☎ *390777*) near Oxwich Bay, open April to September, you can pitch a tent for £5 to £10. The village has a number of snug B&Bs, including *Woodside Guest House* (☎ *390791, Woodside*), open February to November with rooms from £20 per person. The beachside *Oxwich Bay Hotel* (☎ *390329, fax 391254, Oxwich Bay*) has overpriced rooms from £30 per person.

Port Eynon

The 30-bed *Port Eynon Youth Hostel* (☎ *390706, Old Lifeboat House*), down a footpath from the car park, is right on the fine beach at Port Eynon Bay. It opens Monday to Saturday from April to October, and daily from mid-July to August and at bank holiday weekends. Beds cost £9.25/6.50 per night; bring your own food. Reception opens from 5 pm.

The village has several B&Bs, including the *Culver House Hotel* (☎ *390755, fax 390735*), with en-suite rooms from £26. Beachside eateries include the *Captain's Table* restaurant, a chippy called the *Seafarer* and, just inland, the *Smugglers Haunt* pub.

Arthur's Stone

Cefn Bryn is the name for the peninsula's windy, 185m-high central uplands. Above the village of Reynoldston is an immense, 25-ton quartz boulder, the fallen capstone of a Neolithic burial chamber known as Arthur's Stone (Coeten Arthur). In legend it's the pebble Arthur removed from his boot and flung across the Burry Inlet while on his way to the fateful Battle of Camlan in AD 539. Local lore also said that a woman who crawled on her hands and knees around the stone at midnight of a full moon would be joined by her lover if he was faithful.

The best part of making your way up here is the view from the top – you can see out to the edges of the Gower in every direction, as if you were floating above it. On a clear day you can see south to Lundy Island and the Devon and Somerset coast.

To reach Arthur's Stone from Reynoldston (about 11 miles west of Swansea and 1 mile north from the A4118), take the road east and upwards for ½ mile to the village commons and a parking area. The stone is visible to the north. You can also climb southwards for about 1¼ miles from the village of Llanrhidian. This is a good area for mountain biking.

Rhossili

pop 250

You could stay a day or more at the peninsula's western tip. The flinty village of Rhossili looks south-westwards to the wave-blasted tidal islands of Worms Head (from the Old English *wurm*, dragon), and northwards along the full 3-mile length of Rhossili Bay, the Gower's biggest and finest beach. You can see the ribs of the *Helvetica*, a Norwegian barque wrecked in an 1887 storm, sticking out of the sand.

Hang-gliders soar off Rhossili Down (59m), the heath-covered glacial ledge above the beach. At the top are numerous Iron Age earthworks, a burial chamber called Sweyne's Howes, and the remains of a WWII radar station. At its foot, behind the beach, is The Warren, the sand-covered remains of old Rhossili village.

You can walk out across the causeway onto Worms Head only during the two-hour period either side of low tide (see the boxed text 'The Worm Turns – the Tide Too' later). A seabird colony on the Outer Head includes razorbills, guillemots, kittiwakes, fulmars, puffins and oystercatchers, but be considerate and stay away from them during nesting season (April to July). There are also seals here.

South of the village is The Viel (or Vile), a patchwork of strip-fields first laid out in medieval times.

Information The NT's Rhossili Visitor Centre (☎ 390707), at the start of the path to

SOUTH-EAST WALES

The Worm Turns – the Tide Too

Pay close attention to the tides if you plan to walk out onto the Outer Head! People are regularly rescued after being stranded by the incoming tide. Among those who have spent a cold, nervous half-night trapped there was the young Dylan Thomas, as he relates in 'Who Do You Wish Was With Us?', from *Portrait of the Artist as a Young Dog*.

It is only safe to walk out within the two-hour period either side of low tide. If you do get stranded, do *not* under any circumstances try to wade or swim back. Currents here are fierce, and the layered rocks between the islands can be treacherous.

Check the tide tables at the National Trust (NT) Visitor Centre (they're posted in the window when the centre is closed) or at the coastguard station next door.

Worms Head, has maps and information on NT coastal properties around Wales. Upstairs are pictorial exhibits on local flora and fauna, geology, history and famous shipwrecks. The centre opens 10.30 am to 5.30 pm daily, mid-March to October; 11 am to 4 pm Wednesday to Sunday, November and December; and 11 am to 4 pm at weekends, January to mid-March.

A coastguard house closer to Worms Head is used by the CCW as a wildlife information centre.

For a demanding five- to six-hour tour on foot, start in the car park on the eastern side of Middleton (¾ mile east down the road from Rhossili), walk to Worms Head and back to the visitor centre. Then climb to the top of Rhossili Down (a steep, 2½- to 3-mile slog) and continue down to Hillend, returning along the beach to Rhossili and Middleton.

Places to Stay & Eat Among several B&Bs in the village is cheerful *Hampstead* (☎ 390545, fax 391702, ℮ stay@rhossili .com), charging £20 per person for en-suite rooms. The *Worms Head Hotel* (☎ 390512) has an unrivalled view of Worms Head and the beach; most rooms have sea views. B&B costs £43/66 for en-suite singles/ doubles. The hotel's restaurant opens year round, and there are several summer *cafes* in the village.

The solitary house in the middle of The Warren is the *Old Rectory*. Built in the 1850s, it is now restored and let as self-catering holiday accommodation by the NT (see Short-Term Rentals under Accommo-

dation in the Facts for the Visitor chapter). The NT also rents out one of the coastguard cottages near the visitor centre.

Llangennith
At the northern end of Rhossili Bay is Rhossili's twin parish, Llangennith. There you can take surfing lessons at the Welsh Surfing Federation School (☎ 386426, ℮ surfwsf@aol.com), the Croft, for £18/ 28 per half-/full day, including wetsuit and board.

The Iron & Coal Valleys

It was from the valleys of Glamorgan and Monmouthshire, fanning northwards from Cardiff and Newport, that eldorado seams of iron and coal were extracted and processed with growing ruthlessness from the mid 18th to the early 20th centuries. These valleys became a laboratory for state-of-the-art mining and smelting techniques – the Silicon Valley of Britain's Industrial Revolution. At first the iron trade dictated the need for coal, but by the 1830s coal was finding its own worldwide markets and people poured in looking for work.

The most intensive development took place near the heads of the valleys, almost a stone's throw from the serene Brecon Beacons. The hills rise up to form Wales' most abrupt and profound watershed – physically, economically and aesthetically.

Even today it's easier to travel down to the ports to which these valleys were once indentured, than to the much nearer towns of the Beacons.

Today the region is long on socio-historical interest and short on beauty. A landscape chopped and scarred, its towns down-at-heel, it serves as a memorial to what intensive industrialisation and Britain's colonial mentality did right at home.

MERTHYR TYDFIL
☎ 01685 • pop 55,000

There were already settlements around what is now Merthyr Tydfil (pronounced **mur**-thir **tid**-vil) in Mesolithic times, but its role in the Industrial Revolution is what put it on the map. This town at the head of the Taff Valley is as scarred as the rest, but surprisingly rich in the artefacts of the Industrial Age.

History

The town name means something like 'Tydfil the Martyr', referring to a Welsh princess murdered for her Christian beliefs in the 5th century. She was later canonised, and St Tydfil's Church is said to mark the spot where she died.

In 1286, Gilbert de Clare, Norman lord of Glamorgan and master of Caerphilly Castle (see Around Cardiff in the Cardiff & Around chapter), started building a castle at Morlais, but the earl of Hereford claimed it was on his land, and after the two fought over the unfinished castle, it went to ruin.

Merthyr remained a minor village until the late 18th century, when its proximity to iron ore, limestone, water and wood pushed it into position as a centre of iron production. The subsequent discovery of rich coal reserves upped the ante, and by 1801 a string of settlements, each growing around its own ironworks – Cyfarthfa, Penydarren, Dowlais, Pentrebach and others – had fused into the biggest town in Wales. Immigrants flooded in from all over Europe in search of work.

By 1803, Cyfarthfa was the world's biggest ironworks, overtaken by Dowlais by 1850. Each works had its dynasty of wealthy ironmasters – the Crawshays at Cyfarthfa,

the Guests at Dowlais, the Homfrays at Penydarren. To shift all this metal, the Crawshays built the Glamorganshire Canal from Cyfarthfa to Cardiff, and the Homfrays laid a tram from Penydarren to Abercynon. The earliest steam locomotive, developed by Richard Trevethick, was tested on the Homfrays' tramline in 1804.

Ever more efficient ways to make iron were pioneered – on the backs of labourers (including, until 1842, women and children as young as six) who lived in appalling, disease-ridden conditions and were literally worked into the ground. By the 19th century Merthyr was a centre of political radicalism. The Merthyr Rising of 1831 was the most violent uprising in Britain's history: 10,000 ironworkers, angry over pay-cuts and lack of representation, faced off against a handful of armed soldiers, and rioting continued for a month.

In 1900 Merthyr sent Britain's first-ever Labour MP, a pacifist Scots preacher named Keir Hardie, to parliament in London.

As demand for iron and steel dwindled in the 20th century, one by one the ironworks closed down. Unemployment soared (as high as 60% in 1935) and has been disproportionately high ever since, though the town is slowly getting back on its feet.

Orientation & Information

Merthyr is strung out along the upper Taff Valley, and you'll need to do a bit of walking or cycling to see the sights (you can hire a bike at Cyfarthfa Castle). A convenient axis for this is the Taff Trail, the Cardiff-to-Brecon walking and cycling trail, running up the valley along the west side of town.

The TIC (☎ 379884, fax 350043, ⓔ merthyrtic@tsww.com), beside the bus station, opens 9.30 am to 5.30 pm Monday to Saturday. Here you can pick up a series of free brochures about historical walks in and around Merthyr. There is a post office on Penydarren Rd.

Cyfarthfa Castle

For a measure of the wealth that accumulated at the top of the industrial pyramid, check out this castle, built in 1824 by

SOUTH-EAST WALES

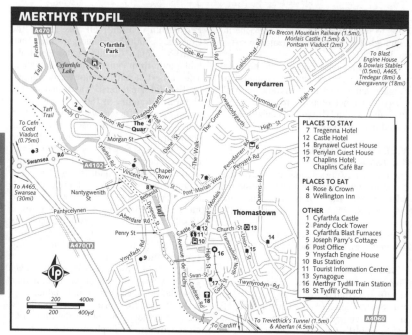

MERTHYR TYDFIL

PLACES TO STAY
7 Tregenna Hotel
12 Castle Hotel
14 Brynawel Guest House
15 Penylan Guest House
17 Chaplins Hotel;
    Chaplins Café Bar

PLACES TO EAT
4 Rose & Crown
8 Wellington Inn

OTHER
1 Cyfarthfa Castle
2 Pandy Clock Tower
3 Cyfarthfa Blast Furnaces
5 Joseph Parry's Cottage
6 Post Office
9 Ynysfach Engine House
10 Bus Station
11 Tourist Information Centre
13 Synagogue
16 Merthyr Tydfil Train Station
18 St Tydfil's Church

Cyfarthfa's boss, William Crawshay II, overlooking his ironworks. Across Brecon Rd is the Pandy Clock Tower, built by Crawshay with clocks on only three sides.

The castle has been restored as an art gallery and museum (☎ 723112) of Merthyr's industrial history. It opens 10 am to 5.30 pm daily, April to September, and 10 am to 4 pm Tuesday to Friday and noon to 4 pm at weekends, the rest of the year. Admission costs £2/1. The surrounding 160 acres of gardens are now a public park (free admission).

Joseph Parry's Cottage

Along Chapel Row are several 19th-century ironworkers' houses, built by the Crawshays and standing in bald contrast to Cyfarthfa Castle. No 4, now restored and open to the public as a museum (☎ 723112), was the birthplace of Welsh composer and songwriter Joseph Parry. It opens 2 to 5 pm Thursday to Sunday, April to September. Admission costs 60/50p.

Industrial Sites

Most of the old ironworks buildings have been demolished. Those that remain are not presently open as public attractions, although the **Cyfarthfa Blast Furnaces**, across the river from the castle, are under restoration. For a better idea of what these ironworks looked like, visit the one at Blaenafon (see Blaenafon later).

The **Ynysfach Engine House** on Ynysfach Rd and the **Blast Engine House** on High St in Dowlais once housed huge beam engines to blow the furnaces at their respective ironworks; both buildings have been restored on the outside. **Dowlais Stables**, for the horses that pulled the factory trams, have been converted into flats. You can still make out the tramline nearby.

Brecon Mountain Railway

A 2-mile section of this narrow-gauge railway, which once hauled coal and passengers, has been restored. From Pant Station

(☎ 722988), 3½ miles north-east of Merthyr town centre, you can ride behind a vintage steam locomotive past Pontsticill Reservoir to Dol-y-Gaer, within the Brecon Beacons National Park.

Trains depart at 10.45 am, noon, 1.15, 2.30 and 3.45 pm (and 5 pm on some days) Easter to October (except some Fridays and Mondays in May and October). The Merthyr TIC has the current timetable. The return journey takes one hour 5 minutes and costs £6.80/3.40.

There's a cafe at the station, or you can get off at the reservoir for a picnic and catch a later train back. At the station you can have a look at several more locomotives and the workshops where volunteers labour at their restoration. For more information check out the Web site at www.breconmountainrailway.co.uk.

From the bus station, take bus No 35 (£1.75 return, 18 minutes, four hourly) or No 30 or 31 (25 minutes, hourly) to the Pant Cemetery stop, from where the train station is a five-minute walk. The Beacons Roundabout bus (see Getting There & Around in the Brecon Beacons National Park section later) stops at Pant Station in the summer.

Other Things to See & Do
St Tydfil's Church, on High St, is a 19th-century replacement of a Norman church built in honour of Merthyr's local saint. On Bryntirion Rd, at the end of Church St, is the town's former **Synagogue**, built in the 1870s.

The Taff Trail crosses two handsome railway viaducts, both completed in 1866, at **Cefn Coed** (the third biggest in Wales) and at **Pontsarn**. There's little left of **Morlais Castle** except for an underground vaulted chamber (one of the finest in Britain though).

Trainspotters may want to have a look at **Trevethick's Tunnel**, site of the first test of Trevethick's steam-powered locomotive – it's off the A470 in Pentrebach, 1¼ miles south of Merthyr town centre (though poorly signposted).

Places to Stay
Two B&Bs within walking distance of the TIC are *Penylan Guest House* (☎ 723179, *12 Courtland Terrace*), off Union St, with rooms for £16 per person, and cycle-friendly *Brynawel Guest House* (☎/fax 722573, *Queens Rd*) with en-suite rooms at £20.

Castle Hotel (☎ 386868, fax 383898, *Castle St*) and *Tregenna Hotel* (☎ 723627, *Park Terrace*), off Pont Morlais West, have wheelchair-accessible, en-suite rooms at around £40 per person. *Chaplins Hotel* (☎ 387272, *Swan St*) has comfortable en-suite singles/doubles from £38/55 and a cafe-bar next door.

The independent, nonsmoking *HoBo Backpackers* hostel (☎ 01495-718422, *Plas-y-Gwely, Central Chambers, Morgan St*) in Tredegar, a small town 7 miles east of Merthyr, is a welcome place for walkers and cyclists to decompress at the interface between the industrial valleys and the Brecon Beacons. Dormitory beds are £10. It's a five-minute walk from Tredegar bus station, half a block past 'The Clock', a prominent clocktower on a roundabout. It closes during the day but you can leave your bags for a few hours at the library or the Cambrian Pub, both by The Clock. Stagecoach bus No X4 or X40 runs from Merthyr twice hourly daily except Sunday.

Places to Eat
Chaplins Café Bar (☎ 387272, *High St*) serves food and drink all day, including children's menus. The *Wellington Inn* (☎ 370665, *Bethesda St*) offers mainly Italian food but only opens in the evening. One of Merthyr's oldest pubs is the *Rose & Crown* (☎ 379766, *Morgan St, The Quar*).

Getting There & Away
Stagecoach (☎ 01633-244744) bus No X4 or X40 runs every 30 minutes from Cardiff (£3 single, 45 minutes) and hourly from Abergavenny (£3.50, 1½ hours). No X78 (£3, one hour) from Cardiff and No X75 (£3.90, one hour) from Swansea both run hourly. No 43 (£2.70, 35 minutes) comes from Brecon every hour or two. All routes stop at Merthyr bus station.

Services are limited or nonexistent on Sunday, with the exception in summer of the Beacons Bus (route B3); see Getting

SOUTH-EAST WALES

There & Around in the Brecon Beacons National Park section.

Merthyr is linked to Cardiff (£3.50/4 single/cheap day return, 55 minutes) by Valley Lines trains (☎ 029-2044 9944) running about every hour (every two hours on Sunday). Call National Rail Enquiries on ☎ 0845 748 4950 for information.

AROUND MERTHYR TYDFIL
Aberfan
On 21 October 1966 in the town of Aberfan (pronounced **ab**-er-van), 4 miles south of Merthyr Tydfil, a poorly secured, rainsoaked mountain of slag (coal mine waste) gave way, burying Pantglas primary school and 144 people, 116 of whom were children.

A tragedy of such magnitude and senselessness beggars comprehension, and still haunts and embitters the Welsh as if it happened yesterday. The lost children, all aged seven to 10, are buried beneath a double row of matching gravestones at the top of Aberfan's cemetery, on the slopes west of the village. It is impossible not to be shaken by this mute memorial.

If you want to visit the cemetery – as thousands still do every year – take the A470 to Pentrebach, the A4054 on to Troedyrhiw and the B4285 across the River Taff and south to Aberfan. The cemetery is also just above the Taff Trail. Stagecoach bus No 78, X78 or 81 makes the 15-minute trip from Merthyr bus station about four times hourly.

BLAENAFON
☎ 01495 • pop 6000
In November 2000 the gritty town of Blaenafon (pronounced blye-**nahv**-on) received worldwide recognition for the role it played in the Industrial Revolution, when UNESCO awarded World Heritage status to a 6km by 8km area of its 18th- and 19th- century ironworks, railways, waterways, mines, quarries and workers' houses.

What is now officially called the Blaenafon Industrial Landscape is one of the best places on earth to see the course and consequences of headlong industrialisation. Focal points include the remains of the Blaenafon Ironworks, Big Pit Mining Museum, Blaenafon town itself, a section of the Brecknock & Abergavenny Canal – and a vast landscape shattered by iron and coal excavation.

UNESCO recognition elevates Blaenafon to the same level of universal cultural importance as, say, Stonehenge or the Great Barrier Reef. The surrounding communities never really recovered from the collapse of the iron and coal industries and will benefit from annual investment of around £1 million a year for a decade plus overnight fame as an important tourist destination.

Orientation & Information
Blaenafon is at the head of the Llwyd Valley, 16 miles north of Newport. Most buses stop at Lion St, off High St, in the town centre. From here Blaenafon Ironworks are a five-minute walk: at the west end of Lion St turn right (north) into High St, which turns left and becomes Upper Waun St; at the end of this, cross North St to the Ironworks entrance. The TIC (☎ 792615), part of the visitor centre at the Ironworks, opens 9.30 am to 4.30 pm daily, Easter to October.

Big Pit Mining Museum and the Pontypool & Blaenafon Railway are several miles west beyond the Ironworks.

Blaenafon Ironworks
When it was completed in 1789, Blaenafon's was one of the most advanced ironworks anywhere. Its original three huge, coal-fired furnaces were blasted with air from a steam engine – an innovation over older, smaller furnaces fired with charcoal and blasted, one at a time, with a water wheel and bellows. Within a few years it was the second-biggest ironworks in the world, after Cyfarthfa at Merthyr Tydfil. Innovation and development continued here until 1904, when the last furnace was shut down, prey to a slumping iron and steel industry.

Today the site, though rundown, is one of the best-preserved of all Industrial Revolution ironworks and is in the midst of restoration by its owner, Cadw. You can make out the remains of all five blast furnaces and the tall shell of a water-balance lift built to raise wagons full of pig-iron up to a tram road running to distant forges. It's not hard to trace the whole process, from the charging of the furnaces (from high ground at the rear) with coal, iron ore and limestone to the casting of molten iron in the yard below.

Nearby are terraced cottages for the iron-workers. The surrounding hillsides are peppered with old tramlines, adit (horizontal) mines, tunnels and 'scouring' sites (where water released from holding ponds washed away topsoil to expose ore seams).

Parts of the site can be visited now, though it will be some time before it's fully restored. It opens 9.30 am to 4.30 pm daily, Easter to October. Admission costs £2/1.50. The visitor centre (☎ 792615) in the old Pay Office has detailed information about this and the rest of the UNESCO zone around Blaenafon.

Big Pit Mining Museum

A mine was in operation here by 1812 to supply coal for the Blaenafon Ironworks, but was not sunk to its present level until 1880. Exactly 100 years later it was shut down by the National Coal Board. In 1983 the Big Pit Mining Museum was created inside the mine, not only as a tourist attraction but also as a kind of memorial to the coal era in south-west Wales. All the staff have a direct connection with the coal industry; some of the guides once cut coal here themselves. In the long run this is to become the National Mining Museum of Wales.

Visitors can descend 90m to the pit floor in an old mine lift and inspect tunnels and coalfaces. This is not a simulation (as at Rhondda Heritage Park near Cardiff) but the real thing, and it's not for the claustrophobic. Topside, you can see the pithead baths, blacksmith's workshop and other colliery buildings.

As Big Pit is still classed as a working colliery and must comply with mine safety legislation, you'll be decked out in hard hat, power pack and other safety gear weighing some 5kg, and won't be allowed to take matches or anything electrical (including photo equipment and watches) down with

you. It's cold at the bottom of the mine so take extra layers, and you'll need sturdy shoes.

Big Pit (☎ 790311) opens 9.30 am to 5 pm daily, March to November, with one hour underground tours from 10 am (last tour at 3.30 pm). Admission costs £5.75/3.95 (free with a Cardiff Card; see Information in the Cardiff & Around chapter).

Pontypool & Blaenafon Railway

This standard-gauge railway was built from Pontypool to Brynmawr, to haul coal and passengers up and down the valley. Passenger traffic ceased in 1941, and coal haulage stopped when the Big Pit was closed in 1980.

Since then a ¾-mile section, running north-westwards from Furnace Sidings near Big Pit, has been restored and maintained by local volunteers. Whistle Halt, the far terminus, is the highest train station in England and Wales at 396m. The Whistle Inn Pub beside the station has a huge collection of miners' lamps.

You can board every 30 minutes from 11.30 am to 4.30 pm at weekends and bank holidays, Easter to September. A ticket costs £2.20/1.10. For further information call ☎ 792263 or ☎ 760242.

Places to Eat

From the bus stop on Lion St in the town centre, head east and turn right into Broad St, where basic cooked meals are on offer at *Coffee Corner* (☎ 791512) and the *Burger Bar* (☎ 790330). A five-minute walk uphill from the ironworks is the *Rifleman's Arms* (☎ 792297, North St), which serves bar meals.

Getting There & Away

The only direct buses are from Newport with Stagecoach Red & White (☎ 01633-244744). No 30 goes via Lion St in Blaenafon town centre out to Big Pit (£6.45 return, 40 minutes, every two hours, no service on Sunday). No 23 or X23 runs only to Lion St (£4, one hour, twice hourly except hourly on Sunday). If you're going to Big Pit it's cheaper to buy a Network Rider pass (see Getting Around at the beginning of the chapter for details).

By car from Newport, take the A4042 to Pontypool and the well-signposted A4043 or B4246 on to Blaenafon.

Blaenafon is also 8 miles south-west of Abergavenny, which is easy by car (take the B4246 with fine views across the Vale of Usk) but awkward and tedious by public transport. A taxi from Abergavenny costs £8.50 each way. There's no direct transport from Cardiff.

The UNESCO designation is certain to radically improve ease of access in the coming few years.

The Lower Wye Valley

The River Wye flows 154 miles from its source in Mid Wales to meet the River Severn at Chepstow. From a mossy spring at Plynlimon it descends via Rhayader and Builth Wells (see the Mid Wales chapter) to Hay-on-Wye (see Brecon Beacons National Park later in the chapter). From there it makes a wide loop into England, returns to Wales at Monmouth and flows down to Chepstow.

Arguably the river's most beautiful stretch, from Monmouth down to its mouth at Chepstow, is the subject of this section. Most of it lies within an officially designated AONB (see Ecology & Environment in the Facts about Wales chapter), and in fact the best reason to come here is to explore the area on foot.

Activities

The Wye Valley Walk is a 107-mile way-marked trail running beside the Wye from Rhayader to Chepstow. From Monmouth downstream the trail runs mainly along the west side of the river, past the splendid ruins of Tintern Abbey (see Around Chepstow later). Chepstow and Monmouth TICs have lots of information and maps. Monmouthshire County Council's good *Wye Valley Walks* (£3.95) includes details of accommodation along the way, and its free *Enjoying the Countryside* leaflet lists activ-

ities and guided walks. Two other freebies are *The Wye Valley Walk*, with details on public transport and accommodation, and *Discover the Wye Valley on Foot & by Bus*.

Offa's Dyke Path is a national trail that zig-zags up the entire Wales-England border. At this end it runs along the east side of the Wye Valley, though it's no match for the gentler and more beautiful Wye Valley Walk. See under Activities in the Facts for the Visitor chapter for details of the Offa's Dyke Path or pick up Lonely Planet's *Walking in Britain*.

The Wye is one of the UK's finest canoeing rivers. From Hay-on-Wye to Chepstow there is a public right of navigation on the river, though in most places permission is still needed to launch or land. Note that below Bigsweir Bridge, and especially below Tintern (where the A466 crosses the Wye between Whitebrook and Llanogo), the Wye is tidal – river levels can vary by up to 12m at Chepstow! – and can be very dangerous for inexperienced canoeists. On no account should you canoe below Chepstow.

Outfits offering guided river trips are noted in local listings. Two good resources, available at Chepstow and Monmouth TICs, are the *Canoeists' Guide to the River Wye*, with access points and other information, and the Wye Management Advisory Group's free *River Wye Handbook*.

CHEPSTOW (CAS-GWENT)
☎ 01291 • pop 11,000

Chepstow is an attractive, pocket-size town at a big S-bend in the Wye, close to where it empties into the River Severn, and just over the border from England. Its main attraction is its splendid Norman castle – though it's popular locally for its racecourse. Half a day is sufficient to look around, though the town can also serve as a base for exploring the lower Wye.

Chepstow first developed as a base for the Norman conquest of south-east Wales, later prospering as a port for the timber and wine trades. As river-borne commerce gave way to railways, Chepstow's importance diminished to that of a typical market town (the Old English name means 'marketplace').

Orientation & Information

Chepstow sits right on the A48, the main road along the west side of the Severn. The town centre tapers south-westwards up from the river, with the castle on a bluff to the north. The bus station is south-west of the centre on Thomas St; the train station is south-east of the centre on Station Rd.

The TIC (☎ 623772, e chepstow-tic@ tsww.com), in the castle car park, opens 10 am to 5.30 pm daily, Easter to October, and 10 am to 1 pm and 2 to 4 pm daily, the rest of the year. In summer they'll keep a watch on your backpack while you visit the castle and town. Major banks cluster around Beaufort Square. The best local bookshop is Chepstow Bookshop at 13 St Mary St.

Chepstow Castle

This well-preserved slab of a castle perches dramatically on limestone cliffs above the Wye. It looks its best from the English side of the river: cross the 1816 Old Wye Bridge, take the pedestrian lane uphill and turn right.

Construction had begun by 1069 – just three years after the Norman conquest – making this Wales' oldest stone castle. The really massive bits were added in the 12th

century, and posh living quarters were built by the earl of Norfolk a century later. The castle was twice besieged during the Civil War and ended its military life in 1690. A cave below the castle is one of many places where legend says King Arthur and his knights sleep until the day they're needed to save Britain.

The castle (☎ 624065, Cadw) opens 9.30 am to 6 pm (to 4pm in winter) daily in summer. Admission costs £3/2.

Port Wall

The 13th-century city wall (the Port Wall, or Customs Wall), running from the castle right across to the other side of the river's loop, was intended more to control entry than for defence. It's best viewed from the Welsh St car park or from near the train station. The Gate House – originally the walled town's only entrance – was much restored in the 16th century.

Chepstow Museum

The museum (☎ 625981), in an 18th-century town house near the TIC, is mostly devoted to the history of the port. It also has a collection of 18th- and 19th-century prints

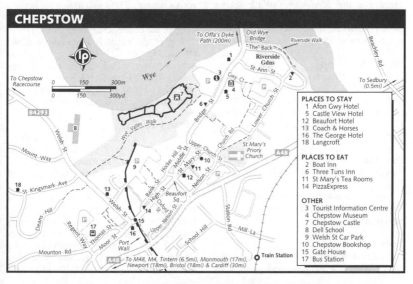

CHEPSTOW

PLACES TO STAY
1 Afon Gwy Hotel
5 Castle View Hotel
12 Beaufort Hotel
13 Coach & Horses
16 The George Hotel
18 Langcroft

PLACES TO EAT
2 Boat Inn
6 Three Tuns Inn
11 St Mary's Tea Rooms
14 PizzaExpress

OTHER
3 Tourist Information Centre
4 Chepstow Museum
7 Chepstow Castle
8 Dell School
9 Welsh St Car Park
10 Chepstow Bookshop
15 Gate House
17 Bus Station

and drawings of the Wye Valley. It opens 11 am to 1 pm and 2 to 5 pm daily (afternoon only on Sunday); it opens half an hour earlier and closes half an hour later in July, August and September. Admission costs £1 (free for kids).

Chepstow Racecourse

Set in parkland alongside the River Wye, just north of the town centre, is Wales' premier racecourse (☎ 622260), home to the Welsh National. The racecourse is a 20-minute walk from the train station, up Welsh St and onto the A466. Admission costs from £11 (£6 for seniors and those aged 16 to 24). Visit the Web site at www.chepstow-racecourse.co.uk for more information.

Walking Routes

A fine but strenuous walk goes upriver to Tintern Abbey (see Around Chepstow later) on Offa's Dyke Path and back on the Wye Valley Walk (about 11 miles; six hours). Offa's Dyke Path offers fine, high views from the heights just over on the English side of the river, before dropping down to Brockweir. Cross the bridge and head back downstream via the Wye Valley Walk on the western bank, to Tintern Abbey. From there the well-marked route back to Chepstow again climbs up for fine views east and west.

River Wye Trips

The Severn Princess Restoration Group (☎ 623560) is a group of volunteers who spend their Sundays restoring an old River Severn ferry, abandoned in Ireland in 1969. To pay for this labour of love, they run river trips up to Tintern in the summer from the mooring outside the Boat Inn (see Places to Eat). The schedule is a bit ad hoc, though trips go at least every few days. Ask at the Boat Inn for details.

You can follow the progress of the *Severn Princess'* restoration online at www.severnprincess.co.uk.

Special Events

The Chepstow Festival takes place during most of July in even-numbered years, with

outdoor art exhibits, Shakespeare in the castle, medieval pageantry, male voice choir singing, comedy, street entertainment and special town tours.

July is busy in odd-numbered years too, with a dramatic weekend sound-and-light show at the castle, featuring local folk in period costumes.

On the last Sunday of each month, the Chepstow Garrison does some fancy footwork in Stuart costume, at the castle.

Contact the TIC for details.

Places to Stay

The *Coach & Horses* (☎ 622626, *Welsh St*) has rooms for £20 and does excellent pub grub. *Langcroft* (☎ 625569, *71 St Kingsmark Ave*) offers B&B for £20 per person, though it's ½ mile from the TIC. *Upper Sedbury House* (☎ 627173, *Sedbury Lane, Sedbury*), a mile outside town, does B&B for £22/37 per single/double and has an outdoor swimming pool.

Afon Gwy Hotel (☎ 620158, *28 Bridge St*) has en-suite rooms with Wye views for £36/49 and a recommended restaurant. Near the TIC and castle is *Castle View Hotel* (☎ 620349, *16 Bridge St*) where rooms start at £37/51 (excluding breakfast). *Beaufort Hotel* (☎ 622497, *Beaufort Sq*), bang in the centre, charges from £35/45.

Top of the range is *The George Hotel* (☎ 625363, *fax 627418, Moor St*), beside the city gate, in a building which itself dates back to 1610. Comfortable en-suite rooms cost £70/80 (full breakfast is an extra £9), with a weekend B&B rate of £45 per person.

Places to Eat

If you're on a tight budget there's a *Pizza Express* (☎ 630572, *29 High St*) in the centre. *St Mary's Tea Rooms* (☎ 621711, *5 St Mary St*) does good snacks, cakes and modestly priced meals.

The *Boat Inn* (☎ 628192, *The Back*) is recommended for its good vibes, riverside location and attractive menu (lunch/evening mains from £5/10), including vegetarian options. Bar meals are also available at the *Coach & Horses* (see Places to Stay) and the *Three Tuns Inn* (☎ 623497, *32 Bridge St*).

The fine restaurant at *Afon Gwy Hotel* (see Places to Stay) offers a three-course set menu for £13.

Entertainment
Chepstow has a number of pubs (see Places to Eat). The Chepstow Male Voice Choir rehearses from 7.30 to 9.15 pm on most Mondays and Thursdays at Dell School on Welsh St.

Getting There & Away
Stagecoach and Badgerline (☎ 0117-955 3231) jointly run bus Nos X10, X11 and X14 to Chepstow from Bristol (£2.70, 50 minutes, hourly). Stagecoach's No 65 or 69 runs to/from Monmouth (£2.75, 50 minutes) about hourly; only the No 69 stops at Tintern. No 73 arrives hourly from Newport (£3.40, 45 minutes). There are no Sunday services.

There are daily direct train services to Chepstow from Newport (£4.20, 20 minutes) and Cardiff (£6.30, 35 minutes).

Chepstow is a short drive up the A466 from the M48, which connects England and Wales via the old Severn bridge.

AROUND CHEPSTOW
Tintern Abbey
The tall walls and huge, empty Gothic windows of this 14th-century Cistercian abbey on the banks of the Wye have been painted by Turner and lauded by Wordsworth. It's one of the most hauntingly beautiful ruins in Wales.

This Cistercian house was founded in 1131 by Walter de Clare, though the present building dates largely from the 14th century. It lasted until the dissolution of the monasteries and, compared to other religious sites that were laid to waste at this time, a remarkable amount remains.

Naturally, the village of Tintern swarms with visitors in summer. The abbey ruins are indeed an awe-inspiring sight, though best visited towards the end of the day, after the crowds have dispersed. The abbey (☎ 01291-689251, Cadw) opens 9.30 am to 6 pm daily, late May to late September; 9.30 am to 5 pm, March to May and October; and 9.30 am

(11am on Sunday) to 4 pm daily, November to March. Admission costs £2.50/2.

Tintern town, 6½ miles north of Chepstow or 10½ miles south of Monmouth, is strung out along the River Wye, with the abbey ruins at the downstream (southern) end. Its TIC (☎ 01291-689566) is upstream (north) of the town at the old station, almost a mile from the abbey, though you can find out all you need to know from the Cadw office and shop at the abbey.

Stagecoach bus No 69 runs every 1½ to two hours from Chepstow (£2, 20 minutes) and from Monmouth (£2.55, 30 minutes), Monday to Saturday, stopping right in front of the abbey.

MONMOUTH (TREFYNWY)
☎ 01600 • pop 12,000
This prosperous market town at the confluence of the Rivers Wye and Monnow has been in and out of Wales over the centuries, as alliances shifted and the border with England was defined and redefined. In any case it's a thoroughly English town – you need to go west at least to Raglan, 8 miles away, to hear Welsh spoken in the streets – though that doesn't prevent it from being an agreeable stopover.

Its trademark and single architectural distinction is a striking 13th-century stone-gated bridge. Beside the Monnow Bridge, on the right day, you can also see the town's bustling cattle market.

On this easily defendable location between the two rivers, the Norman baron William FitzOsborn built a castle in 1068, which was later the birthplace of Harry of Monmouth, the future King Henry V, conqueror of Normandy at the Battle of Agincourt in 1415. Perhaps the town's most everlastingly famous son was Geoffrey of Monmouth (see the boxed text 'Geoffrey of Monmouth' later). A more recent Monmouthite was Charles Stewart Rolls, co-founder of the Rolls-Royce car and aeroplane engine company.

Orientation
Central Monmouth sits in a cleft formed by the Rivers Wye and Monnow. The heart of

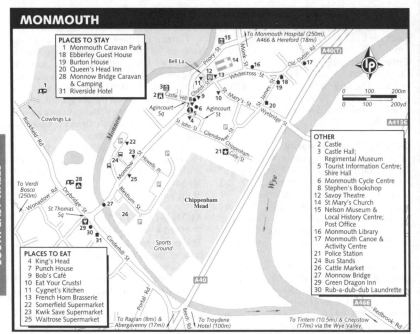

MONMOUTH

PLACES TO STAY
1 Monmouth Caravan Park
18 Ebberley Guest House
19 Burton House
20 Queen's Head Inn
28 Monnow Bridge Caravan & Camping
31 Riverside Hotel

PLACES TO EAT
4 King's Head
7 Punch House
9 Bob's Café
10 Eat Your Crusts!
11 Cygnet's Kitchen
13 French Horn Brasserie
22 Somerfield Supermarket
23 Kwik Save Supermarket
25 Waitrose Supermarket

OTHER
2 Castle
3 Castle Hall; Regimental Museum
5 Tourist Information Centre; Shire Hall
6 Monmouth Cycle Centre
8 Stephen's Bookshop
12 Savoy Theatre
14 St Mary's Church
15 Nelson Museum & Local History Centre; Post Office
16 Monmouth Library
17 Monmouth Canoe & Activity Centre
21 Police Station
24 Bus Stands
26 Cattle Market
27 Monnow Bridge
29 Green Dragon Inn
30 Rub-a-dub-dub Laundrette

town is Agincourt Square, from where Monnow St, the principal thoroughfare and shopping area, descends to the Monnow Bridge. Regional buses use several stands just off Monnow St near the Somerfield supermarket car park.

Many house numbers here run up one side of the street and down the other.

Information

The TIC (☎ 713899, fax 772794, e monmouth-tic@tsww.com) is under the portico of the Shire Hall on Agincourt Square. It opens 10 am to 5.30 pm daily, Easter to October, and 10 am to 1 pm and 2 to 5 pm daily, the rest of the year.

All major UK banks (with ATMs) are represented around Agincourt Square or on Monnow St. The post office shares space with the Nelson Museum on Priory St. Internet access is available for £1.25/2 per half/full hour at Monmouth Library (☎ 775215) on Whitecross St – book ahead. The library

opens 9.30 am to 5.30 pm (until 8 pm Thursday, until 4 pm Saturday) and closes Wednesday and Sunday.

The police station (☎ 712321) is on Chippenham Gate St near the TIC, and Monmouth Hospital (☎ 713522) is north of the centre on Hereford Rd, but for emergency services you must go to Abergavenny.

Stephen's Bookshop at 3 Church St is what bookshops are meant to be, a seemingly endless warren of floor-to-ceiling second-hand books.

You can do your laundry at Rub-a-dub-dub, a laundrette on Cinderhill St.

Things to See & Do

The town's symbol and main attraction is **Monnow Bridge**, the UK's only complete example of a late-13th-century fortified bridge. Much of what you see now, including the roof, is the result of a beefing-up in 1705.

Beside the bridge, the **cattle market** comes alive on Monday (and sometimes on Friday),

Entering Wales via the 3-mile-long Severn Bridge near Chepstow

Waterfall walk, Brecon Beacons

Walk, paddle, cycle or cruise along the Wye Valley – with some climbing and caving on the side...

...or, for views like this, take the Taff Trail past the Pontsticill Reservoir, near Merthyr Tydfil.

Monmouthshire & Brecon Canal

Contemplate the haunting ruins of Tintern Abbey, Wye Valley.

Any idea what attracts visitors to the Brecon Beacons National Park?

The ruins of Llanthony Priory, Brecon, just off Offa's Dyke Path

Lôn Las Cymru tour markers

year round. Centuries back, farmers used to drive their animals here from across the Monnow Bridge. A touchy issue at the time of writing was a plan for a new, high-traffic bridge near the old one, requiring the closure of the cattle market and its consolidation, at Raglan, with Abergavenny's Tuesday sheep market.

The focus of the town is **Agincourt Square**, an irregular plaza dominated by the arcade of the 1724 Shire Hall. Within a stone's throw at **Castle Hill** are the foundations of Monmouth's Norman castle. Except for one tower, its remains were dismantled in the 17th century to build the adjacent Castle Hall, now headquarters of the Royal Monmouthshire Regiment. A little **Regimental Museum** here opens 2 to 5 pm daily, April to October, and 2 to 4 pm at weekends, the rest of the year. Admission is free.

Admiral Horatio Nelson visited Monmouth several times, officially en route to inspect Pembrokeshire forests for wood for his ships (though he had a fling with a local heiress, Lady Emma Hamilton). Lady Llangattock, mother of Charles Stewart Rolls, became an obsessive collector of 'Nelsoniana', the basis for the curious **Nelson Museum & Local History Centre** (☎ 713519) on Priory St. It opens 10 am to 1 pm and 2 to 5 pm daily (afternoon only on Sunday), year round. Admission costs £1/75p.

Activities

Monmouth Canoe & Activity Centre (☎/fax 713461), Castle Yard, Old Dixton Rd, runs half-day/full-day/week-long trips on the Wye by canoe (£16/20/130) or kayak (£12/14/98), as well as climbing and caving trips.

Note that the Monmouthshire & Brecon Canal does not come through Monmouth (see Brecon later in the chapter).

Places to Stay

Monmouth has two camp sites within walking distance of the Monnow Bridge. Just over the bridge is riverside *Monnow Bridge Caravan & Camping* (☎ 714004, *Drybridge St*), charging £6 for a tent and two people and open year round. To the north is *Monmouth Caravan Park* (☎ 714745, *fax*

Geoffrey of Monmouth

The 12th-century Benedictine monk and chronicler Geoffrey of Monmouth is famous for having written one of the most influential pieces of historical fancy in British annals, the *Historia regum Britanniae* or History of the Kings of Britain. In it he culled ancient legends of King Arthur and dressed them up as history, claiming they came from a 'very old book' found in Brittany. In so doing he single-handedly brought the figure of Arthur into the heart of European literature.

It's likely Geoffrey was born in Monmouth, possibly of Breton parents, around 1100. For most of his life he lived in Oxford, where he wrote his medieval best-seller. No serious historian of the time was fooled but his images of Arthur's great quests and conquests, and the prophecies of Merlin (or Myrddin) the sorcerer, have become firmly lodged in the collective European imagination. For more on these stories, see the Myths & Legends special section.

In 1140 Geoffrey was made archdeacon of Llandaff Cathedral in Cardiff, and by the time of his death in 1155 he was bishop of St Asaph in north-east Wales.

716690, Cowlings Lane), charging £7.50 and open March to October.

Two B&B options on St James St, with rooms from £18 per person, are child-friendly *Burton House* (☎ 714958, *fax 772498*) at No 20 and *Ebberley Guest House* (☎ 713602) at No 23. *Troydene* (☎ 712260, *16 Beech Rd*) charges from £17, and *Verdi Bosco* (☎ 714441, *65 Wonastow Rd*) from £15.

The *Queen's Head Inn* (☎ 712767, *St James St*) is recommended for friendly service and good food; singles/doubles cost £25/35, with breakfast. Another good-value option is *Bob's Café* (see Places to Eat later), with en-suite rooms for £30/45.

Riverside Hotel (☎ 715577, *fax 712668, Cinderhill St*), across the Monnow, is the smartest place in town; rooms with bathroom cost £48/68 (£40/55 in winter).

Places to Eat

Cygnet's Kitchen (☎ *715555, 10 White Swan Court*), on Bell Lane, is a good choice, with original and tasty light meals including fine stews (£5), as well as sandwiches and a long wine list. Sit on the patio in summer or by a log fire in winter. *Bob's Café* (☎ *712600, 7 Church St*) is a laid-back cafe and licensed restaurant with eclectic decor and lots of pasta and other imaginative dishes for under £5. *Eat Your Crusts!* (☎ *772977, 5 St Mary's St*) is a tiny sandwich shop with nothing over about £2.50.

Monmouth has at least 10 pubs serving food: two on Agincourt Square are *Punch House* (☎ *713855*) and the JD Wetherspoon franchise *King's Head* (☎ *713417*). Or you can dine in (French) style at the *French Horn Brasserie* (☎ *772733, 24 Church St*) with a mid-week, two-course dinner special for £10.

For self-caterers, *Kwik Save* is at 85 Monnow St, and *Somerfield* is behind it. There's a *Waitrose* supermarket just across Monnow St.

Entertainment

A jolly bar with live music (jazz, folk and so on) on Wednesday evening is the *Green Dragon Inn* (☎ *712561, St Thomas Square*), just across Monnow Bridge.

St Mary's Church is often the venue for choral concerts. The *Savoy Theatre* (☎ *772467, Church St*) has been a drama and cinema venue since 1928, though there has been a theatre on the site for at least 150 years.

Getting There & Away

Stagecoach's No 65 or 69 runs to/from Chepstow (£2.80 single, 50 minutes) about hourly; only the No 69 stops at Tintern. No 83 runs about every two hours from Abergavenny (£2.70, 40 minutes) via Raglan. The cheapest one-day return journeys to either Chepstow or Abergavenny are with a Network Rider pass (see Getting Around at the beginning of the chapter for details).

National Express has a daily coach from Birmingham (£14/17 single/return); the local agent is Cleeve's DIY Shop, 14 Monnow St.

Getting Around

Monmouth Cycle Centre (☎ 772779) at 5 Beaufort Arms Court, a shopping mews around the corner from the TIC, rents mountain bikes for £15/50 per day/week from Easter to April. It opens daily except Thursday afternoon and on Sunday.

AROUND MONMOUTH
Raglan Castle

Raglan was Britain's last medieval castle, built in the 15th and 16th centuries by Sir William ap Thomas and his son, the earl of Pembroke. It is now – despite its gargoyles, heraldic stonework and other architectural fripperies – a moody little ruin, with a savage wound to its Great Tower, which was pulled open by parliamentary soldiers during the Civil War and never used again.

The castle (☎ 01291-690228) opens 9.30 am to 4 pm daily (from 11 am on Sunday). Admission costs £2.40/1.90.

Raglan village is 8 miles from Monmouth and 9 miles from Abergavenny. Stagecoach bus No 83 between Monmouth (£3.30 return, 20 minutes) and Abergavenny (£3.80, 25 minutes) runs every two hours all day, stopping at the Beaufort Hotel in the centre of the village, a five-minute walk from the castle.

The Brecon Beacons

BRECON BEACONS NATIONAL PARK

Founded in 1957, the Brecon Beacons National Park (Parc Cenedlaethol Bannau Brycheiniog) covers some 520 sq miles of high, grassy ridges interspersed with wooded valleys, moorland and farmland. Most of the park is privately owned, and the slopes provide grazing for tens of thousands of sheep. Over 32,000 people live here too, and none of the park is 'wilderness'. Even the highest peaks are used for grazing.

They're called 'mountains', but the Brecon Beacons are really just muscular sandstone hills – less dramatic than Snowdonia but undeniably beautiful, rising in great, green waves above the former mining valleys to the south and the plains to the north. Pen-y-Fan, at 886m, is the highest point in the park (and in southern Britain), and the 3200 hectares surrounding it are in the hands of the NT.

Though named after the Brecon Beacons, the park includes three other blocks of the glacially carved red sandstone that gives them their trademark burgundy hue: Black Mountain to the west, with the lovely glacial lakes of Llyn y Fan Fach and Llyn y Fan Fawr and the 802m escarpment of Fan Brycheiniog; Fforest Fawr (Great Forest), whose rushing streams and spectacular waterfalls form the headwaters of the River Neath, emptying into Swansea Bay; and the Black Mountains, the park's eastern boundary, reaching to 811m at Waun Fach.

Don't confuse little-visited Black Mountain with the popular Black Mountains (though when the weather is bad, any bare piece of high ground in the park deserves the name).

Most visitors come here to walk or cycle, and with good reason. Offa's Dyke Path runs along the park's eastern border. The Taff Trail, for walkers and cyclists, penetrates to Brecon from the south. Lôn Las Cymru, the Welsh National Cycle Route, slips through on quiet minor roads and cycling paths.

But there are many other outdoor options. This is prime pony trekking country. You can go fishing, mountaineering, hanggliding, gliding, canoeing or canal boating. In the south, cavers are attracted to some of the UK's longest, deepest black holes.

Among the park's biggest attractions in terms of visitor numbers are Pen-y-Fan and the Brecon Beacons themselves (see Walking & Cycling Routes later in the section), the Dan-yr-Ogof Showcaves (see Caving later in the section) and Llangorse Lake (see Around Brecon later). Brecon, Abergavenny and other towns around the periphery offer further attractions. For information about Carreg Cennen castle see Around Carmarthen in the Pembrokeshire & Carmarthenshire chapter.

The best bases are Brecon and Abergavenny, though Hay-on-Wye also has a wide range of accommodation. The closest train stations are at Abergavenny and Merthyr Tydfil.

Information

The Mountain Centre (☎ 01874-623366, fax 624515, e mountain.centre@breconbeacons .org), the park's main visitor centre, is in open countryside 5¼ miles south-west of Brecon off the A470, via the village of Libanus. It opens 9.30 am to 6 pm daily, July and August, until 5 pm March to June and September to October, and until 4.30 pm the rest of the year. The Beacons Roundabout bus (see Getting There & Around later in the section) stops at the centre in the summer, and Stagecoach's Merthyr–Brecon bus No 43 goes as far as Libanus (2½ miles from the centre) five or six times daily.

The Mountain Centre itself is the park's most popular attraction, with interpretive trails and other gentle walks, an award-winning tearoom and restaurant, fine views of Pen-y-Fan and Corn Du (823m), and easy disabled access. During school holidays there's a kids' program of guided walks, craft activities and minibus tours.

Another year-round visitor centre with similar hours is the Forest Centre (☎ 01639-730395, e cyncp@breconbeacons.org) at Pen-y-cae, in the Craig-y-Nos Country Park (an older protected area, now part of the park).

A combined park centre and TIC at Llandovery (☎ 01550-720693) opens all year. Park centres at Brecon (☎ 01874-623156) and Abergavenny (☎ 01873-853254) open Easter to October, but share space with local TICs which open year round with park information.

A very useful first step is to pick up Beacons/Bannau, the park's free annual visitor newspaper, bulging with details on using the park, getting around it, events, outfits giving tours and hiring gear and so on. It's available at TICs and some newsagents. The £1.50 Brecon Beacons National Park Map & Information is good value, and the park's own walking booklets cover the main areas in enough detail for those spending a few days here. Harveys Superwalker maps cover the park in two 1:25,000 sheets.

An excellent Web site with news, events and practicalities is the Beacons Mountain Hut at www.brecon-beacons.com.

Walking & Cycling Routes

There's a near-infinite number of walks in the park, ranging from strenuous mountain climbs to gentle strolls along canal tow-paths.

Check the weather forecast before heading into the hills. Take a sweater and waterproof clothing with you, even if it's hot and sunny when you start, and be prepared to turn back if the mist comes down. Whatever the weather, the wind tends to howl across exposed ridges. Bring snacks, but resist the temptation to share them with sheep or ponies, especially in unfenced areas, as this encourages them to move dangerously near to the roads.

The park organises good guided walks and other active events throughout the summer. Guiding Services (☎ 01443-453494, fax 453491, ℮ mwguiding@cix.co.uk), Bwthyn Trydydd, 5 Shingrig Rd, Nelson, Treharris (near Merthyr Tydfil) organises guided walks, mountaineering trips and navigation courses.

In summer, traffic on A-roads can make cycling hazardous, so stick to B- and smaller roads. Lôn Las Cymru (and the Taff Trail where it coincides with it from south of Brecon to Cardiff) is the best known of the park's cycle routes, linking canal tow-paths, disused railway lines and dedicated paths. Cycle hire is available in Brecon, Abergavenny and a few Mid Wales towns adjacent to the park. Two regional bike-tour operators are Brecon Cycle Centre (see Brecon later in the chapter) and Bicycle Beano (see Builth Wells in the Mid Wales chapter).

Following are a few moderately difficult walks/rides. See the later town sections for details of additional local trails.

Pen-y-Fan & Corn Du The park's classic walk – and its most crowded and intensely overused trail – is a 1½-mile climb to the top of Pen-y-Fan or Corn Du from the car park at Storey Arms (no longer a pub) on the A470 (the Merthyr-Brecon road). Park staff call this trail 'the motorway', and urge walkers to try alternatives – for example, the three-hour return trip from the Llwyn-y-Celyn Youth Hostel or the five- to six-hour return trip from Brecon. These and other routes are covered in the leaflet *Walks in the Brecon Area* (see Walking Routes under Brecon later in the chapter).

Directly north of Corn Du in a glacial amphitheatre formed during the last Ice Age, you can take less strenuous walks around the small lake with the tongue-twisting name of Llyn Cwm Llwch (pronounced hlin-coom-**hlooch**).

Taff Trail From Cardiff the waymarked route follows the River Taff north through Merthyr Tydfil, past the Pontsticill Reservoir and Talybont-on-Usk to the Monmouthshire & Brecon Canal (see Brecon later in the chapter) at Pencelli. From there to Brecon you can walk or cycle along the canal or follow the back roads via Llanfrynach. You can pick up a £2 packet of annotated maps from TICs along the way, including at Cardiff, Caerphilly (see Around Cardiff in the Cardiff & Around chapter), Merthyr Tydfil and Brecon.

Canal Walks The least demanding walks in the park are along the towpath of the Monmouthshire & Brecon Canal, which follows the valley of the River Usk. It's possible to walk the full 33-mile length of the canal between Brecon and Pontypool. Crickhowell, just north of the canal and about halfway between the towns, makes a good overnight stop, but there are numerous other villages along the route offering B&B or pub accommodation. Most walkers just hike the 20-mile Abergavenny to Brecon section.

Black Mountain This western section of the park contains the wildest, least visited walking country. The highest point, Fan Brycheiniog, can be reached from the youth hostel at Llanddeusant or along a path that leads off the side road just north of the Dan-yr-Ogof Showcaves (see Caving later).

Fforest Fawr & Waterfall Walks This area, once a Norman hunting ground, offers a great variety of scenery. The youth hostel at Ystradfellte makes a good base. To the north there are mountain walks in terrain similar to that of the Brecon Beacons, and the wooded south has many waterfalls, the finest being Sgwd-yr-Eira (Snow Spout), where you can actually walk behind the falls. This waterfall is an easy 2-mile walk south of Ystradfellte along the River Hepste. There are other falls at Pontneddfechan and Coelbren. Look for the leaflet *Waterfall Walks* at TICs.

Black Mountains Some of the best views on the entire Offa's Dyke Path are from a 17-mile section running through the Black Mountains from Pandy to Hay-on-Wye. Pandy is on the A465, on the bus route between Abergavenny and Hereford. From the high, exposed ridge route you can drop down to the ruins of Llanthony Priory, beside a pub and an atmospheric hotel. Farther north up this valley is the Capel-y-Ffin Youth Hostel. A less strenuous alternative is to follow the River Honddu (**hon**-thee) from Llanfihangel Crucorney, lower down in the valley. TICs stock the two leaflets that cover walks in the north and south parts of this area.

Pony Trekking & Horse Riding

The open hillsides make this ideal pony trekking country, and the park has about two dozen licensed riding centres, concentrated in the Black Mountains. Typical charges are from £12 to £18 for two hours or £25 for a full day. Many centres are on farms that also offer B&B accommodation, including the Grange Pony Trekking Centre (☎ 01873-890215) at Capel-y-Ffin and Llangorse Riding Centre (☎ 01874-658272) near Brecon. The latter also caters to serious riders interested in a superior mount, as does Cwmfforest Riding Centre (☎ 01874-711398) at Talgarth, which offers a range of riding holidays.

Caving

Limestone cave systems in the south of the park – mainly at Llangattock Hillside and in

the upper Swansea Valley – include some of the longest and deepest holes in the UK. Ogof Ffynnon Ddu (Cave of the Black Spring) was the country's first underground National Nature Reserve.

The most accessible site is probably Porth yr Ogof (White Horse Cave) near Ystradfellte, about 20 miles south of Brecon. Pick up a copy of the leaflet *Caving* from TICs. Unless you're an experienced spelunker you should visit the caves through one of the outdoor activity centres, such as Talybont Venture Centre (see Other Activities later).

If a subterranean sound-and-light show with stalagmites illuminated in pretty colours is more your idea of going underground, the family-run Dan-yr-ogof Showcaves (☎ 01639-730284), just off the A4067 north of Abercraf, 20 miles south of Brecon, are for you. This makes a great kids' day out, with three major caves, a dinosaur park, a reconstructed Iron Age farm, a shire-horse centre, dry ski slope and a restaurant. It opens 10 am to 3 pm (last admittance) daily, Easter to October, and occasionally the rest of the year (phone for exact times), and the Beacons Bus (route B2) stops here (see Getting There & Around later in the section). Visit the Web site at www.dan-yr-ogof-showcaves.co.uk.

Canal Cruising

The Monmouthshire & Brecon Canal follows the valley of the River Usk from Brecon to Abergavenny, continuing on to Pontypool. There are just six locks along its 33-mile length and one lock-free section of 22 miles. Built for the iron industry in the early 19th century, it fell into disuse in the 1930s but has now been restored and opened to recreational traffic. See Brecon later in the chapter for information on cruises and narrow-boat hire.

Fishing

Just north of the park and flowing through Hay-on-Wye, the Wye is the finest salmon river in England and Wales. The River Usk, flowing across the north of the park, is among Wales' best waters for brown trout and salmon. Llangorse Lake (see Around Brecon later in the chapter) and the park's 18 reservoirs are good for coarse fishing. You'll need a permit from the owner of the fishing rights, as well as an Environment Agency licence (see Activities in the Facts for the Visitor chapter for details).

Other Activities

The Talybont Venture Centre (☎ 01874-676458) in Talybont-on-Usk, 5 miles southeast of Brecon, offers a range of activities, including abseiling, caving, rock climbing, mountain biking and orienteering. The Beacons Roundabout bus (see Getting There & Around) stops in Talybont in the summer.

Climbing sites are limited in the park; adventure centres tend to be at Llangattock, Craig-y-Dinas (or Dinas Rock) near Pontneddfechan and Morlais Quarry near Merthyr Tydfil. See Around Brecon later in the section for details of the Llangorse Rope Centre (☎ 01874-658272), a fine indoor climbing and caving facility.

Axis Paragliding, based in Abergavenny, offers beginners courses in hang-gliding and paragliding (see Activities under Abergavenny for details). Gliders can be hired from the Black Mountains Gliding Club (☎ 01874-711463), which offers introductory gliding courses from £45. It's on the A479 between Talgarth and Pengenffordd.

The best place in the park for water sports is Llangorse Lake, with facilities for sailing, windsurfing, flatwater canoeing and waterskiing.

Places To Stay & Eat

The park has five YHA/HI youth hostels – Ty'n-y-Caeau (2½ miles from Brecon), Llwyn-y-Celyn (by the A470 Merthyr to Brecon road), Capel-y-Ffin (8 miles south of Hay-on-Wye, attached to a riding school; see Around Abergavenny later in the chapter), Ystradfellte (in the waterfall and caving district) and isolated Llanddeusant (below the Black Mountain).

Recommended independent hostels in the region are Blacksheep Backpackers (see Abergavenny later in the chapter), Joe's Lodge (see Around Brecon later in the chapter) and HoBo Backpackers (see Merthyr Tydfil under The Iron & Coal Valleys earlier in the chapter).

There are some 15 independent bunkhouses in the area, of widely varying quality. This walkers' budget alternative to hostels got its start in the Brecon Beacons, and most of them are concentrated around the park. This book mentions some good ones; a full listing is available on the Web site of the Association of Bunkhouse Operators at www.hostelswales.com.

With the permission of the farmer or landowner, it's possible to camp almost anywhere in the park, though not on NT land. TICs have lists of camp sites with full facilities.

There's a good range of B&Bs and hotels in and around the main centres of Brecon, Abergavenny and Hay-on-Wye, as well as in the villages along the Usk Valley. Some hotels offer all-inclusive activity holidays, including fishing or riding. See those sections later in the chapter for details.

Getting There & Around

Most regional buses to and around the national park are operated by Stagecoach, with a few by Crossgates Coaches (☎ 01597-851226) and Roy Brown's Coaches (☎ 01982-552597). Useful routes (with single fares) include:

Crossgates No 299 Llandovery to Brecon (£1.60, 40 minutes, five daily)
Roy Brown's No 47 Llandrindod Wells to Brecon (£2.50, one hour, two to three daily)
Stagecoach No X4 Cardiff via Merthyr Tydfil to Abergavenny (£4.30, 2¼ hours, hourly)
Stagecoach No 21 Abergavenny to Brecon (£3.45, one hour, every two hours)
Stagecoach No 39 Hay-on-Wye to Brecon (£2.90, 45 minutes, every 2½ hours)
Stagecoach No 43 Merthyr Tydfil to Brecon (£2.70, 40 minutes, every two hours)
Stagecoach No 63 Swansea to Brecon (£4.05, 1½ hours, three daily)

These routes have almost no Sunday services (see the next section for what to do on a Sunday). See Getting Around at the beginning of the chapter for details of money-saving day passes.

Useful rail services are limited to Cardiff-Merthyr Tydfil (£3.50 single, 55 minutes, hourly) and Newport-Abergavenny (£4.80, 25 minutes, hourly). Sunday services are less frequent.

Public transport between smaller villages is limited, and nonexistent on Sunday. If you're not prepared to walk it's worth considering a taxi.

Explore the Brecon Beacons is a useful free guide available from TICs, listing bus and train timetables plus walks that can be linked to public transport routes.

The Beacons Bus & Beacons Roundabout On Sundays and bank holidays from late May to early September, the national park runs a shuttle bus service called the Beacons Bus. Routes tend to converge on Brecon at 11 am and/or 5.30 pm. The routes are (with selected towns and frequencies per day):

Route B1 Swansea, Storey Arms (one)
Route B2 Bridgend, Craig-y-Nos, Dan-yr-Ogof Showcaves (one)
Route B3 Cardiff, Merthyr Tydfil, Storey Arms (one)
Route B4 Carmarthen, National Botanic Garden, Llandovery (one to two)
Route B5 Abergavenny, Crickhowell (two)
Route 40 Hereford, Hay-on-Wye, Talgarth (three)

A more useful circular Sunday service called the Beacons Roundabout allows you to tour the park, or to get off at one place, walk to another and get back on. Useful stops include the Brecon Mountain Railway, Talybont-on-Usk, Llanfrynach, the Ty'n-y-Caeau Youth Hostel and the Mountain Centre. It runs three to five times *daily* from late July to August.

On the first Beacons Bus or Beacons Roundabout bus you board, you buy a ticket (£4.60/3.10, seniors £3.60, families £9.20) good for all services for the rest of the day. The Cardiff to Merthyr, Swansea and Abergavenny services tow a bicycle trailer big enough for 24 bikes (£2.50 extra). You can pick up a detailed timetable free from any TIC along these routes or call ☎ 01873-853254 for information.

HAY-ON-WYE (Y GELLI)
☎ 01497 • pop 1400
On 1 April 1977, Hay-on-Wye declared independence from Britain – just one publicity stunt this eccentric bookshop town has used to draw attention to itself. Most of the publicity has been generated by bookseller Richard Booth, the colourful, self-styled king of Hay (see the boxed text 'Richard Booth, King of Hay' later), who was largely responsible for Hay's evolution from just another market town on the Welsh-English border to the second-hand bookshop capital of the world.

Hay may lie this side of the border, and may consider itself an independent kingdom, but a more determinedly English town you will not find in Wales. A day browsing among its shops is definitely recommended. With a small centre made up of narrow sloping lanes, the town itself is also interesting – and the people it attracts certainly are.

On the north-eastern corner of the national park, Hay is also a good base for exploring the Black Mountains. Offa's Dyke and the Offa's Dyke Path run right through the town.

History
The high points in Hay's history are mainly associated with its position in the Marches, the lowlands of South and Mid Wales along the English border. Indeed, during the Norman conquest it was administered separately as English Hay (the town proper) and Welsh Hay (the countryside to the south and west).

William de Braose II – one of the Norman barons (or Lords Marcher) who was granted vast tracts of border lands to help consolidate conquered territory – built a castle here in about 1200, on the site of an earlier one. For the next three and a half centuries Hay changed hands many times. Following the Acts of Union (see The Tudors & the Acts of Union under History in the Facts about Wales chapter) it settled down as a market town, and became a centre of the flannel trade by the 18th century.

Hay's first big second-hand bookshop opened in 1961, the vanguard of a new

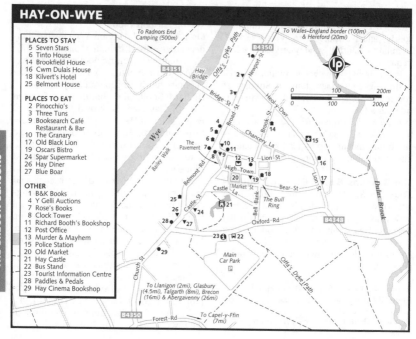

HAY-ON-WYE

PLACES TO STAY
5 Seven Stars
6 Tinto House
14 Brookfield House
16 Cwm Dulais House
18 Kilvert's Hotel
25 Belmont House

PLACES TO EAT
2 Pinocchio's
3 Three Tuns
9 Booksearch Café
  Restaurant & Bar
10 The Granary
17 Old Black Lion
19 Oscars Bistro
24 Spar Supermarket
26 Hay Diner
27 Blue Boar

OTHER
1 B&K Books
4 Y Gelli Auctions
7 Rose's Books
8 Clock Tower
11 Richard Booth's Bookshop
12 Post Office
13 Murder & Mayhem
15 Police Station
20 Old Market
21 Hay Castle
22 Bus Stand
23 Tourist Information Centre
28 Paddles & Pedals
29 Hay Cinema Bookshop

'industry'. In 1971 Richard Booth bought Hay Castle, complete with a Jacobean mansion built within its Norman walls, but a fire in 1977 left it in its present dilapidated state.

Orientation & Information

Hay's compact centre contains the castle and most of the bookshops. The border with England runs along Dulas Brook, which crosses under Newport St about 300m north of the town centre.

The TIC (☎ 820144, fax 820015) is on Oxford Rd, on the edge of town and beside the main car park. It opens 10 am to 1 pm and 2 to 5 pm daily, Easter to October; 11 am to 1 pm and 2 to 4 pm daily, the rest of the year. The TIC stocks a free guide and a town map showing all its bookshops (most bookshops have the map too).

Bookshops

There are now approximately 45 bookshops in Hay, with literally hundreds of thousands of books, most of them secondhand – 400,000 alone in Richard Booth's Bookshop. Quantity tends to rule over quality.

Many bookshops cover all subjects. The most famous, and still the best, are Richard Booth's Bookshop, aka Booth's Books (☎ 820322), 44 Lion St, and Hay Cinema Bookshop (☎ 820071), Castle St, in a converted cinema. Booth's has a sizeable Anglo-Welsh literature section, and a separate section on Wales as a travel destination. The Booksearch Café Restaurant & Bar (☎ 821932), The Pavement, is one of several places that will search for out-of-print books for you. It opens Tuesday to Sunday. You can also enquire by post (Hay-on-Wye, Hereford HR3 5EA) or through their Web site at www.booksearch-at-hay.com.

Some bookshops have esoteric specialities. B&K Books (☎ 820386) on Newport St boasts the world's finest stock of books

Richard Booth, King of Hay

English eccentrics are a sparse breed and to be cherished for their contribution to British culture. Richard Booth, king of Hay, is one of that quintessential species.

As a pioneer anti-globalisation campaigner, Booth has railed against the causes of rural decline. He accuses the rural development boards of investing in failures, in supermarkets that kill off local shops, and in factory farming. For his part he's turned a declining Welsh border town into a prosperous and eminent book town.

A controversial and provocative character, he's in turn been called a monarchist, anarchist, socialist and separatist. Not that this matters, as all roles fit and if nothing else he's a superb self-publicist.

Booth discovered the profitability of second-hand book dealing while still at school and later at university in Oxford. Returning home to Hay in the early 1960s he set up a bookshop in the town's former fire station.

At the time many institutions and country houses were shedding their libraries. Booth bought with gay abandon, stretching his resources to include the USA, Ireland and Australia in his buying sprees. He's lurched in and out of financial ruin, and bankruptcy emptied his coffers in 1984, but he's always bounced back.

Despite financial problems, he established the world's largest bookshop, initially in Hay's former cinema on Castle St but now on Lion St. He owns the 900-year-old Hay Castle, and in the grounds is the Honesty Bookshop. It opens all hours, all days and all weathers (though mainly in the summer); honest readers place 50 pence per book in an 'honesty box'.

Booth's success attracted other booksellers to town, and his former employees have also set up their own shops. Currently 45 bookshops peddle their wares covering 2000 different categories. Such is the knowledge vested in Hay's specialist booksellers that Booth claims they're more important than trained librarians.

The city states of Greece and Italy had been centres of civilisation and so, reasoned Booth, why not Hay. The idea blossomed in early 1976 during a liquid lunch with some journalists who were in town chasing Marianne Faithfull, who had been staying at Hay Castle. Booth announced that Hay would

ASA ANDERSSON

declare its independence on 1 April (which happens to be April Fools' Day). It aroused national interest despite – or perhaps because of – a fierce dismissal by Breconshire Council as a Booth publicity stunt.

Come the declaration, three TV stations, eight national newspapers and the world's press covered the event. Booth was crowned king in the castle grounds and the Hay Navy sent a gunboat (a rowing boat) up the Wye firing blanks from a drainpipe. Many of the king's drinking pals gained cabinet posts.

Subsequently Booth has been involved in setting up other book towns in Europe, Japan and the USA, and in recognition of his role his Hay subjects have elevated him to emperor.

Patrick Horton

on bee-keeping. Rose's Books (☎ 820013) at 14 Broad St stocks rare and out-of-print children's books. Murder & Mayhem (☎ 821613), 5 Lion St, is filled to the brim with detective fiction, true crime and horror.

There are regular book auctions at Y Gelli Auctions (☎ 821179), Broad St.

Paddling the Wye

For a change of pace, open canoes (for two or three people) can be hired year round from Paddles & Pedals (☎ 820604), Castle St, for £15/25 per canoe for a half/full day. Despite the name, there aren't any bikes for rent.

In nearby Glasbury, the Wye Valley Canoe Centre (☎ 847213) rents kayaks for £7/12 and open canoes for £13/20 per half/full day, plus 50p per mile to drop you off or collect you. Another canoe outfitter there is Black Mountain Hire (☎ 847897).

Special Events

Hay's week-long Festival of Literature in late May or early June is a popular and entertaining annual affair, with readings, workshops, guest appearances and book signings – and now a subsidiary children's literature festival – along with music and other entertainment. For further information call ☎ 821217.

Places to Stay

Radnors End Camping (☎/fax 820780), ½ mile north-west on the road to Clyro, charges £3 per person. The nearest youth hostel is at Capel-y-Ffin, 8 miles south in the Vale of Ewyas (see Around Abergavenny later in the chapter). A small independent hostel called Joe's Lodge is at Talgarth (see Around Brecon later in the chapter), 8 miles south-west on the A438 and A4078.

Hay is awash with B&Bs. *Brookfield House* (☎ 820518, Brook St) is a listed 16th-century house with quiet singles/doubles from £18/32. Another good-value choice is *Seven Stars* (☎ 820886, fax 821488, 11 Broad St), with comfortable rooms from £22/37 (£28/45 en suite) and a swimming pool and sauna; booking ahead is wise. Almost next door, pleasant *Tinto House* (☎ 820590, Broad St) has a secluded garden and rooms for £30/40.

Belmont House (☎ 820718, Belmont Rd) has big rooms for £20/32 (£38 for an en-suite double). At friendly *Cwm Dulais House* (☎ 820179, Heol-y-Dwr), B&B costs £25/38. *Kilvert's Hotel* (☎ 821042, fax 821580, The Bull Ring) has rooms from £35/65, and a pub and a-la-carte restaurant.

Two miles south-west of Hay at Llanigon (and near Offa's Dyke Path) is *The Old Post Office* (☎ 820008), a first-rate vegetarian B&B with rooms for £17 per person (£25 en suite). At Glasbury, on the A438 to Brecon, is *The Forge* (☎ 847237), a 15th-century Welsh long house with rooms from about £20 per person.

Places to Eat

You're spoilt for choice here. Recommended is *The Granary* (☎ 820790, Broad St), with carefully prepared vegetarian and other dishes (try the Hungarian goulash at £7.50), and classic summer pudding, made with raspberries and blackberries. It opens 10 am to 10 pm daily in summer and during the festival, and until 5.30 pm in winter.

Sit down for a meal or a drink at the *Booksearch Café Restaurant & Bar* (see Bookshops earlier) while staff search the town or the Internet for your out-of-print book. Central *Oscars Bistro* (☎ 821193, High Town) offers reasonably priced dishes (including vegetarian options), plus good filled baguettes for £3.50. *Pinocchio's* (☎ 821166, 2 Broad St) is a good Italian restaurant. The *Hay Diner* (Castle St) is good for a coffee or a full meal, even takeaway. It opens 10 am to 10 pm daily and has some garden seating.

Tiny *Three Tuns* (Broad St) is a popular old pub and cider house serving bar meals. The *Blue Boar* (☎ 820884, Castle St) has a big bar menu, and there's upmarket pub grub at the *Old Black Lion* (Lion St).

There's a *Spar* supermarket on Castle St for self-caterers (and picnic material).

Getting There & Away

Buses use a stand near the TIC on Oxford Rd. Services with Stagecoach (☎ 01633-244744) include the No 39 from Hereford (£4 single, one hour 5 minutes) and from Brecon (£2.90, 55 minutes), running six times daily (two or three times on Sunday). The Beacons Bus (route 40) also serves Hay (see Getting There & Around in the Brecon Beacons National Park section).

The nearest train station is in Hereford.

ABERGAVENNY (Y-FENNI)
☎ 01873 • pop 11,000

Standing just outside the Brecon Beacons National Park (though the hills surrounding it are all within the park), Abergavenny styles itself as the 'Gateway to Wales'. That may be stretching a point, but it's certainly the best base for walks in the Black Mountains and one of only two towns with access to the park by train (the other is Merthyr Tydfil).

It's a busy market town, and in contrast to its eastern neighbour, Monmouth, self-consciously Welsh. Its ancient name, Y-Fenni (pronounced uh-**ven**-ni; Welsh for 'place of the smiths') was given to a stream that empties into the River Usk here, and later anglicised to Gavenny – Abergavenny means 'mouth of the Gavenny'.

Abergavenny's history goes back 4000 years to a Neolithic settlement. The Romans established Gobannium Fort – exactly a day's march from their garrison at Caerleon, near Newport – and stayed from AD 57 to 400. But the town only grew appreciably after a Marcher lord, Hamelin de Ballon, built a castle here around 1090. Owain Glyndŵr's forces wrecked Abergavenny in 1404.

Though walking may be on many visitors' minds, it's worth visiting the parish church as it contains a quite remarkable collection of medieval tombs – one of the finest in the UK.

Among relatively recent visitors taking advantage of the town's rural position was Rudolf Hess, although of course he wasn't on holiday. After his self-styled peace mission to Britain in 1941, Hitler's former deputy was jailed for a time at Maindiff military hospital, north-east of Abergavenny, and was allowed out for weekly walks in the hills.

Orientation
From the train station it's a 10-minute walk along Station Rd, Monmouth Rd and across the River Gavenny to the TIC in Swan Meadow, on Cross St. The bus station is beside the TIC. From here Cross St, which becomes High St, runs uphill through the central shopping area. A very visible landmark is the copper-green roof of the clock tower on the Market Hall on Cross St.

Information
The TIC (☎ 857588, fax 850217, e aber gavenny-tic@tsww.com) opens 10 am to 5.30 pm daily (until 4 pm November to Easter). In the same building is a national park visitor centre (☎ 853254), open 10 am to 5 pm daily, Easter to October.

All major UK banks (all with ATMs) are represented on Cross St or High St. The main post office is on Castle St. Internet access is available for free at the library on Victoria St, open 9.30 am to 5.30 pm (to 8 pm Thursday, to 4 pm Saturday) daily except Wednesday and Sunday, for £1 per quarter-hour at Blacksheep Backpackers (see Places to Stay later) and for £5 per hour at Celtic Computer Systems (☎ 858111), 20 Monk St, open Monday to Saturday.

The rather non-central police station (☎ 852273) is on Tudor St. Nevill Hall Hospital (☎ 732732), with 24-hour emergency services, is ¾ mile west of the centre, on Brecon Rd.

If you can't find the book you want at the TIC, try the Abergavenny Bookshop (☎ 850380) at 1 High St.

St Mary's Parish Church
This modest-looking church, founded as part of a Benedictine priory about the time the castle was built (1090), is worth a stop even on a sunny day for its remarkable treasury of carved oak, stone and alabaster tombs – the church has the second-biggest church-based assemblage of medieval tombs in the UK.

In the northern transept is one of the most important medieval carvings in Europe – the remains of a beautiful 15th-century carving of the biblical figure of Jesse, which was once the base of an altarpiece in the form of a huge, intricately carved 'family tree' showing the lineage of Jesus.

Most of the tombs are of members of the Herbert family, starting with Sir William ap Thomas, founder of Raglan Castle (see Around Monmouth earlier in the chapter).

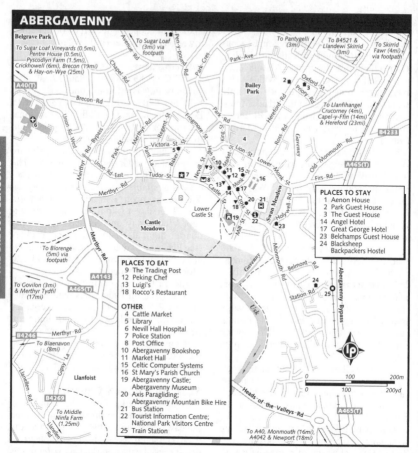

ABERGAVENNY

PLACES TO STAY
1 Aenon House
2 Park Guest House
3 The Guest House
14 Angel Hotel
17 Great George Hotel
23 Belchamps Guest House
24 Blacksheep
   Backpackers Hostel

PLACES TO EAT
9 The Trading Post
12 Peking Chef
13 Luigi's
18 Rocco's Restaurant

OTHER
4 Cattle Market
5 Library
6 Nevill Hall Hospital
7 Police Station
8 Post Office
10 Abergavenny Bookshop
11 Market Hall
15 Celtic Computer Systems
16 St Mary's Parish Church
19 Abergavenny Castle;
   Abergavenny Museum
20 Axis Paragliding;
   Abergavenny Mountain Bike Hire
21 Bus Station
22 Tourist Information Centre;
   National Park Visitors Centre
25 Train Station

The oldest item is a beautiful, carved oak effigy of Sir John de Hastings II, who was probably responsible for the 14th-century restoration of the church. The oldest stone carving is the tomb of 'A Hastings Lady, 1350–90'. The oak choir stalls were carved in the 15th century (note the little dragons at the ends). In the nave is a bell cast in 1308.

It's surprising that this important (and valuable) collection remains in the proud stewardship of parishioners rather than in the grip of Cadw or other heritage agencies. There's always a volunteer warden around to accompany visitors and answer questions. You can pick up a free brochure or a detailed booklet (£5). Leave a donation if you can.

A massive tithe barn beside the church is currently under restoration.

Abergavenny Castle

The castle was the scene of an infamous bit of Norman treachery in 1175 when William de Braose invited the local Welsh prince, Seisyll ap Dyfnwal, and his knights to Christmas dinner – and then slaughtered them all.

The castle was besieged frequently but never taken by force. It was wrecked by royalist forces in 1645 during the Civil War in order to keep it out of parliamentary hands, and it has gone largely untouched since then. The surviving keep, heavy-handedly restored by the Victorians, now houses the small but good **Abergavenny Museum** (☎ 854282). Displays include a Victorian Welsh farmhouse kitchen and a saddler's workshop. It opens 11 am to 1 pm and 2 to 5 pm (afternoon only on Sunday) March to October and closes at 4 pm daily (and all day on Sunday) the rest of the year. Admission costs £1 (free for children).

Activities

The three glacially sculpted hills cradling Abergavenny are 486m Skirrid Fawr, 3 miles north-east; 596m Sugar Loaf, 3 miles north-west; and 559m Blorenge, 3½ miles south-west. Each offers its own rewarding walks and fine views of the Usk Valley and the Black Mountains. See Walking & Cycling Routes in the Brecon Beacons National Park section earlier for information about the area and its weather conditions.

From the TIC, the cone-shaped summit of Sugar Loaf is a steep 9-mile (4½-hour) return trip via heath, woodland and the superb viewpoint of Mynydd Llanwenarth. Less vigorous types can drive to a car park about halfway to the summit (from the A40, turn right for Sugar Loaf Vineyards, then keep to the left at all forks). The Heart of Wales railway line runs right beneath the mountain (see Llandrindod Wells in the Mid Wales chapter).

The summit of Blorenge – also popular as a hang-gliding and paragliding launch pad – can be reached in a 12-mile (six-hour) walk that also takes in a reservoir and a tramline that were part of the ironworks complex at Blaenafon (see The Iron & Coal Valleys section earlier in the chapter).

The TIC sells a national park booklet, *Walks from Abergavenny* (£1.80), with details of these and nine other local treks from 3 to 12 miles long. The county council sponsors gentle guided walks around Abergavenny in the summer; the national park (in summer) and Brecon Beacons Park Society (in winter) run more demanding walks – ask the TIC for details.

The Monmouthshire & Brecon Canal passes just south of Llanfoist, south of the town centre. In addition to walking the towpath you can take a cruise or hire your own narrow boat. A local firm with boats to hire by the day (£50) is Beacon Park Boats (☎ 858277) in Llanfoist. The busiest section of the canal is near the northern end (see The Monmouthshire & Brecon Canal under Brecon later in the chapter).

Axis Paragliding (☎ 850910, 37 Cross St) offers one/two-day introductory courses in hang-gliding and paragliding for £84/160, as well as longer courses. Under the name Abergavenny Mountain Bike Hire, they also rent mountain bikes for £15 per day (see Getting Around later).

More down-to-earth types can visit Sugar Loaf Vineyard (☎ 858675) and sip the local produce. The visitor centre – just off the A40, about a mile from town – opens 10 am to 5 pm daily, March to December.

Places to Stay

Camping A couple of miles west on the A40 near the River Usk, *Pyscodlyn Farm Caravan & Camping Site* (☎/fax 853271, Llanwenarth Citra) charges £8 for a tent plus two people.

Hostels & Bunkhouses Opposite the train station, *Blacksheep Backpackers* (☎ 859125, ✉ blacksheep@greatwestern. freeserve.co.uk, 24 Station Rd) is an independent hostel in the old Great Western Hotel. Beds are £10 in dorms (£12.50 in one twin-bedded room), including continental breakfast. Facilities include kitchen, bar, Internet access and mountain bike hire.

Three miles north of Abergavenny in the village of Pantygelli – and at the foot of Sugar Loaf – is *Smithy's Bunkhouse* (☎ 853432, Lower House Farm), down a track opposite Ye Olde Crown Inn. A bed in one of the two comfortable twelve-bed dorms costs £7 per person and there's a laundry, kitchen and basic common room. Breakfast/half-board (by advance arrange-

THE BRECON BEACONS

ment) is £3.50/15; there's little else but bar food at the Crown. A taxi from Abergavenny costs about £3.

On the flanks of Blorenge peak is a comfortable six-bed bunkhouse at cheerful *Middle Ninfa Farm* (☎ 854662, e *middleninfa .farm@ntlworld.com, Llanellen*). Bring your own food. The farm is about 2 miles south of Abergavenny and Llanfoist on the B4269, including ¾ mile up a paved track. A taxi will cost about £4.

The nearest YHA/HI youth hostel is at Capel-y-Ffin, 15 miles north on the road to Hay-on-Wye (see Around Abergavenny later).

All these places open year round.

B&Bs & Hotels The closest good B&B to the town centre is *Belchamps Guest House* (☎ 853204, *Holywell Rd*), within sight of the TIC and charging £21/38 for a single/ double. A 10-minute walk away via Monk St are two well-run places: *Park Guest House* (☎ 853715, *36 Hereford Rd*) has rooms at £18/32 (with private parking) and *The Guest House* (☎ 854823, *2 Oxford St*) charges £20/36 and also offers evening meals.

Rooms at pleasant *Aenon House* (☎ 858708, *34 Pen-y-Pound Rd*), in a 200-year-old building about ½ mile north of the centre, cost £18/35.

Pentre House (☎ 853435, *Brecon Rd*), 1¼ miles west of the centre, has good-value rooms from £20/35.

Great George Hotel (☎ 854230, *49 Cross St*) charges £20 per person (£25 with breakfast).

Tops for luxury in the centre is *Angel Hotel* (☎ 857121, fax 858059, *15 Cross St*) with rooms for £55/70 (and cheaper weekend promotional rates).

Places to Eat
The Trading Post (☎ 855448, *14 Nevill St*) is a coffee house and bistro with a dash of old-worldly atmosphere; carefully prepared pasta, soup and other simple dishes (£5 to £6) are worth the walk. *Rocco's Restaurant* (☎ 857600, *22a Cross St*), above a flower shop, is a first-rate Genoese Italian eatery,

open in the evening with pasta from £7.50 and meaty mains from £10. *Luigi's* (☎ 855103, *10 Cross St*), the best of several coffee shops around Cross St, has light lunches for under £5 and a children's menu. All three open daily except Sunday.

For the region's best Chinese food, go to the *Peking Chef* (☎ 857457, *Bank House, 59 Cross St*) which has a huge menu of dishes from £5 to £7, plus cheaper takeaways. It opens daily.

Three miles north-east of Abergavenny at Llandewi Skirrid (along the A465 and A4521) is the legendary *Walnut Tree Inn* (☎ 852797), considered one of Wales' finest restaurants (and famous enough to have its own cookbook). The cuisine is international and the ingredients, as far as possible, Welsh. The menu might include anything from *vincigrassi* (pasta, bechamel, porcini mushrooms and truffles) to bubble and squeak. Booking ahead is essential in the evening; they also have a bistro and do a popular lunch trade. After a memorable dinner for two, including drinks and service, don't expect any change from £80. It opens Tuesday to Saturday.

Shopping
The Market Hall on Cross St is a lively place, with a weekly market on Tuesday, a flea market on Wednesday, a smaller market Friday and a crafts or antiques fair on some Saturdays. A farmers market fills the hall on the fourth Thursday of each month.

Getting There & Away
Regional services with Stagecoach (☎ 01633-244744) include No X4 from Cardiff via Merthyr Tydfil (£4.30 single, 2¼ hours, hourly); No 21 from Brecon (£3.45, one hour, every two hours) and from Newport (£3.60, 1¼ hours, hourly); and No 83 via Raglan from Monmouth (£2.70, 40 minutes, every two hours). The Beacons Bus (route B5) also serves Abergavenny (see Getting There & Around in the Brecon Beacons National Park section).

There are trains from Cardiff (£7.30, 40 minutes) via Newport (£4.80, 25 minutes) about every hour, with fewer on Sunday.

Getting Around

You can hire a bike from Abergavenny Mountain Bike Hire (see Activities earlier) for £15 per day. Blacksheep Backpackers (see Places to Stay earlier) also rents mountain bikes. Three miles west of Abergavenny, just before Govilon, is PedalAway (☎/fax 01873-830219, e hopyard@diana .fsnet.co.uk), with lots of route information, rigid and suspension bikes (£15 to £25 per day) and bike delivery for an extra charge.

Reliable local taxi companies include TC Cabs (☎ 07773-861750), Lewis Taxis (☎ 854140) and Station Taxis (☎ 857233).

AROUND ABERGAVENNY
Llanfihangel Crucorney

Tourists flock to this little village, 4½ miles north of Abergavenny on the A465 Hereford road, mainly to visit the *Skirrid Mountain Inn* (☎ 01873-890258), which claims to be Wales' oldest pub. From the early 12th century until the 17th century this was the courthouse, where almost 200 prisoners were hanged – you can still see rope marks on one of the beams.

The choice place to stay in the area is the wonderful *Penyclawdd Court* (☎ 01873-890719, fax 890848), a tastefully restored Tudor manor house below Bryn Arw mountain. B&B costs £50/80 for a single/double; booking ahead is essential.

Vale of Ewyas

Offa's Dyke Path runs along the windblown ridge east above this remote and peaceful valley (also called Llanthony Valley) at the eastern edge of the national park.

The ruins of the 13th-century Augustinian priory church and monastic buildings of **Llanthony Priory** (protected by Cadw) are set in a beautiful location by the River Honddu. A superb walk climbs from the car park up to the bare ridge above. Hatterrall Hill (531m), 2 miles south-east, is a favourite hang-gliding and paragliding spot.

The *Abbey Hotel* (☎ 01873-890487), built into some of the surviving abbey buildings, is as richly atmospheric as Penyclawdd Court in Llanfihangel Crucorney. In the vaulted crypt is a public bar that serves basic meals. The hotel opens Easter to October, and at weekends in winter. Rooms, let only as doubles, cost £46 during the week and £110 for a minimum two-night stay at weekends.

Capel-y-Ffin Youth Hostel (☎ 01873-890650) is about 3 miles north of the priory. The complex opening hours mean calling ahead is advisable, though it normally opens Friday to Tuesday from April to October, daily in July and August and closes in December and January. The nightly charge is £8.50/5.75. The adjacent **riding school** offers horse riding lessons and trail rides; bookings can be made through the hostel.

Crickhowell (Crughywel)
☎ 01873 • pop 2000

This prosperous, rather twee village on the Brecon–Abergavenny road (A40) makes a good walking base. An impressive 13th-century stone bridge crosses the River Usk, leading to the neighbouring village of Llangattock (not to be confused with several other Llangattocks around the park). The TIC (☎ 812105, e brecon.tourism@powys .gov.uk), on Beaufort St by the A40, opens 9 am to 5 pm daily, Easter to October.

There's no shortage of pubs, most serving food, and accommodation to suit all budgets. There's a camp site in the village, the *Riverside Caravan Park* (☎ 810397, New Rd), charging £8 for two adults and a tent. The most central B&B is *Mrs Morgan's* (☎ 811177, 2 Greenhill Villas, Beaufort St) with singles/doubles from £20/36. Lovely *T Gwyn* (☎ 811625, Brecon Rd) charges from £35/42. The *Bear Hotel* (☎ 810408, Beaufort St) is the best place to stay, with rooms (some with jacuzzis) from £50/65, excellent bar food and a good restaurant.

Perth-y-Pia (☎ 810164, T Mawr, Llanbedr) is a pair of bunkhouses (one with shared facilities, one with en-suite rooms) above Llanbedr village, 2 miles north-east of Crickhowell on the flanks of Table Mountain. Beds cost a bargain £6.50 and £7.70, though you need to bring your own sleeping bag or sleeping sheet. It's popular with groups, so book ahead if you can.

THE BRECON BEACONS

The Beacons Bus (route B5) serves Crickhowell (see Getting There & Around in the Brecon Beacons National Park section earlier).

Tretower Court & Castle

Three miles north-west of Crickhowell, Tretower combines a Norman motte-and-bailey castle with a 13th-century tower, a 15th-century fortified manor house (the Court) and a fine garden in the style of the period. The house has been considerably restored and was originally the home of the Vaughan family, the best-known member of which was the Metaphysical poet Henry Vaughan.

Tretower Court (☎ 01874-730279, Cadw) opens 10 am to 4 pm daily, March to October (until 6 pm, May to September). Admission costs £2.20/1.70.

BRECON (ABERHONDDU)
☎ 01874 • pop 7000

This good-natured, handsome stone town and market centre is the logistical hub of the national park, and a natural base for exploring it. Attractions within the town are limited, but links – by bus, bicycle, boat and foot – into the surrounding countryside are plentiful. Food is generally unexceptional but there's accommodation for all budgets.

History

An Iron Age hill fort on Pen-y-Crug, 1½ miles north-west of town, confirms that the area was occupied long before the Romans arrived in AD 75. The remains of a Roman camp can be visited at Y Gaer, 3 miles west of the centre (see Walking Routes later). After the Romans left, the area was ruled by – and took its name from – one Brychan or Brechon, the eponymous Irish founder of the kingdom of Brycheiniog, who married into a Welsh royal house in the 5th century.

It was not until Norman times that Brecon began to grow. The local Welsh prince, Rhys ap Tewdwr, was defeated in 1093 by Bernard de Newmarch, a Norman lord, who then built the town's castle and church (which was later made a cathedral). Llewelyn ap Gruffydd, the first and last Welsh Prince of Wales, besieged Brecon unsuccessfully in 1275.

Brecon, astride the main route from London across South Wales to the coast, was recognised in the 16th century as one of the country's most important towns by its designation as the capital of the former county of Brecknockshire (now absorbed into Powys). For centuries it thrived as a centre of the woollen industry and it remains an agricultural centre.

Orientation

Everything in compact Brecon is within walking distance. The town centre is along a short, wide street called The Bulwark, which is also the terminus for long-distance buses. There are B&Bs clustered in two areas: around The Watton and over the bridge in Llanfaes.

Information

The TIC (☎ 622485, fax 625256, ⓔ brectic@powys.gov.uk) is in the Cattle Market car park, about 150m from The Bulwark, up Lion St and Lion Yard. It opens 10 am to 6 pm daily, Easter to November, and 9 am to 12.30 pm and 1.30 to 4.45 pm (10 am to 1 pm and 1.30 to 4 pm on Sunday) in winter. Here you can pick up the free map-brochure A Look at Brecon, outlining a detailed and quite fascinating town tour.

A national park information centre (☎ 623156) shares space with the TIC and opens 9 am to 5 pm daily, Easter to October (park information is available from the TIC at other times). The park's main visitor centre, the Mountain Centre (☎ 623156), is 5¼ miles to the south-west off the A470, via Libanus (see Information under Brecon Beacons National Park earlier in the chapter).

All major UK banks are represented in Lower High St. The post office is on St Mary St, just down from The Bulwark. Internet access is available free at the library on Ship St, open 9.30 am to 5 pm (until 7 pm Tuesday, until 1 pm Saturday) daily except Sunday, and for £1 per half-hour at 123 Computers (☎ 611929), 11 Watergate, open 9 am to 1 pm and 2 to 5 pm Monday to Saturday.

The police station (☎ 622331) is on Lion St. Brecon Hospital (☎ 622443) is on Cerrigcochion Rd, the extension of Free St.

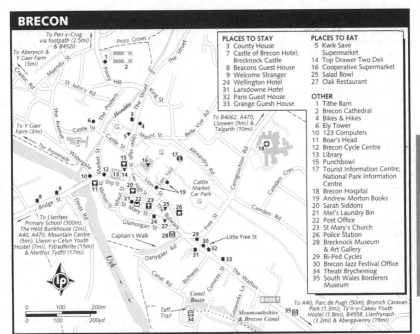

BRECON

To Pen-y-Crug
via footpath (2.5mi)
& B4520

To Aberyscir &
Y Gaer Farm
(3mi)

Priory Groves

Maendu St

Cradoc Rd

St John's Rd

Priory Hill

The Struet

King St

The Watton

To Y Gaer
Farm (3mi)

The Avenue

Castle Sq

The Postern

Honddu

The Struet

To B4062, A470,
Llyswen (9mi) &
Talgarth (10mi)

Belle Vue Rd

Mount St

Castle St

Jardin

The Promenade

Watergate

Market St

Ship St

High St

Lion St

Lion Yard

Alexandra Rd

Ceredigochion Rd

Cattle
Market
Car Park

Camden Cres

Bridge St

Dnas Rd

St Michael St

St Whest St

St Mary St

The Bulwark

Glamorgan St

Free St

Camden Rd

To Llanfaes
Primary School (300m),
The Held Bunkhouse (2mi),
A40, A470, Mountain Centre
(5mi), Llwyn-y-Celyn Youth
Hostel (7mi), Ystradfellte (15mi)
& Merthyr Tydfil (17mi)

Captain's Walk

Danygaer Rd

Little Free St

Usk

Canal Rd

Richway

Conwy St

Gasworks La

The Watton

B4061

Canal
Basin

Taff
Trail

Monmouthshire
& Brecon Canal

To A40, Parc de Pugh (50m), Brynich Caravan
Park (1.3mi), Ty'n-y-Caeau Youth
Hostel (1.8mi), B4558, Llanfrynach
(3.2mi) & Abergavenny (19mi)

0   100   200m
0   100   200yd

PLACES TO STAY
3 County House
7 Castle of Brecon Hotel;
   Brecknock Castle
8 Beacons Guest House
9 Welcome Stranger
24 Wellington Hotel
31 Lansdowne Hotel
32 Paris Guest House
33 Grange Guesh House

PLACES TO EAT
5 Kwik Save
   Supermarket
14 Top Drawer Two Deli
16 Cooperative Supermarket
25 Salad Bowl
27 Oak Restaurant

OTHER
1 Tithe Barn
2 Brecon Cathedral
4 Bikes & Hikes
6 Ely Tower
10 123 Computers
11 Boar's Head
12 Brecon Cycle Centre
13 Library
15 Punchbowl
17 Tourist Information Centre;
   National Park Information
   Centre
18 Brecon Hospital
19 Andrew Morton Books
20 Sarah Siddons
21 Mel's Laundry Bin
22 Post Office
23 St Mary's Church
26 Police Station
28 Brecknock Museum
   & Art Gallery
29 Bi-Ped Cycles
30 Brecon Jazz Festival Office
34 Theatr Brycheiniog
35 South Wales Borderers
   Museum

THE BRECON BEACONS

A bookshop with lots of used and remaindered books is Andrew Morton Books (☎ 620022) on Lion St and in Lion Yard. For OS and other maps go to the TIC or to bike hire outfits (see the Getting Around later).

You can do your laundry at Mel's Laundry Bin in St Mary St, open Monday to Saturday.

Brecon Cathedral

The town's cathedral, above the River Honddu north of the town centre, was founded as part of a Benedictine monastery in 1093, though little remains of the Norman structure except the font and parts of the nave. Gerald of Wales (see the boxed text 'Gerald of Wales' under Books in the Facts for the Visitor chapter) was archdeacon here around 1172, having tossed out his predecessor whom he discovered living comfortably with a mistress. Tower, choir and transepts date from a major rebuilding in the 13th and 14th centuries. The church was

made the cathedral of the Brecon and Swansea diocese in 1923.

At the western end of the nave is the only stone cresset (an ancient lighting device) in Wales: its 30 cups held oil for the cathedral's lamps.

There's an exhibition about the cathedral at the heritage centre (☎ 625222) in the restored tithe barn beside the cathedral. The centre opens 10 am to 4.30 pm Monday to Saturday, April to December. Admission is free.

Brecknock Castle

What remains of Brecon's Norman castle is in two parts. A wall (part of the castle's Great Hall built in the 13th century by the earl of Hereford) and one tower (locked up) are now part of the Castle of Brecon Hotel (see Places to Stay later). You can't go in, but you can wander the hotel grounds for a look. On a hill across the road is Ely Tower (named after the Bishop of Ely who was imprisoned there by Richard III).

Brecknock Museum & Art Gallery

Don't be put off by the dour neoclassical exterior of the former Shire Hall. This is one of the more interesting museums of the old county of Brecknockshire. Inside are an ancient dugout canoe found at Llangorse Lake (see Around Brecon later), a re-created Welsh kitchen, a complete Victorian assize court (there was in fact an assize court here) and a collection of that peculiar Welsh utensil (now reborn as a tourist souvenir), the lovespoon. Also featured are the archaeology, history and natural history of the Brecon area, and an art gallery with changing exhibits.

Museum and gallery (☎ 624121), on Captain's Walk, open 10 am to 5 pm Monday to Saturday year round (closed 1 to 2 pm Saturday; closed at 4 pm Saturday from November to February) and open noon to 5 pm on Sunday, April to September. Admission costs £1/50p.

South Wales Borderers Museum

The Royal Regiment of Wales is based in Brecon. Its predecessor, the 24th Monmouthshire – the South Wales Borderers – fought in the 1879 Anglo-Zulu war in South Africa, and memories are long here. Many members are Gurkhas, often to be seen in their civvies around the town. At its headquarters on The Watton the regiment has a small museum (☎ 613310), open 9 am to 5 pm daily, April to September, and weekdays only the rest of the year.

The Monmouthshire & Brecon Canal

Brecon is the northern terminus of this canal, built between 1799 and 1812 for the movement of coal, iron ore, limestone and agricultural goods. Today much of it – 33 miles from Brecon to Pontypool – is back in business moving tourists around, and the busiest section is around Brecon. The actual terminus is by the Theatr Brycheiniog on Canal Rd.

Several outfits offer boat hire and/or cruises, though the only one operating from Brecon is Dragonfly Cruises (☎ 685222). A 2½-hour return trip costs £5/3, with departures on a complex schedule that more or less boils down to Wednesday, Saturday and Sunday from April to September, plus Thursday in July and August, plus Tuesday and Friday in August; for details ask the TIC or Dragonfly at the canal terminus.

From its tearoom and shop at The Old Storehouse, Llanfrynach, 4 miles south-east of Brecon, Water Folk (☎ 665382) offers 1½-hour horse-drawn cruises (£3.50/2.75) at noon and 3 pm Wednesday, Saturday and Sunday, Easter to October, and daily except Friday in August.

A firm with boats to hire by the day (£28/40/58 for two/four/eight hours) is Brecon Boats (☎ 676401) at Talybont-on-Usk, down the canal from Brecon (about 6 miles away by car or 8½ miles on foot). For weeklong hire, starting at around £700 for a two-berth boat, contact Cambrian Cruisers (☎ 665315) at Pencelli, just south-east of Llanfrynach.

Walking Routes

From the TIC, an 8-mile (3½-hour) walk climbs to Pen-y-Crug (100m) and its Iron Age hill fort, then descends to the remains of a 1st-century AD Roman fort at Y Gaer Farm near the hamlet of Aberyscir, about 3 miles north-west of the town centre.

A flat, peaceful 8½-mile walk takes you along the Taff Trail (which is here the towpath of the Monmouthshire & Brecon Canal) to and from picturesque Talybont-on-Usk. You can ride the Abergavenny bus out or back: either Stagecoach bus No 21 (about every two hours Monday to Saturday) or the Sunday Beacons Roundabout bus (see Getting There & Around in the Brecon Beacons National Park section earlier).

The TIC sells a national park booklet, *Walks in the Brecon Area* (£1.50), with details of these and other local walks from 2 to 10 miles long.

Cycling Routes

Brecon Cycle Centre (☎/fax 622651), 9 Ship St, offers half-day, day and weekend tours around the Brecon Beacons, and can arrange accommodation. It has a Web site at www.breconcycles.enta.net. Bikes & Hikes

(☎ 610071, ⓔ bikes-hikes@brecon.co.uk), The Elms, 10 The Struet, also runs guided trips. Visit its Web site at www.brecon.co .uk/local/bikehike. Both companies rent bikes for around £10/15 per half/full day.

Pony Trekking

Pony trekking is available at the Cantref Riding Centre, Upper Cantref Farm (see Places to Stay later) for £9.50/25 per hour/day.

Special Events

This sober, grey-stoned town seems an unlikely venue for a music festival of any kind but on one weekend in mid-August, the town lets its hair down for the Brecon Jazz Festival. This has become one of Europe's leading jazz festivals, and attracts thousands for what is essentially one long party. For more information, contact the festival office (☎ 625557) at 29 The Watton. Accommodation is hard to find at this busy time, although open areas all over town become makeshift camping grounds.

Previous headlining acts have included Sonny Rollins, Courtney Pine, Dr John, Andy Sheppard and George Melly (who has a house nearby).

Places to Stay

Camping About 1½ miles east of Brecon is *Brynich Caravan Park* (☎ 623325, Brynich). A caravan or tent with two adults costs £8.50/9.50 in low/high season. See the Hostels & Bunkhouses section for transport.

Hostels & Bunkhouses Near Brynich Caravan Park is *Ty'n-y-Caeau Youth Hostel* (☎ 665270), open Monday to Saturday, February to October (daily June to August), and weekends the rest of the year. The nightly charge is £10/6.90 for adults/under-18s. The Beacons Roundabout bus (see Getting There & Around in the Brecon Beacons National Park section) stops at the adjacent camp site in the summer. Alternatively, get off the No 21 bus at the Llanfrynach turning, from where it's a mile north via the village of Groesffordd, or get off the No 39 bus at the Llanddew turning, from where it's a mile south.

Next nearest is the *Llwyn-y-Celyn Youth Hostel* (☎ 624261), 7 miles south on the A470 and 2 miles north of Storey Arms. It opens daily from mid-April to October (except Tuesday and Wednesday in September and October), plus weekends from mid-February. The nightly rate is £9.25/6.50. The No 43 Merthyr–Brecon bus stops outside.

There are several bunkhouses in the area, all charging around £8 to £10 per bed. Three miles south-east of Brecon is *The Held* (☎ 624646, Cantref), first of the Brecon Beacons bunkhouses and probably the most beautiful, with a panoramic view of the escarpments. It's 1½ miles up the road beyond the primary school at Llanfaes (see Entertainment later for directions) and open year round for about £9.

There's more bunkhouse accommodation (from £8.50), plus basic camping (£2.50 per person), B&B (from £17 per person) and a riding centre, at *Upper Cantref Farm* (☎ 665223, Cantref), just south-west of the village of Llanfrynach. The Beacons Roundabout bus (see Getting There & Around in the Brecon Beacons National Park section) stops at Llanfrynach in the summer.

B&Bs With a wide range of rooms, *Beacons Guest House* (☎ 623339, 16 Bridge St) has rooms from £25/36. *Welcome Stranger* (☎ 622188, 7 Bridge St) is a friendly B&B, with a restaurant, charging around £16 per person. The handsome, scrupulously Georgian *County House* (☎ 625844, 100 The Struet) is a former judge's residence with walled garden and parking. Comfortable rooms with B&B cost £35/55, and other meals can be arranged.

East of the centre is a cluster of modest B&Bs. Good value here is nonsmoking *Grange Guest House* (☎/fax 624038, 22 The Watton), with three-star rooms at two-star rates (£17 per person or £20 en suite) and an award-winning garden. *Paris Guest House* (☎ 624205, 28 The Watton) has similar rates.

The excellent *Griffin Inn* at Llyswen (see Places to Eat later) offers B&B from £35 per person.

Hotels Reliable mid-range hotels include the *Lansdowne Hotel* (☎ 623321, 39 The

Watton) with rooms for £27.50/47.50 and the central *Wellington Hotel* (☎ *625225, The Bulwark),* which has a pub, wine bar and coffee shop and offers B&B for £35/55.

At the Best Western *Castle of Brecon Hotel* (☎ *624611, Castle Square),* on the site of Brecknock Castle, rooms (all with bath or shower) cost £54/69 in the main hotel or £45/59 in the adjacent lodge.

Places to Eat
Several tearooms in the centre do modest meals during daytime hours. *Salad Bowl* (☎ *625429, The Bulwark)* is an agreeable source of soups, salads and quiches, plus hot lunch dishes, for under £5.

The small *Oak Restaurant* (☎ *625501, 12 The Bulwark)* offers an imaginative mix of local and Thai dishes from about £7. In peaceful surroundings, including a garden patio in summer, it opens for lunch and dinner daily from March to October (including an evening Thai menu from Wednesday to Saturday) and opens Wednesday to Saturday in winter.

Aside from the Oak, identikit pub meals, overpriced hotel restaurants and takeaways, there is little to choose from after 6 pm. One option is the restaurant at *Beacons Guest House* (see Places to Stay earlier) – it opens to nonresidents and the food is home-made and very good; three-course dinners start at £15.

Self-caterers can shop at supermarkets – the *Cooperative* off Lion St or *Kwik Save* in Upper High St – or at a good deli called *Top Drawer Two,* on High St, which stocks a wonderful range of breads and Welsh cheeses.

The venerable *Griffin Inn* (☎ *754241, fax 754592, Llyswen),* 9 miles north-east on the A470, is a River Wye anglers' haunt with distinctly superior pub grub, including wood pigeon, jugged hare, braised wild duck and partridge. Most main dishes cost from £9.90 to £13.85. It opens daily.

Entertainment
Brecon has lots of pubs. Locals like the lively *Boar's Head (Ship St),* the *Punchbowl (High St)* and the *Sarah Siddons (The Bulwark),* named after the legendary actress Sarah Siddons (1755-1831) who was born in Brecon.

The bar at the *Wellington Hotel* (see Places to Stay earlier) has live jazz some evenings.

The canalside *Theatr Brycheiniog* (☎ *611622, Canal Rd)* is the town's best venue for drama, comedy, classical and pop music, and has an exhibition centre and the Waterfront Bistro & Cafe.

The Brecon Male Voice Choir practices at Llanfaes primary school on Orchard St in Llanfaes from 7.30 to 9.30 pm Friday, and visitors are welcome. The school is just east off the A470 (turn off ¼ mile from the bridge over the River Usk).

Spectator Sports
Fourth-division Brecon RFC is one of Wales' oldest rugby clubs. Matches are played at Parc de Pugh, just south-east of the centre on The Watton.

Getting There & Away
All the Beacons Bus routes come into Brecon (see Getting There & Around in the Brecon Beacons National Park section earlier).

Bus services with Stagecoach (☎ 01633-244744) include No 21 from Abergavenny (£3.45, one hour, every two hours); No 39 from Hereford via Hay-on-Wye (£2.90, 55 minutes, six Monday to Saturday, two to three Sunday); No 43 from Merthyr Tydfil (£2.70, 35 minutes, every hour or two, twice on Sunday); and No 63 from Swansea (£4.10, 1¼ hours, three daily). National Express No 322/509 from London runs daily via Cardiff (£2.75, 1¼ hours).

Getting Around
Mountain bikes can be rented from Bikes & Hikes and from Brecon Cycle Centre (see Cycling Routes earlier) for around £10/15 per half/full day; both also arrange guided bike trips. Another bike hire shop is Bi-Ped Cycles (☎ 622296, mobile ☎ 07970-972186), 4 Free St.

For a taxi, try Brecon Taxis (☎ 623444).

AROUND BRECON
Llangorse
☎ 01874

Llangorse Lake (Llyn Syfaddan), 6 miles east of Brecon, is Wales' second largest natural lake after Llyn Tegid (Bala Lake; see the Mid Wales chapter), and the national park's main venue for flatwater sports (where there are sections of slow-moving water in between rapids), with facilities for sailing, windsurfing, flatwater canoeing and waterskiing. Ironically, it's also an important Site of Special Scientific Interest (SSSI; see Ecology & Environment in the Facts about Wales chapter), which makes for a delicate balancing act.

Llangorse Lake It's a ½-mile walk from Llangorse (Llangors) village on the B4560, via Llangorse Common to the lake's reedy northern shore, where there is a sailing club, a kids' adventure centre and other facilities.

The lake has a unique prehistoric site – some 20–30m offshore is the only trace in Wales of a crannog, a lake dwelling built on an artificial offshore platform made from a wooden palisade filled with brush and stones. Such dwellings or refuges were used from the late Bronze Age until early medieval times. From the amazingly precise technique of tree-ring dating, this one (of which only the base remains) is known to have been built around AD 889-893, probably by the royal house of Brecheiniog, an early Welsh kingdom with roots in Ireland.

The island is privately owned but managed as a scheduled ancient monument, and was excavated between 1989 and 1994. Among items found here was a dugout canoe, now in Brecon's Brecknock Museum. Other artefacts are at the National Museum in Cardiff. Naturally, legends – of submerged cities and churchbells pealing faintly in the middle of the night – abound.

Llangorse Rope Centre This remarkable indoor climbing and caving facility is a good place to conquer any fears you might have before heading up onto (or beneath) the crags in the southern part of the national park. There are synthetic and natural rock climbing surfaces, kids' walls, a high-adrenaline ropes course and even an artificial cave. It costs £11 for a two-hour general instruction session or £4/3 per adult/child

just to use the facilities (plus the cost of renting helmet, harness and so on).

The centre is on the B4560, ¾ mile south of Llangorse village at Gilfach Farm (☎ 658272, fax 658280), which also serves as the village's de facto TIC. It opens 9.30 am to 10 pm (until 6 pm on Sunday) daily, year round. You can visit its Web site at www.activityuk.com.

Also here is a separate riding centre, with an all-weather arena and 24 miles of private tracks.

Places to Stay & Eat The Rope Centre, as *Gilfach Bunkhouse & Farmhouse*, offers nonsmoking bunkhouse accommodation (with full kitchen) in 12th- and 13th-century farm buildings with full kitchen. Bring your own food, sleeping bag/sheet, pillowcase and towel. The cost per person is £10.50/11.50 weekdays/weekends (£1 less if you're booked at the rope centre or riding centre). There's also basic camping for £2.50 per person.

Run by the same family is *Pen-y-Bryn House* (☎ 658606, fax 658215), a rambling old ex-farmhouse in the village, with high-quality B&B from £20 per person. Also in the village is the *Red Lion Hotel* (☎ 658238), where singles/doubles cost from £27/42. At Talgarth, 4½ miles north on the B4560, is a modest independent hostel called *Joe's Lodge* (☎ 711845, Hay Rd), with B&B for £10; book ahead.

At Pengenffordd, 3¼ miles south of Talgarth on the A479, the *Castle Inn* (☎ 711353) has B&B for £20 per person (£23 en suite), bunkhouse accommodation at £12 (meals only at the Inn), spartan camping at £2 per person, and real ales. Also at Pengenffordd is *Upper Trewalkin Farm* (☎ 711349), with B&B for £20 and good evening meals from £13.

Getting There & Away The postbus visits Llangorse from Brecon (35 minutes) twice each weekday; call ☎ 624788 for information. The Beacons Bus (route 40) serves Talgarth (see under Getting There & Around in the Brecon Beacons National Park section).

Pembrokeshire & Carmarthenshire

The south-west is perhaps Wales' most heavily touristed corner, and it's easy to see why. Pembrokeshire's vast 'peninsula of peninsulas', thrusting out into the currents and gales of the Irish Sea, is bordered with perpendicular cliffs, fire-and-brimstone surf and a profusion of coves and sandy bays that can make you feel like you're at the edge of the world. The interface between land and sea is the attraction (most of the coast has been designated a national park), though towns such as Tenby, St David's and Fishguard offer various civilised ways to approach it.

Pembrokeshire is the star; Carmarthenshire is the hinterland you go through to get there, and has fewer attractions of its own – the conspicuous exception being the extraordinary new National Botanic Garden of Wales, which will probably change the way you think about landscapes, and not just Carmarthenshire's.

Getting Around

The region's biggest bus lines are Richards Brothers (☎ 01239-613756), Silcox Coaches (☎ 01646-683143) and First Cymru (☎ 0870 608 2608). Summerdale Coaches (☎ 01348-840270) runs the Puffin Shuttle service (see the Pembrokeshire Coast National Park section later), useful for coastal walkers. Postbuses (see the Getting Around chapter) provide limited but essential connections in remote areas.

The West Wales Rover ticket (£4.60, youth & student £3.40) allows unlimited travel for one day on buses of these and other companies in the region, and on a few services to/from Swansea and Mid Wales (but not the TrawsCambria coach, postbuses nor National Express). Richards Brothers has its own Day Explorer (£3.40/2.30 for adult/child) and Weekly Explorer (£14/9.50) tickets, and a 10-day Coast Path

Highlights

- Strolling by Neolithic monuments, puffin colonies and some of the world's oldest rocks on the clifftop Pembrokeshire Coast Path
- Pausing for thought in St David's Cathedral, Wales' holiest place, simultaneously modest and magnificent.
- Sipping herbal tea in a solarium 122m above the crashing surf, at Pwll Deri Youth Hostel
- Visiting the Mediterranean without ever leaving Wales, at the world-class National Botanic Garden of Wales
- Imagining you are Dylan Thomas, sitting among your papers at the Boathouse at Laugharne

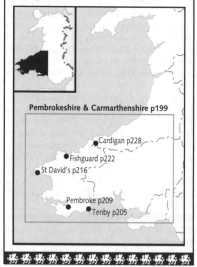

Pembrokeshire & Carmarthenshire p199

Cardigan p228
Fishguard p222
St David's p216
Pembroke p209
Tenby p205

Explorer ticket. All these passes can be bought on the bus.

The railway runs from Swansea via Carmarthen to Milford Haven, branching at

198

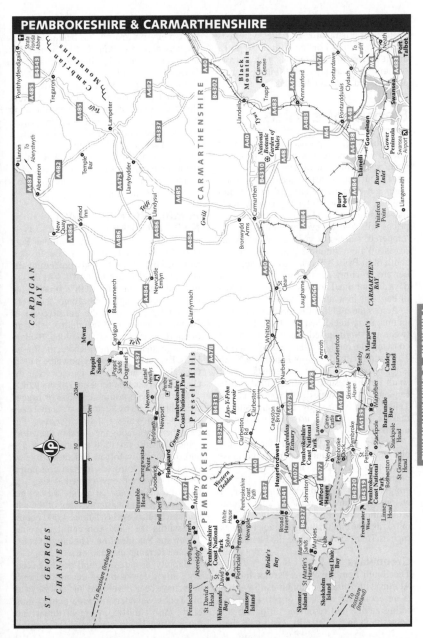

PEMBROKESHIRE & CARMARTHENSHIRE

Whitland for Pembroke Dock and at Clarbeston for Fishguard. But the system is geared to linking London with those ports, and it's awkward and tedious getting from one branch to another, with multiple train changes and poor connections.

Pembrokeshire

Pembrokeshire is probably Wales' most season-sensitive region with its beaches, water sports and general emphasis on 'outdoor' tourism. Tourist areas and coastal roads get desperately clogged in July and August, while in winter the county feels like never-never land and accommodation prices fall. And yet even in winter the sea-tempered weather is good by Welsh standards (Wales' sunniest place is at Dale, south of St Bride's Bay). May and September are probably the best months for clear days and minimal crowds, but there are lots of bargains in winter.

Across the middle of Pembrokeshire runs an imaginary line called the 'Landsker', between the Normanised, castle-dotted south coast and the rural, Welsh-speaking interior. This cultural divide – from Amroth to Newgale, roughly speaking – persists today: south Pembrokeshire is often called 'Little England beyond Wales', and resorts such as Tenby are favoured by English holiday-makers. Many guesthouses here are run by incomers.

Another cultural wrinkle is the region's old Flemish communities. Population pressure and political persecution in early-12th-century Flanders drove many people to emigrate, and the Norman King Henry I encouraged some to settle in south Pembrokeshire, where they practised their weaving skills. The clothmaking tradition in towns such as Tenby owes much to the Flemish.

Greenways

The South Pembrokeshire Partnership for Action with Rural Communities (SPARC) is an economic self-help organisation offering advice and resources to local businesses with an eco-friendly, keep-it-in-the-community angle. One SPARC initiative, the Greenways Project, has begun developing waymarked walking/cycling routes that intersect conveniently with public transport. Greenways Holidays (☎ 01834-860965, e tourism@sparc.org.uk), The Old School, Station Rd, Narberth SA67 7DU, offers flexible walking, cycling, riding and fishing holidays, go-as-you please accommodation and heritage tours. If you're considering a Pembrokeshire holiday, this is a worthy place to start. Check out their Web site at www.southpembrokeshire-holidays.co.uk, which also has links to other useful information on Pembrokeshire.

PEMBROKESHIRE COAST NATIONAL PARK

The Pembrokeshire Coast National Park (Parc Cenedlaethol Arfordir Sir Benfro), established in 1952, is the only predominantly coastal national park in the UK. At 230 sq miles, it's also one of the UK's smallest national parks, though certainly not the shortest, taking in almost the entire coast of Pembrokeshire (about 180 miles), all of its offshore islands, the Daugleddau Estuary and large stretches of moorland in the Preseli Hills. Except in the Preselis, nowhere's more than about 3 miles from the sea. See the chapter introduction for a map of the park.

Most of the coastline consists of rugged cliffs, broken up by stretches of sandy beach – the best in Wales – and rocky coves. The rocks here are among the oldest in the world, some formed over 1500 million years ago and dramatically folded and faulted. Here also is one of Europe's highest concentrations of protected environmental sites. As with the other national parks, this is not 'wilderness' but an interweaving of the natural and human worlds; some 24,000 people live within the park, concentrated around Tenby and Saundersfoot. The biggest activities are farming and tourism.

Happily, despite the mind-bending scenery, only a few parts of the milder south coast have been developed into resorts, with the Tenby–Saundersfoot area getting most of the resort traffic. A bigger threat than tourism may be environmental catastrophes such as the 1996 grounding of the oil tanker *Sea Empress* off Milford Haven (for more on this, see Ecology & Environment in the Facts about Wales chapter).

The more exposed north coast remains unspoilt and offers some of Wales' most dramatically beautiful walking. Indeed most visitors come here to walk, the majority of them along the Pembrokeshire Coast Path, running from Amroth in the south to Poppit Sands in the north. But there's more to the park than walking. The restless sea tempts surfers and sea kayakers, and this coast is the birthplace of another high-adrenaline sport, coasteering (see the following sections for details). Those inclined to quieter waters can explore the secluded inlets and creeks of the Daugleddau Estuary.

The park's only upland area is the Preseli Hills. Ancient trade routes run through them, and hill forts, standing stones and burial chambers are evidence of the prehistoric peoples who once lived here. From these hills in around 2000 BC came the 'bluestone' megaliths that form the inner circle of Stonehenge in England. This is also arguably the park's finest territory for on-road cycling, and prime country for horse riding. The highest point is Foel Cwm Cerwyn, at 536m.

The area is internationally famous for its wildlife. The offshore islands of Skomer, Skokholm and Grassholm support huge breeding populations of Manx shearwaters, puffins, guillemots, razorbills (the emblem of the national park), kittiwakes, fulmars, gannets and gulls. Grey seals breed in coves and caves, especially on Skomer and Ramsey Islands. All of the islands can be visited. Waders and wildfowl use the estuaries as winter feeding grounds. From headlands such as Strumble Head you can see resident bottlenose dolphins and harbour porpoises, and migrating dolphins and Minke whales.

The park's towns have only modest attractions, with the exception of St David's, Britain's smallest city, whose superb cathedral is a shrine to Wales' patron saint. In 2002, the 50th anniversary of the national park, St David's will host the Royal National Eisteddfod (see the boxed text 'The Eisteddfod' under Arts in the Facts about Wales chapter).

Orientation & Information

The park consists of four separate sections, isolated by the peninsula's railway lines (which run to its railheads at Fishguard, Haverfordwest and Pembroke Dock) and the industrial coastline around Pembroke and Milford Haven.

There are effectively about a dozen park information centres, each combined with a county-run Tourist Information Centre (TIC); only two, at St David's and Newport, are actually park-run. On arrival, pick up a copy of *Coast to Coast*, the park's free annual newspaper for visitors, full of information on using and getting around the park, a calendar of events and details of park-organised activities including walks, cycle trips, pony treks, island cruises, canoe trips and minibus tours. It's available at park centres, TICs and some newsagents.

The park's head office (☎ 01437-764636, fax 769045, ℯ pcnp@pembrokeshirecoast .org.uk) is on Winch Lane, Haverfordwest – though this is not a public enquiries office. The park has its own Web site at www.pembrokeshirecoast.org, and its own weather service (☎ 01834-812516) for next-day forecasts during Easter fortnight and from June to August.

Walking & Cycling Routes

The big walk here is the 186-mile, cliff-top Pembrokeshire Coast Path, opened in 1970 and one of Wales' three national trails. You should consider walking at least one section. You don't have to take all your baggage along: several outfits (see Guided Walks & Bicycle Tours later) will send it on ahead for you.

If you've only got a few days, a good choice is the segment facing out to Skomer Island, from Dale to Martin's Haven near Marloes. All three towns are easily accessible from Milford Haven or Haverfordwest, and are on the route of the Puffin Shuttle bus (see the Getting There & Around section later). Another suggestion is the stretch from Solva to Whitesands Bay, which is close to St David's and its good transport links. For more information on this superb trail – including guides and maps – see under Activities in the Facts for the Visitor chapter.

National park rangers lead walks along various parts of the trail from April to October; a half-/full-day walk costs from £2/3.50. There is even a 14-day guided walk of the complete path in late May and early June for £120; booking ahead is essential. See the *Coast to Coast* newspaper or contact a TIC for details.

Bikes are not allowed on the Pembrokeshire Coast Path, but there are plenty of quiet lanes and bridleways through isolated hamlets and deep woods, and some coastal tracks. Summer traffic on A-roads – especially the A487 in the north – can make cycling hazardous, so stick to unclassified or B-roads.

The 100-mile Pembrokeshire Park Cycle Trail, developed by Newport Cycle Hire and West Wales Eco Centre (see under Newport later), takes in some of the county's finest scenery. Some or all of it may become part of Lôn Geltaidd, the Celtic Trail (Sustrans route No 4); see Activities in the Facts for the Visitor chapter for more on the national cycle network. If you plan to cycle off-road, check your route with the park's head office (see the preceding Orientation & Information section). There are bike hire places in St David's, Fishguard, Newport, Cardigan and elsewhere, as noted in the text.

Guided Walks & Bicycle Tours Two outfits offering supported walking and cycling holidays (including route guides, accommodation and baggage transfer) in and around the park are Greenways (part of SPARC; see the introduction to the Pembrokeshire section); and Menter Preseli, also called Pembrokeshire Walking Holidays (☎ 01437-760075, ⓔ haverfordwestinformationcentre @pembrokeshire.gov.uk), with a Web site at www.pembrokeshire-walking-holidays .co.uk.

Sea Sports

Coasteering is a sport invented on the Pembrokeshire coast. Equipped with wetsuit, flotation jacket and helmet, you make your way along the coastal cliffs by a combination of climbing, traversing, scrambling, cliff jumping and swimming.

The western tip of the Pembrokeshire coast is also one of the UK's finest sea kayaking areas. Beginners can enjoy coastal trips starting from calm harbours and bays, and work their way up to heavy seas. As the tides surge in and out of the Irish Sea twice daily, powerful currents around the bigger offshore islands give rise to some incredible standing waves to play on.

Neither of these sports is without risk, and you should only try them with a guide who has a good knowledge of the local coastline, water and weather. You must be a reasonably fit, capable swimmer. Adventure centres here won't rent you the gear unless you agree to some training first (for some non-threatening flatwater canoeing, head for the tranquil waters of the Dauggleddau Estuary).

Pembrokeshire's best surfing is at Tenby South Beach, Manorbier, Freshwater West and West Dale Bay (Freshwater West, favoured by caravanners because the car park is close to the beach, has a strong riptide). Along St Bride's Bay, try Broad Haven South and Newgale. St David's immense Whitesands Bay is good but always crowded. Windsurfing is popular off many beaches, and on the sheltered waters of Milford Haven. Most coastal towns have places where you can hire equipment (see local listings).

Two north Pembrokeshire multiactivity centres (see the Multiactivity section later) offer coasteering, sea kayaking and surfing as part of their programs. All gear is provided except trainers (sneakers) to wear in the water.

Boat Trips

Boat trips to see the wildlife on the island nature reserves are highly recommended. Boats to Ramsey, off St David's, depart from Whitesands Bay or the lifeboat station at St Justinian's. Trips to Skomer, Skokholm and Grassholm Islands normally go from Martin's Haven (see under St Bride's Bay later in the chapter). Boats to Caldey Island go from Tenby. As well as trips on small ex-fishing boats, there are also excursions on high-speed inflatables.

Charges vary according to the length of the trip and the number of islands visited, but you should expect to pay between £10 and £20 for a day trip. See local listings under St Bride's Bay and St David's.

Pony Trekking & Horse Riding

This is an ideal area for riding – along beaches, across open moorland, along wood-ed bridleways or down quiet country lanes – and there are a dozen stables in or near the park; see the *Coast to Coast* newspaper for a listing of them. The National Park also or-ganises rides in the Preseli Hills.

Fishing

To fish the rivers you need a rod licence (from £2.50 to £5.50 a day) from the Envir-onment Agency (☎ 01437-760081) and the permission of the land/fishery owner. Clubs or associations may give day tickets. On small rivers, approach local farmers.

There's also good sea fishing – Newgale is one of the best beaches in Wales to fish from. You'll need permission first if you want to fish off dock or harbour walls; sea fishing licences are available from local post offices.

For more information on fishing in Wales, see under Activities in the Facts for the Vis-itor chapter.

Multi-Activity

Two trustworthy activity centres in north Pembrokeshire, both in business since the mid-1980s, offer residential, group-based programs. Both are willing to slot individu-als in on a space-available basis, though they prefer advance booking. Activities on offer include coasteering, sea kayaking, mountain biking, surfing, coastal hiking, horseriding and climbing/abseiling.

Preseli Venture (☎ 01348-837709, fax 837656, e info@preseliventure.com), Par-cynole Fach, Mathry, Haverfordwest, Pem-brokeshire SA62 5HN, is off the A487 between St David's and Fishguard.

Twr-y-Felin (TYF; ☎ 01437-721611, toll-free ☎ 0800 132588, fax 01437-720488, e info@tyf.com), 1 High St, St David's, Pembrokeshire SA62 6SA, is based at its own hotel, the Twr-y-Felin.

Both have Web sites at www.preseliventure .com and www.tyf.com respectively.

All gear is provided, though some may need to be rented. Both have their own dorm-style accommodation, bar and healthy food, and will collect you from the train or bus sta-tion. Typical prices are around £32/60 for a half-/full-day adventure 'module' (with longer all-in packages available), from £4 to £4.50 per person for camping, £20 to £23 for B&B and £37 to £40 for full board.

Other Attractions

If you have children, the largest theme park in the area is Oakwood (☎ 01834-891376), just off the A40 between Carmarthen and Haver-fordwest, at Canaston Bridge. The wooden roller-coaster ride is Europe's largest, topping 55mph and with 11 crossovers and a maxi-mum drop of 25m. You can visit its Web site at www.oakwood-leisure.com.

Places To Stay & Eat

There are 10 YHA/Hostelling International (HI) hostels in the park – at Manorbier, Lawrenny (12 miles from Pembroke), Mar-loes Sands, Broad Haven, Penycwm (Wales' only five-star hostel), St David's, Trefin, Pwll Deri (at a spectacular cliff-top location near Strumble Head), Newport and Poppit Sands (near Cardigan). To book any number of hostels in west Wales – up to two weeks ahead, for 50p per person per night – contact the West Wales Booking Bureau (☎ 0870 241 2314) at the St David's hostel.

A recommended independent hostel in the region is the Hamilton Guest House in Fishguard (see under Fishguard later).

With the permission of the farmer or landowner, it's possible to camp almost anywhere in the park, though not on Na-tional Trust (NT) land. TICs have lists of camp sites with full facilities.

There's a good range of B&Bs and hotels throughout the park, especially along the well-developed south coast.

Getting There & Around

Except on Sunday, bus services between towns in the park are pretty good. Timetables are available from TICs, and the *Coast to Coast* newspaper lists major services. If you'll be using buses a lot, a good investment is *Easy-Access Routes in the Pembrokeshire Coast National Park* (£2.95). See the chapter introduction for contact numbers and information on travel passes.

The Puffin Shuttle (No 400) is a coastal bus service along St Bride's Bay from Milford Haven to St David's, running twice daily in each direction from late May (Whitsun) to September. You can hail it or get off almost anywhere – a boon for coastal path walkers. Fares depend on distance – for example, £1.85 from St David's to Broad Haven or £3.20 from Milford Haven to Newgale. For more information contact Summerdale Coaches (☎ 01348-840270).

Park & Ride bus services at St David's and Tenby allow you to leave your car outside these overcrowded town centres.

Trains are not a useful way to get around the park.

TENBY (DINBYCH Y PYSGOD)
☎ 01834 • pop 5500

The Welsh name for this genteel seaside town on Carmarthen Bay is as charming as Tenby itself – it means Little Fort of the Fishes. Despite its small-town feel, it's the largest town within the boundaries of a national park in the UK.

Unlike many other UK seaside resorts, Tenby has managed to avoid being overtaken either by amusement arcades and fish-and-chippies or by suffocating tweeness – although it's certainly overtaken by visitors in the summer, when its population swells four- or five-fold. Crowds notwithstanding, the town is definitely worth a visit for its mix of gravitas and attitude, as popular with young surfers as with well-heeled tourists.

The Pembrokeshire Coast Path runs through the middle of town.

History

Tenby has done duty as a Norman stronghold, an Elizabethan port and a Victorian and Georgian seaside resort. Naturally the Normans built their castle on the promontory. A community of Flemish clothmakers who settled here in the early 12th century began a tradition that has lasted for centuries. After three shattering attacks by Welsh princes – in 1153 by Rhys ap Gruffyd, in 1187 by his son Rhys Gryg and in 1260 by Llewelyn ap Gruffydd (Llewelyn the Last) – the town and its headland were walled off from the mainland in the 13th century.

A charter from Henry IV brought the town back to life in the 15th century as a port, exporting its cloth in exchange for salt and wine. In 1471 Henry Tudor, the future Henry VII, sheltered here during the Wars of the Roses before fleeing to Brittany in France.

Decline again set in, this time halted by the arrival of the railway in the 19th century and the development of Tenby as a saltwater-therapy spa by William Paxton (who also owned the estate near Carmarthen that's now home to the National Botanic Garden of Wales).

Anxiety over the possibility of a French invasion of Milford Haven led to the construction in 1869 of a fort on St Catherine's Island, the tidal island beside the promontory.

Among writers and artists who have taken inspiration or rest here are George Elliot, Dick Francis, JMW Turner, Beatrix Potter and Roald Dahl. Artists Augustus and Gwen John were born here.

Orientation

The town's main landmark is Castle Hill, site of the Norman stronghold. Behind it is Tenby harbour, and North Beach sweeps away to the, well, north. South beneath the promontory is tiny Castle Beach, and beyond it stretches South Beach.

From the bus stand it's a block north-east to the old town walls, or a 500m walk north to the TIC, above North Beach. From the train station walk up Warren and White Lion Sts to the TIC. The main shopping precinct is High St and Tudor Square, a block inland from the harbour.

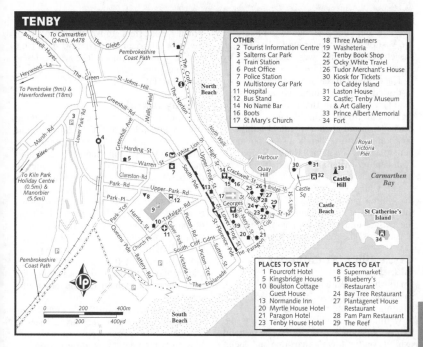

TENBY

OTHER
2 Tourist Information Centre
3 Salterns Car Park
4 Train Station
6 Post Office
7 Police Station
9 Multistorey Car Park
11 Hospital
12 Bus Stand
14 No Name Bar
16 Boots
17 St Mary's Church
18 Three Mariners
19 Washeteria
22 Tenby Book Shop
25 Ocky White Travel
26 Tudor Merchant's House
30 Kiosk for Tickets to Caldey Island
31 Laston House
32 Castle; Tenby Museum & Art Gallery
33 Prince Albert Memorial
34 Fort

PLACES TO STAY
1 Fourcroft Hotel
5 Kingsbridge House
10 Boulston Cottage Guest House
13 Normandie Inn
20 Myrtle House Hotel
21 Paragon Hotel
23 Tenby House Hotel

PLACES TO EAT
8 Supermarket
15 Blueberry's Restaurant
24 Bay Tree Restaurant
27 Plantagenet House Restaurant
28 Pam Pam Restaurant
29 The Reef

Driving and street parking are hellish, though there's plenty of public parking.

Information

The TIC (☎ 842402, fax 845439), on The Croft, above North Beach, opens 10 am to 5 pm daily, Easter to October (to 9 pm, mid-July to August); and 10 am to 4 pm daily except on Sunday the rest of the year. Disabled visitors can hire wheelchairs for their stay (donation requested) through the TIC.

Major UK banks, all with ATMs, have branches on High St or Tudor Square. The post office is on the corner of Greenhill Rd and Warren St. The well-stocked Tenby Book Shop is in Tudor Square. Across the road in Medical Hall is a reliable travel agency, Ocky White Travel (☎ 844133).

The police station (☎ 842303) is on Warren St, and the little Tenby Cottage Hospital (☎ 842040) is south-west of the centre on Trafalgar Rd. Do your laundry at the Washeteria on Lower Frog St, open until 9 pm daily.

Old Tenby

Tall, pastel-painted Georgian houses – most of them now hotels – rise above the pretty harbour, which fills and empties with the tide. The tiny stepped lane of Quay Hill is Tenby at its most atmospheric (and, in summer, its most congested). The old centre is still enclosed by stout walls.

The most interesting building around here is the handsomely restored Tudor Merchant's House (☎ 842279, NT), the town house of a late-15th-century merchant. The remains of three frescoes can be seen inside. The house opens 10 am to 5 pm daily except Wednesday (1 to 5 pm on Sunday), April to October; and 10 am to 3 pm daily except Wednesday and Saturday (noon to 3 pm on Sunday), November. Admission costs £1.80/90p (adult/child).

St Mary's Church

Tenby's parish church is of more interest historically than visually. Its first rector was

Gerald of Wales (see the boxed text 'Gerald of Wales' under Books in the Facts for the Visitor chapter) in around 1210, though the church he knew was later trashed by Llewelyn ap Gruffydd in 1260.

The present church's graceful arched roof is dotted with charming wooden bosses, mainly dating from the 15th century and carved into flowers, cheeky faces, mythical beasts, fish and even a mermaid holding a comb and mirror. There's also a memorial here to a local son named Robert Recorde, a 16th-century writer and mathematician who invented the 'equals' sign.

The young Henry Tudor was hidden in the church before fleeing to Brittany. It's thought that he left by means of a tunnel into the cellars under Mayor Thomas White's house across the road (where Boots is now).

Castle Hill & St Catherine's Island

On this headland are the ruins of the Norman castle, an incongruous memorial to Prince Albert and a grand coastal panorama.

Within the remains of the castle is the Tenby Museum & Art Gallery, with good exhibits on the town's maritime and social history; re-creations of a pirate's cell, an apothecary shop and a Victorian study; and works by Augustus and Gwen John and other artists with local connections. The museum (☎ 842809) opens 10 am to 5 pm daily (closed at weekends, November to March). Admission costs £2/1.50.

William Paxton built saltwater baths above the harbour in what is now Laston House, 1 Castle Square. The Greek writing on the pediment translates as 'The sea will wash away all the evils of man'.

When the tide is out, Tenby is wrapped in immense, flat beaches. At high tide they all disappear, and the harbour fills up. At low tide you can walk across the sand to St Catherine's Island – but it will be a long, cold wait if you get trapped there when the tide comes back in! Check tide tables in the *Coast to Coast* newspaper, buy a table at any newsagent or ask at the TIC. The Victorian fort on the island is not open to the public.

Guided Tours

Town Trails offers guided, themed walks of Tenby's historical sites on most days from mid-June to September. The walks, 1¼ to 1½ hours long, cost £3.25/2.25. For details ask at the TIC or call ☎ 845841.

Caldey Island

A popular boat trip from Tenby harbour crosses to Caldey (or Caldy) Island, home to a community of Cistercian monks and lots of grey seals and seabirds. The monks make a variety of products for sale, including perfume (based on the island's wildflowers), dairy products and chocolate, and do so well that they now employ people from the mainland. There are guided tours of the monastery twice daily and great walks around the island, with good views from the lighthouse. Make sure you visit the old priory and St Illtyd's Church with its oddly shaped steeple. Inside is a stone with inscriptions in Ogham (an ancient Celtic script).

Boats run about every 15 minutes from 9.30 am to 5 or 6 pm weekdays, Easter to October (and 11 am to 4 pm Saturday, mid-May to September). Departure is from the harbour at high tide and from Castle Beach at low tide. The crossing takes 20 minutes. Tickets (£7 return) for the crossing and tour are sold from a kiosk (☎ 844453) at the harbour slipway.

On little St Margaret's Island beside Caldey (landings prohibited) is a nature reserve run by the Wildlife Trust West Wales (☎ 01437-765462), with grey seals and Wales' biggest colony of cormorants.

Special Events

The Tenby Arts Festival (☎ 843839) runs for nine days in late September, with street performances, samba bands, kite flying, sand-castle competitions, choirs, dancing and concerts. Check out the Web site at www.tenbyartsfest.com for further details.

Places to Stay

Camping With a capacity almost equal to the entire population of Tenby, *Kiln Park Holiday Centre* (☎ 844121, *Marsh Rd*) is an immense caravan park – about half a mile south-west of the town centre. Two adults with a tent pay £11, which includes admission to two heated swimming pools, tennis courts, an entertainment centre and various teens' and kids' clubs.

Hostels The closest hostel is 6 miles west along the coast at Manorbier (see Around Tenby later). Older literature refers to a hostel at Pentlepoir, but this is no longer open.

B&Bs & Hotels Every second house seems to be a B&B or vest-pocket hotel, and the area outside the town walls is full of them. Most get booked out during bank-holiday weekends. Prices drop by a few pounds in winter. Many small 'hotels' are indistinguishable from B&Bs.

A comfortable option at the budget end, close to the bus stand, is *Boulston Cottage Guest House* (☎ 843289, 29 Trafalgar Rd), with rooms from about £16 per person. In the droopy neighbourhood near the train station is *Kingsbridge House* (☎ 844148, Warren St), starting at about £20 and with free parking.

The *Paragon Hotel* (☎ 843022, The Paragon) is a long-standing B&B, plain and tidy, whose front rooms have uninterrupted views of Carmarthen Bay. Rooms start at about £23 per person, and there is free off-street parking. Around the corner is the comfortable, nonsmoking *Myrtle House Hotel* (☎ 842508, St Mary's St), at £25 per person (en suite). The *Normandie Inn* (☎ 842227, fax 843318, Upper Frog St), a former coaching inn built into the old town walls, offers B&B, with big en-suite rooms, for £30 per person.

The *Fourcroft Hotel* (☎ 842886, fax 842888, The Croft) is family-run and really *is* a hotel, with traditional comforts and service but accessible prices. Most rooms are en suite, with views of North Beach and the harbour; there's a sauna and, in summer, an outdoor pool. B&B starts at £41 per person from July to September, £35 from Easter to June and in October, and £31 the rest of the year; short-break discounts are also available. The *Tenby House Hotel* (☎ 842000,

The Old Bakery, Tudor Square) offers similar comfort in the centre of town for £55/80 for singles/doubles.

Places to Eat

Restaurants and pubs – plus a glut of overpriced summertime teashops – are concentrated inside the town walls.

Blueberry's Restaurant (☎ 845785, High St), simple, family-friendly and staffed with fresh-faced kids, has a big menu of all-day sandwiches and light meals, available daily until 5 pm.

The Reef (☎ 845258, Vernon House, St Julian's St) is a Mediterranean-style bistro-restaurant with imaginative seafood and pasta dishes for under £6 at lunch and from £6 to £12 in the evening, plus cakes, sweets and good coffee. The bistro-style *Bay Tree Restaurant* (☎ 843510, Tredegar House, Tudor Square) has mains from £7 to £12, and live music at the weekend. Across the street, the pub-style *Pam Pam Restaurant* (☎ 842946, 2 Tudor Square) offers seafood and steaks from £9.

The *Plantagenet House Restaurant* (☎ 842350, Quay Hill, Tudor Square) is beside the Tudor Merchant's House in what is allegedly Tenby's oldest structure. It's worth going in for a gawk at the immense 12th-century Flemish chimney-hearth, or for a light lunch from an equally immense menu. Carefully prepared evening mains cost around £15. It opens daily in summer, and Friday and Saturday (plus Sunday lunch) in winter.

Restaurants in most larger hotels are open to non-guests, and many pubs serve respectable meals, including big Sunday roasts. Best of the pub lot is the *Normandie Inn* (see Places to Stay earlier), its menu including vegetarian and kids' options.

The most central supermarket is *Somerfield*, by the bus stand.

Entertainment

The cheerful, smokey *Normandie Inn* (see Places to Stay earlier) has live bands – everything from folk to rock, including up-and-coming Welsh groups – almost daily in summer and at least on Saturday in winter;

there are also Wednesday jam sessions. Other pubs to check out include the *Three Mariners* (☎ *842834, St George's St)*, the *No Name Bar* (☎ *845941, High St)* and the bar in the *Tenby House Hotel* (see Places to Stay earlier).

Getting There & Away

Useful Silcox (☎ 01646-683143) services to Tenby include the No 381 from Haverfordwest (£2.70, one hour, hourly) and, on Tuesday and Saturday only, the No 390 from Cardigan (£2.70, 70 minutes, three daily). First Cymru (☎ 0870 608 2608). services include the No 349 from Haverfordwest and Pembroke (£3, 40 minutes, hourly), and the No 351 from Carmarthen (£4.20, 1½ hours, four to five daily). Sunday services are very limited.

There's also a direct train service from Swansea (£9 single, 1½ hours, four to seven daily).

Getting Around

To discourage cars from clogging Tenby's narrow streets, the national park operates a free Park & Ride shuttle bus between Salterns car park (west of the train station) and South Parade. It runs every 10 minutes from 10 am to 6 pm daily, mid-July to August. There's also a multistorey car park beside the bus stand.

AROUND TENBY
Manorbier

Above the pretty village of Manorbier (pronounced **man**-er-beer), 5½ miles from Tenby, is a 12th-century castle with superb views over the sea. This was the birthplace of the extraordinary Giraldus Cambrensis, or Gerald of Wales (see the boxed text 'Gerald of Wales' under Books in the Facts for the Visitor chapter). 'In all the broad lands of Wales, Manorbier is the best place by far,' he wrote. The spell is somewhat dented by the TV aerial sticking out of one of the castle's towers. Modern wordsmiths who loved Manorbier include George Bernard Shaw and Virginia Woolf.

In some of the castle's rooms are waxworks in period costume – apparently a job-lot of rejects from Madame Tussaud's in London. Look for two figures that were originally Prince Philip – in one room he's dressed in chain mail; in another he's a 'Welsh Lady' beside a spinning wheel! The castle opens 10.30 am to 5.30 pm daily, Easter to September. Admission costs £2/1.

Manorbier Youth Hostel (☎ *871803)* is 1½ miles east of the village centre, 200m from the beach at Skrinkle Haven. It opens daily, March to October (weekends only from early June to mid-July for some reason). The nightly charge is £11/7.75; you can also camp here. In the village, ¼ mile from the castle, the modest *Castle Inn* does pub meals.

First Cymru's (☎ 0870 608 2608) bus Nos 349 and 359 run between Tenby (20 minutes) and Pembroke (20 minutes), stopping in the village about hourly (every two hours on Sunday).

PEMBROKE (PENFRO)
☎ 01646 • pop 15,400

The pleasant market town of Pembroke, founded over 900 years ago, sprawls at the foot of a muscular, well-preserved Norman castle – the oldest one in west Wales, seat of the Tudor dynasty and birthplace of King Henry VII. This is in fact the only real reason to stop in Pembrokeshire's county town.

Pembroke emerged as a market town after Arnulph de Montgomery (Arnulf of Montgomery) built a castle here in 1093. In 1154 local traders scored a coup when a Royal Act of Incorporation made it illegal to land goods anywhere in the Milford Haven waterway except at Pembroke (actually what is now Pembroke Dock). In 1648 during the Civil War, the castle was besieged for 48 days before it fell, after which Cromwell had the town walls demolished.

Orientation

Central Pembroke is essentially 700m-long Main St. Useful landmarks at the western end are the castle and the orange clock tower of St Mary's Church.

Ferries from Rosslare in Ireland land at Pembroke Dock, the town's busy maritime alter ego, 2½ miles north-west on the Milford

Spot dolphins and Minke whales from Strumble Head, Pembrokeshire.

The Pembrokeshire Coast Path

The beach at immense Whitesands Bay is popular with surfers and sun-seekers alike.

186-miles of cliff-top strolls

High cliffs and sandy beaches along the Pembrokeshire Coast Path

LIZ BARRY

Perching on points for 4500 years – Pentre Ifan burial chamber

JOHN KING

JOHN KING

Two trips to St David's Cathedral once equalled a pilgrimage to Rome.

A Celtic cross, Nevern

IONAS KALTENBACH

Evening lights from the 'Little Fort of the Fishes', Tenby harbour, Pembrokeshire

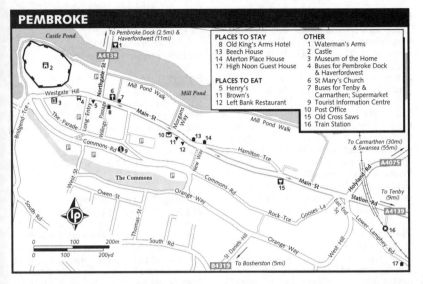

PEMBROKE

PLACES TO STAY
8 Old King's Arms Hotel
13 Beech House
14 Merton Place House
17 High Noon Guest House

PLACES TO EAT
5 Henry's
11 Brown's
12 Left Bank Restaurant

OTHER
1 Waterman's Arms
2 Castle
3 Museum of the Home
4 Buses for Pembroke Dock
   & Haverfordwest
6 St Mary's Church
7 Buses for Tenby &
   Carmarthen; Supermarket
9 Tourist Information Centre
10 Post Office
15 Old Cross Saws
16 Train Station

Haven waterway. For ferry information see Getting There & Away later.

Trains stop at Pembroke train station (just a platform), east of the town centre, and terminate at Pembroke Dock station.

Information

The TIC, called the Pembroke Visitors Centre (☎ 622388), south of the castle on Commons Rd, opens 10 am to 5.30 pm daily, Easter to October. On sale is a *Town Trail* walking guide. Another TIC (☎ 622246), in the Gun Tower on Front St at Pembroke Dock, opens 11 am to 3 pm daily, Easter to September.

Major banks, all with ATMs, cluster at the west end of Main St.

Pembroke Castle

Although a fort was established here in 1093 by Arnulph de Montgomery, the current buildings date mainly from the 12th and 13th centuries. The fort was in use until 1945, and was the home of the earls of Pembroke for over 300 years.

Massive walls enclose a large area of grass and an ugly tarmac parade ground. Passages run from tower to tower, and a plaque in one marks the birthplace (in 1456) of Harry Tudor, who defeated Richard III at the Battle of Bosworth Field in 1485 to become Henry VII. In the centre of the grounds stands the castle's decidedly sinister-looking keep. One hundred steps lead to the top and huge views. If it's windy, the tower is closed.

The castle (☎ 681510) opens 9.30 am to 6 pm daily, April to September; 10 am until 5 pm, March and October; and 10 am until 4 pm, November to February. Admission costs £3/2.

Museum of the Home

This museum at 7 Westgate Hill, opposite the castle, has a great collection of toys and games (allegedly including the first-ever snakes-and-ladders board), cooking and eating implements and other domestic objects of past eras. There are no labels – you're shown around by the enthusiastic owners. The museum (☎ 681200) opens 11 am to 5 pm Monday to Thursday, May to September. Admission costs £1.20/90p. Children under five – perhaps the ones who would take this unintentionally camp place most seriously – are not welcome.

Pembroke Dock

This is all ships and lorries, with little to attract visitors except the Gun Tower, an offshore 'Martello tower' built in 1851 as part of a necklace of defensive works for the protection of the waterway. Inside is the dockland's TIC and exhibits on the lives of the Victorian soldiers who garrisoned these defences. The tower (☎ 622246) opens 10 am to 5 pm Monday to Saturday, April to October (also on Sunday, mid-July to August).

Silcox Coaches (☎ 01646-683143) runs shuttle bus Nos 356 and 357 between Pembroke and Pembroke Dock (80p/£1.35 single/return, 10 minutes) about every 20 minutes during the day (except on Sunday), from opposite the castle entrance.

Places to Stay

Wisteria-clad *Beech House* (☎ 683740, 78 Main St) does B&B in very comfortable surroundings for £15 per person with a generous breakfast – excellent value for money. A few doors up is *Merton Place House* (☎ 684796, 3 East Back, by Main St), eccentric and fussy but equally comfortable, with B&B from £17.50. The *High Noon Guest House* (☎/fax 683736, Lower Lamphey Rd), near the train station, has single/double en suites for £26/42. At the *Old King's Arms Hotel* (☎ 683611, fax 682335, Main St), B&B costs £33/45.

Places to Eat

At *Henry's* (☎ 622293, Westgate Hill), a cafe at the rear of a shop in the unmissable pink building near the castle, lunch plates, including salads, rarebit and stuffed croissants, cost about £4, and traditional cakes cost under £1. *Brown's (Main St)* is a pleasantly retro diner in authentic, tacky 1960s style; the food is unexceptional but you can stodge up for under £5.

The *Old King's Arms Hotel* (see Places to Stay) has the best bar food in town, and a choice of big or bigger helpings; try mussels from £5 or traditional bacon, cockles and laverbread from £6. If you have the dosh for something more imaginative, the *Left Bank Restaurant* (☎ 622333, 63 Main St) offers very good two-course dinners –

for example, Welsh lamb with couscous – for about £20.

Self-caterers can stock up at the *Somerfield* supermarket on Main St.

Entertainment

Drinking seems to be the main night-out activity. Just over the bridge is the riverside *Waterman's Arms*, with an outdoor terrace and fine castle views. A small pub with character is the *Old Cross Saws (Main St)*. The *Old King's Arms Hotel* (see Places to Stay) at the other end of Main St is another good choice.

Getting There & Away

Bus Note that Pembroke is not the same as Pembroke Dock. Some regional bus services go to one or the other but not both.

Most buses heading from Pembroke town to Pembroke Dock and Haverfordwest depart from Westgate Hill near the castle entrance; those bound for Tenby and Carmarthen go from Main St outside Somerfield supermarket. First Cymru's (☎ 0870 608 2608) hourly No 349 runs from Haverfordwest (£2, 40 minutes) and from Tenby (£3, 40 minutes), with limited Sunday services.

If you just want to connect with the ferry service at Pembroke Dock, National Express (☎ 0870 580 8080) has two daily services, Nos 508 and 528, from Tenby (£2 single, 25 minutes), Carmarthen (£3.50, one hour 10 minutes) and Swansea (£5.50, two hours), which bypass central Pembroke.

Train Pembroke is on a branch line from Whitland via Tenby, terminating at Pembroke Dock – though trains to almost anywhere in Pembrokeshire require multiple changes. The main value of this line is for getting to/from Irish Ferries; sample direct Pembroke Dock connections with Wales & West include Tenby (£3.10, 35 minutes), Carmarthen (£5.20, 1¼ hours) and Swansea (£8.20, 1¾ hours), running four to six times daily.

Ferry Irish Ferries (☎ 0870 517 1717) has two ferries crossing daily from Rosslare (Ireland) to Pembroke Dock (four hours).

Single tickets cost £20 for foot passengers and £189 for a car and driver.

AROUND PEMBROKE
Carew Castle & Tidal Mill

Looming romantically over River Carew, its gaping windows reflected in the still water, Carew Castle is an impressive sight. These rambling limestone ruins are a veritable sampler of castle styles, from functional 12th-century fortification (built by Gerald de Windsor, Henry I's constable of Pembroke) to Elizabethan country house.

Abandoned in 1690, the castle is still home to a large number of bats, including the protected greater horseshoe bat. There is a fine Celtic Cross, dating from the 11th century, near the castle entrance. A summer program of events includes battle re-enactments and open-air theatre.

On the causeway nearby is Wales' only working tidal mill, built in Elizabethan times and under restoration by the national park authority, using its original machinery. The rising tide fills the millpond twice daily and, when the tide falls, a head of water is released through a sluice, turning an undershot water wheel, which drives a cornmill inside.

The castle and mill (☎ 01646-651782) open 10 am to 5 pm daily, Easter to October. Admission to the castle costs £1.90/1.40; a combined ticket with the mill costs £2.75/1.80. The nearby *Carew Inn* pub serves food.

Carew is 4½ miles east of Pembroke and 6 miles west of Tenby. First Cymru's (☎ 0870 608 2608) No 349 Pembroke–Tenby bus stops at Carew Cross hourly.

St Govan's & Stackpole
☎ 01646

The very southernmost coast of Pembrokeshire, around St Govan's Head and Stackpole Head, boasts some of the most harshly beautiful coastline in the county. The land arrives here, flat as a tabletop, and just falls off – sheer cliffs drop 50m to churning, thrashing surf. Bizarre rock formations rise offshore like spectres, with self-descriptive names such as Stack

Rocks, Church Rock and the Green Bridge of Wales.

These rocks and the limestone cliffs are rich in coastal birdlife, including a concentration of rare choughs at Stackpole and Pembrokeshire's largest onshore community of guillemots at Stack Rocks. A spume-laden wind howls steadily over the precipices – strong enough to knock you over (including over the cliffs; use extreme caution). But in the lee of St Govan's Head everything goes quiet, and you'll find a couple of lovely, protected beaches, deep woodlands and an 18th-century park full of lily ponds.

So why aren't there caravan parks every half-mile? Much of the area from St Govan's west to Linney Head is within the Ministry of Defence's Castlemartin firing range. No, you won't be dodging artillery shells – in practice the only evidence of military activity are the red flags that go up from time to time, temporarily closing off parts of the coast west of St Govan's. Most of the shooting goes on well to the west, out of earshot, near Linney Head.

St Govan's Chapel This tiny, spartan stone chapel, wedged into a slot in the cliffs just out of reach of the sea, has more legend than history attached to it. It appears that the original chapel was built in the 5th or 6th century, though there has been repeated rework over the centuries.

St Govan may have been an itinerant 6th-century Irish preacher who came here to spend his twilight years in contemplation. The story goes that one day, when he was set upon by thieves, the cliff opened and enfolded him, protecting him from his attackers, whereupon he built this chapel on the spot (a cleft in the rock inside is supposedly the one that held him). The waters from St Govan's well – now dried out – just below the chapel were reputed to cure skin and eye complaints.

A road runs just over a mile south from Bosherston to a car park above the chapel. Access is prohibited if the red flags are up.

Stackpole Estate & Lily Ponds Stackpole Court was the seat of the Campbells, earls of Cawdor, a family with local roots since medieval times; in the church at nearby Cheriton are 14th-century effigies of one Richard de Stackpole and his wife, and one Lord Cawdor, who featured in the French invasion of Fishguard (see the boxed text 'The Last Invasion of Britain' under Fishguard later). In the 18th and 19th centuries they created an elegant park, complete with lily ponds, footpaths, causeways and a handsome eight-arched bridge. In the early 1960s, to everyone's surprise, the family demolished their Georgian mansion here (to avoid inheritance taxes, some say) and moved back to Scotland.

The 800-hectare estate includes woodlands, sand dunes, two fine beaches and 8 miles of cliffs which shelter seabirds and horseshoe bats. Some 230 hectares of the estate are in NT's care, and a quarter of that is a National Nature Reserve, taking in the extravagant lily ponds (at their best in June).

The grounds can be reached from car parks near the church in Bosherston; at Broadhaven South beach; on the north side at Lodge Park Wood and Old Home Farm; or at the tiny harbour of Stackpole Quay. You could take it all in an easy three-hour stroll. Some of the paths are accessible by wheelchair. The woodlands to the north are full of bridleways, open also to mountain bikes.

The site opens year round. For further information contact the warden's office (☎ 661359). The season for coarse fishing in the lakes is mid-March to mid-June; you can buy a fishing licence at the Olde Worlde Café (see Places to Eat later).

Broadhaven South & Barafundle Bay

Two of south Pembrokeshire's finest small beaches are within the NT property. Broadhaven South (not to be confused with Broad Haven on St Bride's Bay) is accessible from Bosherston, and development-free Barafundle Bay from Stackpole Quay.

Places to Stay Emphatically downmarket *St Petrox Caravan & Camping Site* is just north of the church in St Petrox village,

midway between Pembroke and Bosherston, and open year round. You can pitch a tent for £4.50 to £6.50. It's best to bring food, though they'll sell you fresh eggs, milk and bread.

Also at St Petrox is *Bangeston Farm* (☎/fax 683986, @ selina.mathias@talk21 .com), a working farm with B&B for £17.50 per person from March to October. Bike hire is also available.

Trefalen Farm (☎ 661643, fax 661626, @ trefalen@aol.com), almost a mile southeast of Bosherston near Broadhaven South beach, is a restored farmhouse run as a B&B by London refugees. Nonsmoking rooms cost £18.50 per person. They also have two self-catering apartments and basic camping, and will do baggage transfer for coast-path walkers. It's essential to book ahead is essential. The same folks own the *St Govan's Country Inn* (☎ 661311) in Bosherston, where en suites cost £25 per person.

The NT has several holiday properties at Stackpole Quay, which tend to get booked out a year or more in advance. For details contact the NT's Holiday Booking Office (see under Accommodation in the Facts for the Visitor chapter).

Places to Eat Child-friendly *St Govan's Country Inn* (see Places to Stay) serves good home-made food, including venison for £6.50, cawl for £3 and several veggie dishes. Just down the road is *Ye Olde World Café*, basically just the front room and garden of an old coastguard cottage, with cheap, good lunch fare and snacks. There's a good *teahouse* at Stackpole Quay, open daily from Easter to October.

Getting There & Away Bosherston is 5 miles south of Pembroke on the B4319. Bus connections from Pembroke are limited: Silcox Coaches Nos 364 and 365 run twice daily to Stackpole Quay (£1.10, 30 minutes) and Bosherston (£1.25, 35 minutes), on school days only; No 387 runs there and back on Tuesday and Thursday only; and there's a twice-each-weekday postbus.

HAVERFORDWEST (HWLFFORDD)

☎ 01437 • pop 14,000

Haverfordwest was founded as a fortified Flemish settlement beside the River Western Cleddau by the Norman Lord Gilbert de Clare about 1110. Its castle became the nucleus for a thriving market town and its port remained important right up until the railway arrived in the mid-19th century.

Although it's not within the national park, Haverfordwest is Pembrokeshire's commercial hub and a focal point for public transport. The former port area has become one of the town's many huge shopping centres. There's little beyond the decaying castle that's old, and not a lot to do except shop while you're waiting for the next bus out.

Orientation & Information

The TIC (☎ 763110, fax 767738, e haverfordwestinformationcentre@pembrokeshire.gov.uk) is on Old Bridge St, about 150m south of the bus station in a featureless shopping centre. To get there from the train station, walk west for 300m to Salutation Square and north for 300m along Cartlett Rd. It opens 10 am to 5 pm Monday to Saturday, Easter to October; plus 10 am to 4 pm on Sunday, mid-July to August; and 10 am to 4 pm Monday to Saturday, the rest of the year. National park information is available here. The administrative headquarters of the park (☎ 764636, e pcnp@pembrokeshire-coast.org.uk) is in Winch Lane, just under a mile south of the centre, but it's not a public information office.

The traditional shopping zone is High St, about 400m from the TIC (west on Old Bridge St and south on Bridge St).

All major UK banks (with ATMs) are represented on High St. The post office is on Quay St, the southern extension of Bridge St. You can send email from the BIS Computer Centre opposite the TIC, but there's no public Internet access.

The region's main hospital, with accident & emergency services, is Withybush Hospital (☎ 764545) on Fishguard Rd. The police station (☎ 763355) is on Merlin's Hill.

Two reliable travel agencies who can book train, bus and ferry tickets are the Holiday Information Centre (☎ 766330) beside the TIC; and Ocky White Travel (☎ 763046, e mail@ockywhitetravel.com), in the farthest corner of a department store by the same name at 7 Bridge St.

Things to See & Do

The unexceptional ruins of **Haverfordwest Castle** brood over the river above Bridge St. The castle survived an onslaught by Owain Glyndŵr in 1405, but according to one local story was abandoned by its Royalist garrison during the Civil War when its soldiers mistook a herd of cows for Roundheads.

In the old town gaol in the castle's outer ward, The **Castle Museum & Art Gallery** (☎ 763087) has a ho-hum display on town and castle history, plus changing art exhibitions. It opens 10 am to 4 pm daily except on Sunday, Easter to October. Admission costs £1/50p.

Places to Stay & Eat

Villa House (☎ 762977, St Thomas Green) has B&B from £16 per person; there are several other B&Bs in this area, about ¾ miles south of the centre via High St and Market St. The *County Hotel* (☎/fax 762144, Salutation Square) charges £40/60 for comfortable single/double en suites.

Best value for food is the *Moon & Sixpence* (☎ 767851, Swan Square), with cakes and pastries, salads, pitta and tortilla sandwiches with a huge range of fillings, and generous lunches. It's upstairs in a big shop of the same name, 250m west of the TIC, and opens daily except on Sunday. The *Old Bridge Café*, 100m west of the TIC, has a pretty good salad bar. The pub at the *Castle Hotel* (☎ 769322, Castle Square) and the rustic *Olde Three Crowns* on the corner of High and Quay Sts, have bar meals. The *Barking Shark* (Quay St) is a popular watering hole.

A *farmers market* takes over the Riverside Market, just west across the river from the TIC, on the second and fourth Fridays of each month.

PEMBROKESHIRE

Getting There & Away

Bus Services fan out from Haverfordwest all over Pembrokeshire. Richards Brothers' (☎ 01239-613756) No 411 runs from Fishguard (£3.20, 1½ hours, every two hours) and St David's (£3, 45 minutes, hourly). No 412 runs hourly from Cardigan (£3.50, 1½ hours) via Fishguard. First Cymru's (☎ 0870 608 2608) No 349 runs hourly from Pembroke (£2.50, 40 minutes). Silcox Coaches' (☎ 01646-683143) No 322 runs at least twice daily from Carmarthen (£4, one hour). Sunday services are almost nonexistent.

National Express coach No 508 comes twice daily from London Victoria (£21 single, 6¾ hours) via Swansea (£6, 2½ hours). National Express also has a daily No 528 from Swansea. From Cardiff, change at Swansea.

Train Running up to seven times daily, trains link Haverfordwest station (☎ 764361) with Swansea (£8.30 single, two hours), Cardiff (£14, 2¾ hours) and London (£44 or £27 Apex, 4¾ hours). Connections to Tenby, Pembroke or Fishguard are exceedingly tedious, with multiple changes.

ST BRIDE'S BAY (BAE SAIN FFRAID)

St Bride's Bay is at the western end of the 'landsker', the invisible boundary between the Welsh and anglicised parts of Pembrokeshire. The best beaches in Wales line this wide bay, and they're big enough to absorb the crowds of holiday-makers (and surfers) they attract at the height of summer.

The biggest and liveliest resort town is Broad Haven (Aber Llydan; not to be confused with Broadhaven South beach at Bosherston, south of Pembroke). Newgale (Niwgwl) has the bay's biggest beach, which is the main reason to visit this tiny village, popular with swimmers and surfers.

Surfing, Windsurfing & Sailing

Haven Sports (☎ 01437-781354), Marine Rd, Broad Haven, rents windsurfing equipment and runs courses. You can hire surf skis, boards, boogie boards and wetsuits from Newsurf Hire Centre (☎ 01437-721398) at the filling station in Newgale. Another place

for surfing and sailing equipment rental and lessons is West Wales Wind, Surf & Sailing (☎ 01646-636642) at Dale, south of the bay.

Typical rates per hour/day are around £3/7 for a boogie board, £4/9 for a surfboard, £15/30 for a basic windsurfer rig and £80 per day for a Hobie Cat sailboat. Typical rates for a half-/full-day of lessons are around £25/40 for surfing, £50/70 for windsurfing and £60/80 for Hobie Cat sailing.

For more on sea sports in Wales, refer to Activities in the Facts for the Visitor chapter.

Skomer, Skokholm & Grassholm Islands

These islands, lying off the coast south of the bay, are nature reserves populated mainly by colonies of seabirds, busiest between April and mid-August. The *Dale Princess* plies back and forth to the islands in summer, normally from Martin's Haven near Marloes. Trips are booked either through Dale Sailing Co (☎ 01646-601636, e islands@dale-sailing.co.uk), Brunel Quay, Neyland, or the Wildlife Trust West Wales (WTWW; 01437-765462).

Easiest to reach is Skomer, a WTWW reserve which is home to over half a million seabirds, especially puffins and the remarkable, burrow-breeding Manx shearwaters (Skomer and Skokholm together have the largest colony in the world, with 160,000 birds or 40% of the world's population). Trips with a landing (about five hours long) depart at 10 am, 11 am and noon daily except Monday, April to October. Round-island cruises depart at 1 pm on Sunday, Tuesday, Wednesday, Thursday and bank-holiday Mondays. The price is £12/5 with a landing or £6/5 without; book through Dale Sailing. The national park runs round-island cruises at 7 pm each Tuesday and Friday from early May, and frequent guided walks (see the *Coast to Coast* newspaper).

Grey seals are also plentiful on Skomer; contact the WTWW for information on seal watches in the pupping season (September). You may also see porpoises and dolphins en route. The island is surrounded by the Skomer Marine Nature Reserve. Also here is the UK's largest undisturbed Iron Age settlement.

Skokholm is a WTWW reserve known for its storm petrels, Manx shearwaters and puffins. Trips with guided walks depart at 10 am on Monday only from mid-June to mid-August. The fee is £15.50/8.50; book though the WTWW.

The second-largest gannet colony in the northern hemisphere – 33,000 breeding pairs – is on little Grassholm, a distant 11 miles offshore. This is an Royal Society for the Protection of Birds (RSPB) reserve and landings are not permitted, but round-island trips depart at 10 am Monday and noon Friday, and trips with a guide at 5 pm Thursday. The cost is £20; book through Dale Sailing.

It's also possible to stay the night on Skomer and Skokholm; enquire with the WTWW.

Places to Stay & Eat

There are a huge number of caravan parks and camp sites, and most farmers are happy to let you use one of their fields for a few pounds – but ask first. Villages along the bay are loaded with mid-range B&Bs.

The *Marloes Sands Youth Hostel* (☎ *01646-636667, Runwayskiln*), south of Marloes, opens mid-April to October, for £7.50/5.25. The modern *Broad Haven Youth Hostel* (☎ 01437-781688) opens weekends in March, daily from April to October (except on Sunday from mid-September); the nightly charge is £11/7.75.

The year-round *Penycwm Youth Hostel* (☎ *01437-721940, White House, Penycwm*), 1½ miles north of Newgale and the beach, is Wales' only five-star hostel. Dorm beds cost £10/7 (£13/10 B&B); en suites range from about £20 for one adult and one child to £55 for two parents and four kids. There is a games room, two kitchens and a small restaurant (prebooking required) with a respectable beer and wine list. Not surprisingly, advance booking is essential in summer. It's about 1½ miles north of the Penycwm bus stop on the A487.

Getting There & Around

Towns along St Bride's Bay are all accessible by bus from Haverfordwest bus station, Monday to Saturday. For Dale/Marloes take

Edwards Bros No 316 (£2/£1.70, one hour ten minutes/50 minutes, two to three daily). Broad Haven is at the end of First Cymru's (☎ 0870 608 2608) No 311 line (£1.55, 20 minutes, at least three daily). Newgale and Penycwm are stops on Richards Brothers' (☎ 01239-613756) hourly service No 411 between Haverfordwest (£1.54, 25 minutes) and St David's (£1.30, 20 minutes).

The Puffin Shuttle (see under Pembrokeshire Coast National Park earlier in the chapter) stops at all these and more, twice daily in summer.

ST DAVID'S (TYDDEWI)
☎ 01437 • pop 1800

There's something special about St David's that even the crowds of summer holidaymakers fail to extinguish. The magic must have worked for the future St David, who chose to found a monastic community here in the 6th century, only a short walk from where he was born (see the boxed text 'St David'). St David is an iconic figure for the Welsh and the country's patron saint. His relics are kept in a casket in the cathedral named after him; the town's Welsh name means, literally, 'David's House'.

St David's is hardly bigger than a village, a generally unremarkable place with a single square and a few side roads, but the cathedral's presence has bestowed fame, and the right to be called a city (the smallest in Britain), upon it. Interestingly, the cathedral is hardly visible from anywhere in the town, which is as its builders intended, for it was sited down in the vale of the River Alun – known as Glyn Rhosyn (Valley of the Little Marsh) – in the vain hope that passing Norse raiders might miss it. It's a magnificent sight, and if you visit only one cathedral in Wales, make it this one.

Orientation & Information

Buses stop at various points around the centre (see under Getting There & Away later). The centre of town is Cross Square, with the cathedral 200m north-west via The Pebbles.

A combined National Park Visitors Centre and TIC (☎ 720392, fax 720099, e enquiries@ stdavids.pembrokeshirecoast.org.uk) is in

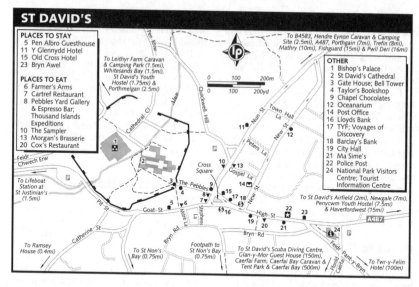

ST DAVID'S

PLACES TO STAY
5 Pen Albro Guesthouse
11 Y Glennydd Hotel
15 Old Cross Hotel
23 Bryn Awel

PLACES TO EAT
6 Farmer's Arms
7 Cartref Restaurant
8 Pebbles Yard Gallery
& Espresso Bar;
Thousand Islands
Expeditions
10 The Sampler
13 Morgan's Brasserie
20 Cox's Restaurant

OTHER
1 Bishop's Palace
2 St David's Cathedral
3 Gate House; Bell Tower
4 Taylor's Bookshop
9 Chapel Chocolates
12 Oceanarium
14 Post Office
16 Lloyds Bank
17 TYF; Voyages of Discovery
18 Barclay's Bank
19 City Hall
21 Ma Sime's
22 Police Post
24 National Park Visitors Centre; Tourist Information Centre

a purpose-built centre 350m east of the square on High St. It's got a good selection of St David's and Pembrokeshire literature and maps, and opens 9.30 am to 5.30 pm daily (10 am to 3 pm daily except on Sunday, November to Easter).

There are Lloyds and Barclay's banks facing the square, and the post office is a block north on New St. Taylor's Bookshop, by the cathedral gatehouse, sells maps and guidebooks on local trails. A part-time police post (☎ 720223) is just east on High St (when it's closed, calls are redirected to Haverfordwest).

St David's Cathedral

This is Wales' holiest place. In 1124 Pope Calixtus II declared that two pilgrimages to St David's were equivalent to one to Rome, and three to St David's were equal to one to Jerusalem itself. The cathedral has seen a constant stream of visitors ever since, and is the only one in the UK with a permanently reserved stall for the reigning monarch.

There has been a church in the valley since the 6th century, though the severe, granite-grey cathedral you see now dates in its simplest form from the late 12th century.

Ireland-based Norse pirates ransacked it at least seven times, and various bishops have added chapels, extensions and other modifications.

Inside there's an atmosphere of great antiquity. The floor slopes and the pillars lean drunkenly, the result of an earthquake in 1248. In the Norman nave is a superbly carved oak ceiling, installed in the 16th century. From the richly carved choir in the centre of the cross, illuminated from the tower above, you feel you could be beamed right up to heaven if you sang well enough.

A statue of St David – curiously dressed as a medieval bishop – is in an alcove of the pulpitum (the screen-wall between nave and choir). It would be no surprise if the bird on his shoulder were a rook; the cathedral close seems always full of their argumentative cawing. The saint's shrine (wrecked during the Reformation) is in the north choir aisle, and his relics are kept behind the altar.

Lord Rhys ap Gruffydd, the greatest of the princes of South Wales, and his son Rhys Gryg are known to be buried in the cathedral, although their effigies in the southern choir aisle date only from the 14th century. Gerald of Wales (Giraldus Cambrensis; see the

St David

What little is actually 'known' about St David (Dewi Sant in Welsh) comes from *The Life of St David*, written around 1190 by one Rhygyfarch of Llanbadarn – and elaborated a decade later by Gerald of Wales (Giraldus Cambrensis), though it's clear there's more legend than historical truth here.

The boy David (Dewi) was born during a violent thunderstorm in around 520, to a young girl named Non, in a simple house overlooking what is now called St Non's Bay, less than a mile south of town. In some accounts he is identified as the son of a king of Ceredigion. Some 30 years before his birth, say the legends, St Patrick decided to settle down at Glyn Rhosyn but was moved on to Ireland by an angel directed to keep the place for David.

The 6th century was a busy time for Christian missionaries across Wales. The gentle but hard-working and rigidly self-disciplined David soon became an important figure in the ascetic and simple 'Celtic' church, and founded his own monastic community at Glyn Rhosyn. Despite the area's remote feel it was probably an important spot then, on the intersection of major land and sea routes.

The vale is said to have had no water until David prayed for some, whereupon a spring gushed forth at his feet. According to Rhygyfarch, the area had been the turf of an Irish bandit named Boia, whose wife sent her maidservants to do a striptease at the new monastery. David was untempted, and the other monks presumably followed his example.

After St David's death in 589 his church became a place of pilgrimage. He was not adopted as the patron saint of Wales until the 18th century, when his probable death date, 1 March, was chosen as a national holiday.

---

boxed text 'Gerald of Wales' under Books in the Facts for the Visitor chapter), an early rector of the cathedral who fought hard and fruitlessly to make this an archbishopric of equal status with Canterbury, is often said to be buried here; there is a gravestone, but serious scholars suggest he is actually buried at Lincolnshire Cathedral.

The cathedral is a hodge-podge of other work across the years. The nave and near transept walls are 12th-century, the eastern Lady Chapel 13th-century, the pulpitum, south porch and St Mary's chapel 14th-century, and the buttresses and west wall 16th-century.

Services are held here at 8 am and 6 pm on most days. On Sunday there are services throughout the morning, and a choral evensong at 6 pm on several days each week. Curiously, the choir is made up of men and girls, but no boys. At the time of writing there were Welsh-language services at 9.30 am on Sunday and 8 am on Wednesday.

The cathedral opens 8 am to 6 pm (except 12.45 to 5.45 pm on Sunday). Admission is free, although a donation of £2/1 is suggested. There are also photography charges.

Guided tours are available by arrangement (☎ 720691, fax 720691); highly recommended is the one by the dean himself, a serious student of history and archaeology. This is a regular venue for classical music concerts. Ask at the TIC for details.

On the hill above the cathedral is a massive 13th-century bell tower; the adjacent gatehouse will eventually house a visitor centre and an exhibit of early Christian stone monuments. This is the only surviving gate out of four in the run-down 12th-century wall that surrounds the cathedral close.

Bishop's Palace

Don't overlook the adjacent Bishop's Palace just because it's a ruin – it's a splendid, stately ruin, easily a match for the cathedral, and an eloquent testament to the wealth and power of the medieval Church. The vast interior – including a 30m-long great hall with a huge circular steel window – is actually a bit of a letdown by comparison with the outside.

The palace was begun in the 12th century, at the same time as the cathedral, though its final, imposing form – including the arcades on the parapet – owes most to Henry de Gower, bishop from 1327 to 1348. It served as a residence until the 16th century.

The palace (☎ 720517), run by Cadw, the Welsh historic monuments agency, and two small exhibitions open 9.30 am to 6 pm daily, June to September; to 5 pm in April, May and October; and to 4 pm (noon to 2 pm on Sunday), November to March. Admission costs £2/1.50. This also provides a spectacular setting for open-air plays held in the summer. Ask at the TIC for details.

St Non's Bay

St David's alleged birthplace is ¾ mile south of the cathedral, beside the bay that now bears his mother's name. A small spring at the site is said to have emerged just as he emerged into the world. The shrine still attracts pilgrims, and the water is believed to have curative powers. Also here are the 13th-century ruins of St Non's Chapel, plus a modern chapel and retreat centre.

Oceanarium

The Oceanarium (☎ 720453), 42 New St, is a modest public aquarium and research facility with tanks of large sea fish, small sharks and other creatures. It opens 10 am to at least 4 pm year round. Admission costs £3/1.80. In summer, if there are enough visitors, staff offer one-hour 'hands-on' talks for kids at 11 am and 12.30, 2 and 3.30 pm daily except Saturday.

Beaches

Two miles north-west of St David's is Whitesands Bay (Porth Mawr), one of the finest of south-west Wales' beaches, and popular with surfers. It gets quite crowded in summer. At extremely low tides you can see the wreck of a paddle tugboat that went aground here in 1882, and the fossil remains of a prehistoric forest. The local Park & Ride shuttle bus (see Getting Around later) diverts to Whitesands at about 9.30 am from the car park by the TIC, and diverts again to depart Whitesands at about 4 pm.

There's a small, secluded beach at Porthmelgan, 15 minutes' walk north of Whitesands.

Activities

TYF (☎ 721611), 1 High St, organises coasteering, surfing, sea kayaking and climbing trips around the region; for details see under Multiactivity in the Pembrokeshire Coast National Park section earlier. They also have a gear shop and a cafe here.

Two local outfits that run trips out to Ramsey Island (see Around St David's later) are Voyages of Discovery (☎ 721911), 1 High St; and Thousand Islands Expeditions (☎ 721686), The Pebbles.

Ma Sime's is a surf shop at 28 High St. St David's Scuba Diving Centre (☎ 721788) is a PADI and BSAC school offering courses to anyone aged over 12, from half-day 'discovery' courses to instructor-level courses, plus diving trips for experienced divers. It's at the Glan-y-Mor Guest House on Caerfai Bay Rd.

Special Events

The St David's Cathedral Festival takes place over 1½ weeks culminating on the spring bank-holiday weekend, with classical music in the cathedral – a venue whose 16th-century Irish oak ceiling gives it fine acoustics. For details contact the festival committee (☎ 720271, fax 721885, ℮ festival@ stdavidscathedral.org.uk). Many other concerts are scheduled at short notice at the cathedral. Ask at the TIC for details.

The St David's Arts Festival, held during the first two weeks in August, features Shakespeare at the Bishop's Palace, prose and poetry readings and a very child-friendly program. August also sees a sand-castle – or rather sand-church – competition at Whitesands Bay, judged by the dean of the cathedral (dates are weather-dependent).

The Royal National Eisteddfod (see under Arts in the Facts about Wales chapter) is to be held here on 3–10 August 2002, at the St David's airfield, 3 miles east of town.

Places to Stay

Camping There are plenty of camp sites along Caerfai Bay Rd. The closest is at *Caerfai Farm (☎ 720548)*, an organic farm and shop, with tent sites (no caravans) for £3.50 per person, open May to September.

Don't confuse this with *Caerfai Bay Caravan & Tent Park* (☎ 720274), the area's biggest site, open Easter to October at £2 per tent for walkers or £6 for a frame tent with car; it's at the end of the road, ½ mile from the TIC. In between is *Glan-y-Mor* (☎ 721788), open March to October for £3.50 per person (shower 10p). The *Twr-y-Felin Hotel* (see B&Bs) has camping for £4 per person.

Lleithyr Farm Caravan & Tent Park (☎ 720245), near Whitesands Bay and open Easter to October, charges £2.50/5.50 for two people with a small/frame tent. *Hendre Eynon Caravan & Camping Site* (☎ 720474), 2½ miles north-east of St David's on the B4583, opens Easter to September and charges £2.70/8.75 per person with a small/big tent.

Hostels The *St David's Youth Hostel* (☎ 720345, *Laethdy*) is 1¾ miles north-west of St David's near Whitesands Bay. It opens daily except Monday and Tuesday, from Easter to October (daily from mid-July to August). The charge is £8.50/5.75 for adults/under-18s. There's no transport but it's worth the walk; a taxi only costs a few pounds – cheap if shared.

B&Bs & Hotels No-frills *Pen Albro Guesthouse* (☎ 721865, *18 Goat St*), around the block from the cathedral, charges £14.50 per person for B&B. *Bryn Awel* (☎ 720082, *45 High St*), near the TIC, has small en suites for £20 per person, and organically raised meat at breakfast. TYF's *Twr-y-Felin Hotel* (☎ 721611, fax 721838), just east of the TIC, has bright, dorm-style rooms at £20 B&B, plus half- and full-board options.

At the good-value *Y Glennydd Hotel* (☎ 720576, fax 720184, *51 Nun St*), B&B in big en suites costs £22 per person; the hotel also has a restaurant and bar. The *Old Cross Hotel* (☎ 720387, fax 720394, *Cross Square*) has en suites for £41 B&B, plus a restaurant and bar.

The dormer-bungalow *Ramsey House* (☎ 720321, *Lower Moor*), on the Porth Clais road, offers only half-board in summer, for £46 per person.

Places to Eat

The best of many cafes is *The Sampler* (*Nun St*), with lots of homemade goodies. *Pebbles Yard Gallery & Espresso Bar* (☎ 720122, *The Pebbles*) has filled baguettes, fresh juice presses and cakes. Among the few places in Wales that know how to make a proper hamburger is the *Farmer's Arms* (see Entertainment).

At *Cartref Restaurant* (☎ 720422, *Cross Square*), lunch options include home-made pasta dishes for around £6 and meaty standards for up to £10. The menu at *Cox's Restaurant* (☎ 720491, *22 High St*) includes a range of Asian specialities for around £12 per dish. Top of the line seems to be *Morgan's Brasserie* (☎ 720508, *20 Nun St*), whose imaginative menu includes fresh seafood, Welsh duck, beef, lamb and vegetarian options; main dishes start at £10.

For a pricey, high-calorie snack, don't miss *Chapel Chocolates* on The Pebbles.

Entertainment

The only pub worth mentioning is the relaxed *Farmer's Arms* (*Goat St*).

Getting There & Away

There's no bus station. Buses from Haverfordwest stop in front of city hall. The stop for buses to Haverfordwest and to/from Fishguard is by the Oceanarium. Richards Brothers' (☎ 01239-613756) No 411 runs from Haverfordwest (£3, 45 minutes, hourly) and from Fishguard (£2.25, 50 minutes, every two hours). Both routes have limited Sunday services.

St David's is also the northern terminus for the twice-daily, summertime Puffin Shuttle bus (see under Pembrokeshire Coast National Park earlier in the chapter) which stops by the TIC and also at the top of New St, near the Oceanarium.

Getting Around

To discourage cars from clogging St David's streets, the national park operates a free Park & Ride shuttle bus between car parks beside the TIC and near the Bishop's Palace. It runs every 15 minutes from 10 am to 4 pm daily, mid-July to August.

PEMBROKESHIRE

Voyages of Discovery (see under Activities earlier in the section) rents bikes for £5/8 per half-/full day.

For a taxi, call ☎ 720931 or ☎ 721731.

AROUND ST DAVID'S
Ramsey Island Trips

Ramsey Island, off St David's Head, is an RSPB reserve with beautiful cliff scenery and varied bird life – including a healthy population of choughs – though the main attraction is its grey seals. If you're there between late August and mid-November, you may also see seal pups. The national park organises frequent guided trips (see the *Coast to Coast* newspaper).

Voyages of Discovery (☎ 721911, toll-free ☎ 0800 854367; winter ☎ 721802), 1 High St, St David's, runs trips around Ramsey for a look at its wildlife and sea-caves. Trips by high-speed inflatable boat (one to two hours) cost £12/7 for adults/children (£20/10 from November to March); more sedate journeys by conventional boat (1½ hours) cost £10/6, in summer only.

Thousand Islands Expeditions (☎ 721686, toll-free ☎ 0800 163621), The Pebbles, St David's, offers similar trips by high-speed inflatable for £20/10. This is the only operator permitted to bring day-visitors onto Ramsey, in strictly limited numbers, by conventional boat – though you'll probably see more wildlife from the boat. The various options cost from £10/5 to £18/9 (no trips go on Tuesday). They also offer high-adrenaline jet-boat trips to The Bitches, remarkable tidal standing waves in Ramsey Sound, for £20 (adults only). These trips operate in summer only.

See the following St David's to Fishguard section for another boat operator, based in Porthgain.

Walking Routes

Incorporating sections of the coast path, there are some excellent half-day walks around St David's peninsula, the site of some of the oldest exposed rocks in the world.

A 5-mile loop around Carn Llidi (87m) can start at the youth hostel or the White-sands Bay slipway, rounding St David's Head on the coast path as far as Penllechwen and returning inland. On St David's Head are the remains of an Iron Age fort, including a protective dyke and hut circles, and a short way inland is a Neolithic burial chamber known as Coetan Arthur (Arthur's Quoit). A climb up the western side of Carn Llidi will take you to some stirring views and several more burial chambers.

Another walk of a similar length goes from the lifeboat station at St Justinian's, south along the coast path – with good views out to Ramsey Island – to Porth Clais (St David's tiny, ancient harbour), and back to the St David's–St Justinian's road. By a sandstone arch just south of St Justinian's is the Iron Age fort of Castell Heinif. At Penmaen Melyn – the westernmost point of mainland Wales – are the remains of a 19th-century copper mine.

Or, from St David's, you could walk south-westwards to Porth Clais, east to Caerfai Bay and back to St David's in under two hours.

ST DAVID'S TO FISHGUARD

The coast from St David's to Fishguard (and beyond) is far less touristy than southern Pembrokeshire. The coves and beaches, if they're accessible at all, are reached by winding lanes and footpaths. If you're only going to walk part of the Pembrokeshire Coast Path, this is an excellent section to tackle. On the way are two splendidly located hostels and numerous farmhouse B&Bs.

Porthgain

For centuries this old coastal village was little more than a few sturdy cottages wedged into a rocky cove. In the mid-19th century it began to prosper as the port for slate quarried just down the coast at Abereiddy, and by the 1870s its own deposits of granite and fine clay had put it on the map as a source of building stone and bricks. The post-WWI slump burst the bubble, and today the brick-works are in ruins.

People now come here primarily to eat and drink. In an age of theme pubs, the

Sloop Inn (☎ 831449) is famous for its old-fashioned ordinariness. Photos on the walls show the village in its industrial heyday. Across the car park is the trendier *Harbour Lights Restaurant (☎ 01348-831549)*, good for light lunches or, at weekends in summer, a three-course evening meal for £25. Several interesting small art galleries are also dotted around.

A fishing boat called the *Carolina* does coastal cruises (£9/5 for adults/children aged under 16), fishing trips and 'potting' trips (when lobster traps are retrieved). Call in at the yellow house four doors inland from the Sloop Inn, or call ☎ 01348-831518. This is the area's only cruise operator which can accommodate disabled passengers.

The Porthgain turning is at Croes-goch, 6 miles north-east of St David's on the A487. The No 411 St David's–Fishguard bus calls in every two hours at Llanrhian, a mile inland.

Trefin

The *Trefin Youth Hostel (☎ 01348-831414)* is in the old school in the centre of Trefin (Trevine; pronounced **trev**-in); the nightly rate is £8.50/5.75. Also in the village is the *Old Court House (☎ 01348-837095)*, a vegetarian guesthouse offering B&B for £22.50 per person and delicious veggie dinners for £14.50 most nights.

The village is ½ mile from the sea, 2½ miles from Porthgain, 8 miles from St David's or 11 miles along the coast path from Whitesands Bay. The No 411 St David's–Fishguard bus calls in every two hours.

Mathry

About a mile north-east of Mathry at Parcynole Fach is the Preseli Venture activity centre (☎ 01348-837709; see under Multi-activity in the Pembrokeshire Coast National Park section earlier). If you don't fancy sea sports, this is also a good base for walking, mountain biking or horseriding. They'll help you with these too, and have mountain bikes for hire for £15/20 per half/full-day. Even perfect couch potatoes can camp for £4.50 per person or stay in the

attractive dorms for £23 B&B (with half- and full-board options).

Pwll Deri

Eight miles farther east from Trefin along the coast path is the *Pwll Deri Youth Hostel (☎ 01348-891233, Castell Mawr, Trefasser)*, in a truly stunning location with a solarium at the edge of a 120m drop to the sea, and an immense panorama of coastal cliffs as far as St David's. Behind it is the summit called Garn Fawr (64m), and Strumble Head is 2 miles away.

It opens daily except Tuesday and Wednesday, Easter to October (daily, mid-July to August). It's popular with walkers, so call ahead in summer. Nightly rates are £8.50/5.75 for adults/under-18s. By car it's 4½ miles west of Goodwick (Fishguard). No buses come anywhere nearer than that, though it's not too expensive to take a taxi if you share it.

Strumble Head is a good vantage point to see migratory birds, seabirds around their nesting areas, and passing whales and dolphins.

FISHGUARD (ABERGWAUN)
☎ 01348 • pop 3200

Ferry ports tend to be dreary places, but Fishguard – its older bits at any rate – is a modest, agreeable town, set where the pretty River Gwaun (pronounced gwine) empties into the Irish Sea. Once a fishing port, it was for a time mooted as a terminus for trans-atlantic ocean-liners, but has settled for being one of Wales' four rail-ferry ports to Ireland. Harbour development is what kept it from being included in the national park, though the coast path comes right through town.

The town itself is something of a film star. The 1971 film version of *Under Milk Wood* (with Richard Burton, Peter O'Toole and Elizabeth Taylor) was shot in Lower Fishguard; older locals still talk about it as if it happened yesterday. Fishguard also featured for two minutes in *Moby Dick* (with Charlton Heston).

This area is also the improbable setting for the last foreign invasion of Britain (see the boxed text later).

PEMBROKESHIRE

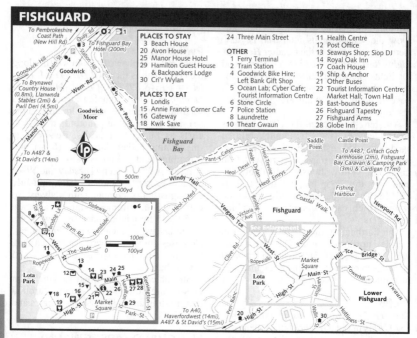

FISHGUARD

PLACES TO STAY	24 Three Main Street	11 Health Centre
3 Beach House		12 Post Office
20 Avon House	OTHER	13 Seaways Shop; Siop DJ
25 Manor House Hotel	1 Ferry Terminal	14 Royal Oak Inn
29 Hamilton Guest House	2 Train Station	17 Coach House
& Backpackers Lodge	4 Goodwick Bike Hire;	19 Ship & Anchor
30 Cri'r Wylan	Left Bank Gift Shop	21 Other Buses
	5 Ocean Lab; Cyber Cafe;	22 Tourist Information Centre;
PLACES TO EAT	Tourist Information Centre	Market Hall; Town Hall
9 Londis	6 Stone Circle	23 East-bound Buses
15 Annie Francis Corner Cafe	7 Police Station	26 Fishguard Tapestry
16 Gateway	8 Laundrette	27 Fishguard Arms
18 Kwik Save	10 Theatr Gwaun	28 Globe Inn

Orientation

Fishguard has three parts. The main town is centred on a traffic roundabout called Market Square (also known as Fishguard Square and The Square). Eastwards, the road winds down around the picturesque fishing harbour of Lower Fishguard. A mile north-west, Goodwick (Wdig Welsh; pronounced **oo**-dick) is a mainly residential area near the train station and the terminal for ferries to Ireland.

Information

The TIC (☎ 873484, fax 875246), in the Town Hall on Market Square, opens 10 am to 5.30 pm daily, Easter to October; and 10 am to at least 4 pm daily except Sunday, the rest of the year. It's also a sales agent for P&O Stena Lines, National Express and Richards Bros buses (but not trains).

There's another TIC (☎ 872037) at Ocean Lab (see the following section), open 10 am to 6 pm daily (to 5 pm winter week-ends, to 4 pm winter weekdays); you can also access the Internet for £2 per half-hour at the Cyber Cafe (☎ 874737) there. The post office is on West St.

The Seaways Shop on West St has a first-rate selection of books and maps (including OS) for the region; watch out for an entertaining series of booklets on Pembrokeshire walks and history – including one about the invasion – by the late Tony Roberts of Fishguard (whose son now runs Hamilton Backpackers).

The police station (☎ 872835) is along Brodog Lane, and a small health centre (☎ 873041) is on Ropewalk. There's a laundrette on Brodog Terrace, open daily except on Sunday. If you're a guest at Hamilton Guest House (see Places to Stay later) you can do your wash for £3 per load.

Things to See & Do

Ocean Lab (☎ 872037), on the waterfront near Goodwick, has a striking Animatronix

The Last Invasion of Britain

On the afternoon of 22 February 1797, a band of 1400 French mercenaries and convicts landed at Carregwastad Point, 4 miles west down the coast from Fishguard. Under the leadership of an American named William Tate, this improbable force had intended to land at Bristol and march to Liverpool, diverting English troops so that France could mount an invasion of Ireland.

Things went wrong from the start. Bad weather diverted them to Carregwastad, where they had to haul themselves up a steep cliff. They then set about looting the Pencaer peninsula for something to eat and drink – and succeeded so well that many were ill for weeks afterwards.

The Pembrokeshire Militia was away on duty. A landowner's son named Thomas Knox was put at the head of a group of local volunteers, and Lord Cawdor of Stackpole set off for Fishguard with his own Castlemartin Yeomanry. Fortunately for all, the beleaguered Tate decided to surrender, at a meeting with Cawdor at a private Fishguard house that is now the Royal Oak Inn. Two days after their arrival, the French laid down their weapons at Goodwick and were sent off to jail at Haverfordwest. Cawdor was the man of the hour.

But there's a nice local twist. Local people had gathered around the French encampment – some curious, some angry and armed with whatever they could find. From a distance the Welsh women in their red cloaks and traditional tall black hats had perhaps resembled English reinforcements, giving the invaders a fright and perhaps encouraging Tate to cave in. One woman in particular, a sturdy cobbler named Jemima Nicholas, is said to have rounded up a dozen unruly Frenchmen with a pitchfork.

In 1997 Fishguard commemorated the bicentenary of the invasion with the creation by 70 local stitchers of a 30m tapestry telling the whole story, Bayeux-style. The *Fishguard Tapestry* is now on display at the old St Mary's Church Institute (☎ 874997) on Main St. It opens 10 am to 5 pm daily (2 to 5 pm Sunday), April to October; and 11 am to 4 pm (2 to 4 pm Sunday), the rest of the year. Admission costs £1.50/50p.

ASA ANDERSSON

(computer animation) show about ancient creatures of the ocean. It opens 10 am to 6 pm daily, Easter to October. Admission costs £2.

On Market Square is the **Royal Oak Inn** (see Entertainment later), scene of the 1797 surrender and full of invasion memorabilia. In the parish churchyard behind it is the grave of local heroine Jemima Nicholas (see the boxed text 'The Last Invasion of Britain'). Walk along Penslade for a good **view** over the old harbour, from a small park with a Gorsedd stone circle commemorating the holding of an eisteddfod here.

At Llanwnda, 2 miles north-west of Goodwick, you can go **horse riding** at Llanwnda Stables (☎ 873595), Penrhiw Fach.

Places to Stay

Camping You can camp at *Fishguard Bay Caravan & Camping Park* (☎ 811415, *Garn Gelli*), 3 miles east, between Fishguard and Newport on the headland at Dinas Cross. It's well situated for the coastal path, and opens March to mid-January. It charges from £8 for a tent, or from £9.50 with a car.

Hostels Relaxed, nonsmoking, cheerfully downmarket *Hamilton Guest House & Backpackers Lodge* (☎ 874797, 21 Hamilton St) is near the TIC in Fishguard. It opens 24 hours, with 20 beds in small dorms for £10 per person; double rooms cost £24. There's a kitchen for self-caterers, a TV lounge and laundry. The helpful owner knows north Pembrokeshire very well.

The nearest YHA/HI *youth hostel* is a splendid one at Pwll Deri, 4½ miles west of Goodwick (see under St David's to Fishguard earlier in the chapter).

B&Bs and Guest Houses Modest *Avon House* (☎ 874476, 76 High St) charges from £16 per person for B&B. *Cri'r Wylan* (☎ 873398, Wallis St), nearer the TIC, charges from £20. The *Manor House Hotel* (☎/fax 873260, Main St) charges £24 for B&B (£30 for back rooms with a sea view). *Three Main Street*, known chiefly as a top-flight restaurant (see Places to Eat), also has three tastefully modern double rooms with bathroom for £60 and £70 (the latter with a sea view), including a gorgeous breakfast.

At Goodwick the welcoming *Beach House* (☎ 872085), off Quay Road above the railway line, a five-minute walk from the ferry, charges £15 for B&B. There are other B&Bs in the area, plus the big *Fishguard Bay Hotel* (☎ 873571, Quay Rd), with single/double en suites for £45/65.

If you prefer the countryside, prize-winning *Brynawel Country House* (☎/fax 874155, Llanwnda), just under a mile northwest of Goodwick, has smashing views, B&B for a bargain £17 per person, and a self-catering annexe. Coast-path walkers are welcome and shuttle help is available. *Gilfach Goch Farmhouse* (☎ 873871), 2 miles east on the A487, has six B&B rooms for £23 and a lovely garden. It opens March to November, and the Fishguard–Cardigan bus stops at the gate.

Places to Eat

The smoky but cheerful *Annie Francis Corner Cafe* (Market Square) opens 7 am to 6 pm (from 10 am Sunday). It can do breakfasts from continental to massive English fry-ups, but is best known for its good (and good-value) seafood meals from £6 to £15.

Three Main Street (☎ 874275, 3 Main St), in a Georgian townhouse, is one of Wales' finest restaurants – quite pricey but a treat for the palate, with original, carefully prepared dishes using fresh local meat,

seafood and other ingredients, including vegetarian choices and gorgeous homemade puddings. Lunch dishes go for around £7 and dinner for £23/28 for two/three courses. Book ahead in the evening.

The *Royal Oak Inn* (see Entertainment) has a wide choice of pub grub including vegetarian. The *Coach House* (see Entertainment) is good for Italian food.

Supermarkets include *Kwik Save* and *Gateway* on High St and *Londis* on West St. A general market takes place every Thursday in the market hall, through the town hall on Market Square. A bigger *farmers market* occupies the car park in front of Kwik Save every other Saturday in summer, and in the market hall in winter.

Entertainment

The *Globe Inn* (☎ 872500, Main St) has local rock bands on Friday and Saturday, and the historic *Royal Oak Inn* (☎ 872514, Market Square) has live Irish music on Tuesday.

Beside the Globe is the *Fishguard Arms* (☎ 872763, Main St), an all-round good pub with real ales from the barrel. The *Coach House* (☎ 875429, High St) has a young clientele and good Italian grub. The *Ship & Anchor* (☎ 874844, High St) is more Welsh than the others, with sing-alongs on Saturday nights.

Theatr Gwaun (☎ 873421, West St) is a cinema as well as the local drama and musical theatre.

Shopping

A good shop for all things Welsh (music, books, handicrafts, even light meals) is Siop DJ, next door.

Getting There & Away

Richards Brothers' (☎ 01239-613756) bus services to Market Square include No 411 every two hours from Haverfordwest (£3.20, 1½ hours) and from St David's (£2.25, 50 minutes); and No 412 from Haverfordwest and from Cardigan (£2.30, 50 minutes, hourly) – all with limited Sunday services. Few if any stop at the ferry terminal. For National Express coaches (and extra train services) to London you must go to Haverfordwest.

Fishguard is the northern terminus of a branch railway line across south Wales, although trains are an awkward way to get around Pembrokeshire. Trains run in service of Ireland ferries – twice daily from Goodwick to London (£44 Super Saver single or £27 Apex, five hours). The 'station' is just a platform (buy tickets on board).

From Rosslare (Ireland) Stena Line (☎ 0870 570 7070) runs ferries (£44 per foot passenger or £184 for a car and driver, 3½ hours, two daily) and catamarans (£60/219, two hours, two to four daily) to the terminal at Goodwick.

Getting Around

Bus No 410 (50p) runs a regular circuit from Market Square to Goodwick Square, Fishguard Harbour and back about every half-hour (except on Sunday).

Goodwick Bike Hire, at the Left Bank Gift Shop (☎ 872050) on Main St in Goodwick, rents mountain bikes for £6/10/45 per half-day/day/week.

NEWPORT (TREFDRAETH)
☎ 01239 • pop 1200

This small, pretty, now middle-class town (not on any account to be confused with the industrial town of the same name east of Cardiff; see the Cardiff chapter) grew up around a small castle at the foot of Carn Ingli (347m), a massive bump on the seaward side of the Preseli Hills, in what tourist brochures call 'bluestone country'. The castle is Norman but there's evidence of much earlier settlements in the area.

Newport makes a pleasant base for forays onto the coast path along this very rugged stretch, or south into the Preseli Hills. From Carn Ingli itself there are fine views north across the estuary of the River Nevern (Nyfer) and Newport Bay. Just north of the town is little Parrog Beach, dwarfed by Newport Sands (Traeth Mawr) across the river.

Orientation & Information

There's little more to the town than four intersections on a ½-mile stretch of the A487, which is clogged almost to a standstill with tourist traffic in July and August. The intersection of the A487 with Long St (to the north) and Market St (to the south) is called The Square (though it isn't one). The A487 is called Bridge St (and other names farther out) west of The Square, and East St to the east.

A little National Park Visitors Centre and TIC (☎ 820912, fax 820412) at Bank Cottages, a block down Long St from The Square, opens daily except on Sunday, Easter to October. In winter, information on accommodation and other practicalities is posted in the window.

The only bank is a Lloyds at The Square. The post office is in the newsagents a few steps down Long St. The Book Shop, an excellent place just up Market St, is chock-a-block with OS and other maps and books of local interest. There's a laundrette 1½ blocks along East St.

Things to See & Do

There's a little **dolmen** (Neolithic burial chamber) called Carreg Coetan right in town: from The Square walk east for two blocks and north up Pen-y-Bont for 200m; it's on the left. Don't miss its big brother, Pentre Ifan (see Around Newport later).

The striking **castle** – now a private residence – overlooking the town was founded by a Norman nobleman named William Fitz-Martin, married to a daughter of Lord Rhys ap Gruffydd, after his father-in-law drove him out of nearby Nevern (see Around Newport later) in 1191. Newport grew up around the castle, initially as a garrison town.

On Lower St Mary's St, a block east and a block north from The Square, is the **West Wales Eco Centre** (☎ 820235, fax 820801), an environmental education and resource centre whose energy-efficient stone home is also the UK's smallest solar-electric generating station. Visitors are welcome; it opens on weekdays, Easter to October. See the Web site at www.ecocentre.org.uk.

Walking & Cycling Routes

Stroll on down Pen-y-Bont for just over ¾ mile to an iron bridge over the **Nevern**

Estuary, flush with bird life especially in the winter season. A 3-mile circular walk runs from the north side of the bridge and along the estuary and beach.

There are lots of fine possibilities for longer walks around **Carn Ingli**. Ask at The Book Shop (see under Orientation & Information earlier) for a series of *Newport Walks* brochures by local resident David Vaughan. The longest and most rewarding is a 9-mile loop that includes a climb to the summit, where there's a 3½-hectare Iron Age hill-fort, which includes several dozen hut foundations.

The back roads south and west of Carn Ingli, dotted with farmhouse B&Bs and cheerful pubs, offer some of the loveliest on-road cycling in south-west Wales. Call in at the Llysmeddyg Guest House, aka Newport Mountain Bike Hire (see Places to Stay & Eat), for some wheels and detailed information on self-guided circular trips – including a fine one along the Cwm Gwaun valley south-east of Carn Ingli.

Places to Stay & Eat

Morawelon Caravan & Camping Park (☎ 820565, *Parrog Beach*), north-west of the town, charges £4.20 per person with tent. Turn off the A487 just west of the Royal Oak Inn. There's also a caravan/camp site around a mile east of town at *Llywngwair Farm*.

The newish *Trefdraeth Youth Hostel* (☎ 820080, *Lower St Mary's St*), behind the Eco Centre, opens daily from mid-April to August; nightly charges are £9.25/6.50 for adults/under-18s. Reception opens at 5 pm.

Soar Hill (☎ 820506, *Cilgwyn Rd*) is ½ mile south off the A487 (turn 200m east of The Square); rooms cost £18 per person (en suites £22). *Hafan Deg* (☎ 820301, *Long St)* is a modern house with garden; singles/doubles cost from £20/45.

Recommended for its interest in budget and 'self-propelled' travellers is the well-run *Llysmeddyg Guest House* (☎ 820008, fax 820801, *East St*), with four spacious singles/doubles for £25/44 (en suites for £35/50), a self-catering flat, and dinner by arrangement for £15. You can also rent bikes here. The *Golden Lion Hotel* (☎ 820321, *East St)* does

en suites from £20/35, and has a bar and restaurant. The pink *Cnapan Country House* (☎ 820575, *East St*) has five rooms for £28 per person, and one of the region's best restaurants, with set dinners for under £20. It opens daily except Tuesday.

The *Fronlas Café* (☎ 820351, *Market St)* does homemade patés, soups and sandwiches for around £3 to £4, plus herbal teas, coffees, scones and cakes; evening meals are pricey at £11 upwards per course. *Café Fleur* (☎ 820131, *Market St*) has delicious crepes and waffles from £3, and good coffee. Budget eaters can shop at the *Spar* on Market St.

Getting There & Away

Richards Brothers' (☎ 613756) hourly No 412 bus runs via Fishguard (£1.45, 20 minutes) between Haverfordwest (£2.55, one hour and five minutes) and Cardigan (£1.90, 20 minutes), daily except on Sunday.

Getting Around

Bikes can be hired for £5/13/65 per hour/day/week from Newport Bike Hire at Llysmeddyg Guest House (see Places to Stay earlier). Kids' bikes and baby seats are also available.

AROUND NEWPORT
Nevern (Nanhyfer)

With its overgrown castle and atmospheric **Church of St Brynach**, this little village (Nanhyfer in Welsh) 2 miles east of Newport makes an easy and worthwhile excursion. St Brynach was a 5th-century Irish holy man who lived in a hut on Carn Ingli, above Newport.

You approach the church up a supremely gloomy alley of English yews, estimated to be six centuries old. Second on the right as you enter is the so-called 'bleeding yew', named after the curious reddish-brown sap that oozes from it. The beautifully melancholy churchyard dates from around the 6th century, predating the church.

Among the gravestones is a tall Celtic cross, one of the finest Celtic crosses in Wales, dating from perhaps the 10th or 11th century. According to one tradition, the first cuckoo that sings each year in Pembrokeshire does so from atop this cross on St Brynach's day, 7 April.

Two other ancient carved stones are inside the church. The so-called Maglocunus Stone, thought to date from the 5th century and engraved with writing in Latin and in Ogham (an ancient Celtic script), forms one windowsill in the south transept. Another bears an elongated Celtic cross.

Castell Henllys

Some 2000 years ago there was a thriving Celtic settlement at what's now called Castell Henllys, 4 miles east of Newport. York University archaeology faculty and students have been digging and sifting at the site every summer for years, and have learned enough to generate a remarkable facsimile of the settlement on its original foundations, complete with educated guesses about the clothing, tools, ceremonies and agricultural life of that time.

The **Castell Henllys Iron Age Settlement** (☎/fax 891319), owned and managed by the national park on 9 hectares of woodland and river meadow, is a bit like time travel. There are reconstructions of the settlement's actual buildings – four thatched roundhouses, animal pens, a smithy and a grain store – and a purpose-built education centre with exhibits about the site. Crafts demonstrations, Celtic festivals and other events bring it to life, and staff are careful and patient with their explanations.

The site opens 10 am to 5 pm daily, Easter to October. Admission costs £2.70/1.80. Take the hourly No 412 Newport–Cardigan bus and get off at the Melina Road stop, from where it's a ¾-mile walk.

Pentre Ifan

Pentre Ifan is a 4500-year-old dolmen on a remote hillside south-east of Newport, with grand views across the Preseli Hills and out to sea. With a 5m-high capstone delicately supported by 2m-high boulders, this is thought to be the finest and best-preserved Neolithic burial chamber in Wales.

There are several ways to get to it, including on foot from Newport. By car or bus, get off at a turning nearly 1½ miles east of The

Square in Newport, then follow signposted back roads for 2½ miles to a gate, from where it's a 150m walk. If you come this way, your first glimpse of the dolmen will have Carn Ingli as a backdrop.

CARDIGAN (ABERTEIFI)
☎ 01239 • pop 4500

Cardigan was the county town of pre-1974 Cardiganshire, though it lost that status to Aberaeron in the county's essentially identical post-1996 reincarnation, Ceredigion. In any case it sits so much closer to Pembrokeshire – 2 miles, to be precise – than to anything of interest in Ceredigion that it only makes sense to include it in this chapter.

The Welsh name refers to the town's position near the mouth of the Teifi, where it was in Elizabethan times the second most important port in Wales after Milford Haven, and by the late 18th century one of Britain's most important seafaring and trading centres. But by the end of the 19th century the railway was displacing sea transport, and when the river began silting up, Cardigan slipped into obscurity.

Cardigan Castle was the venue for the first-ever competitive National Eisteddfod (for more on this Welsh cultural jamboree, see the boxed text under Arts in the Facts about Wales chapter), held in 1176 under the aegis Lord Rhys ap Gruffydd. A strong local interest in the arts continues, and the town has a good alternative theatre and arts centre.

This, some good walks (and a walking festival) and the town's position at the northern end of the Pembrokeshire Coast Path are the only real reasons to pause here.

Orientation & Information

From the Finch Square Café on Finch Square, by the bus stand, it's a 200m walk up Priory St to the town's axis – High St if you turn left towards the river (300m away) or Pendre if you turn right.

The first left off Pendre is Bath House Rd, where a little TIC (☎ 613230, ✉ cardigan tic@ceredigion.gov.uk) is in the lobby of the Theatr Mwldan (see Entertainment later). It opens 10 am to 6 pm daily, mid-July to

August; and 10 am to 5 pm daily (except Sunday) the rest of the year (to 6 pm in September).

The post office and all major UK banks are along High St. Free Internet access is available at the library (☎ 612578) on Pendre; it opens 9.30 am to 6 pm (to 1 pm Wednesday and Saturday) daily except on Sunday.

The police station (☎ 612209) is on Priory St. The Cardigan Memorial Hospital (☎ 612214) is on Pont-y-Clefion just east of Finch Square.

Things to See & Do

Cardigan Castle was founded on a bluff above the river in 1093, by the Norman Lord Roger de Montgomery. Lord Rhys captured it in 1165, and 11 years later ordered the first competitive eisteddfod to be held here to celebrate its reconstruction. Damaged by parliamentary cannonballs in 1644, it's now in a state of collapse, shored up from below and off-limits to the public.

A more interesting destination is to the restored 18th-century granary on the Teifi Wharf, just across the Cardigan Bridge. Done up as the **Cardigan Heritage Centre** (☎ 614404), it features Cardigan history, interactive computer learning for kids and a riverside cafe. It opens 10 am to 5 pm daily, Easter to October; and noon to 4 pm daily except Wednesday and Saturday, the rest of the year. Admission costs £1.50.

A prominent High St landmark is the neo-Gothic 1860 **Guildhall**, with its vaulted ceilings. Nowadays it's the venue for a produce and crafts market, which takes place daily except Wednesday and Sunday (daily except Sunday in July and August). From 9.30 am to 3.30 pm Thursday and Saturday in summer there are extra stalls upstairs, including specialist artisan stalls. The field cannon outside commemorates the Charge of the Light Brigade, which was led by Lord Cardigan.

Special Events

The Cardigan Festival of Walking takes place over a long weekend in early October, with themed linear and circular walks all round the area, plus culture and beer in the evenings. Booking ahead is recommended.

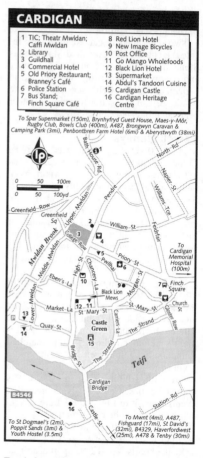

CARDIGAN

1 TIC; Theatr Mwldan;	8 Red Lion Hotel
Caffi Mwldan	9 New Image Bicycles
2 Library	10 Post Office
3 Guildhall	11 Go Mango Wholefoods
4 Commercial Hotel	12 Black Lion Hotel
5 Old Priory Restaurant;	13 Supermarket
Branney's Café	14 Abdul's Tandoori Cuisine
6 Police Station	15 Cardigan Castle
7 Bus Stand;	16 Cardigan Heritage
Finch Square Café	Centre

For information call Theatr Mwldan (see Entertainment later).

Places to Stay

The small **Brongwyn Caravan & Camping Park** (☎ 613644), 3 miles from Cardigan, just north off the A487 at Penparc, has tent sites from £5 for two people.

The good **Poppit Sands Youth Hostel** (☎ 612936) is 3½ miles from Cardigan, at the start of the Pembrokeshire Coast Path and overlooking the mouth of the Teifi. It opens daily except on Sunday and Monday, Easter to October (daily from mid-July to

August); beds cost £9.25/6.50 for adults/ under-18s. Bus No 407 runs from Finch Square to Poppit Sands beach car park (60p, 15 minutes, five daily except on Sunday), from where it's a ½-mile walk to the hostel.

Two quiet B&Bs on Gwbert Rd, 600m north of the centre (turn left at the Spar), are *Brynhyfryd Guest House (☎/fax 612861, Park Place, Gwbert Rd)* with singles/ doubles for £18/36 (en suites for £25/40), and *Maes-y-Môr (☎ 614929, Gwbert Rd)* at £20 per person (rooms are en suite). Buses from Aberystwyth will drop you on the A487 here. In the centre the *Black Lion Hotel (☎ 612532, High St)* has comfortable en suites for £30/40 B&B, and a restaurant and pub.

Six miles east of Cardigan off the A487 is the very comfortable *Penbontbren Farm Hotel (☎ 810248, fax 811129, Glynarthen)*, with double en suites for £86 B&B; bed and full board costs £58 per person.

Places to Eat

The *Old Priory Restaurant (☎ 615167, Priory St)*, upstairs from ho-hum Branney's Café, opens daily for lunch and dinner with inventive specials from £5, big helpings and vegetarian options. *Caffi Mwldan (☎ 612687)* at Theatr Mwldan serves soups, salads and light meals for around £4; it opens 10 am to 5.30 pm weekdays and to 4 pm Saturday – plus Sunday evenings when there are film society screenings.

Most people agree that the best food in town is at *Abdul's Tandoori Cuisine (☎ 621416, 2 Royal Oak, Quay St)*, opposite Somerfield. It opens from 5 pm daily, with £7 four-course early-bird dinners until 7 pm except Saturday.

The *Red Lion Hotel* (see Entertainment) pulls a good pint and has reasonable grub. *Go Mango Wholefoods (Black Lion Mews)* is a wholefood shop with snacks to take away (closed on Sunday). Supermarkets include a *Spar* on North Rd and a *Somerfield* on Quay St.

Entertainment

Theatr Mwldan (☎ 621200), in a former slaughterhouse on Bath House Rd, is the general venue for comedy, drama, dance, music and both alternative and first-run films.

High St has lots of pubs but it's a bit of a teenage scene. The *Red Lion Hotel (☎ 612482, Pwllhai)* has a good party atmosphere and an off-the-wall mix of entertainment. A quieter option is the *Commercial Hotel* on Pendre. Small bars at the *rugby club* and *bowls club* opposite the B&Bs on Gwbert Rd are open to the public.

Getting There & Away

Richards Brothers'(☎ 613756) No 412 bus runs hourly from Haverfordwest (£3.50, 1½ hours) and Fishguard (£2.30, 50 minutes). First Cymru's (☎ 0870 608 2608) No 460 comes from Cardigan (£3.40, 1½ hours) about hourly. None run on Sunday.

Richards Brothers and Arriva Cymru (☎ 01970-617951) jointly run the No 550 from Aberystwyth (£3.60, two hours, hourly), with a change of bus near New Quay. There are about five services on Sunday.

Getting Around

New Image Bicycles (☎ 621275) on Pwllhai rents mountain bikes for around £10/15/ 30 per half-day/day/week, and also has kid seats and trailers.

AROUND CARDIGAN
Mwnt Church

Alone on a wind-raked headland north of Cardigan is the Eglwys Y Grog (Church of the Holy Cross), a tiny 13th-century chapel on the site of a 6th-century monk's cell, and a stop for pilgrims en route to Bardsey Island. The place and the church give a rather touching glimpse of the earliest days of Wales' spartan brand of Christianity – something to ponder as you explore this atmospheric spot. Services are held in the church on the morning and evening of the first Sunday of June, July and August.

There's little else in sight but scattered farms and a small caravan park. The heather-covered headland, 250m Foel-y-Mwnt (pronounced foil-ee-moont), and its little glacier-scoured cove – though not the church – are owned by NT. Above the cove are an old

PEMBROKESHIRE

limekiln and a small, summer-only Ceredigion Heritage Coast information centre.

Grey seals congregate here (with pups from August to mid-November). The headland is also a good place from which to see Cardigan Bay's bottlenosed dolphins feeding close inshore, especially in June and October. A patch of the bay from here up the coast to Aberaeron, and offshore for about 10 miles, is a marine reserve called the Cardigan Bay Special Area of Conservation.

The site is 4 miles from Cardigan, out the Gwbert Rd. The nearest local bus, the No 408, runs twice daily to Ferwig (15 minutes), 2 miles away.

Teifi Valley Railway
One of Wales' 'Great Little Train' journeys is this 2-mile stretch of narrow-gauge line from Henllan, 14 miles from Cardigan or 4 miles from Newcastle Emlyn, just off the A484 (Carmarthen Rd). The train (☎/fax 01559-371077) runs from Easter to October on a complicated timetable (check with the Cardigan TIC). A ride costs £5/3; those not planning to ride still pay £2 per car to visit.

Richards Brothers' (☎ 01239-613756) bus No 460/461 from Cardigan to Henllan (£2.40, 45 minutes, 10 daily) runs Monday to Saturday.

Carmarthenshire

Parts of Carmarthenshire are within or adjacent to the Black Mountain region of the Brecon Beacons National Park. This includes Carreg Cennen Castle, which is treated in this section because it's easiest to reach from here; and the Llandovery area, which has been included in the Mid Wales chapter.

CARMARTHEN (CAERFYRDDIN)
☎ 01267 • pop 15,000
Carmarthenshire's stodgy county town is where legends locate the birthplace of Merlin, the famous wizard of the Arthurian legends. In Welsh versions of his story, Merlin (Myrddin to the Welsh) wandered the countryside in misery for 50 years with a pig as his companion. Perhaps he was looking for somewhere else to live; certainly nowadays there's little reason to stop here, but since Carmarthen is an important transport hub for south-west Wales – including Laugharne and the National Botanic Garden – you may have to.

Merlin manifests himself here mainly as the namesake for barbershops, car repair shops and the like. An oak tree planted on Priory St in 1659 to mark the coronation of Charles II came somehow to be known as 'Merlin's Tree' and linked to one of the magician's prophecies, that the tree's death would signal the end for the town too. But after the tree died peacefully in the 1970s, the town limped on. Pieces of the tree are kept under glass at Carmarthen's civic centre and at the Carmarthen Museum in Abergwili.

Orientation
Central Carmarthen is on the northern bank of the River Tywi (often anglicised to Towy). Buses stop along Blue St, from where it's about 200m around the block to the TIC. From the train station across the river, it's a 500m walk to the buses (cross the bridge and turn left on The Quay or Coracle Way, then take the first right into Blue St).

Information
The TIC (☎ 231557, fax 221901), 113 Lammas St, opens 9.30 am to 1 pm and 2 to 5.30 pm Monday to Saturday (open with no lunch break, and on Sunday too, from June to August; opening 30 minutes later and closing 30 minutes earlier in winter).

In unit 14 of Greyfriars Shopping Centre, between the bus stands and the TIC, is Travel House (☎ 221700), where you can book trains, National Express and TrawsCambria coaches. In Mansel St (across Lammas St from the TIC), Carmarthen Books has a selection of maps and local lore.

County Hall & Carmarthen Castle
The hulking County Hall, above the River Tywi bridge, was designed in the 18th century – apparently as a jail – by John Nash, better known for Buckingham Palace and thank goodness for that. It's on the site of Carmarthen's Norman Castle (destroyed in

the Civil War, though there are sorry remnants just west of the county hall) and an earlier Roman fort.

Places to Stay

An agreeable B&B near the centre is that of *Mr & Mrs Rees* (☎ 233095, 4 Morfa Lane), where single/double en suites cost £20/32; the TIC keeps a list of others. The plain *Spilman Hotel* (☎/fax 237037, Spilman St), 500m east of the TIC via Nott Square and Queen St, has en suites from £30/45 (or £24/36 with shared facilities in a dreary annexe).

Pub-hotels along Lammas St are central but overpriced – for example, the *Rose & Crown* (☎ 237712) at £25/35 (with breakfast) and the *Boar's Head* (☎ 222789) at £30/40 (en suite, plus £5 for breakfast). The twee *Falcon Hotel* (☎ 237152, fax 221277, Lammas St) has en suites for £48/63.

Places to Eat

The top choice is *Caban Y Dderwen* (☎ 238989, 11 Mansel St), with cawl, sandwiches, salads and hot lunches for £4 to £5, and a range of good fish dishes. The biggest menu of traditional Welsh dishes is at *Pantri Blakeman* (mobile ☎ 07977-901367, Blue St), opposite the bus station and upstairs from a carpet shop. *Waverly Stores* (☎ 236521, Lammas St) is a health-food shop with a modest vegetarian restaurant at the back. All open to 5 pm daily except on Sunday.

Supermarkets include the *Cooperative* on King St behind the Spilman Hotel, and *Tesco* a block south of the TIC.

Entertainment

Carmarthen's male voice choir rehearses at 7 pm Tuesday (except in August) at Zion Chapel on Mansel St.

Getting There & Away

First Cymru (☎ 0870 608 2608) services include the No X11 from Swansea (£3.90 single, 1½ hours, hourly) and the No 460 from Cardigan (£3.40, 1½ hours, about hourly). Silcox Coaches No 322 runs from Haverfordwest (£3.90, one hour, at least twice daily). Sunday services are limited or nonexistent.

The Beacons Bus (route B4) links Carmarthen with Brecon on summer Sundays (see Getting There & Around under Brecon Beacons National Park in the Brecon Beacons chapter). Arriva Cymru's Traws Cambria service No 701 (Cardiff–Holyhead; see the Getting Around chapter) passes through daily, as does National Express No 508/528 (Haverfordwest–Swansea).

Trains run to Carmarthen from Cardiff (£10.60, two hours, six daily).

AROUND CARMARTHEN
Carmarthenshire County Museum

This museum of regional history – with Roman gold, Welsh furniture and a re-created country schoolroom – is at least as interesting for its home: the Palace of the Bishops of St David's from the Reformation until 1974. The museum (☎ 01267-231691) is set in peaceful grounds in Abergwili, 1½ miles east of Carmarthen on the A40, and opens 10 am to 4.30 pm daily except on Sunday. Admission is free. Take First Cymru's (☎ 0870 608 2608) bus No 280/281 (£1.15 day return, 12 minutes, every two hours).

Gwili Steam Railway

Fans of Wales' reincarnated steam railways can ride a short section of the standard-gauge Gwili Steam Railway (☎ 01267-230666) along the valley of the River Gwili, starting at Bronwydd Arms, 3 miles out on the A484 towards Cardigan. It only runs a few days of each week except in August when it runs daily. Ask at the Carmarthen TIC for the current timetable, or visit their Web site at www.gwili-railway.co.uk.

Horse Fair

The village centre of Llanybydder (or variant spellings such as Llanybuther) is the site of a huge horse fair on the last Thursday of every month, from around 10 am to mid-afternoon. It's 18 miles north on the A485 to Lampeter. For information call ☎ 01570-480444. First Cymru's (☎ 0870 608 2608) bus No 202 (£4.20 day return, 55 minutes) runs every hour or two from Carmarthen.

CARMARTHENSHIRE

THE NATIONAL BOTANIC GARDEN OF WALES

One of Wales' newest and finest attractions is carefully concealed in rolling countryside in the valley of the River Twyi. The National Botanic Garden of Wales (NBGW), a world-class botanical attraction rivalling London's Kew Gardens and twice its size, is set in 72 hectares in a 227-hectare former regency estate called Middleton Hall, 7 miles east of Carmarthen. Its centrepiece is the Great Glasshouse, a gigantic, high-technology domed greenhouse designed by Lord (Norman) Foster, whose other recent projects include the dome of the restored Reichstag in Berlin.

Opened in May 2000, the garden is dedicated to the broad study of biodiversity and plant conservation, and to education and public awareness – motivated, in the words of its publicity materials, by a vision of 'a world where we understand, value, use, enjoy and sustain plant life to create a balance of life on earth'.

History

The first Middleton Hall was built in the early 1600s by Henry Middleton, high sheriff of Carmarthenshire. Some 800 hectares were sold in 1789 to one William Paxton, who turned the old mansion into a farmhouse and built himself a grand new one. In later years the house fell into decay, and in 1931 was destroyed by fire. The county bought some of the property and leased it to tenant farmers.

The idea for a national botanical garden was the brainchild in 1980 of a local painter named William Wilkins, who founded the Welsh Historic Gardens Trust to pursue the matter. In 1996 the trust was awarded a generous grant by the UK's Millennium Commission, and given a 999-year lease by the county on 227 hectares of the estate. Some 72 hectares have been opened to the public, and more plans are on the boil.

Information

The NBGW (☎ 01558-668768) opens 10 am to 4.30 pm daily (to 5.30 pm in September and October, and to 6 pm from about Easter

to August); last admission is one hour before closing time. Admission costs £6.50 for adults, £3 for those aged five to 16, and £16 for a family. A concession price of £5 is available to anyone who arrives by public bus (show your ticket), bicycle or on foot.

For more infomation, check out the Web site at www.gardenofwales.

Great Glasshouse

The immense domed greenhouse is the world's largest single-span glass house, a 99m by 55m oval with 5000 sq metres of double-glazed, reinforced glass – over 780 panes, 20% of which can be opened and shut by computers to maintain air flow and a 5°C differential between inside and outside. This amazing glass bubble manages to fit into the landscape as if it grew here.

The temperature and humidity inside simulate a Mediterranean ecosystem, sustaining some of the world's most endangered plants – not only from the Mediterranean basin but from South Africa's Cape region, south-western Australia and parts of Chile and California – amongst modernistic rock terraces, pools, waterfalls and fountains. The faint, intermittent whine is the sound of 147 tiny electric motors constantly adjusting the window openings.

Wales' greenery is at its best in May, while the foliage inside the glasshouse is at its most beautiful from late June to early July.

Other Attractions

Other highlights on the site include:

- A 220m promenade from the entrance, flanked by a continuous herbaceous border and dotted with rocks forming a geological walk through the ages – all of them from Wales.
- An interactive exhibit on herbal medicine traditions in Wales and worldwide, with a time-line leading right up to today's debates on genetic manipulation; and a turn-of-the-century apothecary shop (for more on traditional medicine in west Wales, see the boxed text 'The Physicians of Myddfai' under Llandovery in the Mid Wales chapter).
- A look-in at present and planned ways for the NBGW to minimise resource use by recycling its wastes and producing its own heat and, even-

tually, its own electricity (the glasshouse and office/restaurant/shop complex are heated by burning wood from the estate's managed woodlands; sewage and wastewater are treated organically on site and the resulting 'greywater' used to flush toilets, water plants etc).

Around the site are various educational facilities. The non-public two-thirds of the estate are being managed organically. In future, visitors will be able to follow trails among the seven lakes laid out by William Paxton, picnic in temperate-climate woodlands from various parts of the world and explore what is expected to be a nearly self-sustaining environment.

Paxton's Tower

The triangular tower visible on a hilltop east of the garden was built around 1808 by the eccentric Paxton, with a banquet hall, apartment and stained-glass windows depicting the life of his friend Admiral Nelson. One story goes that after losing a parliamentary election in which he promised to build a bridge across the Tywi, a spiteful Paxton spent the money on this instead. Managed by the NT, it's presently closed to the public.

Places to Eat

The only choice is a very good on-site restaurant, with modestly priced but good Welsh and other dishes, including plenty for vegetarians.

Getting There & Away

The garden is on the B4310 about 7 miles east of Carmarthen – reached most easily via the B4300 towards Llanarthne or the A48 towards Swansea. If you're on the A40 Llandeilo road, turn south at Nantgaredig.

First Cymru's (☎ 0870 608 2608) bus No 100 – running only from late June to late September – stops at the NBGW twice daily (once on Sunday) en route from Cardiff (£10 day return, 1½ hours), Swansea (£5, 40 minutes) or Carmarthen (£2.80, 25 minutes). The Beacons Bus (route B4) links the NBGW with Brecon on summer Sundays (see Getting There & Around under Brecon

Beacons National Park in the Breacon Beacons chapter).

The nearest train station is at Llandeilo, on the Heart of Wales line.

CARREG CENNEN

This has to be the most splendidly sited castle ruin anywhere in Wales, visible for miles in every direction on its magnificent Black Mountain escarpment, floating above the green landscape like a dark mirage.

Its remoteness meant that the castle never played much of a military role, though as a symbol of power it has few equals. There was probably a Welsh stronghold here in the time of Rhys ap Gruffydd, ruler of the kingdom of Deheubarth, who in the 12th century reversed many of the territorial gains of the Normans. This castle, and others at Lord Rhys' royal seat of Dinefwr and at Dryslwyn, would have faced down the Tywi valley towards the Norman castle at Carmarthen.

The castle you see today, however, was built at the end of the 13th century in the course of Edward I's conquest of Wales. It was not wrecked in battle, but dismantled in 1461 by Yorkists during the civil war known as the Wars of the Roses.

The breathless walk to the moody ruins at the summit, 90m above the valley of the River Cennen, is rewarded with huge views all round. The so-called Cliff Gallery is a dark, stone-vaulted passage running along the top of the sheer southern cliff to a natural cave (bring a torch, or hire one from the farm shop on the way up).

The castle (☎ 01558-822291, Cadw) is about 4 miles south-east of Llandeilo, near the village of Trapp. It opens daily and admission costs £2.50/2 (pay at the farm shop). Take the A483 south from Llandeilo, or north from the end of the M4, to Derwydd; from there it's a well-signposted 3½ miles east to a car park at Tir-y-Castell Farm. First Cymru's (☎ 0870 608 2608) Wales–Llandeilo bus No X13 stops at Derwydd about hourly (except on Sunday).

Though this area is actually within the Brecon Beacons National Park, access is easiest from Carmarthenshire.

LAUGHARNE (LACHARN)
☎ 01994 • pop 1200

Pilgrims on the Dylan Thomas trail come to this little town on the western side of the Tywi estuary to see the house where he lived, the pub where he perfected the drinking habit that finally killed him and the churchyard where he is buried. Even if you're not a fan, it's a lovely place.

Though born in Swansea, Thomas' family roots were in Carmarthenshire. He was drawn to Laugharne (pronounced larn) towards the end of his life – 'And some, like myself,' he wrote in *Quite Early One Morning*, 'just came, one day, for the day, and never left; got off the bus, and forgot to get on again.' While living in the Boathouse he produced some of his most inspired work, including *Under Milk Wood*. The play's fictional Llareggub was modelled on Laugharne.

Laugharne is a pretty town of Georgian houses, built by wealthy merchants, shipowners and retired sea-captains in the 16th and 17th centuries. The remains of a 12th-century castle stand on the estuary about 500m south of the Boathouse. Thomas and his widow Caitlin are buried in a simple grave in the churchyard of St Martin's Church.

Dylan Thomas Boathouse

Built into the hillside, the boathouse is a leafy five-minute walk from the centre of Laugharne. Thomas spent the last four years of his life (1949–53) living here with Caitlin and their three children, and the house has been preserved as a shrine, with original furnishings, photographs, manuscripts and recordings of the poet reading from his own works.

Above the house, you can look out from the old wooden garage – he called it 'The Shack' – where he wrote *Under Milk Wood*. Next door is a tearoom, from whose terrace you can gaze across his 'heron priested shore'.

The Boathouse (☎ 427420) opens 10 am to 5 pm daily, Easter to October, and 10.30 am to 3 pm in winter. Admission costs £2.75/1. The last few hundred metres down Cliff Rd is pedestrian-only, and not suitable for wheelchairs.

Places to Stay & Eat

Stately *Castle House* (☎ 472616, Market Lane), a pleasant B&B beside the castle, charges £30/50 for an en-suite single/double. The *Stable Door Wine Bar & Brasserie* (☎ 427777, Market Lane) is a lovely old building with a garden facing the castle; try their salmon in filo pastry for £10 or one of many vegetarian dishes for under £8. The atmospheric *Brown's Hotel* (no accommodation) was where Thomas drank, and it's still a serious place for that – no Dylan Thomas cocktails here for the visitors.

Getting There & Away

First Cymru's (☎ 0870 608 2608) bus No 222 runs from Carmarthen (£3.40 day return, 30 minutes) every hour or two (less often on Sunday and in winter). From Swansea you must change at either Carmarthen or St Clears; the cheapest way to do this is with a West Wales Day Rover pass, which you can buy on the bus (see the introduction to the chapter for details).

Mid Wales

In the 1974 reorganisation of Welsh local government, Brecknockshire, Radnorshire and Montgomeryshire were combined into the vast new county of Powys, while Cardiganshire kept its boundaries but got back its ancient name, Ceredigion. This is Wales at its least demonstrative, least accessible, least populated and most thoroughly rural, a low-rise landscape of impossibly green vistas and inward-looking market towns. Welsh is the mother-tongue for three out of every five of Mid Wales' people, although in its eastern parts – the Marches – the area can be quite indistinguishable from England, perhaps because it changed hands so frequently in medieval times.

Powis Castle (Welshpool) and the Centre for Alternative Technology (Machynlleth) are probably the main tourist attractions. The ultra-scenic Heart of Wales railway line crosses southern Powys, and several quite ordinary towns sit in the middle of some fine walking, cycling and riding country. The arts are alive and well here too; if you don't believe it, check out the free monthly *Broad Sheep*, Powys' entertaining rural what's-on, available at Tourist Information Centres (TICs).

But there's little else – beyond some important history – to detain most visitors until they reach the Cambrian Mountains and the Cardigan Bay coastline of Ceredigion (Cardiganshire). Ceredigion's capital, the university town and seaside resort of Aberystwyth, is certainly the most happening place in Mid Wales, and the trip to Devil's Bridge is one of Wales' best steam-train journeys.

Walking & Cycling Routes

This is unspoilt walking country. The region's best-known walk is Offa's Dyke Path, the 178-mile national trail that runs the length of the Wales-England border, constantly nipping from one side to the other. Wales' newest national trail is the 132-mile Glyndŵr's Way, running in a

Highlights

- Riding a bike and drinking beer simultaneously at the Real Ale Wobble, Llanwrtyd Wells

- Watching 20 rare red kites do aerobatics for a scrap of meat at Gigrin Farm, Rhayader

- Riding from Aberystwyth to Devil's Bridge on one of Wales' finest narrow-gauge railways

- Playing Clive of India among the yews at Wales' most famous garden, Powis Castle, Welshpool

- Having a little green fun at the Centre for Alternative Technology, Machynlleth

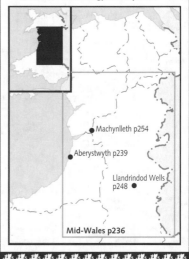

Machynlleth p254

Aberystwyth p239

Llandrindod Wells p248

Mid-Wales p236

great arc – all within Powys – from Knighton to Machynlleth and back to Welshpool. It takes in some fine and relatively unsung countryside and, at least as interestingly, follows in the footsteps of the Welsh hero Owain Glyndŵr. A major walking path that crosses Ceredigion is the

MID WALES

MID WALES

Porthmadog
Penrhyndeudraeth
Tremadog Bay
Talsarnau
Llyn Trawsfynydd
Trawsfynydd
Eden
Llyn Celyn
Trweryn
Llyn Tegid (Bala Lake)
Bala
Llangollen
Chirk Castle
Chirk
A487
A4212
B4402
B4401
A5
Harlech
Llanfair
Coed-y-Brenin Forest Park
Berwyn Mountains
B4391
Oswestry
SNOWDONIA NATIONAL PARK
A496
Cefn
B4580
A483
A5
Dyffryn Ardudwy
A496
Mawddach
A494
Llyn Efyrnwy (Vyrnwy Lake)
B4393
B4396
Tanat
A495
Barmouth
Barmouth & Fairbourne Railway
Cader Idris (889m)▲
Dolgellau
A487
A470
Dovey
Torch
B4391
B4393
Meifod
Cain
Vyrnwy
Severn
Castell Y Bere
Fairbourne
A493
B4405
Corris
Abergynolwyn
Mallwyd
A458
Vyrnwy
A495
A490
A458
Dolgoch
Dovey Valley
A487
Vyrnwy
Llanfair Caereinion
Welshpool & Llanfair Light Railway
Welshpool
Talyllyn Railway
Dysynni
Dolgoch
Tywyn
Dovey
A489
Machynlleth
A470
B4389
A490
A488
Aberdovey
A493
Carno
Montgomery
Church Stoke
CARDIGAN BAY
Plynlimon Fawr
B4518
Gregynog Hall
A483
A489
Lydham
Nant-Y-Moch Reservoir
Llyn Clywedog
B4569
Newtown
Severn
Aberystwyth
A4159
Severn
Llanidloes
A483
B4355
ENGLAND
A44
Ponterwyd
Wye
Vale of Rheidol Railway
A4120
Devil's Bridge
B4574
Ystwyth
B4518
Llanbadarn Fynydd
B4356
Knighton
A4113
A487
A485
B4343
B4340
Craig-Goch Reservoir
Elan Valley
A470
Rhayader
Llanddewi Ystradenny
A488
B4355
Pontrhydfendigaid
Strata Florida Abbey
B4343
Claerwen Reservoir
B4518
Elan Valley Visitor Centre
Cross Gates
B4372
Caban Coch Reservoir
A4081
Llandrindod Wells
A44
B4594
Tregaron
A485
Cambrian Mountains
B4358
A483
Llanelwedd
A481
Kington
A44
Temple Bar
Abergwesyn
Cilmery
A470
A482
Llyn Brianne
A483
A483
Builth Wells
A4111
Lampeter
A485
Llanwrtyd Wells
Llangamarch Wells
B4594
Willersley
A438
A482
Teifi
B4520
B4567
A485
A470
Hay-on-Wye
B4350
B4337
Tywi
Mynydd Eppynt
Glasbury
ENGLAND
Llandovery
Nant Bran
Talgarth
Waun Fach (811m)
Capel-Y-Ffin
Llanthony Priory
A482
A4069
A40
Usk Reservoir
Usk
A470
B4560
Llanthony
B4302
Myddfai
Sennybridge Mountain Centre
Brecon
Ty'n-Y-Caeau
A40
Llangorse Lake
Llangorse
A40
Black Mountain
BRECON BEACONS NATIONAL PARK
Libanus
Llanfrynach
Black Mountains

0   5   10km
0   3   6mi

Cambrian Way. For more on these trails see Walking under Activities in the Facts for the Visitor chapter.

Lôn Las Cymru, the Welsh National Cycling Route (Sustrans route No 8), comes down through the Cambrian Mountains, and the backroads of Mid Wales are a tourer's dream.

Three outfits offering guided rides and cycling holidays in the Cambrians and elsewhere are:

Bicycle Beano (☎ 01982-560471, @ mail@bicycle -beano.co.uk) Erwood, Builth Wells, Powys
Web site: www.bicyclebeano.co.uk
Clive Powell Mountain Bikes (☎ 01597-810585) East St, Rhayader; open April to October
Red Kite Mountain Biking Centre (☎ 01591- 610236) Neuadd Arms Hotel, Llanwrtyd Wells

Getting There & Around

Mid Wales' railway lines – all with daily services – are the Cambrian main line from Shrewsbury (England) to Aberystwyth via Welshpool, Newtown and Machynlleth; and the Heart of Wales Line from Shrewsbury to Swansea via Llandrindod Wells, Builth Wells, Llanwrtyd Wells and Llandovery. Two of Wales' narrow-gauge lines are in Mid Wales.

Bus transport is patchy, especially in Powys, and almost nonexistent on Sunday. Mid Wales' major companies are Arriva Cymru (☎ 01970-624472) in Aberystwyth, and Roy Brown's Coaches (☎ 01982- 552597) in Builth Wells. The West Wales Rover ticket (£4.60/3.40) is good for a day's unlimited travel with major companies in Ceredigion, Pembrokeshire and Carmarthenshire (but not the TrawsCambria coach, postbuses nor National Express). Arriva also has its own one-day (£5/3.50 adult/child), three-day (£10/7) and five-day (£15/10) passes. You can buy these passes on board the bus.

Ceredigion

Although it's just within Ceredigion, Cardigan is included in the Pembrokeshire & Carmarthenshire chapter.

ABERYSTWYTH
☎ 01970 • pop 16,000

Aberystwyth has two things going for it. It's a university town, with the open-mindedness and attitude that go with university towns, plus a bit of student cheer – at least during term-time – and a scattering of international faces untypical of most of Wales. And it's by the sea, which makes any town look good and has given this one some of the airs and graces of a spa.

In spite of all this leavening it still feels rather stuffy and old-fashioned, a wannabe seaside resort – and you couldn't call its people warm-hearted. But this is as cosmopolitan as Mid Wales gets, a bracing place on a sunny day, and definitely worth a night's stopover.

The tourist season barely overlaps with the student season, so your impressions will depend on when you arrive. Welsh is widely spoken, by the young as well as the old.

History

Like many other towns in Wales, Aberystwyth is a product of Edward I's castle-building mania. The castle here was begun in 1277, and like many other castles in Wales it was captured by Owain Glyndŵr at the start of the 15th century, and wrecked by Oliver Cromwell's forces during the Civil War. By the beginning of the 19th century, the town's walls and gates had disappeared.

The town developed a fishing industry, and silver and lead mining were also important here. With the arrival of the railway in 1864, it reinvented itself as a resort. In 1872 Aberystwyth was chosen as the site of the first college of the University of Wales, and in 1907 it became home to the National Library of Wales.

Orientation

Aberystwyth sits where the River Rheidol and the smaller River Ystwyth empty into Ceredigion Bay, at the end of the railway line across Mid Wales. Beaches make up its entire western side. Regional and national buses arrive beside the train station on Alexandra Rd.

MID WALES

Information

The TIC (☎/fax 612125, ⓔ aberystwythtic@ceredigion.gov.uk), at the corner of Terrace Rd and Bath St, opens 10 am to 1 pm and 2 to 6 pm daily except Sunday (to 5 pm from September to May). Here you can pick up the monthly *What's On*, which lists forthcoming events.

All major UK banks have branches (with ATMs) on Great Darkgate St or around the corner on Terrace Rd.

The main post office is at 8 Great Darkgate St. The county library (☎ 617464) on Corporation St has free Internet access but you must book ahead. It opens 9.30 am to 6 pm weekdays and to 1 pm on Saturday. Biognosis (☎ 636953), 21 Pier St, has Internet access for about £3 per hour. It opens 9.30 am to 9 pm (10 am to 6 pm on Saturday, noon to 6 pm on Sunday).

A good, small bookshop with some Welsh language and lore is Llên A Cherdd, at the corner of Terrace Rd and Great Darkgate St.

There are two campuses of the University of Wales here, with some 6800 students – at Penglais, about half a mile north-east up Penglais Rd (A487) from the centre, and at Llanbadarn, a mile south-east of the centre. Facilities of use to visitors are all at the Penglais campus. These include a student travel agency, Guild Travel (☎ 621711, ⓔ guild.travel@aber.ac.uk), and a gay/lesbian student office (ⓔ union.lgb@aber.ac.uk, or via the university's general office at ☎ 621700), both in the student union building. The Aberystwyth Lesbian Gay & Bisexual line (☎ 621707) opens 6 to 8 pm Monday and Thursday.

Laundrettes near the centre all open daily and include Maes-y-Mawr on Bath St near the TIC, Wash 'n Spin 'n Dry on Bridge St and an unnamed one at 75 North Parade.

Bronglais Hospital (☎ 623131) is about 500m from the centre on Caradoc Rd, just off the Llanbadarn Rd (A44). The police station (☎ 612791) is on Blvd St Brieuc.

Along the Waterfront

The **castle** is an unimpressive ruin by day, though a treat for kids, and attractive when floodlit at night.

The **Old College** was designed by one JP Seddon as a seaside hotel complex but it never opened due to financial problems. It was bought by the founders of the University of Wales, and the college was founded in this building in 1872.

Along **North Beach** are the cheerfully tacky Royal Pier, complete with amusements arcade, a bandstand beside the windblown Promenade and a long row of tattered old Georgian hotels on Victoria Terrace.

Constitution Hill

At the end of North Beach is Aberystwyth's headland, Constitution Hill (148m). Victorian tourists enjoyed a stately ride to the summit, and you can too, on the **Cliff Railway** (☎ 617642), the UK's longest electric funicular. It departs from the northern end of the promenade every few minutes from 10 am to 6 pm daily, Easter to October. Tickets cost £2/1 return.

From the top Aberystwyth is at its most photogenic, and there are long coastal views. Up here is another Victorian plaything – a **Camera Obscura** (like an immense pinhole camera or projecting telescope) – allowing you to practically look into the windows of the houses below.

The Vale of Rheidol Railway

One of Aberystwyth's most popular attractions is this narrow-gauge railway, one of the most scenic of Wales' many 'little trains'. Old steam locomotives, lovingly restored by volunteers, chug for almost 12 miles up the valley of the River Rheidol to Devil's Bridge (see Around Aberystwyth later). The line was opened in 1902 to bring lead and timber out of the valley, and the engines, once owned by the Great Western Railway, date from 1923.

Trains normally run daily except Friday, Easter to October (daily, June to August), with two departures daily (four departures Monday to Thursday, mid-July to August). Don't miss the last train back! For the current schedule ring the little ticket office (☎ 625819) by the main train station or check out the Web site at www.rheidolrailway.co.uk.

ABERYSTWYTH

PLACES TO STAY
3 Richmond Hotel
7 Brendan Guest House
11 Four Seasons Hotel
20 Groves Hotel & Restaurant
26 Aisling
37 Yr Hafod
38 Shoreline Guest House
39 Glyn Garth Guest House
48 Fountain Inn

PLACES TO EAT
13 Y Popty
14 Treehouse
15 Spar
17 Oasis Café Bar
18 Sunclouds
19 Agra Restaurant
21 Little Italy
24 Spar
31 Ancient Rain
41 Gannets Bistro
46 Somerfield

OTHER
1 Cliff Railway Station
2 On Your Bike
4 Bandstand
5 Commodore Cinema
6 Maes-y-Mawr Laundrette
8 Library; Internet Access
9 The Varsity
10 Tourist Information Centre; Ceredigion Museum
12 The Bar Essential
16 Llên A Cherdd
22 Summit Cycles
23 Laundrette
25 Coopers Arms
27 Bus Stand for Trawscambria & National Express
28 Bus Stand
29 Vale of Rheidol Railway Station
30 Aberystwyth Train Station
32 Post Office
33 Biognosis
34 Royal Pier
35 Old College
36 Castle
40 Flannery's
42 Market Hall
43 Wash 'n Spin 'n Dry
44 Tabernacle Chapel
45 Rummers Wine Bar
47 Police Station

To Constitution Hill

Cliff Tce

Brynmor Rd

Victoria Tce

Pen-y-Graig

Albert Pl

Queen's Ave

Bryn Rd

Cardigan Bay

Bowling Greens & Tennis Courts

North Rd

Trefor Rd

Loveden Rd

North Beach

Queen's Rd

Bath St

Portland St

Portland Rd

To A487, Bronglais Hospital (400m), National Library of Wales, Penglais Campus, Aberystwyth Arts Centre (0.5mi) & Borth Youth Hostel (7mi)

Northgate St

Thespian St

To A44 & Llanbadarn Campus (1mi)

Marine Tce

Corporation St

Terrace Rd

North Pde

Baker St

Eastgate

Market St

Pier St

New St

Great Darkgate St

Chalybeate St

Cambrian St

Alexandra Rd

Elm Tree Ave

Stanley Rd

Trinity Rd

Union St

King St

Castle St

Laura Pl

St James Sq

Queen St

Gray's Inn Rd

Park Ave

New Promenade

South Marine Tce

Sea View Pl

Vulcan St

Prospect St

Princess St

High St

Bridge St

George St

Powell St

Mill St

Clyndwr Rd

Rheidol Tce

South Rd

Quay Rd

Trefechan Rd

Riverside Tce

Greenfield St

Boulevard St Breuc

South Beach

Harbour

To Tanybwlch Beach & Pen Dinas (600m), A4120, Devil's Bridge (12mi), B4340, Strata Florida Abbey (16mi), A485, Tregaron (18mi), A487 & Cardigan (38mi)

A487

Rheidol

0   100   200m
0   100   200yd

MID WALES

The return fare costs £11 per adult, £2 each for the first two children and £5.50 for each additional child. For an extra £1 you can sit in the 1st-class section.

National Library
Half a mile east of town, the National Library of Wales (☎ 623800) holds over five million books in a variety of languages. Among its ancient manuscripts is the oldest existing text in the Welsh language, the 12th-century *Black Book of Carmarthen* (see Wales Under the Normans under History in the Facts about Wales chapter). The library opens 9.30 am to 6 pm Monday to Friday, and until 5 pm on Saturday. The turning is on Penglais Rd, just beyond the hospital.

Ceredigion Museum
The little Ceredigion Museum (☎ 617911) is in the Coliseum, a restored Edwardian music hall on Terrace Rd, beside the TIC. Inside is an entertaining collection of folk material based on the three main traditional occupations of the people of Ceredigion – agriculture, seafaring and lead mining – and temporary exhibitions of works by local artists. It opens 10 am to 5 pm Monday to Saturday. Admission is free.

Beaches
The main swimming beach is North Beach, with lifeguards and an EU blue flag rating. South Beach has few facilities and is mainly for sailing and other watersports. Both are walking distance from the centre.

Many local people prefer the gravelly but emptier Tanybwlch Beach, just south of the River Ystwyth. From here you can also walk up onto Pen Dinas, topped with a cannon pointing heavenwards – a memorial to the Duke of Wellington.

Places to Stay
Borth Youth Hostel (☎ 871498, *Morlais*) is in an Edwardian house 7 miles north up the B4572 at Borth, overlooking a wide sandy beach (also with a blue flag rating). The hostel opens daily except Sunday and Monday, April to October. The nightly charge is £10/6.90. Take bus No 512 (17 minutes,

hourly). There's also a spartan hostel east of Tregaron (see Around Aberystwyth later).

Recommended B&Bs in the teeth of the sea wind off South Beach include *Yr Hafod* (☎ 617579, *1 South Marine Terrace*) at £18 to £25 per person and *Shoreline Guest House* (☎ 615002, *6 South Marine Terrace*) at £17.

Near the train station, the friendly *Aisling* (☎ 626980, *21 Alexandra Rd*) has B&B for £19 per person. *Brendan Guest House* (☎ 612252, *19 Marine Terrace*) is a simple, clean place charging £20/22 per person for rooms without/with bathroom; most rooms have sea views. *Glyn Garth Guest House* (☎ 615050, *Castle Terrace*) is a comfortable place with B&B from £20 to £26 per person.

The *Groves Hotel & Restaurant* (☎ 617623, *fax 627068,* e *info@ghotel .force9.co.uk, 44 North Parade*) has comfortable en-suite singles/doubles for £45/60, with breakfast. The *Richmond Hotel* (☎ 612201, *44–5 Marine Terrace*) has B&B for £48/70. The *Four Seasons Hotel* (☎ 612120, *50–4 Portland St*) has 14 posh en-suite rooms for £55/82.

Places to Eat
The student presence guarantees plenty of good, cheap food. At the bottom end, there are Chinese and kebab *takeaways* in the area around the pier. Most *pubs* have plain, meaty menus, though few serve food on Saturday nights.

Top marks go to the bistro-style *Oasis Café Bar* (☎ 626040, *20 North Parade*), with lots of coffees and teas, imaginative sandwiches from £3, good paninis (Italian bread with cooked fillings) from £4, and rich, freshly concocted lunchtime specials from £5. It opens daily. Across the road, *Sunclouds* (☎ 617750, *25 North Parade*) does light lunches, and *Little Italy* (☎ 625707, *51 North Parade*) has pizza and pasta from £5.

Both vegetarians and carnivores will like *Treehouse* (☎ 615791, *14 Baker St*), an organic restaurant using locally grown produce. It opens during daytime hours Monday to Saturday and evenings Thursday to Saturday, and is upstairs from an equally good

St David's birthplace, St Non's Chapel

See Prince Phillip in a dress at Manorbier Castle.

Farmers markets in the town square, Caernarfon

Laugharne Castle watches over the River Taff.

St Govan's Chapel beside the sea at Bosherston

The historic Royal Oak Inn, Fishguard

Promenade along the North Beach, Aberystwyth

The hallowed halls of Old College, Aberystwyth

Climb the hill the easy way in Aberystwyth.

The mock-Tudor Gregynog Hall, Powys

Disappearing into the sunset, Dovey Estuary

Call in at the innovative CAT, Machynlleth.

takeaway shop with salads, soups, pizza and other snacks. Another veggie place, with lunch platters for around £5, is *Ancient Rain* (☎ 612363, 13 Cambrian Place). It opens daily except Sunday.

The best of several Indian restaurants is the *Agra Restaurant* (☎ 636999, 36 North Parade), open for lunch and dinner; bring your own wine.

Gannets Bistro (☎ 617164, 7 St James Square) has evening main dishes – including seafood and Welsh black beef – for under £11, and good-value lunches. It opens daily except Sunday.

Y Popty (☎ 627385, 41 Terrace Rd) is a bakery with savoury snacks, baguettes and spit-roast chicken. A 24-hour *Spar* supermarket is just across the road. There's another *Spar* on Northgate St and a *Somerfield* supermarket beside the train station.

A big *farmers market* (and crafts fair) occupies the streets around the Market Hall, St James Square, on the third Friday of the month.

Entertainment

Bars & Clubs The hippest place in town is *The Bar Essential* (☎ 623318, Portland St) at the corner with Terrace Rd, loud and lively and Welsh, with extra space on the mezzanine. Diagonally opposite is *The Varsity* (☎ 615234, Portland St), spacious, simple and student-friendly. *Rummers Wine Bar* (☎ 625177, Bridge St) is right by the river and has seats outside. It opens 7 pm to midnight.

Flannery's (☎ 612334), at the corner of Vulcan and High Sts, has Irish folk music on Wednesday nights, and the *Coopers Arms* (☎ 624050, Northgate St) has live folk music on Tuesday evenings.

Gay & Lesbian Venues Tuesday is gay night at the *Fountain Inn* (☎ 612430, Trefechan Rd, Trefechan), just over the River Rheidol bridge, with a £1.50 door charge after 9.30 pm.

Str8 Up! is a gay/lesbian club night in the upstairs bar at the student union at the university (Penglais campus) on some Tuesdays. The door charge is around £1.50. For

information and current dates call the university's General Office (☎ 621700).

Other Entertainment The university's *Aberystwyth Arts Centre* (☎ 623232, Penglais Rd) is the town's main arts venue, with mainstream films and drama, dance and music programs (all of which can also be booked at the TIC), plus a bookshop, gallery and good cafe. The small *Commodore Cinema* (☎ 612421, Bath St) shows current releases in the evening and has a weekend matinee.

The Aberystwyth Male Voice Choir rehearses at the Tabernacle Chapel at 7.45 pm on most Thursdays; for information call ☎ 828001.

Getting There & Away

Bus Local and regional buses use a stand in front of the B'Wise store on Alexandra Rd, beside the train station. TrawsCambria and National Express coaches have their own stand half a block east.

Arriva Cymru and Richards Brothers (☎ 01239-613756) jointly run the No 550 from Cardigan (£3.40, two hours, hourly), with a change of bus near New Quay; there are about five services on Sunday. Arriva's No 514 comes from Dolgellau (£4.30, one hour 20 minutes) and Machynlleth (£2.90, 45 minutes) every two hours (twice on Sunday).

Arriva's long-haul TrawsCambria service (No 701) arrives daily – twice from Cardiff (£11.35, four hours) and once from Bangor (£11.70, three hours). National Express coach No 420 runs once daily from London via Birmingham.

Train Aberystwyth is the terminus of the Cambrian line across Mid Wales from Birmingham via Shrewsbury, Welshpool, Newtown and Machynlleth. Central Trains has services every two hours (less frequently on Sunday); a single ticket costs £11.40 from Shrewsbury or £16.60 from Birmingham.

Getting Around
The quickest bus to/from the Penglais campus (five minutes, every 15 minutes) is the No 504/505.

MID WALES

On Your Bike (☎ 626996), in the Old Police Yard, Queen's Rd, rents mountain bikes for £10 a day. It opens weekdays only. Summit Cycles (☎ 626061) on Great Darkgate St also rents bikes.

AROUND ABERYSTWYTH
Devil's Bridge
☎ 01970

Devil's Bridge spans the Rheidol Valley on the lush western slopes of 752m Plynlimon (Welsh Pumlumon), source of the rivers Wye and Severn. At Devil's Bridge the rivers Mynach and Rheidol tumble together in a narrow gorge below the village of Devil's Bridge (Pontarfynach).

Just above the confluence, the Rheidol drops 90m in a series of spectacular waterfalls. The Mynach is spanned by three famous stone bridges, built one on top of the other over the centuries. The lowest and oldest is believed to have been built by the Knights Templar before 1188, the next one up in 1753 and the top one, presently carrying the A4120, in recent times.

Access to the waterfalls and the old bridges is beside the topmost bridge, which is itself 300m downhill from the terminus of the Vale of Rheidol Railway. Unfortunately this access is controlled by the nearby Woodland Caravan Park, who charge a stiff £1 to climb down and look at the bridges (a 10-minute return trip) and a further £2 to walk out to the waterfalls (half-an-hour there and back). The terrain is too steep to permit any sort of do-it-yourself access, and you can't see much unless you pay up.

Places to Stay & Eat The nonsmoking *Mount Pleasant Guest House* (☎ 890219, fax 890239), 200m uphill from the railway terminus, charges £29/42 per excellent en-suite single/double, with continental breakfast (£4 extra for a cooked breakfast).

Right beside the bridge itself is the *Hafod Arms Hotel* (☎ 890232), a former shooting lodge where B&B costs £35/56. Across the bridge and about 300 metres farther is the year-round *Woodlands Caravan Park* (☎ 890233), where two people can pitch a tent for £7.50.

Getting There & Away The Vale of Rheidol Railway (see under Aberystwyth earlier) is the most delightful way to reach Devil's Bridge. The postbus (No 596) also runs to Devil's Bridge (30 to 40 minutes) twice daily except Sunday.

A fine alternative is a bicycle: the lovely A4120 roller-coasters along the southern rim of the Vale of Rheidol for 12 miles to Devil's Bridge (with striking views of the Rheidol Windfarm across the valley). See Getting Around in the Aberystwyth section for details of bike hire companies.

Strata Florida Abbey

On an isolated, peaceful site south-east of Aberystwyth are the eloquently simple ruins of a 12th-century Cistercian abbey. The Cistercians were a monastic order with roots in late-11th-century France, and the community at Strata Florida (Ystrad Fflur or 'Valley of the Flowers') was founded in 1164 by a Norman lord named Robert FitzStephen.

But after Welsh resurgence in the south-west, the independent, self-sufficient Cistercians won the support of the Welsh princes. Their abbeys also became a focus for literary activity and influence. The present site was established under Lord Rhys ap Gruffydd, and a number of princes of Deheubarth, as well as the great 14th-century poet Dafydd ap Gwilym, are buried here.

Little remains except for wall foundations and one shapely portal. In a small roofed area are the foundations of three chapels with surviving polychrome floor tiles, probably 14th-century, in a wide variety of styles. The hill to the south-east offers a fine view of the whole area.

Strata Florida (☎ 01974-831261), run by Cadw, the Welsh historic monuments agency, opens 10 am to 5 pm daily, Easter to late September; and 10 am to 4 pm in winter. Admission costs £2/1.50 (free in winter). The site is a mile down a farm road from the village of Pontrhydfendigaid on the B4343; the village is 15 miles from Aberystwyth or 9½ miles south of Devil's Bridge. Arriva's bus No 561 (£2.05, 45 minutes) departs at about 9 am from Aberystwyth, returning from Pontrhydfendigaid at about 2.15 and 6.25 pm daily except Sunday.

Tregaron
☎ 01974

The only reasons to visit this unexciting but decidedly Welsh market town are to watch the region's threatened but resurgent red kites (see the boxed text 'Kite Country' in the Facts about Wales chapter) being fed just to the north-west, or to visit the peat-bog habitat of the Cors Caron Nature Reserve just to the north-east.

Tregaron prides itself as the birthplace in 1812 of Henry Richard, the Welsh 'Apostle of Peace' and an early advocate of the League of Nations. His statue is in The Square, just east of the bridge over the River Brennig. At the Rhiannon Gold Centre (☎ 298415) on The Square, you can buy Celtic-motif, designer jewellery made on site.

The Tregaron Kite Centre (☎ 298977), in a converted schoolhouse 300m along the Llandewi Brefi road, is a quaint regional museum and unofficial TIC where you can view a video on Wales' red kites. It opens 10.30 am to 4 pm daily, Easter to September; and noon to 4 pm at weekends, the rest of the year. Admission is free. The kites themselves are fed meat scraps in an unsignposted field 1¼ miles out on the Aberystwyth road (A485) at 3 pm (4 pm in summer) daily (for details on another feeding station, see Rhayader & Around later in the chapter).

Fro Villa (☎ *298817, Doldre*), about 200m from the kite centre, has B&B singles/doubles for £15/28. The primitive *Blaencaron Youth Hostel* is in the middle of nowhere east of Tregaron; a few hundred metres along the Devil's Bridge road, turn east on a track for 2 miles to Glan-yr-Afon Isaf farm (☎ 298441) where the warden, Mrs Jones, lives. The hostel is half a mile farther and opens Easter to September. Beds cost £6.75/4.75.

Arriva bus No 516 (£2.05, 55 minutes) departs Aberystwyth at about 9.15 am, returning from Tregaron at about 2.15 pm, daily except Sunday.

Southern Powys

LLANDOVERY (LLANYMDDYFRI)
☎ 01550 • pop 2000

Poor Llandovery, geographically drawn and quartered – a 'gateway town' to the Brecon Beacons National Park (and with a park information centre), on the Heart of Wales line and temperamentally part of Mid Wales, but officially within Carmarthenshire. About all it has to offer the traveller is its history, especially the story of the Physicians of Myddfai (see the boxed text later). It also makes a fair base for walks in the Tywi Valley.

Orientation & Information
A combined TIC and Brecon Beacons National Park information centre (☎/fax 720693) is on Kings Rd, a block west of the bus stop, or about 600m south-east of the train station. It opens 10 am to 1 pm and 1.45 to 5.30 pm daily (to 4 pm daily plus Sunday afternoons, November to Easter). A small but good bookshop for local lore and Welsh culture, The Bookshop, is on High St, 1½ blocks east of the TIC.

Things to See & Do
Even the TIC admits there isn't much to see. Behind the TIC and beside the River Brans are the sad ruins of a little motte-and-bailey **castle** built in 1116. It took a beating and changed hands repeatedly after that – between the Normans and the Welsh, and between one Welsh prince and another – and was finally left to decay after Owain Glyndŵr had a go at it in 1403.

The town's pride is its restored 1840 **Market Hall**, now a handicrafts centre, a block east of the TIC and across Kings Rd.

Upstairs from the TIC is a pretty good exhibit, complete with soundtrack, on regional history.

Places to Stay & Eat
Several pubs near the centre do B&B for under £20 per person, and the *Castle Hotel* (☎ *720349, Kings Rd*), a few doors west of the TIC, has doubles from £35. *Llwyncelyn Guest House* (☎ *720566, Towy Ave*), ¼-mile

The Physicians of Myddfai

From the Llandovery area comes one of the most enduring legends in a country whose very history begins in legend. About 8 miles south-east of the town in the Black Mountain area – now part of Brecon Beacons National Park – is a tiny lake called Llyn y Fan Fach (Lake of the Little Peak), said to be haunted by fairies. In the mid-13th century a young man grazing his cattle beside the lake sees a woman – the loveliest woman he has ever seen – sitting on the surface of the water, combing her hair.

ASA ANDERSSON

He falls madly in love with her, coaxes her to the shore with some of his bread and begs her to marry him. Her fairy-father agrees, on the condition that if the young man strikes her three times she will return to the fairy world. As dowry she brings a fine herd of magic cows and for years the couple lives happily on a farm near Myddfai (3½ miles south of Llandovery), raising three healthy sons.

Naturally the three-strikes-and-you're-out story ends sadly. After reproving taps on three separate occasions – for making them late to a christening, for weeping at a wedding and for laughing at a funeral – she and her wondrous cattle return forever to her father in the lake.

The grieving sons return often to the lake and one day their mother appears again. To the eldest son, Rhiwallon, she hands a leather bag containing the secrets of the lake's wild plants as medicines, telling him that it is his mission in life to heal the sick.

From this point, legend shades into fact. Historical records confirm that one Rhiwallon, and his sons Cadwgan, Gruffydd and Einion, were well-known physicians in the 13th century, living at Myddfai under the patronage of Rhys Gryg, lord of Dinefwr and son of Lord Rhys ap Gruffydd. The descendants of these men continued to practice medicine long after the defeat of the Welsh princes.

The last of the line known to practice at Myddfai was one Rhys Williams in the 18th century, though others in the family are said to be doctors around Wales even today. The Pant-y-Meddygon or 'Physicians' Valley' on Mynydd Myddfai, where the doctors gathered many of their ingredients, is still rich in bog plants, herbs and lichens.

north-west of the train station, has singles/doubles from £21/36, including breakfast.

The *Coffee House*, two blocks east of the TIC on High St, does light meals and all-day breakfasts.

Getting There & Away

Crossgates Coaches' (☎ 01597-851226) No 299 comes from Brecon (£1.60, 40 minutes) five times daily. First Cymru service No 280/281 comes from Carmarthen (2¾ hours) eight times daily except Sunday. From Swansea, change at Llandeilo. The Beacons Bus (route B4) also serves Llandovery (see Getting There & Around under Brecon Beacons National Park in the Brecon Beacons chapter).

Llandovery is on the Heart of Wales railway line, with at least three daily trains (fewer on Sunday). Links include Llanwrtyd Wells (£1.80 single, 30 minutes), Llandrindod Wells (£4.90, one hour) and Swansea (£7.20, 1½ hours).

LLANWRTYD WELLS (LLANWRTYD)

☎ 01591 • pop 600

Llanwrtyd Wells came out of nowhere as a spa town in the 18th and 19th centuries, when the health benefits of the local ferrous and sulphurous cold springs were 'discovered'. The fad gradually faded and Llanwrtyd's wells have been capped but the place retains its prim, gabled guesthouses and the agreeably somnolent air of a spa town. With all the historical prerequisites for a town – a royal charter, a market, and a mayor and council – it is, according to the *Guinness Book of Records*, the UK's smallest town.

While Llanwrtyd (khlan-**oor**-tid) is not intrinsically riveting, it sits in the middle of some very fine (and largely unsung) walking, cycling and riding country – the Cambrian Mountains to the north-west and the Mynydd Eppynt to the south-east – in what could be regarded as one of the remotest parts of Wales. A few clever citizens have put it back on the map with a huge menu of unorthodox but genuinely popular events (see the boxed text 'Off the Wall in Llanwrtyd' later).

Orientation & Information

The de facto town centre is Y Sgwar (The Square), the five-way intersection by the old bridge on which the A483 crosses the River Irfon. The TIC is here, and nothing else is much more than a stone's throw away.

The switched-on TIC (☎/fax 610666, e tic@celt.ruralwales.org), Irfon Terrace, opens 10 am to 5.30 pm daily, Easter to October; and 10 am to 4 pm Monday to Saturday, the rest of the year. It sells its own walking and cycling leaflets, and can show you a video on the endangered red kite, making a comeback in the Cambrian Mountains (see the boxed text 'Kite Country' in the Facts about Wales chapter). Visit Llanwrtyd online at llanwrtyd-wells.powys.org.uk.

Barclays, opposite the TIC, is the only bank in town but the post office across the bridge acts as an agent for Lloyds TSB. There's a laundrette behind the Neuadd Arms on Y Sgwar.

Activities

The hills around Llanwrtyd are a poorly kept secret among horse riders and mountain-bikers – criss-crossed with fire roads, country lanes, bridlepaths and footpaths, and with distractingly beautiful scenery. And what's good for them is also good for ramblers. See Around Llanwrtyd Wells later for a few ideas.

The Cyclists' Touring Club (CTC; see Activities in the Facts for the Visitor chapter) has been involved with local people in a program of trail-marking. You can hire bikes from the Red Kite Mountain Bike Centre at the Neuadd Arms (see Places to Stay later) for £12 per day. Cycles Irfon (☎ 610710) on Beulah Rd, off the A483 just north of the centre, is a big shop with bike rental (£10/15 per half/full day) and repair, plus sales of gear and clothing. It opens daily except Sunday and Monday.

Pony trekking has been going on here for over 40 years; Llanwrtyd was even a founding centre of the Pony Trekking Society of Wales. Two local riding centres are Ffos Farm (☎ 610371) on Ffos Rd at the northern end of town (which also offers modest, child-friendly B&B); and Maes Gwaelod Riding Centre (☎ 610209).

Places to Stay & Eat

Irfon River Camping & Caravan Park (☎/fax 620310, Upper Chapel Rd, Garth), 6 miles west of Llanwrtyd on the A483, opens Easter to October.

Best value in town seems to be the Australian-owned *Stonecroft Inn* (☎ 610332, fax 610304, e party@stonecroft.co.uk, Dol-y-coed Rd) – a comfortable hostel and a friendly pub with good, imaginative food, a block west of Y Sgwar. Beds cost £12.50 in rooms of all sizes, including doubles, all with shared facilities. There's bike storage, and a kitchen and lounge in each of the two buildings. But plan ahead: it's booked up on most summer weekends.

The *Neuadd Arms Hotel* (pronounced ney-ath; ☎/fax 610236, Y Sgwar) does B&B from £24 per person (£27 en suite). This place is owned by Gordon Green, instigator of most of the oddball events that make Llanwrtyd so interesting in the summer.

Carlton House (☎ 610248, fax 610242, Dol-y-Coed Rd), just off Y Sgwar, is a three-star B&B with four-star rooms at £58 per person (£65 at the weekend and throughout August) and an award-winning chef in its restaurant. The restaurant opens for dinner daily except Sunday.

Overlooking the Irfon Valley, a mile along

MID WALES

Off the Wall in Llanwrtyd

Many of the following events for walkers, riders, cyclists and/or beer drinkers were dreamt up by Gordon Green, owner of the Neuadd Arms. Schedules are subject to revision so contact the TIC or see its monthly *What's On* booklet.

Folk 'n' Ale Weekend
Real Ales plus live folk music in the town's pubs and a Sunday jam session (second weekend in March)

Man vs Horse Marathon
22-mile overland race with a £20,000 prize for any runner who can beat the fastest horse (in 1982, sponsors very nearly had to hand the money over, as the horse won by only four minutes); also a relay team event and a mountain bike endurance race the same day (first Saturday in June)

Morris in the Forest
Forest walk, Morris dancers and a Saturday barn dance (three days in June)

Llanwrtyd Wells Festival Weekend
Fun run, disco, treasure hunt and carnival (first weekend in August)

Mountain Bike Festival
Four days of guided rides, orienteering, night rides, a chainless downhill race and more (four days in early August)

World Bog Snorkelling Championships
This is surely the most 'alternative' of all the alternative events on offer, the weirdest and the most famous (since 1986): competitors equipped with fins and snorkel swim two lengths of a 55m trench dug in a nearby bog, surfacing only twice for navigational purposes (August bank holiday); as if this weren't enough, there's another 'championship' in mid-July in which competitors cycle up and down the bog

Welsh International Four Days Walks
A walking festival with daily short and long walks from the town, plus evening entertainment (mid-September)

Welsh International Cycle Rides
Ditto for cyclists: short and long rides plus evening entertainment (mid-October)

Mid Wales Beer Festival
Taste 80 different Real Ales in the town's pubs and listen to the local Male Voice Choir; also during the festival there's the Real Ale Wobble, off-road cycle races with free beer at checkpoints, and the Real Ale Ramble with free beer for runners (10 days in late November)

ASA ANDERSSON

Dol-y-Coed Rd, is good-value, nonsmoking *Kilsby Country House* (☎ *610281, fax 610873,* e *kilsbybb@aol.com, Kilsby*) with two B&B doubles for £20 per person or £32.50 for two nights.

The TIC keeps a list of other good B&Bs in the area.

Getting There & Away

There are few useful bus services. Roy Brown's Coaches No 57 (20 minutes) runs from Aberystwyth (£4.40, 2¼ hours), Rhay-ader (£3, one hour and five minutes), Llandrindod Wells (£2, 50 minutes) and Builth Wells (£1.70, 30 minutes) on Thursday in July and August, and No 54 runs from Builth Wells on Monday.

The best way to reach Llanwrtyd is on the Heart of Wales railway line, as spa guests did a century ago. There are at least three trains daily (fewer on Sunday); Llandrindod Wells (£2.90) is 25 minutes away, Swansea (£9.30) 1¾ hours. The station is a five-minute walk from the TIC.

AROUND LLANWRTYD WELLS

Forest tracts north-west of town provide an easy introduction to the Cambrian Mountains. In the Irfon Forest – through which Llanwrtyd's own river flows (to join the Wye at Builth Wells) – is the valley of a tributary called the Abergwesyn. It's 5 pretty miles from Llanwrtyd up through the Irfon Valley to a turning by a white farmhouse at Abergwesyn, then down the turning for a mile or so past unsightly pine plantations into the yawning, heather-blanketed Abergwesyn Valley, gorgeous in any weather. A postbus meanders as far as the turning, departing Llanwrtyd at about 9.15 am and returning via the turning at about 4.30 pm, Monday to Saturday.

After 4 or 5 miles the road through the Abergwesyn Valley reaches Llyn Brianne, Wales' newest reservoir, created in 1973 by a dam across the steep gorge of the River Tywi, which rises here in the Tywi Forest. The road roller-coasters along the lake shore, making this a great favourite of bus tours – but it's also a fine place for beautiful, level walking. Just south of the dam is the cave-hideout of Twm Siôn Catti, the 'Welsh Robin Hood' (see the boxed text).

LLANDRINDOD WELLS (LLANDRINDOD)

☎ 01597 • pop 5200

Of the four old Mid-Wales spa towns with names ending in 'Wells', tongue-twisting Llandrindod (khlan-**drin**-dod; meaning Church of the Trinity) has best preserved (or re-created) some of the atmosphere of Victorian and Edwardian times, when this was a fashionable place to take to the waters. With its generous parks and gardens, its wrought iron and red brick, its primary colours and copper-topped turrets, it really looks the part. This is also the county town of Powys.

Roman remains at nearby Castell Collen show that it wasn't the Victorians who first discovered the healthy effects of local springs. In 1749 an entrepreneur named Grosvenor built a hotel (now long-gone) by Llandrindod Lake but development only took off when the Central Wales Railway

Twm Siôn Catti

One of Mid Wales' most colourful legends is in fact largely true. Thomas Jones was born in 1530, the bastard son of a landowner of Tregaron (see Around Aberystwyth earlier in this chapter). According to the favoured version of the story, Jones – living with his mother in near-poverty – turned outlaw at the age of 18 to save the two of them from starvation.

His banditry was a thumping success and soon developed into a Robin-Hood-style crusade to redistribute regional wealth. A master of disguise with a sense of humour, he relied on trickery rather than violence, retreating when necessary to a secret hide-out near the headwaters of the River Twyi. His speciality was sheep and cattle rustling. He was never caught and in later life he bought himself a Royal Pardon and turned over a new leaf, writing poetry (winning a prize at the Llandaff eisteddfod) and stories (including many about his own exploits), marrying the daughter of the high sheriff of Carmarthenshire and even serving as mayor of Brecon.

Welsh kids still grow up with stories about Twm Siôn Catti, most of them unrelated to historical fact.

(now the Heart of Wales Line; see the boxed text later) arrived here in 1865. The most appropriate and appealing way to visit Llandrindod is still by train.

You could spend a slow, pleasant, if rather tame, day here.

Orientation & Information

The town sits on the eastern bank of the River Ithon but hardly seems to notice it. The A483 (as Temple St) and the railway plunge through the town centre. Between the two is the main shopping zone, one-block-long Middleton St. Most regional buses stop on High St by the footbridge to the train station.

There's a TIC (☎ 822600, fax 829164, e llandtic@powys.gov.uk) in the Old Town Hall on Temple St. It opens 9.30 am to 5.30 pm daily, April to October; 9 am to 4.45 pm daily except Sunday, November and

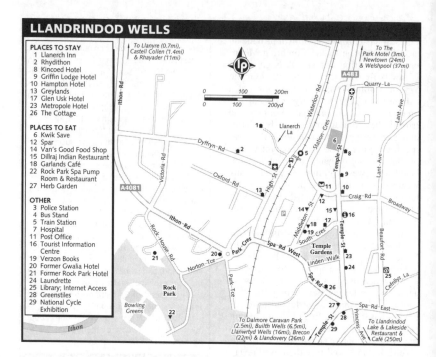

LLANDRINDOD WELLS

PLACES TO STAY
1 Llanerch Inn
2 Rhydithon
8 Kincoed Hotel
9 Griffin Lodge Hotel
10 Hampton Hotel
13 Greylands
17 Glen Usk Hotel
23 Metropole Hotel
26 The Cottage

PLACES TO EAT
6 Kwik Save
12 Spar
14 Van's Good Food Shop
15 Dillraj Indian Restaurant
18 Garlands Café
22 Rock Park Spa Pump Room & Restaurant
27 Herb Garden

OTHER
3 Police Station
4 Bus Stand
5 Train Station
7 Hospital
11 Post Office
16 Tourist Information Centre
19 Verzon Books
20 Former Gwalia Hotel
21 Former Rock Park Hotel
24 Laundrette
25 Library; Internet Access
28 Greenstiles
29 National Cycle Exhibition

December; and on weekdays only, January to March. Its free *Town Guide* has a do-it-yourself walking tour.

All major UK banks (with ATMs) are represented along Middleton St. The post office is on Station Crescent. Free Internet access (one hour maximum) is available at the county library (☎ 826870) on Beaufort Rd but book ahead. The library opens 9.30 am to 5 pm (to 1 pm Wednesday and Saturday, to 7 pm Thursday) daily except Sunday.

The best bookshop in the centre is Verzon Books, on Middleton St.

The Llandrindod Wells Memorial Hospital (☎ 822951) is on Temple St just north of the centre. The police station (☎ 822227) is on High St.

A laundrette on Temple St opens daily.

Rock Park

The old spas have been closed and their buildings converted for other uses. Among the handsome has-beens are the old Rock

Park Hotel and Gwalia Hotel, now county offices.

Though treatment programs are no longer on offer, you can still soothe your nerves beside Arlais Brook, in the serene forested grounds of Rock Park. This is the site of the earliest spa development, though all that remains is the restored Rock Park Spa Pump Room (see Places to Eat later) and a small alternative-medicine consultancy. Fill your bottle at the Chalybeate Spring beside the brook – good for gout, rheumatism, anaemia and more (chalybeate refers to its iron salts).

Llandrindod Lake

Just south-east of the centre is a 6-hectare lake, built at the end of the 19th century to allow Victorians to take their exercise without actually appearing to do so. The original boathouse is now a private residence but you can still rent a boat, fish for carp, look at the ducks and swans, shop for souvenirs, or take lunch at the Lakeside Restaurant & Café (see Places to Eat later). Up the hill is an 18-hole golf course, at 300m one of the highest in the UK.

National Cycle Exhibition

Llandrindod Wells has an original here: a collection of 250 bicycles down through the centuries – including some of the latest – plus re-created Victorian and Edwardian cycle shops and a video history of cycling. It's in the Automobile Palace, a listed Art Nouveau building on Temple St that once housed an auto (and aeroplane!) showroom. The museum (☎ 825531) opens 10 am to 4 pm daily; admission costs £2.50/1.

Castell Collen

Across the River Ithon, about a mile northwest of the town centre at a site called Castell Collen, are the excavated remains of a Roman auxiliary fort and bath-house. It's on private land but is accessible via a public footpath north of Llanyre village (take Ithon Rd across the river and turn right at the village; the footpath begins on the right, half a mile from the village, and the site is about quarter of a mile along the path).

Special Events

Llandrindod Wells gets historical during its Victorian Festival, a week of Victorian dressing-up, street entertainment and high-jinks at the end of August (the last full week before the bank holiday). Just about everybody puts on period costumes, and transport is by horse and carriage. For more information phone ☎ 823441.

The town also hosts a Jazz Weekend (information ☎ 823700) in mid-November, and a popular Drama Festival (☎ 825677) during the first full week of May.

Places to Stay

The closest camping is at *Dalmore Caravan Park* (☎ 822483, Howey), 2½ miles south on the A483, and *The Park Motel* (☎/fax 851201, Crossgates), 3 miles north, both for about £7.50. The Park also has motel rooms for £25; it closes in January and February.

The Heart of Wales Line

The Heart of Wales railway between Swansea and Shrewsbury is one of Wales' most beautiful train journeys, skirting along the Brecon Beacons National Park and crossing the lush, hilly landscape of southern Mid Wales. It's a lifeline to the many towns and villages along its 120-mile length, but in summer, at least, has become as much a tourist attraction as serious transport.

The line was put together by seven different railway companies in the 29 years it took to build it (1839–68). Meant as a link between the factories of north-west England and the booming ports of South Wales, it soon became a Victorian holiday route as well, linking the area's spa towns and accelerating their own growth. Services suffered in the government-led massacre of the rail system in the 1960s; it's a stroke of good fortune that the line wasn't axed completely.

For more information on the line contact the Heart of Wales Line Travellers' Association (HOWLTA, Frankville, Broad St, Llandovery SA20 0AR), a 'user group' dedicated to the line's promotion and improvement. See also the Web site at www.heart-of-wales.co.uk.

The *Hampton Hotel* (☎ 822585, Temple St) is a pub with a vaguely unsavoury look but plain en-suite rooms are just £12.50 per person, including breakfast.

Reliable, central B&Bs with singles/doubles for around £18/34 include *Greylands* (☎ 822253, High St), *Rhydithon* (☎ 822624, Dyffryn Rd) and *The Cottage* (☎/fax 825435, Spa Rd); all have pricier en-suite rooms too. Hotels with B&B from about £16 per person are the good *Griffin Lodge Hotel* (☎ 822432, Temple St), closed in January, and the *Kincoed Hotel* (☎ 822656, Temple St).

The *Llanerch Inn* (☎ 822086, fax 824618, @ llanerchinn@ic24.net, Llanerch Lane), a 16th-century coaching inn (and probably the town's oldest building), has en-suite rooms for £35/55 and first-rate bar food; it's set back half a block from High St.

If you fancy a splurge, one of the old spa hotels will do – eg, the *Glen Usk Hotel*

MID WALES

(☎ 822085, fax 822964, South Crescent) from £28 to £65 per person; or the mammoth *Metropole Hotel (☎ 823700, fax 824848, ⓔ info@metropole.co.uk)*, now a Best Western establishment, from £69/92 (with sauna and indoor swimming pool).

Places to Eat

The best bet among numerous tearooms/cafes is *Garlands Café (☎ 824132, Middleton St)*.

Recommended for both food and atmosphere is a vegetarian restaurant called the *Herb Garden (☎ 824737, Spa Rd)*, with lunches under £4, plus sandwiches and soups; it opens to 5.30 pm in summer and 4 pm in winter, daily except Sunday. Indeed a great many places stay open only until 5 or 6 pm, after which the choice narrows.

The nonsmoking *Rock Park Spa Pump Room & Restaurant (☎ 829267, Rock Park)*, once part of the spa, is still good for a healthy meal, with carefully prepared, good-value lunches for under £5, and an outdoor pavilion in the warm months. It opens daily. Another peaceful spot is the *Lakeside Restaurant & Café (☎ 825679)*, south-east of the centre by Llandrindod lake.

The *Llanerch Inn* (see Places to Stay earlier) has good-value bar food. The *Dillraj Indian Restaurant (☎ 823843, Emporium Bldg, Temple St)* has a big menu of mains from £5 to £7; there's more service than food but it opens every evening.

Van's Good Food Shop (Middleton St) is a wholefood shop and vegetarian deli. Supermarkets include a *Spar* on Station Crescent and a bigger *Kwik Save* on Temple St.

Getting There & Around

Bus connections are pretty limited. Roy Brown's Coaches No 17/47 runs two to three times daily from Brecon (£2.50, one hour), with no Sunday services. Crossgates Coaches' (☎ 851226) bus No 19 runs seven times daily to Rhayder (£1.20, 25 minutes).

Llandrindod Wells (station ☎ 822053) is on the Heart of Wales line, with at least three trains daily (fewer on Sunday). Llanwrtyd Wells (£2.90) is 25 minutes away, Swansea (£11.20) 2½ hours. A day-trip from Swansea to Llandrindod Wells (£12/15 return in summer/winter) is quite feasible; if you set off early (departure about 9 am) you'll have three hours here.

Greenstiles (☎ 824594), in the National Cycle Exhibition building, rents mountain bikes for £8/12 per half/full day.

BUILTH WELLS (LLANFAIR-YM-MUALLT)
☎ 01982 • pop 2000

The tired former spa town of Builth (pronounced bilth) Wells roars to life once a year for Mid Wales' premier event, the Royal Welsh Show. This is a genuine farmers' holiday, and they come from every corner of the country for livestock judging, sheepdog trials, horse jumping, Welsh Guards bands, lumberjack competitions, fishing demonstrations and more.

The venue is the Royal Welsh Showgrounds at Llanelwedd, across the River Wye from Builth. The show runs from Monday to Thursday at the end of July, and accommodation is tight across the entire region. For more information call the Royal Welsh Agricultural Society (☎ 01982-553683).

Cilmeri, 2 miles up the Llandovery road, is where Llewelyn ap Gruffydd, last of the Welsh Princes of Wales, was killed in a chance encounter with a lone English soldier in 1282. The spot is marked with a sad obelisk of Caernarfon granite.

The Builth Wells TIC (☎ 553307, ⓔ builtic@powys.gov.uk) is on the Strand, near the 18th-century arched bridge across the Wye. It opens 9 am to 5 pm daily, Easter to October; and 9 am to 4.45 pm Monday to Saturday, the rest of the year.

If you're determined to stay the night, there's a clutch of B&Bs for a block along Church St, the extension of the Strand westwards from the TIC; *Bron Wye (☎ 553587, 5 Church St)* costs about £18 per person. A pub with tidy rooms (£17; en suite £23) and decent bar food is the *Greyhound Hotel (☎ 553255, Garth Rd)* – take the first left off Church St, for a block. There's also good bar food at the *Llanelwedd Arms (☎ 553292)*, just over the river bridge.

Roy Brown's Coaches (☎ 552597) bus Nos 17/47 and 21 each run two to three times daily from Llandrindod Wells (£1.10, 20 minutes); there are no Sunday services. Crossgates Coaches (☎ 851226) bus No 20 runs three times daily to Rhayader (£1.20, 30 minutes).

Builth Wells is on the Heart of Wales railway line, though the nearest stations are both over 2 miles away: Builth Road station up the Rhayader road (A470), and Cilmeri station up the Llandovery road (A483). A taxi (☎ 553142) from either station costs about £1.50.

RHAYADER (RHAEADR)
☎ 01597 • pop 2000

Rhayader itself is of interest only as a base for visiting the surrounding countryside, and in particular the Elan Valley. It's also the northern terminus of the Wye Valley Walk (see under The Lower Wye Valley in the Brecon Beacons & South-Eastern Wales chapter), a 107-mile walk from Chepstow – about 35 miles of it within Powys.

The town centre – marked by a clock tower – is at the intersection of North St (A470), East St (A44), South St (A470) and West St (B4518). The TIC (☎ 810591, e rhayader@lrc.ruralwales.org), 150m away in the Rhayader Leisure Centre off North St, opens 9.30 am to 5.30 pm daily, April to October; and 10 am to 4.30 pm on weekdays in winter. Buses set you down at the Dark Lane car park opposite the TIC.

Places to Stay & Eat
The *Wyeside Caravan & Camping Park* (☎ 810183, e info@wyesidecamping.co .uk, Llangurig Rd), a third of a mile from the town centre, charges £3 per person in a tent; it closes in January.

Among many B&Bs in town, three good ones near the centre are *Bryncoed* (☎ 811082, Dark Lane) by the TIC, with singles/doubles for £20/32 (£30/44 en suite); *Brynteg* (☎ 810052, East St) at £16/32; and *Liverpool House* (☎ 810706, East St) at £17/30 (en suite). The *Elan Valley Hotel* (☎ 810448, e hotel@elanvalley.demon .co.uk), by itself 2½ miles out on the B4518

in the Elan Valley, has en suites from £32/55 and evening meals by arrangement.

Several *pubs* at the centre have adequate food, and the little *Strand Restaurant* (☎ 810564, East St) has grills for under £5, plus salads, sandwiches, pasties and pastries.

The Red Kite Feeding Station (see the following section) also has camping and B&B.

Getting There & Around
Crossgates Coaches (☎ 851226) buses include the No 19 from Llandrindod Wells (£1.20, 25 minutes, seven daily) and the No 20 from Builth Wells (£1.20, 30 minutes, three daily). There are no Sunday services.

You can hire an off-road bike for £8/12 per half/full day from Clive Powell Mountain Bikes (☎ 810585) on East St, open April to October. They also organise guided rides and cycling holidays.

AROUND RHAYADER
Red Kite Feeding Station
The dramatic Mid Wales resurgence in the UK's threatened population of red kites (see the boxed text 'Kite Country' in the Facts about Wales chapter) makes great environmental news. But these handsome raptors have not quite re-established themselves, and feeding programs are still an unfortunate necessity.

Red kites are fed at the Gigrin Farm Red Kite Feeding Station (☎ 01597-810243, e kites@gigrin.co.uk), at a working farm on the A470 half a mile south of Rhayader town centre (or 1 mile from the Wye Valley Walk). At 2 pm GMT (ie, 3 pm during summer daylight saving time) meat scraps (from local butchers and a local abattoir) are spread on a field. Up to 60 kites may partake, though usually less than 20 at a time. First come crows, then ravens, then the acrobatically swooping kites – often grabbing meat in their talons and eating it in flight – and later ravens and buzzards. You can watch from a wheelchair-accessible hide just 50m away.

An interpretive centre, with information on red kites and other local wildlife, and a user-controlled remote camera overlooking the feeding site, opens 10 am to 5 pm daily. There are also marked nature trails around the property. Admission to the site costs £2.50/1. See the Web site at www.gigrin .co.uk.

The farm also has camping (£6 for a big tent) and two B&B rooms (£20/35 per single/double).

Elan Valley

In the early years of the 20th century three dams were built on the River Elan (pronounced ellen), west of Rhayader, mainly to provide a reliable water supply for the city of Birmingham. In 1952 a fourth, large dam was inaugurated on the tributary River Claerwen. Together their reservoirs now provide over 70 million gallons of water a day for Birmingham and parts of South and Mid Wales.

Though not a project likely to win the hearts of the Welsh, the need to protect the 70 sq mile watershed, called the Elan Valley Estate, has turned it and adjacent areas into an important wildlife conservation area. The dams and associated projects also produce some 4.2MW of hydroelectric power.

Just downstream of the lowest dam, 3 miles from Rhayader on the B4518, is Welsh Water's Elan Valley Visitor Centre (☎ 01597-810898). It opens 10 am to 5 pm daily, March to October, with an exhibit on the water scheme, wildlife and local history, information on frequent guided walks and birdwatching trips, and leaflets on the estate's 80 miles of footpaths and nature trails.

The Elan Valley Trail is a traffic-free walking, riding and cycling path that mostly follows the line of the long-gone Birmingham Corporation Railway for 8 miles alongside the River Elan and its reservoirs, starting just west of Rhayader at Cwmdauddwr. At the top of the lowest reservoir, Caban Coch, you can digress via a causeway to the big Caerwen dam.

You can also drive up on the adjacent road. A postbus comes along here once each weekday on a loop from Rhayader and Llandrindod Wells.

KNIGHTON (TREF-Y-CLAWDD)
☎ 01547 • pop 3000

Literally a stone's throw from England, Knighton's importance rests solely on its association with two of the UK's national trails: it's the headquarters for the Offa's Dyke Path, and lies at the midpoint of the path and at one of two junctions of this and Glyndŵr's Way. Offa's Dyke itself runs through the middle of town.

Knighton itself is rather pretty but hardly worth a diversion. Don't confuse it with the English town of Kington, 12 miles to the south – though it's certainly no more Welsh.

Orientation & Information

The town is centred on a handsome, 1872 stone clock tower on the main thoroughfare, Broad St. The train station is actually in England, five blocks to the north-east via Station Rd. Buses stop by the clock tower.

The Offa's Dyke Centre and TIC (☎ 528753, fax 529242, ⓔ oda@offasdyke .demon.co.uk), three blocks up West St from the tower, opens 9 am to 5.30 pm daily, Easter to October; and 9 am to 5 pm weekdays, the rest of the year. Here you can find out anything you want to know about the Offa's Dyke Path (for more on the path see Walking under Activities in the Facts for the Visitor chapter).

There are branches of Barclays and HSBC banks near the tower. The post office is in the Star's shop opposite the tower.

Things to See & Do

From the clock tower you may stroll for a few minutes up the steep, picturesque and traffic-free lane called The Narrows. Across Broad St and two blocks down Church St is St Edward's Church, with an unusual, rather stumpy 18th-century belltower, though there's little to note inside.

Knighton's livestock market on Station Rd comes alive every Thursday (and sometimes Friday).

Places to Stay & Eat

Three places within a block of the clock tower are *Offa's Dyke House* (☎ 528634, 4 High St) with B&B for £16 per person; *The*

Fleece House (☎ 520169, Market St) at the top of The Narrows, at £20 to £34; and the *Knighton Hotel (☎ 520530, Broad St)*, where rooms start at £45 per person.

Decent bar meals are available at the *Red Lion (☎ 528231, West St)* opposite the clock tower, and the *George & Dragon (☎ 528532, Broad St)*.

Getting There & Away
Knighton is a stop on the Heart of Wales Line, with at least three trains daily (fewer on Sunday). Llandrindod Wells (£3.30 single) is 40 minutes away, Shrewsbury (£4.70) 25 minutes.

It would be hard to get here by coach from anywhere worthwhile in Wales. The only useful regional service is from Ludlow (England) on Whittle Coaches (☎ 01562-820002) No 738/740 (£2, one hour, five daily except Sunday).

Getting Around
The nearest places to rent bikes are Wheely Wonderful (☎ 01568-770755), Petchfield Farm, Elton (5 miles west of Ludlow), where off-road bikes go for £3/12 per hour/day; and Offa's Bikes (☎ 01544-230534), Church House, Church Rd, Kington, at £8/15 per half/full day.

Northern Powys

MACHYNLLETH
☎ 01654 • pop 2000
This rugged, conspicuously upbeat town is best known as a counter-cultural magnet and centre for green living, thanks to the steadily growing fame of the Centre for Alternative Technology (CAT), north of town (see Around Machynlleth later). But Machynlleth (ma-**khun**-khleth) also has a place in the Welsh collective memory, for it was here that the rebel-hero Owain Glyndŵr set up his first parliament in 1404. This is also the home of the first-ever research and exhibition facility devoted to Celtic culture.

It's not your typical Welsh country town. Among the stoic slate homes typical of this former slate-mining region are a number of idiosyncratic 19th-century buildings and a few newer ones dressed up in startling primary colours. There's an important modern-art museum here and several galleries.

Edward I gave Machynlleth its charter as a market town in 1291 but it was Glyndŵr's parliament that put it on the historical map. The town was comfortably endowed by the marquises of Londonderry, who prospered from coal mines in County Durham, married into a lead-mining fortune and made the town their permanent home from the late 19th century until around 1920.

The charm is periodically shattered as RAF jets scream over, almost at treetop height, though local people hardly seem to notice.

Orientation & Information
From the train station it's a 600m walk down Doll and Penrallt Sts to the centre of town, at the Castlereagh Clock Tower (erected by the townspeople to celebrate the coming of age of Charles Stewart, the future sixth marquis, in 1873). Buses set you down at the clock tower.

The town's TIC (☎ 702401, fax 703675, e mactic@mail.powys.gov.uk), Maengwyn St, opens 10 am to 6 pm daily, Easter to September; and 9.30 am to 5 pm daily, the rest of the year.

There are three banks within a few steps of the clock tower, and a post office in the Spar supermarket on Maengwyn St. Internet access is free at the county library (☎ 702322), open 10 am to 1 pm and 2 to 5 pm (to 7 pm Monday and Friday, to 1 pm Saturday) daily except Thursday; and £4 per hour at Cyber Space (☎ 703953), 6 Penrallt St, open daily except Sunday.

Maps and books on local lore are on sale at the TIC, Celtica (see the following section) and the small Machynlleth Book Shop on Maengwyn St. Nigels Launderette is around the corner from the Spar. It opens daily.

Owain Glyndŵr Centre
Beside the TIC, in a rare example of a late-medieval Welsh townhouse, is the Owain

Glyndŵr Centre (☎ 702827), with displays on life in medieval Wales and on the fight for Welsh independence. It opens 10 am to 5 pm, Easter to September. Admission is free. This building was probably built somewhat later than Glyndŵr's parliament but is believed to closely resemble the actual venue, now long-gone.

Celtica

Despite the Celts' defining role in European culture and history, the first 'museum' devoted solely to them was opened only in 1995, at Y Plas, former home of the marquises of Londonderry, just south of the town centre.

Celtica, run by Powys county council, blurs the line between education and entertainment. There are conventional exhibits on Celtic traditions around Europe (including changing ones on specific cultures outside Wales), and a computer research room called the Historium – all free of charge.

The main attraction is an extraordinary, computer-driven, walk-through multimedia show, full of coloured lights and smoke, sound and computer images – theatrical but evocative, giving a sense of daily life as it might have been for the Celts of Wales. Viewers wear headsets with a choice of language options, plus a kids' version for the spooky bits. The show takes just over an hour; admission costs £4.95/3.80.

Special facilities are available for the disabled. There are also indoor and outdoor children's play areas, a book and souvenir shop and a good restaurant. Celtica (☎ 702702) opens 10 am to 6 pm daily (last admission is at 4.40 pm). See the Web site at www.celtica.wales.com.

MOMA for Wales

On Penrallt St is the town's only neoclassical building, a former Methodist chapel (1880), restored and now part of a visual and performing arts centre called The Tabernacle, which subtitles itself the Museum of Modern Art for Wales (MOMA; ☎ 703355). There's a year-round schedule of shows by Welsh artists, both established and up-and-coming, and there's also a small permanent

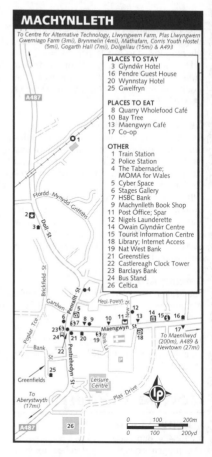

MACHYNLLETH

To Centre for Alternative Technology, Llwyngwern Farm, Plas Llwyngwern Gwerniago Farm (3mi), Brynmelin (4mi), Mathafarn, Corris Youth Hostel (5mi), Gogarth Hall (7mi), Dolgellau (15mi) & A493

PLACES TO STAY
3 Glyndŵr Hotel
16 Pendre Guest House
20 Wynnstay Hotel
25 Gwelfryn

PLACES TO EAT
8 Quarry Wholefood Café
10 Bay Tree
13 Maengwyn Café
17 Co-op

OTHER
1 Train Station
2 Police Station
4 The Tabernacle;
    MOMA for Wales
5 Cyber Space
6 Stages Gallery
7 HSBC Bank
9 Machynlleth Book Shop
11 Post Office; Spar
12 Nigels Launderette
14 Owain Glyndŵr Centre
15 Tourist Information Centre
18 Library; Internet Access
19 Nat West Bank
21 Greenstiles
22 Castlereagh Clock Tower
23 Barclays Bank
24 Bus Stand
26 Celtica

collection. Many of the works are for sale. The gallery opens 10 am to 4 pm daily except Sunday. Admission is free. See the Web site at www.tabernac.dircon.co.uk.

There are also several small private galleries in the town centre.

Special Events

The Gŵyl Machynlleth (Machynlleth Festival) takes place during the third week of August at The Tabernacle (see the preceding section), with music ranging from recitals for kids to serious jazz performances, plus a lively Fringe Festival.

MID WALES

Places to Stay

Nearby camp sites include tents-only *Gwerniago Farm* (☎ *791227, Pennal*), 3 miles west on the A493, which costs £5 for two people; *Llwyngwern Farm* (☎ *702492, Corris*), 3 miles north on the A487 by the CAT, charging £6.50/8.50 for a tent/caravan; and *Brynmelin* (☎ *01650-511501, Llanwrin*), 4 miles north on the A487, at £4 per tent or caravan.

The pioneering, energy-efficient *Corris Youth Hostel* (☎ *761686, Old School, Corris*), 5 miles north of Machynlleth, opens daily from mid-March to October; and at weekends most of the rest of the year. The nightly charge is £9.25/6.50 for adults/under-18s.

Pleasant B&Bs in town, with rooms for £18 to £20 per person, include *Maenllwyd* (☎ *702928, Newtown Rd*), where vegetarian breakfast is available; *Pendre Guest House* (☎ *702088, Maengwyn St*), with some en-suite rooms; and *Gwelfryn* (☎ *702532, 6 Greenfields*). The owner of *Stages Gallery* (☎ *703168 or 703001, 7 Penrallt St*) has one twin room near the centre, fine value at £15 per person B&B.

The *Glyndŵr Hotel* (☎ *703989, 14 Doll St*) offers basic B&B from £16 per person. The *Wynnstay Hotel* (☎ *702941, fax 703884, Maengwyn St*) is an old coaching inn with en-suite singles/doubles from £45/70, plus short-break discounts.

Two good farmhouse B&Bs, with rooms from £20 per person, are *Mathafarn* (☎ *01650-511226, Llanwrin*), 5 miles north; and *Gogarth Hall* (☎ *791235, Pennal*), 7 miles to the west. *Plas Llwyngwern* (☎ *703970, Pantperthog*), 250m from the CAT, charges £17.50 per person.

Places to Eat

There's plenty to choose from during the day. CAT-run *Quarry Wholefood Café* (☎ *702624, Maengwyn St*) has delicious, down-to-earth vegetarian lunch specials, using mostly organic ingredients, from about £4.50. *Maengwyn Café* (☎ *702126, 57 Maengwyn St*) uses local produce, including Welsh lamb, in specials from £4. The *Bay Tree* (☎ *703679, 39 Maengwyn St*)

is a prim tearoom with sandwiches and light lunches. Celtica also has a good *tearoom* (☎ *702702*).

In the evening there's little but takeaways, pub food or the excellent but rather pricey bar food (£6 and upwards per dish) at the *Wynnstay Hotel* (see Places to Stay earlier).

Supermarkets include a *Spar* and *Co-op* on Maengwyn St. The town's Wednesday *farmers market* in Maengwyn St has been going on for over seven centuries.

Getting There & Away

The bus stand is on Pentrebedyn St near the junction with Maengwyn St. Bus services of Arriva Cymru include the No 32/514 from Aberystwyth (£2.90, 40 minutes) and from Dolgellau (£2.45, 30 minutes) every two hours (twice on Sunday); and the daily TrawsCambria service No 701 from Cardiff (£14.50, 5¼ hours) and from Bangor (£9.10, 2½ hours).

Machynlleth is on the Cambrian main line across Mid Wales, with services from Aberystwyth (£4 single, 30 minutes), Shrewsbury in England (£10.90, 1¼ hours) and Birmingham in England (£12.10, 2¼ hours), about every two hours. From here the Cambrian Coaster also runs up the coast via Harlech Castle to Pwllheli (£6.50, two hours) six times daily (three Sunday).

Getting Around

Mountain bikes can be hired from Greenstiles (☎ *703543*) on Maengwyn St for £12 (50% off for visitors to the CAT) from Easter to October.

AROUND MACHYNLLETH
Centre for Alternative Technology

If 'environmentally friendly' makes you yawn, you're in for a few surprises. How about a wind-powered telephone box, a cable car that runs on gravity, or a recycling toilet?

Since its founding in 1974, the Centre for Alternative Technology (CAT) has gone from strength to strength as a laboratory and information source for ecologically sound technologies and lifestyles – and manages to be interesting and child-friendly too. There are over 50 exhibits, including working displays of wind, water and solar power; low-energy buildings; a smallholding with live animals; and an underground display on the world of soil (complete with giant plastic mole). There's a high-tech information centre, a theatre made of straw bales, a shop (including the CAT's own huge selection of publications and learning resources) and a good vegetarian restaurant. The complex runs mainly on wind, water and solar power, and generates almost no waste.

From the car park you ride 60m up to the site on a funicular railway powered by gravity (its two carriages are connected by a cable over a winding-drum; water fills a tank beneath the upper one until it's heavier than the other, and they gently swap places).

The centre (☎ 01654-702400, fax 702782, ⓔ info@cat.org.uk) is 3 miles north of Machynlleth on the A487, on 16 hectares of a disused slate quarry, with about 3 hectares open to the public. It opens 10 am to 5 pm daily (to 4 pm November to March) except at Christmas and for two weeks in January; the funicular is closed in winter. Admission costs £7 for adults, £5 for students and seniors, and £3.60 for children (£5/4/2.60 in winter); there are also good-value family tickets. These costs form a big share of the centre's funding. Arrive by bike and get a 50% discount; or show your bus or train ticket and get 10% off. Check out CAT's Web site at www.cat.org.uk for a virtual tour.

The centre is run as a workers' cooperative. If you're interested in joining in, you can stay for a week or two at just £4 per day plus the sweat of your brow, for bed and board. Those with a more serious interest can book a no-cost 'trial week' in a particular department of the centre, with the aim of staying as a long-term volunteer (six months or more). CAT also runs residential courses on subjects ranging from birdwatching to waterless toilets, as well as family holidays, with basic accommodation and meals provided.

Direct bus services include Arriva's No 30/32/34 (£1.25, 7 minutes, once or twice hourly) from Machynlleth, and No 32 (£2.05, 27 minutes, every two hours) from Dolgellau, Monday to Saturday.

NEWTOWN (Y DRENEWYDD)
☎ 01686 • pop 13,000

This low-key former mill town is more famous for its past than its present, and its past is all about commerce and industry. Most importantly to the greatest number of people, it was the birthplace (in 1771) of Robert Owen – factory reformer, founder of the cooperative movement, 'father of Socialism' – though he left at the age of 10 and only returned just before his death in 1858.

This was once the home of Welsh flannel, and a major UK textile centre. When competition began driving wages down, Wales' first Chartist meeting was held here in October 1838. Pryce Jones, the world's first-ever mail-order firm, got its start here, on the back of the textile trade. Newtown is even – almost – the home of Laura Ashley (she opened her first shop at her home in Carno, 10 miles to the west). There are several little museums devoted to these memories, and even one on the WHSmith retail chain.

There you have it. Only pilgrims and history buffs need go out of their way.

Orientation & Information

Newtown sits in a bend of the River Severn (Afon Hafren), alongside the Welshpool-Aberystwyth road. The town centre is The Cross, at the intersection of Broad, High, Severn and Shortbridge Sts. The TIC is on Back Lane, a block west of Broad St, and the bus station is right behind it. From the train station it's a 600m walk via Old Kerry Rd, Shortbridge St and The Cross, to the TIC.

The TIC (☎ 625580, fax 610065, ⓔ newtic@powys.gov.uk) opens 9.30 am to 5.30 pm Monday to Saturday (daily from June to August; to 5 pm November to March). All major UK banks are represented on The Cross or Broad St.

Puffing Billy on the Welshpool & Llanfair Railway

The curative waters of Llandrindod Wells

The awe-inspiring Afon Mawddach estuary, an RSPB nature reserve, is a twitcher's treat.

EOIN CLARKE

GRANT DIXON

BRYN THOMAS

PETER HINES

EOIN CLARKE

Go go go! To reach Snowdon's peak, struggle up on foot or chug up on the narrow-gauge railway. A word of warning though: rescue by RAF helicopter isn't the most economical way back down.

Things to See & Do

Newtown's days as the 'Leeds of Wales' are recalled at its **Textile Museum** (☎ 622024) in a former weavers' workshop on Commercial St, just north across the river. Displays include old handlooms, re-created shopfronts and flannel and wool samples. It opens 2 to 5 pm Tuesday to Saturday, May to September.

Back on the southern side of the river, at the end of Church St, are the remains of the Church of St Mary, where Robert Owen is buried. The tiny **Robert Owen Museum** (☎ 626345), on the ground floor of the town-council building at The Cross, has a 25-minute video on Owen but will otherwise be of interest mainly to history students. It should be open 9.30 am to noon and 2 to 3.30 pm weekdays and 9.30 am to 11.30 am Saturday, but being volunteer-run it sometimes isn't. Admission is free.

The brick-and-timber WHSmith newsagent and stationery shop at 24 High St looks much as it did when it opened in 1927. Upstairs is a little company **museum** (☎ 626280), open during normal business hours. There is a **Pryce Jones Museum** (☎ 626911) too, at Station Yard near the train station, but at the time of writing it was closed to the public, and its future was in doubt.

A mound in the riverside park south-west of the TIC is all that remains of Newtown's 13th-century motte-and-bailey **castle**. The *gorsedd* circle of stones in the park was erected when the National Eisteddfod was held here in 1965.

Places to Stay & Eat

Charming *Plas Canol Guest House* (☎ 625598, 32 New Rd), set back from the road about 250m west of the train station, has B&B from £18 per person. There are other B&Bs in the area between here and the town centre. At the *Elephant & Castle Hotel* (☎ 626271, Broad St), plain singles/doubles cost £39/58 (£25/50 at the weekend).

Nonsmoking *Yesterdays* (☎ 622644, fax 625992, Severn Square), a block east of The Cross, offers a few good-value en-suite rooms upstairs for £28/39. It also serves

'traditional English food' (roasts, steak-and-kidney pie, fried fish) for around £6 at lunch. It closes for Sunday dinner and Monday lunch.

Popular *Evans Cafe* (☎ 626203, Broad St), at the corner with Turners Lane, has simple but freshly made snacks and lunches. It opens daily except Sunday.

Getting There & Away

Arriva Cymru's regional routes, with negligible Sunday services, include No G8A from Llandrindod Wells (£2.10 single, one hour, three daily), No 522 from Machynlleth (£2.80, one hour, five daily) and No D75 from Shrewsbury (£2.80, 1½ hours, every two hours). National Express' daily coach No 420 stops en route between Shrewsbury (£4.50, 55 minutes) and Aberystwyth (£7.50, one hour 20 minutes).

Newtown is on the Cambrian main line, with trains every hour or two from Machynlleth (£4.40 single, 35 minutes), Aberystwyth (£6.70, one hour 10 minutes) and Shrewsbury (£5.20, 40 minutes).

AROUND NEWTOWN
Gregynog Hall

This splendid, 19th-century, imitation-timber-framed mansion was from 1924 the home of the Davies sisters, Gwendoline and Margaret, best known for the extraordinary collection of impressionist and postimpressionist paintings they bequeathed to the National Museum & Gallery (see the Cardiff & Around chapter) in 1952 and 1963. Their grandfather was David Davies, a sawyer who turned to mining and who, when prevented by the Bute family from exporting his coal from Cardiff, built his own docks at Barry and made a pile.

The sisters intended to make the house a centre for the arts in Wales, founding a fine-arts press and during the 1930s holding an annual Festival of Music and Poetry. In 1960 the estate was given to the University of Wales (Aberystwyth), which now uses it as a residential conference and education centre. The successor to the sisters' festival is the week-long Gregynog Music Festival (☎ 650224) held here in mid-June, with a

MID WALES

program of operatic, choral, orchestral and instrumental music.

The 300-hectare grounds, including an immense golden yew hedge, are open year round. Admission is free. The house only opens for group tours by appointment. It's 5 miles north of Newtown on the B4389, near the village of Tregynon.

WELSHPOOL (TRALLWNG)
☎ 01938 • pop 8000

This Severn Valley town was originally called Pool – after the 'pills' or boggy, marshy ground along the river where it was founded (these have long since been drained). The town was chartered in 1263 as Pool or Poole but this was changed in 1835 to Welch Poole or Welshpool, possibly to distinguish it from Poole in Dorset.

The only real reasons to stop here are to explore Powis Castle and its gardens and to ride the narrow-gauge railway or tootle along the Montgomery Canal.

Orientation & Information
The centre of Welshpool is a four-way intersection called The Cross. From Raven Square train station it's a 700m slog east down Raven St (and its extensions, Mount, Broad and High Sts) to The Cross, then left at Church St and right at the Spar supermarket for 200m to the TIC, in the Vicarage Gardens car park. Regional buses stop on High St, about 400m from the TIC. National Express coaches stop by the TIC.

Welshpool's TIC (☎ 552043, fax 554038, e weltic@powys.gov.uk) opens 9.30 am to 5 pm daily. From The Cross, the police station (☎ 552345) is 300m east on Severn St, and the Victoria Memorial Hospital (☎ 553133) is 400m north on Church St and its extension, Salop Rd.

Powis Castle
South of town, just under a mile from The Cross, is a huge, unexpectedly red-brick castle, originally built by Gruffydd ap Gwenwynwyn, prince of Powys, and subsequently enriched by generations of the Herbert and Clive families. Inside is one of Wales' finest collections of furniture and paintings, and a cache of jade, ivory, armour, textiles and other treasures brought back from India by Baron Clive (British conqueror of Bengal at the Battle of Plassey in 1757).

The spectacular terraced gardens, overhung with enormous clipped yew hedges and concealing statues, an aviary and an orangery, are among the finest in Wales, and at least as great an attraction as the castle – so there's no need to be disappointed if you find the latter closed.

The castle and museum (☎ 557018), run by the National Trust (NT), open 1 to 5 pm, and the gardens 11 am to 6 pm, daily except Monday and Tuesday, Easter to October, plus Tuesday in July and August. Admission costs £7.50/3.75 (£5/2.50 for the gardens only).

Welshpool & Llanfair Light Railway
This narrow-gauge railway was completed in 1902 to help people bring their sheep and cattle to market. The line was closed in 1956 but reopened four years later by enthusiastic volunteers.

Trains make the 8-mile journey from Raven Square Station to Llanfair Caereinion (50 minutes each way, with a 55-minute stop), on a complex timetable that includes weekends from Easter to October plus *most* weekdays from June to August, with departures *usually* at 11.30 am and 2.30 pm (for details ring ☎ 810441 or visit the Web site at www.wllr.org.uk). The return fare is £8.30 per adult, plus £1 for the first child per adult and £4.15 for each additional child.

Montgomery Canal
The Montgomery Canal originally ran for 35 miles from Newtown to Frankton Junction in Shropshire, where it joined the Llangollen Canal. After part of its banks burst in 1936, it lay abandoned until a group of volunteers and the British Waterways Board began repairing it in 1969.

From the Severn St wharf, 200m east of The Cross, Montgomery Canal Cruises (☎ 553271, e montycanal@aol.com) will take you on a 1½-hour narrow boat trip at 1 or 3 pm daily, Easter to October (also at 11 am, June to August). Trips cost £3.50/2.50. The

Heulwen Trust is a charity which provides free weekday canal trips for disabled people and even has a specially adapted narrow boat for the purpose; for details call ☎ 552563.

Other Things to See

Beside the canal wharf is the little **Powysland Museum** (☎ 554656) featuring the archaeology and social history of Montgomeryshire County. It opens 11 am to 1 pm and 2 to 5 pm (from 10 am at weekends) daily except Wednesday, Saturday morning and Sunday from October to April. Admission costs £1.

There are several attractive 16th-century **timber-framed houses** along High St near the bus stand, including the Talbot Inn and Mermaid Inn.

Every Monday, east across the canal from the TIC, there's a **sheep market** which dates back to the granting of the town's charter in 1263.

Special Events

On the third Sunday in July, Welshpool hosts a one-day Country & Western Music Festival complete with spit roast, food stalls and line dancing, at the county showground near Powis Castle, about half a mile from The Cross. Admission costs £4 for adults, £3 for seniors and £1 for those aged under 16. Proceeds benefit the Heulwen Trust (see Montgomery Canal in this section). Accommodation is tight but camping is allowed at the showgrounds for £4 per tent or caravan per night. For more information ring ☎ 552563.

Places to Stay & Eat

Montgomery House (☎ 552693) and *Hafren* (☎ 554112), two neighbouring B&Bs on upper Church St (about 300m from the TIC), have comfortable rooms for around £20 per person.

The Corn Store (☎ 554614, 4 Church St) is a cafe-bar and restaurant open for lunch

and dinner from Tuesday to Saturday, with variants on the usual standards – eg, turkey and mushroom lasagne – for £7 to £10, and a big dessert menu. The *Royal Oak Hotel & Restaurant* (☎ 552217, 7 The Cross) has mains for £10 and up. *The Mermaid* (☎ 552027, 28 High St) does pretty good pub meals.

There's a *Spar* supermarket within sight of the TIC and a *Somerfield* on Berriew St just south of The Cross.

Getting There & Away

Arriva Cymru's bus No D75 comes from Shrewsbury (£2.50, 50 minutes) and Newtown (£2.50, 45 minutes) about every two hours Monday to Saturday. National Express coach No 420 stops daily en route from London, Birmingham and Shrewsbury to Aberystwyth (£9.50, 1¾ hours).

Welshpool is on the Cambrian railway line from Shrewsbury (£4.40 single, 30 minutes), Machynlleth (£6 cheap day single, 55 minutes) and Aberystwyth (£7.70, 1½ hours), with services about every two hours (fewer on Sunday).

AROUND WELSHPOOL
Andrew Logan Museum of Sculpture

Andrew Logan is one of Britain's top modern sculptors and perhaps the only artist ever to have successfully opened a museum dedicated to his own work, which he calls the 'art of popular poetry and metropolitan glamour'. This exuberant, slightly camp collection is definitely worth a visit, just for the fun of it.

The museum (☎ 01686-640689) is 5 miles south at Berriew and opens noon to 6 pm on bank-holiday weekends in April and May, Wednesday to Sunday from June to August and noon to 4 pm at weekends in September and October. Admission costs £2/1. Take the Newtown-bound No D75 bus (£1.25, 14 minutes).

Asked to say something about Wales, the average non-Brit is apt to mention either the coal valleys of the south-east or, more likely, Mt Snowdon. Because it boasts the UK's finest mountain landscapes outside Scotland, the north-west is perhaps the best-known part of Wales. It may be no coincidence that the north-west is also the most traditionally minded and heavily Welsh-speaking corner (modern Gwynedd is something like 70% Welsh-speaking).

Old Gwynedd was a stronghold of the Welsh princes, and Snowdonia – the Snowdon highlands – sheltered Llywelyn ap Gruffydd in the 13th century and Owain Glyndŵr in the 15th during their struggles against the English. Edward I clamped a ring of iron around the mountains but there was no sweeping the Welsh out of them. And with such a formidable mountain shield, it's little wonder that the Llŷn has held with even greater confidence to old Welsh ways.

That doesn't mean English speakers are unwelcome, only that Welsh speakers are proud of themselves. The welcome is as warm as anywhere in the country, and there's more to see than just mountains – Edward's formidable castles at Harlech and Caernarfon, part of a joint UNESCO World Heritage Site with those at Beaumaris and Conwy (see the Anglesey & North Coast chapter); the evocative remains of Snowdon's own industrial heritage at Blaenau Ffestiniog; Wales' finest seaside railway journey (the Cambrian Coast line) and finest narrow-gauge railways; one of its loveliest estuaries, the Mawddach; and a grand and user-friendly national park.

Getting Around

The region's biggest bus operator is Arriva Cymru (Aberystwyth ☎ 01970-624472), while most of the services in Snowdonia National Park are by a consortium of local outfits called the Snowdon Sherpa. Railway travel is more important here than in many parts of the country, thanks to the Cambrian

- Rising with the sun and having lunch on the summit of Mt Snowdon
- Picnicking on the hill of the red dragon and then panning for gold at Sygun Copper Mine
- Daring to cycle the Red Bull Run at Coed y Brenin, near Dolgellau
- Riding some of Wales' biggest rapids on the River Treweryn, near Bala
- Communing with 20,000 saints on Bardsey Island

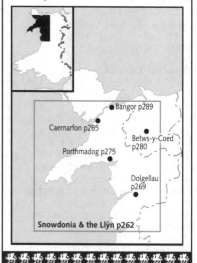

Bangor p289

Caernarfon p285

Betws-y-Coed p280

Porthmadog p275

Dolgellau p269

Snowdonia & the Llŷn p262

Coast line in the south, the Conwy Valley line in the north and the Ffestiniog narrow-gauge railway between them.

Arriva has one-day (£5/3.50 per adult/ child), three-day (£10/7) and five-day (£15/ 10) passes, good for unlimited travel on all its services, and Express Motors has its own one-day Gwynedd Rover (£4.80/2.40) – buy on board. The Freedom of North & Mid Wales Flexi-Rover pass (£28) is good for any three in seven days of bus and train travel (see the introduction to the Getting Around chapter for details). The best collection of transport information is the *Gwynedd Public Transport Maps & Timetables*, published by Gwynedd Council and available on request from Tourist Information Centres (TICs).

Snowdonia

SNOWDONIA NATIONAL PARK (PARC CENEDLAETHOL ERYRI)

There's hardly a place in Wales you could call flat – the land rises and falls almost wherever you go. And yet the first sight of the knot of peaks around Mt Snowdon – at 1085m the tallest mountain in Wales and England – is breathtaking from any direction, rising so abruptly and majestically from the landscape that they seem to have been imported from somewhere else.

Snowdonia National Park was founded in 1951 (Wales' first national park), not so much to call attention to these mountains as to keep them from being loved to death. This is Wales' best-known and most heavily used national park, and the busiest part of the park is, naturally, around Snowdon. Half a million people climb, walk or take the train to the summit each year, and all those sturdy shoes make trail maintenance and repair a frantic job for park staff. It was here that members of the first successful ascent of Mt Everest trained, and this has been the proving ground for Britain's best mountaineers ever since.

The park's coverage is admirably wide – at 827 sq miles it's the UK's second-largest national park after the Lake District in England – though there are omissions so blatant as to seem almost spiteful, most conspicuously a great hole around the old slateworks at Blaenau Ffestiniog. The notion that Wales' industrial landscapes are as much a part of its heritage as its castles didn't seem to cross anyone's mind in 1951.

The Welsh name for Snowdonia, the Snowdon highlands, is Eryri (pronounced eh-**ruh**-ree). The Welsh call Snowdon itself Yr Wyddfa (pronounced uhr-**with**-vuh), meaning Great Tomb – according to legend a giant called Rita Gawr was slain here by King Arthur, and is buried at the summit (see the Myths & Legends special section for more on this).

However, there's more to Snowdonia than mountain peaks. The park embraces innumerable tumbling rivers, a dozen sizeable lakes and reservoirs (one of them, Llyn Celyn, now an enduring symbol of English colonialism; see Around Bala later in the chapter), and landscapes from moorland to gorgeous sprawling estuaries to castled coastline.

Like Wales' other national parks, this one is very lived-in, with a human population of about 27,500 and sizeable towns at Dolgellau, Bala, Harlech, Aberdovey and Betws-y-Coed. Two-thirds of the park is privately owned, with over three-quarters in use for raising sheep and beef cattle. While the most popular reason for visiting the park is to walk, you can also go climbing, white-water rafting, pony trekking, even windsurfing. There are more National Nature Reserves here than in any other UK national park. There are Stone Age burial chambers (eg at Dyffryn Ardudwy near Barmouth and Capel Garmon near Betws-y-Coed), Bronze Age burial cairns (eg at Talsarnau north of Harlech), Roman forts (eg Segontium at Caernarfon) and of course several splendid castles. Many of the region's old slate quarries and gold and copper mines have been reinvented as visitor attractions, along with the narrow-gauge railways – including the famous Ffestiniog Railway – that once served them.

The park is the only home to two endangered species, an arctic/alpine plant called the Snowdon lily *(Lloydia seotina)* and the rainbow-coloured Snowdon beetle *(Chrysolina cerealis)*. The gwyniad is a species of whitefish found only in Llyn Tegid (Bala Lake), which also has what is probably the UK's only colony of glutinous snails *(Myxas glutinosa)*.

Orientation & Information

Although the focus is on Snowdon, the park – some 35 miles east to west and over 50 miles north to south – extends all the way from Aberdovey to Conwy. There are well-stocked

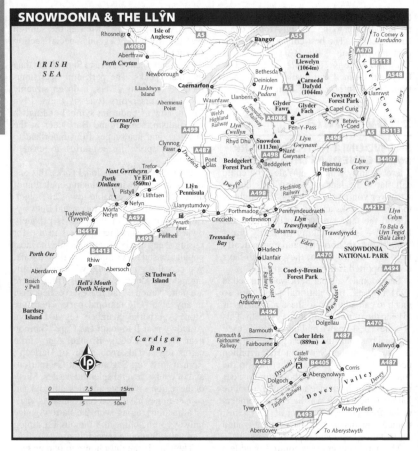

SNOWDONIA & THE LLŶN

park information centres, combined with local TICs, at Betws-y-Coed and Dolgellau (open year round), Aberdovey, Blaenau Ffestiniog and Harlech (summer only). TICs in other towns, including Llanberis (open year round, though not daily in winter), Barmouth and Tywyn (summer only) – as well as Machynlleth in Mid Wales – also have park maps and information. The park's head office (☎ 01766-770274, fax 771211, ℮ info@eryri-npa.gov.uk) is at Penrhyndeudraeth, east of Porthmadog – though it's not a public enquiries office. At your first TIC or park office, pick up a copy of *Eryri/*

Snowdonia, the park's free annual visitor newspaper, which includes information on getting around the park, as well as on park-organised walks and other activities. See also the Web site at www.eryri-npa.gov.uk.

The park maintains its own 24-hour weather service at ☎ 0891-500449 (premium rate). Most TICs also display weather forecasts, as do several outdoor gear shops in the area.

Walking Routes

Mt Snowdon is the main destination for walkers (see the boxed text 'Scaling Snowdon' later), and Llanberis the favoured base. Also popular are the Carneddau – 1044m Carnedd Dafydd and 1064m Carnedd Llewelyn – to the north-east. Above Dolgellau, Cader (or Cadair) Idris rises to 889m. But these peaks get the park's heaviest traffic, so unless you like crowds you might consider alternatives. There are also gentler walks in the forests and hills around Betws-y-Coed, and the later town sections have details of additional trails.

Park information centres and some TICs stock useful brochures (40p) on each of the six main routes up Snowdon (see the boxed text 'Scaling Snowdon' later), and Dolgellau and a few other offices have a similar set on the three main routes up Cader Idris. TICs also have numerous independent publications on these and other walking routes in the park. Staff at Llanberis TIC include some keen local walkers who can offer advice on routes and maps.

Be prepared to deal with hostile conditions at any time of the year; sudden low cloud and mist are common, even on days that start out clear and sunny. Never leave without food, drink, warm clothing and waterproofs, whatever the weather. Carry, and know how to read, the appropriate large-scale OS map for the area, and consider carrying a compass. Call for weather information before setting out; see the preceding Orientation & Information section for the park's own 24-hour weather number. Unless you have the appropriate skills and equipment, most high-level routes are not recommended in the winter as they may be partly covered by snow or ice. Be aware that even some walks described as easy may follow paths that go near very steep slopes and over loose scree; take the Pyg Track up Snowdon, for example, and you'll find yourself scrambling up parts of it.

Inevitably, with so many people on the mountains, accidents happen – usually on the way down. Every year an average of 70 serious incidents occur up here, and about 10 people die. If you're in any doubt about your abilities, the national park organises a variety of two- to four-hour guided walks at various levels of difficulty; ask at TICs or check the *Eryri/Snowdonia* newspaper. Charges are usually £2.50/50p (but free if you get there

on the Snowdon Sherpa bus and show your ticket).

Among dozens of private outfits offering guided or self-guided Snowdonia walks and walking holidays, often with luggage transport, are the following:

High Trek (☎ 01286-871232, fax 870576, e high.trek@virgin.net) Tal-y-Waen, Deiniolen, Gwynedd LL55 3NA
Web site: www.hightrek.co.uk

Plas Y Brenin National Mountain Centre (☎ 01690-720214, fax 720394, e info@pyb .co.uk) Capel Curig, Gwynedd LL24 0ET – offers residential courses (two to five days) in hillwalking, climbing and mountain navigation
Web site: www.pyb.co.uk

Snowdonia Adventures (☎ 01286-871179) Heights Hotel, Llanberis LL55 4HB
Web site: www.heightshotel.co.uk

Turnstone Tours (☎/fax 01286-677059, e info@turnstone-tours.co.uk) Waterloo Port, Caernarfon, Gwynedd LL55 1LP
Web site: www.turnstone-tours.co.uk

Many of the YHA hostels in the area also offer activity courses.

Cycling Routes

There are good routes through Coed Y Brenin Forest Park (☎ 01341-422289) near Dolgellau, Gwydyr Forest Park (Llanrwst ☎ 01492-640578) near Betws-y-Coed, and Beddgelert Forest Park (same telephone number).

The best of them are at Coed Y Brenin; see Around Dolgellau later. Check out the Web site at www.bikeworld.uk.com for additional local cyclists' information.

Lôn Las Cymru, the Welsh National Cycle Route (Sustrans route No 8), runs from Dolgellau, via Porthmadog and Criccieth, to Caernarfon and Bangor. Much of it coincides with two county-built, dedicated walking and cycle paths on either side of Caernarfon (see Activities under Caernarfon later in the chapter). The North Wales Coastal Route (Sustrans route No 5), which in Snowdonia will link Bangor and Conwy, is in the planning stages.

The heavy use of bridleways for off-road cycling to the summit of Snowdon has led to erosion and fears for walkers' safety. A ban is now in place and cycling is not allowed

Scaling Snowdon

Despite the fact that half a million people tramp up Snowdon every year, it's still an amazing hike to the top. Views are stupendous on a clear day, with the peak's fine ridges dropping away in great swoops to sheltered *cwms* (valleys) and deep lakes. Even on a gloomy day you could find yourself above the clouds, which may occasionally part to give glimpses of the world below. Try to avoid going on a midsummer weekend or you may end up agreeing with Prince Charles who, on seeing the crowds, the litter and the summit cafe, declared it the 'highest slum in Europe'.

There are six main routes to the top. Easiest – and least interesting – is the Llanberis Path, southwards from Llanberis along the Snowdon Mountain Railway line (five hours up and back). Almost as easy, shortest of all and safest in winter, is the Snowdon Ranger Path, northwards from the Snowdon Ranger Youth Hostel near Beddgelert (five hours).

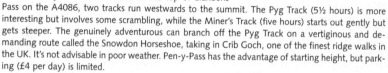

ASA ANDERSSON

From Pen-y-Pass Youth Hostel at the top of Llanberis Pass on the A4086, two tracks run westwards to the summit. The Pyg Track (5½ hours) is more interesting but involves some scrambling, while the Miner's Track (five hours) starts out gently but gets steeper. The genuinely adventurous can branch off the Pyg Track on a vertiginous and demanding route called the Snowdon Horseshoe, taking in Crib Goch, one of the finest ridge walks in the UK. It's not advisable in poor weather. Pen-y-Pass has the advantage of starting height, but parking (£4 per day) is limited.

The undemanding Rhyd Ddu Path, the least-used route, runs eastwards from the A4085 Caernarfon–Beddgelert road (five hours). The most challenging route, with an ascent of over 1000m, is the Watkin Path, northwards from Nant Gwynant, 3 miles north-east of Beddgelert on the A498 (seven hours) – though trailhead parking is plentiful.

You could combine the Miner's Track and the Pyg Track for a high-elevation loop, or any other two for a day-long traverse; for some fine variants see the Snowdonia chapter of Lonely Planet's *Walking in Britain*. The Snowdon Sherpa bus (see Getting Around in this section) stops regularly at trailheads for all of these walks, and there are options for basic accommodation near each trailhead. If you feel like cheating, the Snowdon Mountain Railway will take you right to the summit (see under Llanberis later in the chapter).

---

from 10 am to 5 pm daily, June to September. Traffic on A-roads in summer can make cycling hazardous, so stick to B- or unclassified roads.

Beics Eryri (☎ 01286-676637) at 44 Tyddyn Llwydyn, Hendre, Caernarfon, runs weekend and longer breaks around Snowdon, the Llŷn and Anglesey. See the Web site at www.beicseryri.clara.net. Snowdonia Mountain Biking (☎ 01248-353789) at Eryl Môr Hotel, 2 Upper Garth Rd, Bangor, does guided tours and baggage transfer in the Snowdon area.

Canoeing & Whitewater Rafting

Canolfan Tryweryn, the National Whitewater Centre (☎ 01678-521083, fax 521158, e welsh.canoeing@virgin.net), near Bala, runs safety courses and rafting trips on a stretch of the River Tryweryn. For details see under Bala later in the chapter.

Pony Trekking & Horse Riding

Snowdonia Riding Stables (☎ 01286-650342), at Waunfawr near Caernarfon, offers escorted rides for £12/45 per hour/day; the Snowdon Sherpa bus stops nearby. Meifod Isaf Riding

& Trekking Centre (☎ 01341-247651) in Dyffryn Ardudwy, north of Barmouth, opens Easter to October (closed Saturday in July and August) and offers rides from £9 for one hour to £17 for an afternoon.

Narrow-Gauge Railway Journeys
One of the attractions of this area is the large number of narrow-gauge railways, many of them originally built to haul slate out of the mountains. The scenic Ffestiniog Railway runs from Porthmadog up to Blaenau Ffestiniog (see Porthmadog later in the chapter); the rack-and-pinion Snowdon Mountain Railway from Llanberis to the summit of Snowdon (see Llanberis); and the Talyllyn Railway from Tywyn inland to Abergynolwyn, on the southern side of Cader Idris (see Tywyn). Shorter lines include the Llanberis Lake Railway (Llanberis), the Fairbourne & Barmouth Railway (Barmouth), the Bala Lake Railway (Bala) and the Welsh Highland Railway (Caernarfon).

Places To Stay & Eat
There are over a dozen YHA/HI hostels, including some of the UK's best, at or near Bala, Bangor, Beddgelert, Capel Curig, Dolgellau, Harlech and Llanberis. These, plus good independent hostel accommodation at Caernarfon, Llanberis and Porthmadog, are noted in local listings. With the permission of the farmer or landowner it's possible to camp almost anywhere in the park, though not on National Trust (NT) land. TICs have lists of camp sites with full facilities.

Betws-y-Coed is the town within the park with the most B&Bs and guesthouses.

Getting There & Around
Mainline railways into the park region are the Cambrian Coast Line from Machynlleth up the coast to Porthmadog and Pwllheli, and the Conwy Valley Line south from Conwy to Betws-y-Coed – linked together by the Ffestiniog Railway.

Regional bus connections are adequate (except on Sunday) between major towns. With the help of the narrow-gauge railways (especially the Ffestiniog, Welsh Highland and Talyllyn) and the Snowdon Sherpa spe-

cial bus service (see the following section), you can get to Snowdonia's remotest hostels and most popular trailheads.

Snowdon Sherpa A park-run association of local companies whose dedicated, blue-liveried buses run on a network of routes around the park, Snowdon Sherpa makes it easier for people to leave their cars outside the park. Routes include the park towns of Beddgelert, Betws-y-Coed, Capel Curig and Llanberis, and a new interchange at Pen-y-Pass (under construction at the time of writing); and the surrounding towns of Bethesda, Caernarfon, Llandudno, Llanrwst, Porthmadog and Pwllheli. Buses run on fixed schedules, every hour or two (less often on Sunday) and typically from about May to September, but varying between routes; timetables are available from TICs (or call ☎ 01286-870880 for information). Buses will stop on request at any safe place within the park. A £2/1 Snowdon Ranger ticket lets you use the whole network all day. Routes include:

Bws Ffestiniog (Porthmadog, Beddgelert, Caernarfon)
No 65 (Bangor, Bethesda, Capel Curig, Betws-y-Coed, Llanrwst)
No 95/95A (Llanberis, Beddgelert, Pen-y-Pass, Caernarfon)
No 96 (Llanberis, Pen-y-Pass, Capel Curig, Betws-y-Coed, Llandudno)
No 97 Snowdon Link (Porthmadog, Beddgelert, Pen-y-Pass, Betws-y-Coed)

TYWYN & AROUND
☎ 01654
The seaside town of Tywyn is known best – and probably only – for the narrow-gauge Talyllyn Railway, which runs inland to the village of Abergynolwyn on the southern flanks of Cader Idris. Note that this is one way to reach the Llanfihangel y Pennant route up Cader Idris (see the boxed text 'Climbing Cader Idris' under Dolgellau later in the chapter).

Orientation & Information
The A493 Dolgellau–Machynlleth road passes through town as High St. Buses stop beside the Cambrian Coast mainline station. From here the summer-only TIC (☎ 710070) is

about 200m in the Dolgellau direction, and the Talyllyn Railway terminal is 300m in the Machynlleth direction (south).

Talyllyn Railway & Abergynolwyn

The Talyllyn Railway was opened in 1865 to carry slate from the Bryn Eglwys quarries near Abergynolwyn. In 1950 the line was saved from closure by the world's first railway preservation society. It now runs for 7¼ scenic, steam-powered miles up the Fathew Valley to Abergynolwyn. There are five stations along the way, each with way-marked walking trails (and waterfalls at Dolgoch and Nant Gwernol); leaflets on these are available at the stations.

About 3 miles from Abergynolwyn are the scattered remains of Castell y Bere, begun by Llywelyn ab Iorwerth (Llewelyn the Great) in 1221 and later seized by the Normans – though what little is left is quite over-shadowed by the mountainous backdrop of the Dysynni Valley. Some 300m down the road is the 12th-century St Michael's church; note the window through which local lepers, in less salubrious times, were allowed to observe the sacraments.

The railway (☎ 710472, fax 711755, e enquiries@talyllyn.co.uk) runs more or less daily, Easter to October, with as many as 10 departures in August, but it's wise to call ahead. A £9 Day Rover ticket lets you get on and off all day; children with/without an adult pay £2/4.50. See the Web site at www.talyllyn.co.uk. At the lower terminus is a museum with half a dozen shiny narrow-gauge steam locomotives. It opens 9.30 am to 5 pm daily, Easter to October. Admission costs £50p/20p.

Special Events

Every year in mid-August, the Tywyn Rotary Club sponsors a 'Race the Train' footrace up the valley, plus a 6-mile race, a fun run and lots of entertainment. For information call ☎ 711976.

Places to Stay

Opposite the TIC is the *Greenfield Hotel* (☎ *710354, High St)* where singles/doubles start at £17/32.

Getting There & Away

Arriva's No 28 bus comes from Dolgellau (55 minutes) nine times each weekday (fewer at weekends). From Machynlleth the No 29 comes up the coast (35 minutes) about as often, while the No 30 runs less often via Abergynolwyn (45 minutes).

The Cambrian Coaster train comes from Machynlleth (30 minutes) every two hours or so.

BARMOUTH (Y BERMO)

☎ 01341 • pop 2500

The modest fishing port of Barmouth clings to a headland at the mouth of the immense Mawddach Estuary. In the 19th century the railway gave it a second persona as a seaside resort, complete with funfair and promenade, and boarding houses in a row along Marine Parade, behind a vast clean beach – and everything under surveillance by the large and very English St John's Church on the hill.

It remains an enjoyable place to stop – for the pleasure of being bitten by the salty wind, for views out to the sea and back across the estuary to a tableau of Snowdon's peaks, and for breezy trips by ferry or fishing boat. Behind the town rises Dinas Oleu (pronounced **dee**-nas **oh**-lay), the 'Welsh Gibraltar', the first property ever bequeathed to the NT (in 1895) and an irresistible temptation for walkers. Barmouth Bridge, Wales' only surviving wooden rail viaduct, spans the estuary, complete with a pedestrian walkway that brings it all within reach.

Orientation & Information

Buses stop on Jubilee Rd, right across Beach Rd from the train station. From the train station it's a block up Station Rd past the police station to the summer-only TIC (☎ 280787, e barmouth.tic@gwynedd.gov.uk) where you can buy leaflets on local walks. The main commercial area is High St and its southern extension, Church St.

Walking Routes

From below you'd never know there was an 'Old Barmouth', but scramble up any one of several alleys running uphill off Church St and you'll find the town gets more and more vertical, with better and better views, and old houses nearly on top of one another.

Carry on up to a network of trails all across 265m Dinas Oleu. Bear eastwards around the headland – on one of these paths or from the far end of Church St – to the popular Panorama Walk with the best of the estuary views. Alternatively, follow Church St right out onto the Barmouth Bridge and cross the estuary on its pedestrian walkway which joins up with the Mawddach Trail (see under Mawddach Valley Nature Reserve in the Around Dolgellau section later).

Fairbourne

From April to September ferries run regularly across the estuary to another sandy beach, at Penrhyn Point (£2/1.50 return). From there you can ride Wales' only seaside narrow-gauge railway, the Fairbourne & Barmouth (☎ 250362), south along the coast for 2½ miles to Fairbourne. This line was built in 1895 for moving materials for the construction of Fairbourne village. The return fare is £5.50/3.80. There's a restaurant at Penrhyn Point, and a cafe and a take-it-or-leave-it mini-zoo at Fairbourne station. Admission to the zoo is free. See also the Web site at www.fairbourne-railway.co.uk.

Quayside

Another bit of old Barmouth is down around the quay. Here is where the ferry departs for Penrhyn Point and where you can book a deep-sea or pleasure cruise, eg with Cambrian Coastal Cruisers (☎ 281398). The little round house is Ty Crwn, apparently once a gaol where unruly sailors could be chilled until morning.

Special Events

The international Three Peaks Yacht Race (☎ 280298) held in late June has been an annual event for almost a quarter-century. Contestants sail to Caernarfon where two crew members run to the summit of Snowdon; then to Whitehaven in England and a run up Scafell Pike; and finally to Fort William in Scotland, with another run up Ben Nevis – 390 nautical miles of sailing and 75 miles of

fell running. The record so far is an astonishing two days and nine hours.

More local but equally novel and demanding is the 20-mile Mawddach Wool Race (☎ 281565) held in mid-July, in which teams carry a barrel of ale upriver to Penmaenpool and overland to Dolgellau, and return by the same route with a bale of wool.

During the first three weekends in August the Barmouth Harbour Festival features bands, street theatre, music, fireworks and more.

Places to Stay

Modest B&Bs line Marine Parade, across the tracks from the train station; rooms at the *Wavecrest Hotel* (☎ *280330, 8 Marine Parade*) cost from £18 to £27 per person. At *The Gables* (☎ *280553, Mynach Rd*), a friendly place with sea views, half a mile north of the town centre, B&B starts at £18 per person. On the A496, 2 miles north of town, *Llwyndu Farmhouse* (☎ *280144*) is a 16th-century house with a garden overlooking the sea, a restaurant and B&B for £30 to £35 per person. Over at Fairbourne, the *Fairbourne Hotel* (☎ *250203*), a few hundred metres from the narrow-gauge station, offers B&B from £25 per person.

Places to Eat

The *Inglenook Restaurant* (☎ *280807, Harbour Lane*), in a 17th-century building off Church St, offers good seafood main courses for under £8. *The Bistro* (☎ *281009, Church St*) is a cosy place with an international choice of evening meals from £7 to £10 and good vegetarian meals from £6. The *Indian Clipper* (☎ *280252, Church St*) offers sitdown meals from £6 and a big menu of vegetarian dishes from £5; bring your own (BYO) wine.

Self-caterers can shop at the *Co-op* supermarket by the train station.

Getting There & Away

Barmouth is the western terminus of Arriva's No 94 inter-regional service from Wrexham via Llangollen, Bala (£2.75, one hour) and Dolgellau (£1.80, 20 minutes), running seven times daily (two on Sunday).

No 38 runs from Blaenau Ffestiniog (£1.95, one hour five minutes) at least four times daily from Monday to Saturday.

Barmouth is on the Cambrian Coast railway line, with trains from Machynlleth (£6.40 single, 55 minutes) and Porthmadog (£4.90, 45 minutes) every two or three hours (fewer at weekends).

DOLGELLAU
☎ 01341 • pop 3500

For some visitors, Dolgellau (pronounced doll-**geth**-lye) is the ideally situated, if somewhat dour, base for a climb up 889m Cader Idris or for an exploration of the lovely Mawddach Estuary. For others this handsome, slate-grey market town is itself reason enough for a visit – no other town in Wales has such a concentration of listed buildings (over 200). It's thought the Welsh hero Owain Glyndŵr met with fellow rebels here, though the most likely venue (on Bridge St) was replaced with an ironmongery at least a century ago.

The Dolgellau area has historical links with the Society of Friends or Quaker movement. After George Fox – the most influential exponent of the Friends' philosophy of direct communication with God, free of creeds, rites and clergy – made a visit in 1657, a Quaker community was founded here. Converts ran the gamut from simple farmers to local gentry. They were persecuted with vigour because their refusal to swear oaths – in particular to the king – was considered treasonous. Many eventually emigrated to William Penn's Quaker community in America.

Dolgellau was the main town and market centre for the old county of Meirionnydd (Merionethshire), and in the late 18th and early 19th centuries was a regional centre for the prosperous Welsh woollen industry. Many of the town's finest buildings, sturdy and unornamented, were built at that time, and the town centre hasn't changed all that much since then. Local mills failed to keep pace with mass mechanisation, however, and decline set in after about 1800.

The region bounced back when the Romantic Revival of the late 18th century made

Wales' wild landscapes popular with genteel travellers. Indeed Dolgellau can claim to have been a tourist centre longer than most towns in Wales.

Orientation & Information

Dolgellau sits at the confluence of the River Wnion (a tributary of the Mawddach) and the smaller River Arran. The Wnion and the A470 both pass just north of the town centre, both spanned by the Bont Fawr (Big Bridge; 1638).

Buses stop on Eldon Square, the heart of the town. The combined TIC and National Park Information Centre (☎ 422888, fax 422576, e ticdolgellau@hotmail.com), also on Eldon Square, opens 10 am to 6 pm daily, Easter to September; and 10 am to 5 pm daily except Wednesday and Thursday, the rest of the year. Upstairs is a permanent exhibition (free admission) on the region's Quaker heritage; this office also offers themed walks around various Quaker sites in the summer (see the park's *Eryri/Snowdonia* newspaper). UK banks here are HSBC on Eldon Square, Barclays on Lion St just off Queen's Square and NatWest on Bridge St. If you find the TIC closed, a small bookshop on Eldon Square, Siop Y Dydd, has maps and some local information. The post office is in the Spar supermarket on Smithfield St. There's also a laundrette on Smithfield St.

Walking Routes

If you're interested in Dolgellau's architectural heritage then pick up the good *Dolgellau Town Trail* map-brochure (75p) from the TIC. Also for sale is *Local Walks Around Dolgellau* (£3.95), describing 15 local trails of varying difficulty.

The beautiful Mawddach Trail is a flat (and in places wheelchair-accessible) path through woods and past wetlands on the southern side of the Mawddach Estuary. It begins at the reserve's information centre, 2 miles west of Dolgellau (see under Mawddach Valley Nature Reserve in the Around Dolgellau section later), though you can also get there on a 2-mile walk starting from Industrial Rd. The TIC also stocks three leaflets (40p each) on the main paths up

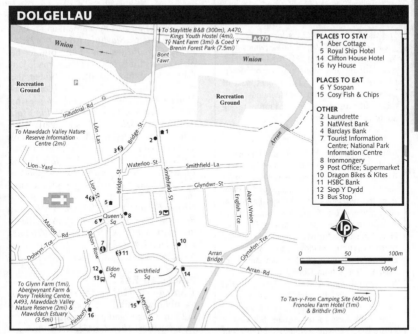

DOLGELLAU

PLACES TO STAY
1 Aber Cottage
5 Royal Ship Hotel
14 Clifton House Hotel
16 Ivy House

PLACES TO EAT
6 Y Sospan
15 Cosy Fish & Chips

OTHER
2 Laundrette
3 NatWest Bank
4 Barclays Bank
7 Tourist Information Centre; National Park Information Centre
8 Ironmongery
9 Post Office; Supermarket
10 Dragon Bikes & Kites
11 HSBC Bank
12 Siop Y Dydd
13 Bus Stop

Cader Idris (see the boxed text 'Climbing Cader Idris'). Sudden storms are not usually a problem on Cader Idris but sudden low cloud and mist definitely are, even if it's clear when you set out – so pack for the cold and the wet, and check the weather before you set off (the national park's weather service is on ☎ 0891-500449).

Pony Trekking

Abergwynant Farm & Pony Trekking Centre (☎ 422377) beside the Mawddach Estuary, 3½ miles south-west of Dolgellau on the A493, offers hourly treks through forests and around the foot of Cader Idris from £10. You can also fish for trout and salmon in the River Gwynant there, for £2 a day.

Special Events

Sesiwn Fawr Dolgellau (☎/fax 423355, ✉ myfyr@sesiwnfawr.demon.co.uk) is one of Wales' best free festivals, a three-day jamboree of Welsh folk music and beer in the streets of Dolgellau on the third weekend in July. For more information check out the Web site at www.sesiwnfawr.demon.co.uk.

Places to Stay

Local legend says anyone who spends the night on top of Cader Idris will awake either mad or a poet (see the special section 'Myths & Legends' for more along these lines). If you're looking for something a little more conventional, there's a wide choice.

The nearest camping is at *Tan-y-Fron* (☎ 422638), a third of a mile east on Arran Rd, charging £10 for two people; they also have B&B for £22 per person. Two camp/caravan sites at Brithdir, 3 miles east of Dolgellau off the A470, are *Llwyn yr Helm* (☎ 450254) and *Dolgamedd* (☎ 422624); both have hot showers and charge about £6 for a tent plus two people. All these sites are open April to October.

The *Kings Youth Hostel* (☎ 422392) is in a country house west of Dolgellau (get off

Climbing Cader Idris

The standard way up Cader Idris is the 'Dolgellau' or Ty Nant Path, south-eastwards from Ty Nant Farm on the A493. The farm (which has camping and bunkhouse accommodation; see Places to Stay) is 3 miles west of Dolgellau, just beyond Penmaenpool. It's a rocky but safe, straightforward route, taking about five hours there and back.

The easiest but longest route (5 miles each way, six hours return) is the 'Tywyn' or Llanfihangel y Pennant Path, a gentle pony track that heads north-east from the hamlet of Llanfihangel y Pennant, joining the Ty Nant Path at the latter's midpoint. Llanfihangel is 1½ miles from the terminus of the Talyllyn Railway at Abergynolwyn (see Tywyn & Around earlier).

Shortest (3 miles up) but steepest (an 870m elevation gain) is the Minffordd Path, running north-west from Dol Idris car park, a few hundred metres down the B4405 from Minffordd, itself 6½ miles from Dolgellau on the A487 Machynlleth road. This route, taking around five hours there and back, requires the most caution, especially on the way back down.

None of these routes requires the kind of effort that Snowdon would, though stout shoes are still essential. You could combine two for a traverse, making use of regional buses: Arriva's Machynlleth–Dolgellau No 32/514 stops at Minffordd five times daily (once on Sunday); the Dolgellau-Tywyn No 28 stops at Penmaen nine times each weekday (fewer at weekends), and also connects at Tywyn with the No 30 or the Talyllyn Railway to Abergynolwyn.

---

the No 28 Tywyn bus at Abergwynant, 1½ miles west of Penmaenpool, from where it's a mile walk south). It opens Easter to August only; nightly charges are £9.25/6.50. There's a camping barn and tearoom at *Ty Nant Farm* (☎ 423433, *Ffordd y Gader*), 3 miles west of Dolgellau; beds are £4 (bring your own pad and sleeping bag) and cookers and utensils are available.

The best B&B value in Dolgellau is cheerful *Aber Cottage* (☎ 422460, e *gmullin1@ compuserve.com, Smithfield St*), just south

of the bridge, with snug rooms for £20 per person, and a first-rate tearoom and restaurant downstairs. *Staylittle B&B* (☎ 422355, *Pen-y-Cefn Rd*), north of the bridge, has plain rooms for £16.50 and home-made jams for breakfast; turn left after the bridge, then right and climb for 250m. The *Clifton House Hotel* (☎ 422554, *Smithfield Square*) has doubles from £36. The *Royal Ship Hotel* (☎ 422209, *Bridge St*) is an early-19th-century coaching inn with very comfortable singles/doubles for £25/40 (£35/60 en suite) B&B. *Ivy House* (☎ 422535, *fax 422689, Finsbury Square*) charges £25/37 (£33/49 en suite) and has a good dining room and basement bar. Remoter B&B options include *Glynn Farm* (☎ 422286, *Old Fairbourne Rd*), a mile west of town overlooking the estuary, from £15 per person; and *Fronoleu Farm Hotel* (☎ 422361, *Tabor*), a farmhouse restaurant a mile east, at £27.

Places to Eat

Y Sospan (☎ 423174, *Queen's Square*), in the old town hall, is a lunchtime cafe offering sandwiches and jacket potatoes.

A meal at *Aber Cottage* (see Places to Stay earlier) is like sitting down in your auntie's living room, and the food is super – imaginative lunch specials, freshly-prepared with local ingredients, are great value at £5. It opens daily except Sunday, with pricier evening meals on Monday, Wednesday and Friday.

The dining room at *Ivy House* (see Places to Stay earlier) opens to non-residents during the summer. There aren't many other options after 5 pm, though cheerful *Cosy Fish & Chips* in Meyrick St usually opens late. There's a *Spar* supermarket on Smithfield St.

Getting There & Around

Arriva Cymru bus services include No 2 from Caernarfon (£4.35 single, 1½ hours, four to six daily); No 94 from Barmouth (£1.80, 20 minutes, seven Mon-Sat and two on Sunday), continuing to Bala (£1.85, 35 minutes), Llangollen and Wrexham; and No 32/514 from Aberystwyth (£4.30, one hour 20 minutes) and Machynlleth (£2.45, 30 minutes) every two hours (twice on Sunday).

Bus No 35 runs to/from Blaenau Ffestiniog (£2, 45 minutes, four daily) Monday to Saturday. Dolgellau is also a stop on the long-distance TrawsCambria (No 701) service.

You can hire a bike for £12 a day from Dragon Bikes & Kites (☎ 423008) on Smithfield St.

AROUND DOLGELLAU
Mawddach Valley Nature Reserve

This Royal Society for the Protection of Birds (RSPB) nature reserve is set in oak woodlands along the northern side of the Mawddach Estuary. Permanent residents include ravens and buzzards, and among spring visitors are redstarts, wood warblers and pied flycatchers. There is a 2½-mile trail, and a wheelchair-accessible ½ -mile trail. You can also take a superb 7½ mile walk west along the estuary and across the Barmouth railway bridge to Barmouth. The reserve, 2 miles west of Dolgellau on the A493 (bus No 28), opens year round; admission is free. An information centre (☎ 01341-422071) by the Penmaenpool toll bridge opens 11 am to 5 pm daily during Easter week and late May to August.

Coed Y Brenin Forest Park

This woodland park north of Dolgellau is laced with 25 miles of cycle trails, the best in Wales and among the UK's finest, all purpose-built with the help of the Forest Enterprise Wales (see Flora & Fauna in the Facts about Wales chapter). There are beginner and family routes as well, and this is also a venue for regular rallies. The Forest Park Centre (☎ 01341-422289) is 7½ miles north of Dolgellau on the A470 Blaenau Ffestiniog road.

BALA (Y BALA)
☎ 01678 • pop 2100

The sturdy, good-natured market town of Bala sits at the north-eastern end of beautiful Llyn Tegid (Bala Lake), formed during the last Ice Age when glaciers blocked up the valley of the River Dee (Afon Dyfrdwy) with debris. This is Wales' biggest natural lake – 4 miles long, just three-quarters of a mile wide and in places over 40m deep – and Bala's main attraction. The town is also

a gateway town to Snowdonia National Park and staggers under crowds at the height of summer. Though chartered by the Normans in 1312, Bala is today staunchly Welsh and predominantly (about 80%) Welsh-speaking. Local hero and MP Tom Ellis was prominent with Lloyd George at the end of the 19th century in the movement for an independent Wales. One of Ellis' friends was Michael D Jones, founder of the Welsh colony in Patagonia.

An alternative to the glacial version of events says the valley was the home of a cruel and dissolute prince named Tegid Foel. One night at a banquet thrown by the prince, the harpist kept hearing a small bird urging him to flee the palace. He finally did so, fell asleep on a hilltop, and awoke at dawn to find the palace and principality drowned beneath the lake.

A modern and all too real 'legend' concerns the drowning of the village of Capel Celyn by waters rising behind the Llyn Celyn dam in 1965. The dam, on the River Treweryn which flows into the Dee near the town, was built in part to regulate the flow of the Dee, the main source of drinking water for the city of Liverpool – to the everlasting fury of many Welsh people. On the lakeside 2 miles above the dam is a small chapel of remembrance, and in dry summers Capel Celyn's chapel, school and farms rise above the water like ghosts.

Orientation & Information

Bala is 18 miles north-east of Dolgellau where the River Dee, flowing out of the lake, is joined by the River Treweryn. The town is basically one long street (the A494), called Pensarn Rd at the south-western end, High St through the centre and Station Rd on the other side. The town 'centre' is the intersection of High and Tegid Sts, by the White Lion Royal Hotel; buses stop a block north-eastwards. The TIC (☎/fax 521021, e bala .tic@gwynedd.gov.uk) is in the town's leisure centre on Pensarn Rd, a third of a mile south-west of the centre. It opens 10 am to 1 pm and 2 to 6 pm daily, Easter to October; and 10 am to 4.30 pm Friday to Monday only (to 3.30 pm at weekends) in winter.

Barclays and HSBC banks, and the post office, are on High St opposite the White Lion.

Activities

The Bala Adventure & Water Sports Centre (☎/fax 521059, 24 hour hotline ☎ 521600, ⓔ balawatersports@compuserve.com), Foreshore, Pensarn Rd (behind the TIC by the lakeshore), is Bala's one-stop activities shop. On offer are windsurfing, sailing, canoeing, whitewater rafting, mountain biking, rock climbing and abseiling trips (from £25/41 per half/full day); multi-day courses in the water-based activities; and gear rental.

Llyn Tegid is the only home of the gwyniad, a species of whitefish trapped here at the end of the last Ice Age. Anglers can pick up information from the lake warden (☎ 520626) in the office above the water-sports centre, gear from Siop Yr Eryr (☎ 520370) on High St opposite the post office, and a licence from the post office.

National Whitewater Centre

One result of the damming of the River Treweryn (see the introduction to this section) is that this and the Dee are among the few Welsh rivers with fairly reliable whitewater all summer. Canolfan Tryweryn, the National Whitewater Centre, runs skills and safety courses, and rafting trips, on a 1½-mile stretch of the Treweryn that is almost continuous class-IV whitewater. On offer are single/double runs (20 minutes each) in big rafts for £10/18 per person (or two hours with multiple runs if there are enough of you – four to seven people – to fill a raft), and half/full-day sessions in two-person rafts for £60/100 per person. The centre (☎ 521083, fax 521158, ⓔ welsh .canoeing@virgin.net) is 3½ miles north-west of Bala on the A4212. Bookings are best made at least two days in advance. Trips are subject to cancellation in the event of insufficient releases from the dam; once you're booked call the centre's hotline (☎ 520826) the day before. For more information visit the centre's Web site at www.welsh-canoeing.org.uk.

Bala Lake Railway

The narrow-gauge Bala Lake Railway (☎ 540666) was opened in 1868 to link main-line stations at Bala and Dolgellau. In 1965 the entire route from Barmouth to Llangollen was closed down and Bala station was closed. Volunteers reopened the 4½-mile stretch from Bala to Llanuwchllyn in 1971, with vintage locos departing from a little station half a mile south of town off the B4391. Departures from Bala are at 11.50 am, 1.25 and 3 pm on most days from mid-April to September, and daily in July and August. The 1½-hour return journey from Bala (with a 35-minute stop for coal and water at the other end) costs £6.70 per adult, £6.20 for seniors or £3 per child, with family tickets also available. See the Web site at www.bala-lake-railway.co.uk/index.html.

Other Things to See & Do

The town has hung onto a few of its older buildings, including half-a-dozen chapels. A former minister at the **Congregational Chapel** on Heol y Domen, a block back (south-east) from the bus stop, was Michael D Jones, a founder (in 1865) of the Welsh colony in Patagonia. On Tegid St is a well-preserved, very photogenic Victorian **ironmongery** (hardware shop).

Places to Stay

There are at least three camping grounds/caravan sites within 4 miles of Bala. *Pen-y-Bont* (☎ 520549, Llangynog Rd), almost a mile south-east on the B4391 and close to the lake, charges from £6 for a tent and £11 for a caravan, and opens April to October. For a tent and two people, *Tyn Cornel* (☎ 520759, Frongoch), just west of the National Whitewater Centre, charges £6, open March to October; and *Glanllyn* (☎/fax 540227), 3 miles out on the A494 Dolgellau road, charges £10 (including hot showers).

Bala would be a great place for a hostel but the nearest one is *Cynwyd Youth Hostel* (☎ 01490-412814, The Old Mill, Cynwyd), 10 miles north-east on the A494 and B4401, and open Easter to September. Nightly charges are £7.50/5.25. A modest B&B, open year round for about £18 per person, is *Traian* (☎ 520059, 95 Tegid St), 300m from the White Lion towards the lake. *The Ship* (☎ 520414), a pub at the north-eastern end of

Not to be missed: the peaks of the Snowdonia range glowing in the early-morning sunlight.

The view to Snowdon (1085m) across the plains from The Cob, the railway causeway at Porthmadog

Blaenau Ffestiniog sits surrounded by slate fields.

Pretty Beddgelert village on the River Gwynant

Caernarfon Castle was built in the 13th century.

The long sandy beach of Barmouth, Cardigan Bay

The well-preserved Victorian ironmongery, Bala

The 'Welsh Gibraltar' rises above Barmouth.

High St, offers B&B in plain rooms for £25 per person. At the *White Lion Royal Hotel* (☎ 520314, 61 High St) – 'royal' because Queen Victoria once stayed there – an en-suite double costs £30 Monday to Thursday but £50 at weekends. George Borrow insists in *Wild Wales* (see Books in the Facts for the Visitor chapter) that his breakfast here was the finest of any in his 1854 walking tour of Wales.

Places to Eat

The *Plas-yn-Dre Restaurant* (☎ 521256, High St) looks like the best and priciest in town, although lunchtime prices are reasonable, with roasts and other traditional-style meals for around £6, plus cheaper sandwiches and salads. There's also a *Plas-yn-Dre Cafe* a few doors down.

The licensed *Express Pizzeria* (☎ 520591, Berwyn St), just off High St near Plas-yn-Dre, has a decent selection of pasta and pizzas from £4 to £6. Most of the town's pubs also serve food.

Getting There & Around

Arriva Cymru's No 94 Barmouth–Wrexham coach passes through Bala seven times daily (twice on Sunday) from Barmouth (£2.75, one hour) and Dolgellau (£1.85, 35 minutes), and from Wrexham and Llangollen.

Roberts Cycles (☎ 520252), on High St 200m north-east of the White Lion, rents mountain bikes for £12 per day. It opens daily, except Sunday in winter.

HARLECH

☎ 01766 • pop 1300

Spectacularly astride a hill with Tremadog Bay and the mountains of Snowdonia for a backdrop, the compact, perfectly-rectangular ghost-castle of Harlech is hardly less intimidating than it must have been when Edward I finished it in 1289. This is the southernmost of his 'iron ring' of fortresses designed to put the Welsh firmly beneath his boot. Jointly with his others at Caernarfon, Conwy and Beaumaris, it's part of Wales' first UNESCO World Heritage Site.

It was also to this place that the ships of Matholwch sailed with his armies from Ireland in the tales of *The Mabinogion*.

Orientation & Information

The town – whose oldest parts are uphill and to the north of the castle – seems almost an afterthought. From the train station it's a strenuous 20-minute climb on one of several stepped tracks, or about a mile by road. Buses stop by the car park in the town, from where the castle is a few minutes' walk north on High St, with the TIC on the way. The TIC (☎ 780658) opens daily, April to October.

Harlech Castle

Harlech is sometimes called the Castle of Lost Causes because it has been defended so many times to no avail. Owain Glyndŵr captured it after a long siege in 1404. He is said to have been crowned Prince of Wales during one of his parliaments in the town, before envoys from Scotland, France and Spain. He was in turn besieged here by the future Henry V. During the Wars of the Roses the castle is said to have held out against a siege for seven years and was the last Lancastrian stronghold to fall. It was again besieged in the Civil War, finally giving in to Cromwell's forces in 1647.

The grey sandstone castle's massive, twin-towered gatehouse and outer walls are still intact, and make the place seem impregnable even now. You can climb the gloomy towers onto the ramparts. The castle (☎ 780552), run by Cadw, the Welsh historic monuments agency, opens 9.30 am to 5 pm daily, April to October (to 6 pm, June to September); and 9.30 to 4 pm (11 am to 4 pm on Sunday) the rest of the year. Admission costs £3/2.

The finest exterior view of the castle (with Snowdon as a backdrop) is from a viewpoint a few minutes' walk back past the car park. Also here is a view-map of points over on the Llŷn Peninsula including Porthmadog, Criccieth and Pwllheli.

Places to Stay & Eat

At Llanbedr (pronounced lam-**pet**-er), *Llanbedr Youth Hostel* (☎ 01341-241287, Plas Newydd, Llanbedr) is 3 miles south of Harlech. It opens mid-April to October (closed on Sunday and Monday in September and October) and charges £9.25/6.50.

Godre'r Graig (☎ 780905, New Rd), just below the castle, charges £16 per person for

B&B. On High St beside the church, *Byrdir House* (☎ 780316) has B&B singles/doubles for £16/20. The *Lion Hotel* (☎ 780731), near the castle, charges £21 per person, and does bar meals. Bang opposite the castle is the *Castle Hotel* (☎ 780529, *Castle Square*), with B&B for £25/40; rooms 3 and 4 look straight out at the gatehouse.

Plas Café (☎ 780204, *High St*) boasts the finest view of any restaurant in town – across to the castle and down to the sea; you can also sit outside. They do three meals a day including good vegetarian choices. *Yr Ogof Bistro* (☎ 780888, *High St*) serves a variety of traditional Welsh and vegetarian dishes.

Getting There & Away

Arriva bus No 38 comes from Barmouth (£1.95, 25 minutes) nine times daily and from Blaenau Ffestiniog (£1.95, 35 minutes) at least four times daily, Monday to Saturday. Trains run on the scenic Cambrian Coast line from Machynlleth (£8.40 single, 1¼ hours) and Porthmadog (£2.50, 20 minutes) every two hours or so.

PORTHMADOG
☎ 01766 • pop 4000

The modest former slate port of Porthmadog (pronounced port-**mad**-uk, but called 'Port' by one and all) is the closest Cambrian Coast Line station to the heart of Snowdonia. It's not a bad base if you're staying a while in the national park, though there's little to do but ride the train – this is the southern terminus for one of Wales' finest narrow-gauge train journeys, the Ffestiniog Railway. From here you can also visit the nearby fantasy-village of Portmeirion (see Around Porthmadog later in the chapter).

The town was founded by an 1821 Act of Parliament granting permission to slate magnate William Alexander Madocks, after whom the town is named, to build himself a harbour. Madocks had already begun by laying a mile-long causeway called The Cob across Traeth Mawr, the estuary at the mouth of River Glaslyn. Some 400 hectares of wetland habitat behind The Cob was drained and turned into farmland, and the causeway provided the route Madocks surely had in mind

all along for the Ffestiniog Railway, to bring his slate down to the new port.

Orientation & Information

The Cob is the only direct route from the east, along a hair-raisingly narrow road with a 5p toll (the ticket is good for the whole day). Most things of interest or use are on or near High St, running for half a mile down the middle of town. The TIC (☎ 512981, fax 515312, e Porthmadog.tic@gwynedd.gov .uk), where High St meets The Cob, opens 10 am to 6 pm daily (to 5 pm and closed Wednesday, November to Easter). The Ffestiniog Railway station is just across the bridge, while the Cambrian Coast Line station is right at the other end of town.

NatWest, Barclays and HSBC banks are on High St near its intersection with Bank Place. The post office is at this intersection too. Internet access is available free at the library on Chapel St and for £2.50 per half-hour at The Computer Shop (☎ 514944), 156 High St, and at Snowdon Backpackers (see Places to Stay later). The best bookshop in town is Browsers at 73 High St. European train specialist Ffestiniog Travel (☎ 512340) is at the Ffestiniog Railway office (see the following section); they're also an outlet for the Freedom of Wales Flexi-Pass (see the introduction to the Getting Around chapter). The laundrette at 34 Snowdon St opens daily except Sunday.

The police station (☎ 512226) is at the northern end of High St. The nearest hospital is in Minffordd, 3 miles eastwards.

Ffestiniog Railway & Welsh Highland Railway

The 13½-mile narrow-gauge Ffestiniog Railway (☎ 512340, fax 514715) was built between 1832 and 1836 to haul slate down to port from the mines at Blaenau Ffestiniog. Horse-drawn wagons were replaced in the 1860s by steam locomotives and the line was opened up as a passenger service. Saved from years of neglect, it has now become one of Wales' premier narrow-gauge journeys. Because it links the Cambrian Coast and Conwy Valley mainlines, it also serves as serious passenger transport. Nearly all services are

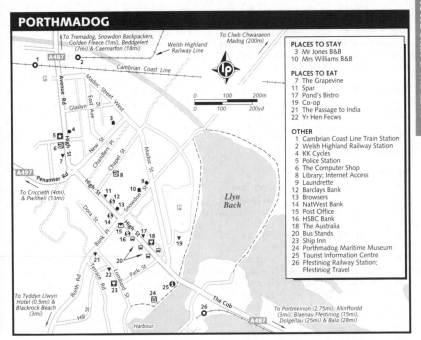

PORTHMADOG

To Tremadog, Snowdon Backpackers, Golden Fleece (1mi), Beddgelert (7mi) & Caernarfon (18mi)

Welsh Highland Railway Line

To Clwb Chwaraeon Madog (200m)

Cambrian Coast Line

To Criccieth (4mi), & Pwllheli (13mi)

Llyn Bach

To Tyddyn Llwyn Hotel (0.5mi) & Blackrock Beach (3mi)

Harbour

The Cob

To Portmeirion (2.75mi), Minffordd (3mi), Blaenau Ffestiniog (15mi), Dolgellau (25mi) & Bala (28mi)

PLACES TO STAY
3 Mr Jones B&B
10 Mrs Williams B&B

PLACES TO EAT
7 The Grapevine
11 Spar
17 Pond's Bistro
19 Co-op
21 The Passage to India
22 Yr Hen Fecws

OTHER
1 Cambrian Coast Line Train Station
2 Welsh Highland Railway Station
4 KK Cycles
5 Police Station
6 The Computer Shop
8 Library; Internet Access
9 Laundrette
12 Barclays Bank
13 Browsers
14 NatWest Bank
15 Post Office
16 HSBC Bank
18 The Australia
20 Bus Stands
23 Ship Inn
24 Porthmadog Maritime Museum
25 Tourist Information Centre
26 Ffestiniog Railway Station; Ffestiniog Travel

steam-hauled. There are from two to a high-summer maximum of six departures daily, April to October, plus limited holiday services in winter. A return ticket costs £13.80 to Blaenau Ffestiniog or £8.40 to Tan-y-Bwlch, halfway up the line. A 1st-class ticket – allowing you to sit in the observation car or in a traditional vintage coach – costs £5 extra. Sizeable discounts apply if you depart before 10 am and return after 3 pm. See the Web site at www.festrail.co.uk for more details.

The same company also runs the sibling Welsh Highland Railway, with a line under construction from Caernarfon to Porthmadog, to link up with both the Ffestiniog Railway station and a narrow-gauge terminus near the mainline train station (see under Caernarfon later for information about trips on that line, presently as far as Waunfawr).

You can use the Freedom of Wales Flexi-Pass or North & Mid Wales Flexi-Rover (see the introduction to the Getting Around chapter) on either line. There are also Rover tick-ets good for travel on these lines and Bws Ffestiniog (the Porthmadog–Caernarfon bus service).

But just to confuse matters, construction is also proceeding in the other direction from the narrow-gauge station near the mainline station, and during the summer a separate Welsh Highland Railway company (☎ 513042) is running trips up to the works – now at Pen-y-Mount, a 45-minute return trip – for £3/2.

Other Things to See & Do
One of the loveliest, most perfectly-framed views of Snowdon – writer Jan Morris calls it 'the classic illumination of Wales' – is up the Glaslyn Estuary (Traeth Mawr) from the middle of The Cob. But walk out there beside the railway track, *not* on the dangerously narrow roadway. It's at its best (and the traffic is minimal) just after sunrise.

In an old slate shed a few doors along the waterfront from the TIC is the little Porthmadog Maritime Museum (☎ 513736), with a pocket history of topsail schooners and other sailing ships. It opens 11 am to 5 pm daily, Easter to September. Admission costs £1/50p.

Beautiful, immense Blackrock Beach is 3 miles west on the Morfa Bychan Rd.

Special Events

Porthmadog hosts a Welsh rock festival called Miri Madog (☎ 512055), usually on the third weekend in August. It's held at Clwb Chwaraeon Madog, the town's sports complex, at the end of Snowdon St.

Places to Stay

One of Wales' better independent hostels is the hospitable *Snowdon Backpackers* (☎ 515354, Lawrence House, Church St) in Tremadog, a 20-minute walk north on the A487. Beds cost £12.50/15.50 in a dorm/private room (£1 less in winter), including light breakfast. A cooked breakfast is £2 more and basic meals are on offer at almost any hour. This is also a good place to swap Snowdonia tips. The hostel is in the house where TE Lawrence (Lawrence of Arabia) was born in 1888.

Among modest, clean B&Bs charging around £17 per person are those of *Mrs Williams* (☎ 513968, 30 Snowdon St) and *Mr Jones* (☎ 514518, 66 New St). *Yr Hen Fecws* (see Places to Eat below) has a few good-value rooms from £22.50 per person.

The *Tyddyn Llwyn Hotel* (☎ 513903, Morfa Bychan Rd), half a mile along Borth Rd in open countryside, is a comfortable, nonsmoking place with en-suite singles/doubles for £30/47, and a camp site charging £7 to £9 per tent or caravan.

Places to Eat

A cheerful, if slightly overpriced, bistro called *The Grapevine* (☎ 514230, 152 High St) offers a range of inventive stir-fries for around £7, vegetarian offerings from £6, and big vegetarian breakfasts. Two other good bistro-style eateries are *Yr Hen Fecws* (☎ 514625, 16 Lombard St), in a restored stone building near the harbour, and *Pond's Bistro* (☎ 512333, 47 High St). The best curries in town are at *The Passage to India*

(☎ 512144, 26 Lombard St), open daily (book ahead at weekends).

Agreeable watering holes with good grub include the *Ship Inn* (☎ 512990, Lombard St) and *The Australia* (☎ 512351, High St) in Porthmadog, and the *Golden Fleece* (☎ 512421, The Square) in Tremadog.

Supermarkets include a *Co-op* near the TIC and a *Spar* at 95 High St; there's also a Spar on the square in Tremadog.

Getting There & Away

Bus The Snowdon Sherpa bus (see Getting There & Around in the Snowdonia National Park section) provides useful links to Snowdon trailheads and elsewhere. Routes serving Porthmadog are the No 97 via Beddgelert from Betws-y-Coed, and the Bws Ffestiniog from Pwllheli and via Beddgelert from Caernarfon.

Express Motors (☎ 01286-881108) bus No 1 runs about hourly (fewer on Sunday) from Blaenau Ffestiniog (£1.60 single, 30 minutes) and from Caernarfon (£2.50, 50 minutes). Arriva's No 2 comes from Dolgellau (£2.85, 50 minutes, four to six daily). Arriva's TrawsCambria coach (No 701) arrives daily from Dolgellau (£4.70, 50 minutes), Aberystwyth and Cardiff, and from Bangor (£4.70, 55 minutes). National Express coach No 545 passes through daily from London via Chester, Llandudno, Bangor and Caernarfon, and on to Pwllheli; it also stops opposite Snowdon Backpackers.

Train Porthmadog is on the Cambrian Coast line, with trains from Machynlleth (£9.70 single, 1½ hours) and Pwllheli (£3.20, 15 minutes) every two or three hours (fewer at weekends). See the preceding Ffestiniog Railway section for links with Blaenau Ffestiniog.

Getting Around

You can rent a mountain bike from Snowdon Backpackers (see Places to Stay earlier) for £15 per day (guests £12.50). From Easter to September, bikes can also be hired from KK Cycles (also known as the Kandy Kitchen sweet shop; ☎ 512310), 141 High St.

Bus No 3 runs between Porthmadog and Tremadog about hourly.

AROUND PORTHMADOG
Portmeirion

Kitsch enthusiasts can head east of Porthmadog to Portmeirion, an Italianate village created in its entirety between 1925 and 1927 by the late Welsh architect Sir Clough Williams-Ellis, on its own tranquil peninsula not far from his ancestral home. Sir Clough wanted to show that architecture could be whimsical and intriguing, and he was right – although summer crowds certainly blunt the experience.

There are 50 buildings around a central piazza, some brought here to save them from destruction elsewhere, most looking like cake decorations. The village has no residents, only guests: Portmeirion is a holiday village, probably the strangest one you'll ever see. Noel Coward wrote *Blithe Spirit* here in the 1940s. Many people know Portmeirion only as the set for the 1960s cult TV series, *The Prisoner;* it still draws the fans, and there's even a Prisoner Information Centre.

The village's Gwyllt Gardens – 28 hectares of immaculate Victorian pleasure gardens and woodlands – include rare Himalayan flowering trees and other exotics, and even a dog cemetery.

You can throw your money away in style here: the *Hotel Portmeirion (☎ 770228)* charges £145 upwards per room in the main building or from £115 for a room in one of the village's cottages; there are also self-catering units. The hotel restaurant does set dinners for £33. The gardens also have a restaurant, an ice-cream parlour and seven shops, one of which sells firsts and seconds of the famous pottery designed by Susan, Sir Clough's daughter, and bearing the Portmeirion label (see Shopping in the Facts for the Visitor chapter) – though these days it's made in Stoke-on-Trent in England.

The village opens to the public from 9.30 am to 5.30 pm daily; admission costs £5/2.50. It's 1¾ mile east of Porthmadog and one mile off the road, an easy walking trip. Bus No 98 runs to the site three times daily from Porthmadog; many more buses and the Ffestiniog Railway run to Minffordd, from where it's about a one-mile walk. A taxi costs £4.50 each way.

BEDDGELERT
☎ 01766 • pop 300

This is one of the prettiest of all Snowdon's villages, posing demurely at the confluence of the Rivers Colwyn and Glaslyn. Scenes from Mark Robson's 1958 film, *Inn of the Sixth Happiness*, starring Ingrid Bergman, were shot here.

The name, meaning 'Gelert's Grave', refers to one of the best known and most heartwrenching of Welsh legends, that of Prince Llewelyn's faithful dog, killed by its owner after he thought it had savaged his baby son, when it had actually killed a wolf that was attacking the baby. If there is a dog's grave here, it was quite probably invented by a canny 19th-century hotelier. More likely the name refers to Celert, a 5th-century missionary preacher from Ireland who is thought to have founded a church here.

The summer-only TIC (☎/fax 890615) at Canolfan Hebog opens 10 am to 6pm daily.

A mile east of the village, on the northern side of the road, is a hill called **Dinas Emrys** where the legendary King Vortigern – son-in-law of the last Roman ruler, Magnus Maximus, and unfortunately remembered for having invited the Saxons over – tried to build a castle. The young wizard Merlin revealed two dragons in a cavern under the hill, a red one representing the Welsh and a white one representing the Saxons, and prophesied that they'd fight until the red dragon was triumphant. As he spoke the dragons set upon one another and have been at it ever since. Vortigern had to build his castle elsewhere.

Right across the road from Dinas Emrys is the **Sygun Copper Mine** (☎ 510100), mined from Roman times and especially in the 19th century, abandoned in 1903 and now reinvented as a tourist attraction, complete with underground tour, special effects and a chance to pan for gold. It opens 10 am (11 am on Sunday) to 5 pm (4 pm Saturday) daily, Easter to September, with shorter hours the rest of the year. Admission costs £4.75/3.

Places to Stay & Eat

Beddgelert Forest Campsite (☎ 890288) is well equipped and well sited, a mile out on the Caernarfon road. Charges start at £4 per person.

The **Snowdon Ranger Youth Hostel** (☎ 01286-650391) is on the A4085, 5 miles north of Beddgelert at the trailhead for the Snowdon Ranger Path up Snowdon. It opens April to October (except Monday and Tuesday in September and October) plus weekends the rest of the year; nightly charges are £10/6.90. Four miles east of Beddgelert, above Llyn Gwynant lake and near the Watkin Path trailhead, is the **Bryn Gwynant Youth Hostel** (☎ 01766-890251, Nant Gwynant), open March to October, plus Friday and Saturday in January and February, with the same charges. This one also has some en-suite double rooms from £27.

Beddgelert has three adjacent B&Bs with similar names and rates (£18 per person or £20 en suite) between the bridge and the Saracens Head Inn on the A4085 Rhyd Ddu road – **Plas Colwyn** (☎ 890458), serving good Welsh food in the restaurant downstairs; **Plas Gwyn** (☎ 890215); and **Colwyn Guest House** (☎ 890276). **Beddgelert Bistro & Tearooms** (☎ 890543), beside the bridge, serves local dishes from £10 and has three rooms from £18. Don't pass **Glaslyn Ices** in the village without trying their award-winning, home-made ice-cream.

Getting There & Around
Snowdon Sherpa bus services (see Getting There & Around in the Snowdonia National Park section) include the No 95 from Caernarfon and Llanberis; the No 97 from Porthmadog and from Capel Curig and Betws-y-Coed; and the Bws Ffestiniog from Caernarfon and from Pwllheli and Porthmadog.

Beics Beddgelert (☎ 890434), 2 miles north on the A4085, rents mountain bikes for £7.50 for two hours or £16 per day. Its Web site is at www.bikeworld.uk.com.

BLAENAU FFESTINIOG
☎ 01766 • pop 6000
Most of the slate used to keep English houses dry came from Wales, and most of that came either from the quarries of Bethesda or the mines of Blaenau Ffestiniog.

Slate was the basis of Snowdonia's wealth in the 19th century.

Only about 10% of mined slate is usable, so for every ton that goes to the factory, nine tons are left as rubble. Despite being in the very centre of the national park, the grey mountains of mine waste that surround Blaenau Ffestiniog prevented it from being officially included in the park – a slap in the face for this impoverished town, in the days before Wales' industrial sites were recognised as part of its heritage. The two main mines are right beside the town, Oakley to the east and Llechwedd to the west. During WWII Llechwedd was used as a top-secret 'warehouse' for Britain's art treasures – and, according to some sources, for the British crown jewels.

Although slate mining continues on a small scale, Blaenau (pronounced **blay**-nye) is now a tourist town, selling history – of the slate industry, of the Ffestiniog Railway (which has its northern terminus here) and of the Tan-y-Grisiau pumped-storage electric power station just down the Dwyryd Valley.

Orientation & Information
From the train station – used by both the narrow-gauge line from Porthmadog and the standard-gauge line from Llandudno – the summer-only TIC (☎/fax 830360) is just across Church St. Buses stop here too. The handiest reference point for local sights is Commercial Square, a roundabout (traffic circle) at the upper (north-western) end of Church St, 350m from the station.

Slate Mines
The Llechwedd Slate Caverns (☎ 830306, fax 831260, e llechwedd@aol.com) are the slate-mine equivalent of the Big Pit coal mine (see under Blaenafon in the South-East Wales & the Brecon Beacons chapter) – a chance to descend into a real slate mine and get a sense of what the work was like. There are two tours, both costing £6.95/4.80 (or £10.50/7.20 for both). Best is the 25-minute Deep Mine tour, including a descent on the UK's steepest passenger railway and a walk through 10 multimedia sequences. If you can't manage a lot of steps, go for the Miner's

Tramway tour, a ride through a network of tunnels, caverns and Victorian tableaux. The site has a cafe, pub, licensed restaurant and plenty of semi-historical kitsch too.

The caverns open 10 am to 6 pm (last tour at 5.15 pm) daily, closing an hour earlier, October to February. The site is just under a mile north of Commercial Square on the A470 Betws-y-Coed road.

Tan-y-Grisiau

The UK's first pumped-storage electric power station – where surplus energy is used to pump water from a lower to an upper reservoir, from where it's released to generate electricity during sudden peak demands – is just down-valley from the slate mines.

Guided tours of the mostly-underground facility are available from Edison Electric's Ffestiniog Visitor Centre (☎ 830465) at Tan-y-Grisiau. From Commercial Square head south for a mile on the A496 Porthmadog road, and west for half a mile from the roundabout.

For an even more switched-on tour, visit the Dinorwig power station ('Electric Mountain') at Llanberis; see that section later for details.

Places to Stay & Eat

Most visitors come here on day trips and accommodation is pretty limited. *Isallt Guest House* (☎ *832488, Church St)*, just up the steps from the train station, has plain en-suite singles/doubles for £20/35. *Dolawel Guest House* (☎ *830511, Rhiwbryfdir)*, 250m up the A470 from Commercial Square, has two en-suite rooms for £17 per person, at least in summer. The *Queen's Hotel* (☎ *830055, Church St)* by the station charges £28.

The best restaurant the town has to offer is the upstairs *Ty Graig* (☎ *831447, 3–4 Commercial Square)*, with sturdy standards for £6 to £7. Downstairs there's a fish-and-chip shop.

Getting There & Away

The Ffestiniog Railway (☎ 512340), one of Wales' finest narrow-gauge journeys, is the preferred way to get here. The 13½-mile line, built in the 1830s to haul slate to port at Porthmadog, is now an important link between Conwy Valley and Cambrian Coast mainlines. There are from two to a high-summer maximum of six trains daily, April to October; a return ticket from Porthmadog costs £13.80. For more information on the line, see under Porthmadog earlier in this chapter.

The standard-gauge Conwy Valley line comes from Llandudno (£4.85 single, one hour five minutes) via Betws-y-Coed (£3, 30 minutes) at least five times daily, Monday to Saturday – with slower, less-frequent fill-in buses (No 84) on Sunday.

Express Motors (☎ 01286-881108) bus No 1 runs from Porthmadog (£1.60 single, 30 minutes) and Caernarfon (£3.40, 1¼ hours) about hourly (fewer on Sunday). Arriva Cymru services include No 35 from Dolgellau (£2, 45 minutes, four daily) and No 38 from Barmouth (£1.95, one hour five minutes, at least four daily) via Harlech, Monday to Saturday.

BETWS-Y-COED
☎ 01690 • pop 700

Betws-y-Coed (pronounced **bet**-us-ee-**coyd**) is a tourist village styling itself the eastern gateway to the national park. The name means Sanctuary in the Wood, so called because of the 14th-century St Michael's Church here. Much of that old wood remains, as the surrounding Gwydyr Forest.

'Betws' has been Wales' most popular inland resort since Victorian days. A nexus of valleys into and around Snowdonia with more tourist accommodation than any other town in the park, it's a logical base for walkers – though somewhat distant from trailheads, rather overpriced and in summer extremely crowded. The quietest days are Monday and Friday, when all the coach parties are en route or homeward bound. There's another small peak in autumn during the fishing season, when the Conwy and Llugwy are rich with salmon and sewin.

Betws is well-served by the Conwy Valley railway and fairly well connected by Snowdon Sherpa buses. The A5, the London–Holyhead highway, is the village's main road.

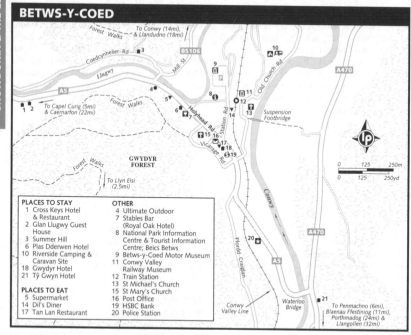

BETWS-Y-COED

PLACES TO STAY	OTHER
1 Cross Keys Hotel & Restaurant	4 Ultimate Outdoor
2 Glan Llugwy Guest House	7 Stables Bar (Royal Oak Hotel)
3 Summer Hill	8 National Park Information Centre & Tourist Information Centre; Beics Betws
6 Plas Dderwen Hotel	9 Betws-y-Coed Motor Museum
10 Riverside Camping & Caravan Site	11 Conwy Valley Railway Museum
18 Gwydyr Hotel	12 Train Station
21 Tŷ Gwyn Hotel	13 St Michael's Church
	15 St Mary's Church
PLACES TO EAT	16 Post Office
5 Supermarket	19 HSBC Bank
14 Dil's Diner	20 Police Station
17 Tan Lan Restaurant	

Orientation & Information

Betws is little more than a few streets off the A5 (which is here called Holyhead Rd). Regional buses usually stop both outside the train station on Station Rd, and on the A5 by Station Rd. The combined National Park Information Centre and TIC (☎ 710426, fax 710665, e ticbetws@hotmail.com), in the former stables of the Royal Oak Hotel, opens 10 am to 6 pm daily (9.30 am to 4.30 pm November to Easter). The TIC has books and maps about the region but for a good selection of specialist references for walkers, climbers and cyclists, check out the Ultimate Outdoor adventure shop (☎ 710555) on the A5.

The only bank is HSBC, also on the A5.

Things to See & Do

There's little to do here except walk and take tea, which in this case is enough. The 14th-century St Michael's Church, which gave Betws-y-Coed its name, is across the train tracks from the TIC (the TIC has the key).

There are two museums, neither of great interest. The little Conwy Valley Railway Museum (☎ 710568), behind the train station, opens 10.15 am to 5 pm daily, Easter to October (weekends only in winter); admission costs £1/50p. There's also a miniature steam train. The Betws-y-Coed Motor Museum (☎ 710760), behind the TIC, usually opens about 10 am to 5.30 pm daily, Easter to October; admission costs £1.50/1.

Walking & Cycling Routes

North-west and south-west from Betws-y-Coed is the 28 sq mile Gwydyr Forest, planted since the 1920s with oak, beech, larch and the inevitable stands of Douglas fir. At its heart is the Gwydyr Forest Park, laced with walking and cycle tracks, old miners' paths and forestry roads. These tend to get very muddy in wet weather. There are also two designated cycle routes within the forest park.

The Llanrwst Forest District publishes a free map-brochure – available at the TIC for

£2 – showing nine graded walks ranging from 300m to 6 miles. Recommended is a steep walk of about 2½ miles from behind St Mary's Church up to a lake at 250m called Llyn Elsi.

Pony Trekking & Horse Riding

There's pony trekking at Ty Coch Farm (☎ 760248) in Penmachno, 6 miles south of Betws-y-Coed. Rides through the Gwydyr Forest start at £10 for one hour and novice riders are welcome. The farm also does a popular pub ride for £26, lasting around four hours. The TIC has a brochure with map.

Places to Stay

The *Riverside Camping & Caravan Site* (☎ 710310, Old Church Rd) has tent and caravan pitches, hot showers and other amenities.

Some B&Bs with modest rates include *Summer Hill* (☎ 710306, Coedcynhelier Rd) and tidy, nonsmoking *Glan Llugwy Guest House* (☎ 710592, Holyhead Rd) half a mile out on the A5 towards Llanberis. Both charge about £18 per person. Next door to Glan Llugwy is the *Cross Keys Hotel & Restaurant* (☎ 710334, Holyhead Rd), charging £30/40 for an en-suite single/double.

Hotels along the Holyhead Rd include the *Plas Dderwen* (☎ 710388) with B&B from £18 per person, and the *Gwydyr* (☎ 710777) from £25. The *Tŷ Gwyn Hotel* (☎ 710383), across the Waterloo Bridge, is a 17th-century coaching inn with B&B from £17 per person (£28 en suite).

Places to Eat

Beside the train station, *Dil's Diner* (☎ 710346, Station Rd) – cheap and cheerful as Betws-y-Coed eateries go – offers filling standards such as fish and chips (around £4.50) until around 8 pm. The *Tan Lan Restaurant* (☎ 710232, Holyhead Rd), beside the post office, includes a bakery with soup and sandwiches, and a separate restaurant with burgers, chicken and pasta dishes, mostly under £5.

Up a notch are Betws' hotel-restaurants, most of which are open to nonguests. The *Cross Keys Hotel & Restaurant* (see Places to Stay

earlier) has good main courses from £7 to £12 and vegetarian choices for around £7.

There's a *Spar* supermarket on Holyhead Rd.

Entertainment

The *Stables Bar* at the left end of the Royal Oak Hotel has live jazz on Thursday nights.

Getting There & Away

The best connections to Betws are by train, with at least five daily services from Llandudno (£3.65 single, 35 minutes) and from Blaenau Ffestiniog (£3, 30 minutes) Monday to Saturday, and slower, less frequent fill-in buses (No 84) on Sunday.

Snowdon Sherpa bus services (see Getting There & Around in the Snowdonia National Park section) include the No 65 from Bethesda and Capel Curig; the No 96 from Llandudno and from Llanberis and Capel Curig; and the No 97 from Porthmadog, Beddgelert and Capel Curig.

Getting Around

Mountain bikes can be hired from Beics Betws (☎ 710829), beside the TIC. The charge is a hefty £16 a day.

AROUND BETWS-Y-COED
Capel Curig
☎ 01690 • pop 180

Little Capel Curig, 5 miles west of Betws-y-Coed, is one of Snowdonia's oldest mountain resorts, now more than ever a popular place with walkers, climbers and other outdoor junkies.

One reason is Plas y Brenin, the National Mountain Centre (☎ 720214, fax 720394, ⓔ info@pyb.co.uk) in the former Eagle Hotel at the western edge of the village. The centre opens year round with an alluring range of residential courses – rock climbing, summer and winter mountaineering, alpine skiing, and whitewater kayaking and canoeing – which, though best booked ahead, are open to walk-in visitors on a space-available basis.

The *Capel Curig Youth Hostel* (☎ 720225, Plas Curig), beside the petrol station just east of the village centre, opens daily from mid-February to October (Friday and Saturday only the rest of the year); the nightly charge is £10/6.90. The *Idwal Cottage Youth Hostel* (☎ *01248-600225, Nant Ffrancon*), 6 miles west of Capel Curig, opens March to August (Friday and Saturday only the rest of the year) and charges £8.50/5.75.

In the village, friendly *Bron Eryri Guest House* (☎ *720240*) has five en-suite rooms for £21 per person B&B. The *National Mountain Centre* also has local B&B accommodation available, even for those not registered for their courses, but it can only be booked a week ahead; it also has a dormitory-style bunkhouse at £5 per bed. In the evenings everyone meets at the *Bryn Tyrch* (☎ *720223*), a hotel (B&B from £21 per person) with a busy pub; *Cobdens Hotel* (☎ *720243*), where B&B costs £32 per person; or at the bar at Plas y Brenin.

Snowdon Sherpa bus services are the same as for Betws-y-Coed.

Perhaps the best-known view of Snowdon is from beside the twin lakes Llynnau Mymbyr, a mile west of Capel Curig on the A4086 Llanberis road.

LLANBERIS
☎ 01286 • pop 2000

Llanberis was originally built to house workers in the nearby Dinorwig slate quarry, whose massive waste tips you can't fail to notice as you approach from the east. Since the quarry shut down in 1969, this cheerful, one-street town – the closest town to Snowdon's summit – has become a magnet for walkers and climbers of every shade, from crusties to the Burberry brigade. With the mountains looming above, it has a vaguely wild-west feel at the height of summer, and if you can find a place to stay (not easy in July and August) it's an easy place to linger and walk your legs off.

Dinorwig, which once boasted the largest artificial cavern in the world, has now become part of Europe's biggest pumped-storage power station. Some of the old quarry workshops have been reincarnated as a good museum of the slate industry, and the narrow-gauge railway that once hauled slate to the coast now tootles along Llyn Padarn. Another train pulls itself right to the top of Snowdon.

Orientation & Information

Llanberis sits right beside the A4086, with High St running parallel to it. Just about everything of use is on High St, so you can't get lost. Across the A4086 are the village's two lakes, Llyn Padarn and Llyn Peris. The TIC (☎ 870765, fax 871924, **e** llanberis .tic@gwynedd.gov.uk), at 41 High St, opens 10 am to 6 pm daily, Easter to October; and 10 am to 4 pm on Wednesday, Friday, Saturday and Sunday in winter. The post office is across the street from the TIC; next door, Pete's Eats (see Places to Eat later) has Internet access for £2 per half-hour and a good notice board. There's an HSBC bank just west of the TIC and a Barclays ATM at the Electric Mountain exhibition centre (see later in the section).

Outside (☎ 871534), a mountain shop at 13 High St, two blocks west of the TIC, has a notice board that includes gear for sale and accommodation.

Snowdon Mountain Railway

Opened in 1896, Snowdon Mountain Railway (☎ 870223) – the UK's highest railway and its only public rack-and-pinion railway – climbs 1085m from Llanberis to the summit of Snowdon, a 5-mile journey that takes an hour. Seven vintage steam locomotives and four modern diesel locomotives haul carriages up and down from 9 am to late afternoon, Easter to October. At peak periods (bank holidays and from mid-July to early September) trains depart every half-hour until 5 pm (until 3.30 pm on Saturday). Departures are weather-dependent and summer queues can be long. A return ride costs £17/12; for those who want to walk one way, a single ticket costs £11/9. Early departures outside peak season may get you a £3/2 discount. See the Web site at www.snowdonrailway.co.uk.

The station is on the A4086 about half a mile south of the TIC.

Electric Mountain

The Dinorwig pumped-storage power station uses surplus energy to pump water from

Llyn Peris 600m up to Marchlyn reservoir. When half the British population switches on their kettles for tea during a break in *Coronation Street*, creating a sudden surge in electricity demand, the water can be released to fall through underground turbines for an ultra-rapid response. Electric Mountain (☎ 870636), the power station's visitor centre, has free interactive exhibits on the history of hydropower. A considerably more interesting guided tour (£5/2.50) into the underground power station also starts here. The centre opens 9.30 am to 5.30 pm daily, Easter to September; and 10.30 am to 4.30 the rest of the year (daily in December and Thursday to Sunday from then to Easter). The centre is located where High St joins the A4086, about a third of a mile south of the TIC.

Welsh Slate Museum

The Welsh Slate Museum (☎ 870630), run by National Museums & Galleries of Wales (NMGW), in old maintenance workshops beside Llyn Padarn, features a huge working waterwheel, demonstrations on splitting slate into tiles and a 3D presentation on the story of slate, among other things. The museum opens 10 am to 5 pm (to 4 pm, November to Easter), daily except Saturday. Admission is £3.50/free.

The turning is on the A4086 between the Electric Mountain centre and the Snowdon Mountain Railway station.

Llanberis Lake Railway

Across the parking lot from the Welsh Slate Museum, a little train departs on a 2-mile jaunt beside Llyn Padarn, part of the route (though not the same track) used from 1843 to 1961 to haul slate to port on the Menai Strait. The rather tame 45-minute return trip through Padarn Country Park costs £4.20/2.50 (with over a dozen family-ticket options). The Llanberis Lake Railway (☎ 870549) opens March to October, with four to a high-season maximum of 11 daily departures. See the Web site at ukhrail.uel.ac.uk/llr.html.

Other Activities

High Trek Snowdonia (☎ 871232) organises guided walks, gorge scrambling, night hikes and abseiling around Snowdon. The Dolbadarn Pony Trekking Centre (☎ 870277) operates from the Dolbadarn Hotel (see the following section on Places to Stay) and charges £10 per hour.

Great for kids is the Padarn Watersports Centre (☎ 870556) at Llyn Padarn offering kayaking, canoeing, raft building, climbing, abseiling and mountain-walking activities for small groups – eg £18 per person per half-day for a group of five. Menai Historical Cruises (☎ 07974 716418) run half-hour boat trips on Llyn Padarn in summer for £3.50/2; the boat leaves from the jetty near the Slate Museum car park.

The ruins of the 13th-century Dolbadarn Castle – little more than a truncated tower with gaping windows – are beside Llyn Peris at the south-eastern end of town. The site opens free of charge.

Places to Stay

Camping Two miles from Llanberis, *Cae Gwyn Camp Site (☎ 870718, Nant Peris)* charges £2.50 for a tent pitch.

Hostels There's dorm accommodation at *The Heights Hotel* (see the following section on B&Bs & Hotels) for £9, or £12.50 with breakfast.

Surrounded by Welsh black cattle and with a view over the top of the slate quarry, *Llanberis Youth Hostel (☎ 870280)* was originally a quarry manager's house. It is half a mile south-west of the town and opens daily, April to October (closed on Sunday and Monday in August), and weekends the rest of the year. The nightly charge is £10/6.90. *The Pen-y-Pass Youth Hostel (☎ 01286-870428)*, superbly situated 5½ miles up the A4086 atop Llanberis Pass (and by the Pyg Track and Miners' Track trailheads), opens Friday and Saturday year round and on *most* days from mid-February to October for £11/7.75 (call ahead).

At *Snowdon House (☎ 870356, 3 Gwastadnant)*, 3 miles towards Pen-y-Pass at Nant Peris, there's bunkhouse accommodation from £5 per person, camping for £2.50 and a cottage to let. On the B4547 Bangor road 3 miles from Llanberis, nonsmoking *Jesse*

James' Bunkhouse (☎ 870521, *Penisa'r Waun*) has been a walkers' base since 1966; JJ is a mountain guide who offers a range of accommodation from £7.50 to £15.

B&Bs & Hotels Three blocks west of the TIC and overlooking Llyn Padarn, *Beech Bank Guest House* (☎ 870414, *3 High St*) has B&B for £15 per person. Next door, the *Alpine Lodge* (☎ 870294, *1 High St*) has doubles/triples from £35/45.

At the eastern end is *The Heights Hotel* (☎ 871179, *74 High St*), with en-suite singles/doubles for £25/40 B&B, plus cheaper dorm beds. This is probably the most enjoyable place in town, with a popular bar and live folk music every Thursday. Other places at this end of High St include the *Dolbadarn Hotel* (☎ 870277), the pleasant *Y Gwynedd Hotel* (☎ 870203) and a guesthouse called *Bron-y-Graig* (☎ 872073, *Capel Coch*), about 150 metres off High St; turn at the Spar supermarket – all charging around £18 per person. Nearby is the *Padarn Lake Hotel* (☎ 870260, *High St*) at £36/59 per single/double.

Top of the lot is the *Royal Victoria Hotel* (☎ 870253), near the Snowdon Mountain Railway station, with en-suite B&B at £47.50 per person and a first-rate restaurant.

The *Pen-y-Gwryd Hotel* (☎ 870211), 7 miles south-east over the Llanberis Pass at the junction of the A498 and A4086, offers B&B from £23 per person. The 1953 Everest team used the inn as a training base – note their signatures on the ceiling. Residents sit round a single table for the evening meal, and bar food is also available.

Places to Eat & Drink

Pete's Eats (☎ 870358, *40 High St*) is the place of choice – a crowded cafe where hikers and climbers swap information over generous sandwiches, salads, chicken, chips and £4 monster breakfasts. For walking fodder, try their Big Jim – a mixed grill for £8.50. There are good vegetarian choices too. It's opposite the TIC.

Y Bistro (☎ 871278, *45 High St*) is the place to go for a splurge – Welsh produce with a rustic French twist. It only opens in the evening, with set dinners from £20.

The people from Snowdon House (see Places to Stay earlier) also run the cosy climber's haunt, the *Vaynol Arms* (☎ 870284, *Nant Peris*), with hot meals and snacks to suit all pockets.

In the evenings, climbers hang out at *The Heights Hotel* (see Places to Stay earlier), whose pub even has its own climbing wall.

Getting There & Away

KMP's (☎ 870880) bus No 88 shuttles between Llanberis and Caernarfon (£1.50, 25 minutes, twice hourly except hourly Sunday); a few runs continue to Nant Peris. From Bangor, take Arriva's No 77 or 86 (£1.20, 40 minutes), each hourly (less often on Sunday). Snowdon Sherpa routes (see under Getting There & Around in the Snowdonia National Park section) to Llanberis are No 95 from Caernarfon and Beddgelert, and No 96 from Llandudno, Betws-y-Coed and Capel Curig.

CAERNARFON
01286 • pop 9700

In 1301 Edward I raised two fingers to the Welsh people by declaring his own infant son the Prince of Wales and installing him in the mighty castle that dominates this town. In 1911, in a bid to involve the crown more closely with his constituency in this part of Wales, Prime Minister David Lloyd George arranged for the investiture ceremony for the heir to the throne – the future Edward VIII – to be held in the castle. Local people were resoundingly unimpressed: Caernarfon is at the heart of Welsh-nationalist Wales and is even now an economically hard-pressed area which the royal connection has done little to help. When Prince Charles was invested here as the next Prince of Wales by his mother in 1969, nationalists made an unsuccessful attempt to blow up his train.

Caernarfon (pronounced care-**nar**-von) is really no more or less than the county town of Gwynedd, though it has the energy of a city. But it will always lie in the shadow of its castle – literally so in the case of the old walled town at its feet.

Orientation & Information

The historical heart of Caernarfon is the group of eight or so square blocks enclosed within stout 14th-century walls, just to the north of the castle, beside the River Seiont where it empties into the Menai Strait. The centre of modern Caernarfon is just east of the castle, at Castle Square (Y Maes). The main shopping area is pedestrianised Pool St, running east from Castle Square. Buses stop at stands along Penllyn, two blocks north of Pool St.

The TIC (☎/fax 672232, ⓔ caernarfon .tic@gwynedd.gov.uk) shares space with the Pendeitsh Gallery on Castle Ditch, directly opposite the castle's main entrance, the King's Gate. The TIC opens 10 am to 6 pm daily, Easter to October; and 9.30 am to 4.30 pm daily except Wednesday, the rest of the year.

Banks include NatWest and HSBC on Castle Square, Lloyds on Pool St and Eastgate St, and Barclays on Bangor St. The post office faces Castle Square. Internet access is available at Dimensiwn 4 (☎ 678777), Bangor St, for £2 per half-hour – along with a cafe serving sandwiches, soups and snacks.

The best source of local books and maps is the TIC. WHSmith on Pool St also has maps and general guidebooks. Pete's Launderette

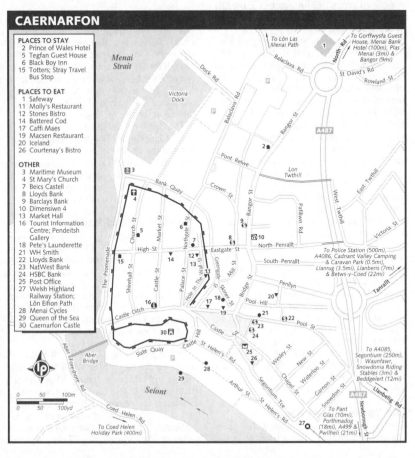

CAERNARFON

PLACES TO STAY
2 Prince of Wales Hotel
5 Tegfan Guest House
6 Black Boy Inn
15 Totters; Stray Travel Bus Stop

PLACES TO EAT
1 Safeway
11 Molly's Restaurant
12 Stones Bistro
14 Battered Cod
17 Caffi Maes
19 Macsen Restaurant
20 Iceland
26 Courtenay's Bistro

OTHER
3 Maritime Museum
4 St Mary's Church
7 Beics Castell
8 Lloyds Bank
9 Barclays Bank
10 Dimensiwn 4
13 Market Hall
16 Tourist Information Centre; Pendeitsh Gallery
18 Pete's Launderette
21 WH Smith
22 Lloyds Bank
23 NatWest Bank
24 HSBC Bank
25 Post Office
27 Welsh Highland Railway Station; Lôn Eifion Path
28 Menai Cycles
29 Queen of the Sea
30 Caernarfon Castle

(☎ 678395) is at 10 Skiner St, just north-east of Castle Square.

The police station (☎ 673333) is on Maesincla Lane, about two-thirds of a mile east of the town centre. The nearest accident and emergency services are in Bangor.

Caernarfon Castle

The site was first fortified in 1090 by the Norman earl of Chester but was soon captured by the Welsh Princes of Gwynedd, who held it until Edward I's defeat of Llewelyn ap Gruffydd in 1282. The present castle was begun the following year and more or less completed around 1330 – part of Edward's 'iron ring' of forts designed to keep the Welsh under control.

This one is stupendously strong and domineering, allegedly modelled on the 5th-century walls of Constantinople, and sure to make its occupants feel quite invincible. Its excellent condition is testament to its impregnability – in 1404 just 28 men successfully defended it against Owain Glyndŵr and his French allies; during the Civil War it was besieged three times, without success.

Caernarfon was also designed to be a palace (Edward's son was born here). Living quarters, fitted out with glass windows and other 14th-century mod-cons, were in the towers; the Eagle Tower at the western end is the finest and biggest.

In a theatre on the first floor, a good film on Edward and his castles runs every half-hour. In the Queen's Tower (named after Edward's wife Eleanor) is a museum of the Royal Welsh Fusiliers, a regiment that seems to have produced more than its share of writers – Robert Graves and Siegfried Sassoon among them. The circular slate dias at the eastern end was cut and shaped at the Dinorwig quarry at Llanberis for the July 1969 investiture of Prince Charles as Prince of Wales.

The castle (☎ 677617; Cadw) opens 9.30 am to 6 pm daily (to 4 pm daily, and from 11 am on Sunday, November to Easter). Admission costs £4.20/3.20.

Old Town & Slate Quay

Don't overlook the pocket-size, walled town beside the castle. St Mary's Church, in the north-western corner of the old town, was founded as a garrison church in 1307, though little remains from this period except the Jesse Window, facing the Menai Strait, and the arcades over the nave. Probably the town's oldest inn is the 16th-century Black Boy Inn in Northgate St (see Places to Stay later). The Market Hall in Palace St dates from 1832. There's no access to the top of the town walls.

Slate Quay, with its little marina beside the castle, is probably Caernarfon's most photographed spot. For the best views cross the footbridge.

Segontium

Just east of the centre are the excavated remains of Segontium, the westernmost Roman legionary fort of the Roman empire. Big enough for 1000 infantry soldiers, it was occupied for a remarkable three centuries, from AD 77. It was from here that the Romans completed their conquest of Wales with the capture of the Isle of Anglesey.

The Cadw-owned site is a 10-minute walk along Llanbelig Rd (A4085), which crosses through the middle of it. A small museum (☎ 675625, NMGW) at the eastern end opens 10 am to 5 pm daily, April to October, and to 4 pm the rest of the year (afternoon only on Sunday). Admission costs £1.25/75p.

Welsh Highland Railway

The narrow-gauge Welsh Highland Railway (Porthmadog ☎ 01766-512340), an amalgamation of several late-19th-century railways used for carrying slate, opened for passenger traffic in 1923 but closed just 14 years later. It reopened as a tourist attraction in 1997 and will eventually run to Porthmadog, making it potentially as useful as the Ffestiniog Railway in encouraging car-free visits to the national park.

The station is on St Helen's Rd. So far, trains go 3 miles up to Waunfawr, a 35-minute trip (1½ hours return). There are departures three to four times daily (twice daily in winter) at weekends, March to December and daily, April to October, with steam-hauled services at least at weekends. A return ticket to Waunfawr costs £7.60; there are also family tickets. The line is expected to reach Rhyd Ddu (about half way between Caernarfon and Porthmadog) by 2003.

You can use the Freedom of Wales Flexi-Pass or North & Mid Wales Flexi-Rover (see the introduction to the Getting Around chapter). There are also Rover tickets good for travel on this line, the Ffestiniog Railway and Bws Ffestiniog (the Porthmadog–Caernarfon bus service). See the Web site at www.whr.co.uk.

Other Things to See & Do
At Victoria Dock there's a small **Maritime Museum** (☎ 675269), usually open 10 am to 4 pm daily, May to September. Admission is £1/free.

The pleasure boat *Queen of the Sea* (☎ 672772) does 40-minute tours up and down the Menai Strait from Slate Quay, beside the castle, from late May (Whitsun) to October. Tickets cost £3.50/2.

Activities
Two dedicated walking and cycling paths established by Gwynedd Council along disused railway lines, are the 12-mile Lôn Eifion south to Bryncir (starting near the Welsh Highland Railway station) and the 4½-mile Lôn Las Menai along the Menai Strait towards Bangor. A map-brochure on these routes is available from the TIC; see under Getting Around for details of bike hire.

Plas Menai, the National Watersports Centre (☎ 01248-670964, e plas.menai@scw.co.uk) at Llanfairisgaer, about 3 miles out the A487 towards Bangor, offers single-activity instruction weekends and multi-activity courses in sailing, windsurfing, canoeing and other sports. Advance booking is suggested. For more information, see the Web site at www.plasmenai.co.uk.

Snowdonia Riding Stables (☎ 650342) at Waunfawr, 3 miles up the A4085 towards Beddgelert, charges £26/45 per half/full day, the latter with a picnic or pub stop; booking is advisable.

Places to Stay
Coed Helen Holiday Park (☎ 672852, *Coed Helen Rd*), just across the river from the cas-

tle, has just five tent pitches amongst the caravans at £3 per person plus a pitch fee of £2 (or £2.50/3.50 with a motorbike/car).

Cadnant Valley Camping & Caravan Park (☎ 673196) is half a mile east of the castle along the A4086 Llanberis road. It opens March to October and costs from £7 to £9 for two people with a tent. *Plas Gwyn Caravan Park* (☎ 672619) at Llanrug, 3½ miles along the same road, has tent sites from £2 per person.

Totters (☎ 672963, *Plas Porth Yr Aur, 2 High St*) is an independent hostel with dorm beds (including bedding and a light breakfast) for £10, laid-back, helpful owners and a 600-year-old pantry. This is also the local stop for the buses of Stray Travel (see under Bus in the Getting Around chapter).

Among B&B options within the old town walls – probably the quietest part of town – is *Tegfan Guest House* (☎ 673703, *4 Church St*), charging £20 per person. The *Black Boy Inn* (☎ 673604, *Northgate St*) is a crusty old pub with B&B in singles/doubles for £20/34 (£23/40 en suite).

The *Prince of Wales Hotel* (☎ 673367, fax 676610, *Bangor St*) is a former coaching inn with B&B from £25 per person. Options farther out include *Gorffwysfa Guest House* (☎ 678981, *North Rd*), charging from £16.50; and the good *Menai Bank Hotel* (☎ 673297, *North Rd*) at £30/50 per single/double.

If you've got wheels, try *Hen Ysgol Guest House* (☎ 660701, *Bwlchderwin, Pant Glas*) in a former schoolhouse just west of the A487, 10 miles south of Caernarfon. Rooms cost from £17 per person B&B, plus £10 for a three-course evening meal.

Places to Eat
Caffi Maes (☎ 673075, *4 Castle Square*) is a snug tearoom with toasties and cakes. The cheap-and-cheerful *Battered Cod* (28 High St) has tasty lunchtime grills and pasta dishes for around £4, plus takeaway fish and chips.

Hole in the Wall St, nestled along the old town wall, is a good place for foodies. At *Stones Bistro* (☎ 671152), at No 4, you can tuck into good roast Welsh lamb and other carefully prepared, meaty dishes from £7 to about £12, or cheaper vegetarian choices. The atmosphere is French, and it's popular so booking ahead is wise. A broader menu – including seafood and game – at higher prices (£11 to £15 per dish) is on offer at *Molly's Restaurant* (☎ *673238*) down the street; it opens every evening except Monday.

Reasonable set restaurant meals and pub grub are available at the *Black Boy Inn* (see Places to Stay earlier). *Macsen Restaurant* (☎ *676464, 11 Castle Square*) specialises in traditional Welsh dishes upstairs, with home-made cakes and snacks served in the airy ground-floor cafe. For quality and value for money, the best choice is *Courtenay's Bistro* (☎ *677290, 9 Segontium Terrace*), with main dishes in the £7 to £9 range and lunches under £5. The emphasis is on local produce such as mussels, sea trout, lamb and Welsh cheeses. It opens daily except Sunday and Monday.

Local supermarkets include *Iceland*, off Penllyn, and a *Safeway* on North Rd. A *farmers market* sprawls across Castle Square every Saturday and, in summer, on Monday too (the Market Hall in the old town is just for handicrafts and other small shops).

Getting There & Away

With the exception of the Welsh Highland Railway (see that section earlier), Caernarfon has been bypassed by the railways, though bus services are plentiful.

Snowdon Sherpa bus services (see Getting There & Around in the Snowdonia National Park section) include the Bws Ffestiniog from Pwllheli, Porthmadog and Beddgelert, and the No 95 from Llanberis and Beddgelert. Express Motors (☎ 881108) bus No 1 runs from Porthmadog (£2.50, 50 minutes, hourly) and from Bangor (£1.40, 25 minutes, three daily); services are less frequent Sunday. Arriva Cymru's No 5/5A/5B/5X runs from Bangor (£1.90, 30 minutes) every 15 minutes and from Llandudno (£3.45, 1½ hours) hourly, Monday to Saturday. Berwyn (☎ 660315) No 12 runs hourly from Pwllheli (£2, 45 minutes), less often on Sunday. For trans-Wales connections, Arriva's TrawsCambria (No 701) coach comes from Holyhead (£5.10, one hour 20 minutes) and from Cardiff, Swansea, Aber-

ystwyth, Machynlleth, Dolgellau (£6.70, 1¾ hours) and other points south.

Getting Around

Bikes are available for hire from Menai Cycles (☎ 713871), Slate Quay, for £12 per day. Beics Castell (☎ 677400), 33 High St, sells bikes and other gear, and hires out bikes by the hour or day. See the Web site at www.bikeworld.uk.com.

BANGOR

☎ 01248 • pop 12,000

Bangor – Gwynedd's only city, in official terms – is one of the campus centres of the University of Wales, attracting about 6500 students from all over the UK, and is at its liveliest during term-time. Things go pretty quiet during the summer, although the town – on the Chester-Holyhead railway – was a popular destination in Victorian times and still has pretensions as a resort. Its Victorian end, including a venerable old pier, occupies bluffs above the Menai Strait.

The first settlement here was probably a monastery established in 525 by St Deiniol, and the small, lopsided, proud cathedral named after him is the town's main attraction.

Welsh opera superstar Bryn Terfel (see Arts in the Facts About Wales chapter) lives about 3 miles outside of town.

Orientation & Information

From Bangor train station it's about a half-mile north-east on Deiniol Rd to the TIC, and another block north-east to the bus stands on Garth Rd. Most university buildings are on Deiniol Rd with older ones on the hill above. To the south-east and parallel to Deiniol Rd is High St, the main shopping area, centred on the Town Clock.

The TIC (☎ 352786, fax 362701, ⓔ bangor .tic@gwynedd.gov.uk) on Deiniol Rd opens 10 am to 6 pm daily, Easter to October (on Friday and Saturday only in November and mid-February to Easter; closed December to mid-February). Across Deiniol Rd is the Student Union.

All major UK banks have offices on High St. The post office is across Gwynedd Rd

The end of another day: the sun casts long shadows across the fields of the Llŷn Peninsula.

Llanberis' beautiful lake, Llŷn Padarn, can be circumnavigated by train or traversed by hire boat.

BRYN THOMAS

The UK's smallest house, Conwy

BRYN THOMAS

The Ladies of Llangollen called this Gothic and Tudor pile home.

PAUL BIGLAND

The Menai Bridge, which links Anglesey with the mainland, was built by Thomas Telford in 1826.

PATRICK HORTON

Not quite at the end of the rainbow – the stately home of Erddig

PETER HINES

Beaumaris Castle, Anglesey

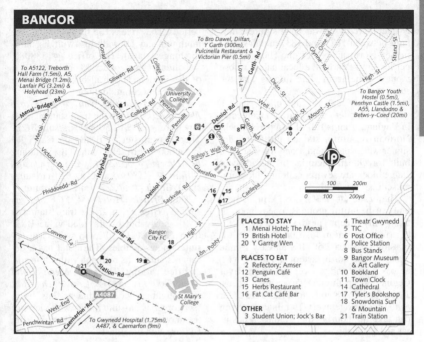

BANGOR

To Bro Dawel, Dilfan,
Y Garth (300m),
Pulcinella Restaurant &
Victorian Pier (0.5mi)

To A5122, Treborth
Hall Farm (1.5mi), A5,
Menai Bridge (1.2mi),
Lanfair PG (3.2mi) &
Holyhead (23mi)

To Bangor Youth
Hostel (0.5mi),
Penrhos Castle (1.5mi),
A55, Llandudno &
Betws-y-Coed (20mi)

University
College

Bishop's Walk

Bangor
City FC

St Mary's
College

To Gwynedd Hospital (1.75mi),
A487, & Caernarfon (9mi)

PLACES TO STAY		4	Theatr Gwynedd
1 Menai Hotel; The Menai		5	TIC
19 British Hotel		6	Post Office
20 Y Garreg Wen		7	Police Station
		8	Bus Stands
PLACES TO EAT		9	Bangor Museum
2 Refectory; Amser			& Art Gallery
12 Penguin Café		10	Bookland
13 Canes		11	Town Clock
15 Herbs Restaurant		14	Cathedral
16 Fat Cat Café Bar		17	Tyler's Bookshop
		18	Snowdonia Surf
OTHER			& Mountain
3 Student Union; Jock's Bar		21	Train Station

from the TIC. The best bookshops, both on High St, are Tyler's at the corner with Lôn Pobty, and Bookland beyond the Town Clock. The police station (☎ 673333) is on Garth Rd by the bus stands. Gwynedd Hospital (☎ 384384) is 2¼ miles south-west of the centre on Penrhos Rd.

For lesbian and gay travellers, the Student Union has a lesbian-gay-bisexual student office (e lgb@undeb.bangor.ac.uk, or ask at reception in the Union).

Cathedral Church of St Deiniol

St Deiniol was made a bishop in about 546 by Prince Maelgwyn of Gwynedd, making his little church a cathedral and Deiniol's see a diocese, perhaps the oldest one in Britain. Vikings burned the church down in 1073. The earliest surviving bits date from the 12th century, and the earliest substantial part is the presbytery (the alcove around the altar) from the early 13th century. The nave dates from the 14th century, the bell tower

from the 16th, and the whole church was much restored in the 19th century.

Opposite the northern entrance is the renowned late-15th- or early-16th-century carved oak figure, almost lifesize, known as the Mostyn Christ. Its origin is uncertain, though it may have come from Rhuddlan Priory near the North Wales coast. The university's main building, up on the hill, is often mistaken for the cathedral, on which it was allegedly modelled.

Victorian Pier

The renovated Victorian pier, built in 1896, stretches 450m out into the Menai Strait – seemingly halfway to Anglesey – with a distant view of Thomas Telford's handsome Menai Suspension Bridge. In high season there's a 25p admission charge to the pier.

Penrhyn Castle

Just east of town is Bangor's other attraction, Penrhyn Castle. Unlike the other high-profile castles in this corner of Wales, this one was not put there by Edward I. It's pure fancy, built between 1820 and 1837 and designed in 'neo-Norman' style by one Thomas Hopper for Lord Penrhyn, a local nabob whose money came from slate mining and the sugar trade.

It's a vast, extravagant place, with a great hall modelled on Durham Cathedral in England, rooms full of Hopper's mock-Norman furniture, stained glass and designer wallpaper – and a one-ton slate bed built for Queen Victoria. In the adjacent stable block are several galleries and mini-museums.

The castle (☎ 353084, NT), in 16 hectares of beautiful grounds, opens noon to 5 pm daily except Tuesday, Easter to October (from 11 am in July and August). Admission costs £5/2.50. It's an easy 2-mile walk – to the north-eastern end of High St, across a footbridge over the little River Cegin, and up through the castle gardens. Arriva bus No 78 goes from Garth Rd as far as the footbridge every 15 minutes, or you can take the hourly No 7 Bethesda bus as far as Llandegai.

Bangor Museum & Art Gallery

This free town museum features 2000 years of local history including archaeological relics and tableaux of domestic scenes of yore. It opens 12.30 to 4.30 pm Tuesday to Friday and 10.30 am to 4.30 Saturday.

Places to Stay

At *Treborth Hall Farm Caravan & Campsite* (☎ 364399, *Treborth Rd*), 2 miles west of town and just west of the Menai Bridge, you can camp for £4 to £7 per person.

The *Bangor Youth Hostel* (☎ 353516, *Tan-y-Bryn*) is three-quarters of a mile east of the town centre, just off the A5122 Llandegai road, with good views of Penrhyn Castle. Take the No 78 bus (every 15 minutes) to the Tan-y-Bryn stop. It opens year round (but closes some weekend nights outside the high season, so call ahead); nightly rates are £11/7.75.

The university's accommodation office lets out *student rooms* on a B&B basis during summer, Easter and Christmas holiday periods. The price is £35 for two nights, the minimum stay for walk-ins (with discounts for longer stays). The office (☎ 388088, @ holidays@bangor.ac.uk) on the 3rd floor of the Student Union also keeps a list of other local accommodation.

Friendly *Y Garreg Wen* (☎ 353836, 8 *Deiniol Rd*), close to the train station, has a few rooms at £12.50 per person B&B. There's a cluster of B&Bs on Garth Rd about 600m north-east of the TIC, including *Bro Dawel* (☎ 355242) at £15 per person, *Dilfan* (☎ 353030) at £18 (£20 en suite) and *Y Garth* (☎ 362277) at £20 en suite.

The *British Hotel* (☎ 364911, fax 370569, *High St*) near the train station is traffic-noisy but offers good-value B&B from £25/36 (£17.50/25 in winter) in en-suite singles/doubles. The hotel has a decent restaurant, its own pub with bar meals, and free parking. The small *Menai Hotel* (☎ 354200, fax 354512, *Craig-y-Don Rd*), in a neighbourhood of student flats, has a few gorgeous en-suite rooms with views of the mountains or the Menai Strait from £45/69, with breakfast.

Places to Eat

If your budget's tight, take your meals at the student canteen upstairs in the refectory building adjacent to the Student Union, or in one of several cheap eateries upstairs in the Union.

The *Fat Cat Café Bar* (☎ 370445, 161 *High St*) pulls in the students with good home-made burgers (£5), filled baguettes and vegetarian plates, plus drinks inside or at the outdoor bar. *Penguin Café* (☎ 362036, 260 High St) has bagels and baguettes, quiche and home-made pasta for around £4. Grills and stir-fries are on offer at *Canes* (☎ 364728, 215 High St).

Herbs Restaurant (☎ 351249, 162 High St) is fully licensed and opens until 9 pm, with sandwiches under £4 and salads under £6.

The Menai, a trendy cafe-bar at the hotel of the same name (see Places to Stay earlier), does burgers, sandwiches, giant salads and other snacks during the day.

Out at the pier, the Italian restaurant *Pulcinella* (☎ 362807) has the best views, plus pizza and pasta from about £5.

Entertainment
A modest nightlife scene centres around the Student Union. In the basement is *Jock's Bar*, usually open Wednesday to Saturday, with gay/lesbian nights on some Thursdays or Fridays (ask at reception at the Union). There's a bar and nightclub called *Amser* (Time) in the refectory building adjacent to the Union, on Monday, Friday and Saturday nights. A favoured haunt in town is the *Fat Cat* (see Places to Eat earlier).

Theatr Gwynedd (☎ 351708, Deiniol Rd), opposite the TIC, is one of four theatres in Wales with a resident acting company, and has a full schedule of drama (Welsh- and English-language), dance, musicals and new-release films.

Getting There & Away
Arriva Cymru's No 5/5A/5B/5X bus runs from Caernarfon (£1.90 single, 30 minutes) four times hourly and from Llandudno (£2.85, one hour) twice hourly. Express Motors (☎ 01286-881108) No 1 comes from Porthmadog (£3.20, 1¼ hours) via Caernarfon (£1.40, 25 minutes) three times daily. Services are less frequent on Sunday.

The shortest route into the heart of the national park is Arriva's No 77 or 86 to Llanberis (£1.20, 40 minutes), each hourly (less often on Sunday).

Bangor is a stop on Arriva's daily trans-Wales TrawsCambria (No 701) coach. National Express coach No 545 comes daily from London (£22, 8½ hours) via Llandudno and Birmingham.

Bangor is on the InterCity line from London's Euston station (£25 if you book in advance, 3 ¾ hours, four daily). It's also on the North Wales coast line from Crewe and Chester (£12.50, one hour 10 minutes), running every hour or two.

Getting Around
Snowdonia Surf & Mountain (☎ 354321), 75 High St, rents good Kona mountain bikes for £16 per day.

Llŷn Peninsula

The Llŷn Peninsula and the Isle of Anglesey were the last places the Romans and the Normans reached, and remain the least tamed. But while Anglesey now has an international port and a European-class motorway, 'the Llŷn' remains untouched by comparison. Over the centuries the heaviest footfalls have been those of pilgrims on their way to holy Bardsey Island.

Few English holidaymakers have pushed beyond Abersoch, and the railway stops at Pwllheli. In its further parts, this crooked finger of land is peaceful and largely undeveloped, with 70 miles of wildlife-rich coastline (much of it in the hands of the NT, and almost 80% of it officially designated an Area of Outstanding Natural Beauty), quiet walking and cycling, some excellent beaches and a handful of small fishing villages. Welsh is the language of everyday life. This is about as Welsh as Wales gets.

CRICCIETH
This seaside town about 4 miles west of Porthmadog likes to call itself the gateway to the Llŷn, though it's probably too English for the job. There are just two attractions: Criccieth Castle and the sea.

The centre, such as it is, is Y Maes, a wide place on High St, the A497 Porthmadog–Pwllheli road. The seaside road running parallel to High St is Castle St. There's a small, summer-only TIC on Y Maes, and the train station is about two blocks west down the A497.

Criccieth Castle can fairly be considered Welsh, having been started in 1239 by Llewelyn ap Iorwerth (Llewelyn the Great), though it was enlarged by Edward I. The ruins are modest but the position is superb, with fine views up and down the Llŷn's southern coast and across Tremadog Bay to Harlech. The castle (☎ 522227, Cadw) and a small information centre open 10 am to 6 pm daily, April to September; admission costs £2.20/1.70. Admission is free the rest of the year.

Just west of the castle on Castle St is the Chapel of Art (☎ 523570), a 19th-century chapel renovated and reborn as an eclectic art gallery and concert venue. It opens 10 am to 6 pm daily except Monday, in summer only. You can't miss the bright pavement tiles out in front – congratulations from far-flung ceramicist-friends.

The week-long Criccieth Festival (☎/fax 522778, ℮ festival@criccieth.freeserve.co .uk) is an equally eclectic sampler of art, lectures, walks, drama, jazz and classical music in venues around the town in the second half of June each year.

The town has lots of accommodation and nothing else to do – the explanation being that for many years this was a favourite English 'how-we-do-love-to-be-beside-the-seaside' resort, easy to reach on the Cambrian Coast line.

There's a line of modest Victorian guesthouses facing the sea on Min-y-Mor (Marine Terrace), the western extension of Castle St. Cyclist-friendly *Budget Accommodation* (☎ 523098, 11 Marine Terrace) opens May to September with just two rooms at £10 per person. B&B is on offer from £14 per person at *Y Rhoslyn* (☎ 522865, 8 Marine Terrace) and from £18 at *Seaspray* (☎ 522373, 4 Marine Terrace). The *Lion Hotel* (☎ 522460), a block north-west of Y Maes, has singles/doubles with views of the castle and sea from £31/55. The very good *Moelwyn Restaurant* (☎ 522500, 27–9 Mona Terrace), two blocks south-east from Y Maes, also has en-suite rooms from £25 per person.

Just over a mile north on the B4411 Caernarfon road, there's bunkhouse accommodation for £5 per person at the *Stone Barn* (☎ 522115, Tyddyn Morthwyl); book in advance.

Besides trains from Machynlleth and from Pwllheli (six a day), there are some useful bus services. Express Motors No 1 runs about hourly (fewer on Sunday) from Blaenau Ffestiniog and Porthmadog (£1.30 single, 10 minutes), and from Caernarfon (£2.30, 40 minutes). Arriva's bus No 3 passes by every half-hour (every two hours on Sunday) en route from Porthmadog and from Pwllheli (£1.40, 25 minutes).

AROUND CRICCIETH
Llanystumdwy

Llanystumdwy (pronounced khlan-uh-**stim**-dwee) is the boyhood home and final resting place of David Lloyd George, one of Wales' finest contributions to Westminster and prime minister from 1916 to 1922 (see the boxed text 'The Rise of Lloyd George' under History in the Facts About Wales chapter). There's a small Lloyd George Museum (☎ 522071) here, full of photos, posters, personal effects and state gifts, plus a library and Internet access. It opens 10.30 am to 5 pm weekdays (plus Saturday in June, and Saturday and Sunday in July), Easter to October. Highgate, the house he grew up in, is 50m away, and for political pilgrims his grave is about 150m away on the other side of the car park.

The turning to the village is 1½-miles west of Criccieth on the A497. The No 3 Porthmadog–Pwllheli bus stops here every half-hour (every two hours on Sunday).

PWLLHELI
☎ 01758 • pop 5000

The only place of any size on the peninsula is the market town of Pwllheli (pronounced poolth-**heh**-lee) – known more for its Welshness than for anything else (it was here in 1925 that Plaid Cymru, the Welsh National Party, was founded, though the building itself is long gone).

There is not, in truth, much to do here but walk on South Beach promenade, look at lobster-pots on the quay or go deep-sea fishing on the *Judy B* (☎ 01766-512464). Being the terminus of the Cambrian Coast railway from Machynlleth, however, Pwllheli is the logical place from which the carless can explore the Llŷn.

The train station, bus stands and harbour are all within a block of one another. The TIC (☎/fax 613000, ℮ pwllheli.tic@gwynedd.gov .uk), opposite the train station, has everything you'll need to know about the peninsula. It opens 10 am to 6 pm daily (to 4.30 pm daily except Sunday and Thursday, October to Easter); the only other TIC on the peninsula is a summer-only one at Abersoch. Y Maes, the central square, doubles as a parking lot and, on Wednesday, as an open-air market. You'll get further here with Welsh street names than English ones – eg Stryd Fawr instead of High St, Ffordd-y-Cob rather than Embankment Rd.

Bank Place (☎ 612103, 29 Stryd Fawr), two blocks north of the TIC, has rooms from £12 per person. *Rhosydd (☎ 612956, Talcymerau)*, three blocks south-west from Y Maes, has B&B for £17 per person, and the *Victoria Hotel (☎ 612834, Ffordd-y-Cob)*, two blocks south of Y Maes along the harbour, charges £18.

The *Chess Restaurant (☎ 612203, 2 Gaol St)*, 1½ blocks north of Y Maes, offers some inventive lunchtime dishes (try the pheasant casserole or vegetarian lasagne) for under £5. Try the *Mariner Bistro (☎ 612245)* beside the TIC for chicken or pizza. The *Village Restaurant (☎ 613198, Y Maes)*, above the *Spar* mini-market, mixes Mexican and traditional fare.

Trains come from Machynlleth via Porthmadog (£3.20 single, 25 minutes) every two or three hours (fewer at weekends). Bus services to Pwllheli include Arriva's No 3 from Porthmadog (£1.70, 40 minutes, every half hour) and Clynnog & Trefor's (☎ 01286-660208) No 12 from Caernarfon (£2.30, 45 minutes, hourly) – both with a less frequent Sunday service.

AROUND PWLLHELI
Penarth Fawr
Just off the A497, 3 miles east of Pwllheli, is a handsome 'hall-house' built for a member of the Welsh gentry in the early 15th century. Faced with plain stone outside, it's a spectacle of carved wood inside. The house, owned by Cadw, opens 9.30 am to 6.30 pm daily, March to October; and 9.30 am to 4 pm (2 to 4 pm on Sunday), the rest of the year; the key is at the ceramics and bookbinding gallery in the adjacent former stables.

ABERSOCH & AROUND
☎ 01758
This fairly anglicised town is a popular resort and marina, and Llŷn's main watersports centre, with two big beaches and seemingly more fast-food than anywhere else on the peninsula.

Offshore, the two privately owned St Tudwal's Islands have colonies of grey seals. The Craft & Angling Centre (☎ 712646) runs excursions around the islands, as well as deep-sea fishing trips. A 3-mile walk south takes you to the beach at Porth Ceiriad, surrounded by cliffs where chough and auks nest. An equal distance west across the headland is 3-mile-long Porth Neigwl (Hell's Mouth), the Llŷn's most popular surfing beach.

Tanrallt Farm (☎/fax 713527) opens year round with dorm-style accommodation at £10 per bed, and bike hire. *Llysfor B&B (☎ 712248)* charges £20 per person in en-suite rooms. Rooms at the *Carisbrooke Hotel (☎ 712526)* start at £24 B&B.

Arriva's No 18 bus runs to Abersoch from Pwllheli (£1.65, 25 minutes) every hour or so (less often on Sunday).

ABERDARON & AROUND
☎ 01758
The Llŷn's most accessible coastal walking centres on the westerly village of Aberdaron, whose whitewashed houses contemplate Aberdaron Bay across a fine sandy beach. The little Gwylan Islands in the bay are North Wales' most important puffin-breeding site. At wind-blasted Braich-y-Pwll, the Llŷn's westernmost mainland point, the NT has a small information post in an old coastguard hut, open most weekends from Easter to September. There are few better views out to Bardsey Island than from here. Inland are strip-fields which preserve many of the patterns of ancient land-use.

Just north of Aberdaron at Porthor are the so-called Whistling Sands, a crescent-shaped beach whose sand squeals unnervingly when you walk on it. From here it's a 2-mile coastal walk west via the twin headlands of Dinas Bach and Dinas Fawr to the cove of Porth Orion.

On the heights near the hamlet of Rhiw, 5 miles east of Aberdaron, is a 17th-century Welsh manor house called Plas-yn-Rhiw (☎ 780219, NT). Restored in the 1930s and 1940s, its ornamental gardens are in startling contrast to the surrounding moorland. It opens noon to 5 pm (last admission 4.30 pm) Thursday to Monday, April to mid-May; Wednesday to Monday, mid-May to September; and at weekends in October. Admission costs £3.20/1.60. The nearby viewpoint of Mynydd Rhiw looks right down the length of Hell's Mouth beach.

Aberdaron guesthouses offering B&B include *Pennant* (☎ 760610) at £17 per person, and *Carreg Plas* (☎ 760308) from £20 to £27 (en suite). Rooms at the *Ship Hotel* (☎ 760204) start at £21 per person. Singles/doubles at the *Ty Newydd Hotel* (☎ 760207) cost from £40/65.

Arriva bus No 17/17B runs to Aberdaron from Pwllheli (£2.05, 40 minutes) every hour or two Monday to Saturday; the No 17B stops twice daily at Plas-yn-Rhiw.

BARDSEY ISLAND (YNYS ENLLI)

The ancient name for this 2-mile-long island, 2 miles off the tip of the Llŷn peninsula, is the Isle of 20,000 Saints. In the 6th or 7th century the obscure St Cadfan founded a monastery here. At a time when journeys from Britain to Italy were long, perilous and beyond the means of most people, three pilgrimages to Bardsey came to have the same value as one to Rome. The 20,000 were probably not so much saints as pilgrims who came here to die.

The island's Welsh name means 'Isle of the Currents', a reference to the treacherous tidal surges in Bardsey Sound which probably convinced medieval visitors that their lives were indeed in God's hands.

Most modern pilgrims to Bardsey are seabird-watchers (the island is home to an important colony of Manx shearwaters) – although there are also some 6th-century carved stones and the remains of a 13th-century abbey tower to mull over. The Bardsey Island Trust (☎ 01758-730740), which looks after the island, organises boat trips from Porth Meudwy (the closest harbour to the island) – 15 minutes each way plus four hours on the island – twice daily from June to August and by arrangement the rest of the year, weather permitting. For information during the summer, call ☎ 01758-760667

between 10 am and 4 pm daily. The trust also maintains some self-catering accommodation and a little shop on the island, along with a retreat centre, an ornithological research station and a 180-hectare sheep farm (when the trust advertised in late 2000 for someone to take out a 20-year lease on this farm, over 1100 people applied).

Bardsey is one of many candidates for the mythical Isle of Avalon, where King Arthur is said to have been taken after the Battle of Camlann. Other legends say the wizard Merlin is asleep in a glass castle on the island.

THE NORTH COAST
☎ 01758

The north coast presents a more modest prospect, with only small villages and a few quiet beaches, the best of them at Tywyn (Tudweiliog) and Morfa Nefyn.

It's hard to believe that the little crescent of sand at Porth Dinllaen – now owned in its entirety by the NT – was once a busy cargo, shipbuilding and herring port, the only safe haven on the peninsula's north coast. It was eyed up by William Madocks (see under Porthmadog earlier in the chapter) as a possible home for ferries to Ireland but in 1839 the House of Commons gave that job to Holyhead. The most agreeable way to get here is on foot along the beach – a mile west from Morfa Nefyn or 2 miles from Nefyn.

For more on the area's maritime history visit the little Maritime Museum in St Mary's Church, Nefyn, open 10.30 am to 4.30 pm Monday to Saturday and 2 pm to 4 pm Sunday, July to September.

St Beuno was to North Wales what St David was to the south of the country, and there's a tiny church dedicated to him – one of the peninsula's many stopovers for medieval pilgrims – at the hamlet of Pistyll, 2 miles east of Nefyn (another St Beuno church is up the coast at Clynnog Fawr). A few miles on from Pistyll are the 100m sea-cliffs of Carreg y Llam, a major North Wales seabird site, with huge colonies of razorbills, guillemots and kittiwakes.

Nant Gwrtheyrn is a 'ghost village'

brought back from the dead when it was purchased and restored as the home of Wales' National Language Centre (see under Courses in the Facts for the Visitor chapter). It's reached from the village of Llithfaen by a path down a steep valley where, according to tradition, the semi-mythical Celtic King Vortigern is buried.

The Llŷn's highest point is the 564m cluster of volcanic peaks called Yr Eifl – anglicised to 'The Rivals' – which plunge spectacularly into Caernarfon Bay just west of the former quarrying village of Trefor. A century ago, mines on the flanks of Yr Eifl were the world's main source of granite paving-stones.

The **Llys Olwen Guest House** (☎ 720493, *Morfa Nefyn*) has rooms for £20 per person. In Nefyn try the **Caeau Capel Hotel** (☎ 720240, *Rhodfar Môr*), with en-suite rooms from £25 per person. Whet your whistle by the sea at Porth Dinllaen's very popular **Ty Goch Inn**.

Nefyn Coaches (☎ 01758-720904) bus No 8 runs to Nefyn from Pwllheli every one to 1½ hours Monday to Saturday, and somewhat less frequently to Tudweiliog. The No 27 goes to Llithfaen every two or three hours, and less frequently to Nefyn. Both have limited Sunday services. The No 12 Caernarfon–Pwllheli bus (see Pwllheli earlier in the chapter) stops at Trefor.

Anglesey & the North Coast

Everything in North Wales plays second fiddle to Snowdonia, with most travellers seemingly bound for the mountains. But don't be in too great a rush on your way from England or from the Ireland ferry at Holyhead, for there are some pleasant surprises and a few places worth lingering in.

The north coast seems to consist mainly of industrial development alternating with vast caravan parks, all strung together by the A548 and the A55 motorway. Only when you get west as far as Llandudno, on its own rather splendid peninsula, and the fine walled town of Conwy, do you feel you've reached into Wales. A slower, more appealing approach from England is up the valley of the River Dee, where Llangollen offers more to detain its guests than any other town in the north-east.

Anglesey Island has a greater concentration of prehistoric sites than anywhere else in Wales, and this is where Britain's Celts made their last stand against the Romans, so it's no surprise that the island is nicknamed 'Mother of Wales'. Get off the thundering Bangor-Holyhead road and you'll find some of the quietest, remotest and least-changed places in the country.

Getting Around
The main bus company on Anglesey is Arriva Cymru (Aberystwyth ☎ 01970-624472). Useful operators in the north-east are Arriva Cymru, Bryn Melyn (Llangollen ☎ 01978-860701) and GHA (Wrexham ☎ 01978-753598).

Arriva has one-day (£5/3.50 adult/child), three-day (£10/7) and five-day (£15/10) passes, good for unlimited travel on all its services (buy on board). The Freedom of North and Mid Wales Flexi-Rover pass (£28) is good for any three in seven days of bus plus train travel (see the introduction to the Getting Around chapter for details).

The North Wales Coast railway line from Chester (England) to Holyhead provides

Highlights

- Checking out cutting-edge Stone Age art at Barclodiad y Gawres (Anglesey)
- Learning to pronounce Llanfairpwllgwyngyllgogerychwyrndrobwllllantysiliogogogoch from the people who live there
- Walking the ramparts of Conwy, one of Europe's finest walled towns
- Taking a cable car up the Great Orme (Llandudno) and counting the peaks of Snowdonia
- Riding a canal boat across the spectacular Pontcysyllte Aqueduct, near Llangollen

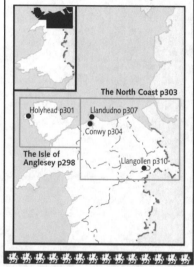

easy access to coastal towns, including Llandudno and Conwy, and via Bangor (Snowdonia) across Anglesey to Ireland ferries at Holyhead. In England, near Wales' eastern border, runs the Birmingham-Shrewsbury-Chester line. The Conwy Valley Line to Llandudno from Betws-y-Coed and Blaenau Ffestiniog allows rail access from the heart of Snowdonia.

The Isle of Anglesey (Ynys Môn)

As the Celts' last refuge in Britain against the Roman advance, Anglesey qualifies as the Welsh heartland, if there is such a thing. The Celts are thought to have arrived on the island around 500 BC. Their artistic and metalworking skills have been confirmed by a famously rich cache of iron tools, slave-chains, jewellery and other objects (now in Cardiff's National Museum) found at the bottom of Llyn Cerrig Bach in west Anglesey.

Within a few centuries the teachings of the druids, the Celts' religious leaders, were washing back into the wider European Celtic amalgam. Anglesey was becoming a kind of spiritual centre, which may be why the Celts defended it with such ferocity against the Romans. It's said the Roman invasion force stood rooted to the ground with fear at the sight of the men and women, half-naked and shrieking hysterically at them, that they saw across the Menai Straits. In the end the Romans crossed the straits in boats and pushed on to Holyhead, and the Celtic infrastructure unravelled.

Anglesey – at 276 sq miles the largest island in Wales and England, with a population of just 71,000 – is today a curious combination of old and new. Here is some of Wales' remotest and most ancient countryside (and its highest concentration of prehistoric sites) – with a European-class motorway belting across the middle of it in the service of an international ferry port. The island is often referred to as *Mam Cymru*, Mother of Wales – as much for the sense of sacred inheritance as for agricultural fecundity. It has for centuries been North Wales' breadbasket, and still produces more than its share of cereal crops and beef. In addition to farming, its inhabitants have relied on smuggling, copper and coal mining and quarrying, as well as the sea, for their income.

The island was only linked to the mainland in 1826, when Thomas Telford built the handsome Menai Bridge, the first ever heavy-duty iron suspension bridge. A mile away is the Britannia Bridge, designed by Robert Stephenson (whose father, George Stephenson, developed the steam-powered *Rocket*, the first passenger locomotive) and which opened in 1850. This now bears most of the traffic, including the train, between Bangor and Holyhead.

Most visitors see little more than what's visible from the A5, or at most venture across the straits to Beaumaris and Plas Newydd. This is the flattest part of Wales, rising to just 219m at Holyhead Mountain, but the coast offers rugged cliffs, some excellent sandy beaches, and coastal watersports centres at Beaumaris and Holyhead. The still-life landscape is tailor-made for cycling and unhurried rambles; the county council publishes a series of useful free map-leaflets, *Circular Walks on the Isle of Anglesey*.

Most of the island's stone monuments, burial chambers and ancient settlements are managed by Cadw, the Welsh historic monuments agency; best known, and one of Wales' finest, is the Bryn Celli Ddu burial mound (see under South Anglesey later in the chapter). The National Trust (NT; see Useful Organisations in the Facts for the Visitor chapter) owns a great deal of coastal property as part of its Neptune Campaign.

The easiest access to the island is from Bangor. The best source of information is the Tourist Information Centre (TIC) at 'Llanfair PG', the town with the famously long name (see under South Anglesey later).

BEAUMARIS (BIWMARES)
☎ 01248 • pop 1500

Beaumaris used to be the island's principal town and chief port. Today it is not even that but is known primarily as the site of the castle that James of St George built here for Edward I, and as a sailing and watersports centre. But the castle and the town's picturesque narrow streets make it a worthwhile excursion from Bangor.

Beaumaris Castle
Beaumaris Castle (☎ 810361; Cadw) overlooks the ancient ferry crossing on the Menai

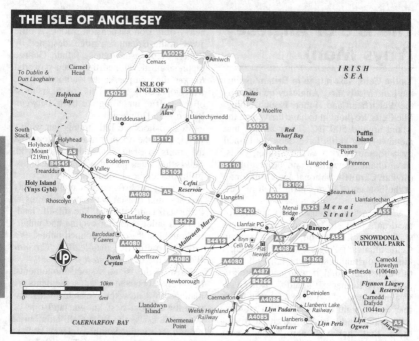

THE ISLE OF ANGLESEY

Strait and is the last, most ambitious and probably finest of Edward's castles in Wales, laid out with geometrical precision. It was begun in 1295 but money and supplies ran out before it was completed, so it's not as tall as it was meant to be and lacks the menace of Edward's other castles. Owain Glyndŵr managed to take it, and it saw action for the last time in 1646 during the Civil War. It opens 9.30 am to 5 pm daily (to 6 pm June to September; to 4 pm, and from 11 am on Sunday, November to March). Admission costs £2.20/1.70 for adults/children.

Other Things to See & Do
Beaumaris Gaol (☎ 810921) was a model prison when it opened in 1829. This and the adjacent 1614 Courthouse open 10.30 am to 5 pm, Easter to October; joint admission costs £2.75/1.75.

For a dose of treacly, overpriced nostalgia, check out the **Museum of Childhood** (☎ 712498), opposite the castle. It opens 10.30 am to 5.30 pm daily (from noon on Sunday), Easter to October; admission costs £3.25/2.

Walking Routes
From the public car park at the northern end of Llangoed (2 miles north up the coast from Beaumaris), a moderate 6-mile (three-hour) walk goes out to Penmon Point, Anglesey's easternmost tip, via Penmon village and an Augustinian priory said to have been founded in the 12th century by St Seiriol, one the island's two important saints (the other, St Cybi, was based at Holyhead).

Boat Trips
Several operators run summer cruises from Beaumaris pier out to Puffin Island, which has a few puffins and lots of seals, or along the Menai Strait. Beaumaris Marine Services (☎ 810746), with a kiosk on the pier, has daily departures from April to October; an hour's cruise to Puffin Island costs £4/3.

Places to Stay & Eat

The *Kingsbridge Caravan & Camping Park* (☎ 490636, Llanfaes) – 'not suitable for teenagers' – has tent sites from £3; it's just north of Beaumaris.

Ye Olde Bulls Head Inn (☎ 810329, fax 811294, Castle St), with 15 en-suite singles/doubles for £53/83, is at least interesting. It dates back to 1472 when it was the borough posting-house. Charles Dickens once stayed here, and the bedrooms are named after his characters. A set three-course meal in the restaurant costs £27.50 and the brasserie has baguettes and hot meals from £4 to £15.

The nearest farmhouse accommodation is at handsome *Plas Cichle* (☎ 810488), 1½ miles from the centre, with B&B for £22 to £25 per person. *Môr Awel* (☎ 490930, Llangoed) charges from £16.

Getting There & Around

Arriva bus No 53/57/58 comes from Bangor (£1.85, 30 minutes) about hourly (every two hours on Sunday).

The Beaumaris Leisure Centre (☎ 811200), Rating Row, right behind the castle, rents bikes from Easter to October; they cost £6 for two hours or £12 per day.

SOUTH ANGLESEY
Llanfairpwllgwyngyllgogerych-wyrndrobwllllantysiliogogogoch
☎ 01248 • pop 2500

The tour buses pour into this nondescript village on the A5 simply because it's in the record books with the UK's longest place name, which means 'St Mary's Church in the Hollow of the White Hazel near a Rapid Whirlpool and the Church of St Tysilio near the Red Cave'. It was dreamt up in the 19th century to get the tourists in and it's been marketed for all it's worth ever since.

The old name, Llanfairpwllgwyngyll, would have been hard enough. Local people call it 'Llanfairpwll' and most tourist and transport officials call it 'Llanfair PG' (khlan-**vyre**-pee-gee). This was Anglesey's first train station, and is still a stop on the Bangor-Holyhead mainline (you can buy a large platform ticket as a souvenir).

The town is of little interest but it's quite literally the gateway to the island, just over the Britannia Bridge. The TIC (☎ 713177, fax 715711, @ llanfairpwll.tic@virgin.net) – the best general source of information on Anglesey – is across the car park from the train station, in one corner of a gift-shop complex. It opens 10 am to 5 pm daily.

The *Penrhos Arms* (☎ 714892, Holyhead Rd), opposite the TIC, has bar meals from £5 and B&B in en-suite singles/doubles for £28/50.

This is a stop on the daily TrawsCambria (No 701) coach from Holyhead (£3.10, 45 minutes) via Bangor (£3.10, 20 minutes) to Cardiff, and something like 10 other Anglesey bus routes from Bangor also call in. Mainline trains from Holyhead (£4.35, 30 minutes) and from Crewe (England) and Bangor (£1.50, six minutes) stop here every two hours.

Plas Newydd

This is one of North Wales' finer stately homes, a mansion renovated by James Wyatt in Gothic style in the late 18th century for Henry William Paget (1768–1854), first marquis of Anglesey and principal commander of the Allied cavalry at the Battle of Waterloo, who also made a bundle from Anglesey copper mines.

There are fine views across to Snowdonia from the landscaped grounds. Inside, a series of paintings by Rex Whistler (who spent several years working here under the patronage of the sixth marquis in the 1930s) culminates in an immense trompe-l'oeil Snowdon dreamscape taking up an entire room. There's also a little cavalry museum featuring the state-of-the-art wooden leg designed for the first marquis, who lost a leg at Waterloo.

Owned by the National Trust (NT), Plas Newydd (☎ 01248-714795) opens noon to 5 pm Saturday to Wednesday, April to October; the gardens open 11 am to 5.30 pm. Admission costs £4.50/2.25. It's 1½ miles from the turning at the southern end of Llanfair PG. Don't confuse this with the less stately house of the same name at Llangollen.

Bryn Celli Ddu

This burial chamber, in which archaeologists

found the remains of Stone Age people, and the surrounding stone circle form one of Anglesey's most important Neolithic monuments. At the centre is a stone chamber roofed by two huge capstones, which was originally covered by a mound of earth. Take a torch and note the spiral design carved into one wall of the inner chamber (this is a reproduction; the original is in the National Museum in Cardiff).

The site is a 600m walk from a car park on the A4080 just west of Plas Newydd and 2 miles west of Llanfair PG.

Llanddwyn Island (Ynys Llanddwyn)

This 24-hectare peninsula in the southern corner of Anglesey, at the western entrance to the Menai Strait, is part of Newborough Warren, a National Nature Reserve around one the UK's finest coastal sand-dune systems. Its main landmark is Twr Mawr, a disused lighthouse built in 1845 to resemble one of Anglesey's (mostly long-gone) windmills. You can also see some of the cottages – one now restored – for pilots who helped boats navigate up the strait and operated a lifeboat station from 1826 to 1903. The cannon here was used to summon lifeboat volunteers.

Legend has it that St Dwynwen, Welsh patron saint of lovers and one of 24 daughters of the Welsh Prince Brychan, founded a chapel here in the 5th century. On the peninsula (it's only an 'island' at very high tides) are the ruins of a chapel built in the 16th century when Dwynwen pilgrimages were at their peak.

This is a wonderfully serene place for walking, with grassy dunes and a long, coarse beach (but please respect the fences placed for dune protection). Its isolation is encouraged by a £2 fee for cars to pass through the Newborough Forest Park, plus a prohibition on coaches and vendors (so bring your own picnic), plus a 1-mile beach walk. The car park is 2 miles from an unmarked turning in the village of Newborough (Niwbwrch), by the Spar supermarket and White Lion Inn; Newborough is on the 4080, 9 miles west of Llanfair PG.

Porth Cwyfan

From Aberffraw village on the A4080, a lane runs for 1½ miles down to this small, wind-blasted cove. On a small, walled island is the so-called 'Church in the Sea', the Church of St Cwyfan, which dates back to the 12th century. The atmosphere is somewhat tarnished by a disused military camp on the far shore.

In a converted farm building in Aberffraw itself is a little Coastal Heritage Centre run by the North Wales Wildlife Trust, with exhibits on local flora, fauna and marine ecology, and a small cafe.

Barclodiad y Gawres

Wales' most important Neolithic site, spectacularly sited at the top of a sea cliff, is a burial chamber some 27m in diameter, with a long entrance flanked by upright stones, a cross-shaped inner chamber and several side-chambers. This tomb (whose name translates, mysteriously, as 'The Giantess' Apron') includes some remarkable upright stones bearing spiral and zig-zag designs, probably related to ceremonial functions of the tomb.

The site is just off the A4080, about a mile south of the village of Llanfaelog. Stop in the Wayside Shop in Llanfaelog for the key (£5 deposit). Bring a torch.

At nearby Rhosneigr is a good camp site, *Ty Hen* (☎ 01407-810331), charging £6 (£7 in peak season) for two people plus a tent; hot showers and other amenities are available. It's advisable to book ahead.

HOLYHEAD (CAERGYBI)
☎ 01407 • pop 12,500

A grimmer, greyer town than the ferry port of Holyhead (pronounced hollyhead) you won't find between here and Glamorganshire. You'll know where you are by the immense phallic stack of the Anglesey Aluminium factory – possibly the highest object on the island – where the A5 approaches the town. The only reason to be here, at the far end of the road and railway line from London, is to be heading to or from Ireland.

It's a pity, because the area around it does have certain charm. Town and port occupy a separate island, Holy Island (Ynys Gybi), 7

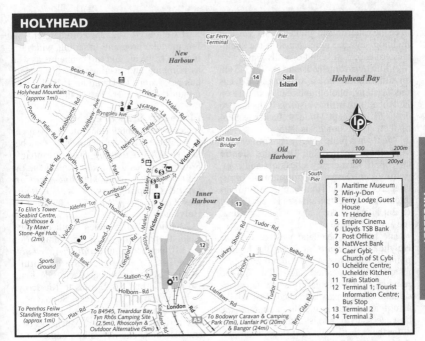

HOLYHEAD

New Harbour

Beach Rd

Prince of Wales Rd

Vicarage La

Vicarage La

Car Ferry Terminal

Pier

Salt Island

Holyhead Bay

To Car Park for Holyhead Mountain (approx 1mi)

Porthy-y-Felin Rd

Seabourne Rd

Walthew Ave

Bryngoleu Ave

Newry Fields

Newry St

Salt Island Bridge

Old Harbour

South Pier

Queens Park

New Park Rd

Porth-y-Felin Rd

Cambrian St

Stanley St

Victoria Rd

Inner Harbour

South Stack Rd

Alderley Tce

Thomas St

Market St

Victoria Tce

Tudor Rd

To Ellin's Tower Seabird Centre, Lighthouse & Ty Mawr Stone-Age Huts (2mi)

Vulcan St

Edmund St

Longford Rd

Victoria Rd

Turkey Shore Rd

Priory La

Belbio Rd

Sports Ground

Mill Bank

Station St

Holborn Rd

Llanfawr Rd

Tudor Rd

Bryn Glas Rd

To Penrhos Feilw Standing Stones (approx 1mi)

Plas Rd

Kingsland Rd

London Rd

To B4545, Trearddur Bay, Tyn Rhôs Camping Site (2.5mi), Rhoscolyn & Outdoor Alternative (5mi)

A5

To Bodowyr Caravan & Camping Park (7mi), Llanfair PG (20mi) & Bangor (24mi)

1 Maritime Museum
2 Min-y-Don
3 Ferry Lodge Guest House
4 Yr Hendre
5 Empire Cinema
6 Lloyds TSB Bank
7 Post Office
8 NatWest Bank
9 Caer Gybi; Church of St Cybi
10 Ucheldre Centre; Ucheldre Kitchen
11 Train Station
12 Terminal 1; Tourist Information Centre; Bus Stop
13 Terminal 2
14 Terminal 3

0   100   200m
0   100   200yd

ANGLESEY

miles long and separated from Anglesey proper by sandbanks and a narrow channel. It's 'Holy' because this was the territory of St Cybi, a well-travelled monk thought to have lived in the 6th century. Arriving in North Wales fresh from a pilgrimage to Jerusalem, he was granted land for a monastic settlement by King Maelgwyn of Gwynedd.

The site, and a little Roman fort, are in the centre of town (Holyhead's Welsh name means 'Cybi's Fort'). Elsewhere on Holy Island are huge colonies of seabirds and a Royal Society for the Protection of Birds (RSPB) observation centre, a two-century-old lighthouse, the foundations of Stone Age dwellings and, on Anglesey's highest point, a Celtic hill-fort (see Things to See & Do later). This must have been quite a special place in St Cybi's time.

Orientation & Information

The A5 (here called the London Rd) and the North Coast railway line begin/end at Holy-head train station, at the end of the Inner Harbour.

There are three ferry terminals. Connected to the train station is Terminal 1 where all foot passengers check in or disembark; regional buses call here too. Further along the Inner Harbour is Stena Line's Terminal 2, and across the harbour, out on the Salt Island peninsula (via a dedicated bridge and roadway), is Irish Ferries' Terminal 3. Foot passengers get a free shuttle-bus ride to/from Terminal 3.

The town's TIC (☎ 762622, fax 761462, e holyhead.tic@virgin.net) is next to the lobby at Terminal 1 and opens 10 am to 5.30 pm daily (to 4.30 pm, and closed Sunday, November to Easter). Lloyds TSB, NatWest and the post office are on Boston St.

Things to See & Do

In the middle of town is **Caer Gybi**, probably a 4th-century Roman outpost (the archway dates from modern times). Inside is the medieval **Church of St Cybi**. This is thought to be the patch of land granted to St Cybi, and tradition says the little chapel in the south-western corner was built over his grave.

A little **Maritime Museum** (☎ 769745) in an old lifeboat house off Beach Rd has model ships, photographs and exhibits on Holyhead's maritime history. It opens 1 to 5 pm daily except Monday, Easter to September. Admission costs £1/50p.

The town's pride and joy is a former convent chapel called the **Ucheldre Centre** (☎ 763361), Anglesey's best arts and community centre, with a program of films, concerts, drama and dance, plus exhibitions and a licensed restaurant (see Places to Stay & Eat later). There's also a small **cinema**, the Empire, on Stanley St.

The bulbous headland west of town is **Holyhead Mountain**, at 219m the highest point on Anglesey. At its summit are a prehistoric hill-fort called Caer-y-Twr and the remains of a 19th-century semaphore station. From a car park at the end of Beach Rd a footpath winds round the mountain; the best access to the site is on the western side.

Farther west, down 400 steps to an offshore rock called South Stack, is a **lighthouse** dating from 1809, now open to the public. Just off the road above it is the RSPB-run **Ellin's Tower Seabird Centre**, originally a private bird-watching refuge, now the ideal place to look down at the island's choughs, fulmars, kittiwakes, guillemots, razorbills, gulls and, from about mid-April to July, puffins. Ellin's Tower (☎ 764973) opens 11 am to 5 pm daily, Easter to September. Take South Stack Rd for about 2 miles to a car park at the road's end, where there is also a cafe. Just inland from the car park are the excavated foundations of a circle of **Stone-Age huts** called Ty Mawr.

About a mile south-west of town at Penrhos Feilw are a pair of 3m-high **standing stones** dating back some 4000 years.

The TIC has a map-brochure showing circular walks to these and other sites on Holy Island.

Trearddur Bay, 2½ miles south of Holyhead on the B4545, is Anglesey's main

watersports centre. The Anglesey Sea & Surf Centre (☎ 762525, Porthdafarch) offers modular programs in sailing, windsurfing, sea kayaking and surf canoeing, as well as climbing and cycling. Arriva's Bangor bus No 4 stops at Trearddur (£1.10, seven minutes) about every half-hour.

Places to Stay & Eat

Accessible camping (tent pitches from £5) is available from about Easter to October at *Tyn Rhôs Camping Site* (☎ 860369, *Ravenspoint Rd, Trearddur Bay*) and at the well equipped, nonsmoking *Bodowyr Caravan & Camping Park* (☎ 741171, *Bodowyr Farm, Bodedern*), 7 miles east of Holyhead.

At Rhoscolyn, 5 miles south of Holyhead, there's bunkhouse accommodation for £10 per person at *Outdoor Alternative* (☎ 860469, *Cerrig-yr-Adar*), beautifully situated 300m from the beach. OR Jones (☎ 730204) bus No 23 runs to Rhoscolyn every two hours, daily except Sunday.

B&Bs in Holyhead are accustomed to late arrivals off the ferry. Much the best, and recommended for walkers and cyclists, is *Ferry Lodge Guest House* (☎ 765276, ⓔ *ferrylodge89@aol.com, 89 Newry St)*, with spotless en-suite singles/doubles for £25/35, plus larger rooms; area tours are also available. Across the road, *Min-y-Don* (☎ 762718, *Newry Fawr*) charges £16 per person. Agreeable *Yr Hendre* (☎ 762929, *Porth-y-Felin Rd*) has B&B from £30/40.

The town centre has an assortment of unexceptional 'caffs' and takeaways. A more appealing spot is the *Ucheldre Kitchen* at the Ucheldre Centre (see Things To See & Do earlier), open 10 am to 4.30 pm weekdays and 2 to 4.30 pm on Sunday.

Getting There & Away

The quickest and most comfortable bus service from Bangor (£4.70 single, 55 minutes) or Caernarfon (£5.10, 1¼ hours) is Arriva's daily TrawsCambria (No 701) coach. Most frequent is the No 4 bus from Bangor (£2.90, 1½ hours, twice hourly) that runs Monday to Saturday; No 44 runs every two hours on Sunday.

Trains arrive here from Chester (England), Llandudno Junction (£7.80 single, 55 minutes) and Bangor (£5.20, 40 minutes) about four times hourly.

Both Irish Ferries (☎ 0870 517 1717) and Stena Line (☎ 0870 570 7070) operate ferries from Ireland. Irish Ferries comes from Dublin with two daily slow ferries (£44 foot passengers, £209 car plus driver, 3¼ hours) and three fast ones (£56/249, 1½ hours). Stena comes twice daily from Dublin (£199, no foot passengers, 3¾ hours) and four times daily from Dun Laoghaire (£56/244, 1¾ hours).

If you fancy a day-trip to Dublin, Irish Ferries sometimes has special offers from as little as £9 return.

The North Coast

The north coast serves as a holiday playground for much of the English North and Midlands, and has little to offer a serious traveller. 'From the train,' wrote Bill Bryson in *Notes from a Small Island*, 'North Wales looked like holiday hell – endless ranks of prison camp caravan parks'. Most travellers pass straight through to Snowdonia, with a stop at Llandudno and Conwy. If you're willing to take less-travelled inland roads – for example, up the valley of the River Dee – there are some other rewards, the biggest one being Llangollen.

CONWY
☎ 01492 • pop 3800
Conwy was just a good place for fishing and mussel gathering until Edward I planted a castle here – one of his iron necklace of fortresses designed to cow the Welsh. Today the castle is a UNESCO-designated cultural treasure. The fine town walls, still intact and chasing over the local hills like a miniature Great Wall of China, give the centre of this otherwise modest seaside town an unexpected dignity, and are what make it worth visiting.

THE NORTH COAST

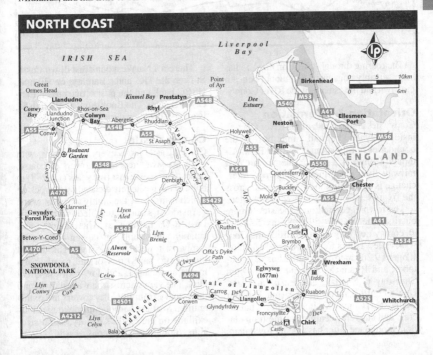

NORTH COAST

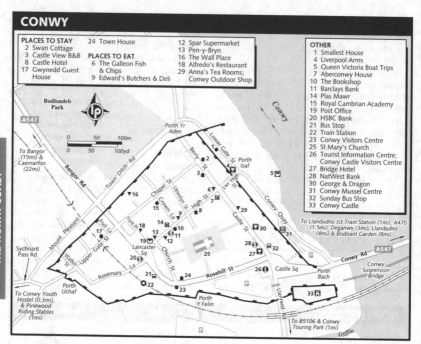

CONWY

PLACES TO STAY	24 Town House	12 Spar Supermarket	OTHER
2 Swan Cottage		13 Pen-y-Bryn	1 Smallest House
3 Castle View B&B	PLACES TO EAT	16 The Wall Place	4 Liverpool Arms
8 Castle Hotel	6 The Galleon Fish	18 Alfredo's Restaurant	5 Queen Victoria Boat Trips
17 Gwynedd Guest	& Chips	29 Anna's Tea Rooms;	7 Aberconwy House
House	9 Edward's Butchers & Deli	Conwy Outdoor Shop	10 The Bookshop

OTHER
1 Smallest House
4 Liverpool Arms
5 Queen Victoria Boat Trips
7 Aberconwy House
10 The Bookshop
11 Barclays Bank
14 Plas Mawr
15 Royal Cambrian Academy
19 Post Office
20 HSBC Bank
21 Bus Stop
22 Train Station
23 Conwy Visitors Centre
25 St Mary's Church
26 Tourist Information Centre;
   Conwy Castle Visitors Centre
27 Bridge Hotel
28 NatWest Bank
30 George & Dragon
31 Conwy Mussel Centre
32 Sunday Bus Stop
33 Conwy Castle

The roaring through-traffic on the A55 has been sensibly consigned to a tunnel beneath the town and the estuary of the River Conwy.

Orientation & Information

Conwy lies at the mouth of the River Conwy, inside Gwynedd but half a mile beyond the boundaries of Snowdonia National Park. Although Conwy is a stop on the North Coast railway line, the region's main rail interchange is at Llandudno Junction, just across the river (see Getting There & Away later).

The town is centred on Lancaster Square but its little TIC (☎ 592248, fax 573545, ⓔ conwy.tic@virgin.net) is inside the Conwy Castle Visitors Centre, on Castle Square. It opens 9.30 am to 5 pm daily, Easter to October; and 10 am to 1 pm and 1.30 to 4 pm Thursday to Sunday, the rest of the year. Don't confuse this with the (much better signposted) Conwy Visitors Centre, a handicraft and souvenir centre near the train station, though the latter has a better town map.

There's a NatWest bank just down Castle St from the TIC, and a Barclays on High St. HSBC bank and the post office are on Lancaster Square. The Bookshop, at 21 High St, is a good browser.

Conwy Castle

Conwy Castle looks every bit the part, with eight massive, crenellated towers of coarse, dark stone. It took just five years (1282–7) to build, its shape largely dictated by the rock on which it sits. Note the faintly tapered towers.

Inside it's more tumbledown than its UNESCO partner at Caernarfon, and smaller and simpler in design – but with ramparts, towers and passages galore, and the fairly grand ruins of the royal apartments and chapel, and now-roofless Great Hall. The views across the walled town and the estuary from the lofty towers are exhilarating. Scattered around inside are various exhibits on the castle's history, and a sizeable community of pigeons.

A train passes the massive Conwy Castle, which was built under order of Edward I in just five years.

The beautiful Menai Straits, as seen from Anglesey, bustling with fishing boats and private yachts

PHILIP GAME

A typical Welsh pub sign

ROB RACHOWECKI

Standing stones in the grounds of the Plas Newydd stately home

IAN DUCKWORTH

...or Llanfair PG for short, holds the record for the longest British place name.

PAUL BIGLAND

Penmon Point's 12th-century Augustinian priory

BRYN THOMAS

Llandudno's Victorian pier

Reached by a footbridge over Llanrwst Rd, the castle (☎ 592358; Cadw) opens 9.30 am to 5 pm daily, Easter to October (to 6 pm June to September); and 9.30 am to 4 pm (and from 11 am on Sunday) the rest of the year.

But it's the town walls – fully intact, three-quarters of a mile long, with 22 towers and three original gateways – that put Conwy up among Europe's handsomest medieval walled communities. You can walk along many sections of the walls.

The best view of the castle is from Deganwy, across the river, with Snowdon providing a dramatic backdrop, when it's not veiled in cloud.

Conwy Suspension Bridge

With its own crenellated Gothic turrets, Thomas Telford's handsome suspension bridge looks at first glance like part of Edward's castle. But it was completed in 1826, the same year as Telford's other milestone bridge over the Menai Strait – both of them intended to speed the movement of people and goods from London to Holyhead. Like its Menai cousin, it was eclipsed a quarter-century later by an adjacent steel bridge designed by Robert Stephenson (who also designed the arch where the railway punctures the old town walls).

You can visit Telford's bridge, now pedestrian-only, and its restored toll house (☎ 573282; NT) from 10 am to 5 pm daily except Tuesday, April to October (daily in July and August). Admission costs £1/50p.

Other Things to See & Do

There are a few other small gems worth seeking out. Conwy's finest historic house is **Plas Mawr** (☎ 580167; Cadw) on High St. Completed in 1585 for a Welsh merchant and courtier named Robert Wynn, it is the UK's finest surviving Elizabethan house, its height and whitewashed outer walls indicating the status of the original owner. Inside, the painted plasterwork is eye-popping. It opens 9.30 am to 5 pm daily except Monday, April to October (to 6 pm mid-May to August, to 4 pm in October). Admission costs £4/3 and includes an audioguide tour.

The timber-and-plaster **Aberconwy House** (☎ 592246; NT) on Castle St is the town's oldest medieval merchant's house, dating from the 14th century. Inside are rooms furnished in period style, and a good audio-visual presentation. The house opens 11 am to 5 pm daily except Tuesday, April to October. Admission costs £2/1.

The **Royal Cambrian Academy**, Wales' top art institute, has a gallery (☎ 593413) on Crown Lane with a full program of exhibitions by members plus visiting shows from the National Museum and elsewhere. It opens 11 am to 5 pm Tuesday to Saturday and 1 to 4.30 pm Sunday.

The small riverside quay makes for a pleasant walk on a sunny morning. A minuscule dwelling here claims to be the UK's **Smallest House**; not surprisingly, there's little to see for your 50/30p.

Also on the quay is the **Conwy Mussel Centre** (☎ 592689), a mini-museum devoted to mussel harvesting on this estuary, which dates back to Roman times. The mussel 'industry' today consists of about a dozen practitioners using traditional raking techniques. They can only gather the mussels in winter, and it's hoped this centre will help supplement their income and sustain a threatened trade. It opens 10 am to 5 pm daily, late March to early September. Admission costs about £1.50.

Horse Riding

Pinewood Riding Stables (☎ 592256) offers rides from £12 for the first hour. It's on Sychnant Pass Rd, about a mile from the town centre.

Boat Trips

Conwy River Trips (mobile ☎ 0777 560 1990) runs trips lasting about half an hour from the quay both out through the estuary and upstream into the Conwy Valley (£3/2), as well as one-hour wildlife-spotting trips upriver (£4.50/3). The *Queen Victoria* departs between 10.30 am and 5 pm daily, mid-March to October (to 7.30 pm June to August). However, note that the River Conwy is tidal here, and consequently timetables are variable.

Places to Stay

At *Conwy Touring Park* (☎ 592856), 1½ miles south of Conwy on the B5106, tent sites cost from £7 to £11 for two people in summer.

The *Conwy Youth Hostel* (☎ 593571, *Larkhill, Sychnant Pass Rd*) is in a converted modern hotel, a 10-minute walk from the town centre. A bed in a small, en-suite dorm costs £12.50/8.50, and there's a cafe in the hostel. The hostel opens February to October, plus Friday and Saturday nights in winter.

B&B options within the town walls include the *Town House* (☎ 596454, *18 Rosehill St*) from £16 per person or £38 per en-suite room; and *Castle View B&B* (☎ 596888, *3 Berry St*) from £14 per person. *Swan Cottage* (☎ 596840, *18 Berry St*) is a small 16th-century house with three rooms from £15 per person. *Gwynedd Guest House* (☎ 596537, *10 Upper Gate St*) has four rooms for £18/32.

The *Castle Hotel* (☎ 592324, *High St*) is an old coach house bang in the centre with singles/doubles from £60/80.

Places to Eat

There are several tearooms dotted about the town, of which the best is the *Pen-y-Bryn* (☎ 596445, *28 High St*), where a full cream tea includes *bara brith* (spicy fruit loaf) and cake; it also does light lunches. *Anna's Tea Rooms*, above the Conwy Outdoor shop on Castle St, is also good for traditional fare. *The Wall Place* (☎ 596326, *Chapel St*), a secluded cottage with garden, doubles as a vegetarian restaurant with excellent dishes under £5, and a gallery with temporary exhibits from Llandudno's Mostyn Gallery.

Alfredo's Restaurant (☎ 592381, *Lancaster Square*) is an Italian place open every evening and for lunch on Saturday, with pasta and pizza dishes from £5. The *Castle Hotel* (see Places to Stay) has a set three-course dinner for £16.

See also Entertainment for pub meals.

For self-caterers, there's the *Spar* supermarket on High St. Nearby is *Edward's Butcher & Deli*, with pies and hot meals to take away. For finger-licking chips try *The Galleon Fish & Chips* on the corner of High and Berry Sts.

Entertainment

The *Liverpool Arms* pub, down on the quay, is where the fishing crowd drinks. The *Bridge Hotel* on the corner of Castle and Rosehill Sts does good-value lunches, especially on Sunday. The *George & Dragon* on Castle St serves reasonable pub grub and has a small beer garden.

Getting There & Away

Arriva Cymru bus No 19 runs twice hourly (hourly on Sunday) between Conwy (train station), the resort town of Llandudno (4 miles to the north) and the railway interchange of Llandudno Junction (1½ miles to the east). No 5 travels to Conwy, Llandudno and Llandudno Junction hourly from Bangor (£2.85, one hour) and Caernarfon (£3.45, 1½ hours); its Sunday version, No 5X, stops instead on Castle St near the TIC.

Conwy's train station is now used only by regional services. Llandudno Junction, a 15-minute walk from Conwy, is the mainline station. There are trains every hour or two between Llandudno Junction and Conwy (£1.90, three minutes).

AROUND CONWY
Bodnant Garden

One of the UK's most splendid gardens is 8 miles south of Conwy. Bodnant Garden (☎ 650460; NT), on 32 hectares of terraced land with commanding views across the Conwy Valley to the peaks of Snowdonia, is a riot of rhododendrons, camellias and magnolias in spring, of roses and water lilies in summer, of hydrangeas and turning leaves in autumn. It opens 10 am to 5 pm daily, Easter to October. Admission costs £5/2.50. It's just off the A470 Betws-y-Coed road. Arriva's bus No 25 passes by hourly from Llandudno, but from Conwy you must change at Llandudno Junction.

LLANDUDNO
☎ 01492 • pop 22,000

As Wales' largest seaside resort, Llandudno (lan-**did**-no) seethes with tourists in summer and attracts a steady stream of pensioners all year round.

Developed as an upmarket Victorian

holiday town, it has retained its graceful architecture and some of its 19th-century atmosphere. There's a stately pier, a grand promenade and suitably antiquated attractions such as donkeys and Punch & Judy shows on the beach. Elegant hotels line the promenade for a full mile, but behind them sprawls a characterless coach-party land.

In its heyday, Llandudno's visitors included many of the Great And Good. In 1861 the Liddell family, whose daughter was Lewis Carroll's model for *Alice in Wonderland*, summered in the house that is now the St Tudno Hotel. They later built their own house, which has since become the Gogarth Abbey Hotel.

Llandudno is on its own peninsula, sandwiched between two immense beaches and dominated by the spectacular, 2-mile-long limestone headland called the Great Orme. This headland, with its Bronze Age mine, tramway, cable car and superb views, is perhaps the town's most absorbing attraction.

Llandudno will have to remember its Welsh in 2002 when it's the venue for the Urdd Eisteddfod, the national youth eisteddfod (see the boxed text 'The Eisteddfod' under Arts in the Facts about Wales chapter for more details).

Orientation & Information

The town straddles the peninsula, with Llandudno Bay and North Shore Beach to the north-east and Conwy Bay and West Shore Beach to the south-west. From the train station it's a three-block walk up Augusta and Madoc Sts to the TIC. National Express and some regional coaches stop on Mostyn Broadway, but there are a dozen more stops for other buses; see under Getting There & Away later for useful ones.

The town's TIC (☎ 876413, fax 872722, e llandudno.tic@virgin.net) on 1–2 Chapel St opens 9.30 am to 5 pm daily, Easter to October; and 10 am to 4 pm daily except Thursday and Sunday, the rest of the year.

THE NORTH COAST

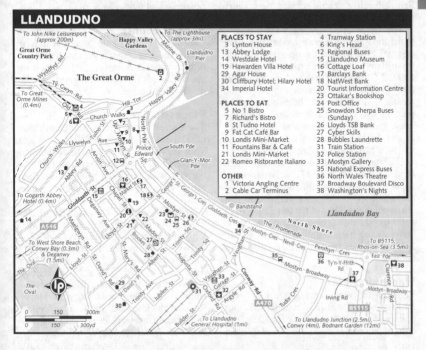

LLANDUDNO

PLACES TO STAY		4 Tramway Station
3 Lynton House		6 King's Head
13 Abbey Lodge		12 Regional Buses
14 Westdale Hotel		15 Llandudno Museum
19 Hawarden Villa Hotel		16 Cottage Loaf
29 Agar House		17 Barclays Bank
30 Cliffbury Hotel; Hilary Hotel		18 NatWest Bank
34 Imperial Hotel		20 Tourist Information Centre
		23 Ottakar's Bookshop
PLACES TO EAT		24 Post Office
5 No 1 Bistro		25 Snowdon Sherpa Buses
7 Richard's Bistro		(Sunday)
8 St Tudno Hotel		26 Lloyds TSB Bank
9 Fat Cat Café Bar		27 Cyber Skills
10 Londis Mini-Market		28 Bubbles Laundrette
11 Fountains Bar & Café		31 Train Station
21 Londis Mini-Market		32 Police Station
22 Romeo Ristorante Italiano		33 Mostyn Gallery
		35 National Express Buses
OTHER		36 North Wales Theatre
1 Victoria Angling Centre		37 Broadway Boulevard Disco
2 Cable Car Terminus		38 Washington's Nights

Mostyn St is the main shopping street where the post office and all major UK banks can be found. Cyber Skills (☎ 874627), 50 Madoc St, opens daily with Internet access at £2.50 per half-hour. The best bookshop looks like Ottakar's on Mostyn St. The Bubbles Laundrette, 25 Brookes St, opens daily. The police station (☎ 517171) is a block east of the train station. Llandudno General Hospital (☎ 860066) is almost a mile south of the centre.

The Great Orme

There's hardly a clue from town as to what's up on the Great Orme (Y Gogarth), but its attractions include some spectacular walks; 360° views which on a clear day include the peaks of Snowdonia, several Neolithic sites and a veritable encyclopaedia of flowers, butterflies and seabirds. The entire headland is a Country Park (☎ 874151), and a designated Site of Special Scientific Interest (SSSI). Two-hour guided walks (£1/50p) are offered at 2.30 pm every Sunday, May to September; for details contact the country park warden at ☎ 874151.

The Great Orme Tramway (☎ 876749), at the top of Church Walks, takes you up in original 1902 tramcars. It operates 10 am to 6 pm daily, Easter to October; tickets cost £3.80/2.60 return. There's also a cable car (☎ 877205) that operates subject to the weather, from Happy Valley, above the pier. Tickets cost £5/2.60 return. At the top are a visitor centre, with leaflets on every aspect of the country park, plus picnic tables, a cafe and gift-shop complex.

Halfway up the tramline are the Great Orme Mines (☎ 870447), a Bronze-Age copper mine, and possibly one of the most important sources of the metal during that era, with over 4 miles of tunnels dating from 1860 to 600 BC. It opens during the same hours as the tram. Admission costs £4.40/2.80, or £7.25/5 for a combined ticket with the tram.

Llandudno Pier

This elegant Victorian pier reaches 670m into the sea. It was first built in 1857 but collapsed in a storm two years later. The current pier was started in 1877 and its main use was as a disembarkation point for passengers from Isle of Man steamers (there are none these days).

You can rent fishing tackle from the Victoria Angling Centre (☎ 530663) at the pier entrance, and you can fish from the pier.

Other Things to See & Do

The Mostyn Gallery (☎ 879201), 12 Vaughan St, is North Wales' leading venue for contemporary art, and a peek-in is likely to be rewarding. It opens 11 am to 6 pm daily except Sunday; admission is free. It also runs short arts workshops.

The Llandudno Museum (☎ 876517) at 17–19 Gloddaeth St has a few local history artefacts on view from 10.30 am to 1 pm Tuesday to Saturday in summer. Admission costs £1.50/75p.

If these make you yawn, there's always the dry ski slope on the flanks of the Great Orme. John Nike Leisuresport (☎ 874707), Happy Valley Rd, offers daily skiing, snowboarding and toboggan tuition.

Special Events

Llandudno's biggest do of the year is its Victorian Extravaganza, over the May bank-holiday weekend (early May), with many streets closed off for steam engines, parades, a funfair and more.

Places to Stay

There are about 400 hotels and guesthouses here, more than any other town in Wales. That's about 15,000 beds, so finding one for yourself is rarely a problem. The TIC goes bonkers with bookings in summer. There are no camping facilities in the immediate area.

St David's Rd is a good place to start looking for rooms in the region of £18 to £20 per person. *Cliffbury Hotel (☎ 877224)* at No 34 is a decent, nonsmoking place. The *Hilary Hotel (☎ 875623)* at No 32 and *Agar House (☎ 875572)* at No 17 are both simple and comfortable. There are also some reasonable places along St Mary's Rd, one block towards the Promenade.

A central, budget place is friendly *Hawarden Villa Hotel (☎ 860447, 27 Chapel St)*, just across from the TIC, with modest, good-value rooms for £20 per person.

At the comfortable *Westdale Hotel* (☎ *877996, 37 Abbey Rd*), B&B costs from £18 per person, or from £22.50 with dinner. The excellent, nonsmoking *Abbey Lodge* (☎ *878042, 14 Abbey Rd*) has a pretty garden and offers B&B from £25 per person. *Lynton House* (☎ *875057, 80 Church Walks*), close to the pier and the tramway, charges £24 per person; all its rooms are en suite.

For an unusual night's rest, try *The Lighthouse* (☎ *876819, Marine Drive*) – which really was one until 1985 – atop a sheer 100m cliff at the end of the Great Orme promontory. Decorated like a ship on the inside, it has three rooms with bath and binoculars, from £48 per person. Book ahead; you'll have a better chance on a weekday.

At the top end of the scale are some of the hotels along the Promenade such as the elegant, Victorian *Imperial Hotel* (☎ *877466, The Promenade*), where B&B costs £65/95 per single/double (try bargaining in the off-season). *Gogarth Abbey Hotel* (☎ *876211, West Shore*), the rather old-fashioned former summer home of Alice Liddell, charges from £50 per person for B&B.

Places to Eat

Like its Bangor cousin, the *Fat Cat Café Bar* (☎ *871844, 149 Upper Mostyn St*) offers a lively bar atmosphere, real ales and a menu you can get your teeth into, including good burgers, filled baguettes, all-day breakfast and vegetarian specials for under £6. Across the street, *Fountains Bar & Café* (☎ *875600*) has similar food and a marginally more sedate atmosphere.

Romeo Ristorante Italiano (☎ *877777, 25 Lloyd St*) does traditional pizzas from £5 and steaks from £10.50 to £12.50.

Two popular, upmarket bistros open nightly with main dishes from £12 upwards are *Richard's Bistro* (☎ *875315, 7 Church Walks*) and the *No 1 Bistro* (☎ *875424, Old Rd*). The restaurant at the *St Tudno Hotel* (☎ *874411, 16 North Parade*) is regarded as the top place to eat in town, with first-class main courses from £15 to £20.

On Mostyn St you'll find a *Londis* mini-market as well as fast-food restaurants, cafes and fish-&-chip takeaways. Another *Londis* is on Upper Mostyn St.

Entertainment

Twentysomethings should head down the beach to *Washington's Nights* (☎ *877974, East Parade*) or the *Broadway Boulevard Disco* (☎ *879614, Mostyn Broadway*). Babyboomers may prefer their drinks at the *Cottage Loaf* (☎ *876753, 1 Market St*) or the *King's Head* (☎ *877993, Old Rd*) by the tramway station.

Opened only in 1996, the *North Wales Theatre* (☎ *872000, The Promenade*) has become a major North Wales performance venue, with everything from West End musicals to Welsh National Opera, plus dance, drama, comedy, pop and classical music, on the UK's second-biggest stage (after Brighton).

If you're willing to go 4 miles east to Rhos-on-Sea you can enjoy a show at the *Harlequin Puppet Theatre* (☎ *548166, The Promenade*), the UK's only permanent marionette theatre. It opens in July and August and at school half-term holidays, with children's shows at 3 pm daily, plus grown-up stuff (variety shows, musicals, plays) at 8 pm on Wednesday. Tickets cost £4/3. The No 12, 14 or 15 bus goes to Rhos from Gloddaeth St about six times an hour (less often on Sunday).

Getting There & Away

Bus Arriva Cymru bus No 19 runs twice hourly (hourly on Sunday) between Conwy, Llandudno and the railway interchange of Llandudno Junction. Arriva's No 5/5X runs hourly from Caernarfon (£3.45, 1½ hours) and Bangor (£2.85, one hour) via Conwy and Llandudno Junction, with a less-frequent Sunday service. All these buses stop on Gloddaeth St.

Connections to/from Snowdonia are run by the Snowdon Sherpa service (see Getting There & Around under Snowdonia National Park in the Snowdonia & the Llŷn chapter): route No 96 arrives via Llandudno Junction three times daily from Betws-y-Coed, Capel Curig and Llanberis. Buses stop on Gloddaeth St (on Mostyn St on Sunday).

THE NORTH COAST

National Express coach No 545 passes through daily from London via Chester, and from Pwllheli, Porthmadog, Caernarfon and Bangor. These coaches use the station on Mostyn Broadway.

Train The Conwy Valley line comes to Llandudno from Blaenau Ffestiniog (£4.85 single, one hour and five minutes) via Betws-y-Coed (£3.65 single, 35 minutes) at least five times daily, Monday to Saturday – with slower, less-frequent buses (No 84) on Sunday.

First North Western has hourly direct services to Llandudno from Manchester (£18, 2½ hours) via Chester. For other destinations on the London-Holyhead mainline you must change at Llandudno Junction, which is itself a short ride from Llandudno by train (£1.35, eight minutes, twice hourly) or No 19 bus (see under Bus earlier).

Llandudno Junction is served three times daily by Virgin Trains direct from London's Euston station (£24 for a ten-day advance-

purchase single, 3½ hours), with many more options if you change at Crewe. From Holyhead and Bangor (£3.50, 20 minutes) there are direct services almost hourly.

LLANGOLLEN
☎ 01978 • pop 3500

This friendly, rather wholesome town is best known outside of Wales for its International Musical Eisteddfod, a six-day jamboree of music and dance that attracts folk groups from all over the world. The town has little in the way of memorable architecture and nothing groundbreaking in its own past, but the Vale of Llangollen is a lovely place, sufficiently appealing and historical (and child-friendly) to linger in for a day or two.

Outdoor activities are at the top of the list, including canal trips by horse-drawn boat, canoe trips on the frisky River Dee (which tumbles through the town centre), steam railway journeys and some fine walks.

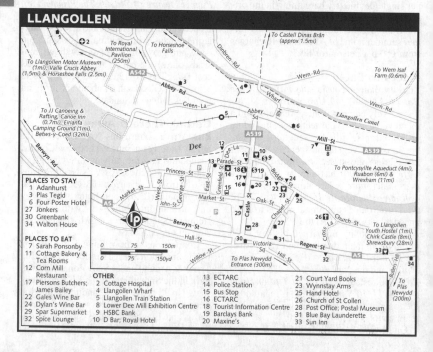

LLANGOLLEN

PLACES TO STAY
1 Adanhurst
3 Plas Tegid
6 Four Poster Hotel
27 Jonkers
30 Greenbank
34 Walton House

PLACES TO EAT
7 Sarah Ponsonby
11 Cottage Bakery & Tea Rooms
12 Corn Mill Restaurant
17 Piersons Butchers; James Bailey
22 Gales Wine Bar
24 Dylan's Wine Bar
29 Spar Supermarket
32 Spice Lounge

OTHER
2 Cottage Hospital
4 Llangollen Wharf
5 Llangollen Train Station
8 Lower Dee Mill Exhibition Centre
9 HSBC Bank
10 D Bar; Royal Hotel
13 ECTARC
14 Police Station
15 Bus Stop
16 ECTARC
18 Tourist Information Centre
19 Barclays Bank
20 Maxine's
21 Court Yard Books
23 Wynnstay Arms
25 Hand Hotel
26 Church of St Collen
28 Post Office; Postal Museum
31 Blue Bay Launderette
33 Sun Inn

The vale was part of the London to Holyhead stagecoach route in the 18th and 19th centuries, when the road ran through the middle of the town (present-day Bridge and Church Sts). Several former coaching inns remain from that time. Close by is the Llangollen Canal which feeds from the Dee just upstream and then crosses right over it in spectacular fashion just downstream.

Orientation & Information

Llangollen (khlan-**gokh**-len) sits astride the River Dee (Afon Dyfrdwy) about 6 road miles from the English border; the nearest big town is Wrexham, 11 miles away. The A5 road, successor to the stagecoach route, skirts the southern edge of town, and the canal is a stone's throw from the river on the other side. Through buses stop on Market St. The town is small enough to walk around.

The town's TIC (☎ 860828, fax 861563, ✉ llangollen.tic@virgin.net), on Castle St, opens 10 am to 6 pm daily, Easter to October; and 9.30 am to 5 pm daily except Wednesday in winter.

Bank branches include Barclays, opposite the TIC, and HSBC on Bridge St. The post office is a few doors from the A5. Internet access is available at the Llangollen Youth Hostel (see Places to Stay later) for £1.50/2.50/4.50 per quarter/half/full hour. Maxine's (☎ 860334), 17 Castle St, is a good browsing bookshop-cum-cafe (with a kids' play area and uninspiring but cheap daytime snacks); it opens daily. Down a nearby alley is the more mannerly Court Yard Books, and on the other side of Castle St, ECTARC (see Other Things to See later) has a small bookshop. Blue Bay Launderette on Regent St opens daily except Sunday.

The police station (☎ 860222) is on Parade St, round the block from the TIC. A small Cottage Hospital (☎ 860226) is on Abbey Rd; the nearest accident/emergency services are in Wrexham.

Plas Newydd

Plas Newydd was the home of the so-called Ladies of Llangollen, Lady Eleanor Butler and Sarah Ponsonby. They lived here for almost half a century, transforming the house

---

The Ladies of Llangollen

The Right Honourable Lady Eleanor Butler and Miss Sarah Ponsonby, the 'Ladies of Llangollen', lived in Plas Newydd from 1780 to 1829 with their maid, Mary Carryl. They had fallen in love in Ireland, but their aristocratic Anglo-Irish families discouraged the relationship. In a desperate bid to be allowed to live together the women eloped to Wales, disguised as men, and set up home in Llangollen to devote themselves to 'friendship, celibacy and the knitting of stockings'.

Their romantic friendship became well known yet respected, and they were visited by many literary and national figures of the day, including the duke of Wellington, the duke of Gloucester, William Wordsworth and Sir Walter Scott. Wordsworth called them 'sisters in love, a love allowed to climb, even on this earth above the reach of time'. He was less accepting of Plas Newydd, which he called 'a low browed cot'.

The ladies' relationship with their maid, Mary, was also close – most unusual for those days. Mary managed to buy the freehold of Plas Newydd, and left it to them when she died. They erected a large monument to her in the graveyard at the Church of St Collen on Bridge St, where they are also buried. Lady Eleanor died in 1829, Sarah Ponsonby two years later.

---

into their own private hybrid of Gothic and Tudor romantic styles, complete with stained-glass windows, carved oak panels and formal gardens. The black-and-white timbering was, however, an alteration made by the next owner. Sir Roy Strong, former director of the Victoria & Albert Museum in London, called Plas Newydd 'an early monument to architectural salvage'.

The house (☎ 861314), quarter of a mile south-east of Victoria Square, opens 10 am to 5 pm daily, Easter to October (last entry 4.15pm). Admission costs £2.50/1.25. Don't confuse this place with the stately home of the same name on Anglesey (see the Isle of Anglesey section earlier in the chapter).

Valle Crucis Abbey & Eliseg's Pillar

In the valley of the River Eglwyseg, a quiet tributary of the Dee, stand the dignified ruins of Valle Crucis Abbey, one of Wales' last Cistercian monasteries, founded in 1201 by Madog ap Gruffydd. In its serene setting and present, largely Gothic form (including a huge rose window) it predates its grander, more famous sibling at Tintern (see the South-East Wales & the Brecon Beacons chapter). It is sadly disfigured by the hideous caravan park next door.

The abbey (☎ 860326; Cadw), 1½ miles north-west of Llangollen on the A542, opens 10 am to 5 pm daily, April to September. Admission costs £2/1.50 (free in winter). Bryn Melyn bus No 98 departs from Llangollen at 7.45 am on school days and at 10.10 am and 1.10 pm on Tuesday and Friday, stopping beside the site.

Beside the road 300m farther on is a much older and more important monument, after which this area – Glyn y Groes, Vale of the Cross – is named. Eliseg's Pillar is a 2.5m-tall stone column, all that remains of a cross almost three times as high erected by Cyngen (died 854), the last independent king of Powys, to the memory of his great-grandfather, famous for his victories over the Saxons in the 8th century. The top was smashed off by Parliamentary soldiers during the Civil War. What remained (now all but eroded away) was copied and translated in 1696:

...annexed the inheritance of Powys...laid waste for nine years...out of the hands of the English with fire and sword...Cyngen son of Cateli; Cateli son of Brochmail; Brochmail son of Eliseg; Eliseg son of Cnoillane; Cyngen, therefore great-grandson of Eliseg, erected this stone to his great-grandfather Eliseg...

Llangollen Canal

Canals and the horse-drawn barge had a 'golden age' in the 18th century as the most efficient way of hauling goods over long distances. With the advent of the railway, most of them fell into disrepair.

The Llangollen Canal fared better than most because it was used for years more to carry drinking water from the River Dee to the Hurleston Reservoir in Cheshire. Today it's again in use, carrying visitors up and down the Vale of Llangollen. In addition, the old towpaths offer miles of peaceful, traffic-free walking. And the canal itself is part of the attraction, thanks to the great civil engineer Thomas Telford (1757–1834).

To collect water for the canal from the River Dee, Telford designed an elegant curving weir called **Horseshoe Falls**. The adjacent riverbank is a tranquil picnic spot. It's about 2½ miles west of Llangollen – on foot along the canal towpath; via the Llangollen Steam Railway (a 15-minute walk from Berwyn station; see Llangollen Railway later); on the No 98 bus (see Valle Crucis Abbey & Eliseg's Pillar earlier); or by car along the A542 (turn left onto the B5103 after about 1½ miles).

However, Telford's real masterpiece is the **Pontcysyllte Aqueduct**, completed in 1805 to carry the canal over the Dee. It is perhaps the most spectacular piece of engineering on the entire UK canal system, 307m long, a dizzy 38m high, and quite beautiful to look at. It is an extraordinary experience to walk across it, and quite surreal to do in a longboat. The aqueduct is about 4 miles east of Llangollen, near the village of Froncysyllte – walk the towpath or drive, most conveniently out on the A539 Ruabon road.

From Llangollen Wharf (☎ 860702) you can take a short (45 minutes return) excursion on the canal by horse-drawn narrowboat for £3.50/2.50. There are regular departures from 11 am daily, Easter to September; and daily except some Thursdays and Fridays in October.

Also on offer are various two-hour journeys by motorised narrowboat: one-way from Llangollen to Froncysyllte, daily from May to August and on most days in April, September and October, for £6/5; and from there, on most days, an option to either return by boat to Llangollen, or cross over the Pontcysyllte Aqueduct and back, for an additional £5.50/4.50. Return transport to Llangollen is also provided. All boats are wheelchair-accessible.

Llangollen Railway

The standard-gauge Llangollen Railway (☎ 860979) was once part of the Ruabon to Barmouth mainline. Closed down in 1968, it was brought back to life seven years later by keen volunteers, and now runs on a 7½-mile stretch up the valley from Llangollen via Berwyn (near Horseshoe Falls) to Glyndyfrdwy and Carrog.

There are departures three to six times daily on most days from Easter to October (and over the Christmas holidays) plus weekends year round except in January. During the summer most trains are steam-hauled. Sample return fares are £2.40/1.20 to Berwyn and £8/3.80 to the end of the line. Fanatics can buy a one-day Rover pass for £15/7.50 and there are also rail/canal combination tickets. The timetable changes from year to year, so call ahead if you're determined to ride. You can visit its Web site at www.llangollen-railway.co.uk.

The station is just across the river from the town centre.

Castell Dinas Brân

On the round hill north of Llangollen, rising 300m above the valley of the Dee, are the remnants of an Iron Age fort and the ruins of a castle whose history is obscure but which may have been built in the late 12th century by Madog ap Gruffydd, the Welsh chieftain credited with the building of nearby Valle Crucis Abbey (see Around Llangollen later). The castle fell to the forces of Edward I in 1283 and remained in English hands for two centuries, after which it went to ruin.

The real attraction though is the view – north-east to the limestone escarpments of Eglwyseg Mountain, south-west to the rounded Berwyn Mountains, west to Snowdonia and east into the flattening Marches. It's an exhilarating 45-minute walk up from near Llangollen Wharf.

Other Things to See

ECTARC (☎ 861514, fax 861804, e ectarc@aol.com) is the European Centre for Traditional and Regional Cultures, promoting Europe's traditional cultures – Wales being one – with an eye on their economic develop-

ment. Its centre, in a former Baptist chapel on Castle St, often mounts interesting exhibits on these regions and peoples, and has a small bookshop; it also has space in a former schoolhouse around the corner. It opens 10 am to 5 pm daily; admission is free.

Llangollen abounds in quaint small museums on peripheral topics. In the Lower Dee Mill Exhibition Centre (☎ 860584) on Mill St there are **exhibits on Dr Who** (a hugely popular British sci-fi TV program) for £5.75/3.50 and on model trains for £4.75/3.75. There's also a little **Postal Museum** at the post office in Castle St.

About a mile out on the A542 is the **Llangollen Motor Museum** (☎ 860324), featuring over 30 vehicles from the 1920s to 1970s. It opens 10 am to 5 pm Tuesday to Sunday, April to October; and 11 am to 5 pm Wednesday to Sunday, November to March (closed January). Admission costs £2/1.

Activities

Depending on whom you ask, the best walk in the area is west along the canal to Horseshoe Falls, or it's up to Castell Dinas Brân; see the Llangollen Canal and Castel Dinas Brân sections earlier. The Offa's Dyke Path also passes within a mile of Llangollen (on the far side of Dinas Brân) and crosses the Pontcysyllte Aqueduct. Hillwalk Wales (☎ 01691-600287) in Llanarmon Dyffryn Ceiriog, south of Llangollen, organises guided walks in the region.

As the Dee has reliable rapids throughout the summer (for the reason why, see under Bala in the Snowdonia & the Llŷn chapter), Llangollen has become a whitewater centre. JJ Canoeing & Rafting (☎ 860763), Mile End Mill, Berwyn Rd, just under a mile west of Llangollen on the A5, offers a range of activities and instruction – for example, two hours of whitewater rafting for £24, an hour of kayak instruction for £15, plus various dryside activities. It opens year round.

The Llangollen Youth Hostel (see Places to Stay later) provides space for Lonely Mountain (☎ 01490-430823), an activity centre based in Glyndyfrdwy, 5 miles west of Llangollen. Though group-oriented, it accepts individuals and families on a space-available basis for programs in climbing, caving, canoeing, cycling, orienteering and other pursuits.

Special Events

The International Musical Eisteddfod (☎ 862000) was first held in 1947. It now takes place in the Royal International Pavilion, a purpose-built pavilion just upriver, for six days each July. It's a massive, multilingual affair, with over 12,000 performers – choirs, musicians, folk singers and dancers – and crowds of more than 150,000. There's even a Fringe Festival (☎ 860030) with talks, poetry, music etc. Check out the Web site at www.inter national-eisteddfod.co.uk.

Another annual event at the Pavilion is the North Wales Hot Air Balloon festival, on the Summer bank-holiday weekend. Admission costs £5/3.

Over a long weekend in mid-May, Llangollen loosens up for its own International Jazz Festival (Liverpool ☎ 0151-339 3367 for information), with top British and some local bands playing at about eight venues around town.

Places to Stay

There are plenty of places to stay, but at Eisteddfod time you should book well in advance.

Eirianfa Camping Ground (☎ 860919, *Berwyn Rd*), a mile west on the A5, charges £6 for a tent and two people. The camp site at *Wern Isaf Farm* (☎ 860632, *Wern Rd*), a mile north-east of the centre, charges £3 per adult in a tent.

For the price of a hostel bed you can spend the night in a manor house. The extraordinary *Llangollen Youth Hostel* (☎ 860330, *Tyndwr Rd*) occupies Tyndwr Hall, a Victorian mansion set in two hectares of woodland, 1 mile south-east of town. It opens year round for a nightly charge of £10/6.90 for adults/under-18s, and also has a small licensed restaurant and an activity centre (see Activities earlier in the section).

The *Canoe Inn* (☎ 869589, *Mile End Mill, Berwyn Rd*), associated with JJ Canoeing & Rafting (see Activities earlier), charges from £7.50 per person for dormitory accommodation.

Front rooms at *Greenbank* (☎ 861835, *fax 860775, Victoria Square*) have views of Castell Dinas Brân; B&B is good value from £23.50/39 in tastefully simple en-suite singles/doubles. *Jonkers* (☎ 861158, *9 Chapel St*) is an antique shop with two well restored old rooms, complete with sloping floorboards, available for B&B at £20/36 per single/double.

Three other B&Bs charging around £20 per person are *Plas Tegid* (☎ 861013, *Abbey Rd*), *Walton House* (☎ 860825, *Queen St*) and the cheerful, one-room *Adanhurst* (☎ 860562, *Abbey Rd*), almost half a mile out on the A542.

The *Four Poster Hotel* (☎ 861062, *Mill St*) specialises in four-poster beds, charging from £32 per person. The very central *Gales Wine Bar* (see Places to Eat) has 15 deluxe rooms for £45/63 and good-value food in the bar.

Places to Eat

Llangollen has plenty of good mid-range restaurants for a town its size.

Dylan's Wine Bar (☎ 869099, *19 Bridge St*) has a menu for the hungry – everything from chilli to steak-and-kidney, chicken curry to seafood lasagne, at very reasonable prices (most dishes under £6). Across the street is *Gales Wine Bar* (☎ 860089, *18 Bridge St*), with similar but pricier offerings. Cheerful, bistro-style *Greenbank* (see Places to Stay earlier) does steak, chicken and fish dishes for £6 to £7.

Up a notch or two is the *Corn Mill Restaurant* (☎ 869555, *Dee Lane*), with a pricey but imaginative selection including game or duck (from £8) and Welsh lamb – plus a few cheaper 'starter' portions and sandwiches for around £5. It opens daily, with food from noon to 9 pm; go outside regular mealtimes to bag a table on the outdoor deck above the river.

Named after one of the Ladies of Llangollen, *Sarah Ponsonby* (☎ 861119, *Mill St*) is a bright, airy riverside bar serving snacks and daily a la carte lunch and dinner. *Spice*

Lounge (☎ 861877, 36 Regent St) is good for tandoori food. *Cottage Bakery & Tea Rooms (Castle St)* does good cream teas.

Piersons Butchers beside the TIC sells hot barbecue chicken, and the adjacent delicatessen, *James Bailey*, does home-made pies – try a Welsh Oggie (meat, potato and onion pasty). A block up Castle St is a *Spar* supermarket open until 11 pm daily.

Tuesday is market day with produce, handicrafts and more in the parking lot on Market St.

Entertainment

The most happening place in Llangollen seems to be the *Sun Inn (☎ 860233, Regent St)*, with an international selection of beers and ales and lots of live music: folk Wednesday, blues or hard rock Friday, easy rock Saturday and jazz Sunday.

Agreeable drinking spots nearer the centre include the *D Bar (☎ 860202, Bridge St)*, open Thursday to Saturday at the Royal Hotel, and the bar at the *Wynnstay Arms (☎ 860710, Bridge St)*.

The *Llangollen Male Voice Choir (☎ 420489)* practises at the Hand Hotel on Bridge St on most Friday evenings and sometimes on Monday.

Getting There & Away

Between them Bryn Melyn Motor Services (☎ 860701) bus No X5 and GHA Coaches (☎ 753598) No 555 run three times hourly to/from Ruabon (95p, 14 minutes) and Wrexham (£1.30, 30 minutes), Monday to Saturday; Arriva Midlands North's (☎ 01543-466124) No 5 service goes four times on Sunday afternoon.

Transport to Snowdonia is limited: take Arriva Cymru's bus No 94 to Corwen (where you can pick up a No 70 to Betws-y-Coed and Llandudno) or to Dolgellau (where you can pick up the No 35 to Blaenau Ffestiniog). National Express coach No 420 runs daily from Wrexham (£2, 30 minutes) and from London via Birmingham and Shrewsbury.

Llangollen's train station only serves the Llangollen Railway. The nearest mainline station is at Ruabon, 6 miles east on the Shrewsbury-Chester mainline, with services every two hours. A taxi (☎ 861018) to/from Ruabon costs about £6.

Getting Around

Bikes can be hired from the Llangollen Youth Hostel (see Places to Stay earlier) for £8/15 per half/full day.

AROUND LLANGOLLEN
Chirk Castle

South-east of Llangollen near the English border, with fine views over the English borderlands, is this fine Marcher fortress built in 1310 and continuously occupied ever since. It was bought in 1595 by the Myddelton family, who adapted it for more comfortable living and still live there today. Its formal gardens are part of the attraction.

The castle (☎ 01691-777701) opens noon to 5 pm daily except Monday and Tuesday, April to October (to 4 pm in October). Admission costs £5/2.50. The gardens open 11 am to 6 pm, for £2.80/1.40. The castle is 2 miles west of Chirk village, itself 6 miles from Llangollen; Bryn Melyn bus No 64 goes to Chirk village (£1.30, 15 minutes), with three useful departures before about 2 pm, Monday to Saturday.

WREXHAM (WRECSAM)
☎ 01978 • pop 43,000

The largely uninspiring town of Wrexham is situated in the Clywedog Valley, near the border with England. Wrexham is famous for its lager – the UK's first lager brewery opened here in 1882 – and for its rugby team, one of Wales' top six. Attractions on a higher plane include Erddig, a fine 17th-century stately home 2 miles south of the town centre, and Chirk Castle, 10 miles to the south (see Around Llangollen earlier).

Orientation & Information

From the bus station on King St it's a five-block walk to the TIC (south for one block to Regent St, east for three blocks to Queen St, and one block north). From the train station it's a similar walk east down Regent St.

There's a TIC (☎ 292015, fax 292467, ⓔ tic@wrexham.gov.uk) on Lambpit St open 10 am to 5 pm Monday to Saturday (to 4 pm November to March). All major UK banks are represented in or around High St. The police station (☎ 290222) is on Bod-hyfryd Rd, north-east of the TIC. Maelor Hospital (☎ 291100) is on Croes Newydd Rd, half a mile south of the train station.

Erddig

Erddig (☎ 355314; NT), home of the Yorke family for over two centuries until 1973, gives an illuminating look into the life of the British upper classes in the 19th cen-tury, and perhaps the best insight in the UK into the 'upstairs-downstairs' relationship that existed between masters and servants.

In the fine staterooms are much of the family's original furniture and furnishings. A wide range of outbuildings includes kitchen, laundry, bakehouse, stables, sawmill, smithy and joiner's shop. A formal walled garden has been restored to its appearance in Victo-rian times and features rare fruit trees, a canal and the National Ivy Collection. The 809-acre property includes extensive wood-land walks.

The Yorkes were known for the respect with which they treated their servants. Below stairs are portraits and photographs of servants through the years and a collec-tion of household appliances of the time.

The house opens noon to 5 pm daily ex-cept Thursday and Friday, April to October (to 4 pm in October; last admission one hour before closing); the grounds open 11 am to 6 pm (from 10 am in July and August, to 5 pm in October). Because this is a pop-ular destination, timed admission tickets may be issued. Admission costs £6/3 to the house and grounds or £2.50/1.50 to the out-buildings and grounds. There are also fam-ily tickets.

Erddig is 2 miles south of Wrexham, off the A483.

Wrexham County Museum

This free museum (☎ 317970) offers a look at the prehistory and history of North Wales' most important industrial town. It's in the county building on Regent St, beside St Mary's Church and near the bus station, and opens 10.30 am to 5 pm daily except Sunday (to 3 pm on Saturday).

Places to Stay & Eat

The *Grove Guest House* (☎ 354288, 36 Chester Rd), about 700m north of the TIC, has B&B singles/doubles from £18/34. The *Wynnstay Arms Hotel* (☎ 291010, Yorke Street), three blocks south from the TIC, of-fers B&B from £27 to £47 per person.

Kristina's (☎ 312312, 56 Chester Rd) is a cafe about a block from the TIC with snacks and light lunches. The *Horse & Jockey* (Hope St), at the eastern end of Re-gent St, has real ales and bar meals.

Getting There & Away

GHA Coaches (☎ 753598) bus No 555 and Bryn Melyn Motor Services (☎ 860701) No X5 together run three times hourly from Llangollen (£1.30 single, 30 minutes), Monday to Saturday; Arriva Midlands North's (☎ 01543-466124) No 5 service goes four times on Sunday afternoon.

Arriva Cymru's cross-Wales coach No 94 has seven services daily (two on Sun-day) from Barmouth via Dolgellau (£4.15, two hours), Bala (£3.35 single, 1½ hours) and Llangollen (£1.50, 30 minutes). Ar-riva's No 1 comes from Chester every 15 minutes (hourly on Sunday). National Ex-press coach No 420 runs daily via Llan-gollen (£2, 30 minutes) and Shrewsbury (£3.50, 1½ hours) from London and Birm-ingham.

Wrexham is on the Chester-Birmingham line, with trains from Chester (£3 single, one hour) and from Shrewsbury (£4.50, 40 minutes) about hourly and Birmingham every two hours.

Language

You can get by almost anywhere in Wales these days without speaking Welsh (although that probably won't be the case in a generation!). But for anyone who's serious about getting to grips with Welsh people and their culture, the ability to speak basic Welsh is immeasurably valuable right now.

Beginners will find lots of resources, including teach-yourself books, videotapes and CD-ROMs; you can even learn Welsh via the Internet. For information on courses – including correspondence courses – see under Courses in the Facts for the Visitor chapter.

The Welsh language belongs to the Celtic branch of the Indo-European language family. Closely related to Breton and Cornish, and more distantly to Irish, Scottish and Manx, it's the strongest Celtic language both in terms of numbers of speakers (over 500,000) and place in society.

Pronunciation

All letters in Welsh are pronounced and the stress is usually on the second last syllable. Letters are pronounced as in English except for the following:

Vowels

Vowels can be long or short. Those marked with a circumflex (eg, **ê**) are always long and those with a grave accent (eg, **è**) short.

a	short as in 'map'; long as in 'margin'
e	short as in 'pen'; long as in 'there'
i	short as in 'bit'; long as in 'police'
o	short as in 'box'; long as in 'bore'
u	as **i** (short and long)
w	short as the 'oo' in 'book'; long as the 'oo' in 'spook'
y	as **i** (short or long); sometimes as the 'a' in 'about', especially in common one-syllable words like *y*, *yr*, *fy*, *dy* and *yn*.

In words of one syllable, vowels followed by two consonants are short – eg, *corff*

(body). If a one-syllable word ends in **p**, **t**, **c**, **m**, or **ng**, the vowel is short – eg, *llong* (ship). If it ends in **b**, **d**, **g**, **f**, **dd**, **ff**, **th**, **ch**, or **s**, the vowel is long – eg, *bad* (boat) – as is any vowel at the end of a one-syllable word, such as *pla* (plague).

In words of more than one syllable, all unstressed vowels are short, such as in the first and final vowels of *cariadon* (lovers). Stressed vowels can be long or short and in general follow the rules for vowels in monosyllables.

Diphthongs

ae/ai/au	as the 'y' in 'my'
aw	as the 'ow' in 'cow'
ei/eu/ey	as the 'ay' in 'day'
ew	as a short 'e' followed by 'oo'
iw/uw/yw	as the 'ew' in 'few'
oe/oi	as 'oy' in 'boy'
ow	as the 'ow' in 'tow'
wy	sometimes as 'uey' (as in 'chop suey'); sometimes as the 'wi' in 'wing' (especially after **g**)

Consonants

The combinations **ch**, **dd**, **ff**, **ng**, **ll**, **ph**, **rh** and **th** count as single consonants in Welsh.

c	always as 'k'
ch	as the 'ch' in Scottish *loch*
dd	as the 'th' in 'this'
ff	as the 'f' in 'fork'
g	always as the 'g' in 'garden', not as in 'gentle'
ng	as the 'ng' in 'sing'
ll	as 'hl' (put the tongue in the position for 'l' and breathe out)
ph	as 'f'
r	rolled, as in Spanish or Italian
rh	pronounced as 'hr'
s	always as the 's' in 'say', never as the 's' in 'busy'
si	as the 'sh' in 'shop'
th	always as the 'th' in 'thin'

Greetings & Civilities

Hello.
Sut mae. *sit mai*
Good morning.
Bore da. *bo-rre dah*
Good afternoon.
Prynhawn da. *pruhn-hown dah*
Good evening.
Noswaith dda. *noss-waith thah*
Goodnight.
Nos da. *nohs dah*
See you (later).
Wela i chi *wel-ah ee khee*
(wedyn). *(we-din)*
Goodbye.
Hwyl fawr. *hueyl vowrr*
Please.
Os gwelwch in *os gwel-ookh uhn*
dda. *thah*
Thank you (very much).
Diolch *dee-olkh*
(in fawr iawn). *(uhn vowrr yown)*
You're welcome.
Croeso. *kroy-ssoh*
Excuse me.
Esgusodwch fi. *ess-gi-so-dookh vee*
Sorry (excuse me; forgive me).
Mae'n ddrwg *main thrroog*
gyda fi. *guh-da vee*
Don't mention it.
Peidiwch â sôn. *payd-yookh ah sohn*
Yes.
Oes. *oyss*
No.
Nac oes. *nag oyss*
How are you?
Sut ydych chi? *sit uh-deekh khee?*
(Very) well.
(Da) iawn. *(dah) yown*
What's your name?
Beth yw eich *beth yu uhch*
enw chi? *en-oo khee?*
My name's ...
Fy enw i yw ... *ne-noo ee yu ...*
Where are you from?
O ble ydych *oh ble uh-deekh*
chi'n dod? *kheen dohd?*
I'm from ...
Dw i'n dod o ... *doo een dohd oh ...*

Language Difficulties

I don't understand.
Dw i ddim in deall.
doo ee thim uhn deh-ahhl
How do you say ...?
Sut mae dweud ...?
sit mai dwayd ...?
What's this called in Welsh?
Beth yw hwn in Gymraeg?
beth yu hoon uhn guhm-raig?

Food & Drinks
Traditional Welsh Dishes

bara brith *(bah-ra breeth)* – rich, fruited tea-loaf

bara lawr *(bah-ra lowrr)* – laver seaweed boiled and mixed with oatmeal and traditionally served with bacon for breakfast

cawl *(cowl)* – broth of meat and vegetables

caws caerffili *(cows kairr-fil-ee)* – Caerphilly cheese, a crumbly salty cheese that used to be popular with miners

ffagots a pys *(fa-gots a peess)* – seasoned balls of chopped pork and liver in gravy served with peas

lobsgows *(lobs-gowss)* – a Northwalian version of cawl

pice ar y maen *(pi-keh ar uh mahn)* – (lit: cakes on the griddlestone) small, fruited scone-like griddle cakes known also as Welsh cakes

In the Pub

I'd like a (half) pint of ...
Ga i (hanner o) beint o ...
gah ee (hann-err oh) baynt oh ...

bitter	chwerw	*khwe-rroo*
cider	seidr	*say-dirr*
lager	lager	*la-gerr*
orange juice	sudd oren	*seeth oh-ren*
water	dwr	*doorr*

Days & Months

Monday
dydd Llun *deeth hleen*
Tuesday
dydd Mawrth *deeth mowrrth*
Wednesday
dydd Mercher *deeth merr-kherr*
Thursday
dydd Iau *deeth yigh*

Friday
dydd Gwener   *deeth gwen-err*
Saturday
dydd Sadwrn   *deeth sad-oorrn*
Sunday
dydd Sul   *deeth seel*

Some names for months are borrowed from Latin. Others are native Welsh.

January	Ionawr	*yon-owrr*
February	Chwefror	*khwe-vrrohrr*
March	Mawrth	*mowrrth*
April	Ebrill	*eh-brihl*
May	Mai	*mai*
June	Mehefin	*me-he-vin*

(lit: the middle of summer)

July	Gorffennaf	*gor-fen-ahv*

(lit: the end of summer)

August	Awst	*owst*
September	Medi	*med-dee*

(lit: reaping)

October	Hydref	*huh-drev*

(the rutting season, lit: stag-roaring)

November	Tachwedd	*tahkh-weth*

(the time for slaughtering animals before winter, lit: slaughter)

December	Rhagfyr	*hrag-virr*

(the shortest day, lit: before short)

Numbers

0	dim	*dim*
1	un	*een*
2	dau/dwy (f)	*dy/duey*
3	tri/tair (f)	*tree/tairr*
4	pedwar/pedair (f)	*ped-wahrr/ped-airr*
5	pump	*pimp*
6	chwech	*khwekh*
7	saith	*saith*
8	wyth	*ueyth*
9	naw	*now*
10	deg	*dehg*

Place Names

Place names are often based on words that describe a landmark or a feature of the countryside.

aber	*ab-berr*	estuary/confluence
afon	*a-von*	river
bach	*bahkh*	small
bro	*broh*	vale
bryn	*brin*	hill
caer	*kairr*	fort
capel	*ka-pl*	chapel
carreg	*karr-ek*	stone
clwn	*kloon*	meadow
coed	*koyd*	wood/forest
cwm	*koom*	valley
dinas	*dee-nass*	hill fortress
eglwys	*eglueyss*	church
fach	*vahkh*	small
fawr	*vowrr*	big
ffordd	*forth*	road
glan	*glahn*	shore
glyn	*glin*	valley
isa (f)	*issa*	lower
llan	*hlan*	church/enclosure
llyn	*hlin*	lake
maes	*maiss*	field
mawr	*mowrr*	big
mynydd	*muhneeth*	mountain
nant	*nahnt*	valley/stream
ogof	*o-gov*	cave
pen	*pen*	head/top/end
plas	*plahss*	hall/mansion
pont	*pont*	bridge
rhos	*hross*	moor/marsh
twr	*toorr*	tower
tŷ	*tee*	house
uchaf	*ikhav*	upper
ynys	*uh-niss*	island/holm/ watermeadow

Glossary

For some additional, specifically Welsh, words and roots, see the boxed text 'Place Names' in the preceding Language chapter.

abe – estuary (Welsh)
afon – river (Welsh)
aka – also known as
almshouse – accommodation traditionally offered to the aged or needy
AONB – Area of Outstanding Natural Beauty
ATM – automatic teller machine

B&B – bed and breakfast
BABA – Book-A-Bed-Ahead scheme
bach – small (Welsh)
bailey – outermost wall of a castle
banger – old, cheap car
bangers – sausages
bara birth – spicy fruit loaf (Welsh)
bent – not altogether legal
bevvied – drunk
bill – restaurant check
billion – a million million, not a thousand million
biscuit – cookie
bitter – beer
black pudding – a type of sausage made from dried blood and other ingredients
bloke – man
bloody – damn
bodge job – poor-quality repairs
bridleway – path that can be used by walkers, horse riders and cyclists
BTA – British Tourist Authority
bus – local bus; *see also* coach
BYO – bring your own

cadair – stronghold/chair (Welsh)
Cadw – the Welsh historic monuments agency (Welsh)
caer – fort (Welsh)
caff – cheap cafe
capel – chapel (Welsh)
car bonnet – hood
car boot – trunk
carreg – stone (Welsh)

cheers – goodbye; *also* thanks; *also* a drinking toast
chemist – pharmacist
chine – valley-like fissure leading to the sea
chips – French fries
clun – meadow (Welsh)
coach – long-distance bus; *see also* bus
coaching inn – inn along an old coaching route at which horses were changed
coasteering – steering your way around the coastline by climbing, jumping, swimming and scrambling
coch – red (Welsh)
coed – forest/wood (Welsh)
couchette – sleeping berth in a train or ferry
courgette – zucchini
crack – good conversation, good fun (originally from Ireland)
crannog – artificial island settlement
crisps – potato chips
cromlech – burial chamber (Welsh)
cwm – valley (Welsh)

de – south (Welsh)
dear – expensive
din (dinas) – fort (Welsh)
DIY – do-it-yourself, as in handyman shop
dolmen – chambered tomb
donkey – engine
dosh/dough – money
downs – rolling upland, characterised by lack of trees
du – black (Welsh)

EH – English Heritage
eisteddfod – festival in which competitions are held in music, poetry, drama and the fine arts (Welsh)
en suite – refers to a room with attached toilet and bath/shower
EU – European Union

fag – cigarette; *also* a boring task
fanny – female genitals, not backside
fawr – big ((welsh))
ffordd – road (Welsh)

fiver – five-pound note
flat – apartment
flip-flops – thongs
footpath – sidewalk

glan – shore (Welsh)
glas – blue (Welsh)
glyn – valley (Welsh)
grand – one thousand (pounds)
greasy spoon – cheap cafe
gutted – very disappointed
gwrydd – green (Welsh)
gwyn – white (Welsh)

hammered – drunk
HI – Hostelling International
hire – rent
hotel – accommodation with food and bar, not always open to passing trade
Huguenots – French Protestants

inn – pub with accommodation

jam – jelly
jelly – jello
jumper – sweater

lager lout – *see* yob
lass – young woman
laver bread – laver seaweed fried as a breakfast food (Welsh)
ley – clearing
lift – elevator
llan – enclosed place or church (Welsh)
llyn –lake (Welsh)
lock – part of a canal or river that can be closed off and the water levels changed to raise or lower boats
lolly – money; *also* candy on a stick (possibly frozen)
lorry – truck
love – term of address, not necessarily to someone likeable

machair – grass- and wildflower-covered sand dunes
manky – low quality
mate – a friend of any sex; term of address
mawr – great (Welsh)
merthyr – burial place of a saint (Welsh)
midge – a mosquito-like insect

motorway – freeway
motte – mound on which a castle was built
mynydd – mountain (Welsh)

naff – inferior, in poor taste
nanat – valley/stream (Welsh)
nappies – diapers
newydd – new (Welsh)
NMGW – National Museums & Galleries of Wales
NT – National Trust

off-licence (offie) – carry-out alcoholic drinks shop
ogof – cave (Welsh)
OS – Ordnance Survey

pee – pence
pen – headland (Welsh)
pint – measure (of beer)
pissed – drunk (not angry)
pissed off – angry
pistyll – waterfall (Welsh)
pitch – playing field
plas – hall/mansion (Welsh)
ponce – ostentatious or effeminate male; *also* to borrow (usually permanently)
pont – bridge (Welsh)
pop – fizzy drink
postbus – minibus, operated by the Royal Mail, which follows postal delivery routes
pub – public house, a bar, usually with food, sometimes with accommodation
punter – customer
pwll – pool (Welsh)

queue – line
quid – pound (money)

ramble – (to go for) a walk in the country-side
return ticket – round-trip ticket
rhiw – slope (Welsh)
rhos – moor/marsh (Welsh)
roll-up – roll-your-own cigarette
rood – alternative word for cross
RSPB – Royal Society for the Protection of Birds
rubber – eraser
rubbish bin – garbage can

sacked – fired
sarnie – sandwich
shag – have sex
shout – to buy a group of people a drinks, usually reciprocated
single ticket – one-way ticket
snogging – kissing
SSSI – Site of Special Scientific Interest
steaming – drunk
stone – 14lb, 6.35kg
subway – underpass
sweet – candy

ta – thanks
TIC – Tourist Information Centre
ton – one hundred
tor – Celtic word describing a hill shaped like a triangular wedge of cheese
torch – flashlight
towpath – a path running beside a river or canal
trainers – tennis shoes, sneakers etc
traveller – nomadic, New-Age hippy
tre – town (Welsh)

twitcher – birdwatcher
twr – tower (Welsh)
ty – house (Welsh)

underground – London's underground railway; subway

VAT – value-added tax, levied on most goods and services, currently 17.5%
verderer – officer upholding law and order in the royal forests

wanker – worthless/hopeless person
way – a long-distance trail
wide boy – ostentatious go-getter, usually on the make
wold – open, rolling country
WTB – Wales Tourist Board

YHA – Youth Hostels Association
ynys – island (Welsh)
yob – hooligan
ystwyth – winding (Welsh)

Lonely Planet Guides by Region

Lonely Planet is known worldwide for publishing practical, reliable and no-nonsense travel information in our guides and on our Web site. The Lonely Planet list covers just about every accessible part of the world. Currently there are 16 series: Travel guides, Shoestring guides, Condensed guides, Phrasebooks, Read This First, Healthy Travel, Walking guides, Cycling guides, Watching Wildlife guides, Pisces Diving & Snorkeling guides, City Maps, Road Atlases, Out to Eat, World Food, Journeys travel literature and Pictorials.

AFRICA Africa on a shoestring • Botswana • Cairo • Cairo City Map • Cape Town • Cape Town City Map • East Africa • Egypt • Egyptian Arabic phrasebook • Ethiopia, Eritrea & Djibouti • Ethiopian Amharic phrasebook • The Gambia & Senegal • Healthy Travel Africa • Kenya • Malawi • Morocco • Moroccan Arabic phrasebook • Mozambique • Namibia • Read This First: Africa • South Africa, Lesotho & Swaziland • Southern Africa • Southern Africa Road Atlas • Swahili phrasebook • Tanzania, Zanzibar & Pemba • Trekking in East Africa • Tunisia • Watching Wildlife East Africa • Watching Wildlife Southern Africa • West Africa • World Food Morocco • Zambia • Zimbabwe, Botswana & Namibia
Travel Literature: Mali Blues: Traveling to an African Beat • The Rainbird: A Central African Journey • Songs to an African Sunset: A Zimbabwean Story

AUSTRALIA & THE PACIFIC Aboriginal Australia & the Torres Strait Islands •Auckland • Australia • Australian phrasebook • Australia Road Atlas • Cycling Australia • Cycling New Zealand • Fiji • Fijian phrasebook • Healthy Travel Australia, NZ & the Pacific • Islands of Australia's Great Barrier Reef • Melbourne • Melbourne City Map • Micronesia • New Caledonia • New South Wales • New Zealand • Northern Territory • Outback Australia • Out to Eat – Melbourne • Out to Eat – Sydney • Papua New Guinea • Pidgin phrasebook • Queensland • Rarotonga & the Cook Islands • Samoa • Solomon Islands • South Australia • South Pacific • South Pacific phrasebook • Sydney • Sydney City Map • Sydney Condensed • Tahiti & French Polynesia • Tasmania • Tonga • Tramping in New Zealand • Vanuatu • Victoria • Walking in Australia • Watching Wildlife Australia • Western Australia
Travel Literature: Islands in the Clouds: Travels in the Highlands of New Guinea • Kiwi Tracks: A New Zealand Journey • Sean & David's Long Drive

CENTRAL AMERICA & THE CARIBBEAN Bahamas, Turks & Caicos • Baja California • Belize, Guatemala & Yucatán • Bermuda • Central America on a shoestring • Costa Rica • Costa Rica Spanish phrasebook • Cuba • Cycling Cuba • Dominican Republic & Haiti • Eastern Caribbean • Guatemala • Havana • Healthy Travel Central & South America • Jamaica • Mexico • Mexico City • Panama • Puerto Rico • Read This First: Central & South America • Virgin Islands • World Food Caribbean • World Food Mexico • Yucatán
Travel Literature: Green Dreams: Travels in Central America

EUROPE Amsterdam • Amsterdam City Map • Amsterdam Condensed • Andalucía • Athens • Austria • Baltic States phrasebook • Barcelona • Barcelona City Map • Belgium & Luxembourg • Berlin • Berlin City Map • Britain • British phrasebook • Brussels, Bruges & Antwerp • Brussels City Map • Budapest • Budapest City Map • Canary Islands • Catalunya & the Costa Brava • Central Europe • Central Europe phrasebook • Copenhagen • Corfu & the Ionians • Corsica • Crete • Crete Condensed • Croatia • Cycling Britain • Cycling France • Cyprus • Czech & Slovak Republics • Czech phrasebook • Denmark • Dublin • Dublin City Map • Dublin Condensed • Eastern Europe • Eastern Europe phrasebook • Edinburgh • Edinburgh City Map • England • Estonia, Latvia & Lithuania • Europe on a shoestring • Europe phrasebook • Finland • Florence • Florence City Map • France • Frankfurt City Map • Frankfurt Condensed • French phrasebook • Georgia, Armenia & Azerbaijan • Germany • German phrasebook • Greece • Greek Islands • Greek phrasebook • Hungary • Iceland, Greenland & the Faroe Islands • Ireland • Italian phrasebook • Italy • Kraków • Lisbon • The Loire • London • London City Map • London Condensed • Madrid • Madrid City Map • Malta • Mediterranean Europe • Milan, Turin & Genoa • Moscow • Munich • Netherlands • Normandy • Norway • Out to Eat – London • Out to Eat – Paris • Paris • Paris City Map • Paris Condensed • Poland • Polish phrasebook • Portugal • Portuguese phrasebook • Prague • Prague City Map • Provence & the Côte d'Azur • Read This First: Europe • Rhodes & the Dodecanese • Romania & Moldova • Rome • Rome City Map • Rome Condensed • Russia, Ukraine & Belarus • Russian phrasebook • Scandinavian & Baltic Europe • Scandinavian phrasebook • Scotland • Sicily • Slovenia • South-West France • Spain • Spanish phrasebook • Stockholm • St Petersburg • St Petersburg City Map • Sweden • Switzerland • Tuscany • Ukrainian phrasebook • Venice • Vienna • Wales • Walking in Britain • Walking in France • Walking in Ireland • Walking in Italy • Walking in Scotland • Walking in Spain • Walking in Switzerland • Western Europe • World Food France • World Food Greece • World Food Ireland • World Food Italy • World Food Spain **Travel Literature:** After Yugoslavia • Love and War in the Apennines • The Olive Grove: Travels in Greece • On the Shores of the Mediterranean • Round Ireland in Low Gear • A Small Place in Italy

Lonely Planet Mail Order

onely Planet products are distributed worldwide. They are also available by mail order from Lonely Planet, so if you have difficulty finding a title please write to us. North and South American residents should write to 150 Linden St, Oakland, CA 94607, USA; European and African residents should write to 10a Spring Place, London NW5 3BH, UK; and residents of other countries to Locked Bag 1, Footscray, Victoria 3011, Australia.

INDIAN SUBCONTINENT & THE INDIAN OCEAN Bangladesh • Bengali phrasebook • Bhutan • Delhi • Goa • Healthy Travel Asia & India • Hindi & Urdu phrasebook • India • India & Bangladesh City Map • Indian Himalaya • Karakoram Highway • Kathmandu City Map • Kerala • Madagascar • Maldives • Mauritius, Réunion & Seychelles • Mumbai (Bombay) • Nepal • Nepali phrasebook • North India • Pakistan • Rajasthan • Read This First: Asia & India • South India • Sri Lanka • Sri Lanka phrasebook • Tibet • Tibetan phrasebook • Trekking in the Indian Himalaya • Trekking in the Karakoram & Hindukush • Trekking in the Nepal Himalaya • World Food India **Travel Literature:** The Age of Kali: Indian Travels and Encounters • Hello Goodnight: A Life of Goa • In Rajasthan • Maverick in Madagascar • A Season in Heaven: True Tales from the Road to Kathmandu • Shopping for Buddhas • A Short Walk in the Hindu Kush • Slowly Down the Ganges

MIDDLE EAST & CENTRAL ASIA Bahrain, Kuwait & Qatar • Central Asia • Central Asia phrasebook • Dubai • Farsi (Persian) phrasebook • Hebrew phrasebook • Iran • Israel & the Palestinian Territories • Istanbul • Istanbul City Map • Istanbul to Cairo • Istanbul to Kathmandu • Jerusalem • Jerusalem City Map • Jordan • Lebanon • Middle East • Oman & the United Arab Emirates • Syria • Turkey • Turkish phrasebook • World Food Turkey • Yemen **Travel Literature:** Black on Black: Iran Revisited • Breaking Ranks: Turbulent Travels in the Promised Land • The Gates of Damascus • Kingdom of the Film Stars: Journey into Jordan

NORTH AMERICA Alaska • Boston • Boston City Map • Boston Condensed • British Columbia • California & Nevada • California Condensed • Canada • Chicago • Chicago City Map • Chicago Condensed • Florida • Georgia & the Carolinas • Great Lakes • Hawaii • Hiking in Alaska • Hiking in the USA • Honolulu & Oahu City Map • Las Vegas • Los Angeles • Los Angeles City Map • Louisiana & the Deep South • Miami • Miami City Map • Montreal • New England • New Orleans • New Orleans City Map • New York City • New York City City Map • New York City Condensed • New York, New Jersey & Pennsylvania • Oahu • Out to Eat – San Francisco • Pacific Northwest • Rocky Mountains • San Diego & Tijuana • San Francisco • San Francisco City Map • Seattle • Seattle City Map • Southwest • Texas • Toronto • USA • USA phrasebook • Vancouver • Vancouver City Map • Virginia & the Capital Region • Washington, DC • Washington, DC City Map • World Food New Orleans **Travel Literature:** Caught Inside: A Surfer's Year on the California Coast • Drive Thru America

NORTH-EAST ASIA Beijing • Beijing City Map • Cantonese phrasebook • China • Hiking in Japan • Hong Kong & Macau • Hong Kong City Map • Hong Kong Condensed • Japan • Japanese phrasebook • Korea • Korean phrasebook • Kyoto • Mandarin phrasebook • Mongolia • Mongolian phrasebook • Seoul • Shanghai • South-West China • Taiwan • Tokyo • Tokyo Condensed • World Food Hong Kong • World Food Japan **Travel Literature:** In Xanadu: A Quest • Lost Japan

SOUTH AMERICA Argentina, Uruguay & Paraguay • Bolivia • Brazil • Brazilian phrasebook • Buenos Aires • Buenos Aires City Map • Chile & Easter Island • Colombia • Ecuador & the Galapagos Islands • Healthy Travel Central & South America • Latin American Spanish phrasebook • Peru • Quechua phrasebook • Read This First: Central & South America • Rio de Janeiro • Rio de Janeiro City Map • Santiago de Chile • South America on a shoestring • Trekking in the Patagonian Andes • Venezuela **Travel Literature:** Full Circle: A South American Journey

SOUTH-EAST ASIA Bali & Lombok • Bangkok • Bangkok City Map • Burmese phrasebook • Cambodia • Cycling Vietnam, Laos & Cambodia • East Timor phrasebook • Hanoi • Healthy Travel Asia & India • Hill Tribes phrasebook • Ho Chi Minh City (Saigon) • Indonesia • Indonesian phrasebook • Indonesia's Eastern Islands • Java • Lao phrasebook • Laos • Malay phrasebook • Malaysia, Singapore & Brunei • Myanmar (Burma) • Philippines • Pilipino (Tagalog) phrasebook • Read This First: Asia & India • Singapore • Singapore City Map • South-East Asia on a shoestring • South-East Asia phrasebook • Thailand • Thailand's Islands & Beaches • Thailand, Vietnam, Laos & Cambodia Road Atlas • Thai phrasebook • Vietnam • Vietnamese phrasebook • World Food Indonesia • World Food Thailand • World Food Vietnam

ALSO AVAILABLE: Antarctica • The Arctic • The Blue Man: Tales of Travel, Love and Coffee • Brief Encounters: Stories of Love, Sex & Travel • Buddhist Stupas in Asia: The Shape of Perfection • Chasing Rickshaws • The Last Grain Race • Lonely Planet ... On the Edge: Adventurous Escapades from Around the World • Lonely Planet Unpacked • Lonely Planet Unpacked Again • Not the Only Planet: Science Fiction Travel Stories • Ports of Call: A Journey by Sea • Sacred India • Travel Photography: A Guide to Taking Better Pictures • Travel with Children • Tuvalu: Portrait of an Island Nation

LONELY PLANET

ON THE ROAD

Travel Guides explore cities, regions and countries, and supply information on transport, restaurants and accommodation, covering all budgets. They come with reliable, easy-to-use maps, practical advice, cultural and historical facts and a rundown on attractions both on and off the beaten track. There are over 200 titles in this classic series, covering nearly every country in the world.

 Lonely Planet Upgrades extend the shelf life of existing travel guides by detailing any changes that may affect travel in a region since a book has been published. Upgrades can be downloaded for free from **www.lonelyplanet.com/upgrades**

For travellers with more time than money, **Shoestring** guides offer dependable, first-hand information with hundreds of detailed maps, plus insider tips for stretching money as far as possible. Covering entire continents in most cases, the six-volume shoestring guides are known around the world as 'backpackers bibles'.

For the discerning short-term visitor, **Condensed** guides highlight the best a destination has to offer in a full-colour, pocket-sized format designed for quick access. They include everything from top sights and walking tours to opinionated reviews of where to eat, stay, shop and have fun.

CitySync lets travellers use their Palm™ or Visor™ hand-held computers to guide them through a city with handy tips on transport, history, cultural life, major sights, and shopping and entertainment options. It can also quickly search and sort hundreds of reviews of hotels, restaurants and attractions, and pinpoint their location on scrollable street maps. CitySync can be downloaded from **www.citysync.com**

MAPS & ATLASES

Lonely Planet's **City Maps** feature downtown and metropolitan maps, as well as transit routes and walking tours. The maps come complete with an index of streets, a listing of sights and a plastic coat for extra durability.

Road Atlases are an essential navigation tool for serious travellers. Cross-referenced with the guidebooks, they also feature distance and climate charts and a complete site index.

LONELY PLANET

ESSENTIALS

Read This First books help new travellers to hit the road with confidence. These invaluable predeparture guides give step-by-step advice on preparing for a trip, budgeting, arranging a visa, planning an itinerary and staying safe while still getting off the beaten track.

Healthy Travel pocket guides offer a regional rundown on disease hot spots and practical advice on predeparture health measures, staying well on the road and what to do in emergencies. The guides come with a user-friendly design and helpful diagrams and tables.

Lonely Planet's **Phrasebooks** cover the essential words and phrases travellers need when they're strangers in a strange land. They come in a pocket-sized format with colour tabs for quick reference, extensive vocabulary lists, easy-to-follow pronunciation keys and two-way dictionaries.

Miffed by blurry photos of the Taj Mahal? Tired of the classic 'top of the head cut off' shot? **Travel Photography: A Guide to Taking Better Pictures** will help you turn ordinary holiday snaps into striking images and give you the know-how to capture every scene, from frenetic festivals to peaceful beach sunrises.

Lonely Planet's **Travel Journal** is a lightweight but sturdy travel diary for jotting down all those on-the-road observations and significant travel moments. It comes with a handy time-zone wheel, a world map and useful travel information.

Lonely Planet's eKno is an all-in-one communication service developed especially for travellers. It offers low-cost international calls and free email and voicemail so that you can keep in touch while on the road. Check it out on **www.ekno.lonelyplanet.com**

FOOD & RESTAURANT GUIDES

Lonely Planet's **Out to Eat** guides recommend the brightest and best places to eat and drink in top international cities. These gourmet companions are arranged by neighbourhood, packed with dependable maps, garnished with scene-setting photos and served with quirky features.

For people who live to eat, drink and travel, **World Food** guides explore the culinary culture of each country. Entertaining and adventurous, each guide is packed with detail on staples and specialities, regional cuisine and local markets, as well as sumptuous recipes, comprehensive culinary dictionaries and lavish photos good enough to eat.

LONELY PLANET

OUTDOOR GUIDES

For those who believe the best way to see the world is on foot, Lonely Planet's **Walking Guides** detail everything from family strolls to difficult treks, with 'when to go and how to do it' advice supplemented by reliable maps and essential travel information.

Cycling Guides map a destination's best bike tours, long and short, in day-by-day detail. They contain all the information a cyclist needs, including advice on bike maintenance, places to eat and stay, innovative maps with detailed cues to the rides, and elevation charts.

The **Watching Wildlife** series is perfect for travellers who want authoritative information but don't want to tote a heavy field guide. Packed with advice on where, when and how to view a region's wildlife, each title features photos of over 300 species and contains engaging comments on the local flora and fauna.

With underwater colour photos throughout, **Pisces Books** explore the world's best diving and snorkelling areas. Each book contains listings of diving services and dive resorts, detailed information on depth, visibility and difficulty of dives, and a roundup of the marine life you're likely to see through your mask.

OFF THE ROAD

Journeys, the travel literature series written by renowned travel authors, capture the spirit of a place or illuminate a culture with a journalist's attention to detail and a novelist's flair for words. These are tales to soak up while you're actually on the road or dip into as an at-home armchair indulgence.

The range of lavishly illustrated **Pictorial** books is just the ticket for both travellers and dreamers. Off-beat tales and vivid photographs bring the adventure of travel to your doorstep long before the journey begins and long after it is over.

Lonely Planet **Videos** encourage the same independent, tough-minded approach as the guidebooks. Currently airing throughout the world, this award-winning series features innovative footage and an original soundtrack.

Yes, we know, work is tough, so do a little bit of deskside dreaming with the spiral-bound Lonely Planet **Diary** or a Lonely Planet **Wall Calendar**, filled with great photos from around the world.

TRAVELLERS NETWORK

Lonely Planet Online. Lonely Planet's award-winning Web site has insider information on hundreds of destinations, from Amsterdam to Zimbabwe, complete with interactive maps and relevant links. The site also offers the latest travel news, recent reports from travellers on the road, guidebook upgrades, a travel links site, an online book-buying option and a lively traveller's bulletin board. It can be viewed at **www.lonelyplanet.com** or AOL keyword: lp.

Planet Talk is a quarterly print newsletter, full of gossip, advice, anecdotes and author articles. It provides an antidote to the being-at-home blues and lets you plan and dream for the next trip. Contact the nearest Lonely Planet office for your free copy.

Comet, the free Lonely Planet newsletter, comes via email once a month. It's loaded with travel news, advice, dispatches from authors, travel competitions and letters from readers. To subscribe, click on the Comet subscription link on the front page of the Web site.

Index

Text

Bold indicates maps.

Boxed Text

MAP LEGEND

BOUNDARIES

╾╌╌╼╌╼	International
╾╌╌╌╌╌	Regional

HYDROGRAPHY

	Coastline, Lake
	River, Creek
	Canal
⊙	Spring, Rapids
⁙	Waterfalls

ROUTES & TRANSPORT

	Motorway
	Major Road
	Minor Road
	Other Road
	Unsealed Road
	Motorway (City)
	Through Route (City)
	Major Road (City)
	Street, Lane (City)
	Pedestrian Mall
⟩╌╌╌	Tunnel
	Path Through a Park
╌╌╌╌╌╌	Walking Track
·············	Walking Tour
┝━┝━━◯━┝	Railway, Station
╌╌╌╌▣╌	Tramway, Stop
┝╌╌╌▣╌┥	Cable Car, Terminus
╌╌╌╌⊐╌	Ferry Route, Terminal

AREA FEATURES

⊛	Park, Gardens		Building
	Cemetery		Market
	Beach, Desert		
	Urban Area		

MAP SYMBOLS

✪ **CARDIFF**	National Capital			⬜	Museum
⦿ **Swansea**	City	❸	Bank	⛱	Park
⊙ **Colwyn**	Town	⬈	Beach	⬜	Parking
○ **Harlech**	Village	▣ ▣	Bus Station, Stop	⊞	Police Station
		⬛	Castle or Fort	⬛	Post Office
●	Point of Interest	⌂	Cave	⬛	Ruins
⬧	Place to Stay	⬛ ⬛	Church	⬛	Shopping Centre
⬛	Camping Ground	⊞	Cinema	⬛	Stately Home
⬛	Caravan Park	⁓	Cliff or Escarpment	⬛	Swimming Pool
		⬛	Embassy	⬛	Synagogue
▼	Place to Eat	⊕	Hospital	⬛	Theatre
⬛	Pub or Bar	▣	Internet Cafe	○	Toilet
		☆	Lighthouse	⬛	Tomb
⬛	Airport	⬣	Monument	❶	Tourist Information
⌒	Ancient or City Wall	▲	Mountain or Hill	⬛	Transport

Note: not all symbols displayed above appear in this book

LONELY PLANET OFFICES

Australia
Locked Bag 1, Footscray, Victoria 3011
☎ 03 8379 8000 fax 03 8379 8111
email: talk2us@lonelyplanet.com.au

USA
150 Linden St, Oakland, CA 94607
☎ 510 893 8555 TOLL FREE: 800 275 8555
fax 510 893 8572
email: info@lonelyplanet.com

UK
10a Spring Place, London NW5 3BH
☎ 020 7428 4800 fax 020 7428 4828
email: go@lonelyplanet.co.uk

France
1 rue du Dahomey, 75011 Paris
☎ 01 55 25 33 00 fax 01 55 25 33 01
email: bip@lonelyplanet.fr
www.lonelyplanet.fr

World Wide Web: www.lonelyplanet.com *or* AOL keyword: lp
Lonely Planet Images: lpi@lonelyplanet.com.au